Introduction to Nursing

Introduction
to Nursing
AN ADAPTATION MODEL

Second Edition

SISTER CALLISTA ROY

Professor, Mount St. Mary's College
Adjunct Professor, University of Portland

Prentice-Hall, Inc., Englewood Cliffs, New Jersey 07632

Library of Congress Cataloging in Publication Data
Main entry under title:
Introduction to nursing.

   Includes bibliographies and index.
   1. Nursing.   2. Nursing—Psychological aspects.
I.   Roy, Callista. [DNLM: 1. Adaptation, Psychological.
2.   Models, Theoretical.   3. Nursing.   WY 100 R888i]
RT41.I57 1984   610.73   83-24496
ISBN 0-13-491274-8

Editorial/production supervision and interior design: Maria McKinnon
Cover design: Edsal Enterprises
Manufacturing buyer: John Hall

Printed in the United States of America

10   9   8   7

ISBN 0-13-491274-8

Prentice-Hall International, Inc., *London*
Prentice-Hall of Australia Pty. Limited, *Sydney*
Editora Prentice-Hall do Brasil, Ltda., *Rio de Janeiro*
Prentice-Hall Canada Inc., *Toronto*
Prentice-Hall of India Private Limited, *New Delhi*
Prentice-Hall of Japan, Inc., *Tokyo*
Prentice-Hall of Southeast Asia Pte. Ltd., *Singapore*
Whitehall Books Limited, *Wellington, New Zealand*

To my family, especially my parents,
    Pirth and Fabien Roy
To my friends, especially
    Cecilia Martinez
To my community, especially
    Sister Annette Debs, C.S.J.
To my colleagues, especially
    Rose Patricia McKay

Contributing Authors

Sue Ann Brown, R.N., M.N.
Consultant, Preventive Mental Health
Portland, Oregon

Marjorie Buck, R.N., M.N.
Former Instructor, Department of Nursing
Mount St. Mary's College, Los Angeles, California

Joan Seo Cho, R.N., M.N.
Assistant Professor, Department of Nursing
Mount St. Mary's College, Los Angeles, California

Marjorie Clowry Dobratz, R.N., M.S.N.
Assistant Professor, Department of Nursing
Mount St. Mary's College, Los Angeles, California

Marie J. Driever, R.N.,M.N.
Doctoral Student, University of Washington
Seattle, Washington

Sheila Driscoll, R.N., M.N.
Assistant Professor, Department of Nursing
Mount St. Mary's College, Los Angeles, California

Joan Hansen, R.N., M.N.
Clinical Instructor, California State University
Fullerton, California and
Formerly Assistant Professor of Nursing
Mount St. Mary's College, Los Angeles, California

Mary E. Hicks, R.N., M.P.H.
Assistant Professor, Department of Nursing
Mount St. Mary's College, Los Angeles, California

Mary Howard, R.N., M.S.N.
Formerly Associate Professor, Department of Nursing
Mount St. Mary's College, Los Angeles, California

Lorraine Ann Marshall, R.N., B.S.N., M.B.A.
Marketing Planning Specialist, Philips Ultrasound
Santa Ana, California

Kathleen Anschutz Nuwayhid, R.N., M.N.
Formerly Instructor, Department of Nursing
Mount St. Mary's College, Los Angeles, California

Nancy Zewen Perley, R.N., M.N., N.P.
Instructor, Women's Health Care
Nurse Practitioner Program
Harbor-UCLA Medical Center,
Torrance, California

Marsha Milton Roberson, R.N., M.N.
Assistant Professor, Department of Nursing
Mount St. Mary's College, Los Angeles, California

Sister Callista Roy, R.N., Ph.D., F.A.A.N.
Postdoctoral Fellow, Robert Wood Johnson Clinical
Nurse Scholars Program,
University of California, San Francisco, California
Professor, Department of Nursing
Mount St. Mary's College, Los Angeles, California (on leave)
Adjunct Professor, Graduate Program, School of Nursing
University of Portland, Portland, Oregon (on leave)

Marsha Keiko Sato, R.N., M.N.
Assistant Professor, Department of Nursing
Mount St. Mary's College, Los Angeles, California

Jane Servonsky, R.N., M.S.N.
Assistant Professor, Department of Nursing
Mount St. Mary's College, Los Angeles, California

Mary C. Sloper, R.N., M.N.
Assistant Professor, Department of Nursing
Mount St. Mary's College, Los Angeles, California

Nancy S. Taylor, R.N., M.S.
Assistant Professor, Department of Nursing
Mount St. Mary's College, Los Angeles, California

Mary Poush Tedrow, R.N., M.S.N.
Assistant Professor, Department of Nursing
Mount St. Mary's College, Los Angeles, California

Sharon A. Vairo, R.N., M.S.
Associate Professor, Department of Nursing
Mount St. Mary's College, Los Angeles, California

Sally Valentine, R.N., M.N.
Clinical Instructor, Department of Nursing Education
Children's Hospital, Los Angeles, California

Joyce Van Landingham, R.N., M.N.
Instructor of Nursing, California State University,
Los Angeles, California and
Formerly Assistant Professor of Nursing
Mount St. Mary's College, Los Angeles, California

Contents

Preface

Since this text was published in 1976, there has been continued growth in the use of conceptual models in nursing education, practice, and research. Along with this growth, the Roy Adaptation Model has continued to develop. Work on the model's theoretical dimensions and practical implementation has been carried out by the original author, her associates, and others in this country and abroad. This work has maintained the focus of the original publications, that is, to specify the nature of nursing according to the Roy model and, through observing that phenomenon, to classify, relate, predict, and prescribe what is currently known about people who cope with health and illness and about what the nurse can do to promote that process of adaptation.

Although many publications and public lectures have resulted from this work, at this point it seemed necessary to look at the definitive work on the Roy Adaptation Model and to revise this text to reflect the growth of recent years. The second edition once again aims to be an introduction to nursing based on the Roy Adaptation Model. It presents what the authors believe to be knowledge essential for basic nursing preparation. At the time the revision was planned, all contributing authors were on the faculty of Mount St. Mary's College. Although innovative uses of the model are going on in numerous other institutions, clearly the demand from our readers was to provide an update on the model's development at the institution of its origin, Mount St. Mary's College in Los Angeles. The faculty of both the associate and baccalaureate degree programs were asked to identify major revisions that were needed based on their own experience in using the text, as well as from their experience in providing consultation on the model in many educational and practice settings.

Because of the continued development of the model and faculty-expressed needs, the second edition of this text is extensively revised. Major revisions focus on: emphasis on health as well as acute and chronic illness; identification of theories basic to the model; clearer guidelines for nursing assessment in all four adaptive modes; inclusion of adaptation problems involving more than one adaptive mode and groups; application of theory in devising general as well as specific nursing approaches; greater integration of content on minority cultures; and application to the family, and group, as well as to the individual. In addition, efforts have been made to refine stylistic approaches such as consistent format, clear terminology, avoidance of sex-role stereotyping, and more use of learning aids and case study examples.

This text may be used appropriately in associate in arts and diploma nursing programs as well as throughout baccalaureate nursing programs. It will be particularly useful to graduate students on masters or doctoral levels who are studying the development of nursing knowledge and of conceptual frameworks. The text can be a valuable resource to nursing service personnel and individual nurses who are implementing the Roy Adaptation Model in various settings for nursing practice.

The book is organized into five parts. Part I introduces the model by showing its relationship to current developments in nursing as a scientific discipline and by describing the components of the model—the person, health, environment, and nursing activities. The nursing process according to the Roy Adaptation Model is discussed, then the major factors influencing adaptive behavior—culture, family, and development—are summarized. Part II focuses on adaptation in the physiological mode and describes assessment of the five basic needs of oxygenation, nutrition, elimination, activity and rest, and skin integrity. The major regulating processes in physiological adaptation—the senses, fluid and electrolytes, neurological function, and endocrine function are discussed in a similar way. Part III is a theoretical section that looks at the basis for and development of each of the psychosocial modes, that is, self-concept, role function, and interdependence. Parts IV and V focus on selected adaptation problems. Problems that are more commonly occurring, can be more easily ascribed to a disturbance in one mode, and can be expected to have more predictable outcomes are covered first. Second, a sample of complex clinical situations that bring about adaptation problems affecting more than one mode and having less predictable outcomes is considered. The last two chapters focus on adaptation in groups, specifically the family and the nursing care group.

It is hoped that this revised presentation of the Roy Adaptation Model of nursing may continue contributing to the improvement of health care at the same time that it advances the development of the science of nursing.

The author and the progress of this work are indebted to many persons for their insights, interest, and help that continue to stimulate the development of the Roy Adaptation Model. This network now extends from those close at home to colleagues around the world. Specifically I want to thank the contributors to this text and all the faculty and students at Mount St. Mary's College for their special and productive role in this development. Ruth A. Garrick has served as the major author's assistant for the work, and Sally Valentine worked with many of the details of the manuscript. Their capable help is greatly appreciated. I would like to express gratitude to my professional colleagues from other countries whose questions often bring me back to the essentials of the nursing model. Interactions with many graduate students, and particularly those at the University of Portland, have served this purpose, too. And lastly, I am grateful for the rewarding relationship I have had with the contemporary nurse thinkers who served with me from 1977 through 1982 on the Nurse Theorist Group of the National Conference on Nursing Diagnoses. Their influence is evident, I believe, in this second edition.

Sister Callista Roy

Introduction to Nursing

Part I

Introduction
to the Nursing Model

This text introduces the student and the practicing nurse to nursing as based on the Roy Adaptation Model. Part I begins this process by discussing nursing as a science and the development of nursing models. The elements of the Roy Adaptation Model are explained and used to provide direction for the nursing process. Finally, in this section some major influencing factors that are relevant in examining the adaptation process of persons and groups are explored.

Chapter 1

Nursing as a Scientific Discipline

BEHAVIORAL OBJECTIVES

After studying this chapter, the reader will be able to:

1. Define the key concepts of the chapter.
2. List five elements of models for nursing practice.
3. Compare and contrast one element of nursing models proposed by three different authors.
4. List briefly the following elements of the Roy Adaptation Model of nursing:
   a. The person
   b. The goal of nursing
   c. Nursing activities

KEY CONCEPTS DEFINED

Nursing Science: a developing system of knowledge about persons that observes, classifies, and relates the processes by which persons positively affect their health status. As the science develops, general laws of the interactions of these processes are stated and tested together with the laws about how nurses diagnose and treat persons' patterns of affecting their health.

Nursing Model: a set of concepts or images that identify and relate the essential elements of nursing practice.

Nursing as a Practice Discipline: nursing's scientific body of knowledge used for the purpose of providing an essential service to people, that is, promoting ability to affect health positively.

Elements of Nursing Practice: the concepts that best describe the essentials of nursing practice. The following elements may be used to compare the writings of the various authors about nursing practice: person, goal, health, environment, and nursing activities.

Nursing has long been considered both an art and a science. Throughout history, family members have skillfully used their traditions and experience in caring for the ill among them and in helping them prevent illness and increase wellness. This art of caring has been combined more and more with the scientific approach to create the field of nursing we know today. In this chapter we focus on the developing science of nursing and show how nursing models, such as the one presented in this text, are contributing to this development.

NURSING AS A SCIENCE

Nurses have studied various sciences, for example, biology, physics, and psychology. In these studies they note that a science observes and classifies particular phenomena, or objects, according to its particular viewpoint. Then the relationships between the phenomena, or the parts of any one object, are identified and the general laws of their interaction are stated and tested. Thus, in biology, living organisms, from the smallest one, now generally considered the invisible virus, to the complex human being are arranged in a hierarchy according to their various characteristics. As biological scientists studied living beings, they identified patterns of the activities of the various species, for example, ingestion and reproduction. In this way, general laws or statements of relationships that are believed to hold true under given conditions are established. Thus the field of biology proposes certain principles about the replication and duplication of genetic material in all living beings. The purpose of science, then, is to observe, classify, and investigate relationships that lead to understanding and control of natural phenomena (see Reynolds, 1971).

The need for science stems basically from our need to understand and deal with the world around us. When we go to a college campus or a medical center for the first time, we ask for a map of the immediate area. We need to lay out the parts of the area without wasting our time to observe, classify, and identify relationships between each building, walkway, and parking lot. Our understanding of the world comes in many ways and many forms. Some of what we know comes from the experience of others, such as a person who drew the map of the campus or medical center. Other things we know from our own experience. If we go to the cafeteria late at school or work, many of us know from experience that we will get a poorer selection of food. But beyond the knowledge of immediate experience, scientific knowledge has accumulated through generations of study and research.[1] Thus we have many branches of systematized knowledge derived from observation, study, and experimentation that seek to explain natural happenings.

Nursing as a science is still in the early stages of development. However, that development has progressed rapidly in the last few decades and can be expected to advance even more quickly in the remaining few years before the year 2000. Since a science focuses on a particular phenomenon and has a particular way of looking at the phenomenon it studies, nurse scholars and practitioners have been working to clarify the phenomenon of nursing and how we view it. This work was summarized by Donaldson and Crowley (1977), who identified the *commonalities in nursing* through the writings of various nurses. These commonalities are:

1. Concern with principles and laws that govern life processes, well-being, and optimum functioning of human beings, sick or well
2. Concern with the pattern of human behavior in interaction with the environment in critical life situations
3. Concern with the processes by which positive changes in health status are effected

Thus nursing focuses on persons and how they maintain well-being and high-level functioning whether sick or well. For example, nurses are concerned with how the developmentally disabled child can reach his or her highest level of functioning, and how the dying cancer patient can maintain rights to make decisions for as long as able to do so. At the same time, nurses look at the pattern of human behavior within a particular environment at various critical periods of life. In the usual flow of life there are times that are more significant for the person because of expected gradual changes, such as adolescence, or because of more abrupt or unexpected changes, such as sudden illness. These significant times are referred to as *critical periods of life.*

Nurses, for example, deal with the life-style of the developing family when a new baby is born and also observe how family members prepare themselves and their home when a loved one is returning to them after suffering a disabling illness, such as a stroke.

Finally, nurses identify ways in which people can bring about positive changes in their health status. Beyond simply learning how certain factors

---

[1]Epistemology is a branch of philosophy that includes the study of ways of knowing. Here we are merely giving two examples of broad types of knowledge, experiential and scientific.

threaten a person's health, for example, cigarette smoking, nursing is more concerned with all aspects of the process of promoting health, for example, the process of habit formation and alteration, of underlying needs, attitudes, and motivation as well as processes of learning such as reinforcement and imitation. Understanding these processes, the nurse hopefully can make a greater impact on the health status of others, for example, the long-time smoker.

We might say that through the years nursing has clarified that the phenomenon of its science is a particular holistic approach to persons. Nursing views persons by looking at their total processes for maintaining well-being and high-level functioning, for interacting with the environment in critical life situations, and for positively changing their health status. In the development of the *science of nursing*, then, nurses observe and classify these processes of the person, the relationships between the processes are identified, and the general laws of their interactions and how nurses can affect them are stated and tested. The work of scholars and students, practicing nurses, and administrators is all contributing to the nursing science of understanding persons in health and illness.

THE VALUE OF THE SCIENTIFIC APPROACH FOR NURSING

We began by saying that nursing has long been considered an art and a science. The art of caring for others is a significant part of what nurses do everyday. It is, moreover, often basic to a person's motivation to choose nursing as a profession. A number of authors in nursing are exploring the caring aspect of nursing (see Paterson and Zderad, 1976). Anyone who has ever been cared for at a time that was critical for them can understand the importance of blending the art of caring into the scientific approach nurses use.

What can we say about the value of the scientific approach for nursing? Earlier we noted that in a science one observes, classifies, and investigates the relationships which lead to understanding natural events. Specifically, nursing as a science studies the natural events of the processes by which persons positively affect their health status. How might an individual nurse use the scientific approach, and what effect can it have on nursing knowledge? Let us take the simple example of a nurse working with mothers of newborn infants. The nurse observes that the behavior of some mothers is different from that of others. These mothers seem more confident, quickly learn, and are comfortable using new skills, such as breast feeding, bathing, and handling their babies. The nurse has observed the behavior and generally classified it as positive mothering. This behavior will affect the health of both the mother and the baby. The baby's physical and emotional needs will be met better at the same time that the mother feels less stress and more satisfaction in what she is doing.

At this point, the nurse might say, "I must be doing something right in working with these mothers; at least some of them have behaviors that will promote their health and that of their child. If I continue what I'm doing, there is at least a chance that some mothers will develop positive mothering." Or she might say, "I'll separate my techniques and use them one at a time by trial and error, until I find the best one." However, as a nurse with a scientific approach, it is not satisfactory that "something is right" or "some will be healthier," or "eventually I'll find the right answer." The nurse wants to go one step further and investigate the relationship between a nursing action and the behavior of the mothers showing the positive effect. In this way, one can hope to affect the behavior, and thereby the health, of more of the mothers in a shorter period of time.

In such an investigation, the nurse might look at nursing actions from the mothers' points of view. Are some teaching approaches effective only with those mothers who share the same values about child care? Are other actions effective only for those who have someone else to support them in their new role, such as their own mother? There are, of course, many possibilities to be considered. The point we are making is that, using a scientific approach, the nurse can identify approaches that will be more consistently effective. Not only can this individual nurse help more people be more healthy, what is learned in this situation can be tested in other situations, such as in a group for teaching new skills of taking care of oneself after a disabling illness. In this way, research can generate new knowledge that can be used by other nurses in practice and can be taught to students who are learning to be effective nurses. Nursing students learn not only what other nurses do, but also what has been scientifically demonstrated to be most effective. In addition, the student learns the skills of examining her own nursing practice and generating new nursing knowledge.

A scientific approach to nursing, blended with our increasing understanding of the caring art of nursing, is essential to being able to affect people's health positively in an understandable and consistent way. Nurses believe that their growing knowledge about people's holistic processes for promoting their own well-being can have a significant influence on levels of health status. Nurses using a science of nursing can help more people be healthier.

The development of knowledge for the science of nursing can be described on three levels: theoretical and philosophical assumptions, nursing model development, and theory construction and testing derived from the nursing models (see Roy and Roberts, 1981, and Roy, 1983a,b).[2] In this text we are dicussing primarily the middle level, nursing models, and the Roy Adaptation Model specifically. Therefore, the next section defines and

---

[2]It should be noted that the distinctions Roy makes between theories and models are based on form and function rather than on levels of abstractions as proposed by Fawcett (1980).

describes what is meant by a nursing model and shows the historical development of a few selected nursing models.

NURSING MODELS

In focusing efforts to describe, to generate, and to verify the science of nursing, various authors have developed *nursing models*. Each model gives a particular focus for the study of human processes as they are viewed by the field of nursing.

A model is defined most simply as a description or analogy used to help visualize something that cannot be directly observed. When scientists work with problems of travel in space, they use models of the galaxies and models of spacecraft. The pieces of the models represent the features of the actual galaxies and spacecraft that are involved. However, these representations are in an abstracted form; for example, most simply they may be built with Styrofoam and glue to some miniature scale of what they stand for, or they may be further abstracted to mathematical formulas or to words denoting concepts and their relationships.

Nursing as a scientific discipline is *practice-oriented*. That is, nursing's scientific body of knowledge is for the purpose of providing a service to people, namely, promoting the ability to affect health positively. Just as any model is made up of the essential parts of what it represents, so a nursing model is made up of essential parts, or elements, of nursing practice. Thus we define a conceptual model for nursing as a set of concepts or images that identify and relate the essential elements of nursing practice.

The *essential elements of a model for nursing practice*, or concepts to be included, are:

1. A description of the *person* or groups receiving nursing care
2. A statement of the specific *goal* or purpose of nursing
3. A definition of *health*
4. A specified meaning for *environment*
5. A delineation of *nursing activities*

A model describes each of these concepts and shows in a general way how the concepts are related to one another.

The writings of nurses from Florence Nightingale (1820–1910) to the present can be analyzed to show how each addresses the broad commonalities of nursing described earlier. This will be done by identifying the elements of nursing models as reflected in the writings of seven selected nurse authors.[3] Historically, at times one element may be emphasized more than

---

[3]It is recognized that there are many more nursing models that might have been selected, but these seven are meant to serve as examples for the beginning student who can later pursue the expanding literature in this field.

another. Cumulatively, these writings show the rich heritage of nursing as a practice discipline.[4] A brief description of the selected authors' views of the person, the goal of nursing, health, environment, and nursing activities are given in Table 1.1 and discussed in the following pages.

Selected Nursing Models

Nightingale.   Florence Nightingale initiated the modern era of nursing by her writings and nursing education programs based on her specific view of the nature of nursing. Nightingale described her concept of nursing in 1859 in a book entitled *Notes on Nursing: What It Is and What It Is Not.* From this work, we can outline the elements of her nursing model.

Nightingale viewed the *person* as a passive instrument of nature. The person, whether healthy or sick, responds to certain laws of nature. Although Nightingale did not explore these laws (and, in fact, did not even make use of the scientific knowledge of her day), her view of the person was historically important for the development of the science of nursing. The Nurse Practice Acts in some states and many nursing scholars today still consider that the person's total response in health and illness is the core of nursing knowledge.

Since the person receiving nursing care was responding to laws of nature, the specific *goal* of nursing, for Nightingale, was to put persons in the best condition for nature to act upon them to restore or preserve health. This function was seen as distinct from that of medicine since surgical or medical treatment was not to cure, but to remove an "obstruction." Then with the help of nursing, nature would cure the person. Health, then, is an ultimate goal for nursing.

From Nightingale's discussions of disease, we can presume that her concept of *health* included the notion of absence of disease. However, she saw disease as a reparative process, in itself, an effort of nature to remedy a process of poisoning or of decay. In addition, Nightingale notes that health is "not only to be well [presumably without disease], but to be able to use well every power we have [possibly a reference to high level functioning]."

The fourth element of nursing models being considered, the *environment*, was central in Nightingale's view of nursing. She believed that nursing should involve the proper use of fresh air, light, warmth, cleanliness, quiet, and the proper selection and administration of diets. Many of Nightingale's later writings focused on these environmental factors in relation to sanitation.

Based on Nightingale's view of the person, the goal of nursing, health, and the environment, we can delineate her view of *nursing activities*. First,

---

[4]For another discussion of the historical development of nursing thought and more focus on shifts in the relationships among the concepts, see Newman (1983).

TABLE 1.1
Comparison of Models of Nursing

	Person	*Goal of Nursing*
Nightingale	A passive instrument of nature responding to the same laws, whether healthy or sick	To put persons in the best condition for nature to act on them to restore or preserve health
Henderson	A whole, complete, and independent being who has 14 basic activities: breathe, eat and drink, eliminate, move and maintain posture, sleep and rest, dress and undress, maintain body temperature, keep clean, avoid danger, communicate, worship, work, play, and learn	To substitute for what persons lack in physical strength, will, or knowledge to make them complete, whole, or independent
Peplau	A developmental being pursuing satisfaction and interpersonal security and contact	To foster forward movement of the personality and other ongoing human processes in the direction of creative, constructive, and productive personal and community living
Johnson	A behavioral system composed of seven subsystems: affiliative, dependency, ingestive, eliminative, sexual, aggressive, and achievement	To restore, maintain, or attain behavioral system balance and dynamic stability at the highest possible level for the individual
Orem	An individual with universal, developmental, and health-deviation-type self-care requisites who may vary in power to engage in self-care	To provide and manage self-care action on a continuous basis in order to help others sustain life and health, recover from disease or injury, and cope with their effects; to move the person toward responsible action in mat-

Health	Environment	Nursing Activities
Condition of living and using every power one has, as well as having no disease	Those factors that affect santitation, such as air, light, warmth, cleanliness, quiet, and diet	Recognize the laws of life, of health, and of sickness; "keep constant watch over the sick"; make proper use of environmental factors to conserve the vital powers of the person Assist persons in daily pattern of living or health-related activities contributing to health, recovery, or a peaceful death and help them be independent of such assistance as soon as possible
A word symbol that implies the forward movement of the personality and other ongoing human processes in the context indicated by the goal	Social Context	Improve social context through therapeutic interpersonal process, which has four clearly defined stages: orientation, identification, exploitation, and resolution; throughout the process the nurse includes the activities of observing, communicating, and recording Assess behavioral stability and the dynamics of behavioral instability; stimulate, protect, restrict, defend, inhibit, or facilitate behavior
Condition of having no self-care purposes that are associated with illness, injury, or disease; these include changes in human structure, physical functioning, and behavior and habits of daily living	External conditioning factors significant for self-care	Diagnose, prescribe, and provide care that compensates for or aids in overcoming the health-related deficits of others by acting or doing for, guiding, supporting, providing a developmental-type environment, and teaching

TABLE 1.1 (continued)

	Person	*Goal of Nursing*
		ters of self-care and members of the family toward increasing competence in making decisions relative to the continuing daily personalized care of the person
Rogers	A unitary, four-dimensional, negentrophic energy field identified by pattern and organization and manifesting characteristics and behaviors that are different from those of the parts and which cannot be predicted from the knowledge of the parts	To promote symphonic interaction between man and environment, to strengthen the coherence and integrity of the human field, and to direct and redirect patterning of the human and environmental fields for realization of maximum human potential
Roy	An adaptive system with cognator and regulator acting to maintain adaptation in the four adaptive modes; physiologic function, self-concept, role function, and interdependence	To promote adaptation in each of the four adaptive modes, thus contributing to the person's health, quality of life, and dying with dignity

it can be presumed that a nurse utilizing this concept of nursing would recognize the laws of life, of health, and of sickness. Second, her interventions would include the proper use of the environmental factors listed above and, Nightingale states, this is to be done at the least expense of the vital power to the patient. Third, because of the nature of these two activities, Nightingale emphasized the nurse's responsibility for observation. Specifically, she stated, "A careful nurse will keep constant watch over her sick." This tradition of the nurse as the observer of the patient remains strong to this day in nursing assessments, whether they be done by monitoring in critical care units, or by interviewing in rural homes.

The influence of Nightingale's model of nursing is seen in the writings of later nursing theorists, who refer frequently to her statements on the nature of nursing.

Health	Environment	Nursing Activities
A state of wholeness or integrity that includes continuing human development		
(A rhythmic pattern of energy exchange which is mutually enhancing and expresses full life potential)	A four-dimensional negentropic energy field identified by pattern and organization and encompassing all that is outside any given human field	Replace rule-of-thumb activities with broad principles to guide practice (e.g., those being developed in time and motion studies)
A state and a process of being and becoming an integrated, whole person	All conditions, circumstances, and influences surrounding and affecting the development and behavior of persons or groups	Assess behavior and factors that influence adaptation level and intervene by managing the focal, contextual, and residual stimuli

Henderson.   Virginia Henderson wrote extensively in the 1950s and 1960s on the nature of nursing. Her writings provided a theoretical approach which influenced the thinking of that day by being included in the 1955, fifth edition, of a popular nursing book, *Textbook of the Principles and Practice of Nursing.* The earliest edition of this book, written by Bertha Harmer, was published in 1922, and it has continued in revisions, with Virginia Henderson as the major author from 1955 through 1978. A monograph containing Henderson's concept of nursing was published by the International Council of Nurses in 1961 and later was translated into 10 languages.

Henderson added to Nightingale's concept of person, the recipient of nursing care, by emphasizing that the *person* is a whole, complete, and independent being. Her view is further specified by her enumeration of the activities the human being must perform. These activities include the following (Henderson, 1964, p.65):

1. Breathe normally.
2. Eat and drink adequately.
3. Eliminate body wastes.
4. Move and maintain desirable posture.
5. Sleep and rest.
6. Select suitable clothes: dress and undress.
7. Maintain body temperature within normal range by adjusting clothing and modifying the environment.
8. Keep the body clean and well-groomed and protect the integument.
9. Avoid dangers in the environment and avoid injuring others.
10. Communicate with others in expressing emotions, needs, fears, and so on.
11. Worship according to one's faith.
12. Work in such a way that there is a sense of accomplishment.
13. Play or participate in various forms of recreation.
14. Learn, discover, or satisfy the curiosity that leads to "normal" development and health, and use the available health facilities.

These activities clearly delineate the aspects of the person that are the focus of nursing.

The specific *goal* of nursing, for Henderson, is to substitute for what the persons lack, to make them complete, whole, or independent. The lack may be of physical strength, will, or knowledge. She sees nursing, then, as primarily complementing the person by supplying what is needed to perform daily activities and also to carry out the treatment prescribed by the physician.

Although Henderson mentioned health and the environment, her major focus was to develop nursing's unique view of persons and their activities, and to show how nursing relates to the person by its specific goal and substituting activities. Thus an explicit definition of *health* and meaning of *environment* do not seem to be included in Henderson's writings. Rather, her particular contribution at this time was to develop the concept of nursing as focusing on meeting particular needs of people.

The last element of her model, *nursing activities*, is implied in Henderson's concepts of the person and the goal of nursing. The nurse is to substitute for what persons lack to be complete in relation to their 14 basic activities. Thus Henderson emphasizes, as did Nightingale, the assessment responsibilities of the nurse. She notes that the nurse makes efforts to *know her patients*, to understand them, "to get inside their skin." Henderson also spelled out more clearly other steps of what became commonly known as the nursing process (a more thorough discussion of which can be found in Chapter 3). After assessment, the nurse *identifies* what the person *lacks* (diagnosis) and helps to *supply* this *lack* (intervention). Finally, Henderson stresses that the nurse *evaluates* her *success* according to the degree to which the person establishes independence in all activities (evaluation). Although Henderson did not provide a scheme of nursing approaches to be used in nursing intervention, the approaches she would consider as nursing interventions are implied in the activities of persons, which the nurse is to facilitate. The nursing process is a broad outline of procedures for nursing activity.

Henderson's contributions to the development of the concept of nursing were not only widespread through her publications, but were long-lasting in their effects on the thinking of nurse writers and teachers for the next several decades.

Peplau. Another important author whose work in the 1950s contributed to nursing model development was Hildegard E. Peplau. With a background in psychiatric nursing, Peplau presented the elements of her model in her 1952 book, *Interpersonal Relations in Nursing.*

Based on her specialty in nursing, Peplau focused attention on the *person* receiving nursing care as a developing personality. The psychoanalytic theorist Harry Stack Sullivan (1953) provided some of the background for describing the dynamic interaction that occurs in the development of early infancy and childhood. The individual pursues satisfaction of physiological demands and interpersonal security and interpersonal contact. In this process, tensions of need, anxiety, and loneliness are created. The energy of these tensions, according to Peplau, can be transformed in positive directions.

Given this view of the person, Peplau's concept of the specific *goal* of nursing can be stated most simply as: to foster forward movement of the personality and other ongoing human processes in the direction of creative, constructive, and productive personal and community living. Peplau notes that nurses facilitate natural ongoing tendencies in human organisms. We may note here a similarity with Nightingale's goal for nursing, although the natural tendencies of growth that Peplau speaks of are quite different from the natural laws of healing referred to by Nightingale. The nurse, according to Peplau, is an educative instrument and a maturing force, aiming at forward movement.

As with Henderson, Peplau emphasizes a unique concept of nursing as an approach to people. Her discussions of health and environment are less explicit. Peplau refers to *health* as a word symbol that implies forward movement of personality and other ongoing human processes in the context noted above. Peplau's meaning for *environment* is the general notion of social context.

Peplau's greatest contribution to the developing science of nursing was her delineation of *nursing activities* as being an interpersonal process. The nurse improves the person's social context by therapeutic interaction with the person. Peplau describes this process as a series of phases involving different roles for the nurse and the person. She emphasizes that the phases and roles are fluid in nature and tend to flow together or move backward or forward as the person moves forward or regresses.

The *orientation* phase involves learning the nature of the person's difficulty and the extent of the need for help. The *identification* phase is the time period in which the person is responding to the nurse and feeling a sense of belonging and identification. The *exploitation* phase occurs when the person identifies with a nurse and proceeds to make full use of the services offered, including the nurse's interpersonal skills. The *resolution* phase generally concludes the process as old ties and dependencies are relinquished. The person prepares to go home or to resume independence. During these phases, the nurse may fulfill a variety of roles, including teacher, resource person, counselor, and surrogate. The person with whom she interacts can fulfill the complementary roles to each of these, or at times may reverse roles with the nurse, who is also a developing personality. Within the nurse's activities of the interpersonal relationship, Peplau also emphasizes the specific skills of observing, communicating, and recording.

Peplau's work had a significant impact not only on the teaching of psychiatric nursing, but also on the shift in models of nursing from a major focus on the person to a focus that included the nurse–patient relationship. In addition, Peplau's influence on nursing has continued through the years since her 1952 book. Notably, she served as President of the American Nurses' Association from 1970 to 1972; in the 1970s, her writings and speeches stressed the role of nursing in the development of health plans, programs, and policies, and involvement in broad and specific social issues such as the rights of young women and the aging; and recently Peplau served on the task force of the Congress for Nursing Practice of the American Nurses' Association, which in 1980 issued a policy statement on the nature and scope of nursing practice.

Johnson.   Toward the end of the 1950s, in several significant journal articles, Dorothy E. Johnson began to write about the nature of a science of nursing and to emphasize the need to clarify what we are trying to do, why, and what scientific knowledge is involved (Johnson, 1959). Johnson held some initial premises about nursing as a direct service provided to individuals or groups under stress of a health/illness nature. By the early 1960s, her nursing model became the basis of the undergraduate nursing curriculum at the University of California at Los Angeles.

Johnson developed a comprehensive view of the *person* as the recipient of nursing care.[5] The person is a behavioral system that has a tendency to achieve and maintain stability in patterns of functioning. Like Nightingale, Johnson sees that similar patterns occur in both health and illness. Johnson postulates that the whole behavioral system of the human being is composed of seven subsystems: affiliative, dependency, ingestive, eliminative, sexual, aggressive, and achievement. The goals of the total behavioral system are the survival, reproduction, and growth of the human organism. To maintain the stability of the system, and thus to meet its goal, each subsystem must receive adequate functional requirements or sustenal imperatives. Johnson defines these as input in the form of protection, nurturance, and stimulation. Problems arise for the person when there are disturbances in the structure or function of the subsystems or the system, or because the level of behavioral functioning is less than optimal.

Based on this concept of the person, the *goal* of nursing is to restore, maintain, or attain the person's behavioral stability. Nursing aims at establishing regularities in behavior so that the goal of each subsystem will be fulfilled. Behavioral stability exists when a minimum expenditure of energy is required, continued biological and social survival are ensured, and some degree of personal satisfaction is accrued. Behavioral instability might be observed either as physiological changes or as behavioral changes such as disorder, purposelessness, or unpredictability.

Once again, we find that although this author frequently mentions both *health* and the *environment*, Johnson's focus on unique nursing knowledge does not include definitions and meanings of these terms.

When we look at *nursing activities*, Johnson outlines more specifically than the earlier theorists the four stages of the nursing process: assessment, diagnosis, intervention, and evaluation. The *assessment* process involves a thorough examination of the behavior of each subsystem and the significant variables that affect it. Johnson categorizes these variables as: biological, sociological, and a general category called level of wellness. If the nurse finds an actual or potential problem, she closely analyzes the unstable subsystem.

The nurse then makes a *diagnosis* by deciding what are the dynamics of the behavioral instability. Johnson outlines four diagnostic categories. The first two, originating within any one subsystem, are manifested by insufficiency or discrepancy. The second two, manifested within more than one subsystem, are either incompatability or dominance. Under each of these categories for each subsystem, specific nursing problems or subcategories can be listed.

[5]This view was initially developed, implemented, and tested in Johnson's teaching and scholarship roles, then later published (1980) in Riehl and Roy's *Conceptual Models for Nursing Practice*.

In regard to nursing *intervention*, according to the Johnson model, the nurse has six choices: to stimulate, protect, restrict, defend, inhibit, or facilitate. Nursing is viewed as an external regulatory force which acts to preserve the organization and integration of the person's behavior. This force can impose external control through attempts to change structural units in desirable directions, or fulfillment of the functional requirements of the subsystems. The outcome of nursing intervention is evaluated according to the goal of behavioral stability.

Even in the early 1960s, Johnson's behavioral systems model was one of the most completely developed models of nursing. Although Johnson's own published description of the model was not available until 1980, her teaching, related writings, speaking, sharing of unpublished materials, and consultation with schools of nursing exerted their influence in the intervening years, and, in fact, did much to establish the trend of the rapid growth of nursing models for education and practice in the decades of the 1960s and 1970s.

Orem.   Also in the late 1950s, another major model of nursing was being developed by Dorothea Orem. Her initial formulations of a self-care framework were published in 1959 by the Department of Health, Education, and Welfare under the title *Guides for Developing Curricula for the Education of Practical Nurses.* In 1965, the Nursing Model Committee of the Nursing Faculty of the Catholic University of America initiated an exploration of the conceptual structure of nursing. This work was carried on by the Nursing Development Conference Group from 1969 to 1973, when the first edition of *Concept Formalization in Nursing: Process and Product* was published. This text, together with Orem's 1971 book, *Nursing: Concepts of Practice*, present the elements of the Orem Self-Care Model of Nursing. The second edition of these books appeared in 1979 and 1980, respectively.

Orem, like Johnson, presents a well-developed concept of the human *person*. The primary term used by the conference group to characterize how the nurse views the person is that of *self-care agency*. Self-care agency is the power of individuals to engage in self-care. Self-care requisites include: the universal type, that is, those that apply for all persons during all stages of the life cycle and which are associated with life processes and with the integrity of human structure and functioning; the developmental type, that is, those that are associated with human development processes and with conditions and events occurring during various stages of the life cycle; and the health-deviation type, that is, those that are associated with disease, injury, disfigurement, and disability, and with medical care measures utilized in medical diagnosis and treatment.

The specific *goal* of nursing is described in Orem's work in relation to this concept of the person. The nurse aims to provide and manage self-care action on a continuous basis in order to help others sustain life and health, recover from disease or injury, and cope with the effects of these. The nurse's ultimate goal is to move the person toward responsible action in matters of self-care. When appropriate, the specific goal may be to increase the competence of family members in making decisions relative to the continuing daily care of the person.

Orem's definition of *health* seems to be implied in earlier discussions of health-deviation self-care requisites and later commentaries on health as a descriptive term and health as a state (Orem, 1980). Health is a condition of having no self-care purposes that are associated with illness, injury, or disease. Such requisites would stem from changes in human structure and physical functioning, as well as changes in behavior and habits of daily living. Furthermore, health is a term that is useful in describing the state of wholeness or integrity of human beings. Health defined as a state of being sound or whole reflects a state of human perfection that includes continuing human development.

The meaning attached to the term *environment*, within the Orem self-care model, can be found in discussions of conditioning factors for the person. Conditioning factors are both internal (such as age, sex, and health state) and external (such as health care system elements and family system elements). The nurse focuses on conditioning factors that are significant for self-care. Thus Orem's meaning for environment is presumably those external conditioning factors which are significant for self-care.

In describing the *activities* of nursing according to Orem, the work to explicate the concept of nursing agency, as parallel with that of self-care agency, is relevant. The nursing agency is the complex set of specialized abilities that enable the nurse to diagnose, prescribe, and provide care for health-related self-care deficits. To come to a diagnosis, the nurse using an Orem model first makes an *assessment* which determines the therapeutic self-care demand and the person's potential for self-care agency. The *diagnosis* is, then, a judgment about the self-care deficit in quality and quantity in relation to therapeutic self-care demand. Based on the diagnoses of one person, or a group of persons, the nurse *designs a system* of assistance for therapeutic self-care that can be wholly compensatory, partly compensatory, or educative/developmental. Specific activities of nursing *intervention* include acting or doing for, guiding, supporting, providing a developmental type of environment, and teaching. The effects of nursing action are evaluated on the basis of the goal of the model; that is, are self-care needs met? Does the person move forward toward responsible action in matters of self-care? Do family members increase in competence in making decisions relative to the continuing daily personalized care of the person?

By the early 1970s, a number of articles began to appear by nurses who were applying the Orem model in practice settings, for example, in a nurse-conducted diabetic management clinic and cardiac clinics (Backscheider, 1974; Crews, 1972). Other publications have focused on the implementing of Orem's framework in nursing education (Piemme and Trainor, 1977). By the late 1970s, articles reporting applications of Orem's work included the development of instruments to measure relevant self-care agency dimensions (Kearney and Fleischer, 1979). This widespread implementation of the model is sure to influence the direction of inquiry in nursing science as well as the practice of nursing for some years to come.

Rogers.   Martha Rogers was involved in the scholarly discussions that were common in the late 1950s and early 1960s of need to clarify the nature of nursing. In her 1961 book *Educational Revolution in Nursing*, Rogers presented the object of nursing as the movement of the person toward maximum health. By 1970, she presented her evolving views on the nature of nursing in a book entitled *An Introduction to the Theoretical Basis of Nursing*. A more recent article, "Nursing: A Science of Unitary Man" (Rogers, 1980), continues the development of these views.

The major focus of Rogers' work has been her revolutionary concept of the human *person.* She identifies unitary man as the recipient of nursing care. This person is a unitary, four-dimensional, negentropic energy field identified by pattern and organization and manifesting characteristics and behaviors that are different from those of the parts and which cannot be predicted from knowledge of the parts. According to Rogers, nursing is the only science or learned profession that truly deals with a unitary view of the total person, since other sciences study various parts of the person or an addition of parts. However, she recognizes that, for nurses who have been taught other basic sciences, it is difficult to think in terms of unitary patterns rather than parts of the person. Within Rogers' conceptual scheme, she defines the specific characteristics of the unitary person that she has identified. The human energy field evolves rhythmically along life's nonlinear, spiraling axis in a way that can be represented by the child's coiled toy known as Slinky.

The specific *goal* of nursing, according to Rogers, is to promote symphonic interaction between the person and the environment. The nurse aims at strengthening the coherence and integrity of the human field and directing and redirecting patterning of the human and environmental fields for realization of maximum potential.

Even though the concept of *health* is included in Rogers' stated goal of nursing, her glossary of terms does not provide a specific definition of health. However, the Nurse Theorist Group of the National Conference on Nursing Diagnoses, meeting periodically since 1978, developed the following related definition of health: a rhythmic pattern of energy exchange which is mutually enhancing and expresses full-life potential.

Rogers is more specific in her discussion of *environment* since this is a major concept of her theoretical formulations. Environment, in Rogers' words, is a four-dimensional, negentropic energy field identified by pattern and organization and encompassing all that is outside any given human field. For Rogers, both the human field and the environmental field are coextensive with the universe.

When we look at *nursing activities*, the Rogers framework can also dictate a nursing process similar to the process used within the frameworks of the other nursing theorists. When the nurse *gathers data* (assessment) she considers the *person in his environmental field* at a given point in space-time. She identifies individual differences in the sequence and patterning of the life process. Based on these data, the nurse makes a nursing *diagnosis* and determines immediate and long-range *goals* for the individual, family, and society. Nursing *interventions* are designed to help the patient reach the goal. Technological activities, manual skills, or human relationships are geared toward *repatterning* man and the environment for the development of the total human potential. Rogers emphasizes that the science of nursing is a prerequisite to the process of nursing. She notes that within this framework nurses will replace rule-of-thumb activities with broad *principles to guide practice*: for example, principles derived from research projects related to human patterns such as studies involving how people pattern themselves in time and motion.

Rogers continues in the mid 1980s to be a much-called-upon speaker to present these innovative ideas about the science of nursing. Her influence is further felt by her almost charismatic effect on the doctoral students whom she teaches. Several of these persons are now publishing their own conceptual models for nursing which utilize some of Rogers's basic assumptions about the person and nursing, for example, Parse (1981).

Roy.   The last model whose elements are presented in Table 1.1 is the Roy Adaptation Model of nursing. This model is the specific focus of this book. The elements of the Roy Model will be discussed in greater detail in the next chapter. At this point, we may summarize these elements so that they can be seen in perspective with the other major nursing models presented.

Roy began her work on the nursing model while she was a graduate student studying with Dorothy E. Johnson from 1963 to 1966 at the University of California, Los Angeles. Her first published work on the model was an article in 1970 (Roy, 1970), the same year the model was implemented as the basis of the baccalaureate curriculum at Mount Saint Mary's College in Los Angeles.

Beginning with a systems theory[6] approach, Roy describes the *person* as an adaptive system. As with any type of system, the person has internal processes that act to maintain the goals of the person. At this time, these

---

[6]For a general introduction to systems theory, see Chapter 2 as well as Hazard (1971).

processes are broadly categorized as a *regulator* subsystem and a *cognator* subsystem. The regulator involves physiological processes such as chemical, neurological, and endocrine responses which allow the body to cope with the changing environment. For example, when a person perceives a sudden threat, such as an oncoming car approaching the crosswalk, a rush of energy is available from an increase of adrenal hormones.

The cognator subsystem involves the psychological processes for dealing cognitively and emotionally with the changing environment. In the example of the person who runs from an oncoming car, the cognator acts to process the emotion of fear. The perceptions of the situation are also processed and the person may come to some new decision about where and how to cross the street safely.

Both the cognator and regulator activity are manifested in four particular ways in each person: in behaviors indicating physiologic function, self-concept, role function, and interdependence. These four ways of categorizing the effects of cognator and regulator activity are called *adaptive modes*.

Roy's view of the *goal* of nursing was the first major concept of her nursing model to be described. Roy began her work by attempting to identify the unique function of nursing in promoting health. Since a number of health care workers have the goal of promoting health, it seemed important for nursing to identify a *unique* goal. As a staff nurse in pediatric settings, Roy had noted the great resiliency of children in responding to major physiological and psychological changes. Yet nursing intervention was needed to support and promote this positive coping. It seemed, then, that the concept of adaptation, or positive coping, might be used to describe the goal or function of nursing. From this initial notion, Roy has developed her description of the goal of nursing as: the promotion of adaptation in each of the four adaptive modes, thus contributing to persons' health, quality of life, and dying with dignity. Roy's particular view of adaptation, together with the other major concepts of the model, will be described in greater detail in the next chapter.

Although her earlier writings had focused mainly on the concept of adaptation, Roy later found it necessary to articulate her concept of health. A nurse promotes adaptation for the purpose of positively affecting health. Roy currently defines *health* as a state and a process of being and becoming integrated and whole.

Roy considers *environment* most broadly as all the conditions, circumstances, and influences surrounding and affecting the development and behavior of persons or groups. Since the person is viewed as an adaptive system, the environment is seen as the input to the system. This input involves both internal and external factors. Roy uses the work of Helson (1964), a physiological psychologist, to categorize these factors further as focal, contextual, and residual stimuli. Once again, the reader will find these concepts explored in greater depth throughout this text.

The final element of a nursing model is the model's description of *nursing activities*. Roy sees nursing activities outlined briefly as *assessment* of behavior and the factors that influence adaptation level and *intervention* by managing[7] the focal, contextual, and residual stimuli. The full description of the nursing process according to Roy is covered in Chapter 3.

In the years since 1970, over 1500 faculty and students working with Sister Callista Roy have contributed to the theoretical development and practical application of the Roy Adaptation Model as presented in both the first (Roy, 1976) and current edition of *Introduction to Nursing: An Adaptation Model*. In addition, with the study of major nursing models becoming a focus for graduate study, there is increasing testing of the Roy Model in a variety of settings (see Wagner, 1976, and Galligan, 1979); implementation in practice, analysis, and expansion of the model (see Mastal et al., 1982; Mastal and Hammond, 1980; Randell et al., 1982; and Rambo, 1983); and research related to the model (see Idle, 1977; Lewis et al., 1978; and Dahlen, 1980).

SUMMARY

Nursing as a science is developing a system of knowledge about persons and their ways of maintaining well-being and high-level functioning, of interacting with the environment in critical life situations, and of positively changing health status. Nurse authors since the time of Florence Nightingale have been developing concepts of the elements of nursing practice, that is, their views of persons, nursing goals, health, environment, and nursing activities. This chapter included a brief presentation of these major elements of a nursing model as reflected in the writings of Nightingale, Henderson, Peplau, Johnson, Orem, Rogers, and Roy. The remainder of this text will focus specifically on the Roy Adaptation Model of nursing and its use in nursing practice.

STUDENT LEARNING ACTIVITY

Read one article from the references which shows the application of a given nursing model to nursing practice. Be prepared to report this approach and compare it with other presentations by your classmates. Evaluate whether or not this approach agrees with your own beliefs about nursing.

---

[7]Use of the term *managing stimuli* to describe nursing intervention was suggested to Roy by Helen Hammond who has been involved actively in implementing the model since 1979.

REFERENCES

Backscheider, J. E. "Self-Care Requirements, Self-Care Capabilities and Nursing Systems in the Diabetic Management Clinic," *American Journal of Public Health*, vol. 64, no. 12, 1974, pp. 1138–1146.

Crews, J. "Nurse Managed Cardiac Clinics," *Cardiovascular Nursing*, vol. 8, no. 4, July/August 1972, pp. 15–18.

Dahlen, Ro Anne. "Analysis of Selected Factors Related to the Elderly Person's Ability to Adapt to Visual Protheses following Senile Cataract Surgery," doctoral dissertation, University of Maryland, 1980.

Donaldson, Sue K., and Dorothy Crowley. "Discipline of Nursing: Structure and Relationship to Practice," in *Communicating Nursing Research*, vol. 10, M. Batey, ed. Boulder, Colo.: Western Interstate Commission on Higher Education, 1977.

Fawcett, J. "A Framework for Analysis and Evaluation of Conceptual Models," *Nurse Educator*, November/December 1980, pp. 10–14.

Galligan, A. C. "Using Roy's Concept of Adaptation to Care for Young Children," *The American Journal of Maternal Child Nursing*, vol. 4, 1979, pp. 24–28.

Harmer, Bertha. *Textbook of the Principles and Practice of Nursing*, 5th ed., revised by Virginia Henderson. New York: Macmillan Publishing Co., Inc., 1955.

Hazard, Mary. "Overview of Systems Theory," *Nursing Clinics of North America*, vol. 6, September 1971, pp. 385–393.

Helson, Harry. *Adaptation Level Theory*. New York: Harper & Row, Publishers, 1964.

Henderson, Virginia. "The Nature of Nursing," *American Journal of Nursing*, vol. 64, no. 8, 1964, pp. 62–68.

Idle, Betty A. "SPAL: A Tool for Measuring Self-Perceived Adaptation Level Appropriate for an Elderly Population." In Sigma Theta Tau, *Clinical Nursing Research: Its Strategies and Findings*. Monograph Series 78-Two. University of Arizona, September 15 and 16, 1977.

Johnson, Dorothy E. "A Philosophy of Nursing," *Nursing Outlook*, vol. 7, 1959, pp. 198–200.

Johnson, Dorothy E. "The Behavioral System Model for Nursing," in J. P. Riehl and C. Roy, *Conceptual Models for Nursing Practice*, 2nd ed. New York: Appleton-Century-Crofts, 1980.

Kearney, B. Y., and B. J. Fleischer. "Development of an Instrument to Measure Exercise of Self-Care Agency," *Research in Nursing and Health*, vol. 2, 1979, pp. 25–34.

Lewis, Frances, et al. "Measuring Adaptation of Chemotherapy Patients," in *Nursing Research, Development, Collaboration, Utilization*, Janelle C. Krueger, Allen H. Nelson, and Mary Opal, eds. Germantown, Maryland: Aspen Systems, 1978.

Mastal, M., and H. Hammond. "Analysis and Expansion of the Roy Adaptation

Model: A Contribution to Holistic Nursing," *Advances in Nursing Science*, vol. 3, July 1980, pp. 7–78.

Mastal, M., H. Hammond, and M. Roberts. "Theory into Hospital Practice: A Pilot Implementaton," *The Journal of Nursing Administration*, June 1982, pp. 9–15.

Newman, M. "The Continuing Revolution: A History of Nursing Science," in *The Nursing Profession: A Time to Speak*, N. Chaska, ed. New York: McGraw-Hill Book Company, 1983, pp. 385–393.

Nightingale, Florence. *Notes on Nursing: What It Is and What It is Not*. Philadelphia: J. P. Lippincott Company, 1966. (A facsimile of the first edition printed in London, 1859, with a foreword by Annie W. Goodrich.)

The Nursing Development Conference Group. *Concept Formalization in Nursing: Process and Product*, Boston: Little, Brown and Company, 1973.

The Nursing Development Conference Group, Dorothea E. Orem, ed. *Concept Formalization in Nursing: Process and Product*, 2nd ed. Boston: Little, Brown and Company, 1979.

Orem, Dorothea E. *Nursing: Concepts of Practice*. New York: McGraw-Hill Book Company, 1971.

Orem, Dorothea E. *Nursing: Concepts of Practice*, 2nd ed. New York: McGraw-Hill Book Company, 1980.

Parse, Rosemarie. *A Theory of Nursing: Man–Living–Health*. New York: John Wiley & Sons, Inc., 1981.

Paterson, Josephine G., and Loretta T. Zderad. *Humanistic Nursing*. New York: John Wiley & Sons, Inc., 1976.

Peplau, Hildegard. *Interpersonal Relations in Nursing*. New York: G. P. Putnam's Sons, 1952.

Piemme, J. A., and M. A. Trainor. "A First-Year Nursing Course in a Baccalaureate Program," *Nursing Outlook*, vol. 25, March 1977, pp. 184–187.

Rambo, B. *Adaptation Nursing: Assessment and Intervention*. Philadelphia: W. B. Sanders Company, 1983.

Randell, Brooke, Mary Poush-Tedrow, and Joyce Van Landingham. *Adaptation Nursing: The Roy Conceptual Model Applied*. St. Louis: The C. V. Mosby Company, 1982.

Reynolds, Paul D. *A Primer of Theory Construction*. Indianapolis: The Bobbs-Merrill Company, Inc., 1971.

Riehl, Joan P., and Sister Callista Roy. *Conceptual Models for Nursing Practice*, 2nd ed. New York: Appleton-Century-Crofts, 1980.

Rogers, Martha E. *Educational Revolution in Nursing*. New York: Macmillan Publishing Co., Inc., 1961.

Rogers, Martha E. *An Introduction to the Theoretical Basis of Nursing*. Philadelphia: F. A. Davis Company, 1970.

Rogers, Martha E. "Nursing: A Science of Unitary Man," in Joan P. Riehl and Sister Callista Roy, *Conceptual Models for Nursing Practice*, 2nd ed. New York: Appleton-Century-Crofts, 1980.

Roy, Sister Callista. "Adaptation: A Conceptual Framework for Nursing," *Nursing Outlook*, March 1970, pp. 42–45.

Roy, Sister Callista. *Introduction to Nursing: An Adaptation Model.* Englewood Cliffs, N. J.: Prentice-Hall, Inc., 1976.

Roy, Sister Callista. "Roy Adaptation Model," in *Family Health: A Theoretical Approach to Nursing Care*, Imelda Clements and Florence Roberts, eds. New York: John Wiley & Sons, Inc., 1983a.

Roy, Sister Callista. "Theory Development in Nursing: Proposal for Direction," in *The Nursing Profession: A Time to Speak*, Norma Chaska, ed. New York: McGraw-Hill Book Company, 1983b.

Roy, Sister Callista, and S. Roberts. *Theory Construction in Nursing: An Adaptation Model.* Englewood Cliffs, N. J.: Prentice-Hall, Inc., 1981.

Sullivan, Harry Stack. *The Independent Theory of Psychiatry.* New York: W. W. Norton & Company, Inc., 1953.

Wagner, P. "The Roy Adaptation Model: Testing the Adaptation Model in Practice," *Nursing Outlook*, vol. 24, 1976, pp. 682–685.

Chapter 2

The Roy Adaptation Model of Nursing

Sister Callista Roy

BEHAVIORAL OBJECTIVES

After studying this chapter, the reader will be able to:

1. Define the key concepts of the chapter.
2. Describe the following elements of the Roy Adaptation Model of Nursing:
   (a) The person
   (b) The goal of nursing
   (c) Nursing activities
3. Identify a coping mechanism that one uses for oneself in a given situation.
4. Apply the concept of adaptation level to a response to an ordinary life experience.

KEY CONCEPTS DEFINED

System: a set of units so related or connected as to form a unity or whole and characterized by inputs, outputs, and control and feedback processes.

Stimulus: that which provokes a response.

Adaptation Level: a constantly changing point, made up of focal, contextual, and residual stimuli, which represents the person's own standard

27

of the range of stimuli to which one can respond with ordinary adaptive responses.

Coping Mechanisms: innate or acquired ways of responding to the changing environment.

Regulator: subsystem coping mechanism which responds automatically through neural–chemical–endocrine processes.

Cognator: subsystem coping mechanism which responds through complex processes of perception and information processing, learning, judgment, and emotion.

Adaptive (Effector) Modes: classification of ways of coping that manifest regulator and cognator activity, that is, physiologic, self-concept, role function, and interdependence.

Adaptive Responses: responses that promote integrity of the person in terms of the goals of survival, growth, reproduction, and mastery.

Ineffective Responses: responses that do not contribute to adaptive goals, that is, survival, growth, reproduction, and mastery.

Health: a state and a process of being and becoming an integrated and whole person.

Environment: internal and external stimuli, or all conditions, circumstances, and influences surrounding, and/or affecting the development and behavior of persons or groups.

A number of nursing authors have included a person's adaptation as basic to a framework for nursing practice (for example, Byrne and Thompson, 1972, and Levine, 1973.) This book will present the theoretical framework of an adaptation model developed by one author, Sister Callista Roy. In Chapter 1 we noted that Roy began her work on the nursing model while she was a graduate student from 1964 to 1966. The elements of the Roy Adaptation Model were introduced briefly in that chapter. This chapter will discuss in greater detail each element of the model: person, goal, health, environment, and nursing activities.

THE PERSON

Nursing care may focus on an individual person, the family or group, a community, or society. At each level, the abstract concept we use to describe the recipient of nursing care is an *adaptive system*, that is, what we can say about the adaptation of people seen one at a time, but always in interaction with other people. Later in this text we will see that our knowledge of an individual as an adaptive system can be applied to groups as adaptive systems. That is, the nurse also can see a family, or other group of persons, as an adaptive system. She may, for example, view the group of people that she works with as an adaptive system with its own way of coping with internal and external demands on the group.

In order to understand persons or groups as adaptive systems, we will first describe the meaning of the term *system*. A broad definition of the term *system* is that it is a set of units so related or connected as to form a unity or whole. We are familiar with the use of the term *system* in such contexts as solar system, traffic system, economic system, and health care system. In each case we could define the parts of the system and show how they are related to make up a whole. A system is a *whole* that functions as a whole by virtue of the interdependence of its *parts*. In addition to having wholeness and related parts, systems also have *inputs, outputs,* and *control* and *feedback* processes. We can illustrate these system characteristics by looking first at a simple mechanical system such as a heating device.

The parts of a mechanical control system are: input, control process, output mechanism, and feedback loop. Figure 2.1 shows these parts in relation to one another. In a simple electrical heating system, these parts function as a whole for the purpose of producing and maintaining heat at a certain temperature. The input for this very simple system has two parts. First,

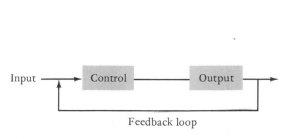

Feedback loop

Figure 2.1   Simple Mechanical Control System. (Reprinted from Sister Callista Roy and Sharon Roberts. *Theory Construction in Nursing: An Adaptation Model.* Englewood Cliffs, N.J.: Prentice-Hall, Inc., 1981, p. 501.)

the input is the location of a preset point on the thermometer indicating the desired temperature. A second form of input is the feedback that comes from the output. This feedback allows the control device to compare the heat produced with the amount of heat needed to reach the temperature that has been preset. Input, in the form of a standard or feedback, often is referred to in systems theory as *information*. The control device is the mechanism that operates the switch according to the environmental temperature. It contains a sensing and regulating thermometer and an electromagnet that will throw the switch for the current. The output device may be a high-resistance wire heated by the passage of an electric current supplied by a central voltage source. The current can be turned on or off by a switch that is open or closed.

We can summarize the notion of a simple mechanical control system by reading the diagram of Fig. 2.1 as follows: Because of the input of a set standard compared with the feedback, the control device instructs the output device as to appropriate action, and the output device produces its output; this output is fed back to the control device. Or, in the familiar terms of a household heating system, we might say: When the heater produces heat, this is fed back into the system and compared with the temperature indicated by our setting of the thermostat to control whether more or less heat is produced.

In moving from the mechanical systems to living systems, we make a transition to more complex and dynamic interaction of parts to make a whole. A living system, however, can also be described as a whole made up of parts that function as a unity for some purpose. The input of living systems involves standards and feedback to direct the functioning of the system.

Roy's description of a person as an adaptive system is illustrated in Fig. 2.2. Inputs for the person as an open system come both externally from the environment outside the person and internally from the self. These inputs have generally been termed *stimuli*.[1] Certain stimuli pool to make up

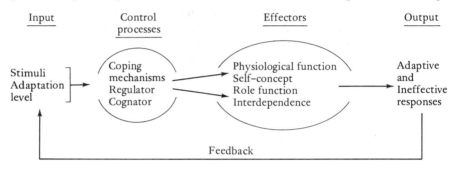

Figure 2.2   Person as an Adaptive System

what Helson (1964) calls the person's *adaptation level*. This level represents a variable standard against which the feedback can be compared. It is like the setting of the thermostat, except that with the living person, the setting does not stay at a fixed point. People constantly have new levels of ability to cope. The adaptation level, then, is a constantly changing point which represents the person's own standard of the range of stimuli that can be tolerated with ordinary efforts.

As we view the control processes of the person as an adaptive system, we consider these by the general term *coping mechanisms*. We know that people have biologic and psychologic abilities to cope with a changing environment. Some biologic mechanisms are genetically determined, such as the amount of antihemophilic factor in the blood, a substance necessary for blood clotting. Other innate mechanisms are common to the species and include such factors as the self-sealing mechanism of the blood vessels. When it is disrupted, the cut end of a blood vessel constricts, thus helping to prevent excessive bleeding. Mechanisms may also be acquired through such

---

[1]A *stimulus* is simply anything that provokes a response. If you prick your finger while sewing, the needle is a stimulus that provokes the response of bleeding and pain.

processes as learning. For example, every student nurse learns how to apply pressure to the site to control local bleeding. Psychological defense mechanisms act in a similar way. If a fact is too anxiety-provoking, one can block it out by the use of mechanisms of denial.[2] Whatever the change in the environment, be it a direct assault that causes injury or a subtle variation in psychological climate, the person has mechanisms to cope with the changing world.

Changes within the environment need not be negative happenings to demand increasing energy to cope with the situation. Daily life is filled with examples of changes that bring about new levels of mastery through extending one's efforts, for example, the challenge to enter a 5-kilometer race or to accept a job promotion. Persons as adaptive systems constantly raise their levels of ability to cope by responding to the challenges of the environment.

Moving from the general notion of coping mechanisms that is common in scientific literature, Roy is developing a nursing science perspective of these adaptive processes. She begins by describing two basic internal processes of the person as a system: the regulator and cognator subsystems.

The *regulator* receives input from the external environment and from changes in the person's internal state. It then processes the changes through neural–chemical–endocrine channels to produce responses. One schematic representation of regulator processes is presented in Fig. 2.3.

In reading Fig. 2.3, the internal and external stimuli are basically chemical or neural and act as inputs to the central nervous system. The chemical stimuli travel through the circulatory system and may be transduced into neural inputs. The spinal cord, brain stem, and autonomic reflexes act through effectors to produce automatic, unconscious effects on the body responses. The chemical stimuli in the circulation influence the endocrine glands to produce the appropriate hormone. The responsiveness of target organs or tissues then effects body responses. By some unknown process, the neural inputs are transformed into conscious perceptions in the brain. Eventually, this perception leads to psychomotor choices of response which activate a body response. These bodily responses, brought about through the chemical–neural–endocrine channels, are fed back as additional stimuli to the regulator system.

An example of a regulator process can be seen by examining the nutritional function of the person. Some of the internal stimuli for maintaining cellular nutrition involve hunger and blood sugar level. The hypothalamus is a center of autonomous control and is responsible for the sensation of hunger. The hypothalamus consists of groups of nuclei that become aggregates of nerve cell bodies. These bodies consist of lateral and medial nuclei which researchers have shown to have important functions in relation to nutrition. According to animal experiments (Langley, 1965), when energy output exceeds energy intake, the lateral nuclei send messages that evoke

---

[2]A complete listing and explanation of common psychological defense mechanisms can be found in any introductory psychology text.

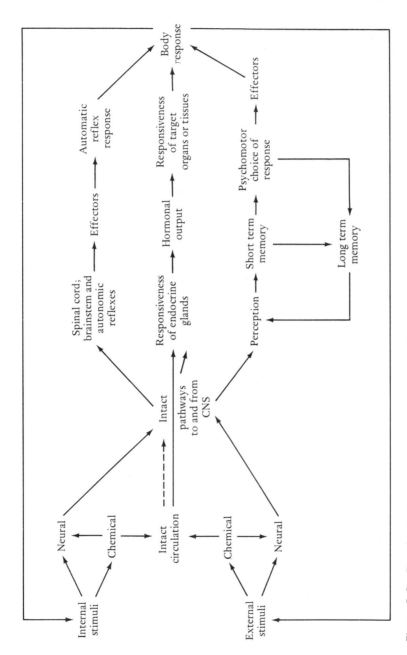

Figure 2.3 Regulator. (Reprinted from Sister Callista Roy and Sharon Roberts. *Theory Construction in Nursing: An Adaptation Model.* Englewood Cliffs, N.J.: Prentice-Hall, Inc., 1981, p. 61.)

hunger contractions. The sensation of hunger then stimulates eating. As food is taken in, the medial nuclei become progressively more active. Messages are then sent to the lateral nuclei, which inhibit the drive for food. When hunger is satiated, the usual response to regulator activity is to stop eating.

The physiological activity involving the blood sugar level's effect on nutrition could be similarly examined as another regulator process. In addition, we know that nutrition is also influenced by such factors as culture, emotional state, appearance of food, and so forth. The regulator mechanisms seldom act alone, but are most often interactive with other human control processes. Developing nursing knowledge will continue to explore this interrelationship, rather than focusing solely on the physiology involved.

The second major adaptive process, according to the Roy Adaptation Model, is the *cognator*. The inputs for the cognator are internal and external stimuli, just as they are for the system as a whole. These inputs vary in intensity and involve psychological and social factors as well as physical and physiological ones, including those that are the output of the regulator mechanisms. These inputs, or changing stimuli, are processed through the various cognitive/emotive pathways. An initial representation of cognator processes was presented by Roy in 1981 and is depicted in Fig. 2.4.

Following the scheme of Fig. 2.4, we will describe the cognator. The internal and external stimuli trigger off four kinds of processes: perceptual/information processing, learning, judgment, and emotion. Within each of these processes, we can place knowledge that is currently known about these human abilities. Under perceptual/information processing, we may consider the person's internal activity of selective attention, coding, and memory. Learning involves such processes as imitation, reinforcement, and insight. The judgment process includes problem solving and decision making. Through the emotional pathways, the person uses defenses to seek relief and affective appraisal and attachment.

These four channels process input stimuli and produce responses. Responses are carried out through the effectors. In this developing theory of a person as an adaptive system, the cognator and the regulator are seen as acting in relation to four *effector modes*: physiologic, self-concept, role function, and interdependence. The modes provide the particular form or manifestations of cognator and regulator activity. Later chapters of this book describe each of these modes in detail and how the nurse observes adaptive and ineffective behavior in each of the four major categories by which people manifest their levels of adaptation.

At this point we can give an example of a cognator process and how it might be manifested in behavior. A student comes to the teacher after the first class of the semester and tells the teacher that she wants to drop the course. As the teacher talks with the student, she learns that the student

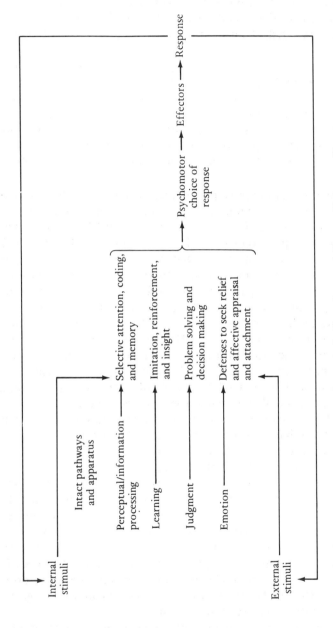

Figure 2.4 Cognator. (Reprinted from Sister Callista Roy and Sharon Roberts. *Theory Construction in Nursing: An Adaptation Model.* Englewood Cliffs, N.J.: Prentice-Hall, Inc., 1981, p. 64.)

perceived an unusual amount and quality of work being demanded as the outline of the course was presented by the teacher. The student has focused attention on this one aspect of the situation and ignored other aspects, such as her abilities, interests, and future goals in this field. Although selective attention is an appropriate mechanism in some situations, in this case it has led to a constricted view of the situation so that the student acts hastily based only on the information to which she is attending. Her behavior manifests one form of cognator activity.[3]

Although the theoretical work on cognator and regulator processes is still in the beginning stages, we can already say that the complex relationships between cognator and regulator can lead us to further understandings of the holistic nature of the human person. Nurses can explore the basic coping mechanisms of each person. Hopefully, they can help persons use their abilities more effectively to promote adaptation. In this way, nursing can contribute to increasing levels of wellness without an overuse of some of the common medications or surgical interventions being used today.

Within these broad coping mechanisms of regulator and cognator, the individual nurse will identify specific coping abilities as used by the person she is working with. One person, for example, may try to cope with anxiety by overeating, while another person may deal with anxiety by feeling unable to eat. Some day we may be able to describe an overall pattern of common coping mechanisms most frequently used, and within this, the nurse may be able to identify a unique combination of mechanisms used by a particular person.

The output of the system comprises *adaptive* and *ineffective responses*. Adaptive responses are those that promote the integrity[4] of the person in terms of the goals of the human system: survival, growth, reproduction, and mastery.

We have been discussing the scientific assumptions about viewing the person as an adaptive system. The Roy Adaptation Model adds humanistic values to this scientific concept. Humanism, in both philosophy and psychology, explores beliefs and values about persons. Maslow (1968, p. iii) notes that humanistic psychology more recently has become an established alternative to behavioristic psychology. Roy finds it important at this time to be more explicit about the humanistic value base of her nursing model. In the process of developing the scientific assumptions of the model, these values received little attention in the earlier writings.

---

[3]This interpretation of the situation is oversimplified for use as an example. Because the person functions as a whole, all the other cognator processes, such as memory or avoidance of anxiety, could also be considered, as well as any regulator influences.

[4]Integrity has to do with soundness, or an unimpaired condition that can lead to completeness and unity.

Historically, nursing has been concerned about the value of the human person. Women of early Christian times took up the work of caring for the sick. Through many changes in health care, concern and caring for persons have been the heritage of nursing. Today, we continue to clarify and express these values in nursing practice.

As humanistic nurses, we believe in the person's own creative power. Roy places emphasis on the person's own coping abilities. Nurses see processes moving purposefully and not merely as chains of cause and effect. Roy views adaptation as an ongoing purposive process. Nursing's holistic approach is rooted in humanism. Roy's theoretical work is attempting to describe persons' functioning holistically and to point out holistic approaches to nursing care of persons. Nursing accepts the humanistic approach of valuing other persons' opinions and viewpoints. We will see later how Roy builds this approach into the nursing process. Nursing has long recognized the significance of interpersonal relatonships. This humanistic value also is basic to the Roy Adaptation Model's nursing process.

Summarizing the Roy Adaptation Model's view of the person, we can say that the person is an adaptive system with cognator and regulator acting to maintain adaptation in regard to the four adaptive modes. Underlying this scientific notion of the person are the humanistic values of nursing which Roy continues to make explicit.

THE GOAL OF NURSING

In Chapter 1 we noted that the second essential element of a model for nursing practice is the goal of nursing. To understand the author's approach to nursing, we must be able to state the specific goal of nursing according to the model. The goal is the outcome of nursing action stated in broad terms.

Since the Roy Adaptation Model views the person as an adaptive system, the *goal* of nursing within this model can be stated most simply as: *to promote adaptation.* There are many descriptions of adaptation in fields such as biology, psychology, anthropology, and others. Waterman (1968), a biologist, states that "organisms are self-regulating, adaptive systems, capable of autoduplication." They acquire energy from the environment to do their biological work and act thermodynamically as irreversible chemical machines. To be self-regulating and adaptive, control and information are essential. Mechanisms must provide at once the basis for the organism's steady state and dynamic activity as well as the adaptiveness required for its survival.

Nursing is dealing with the person, not only as a biological organism, but as a holistic adaptive system. Therefore, Roy attempts to describe adaptation as a process involving holistic functioning to affect health positively.

The work of Helson (1964), a physiological psychologist, provides a beginning point for this description of adaptation.

Helson (1964) states that an adaptive response is a function of the stimulus that is input to the adaptive person and that person's adaptation level. The adaptation level is determined by the pooled effect of three classes of stimuli: (1) focal stimuli, or stimuli immediately confronting persons; (2) contextual stimuli, or all other stimuli present, either within persons as their internal condition or coming as input from the environment; and (3) residual stimuli, such as beliefs, attitudes, or traits which have an indeterminate effect on the present situation. By Helson's definition, then, adaptation is a process of responding positively to environmental changes in such a way as to decrease responses necessary to cope with the stimuli and increase sensitivity to respond to other stimuli.

A person's ability to respond positively, or to adapt, depends on the degree of the change taking place and the state of the person coping with the change. Thus, if the weather changes by the temperature dropping 20 degrees in 24 hours, and the person is normally healthy and has frequently experienced such changes in temperature, the person responds positively, or adapts to the change. On the other hand, if the temperature change is extreme, say 150 degrees in 24 hours (not unheard of when it is possible to fly from the equator to the North Pole in a matter of hours, and soon it may be common to have to cope with temperature changes associated with entering and leaving the earth's atmosphere), the person may not adapt without special efforts or assistance. Similarly, if the change is not so extreme, but a person's ability to adapt is limited, for example, through an illness such as pneumonia or through limited experience such as living only in a very mild climate, there will be difficulty in adapting.

We are equating the degree of change with Helson's notion of the focal stimulus and the person's ability to respond positively with adaptation level. Another researcher (Peak, 1955) noted that the adaptation level sets up a zone within which stimulation will lead to a positive or adaptive response. This is illustrated in Fig. 2.5. On the other hand, stimuli that fall outside the zone lead to negative or ineffective responses, as shown in Fig. 2.6.

Nursing aims to increase the person's adaptive responses and to decrease ineffective responses. We might ask how a nurse is to judge which responses are adaptive and which responses are ineffective. From our discussion thus far, we might say that an adaptive response is one that decreases the amount of energy needed to cope with the given situation and increases energy for other human processes. For example, when a patient has adapted to the change of having a surgical incision, this person's energies are no longer bound up with that one stimulus. Rather than talking about it, protecting it, and being aware of it in every action, the person forgets about it, and puts energies into such things as planning to go home, and

Figure 2.5 Adaptation: positive response.

to return to work. The Roy Adaptation Model assumes that when energy is freed from ineffective behavior, it can be used for promoting health.

The Roy Adaptation Model adds humanistic values to the scientific assumptions of systems theory and adaptation level theory. Based on these values, we can expand the notion of adaptation. Roy believes in a dynamic purpose for human existence. In a general sense, the goals of persons include survival, growth, reproduction, and mastery. Adaptive behavior, then, is behavior that leads to these goals for the individual. Or, as noted earlier, an adaptive response is behavior that maintains the integrity of the individual. An ineffective response is behavior that does not lead to these goals, or that disrupts the integrity of the individual. Throughout this text we will illustrate this definition of adaptation as it is applied in clinical situations. In Chapter 13 we will relate the concept of adaptation to the concept of stress. We may summarize the *goal* of nursing, according to the Roy model, as the promotion of adaptation in the four adaptive modes, thereby contributing to health, quality of life, and dying with dignity.

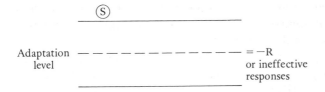

Figure 2.6 Adaptation: ineffective response.

Health

In the discussion of adaptation, we noted that Roy assumes that the person's adapted state frees one to respond to other stimuli. This freeing of energy links the concept of adaptation to the concept of health. When energy is freed from ineffective coping attempts, this energy can promote healing and enhance health.

As the concept of wellness has evolved, it has long meant more than the absence of disease, but has included an emphasis on states of well-being.

The literature about holistic health in recent years has emphasized such dimensions of wellness as the following: self-responsibility, nutritional awareness, physical fitness, stress management, and environmental sensitivity.

The evolving concept of health, according to the Roy Adaptation Model, includes the notion that adaptation is a process of promoting integrity. Integrity implies soundness or an unimpaired condition that can lead to completeness or unity. *Health*, then, is defined as a state and a process of being and becoming an integrated and whole person.

Environment

According to the Roy Adaptation Model, we have described the person's *environment* as internal and external stimuli. Stated more broadly, environment may be considered as all conditions, circumstances, and influences surrounding and affecting the development and behavior of persons or groups. In Chapter 4 some significant factors that act as internal and external environment for the person are discussed.

Nursing Activities

The Roy Adaptation Model of nursing implies a process similar to that which has been developed over the years of nursing history. The nurse first assesses behavior in each of the adaptive modes. This is called *first-level assessment*. Then she selects areas of concern, either ineffective behaviors or adaptive behaviors needing reinforcing. For each of these the nurse moves to *second-level assessment* and determines the focal, contextual, and residual stimuli contributing to each behavior. Based on this assessment, the nurse diagnoses the related adaptation situation. Since the behavior to be changed or reinforced has been identified, the nurse can easily establish a nursing goal. This goal is stated in terms of the anticipated behavioral outcome agreed upon by the person and the nurse. Nursing approaches are then selected to accomplish the nursing goal. In general, these approaches are aimed at managing the focal, contextual, or residual stimuli. In this way, factors that are precipitating ineffective behavior are changed, or the person's ability to cope—as determined by the adaptation level—is broadened. The nurse manages the person's internal and external stimulus configuration by removing, increasing, decreasing, or altering the focal, contextual, and residual stimuli. Behavioral outcomes are then evaluated, and nursing approaches modified as necessary. This total nursing process is explored in detail in Chapter 3.

SUMMARY

In this chapter we have considered the elements of the Roy Adaptation Model of nursing: person, goal, health, environment, and nursing activities. Figure 2.7 is a schematic representation of the relationships between these major concepts. That is, persons or adaptive systems interact with environment and move toward the goal of adaptation and health. The nursing process based on the model influences that movement. In this chapter special emphasis was placed on the model's view of the person as an adaptive system and on the concept of adaptation. Each concept and each relationship will be explored further in the ongoing process of developing nursing knowledge based on this model and in efforts to validate that knowledge through research.

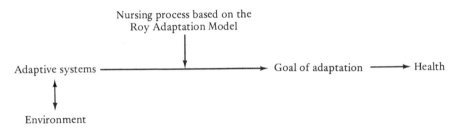

Figure 2-7   Relationships between the major concepts of the Roy Adaptation Model of nursing.

STUDENT LEARNING ACTIVITY

Select another author who has written about the Roy Adaptation Model of nursing, or a nurse who is experienced in using the Roy Adaptation Model, and compare the views expressed about the person as an adaptive system with the views discussed in this chapter. Identify the similarities and the differences you note.

REFERENCES

Byrne, Marjorie, and Leda F. Thompson. *Key Concepts for the Study and Practice of Nursing.* St. Louis: The C. V. Mosby Company, 1972.

Helson, Harry. *Adaptation Level Theory.* New York: Harper & Row, Publishers, 1964.

Langley, L. L. *Homeostasis.* New York: Reinhold Publishing Corporation, 1965.

Levine, Myrna. *Introduction to Clinical Nursing.* Philadelphia: F. A. Davis Company, 1973.

Maslow, Abraham H. *Toward a Psychology of Being*, 2nd ed. New York: Van Nostrand Reinhold Company, 1968.

Peak, Helen. "Attitude and Motivation," in *Nebraska Symposium on Motivation*, Marshall R. Jones, ed. Lincoln: University of Nebraska Press, 1955.

Roy, Sister Callista and S. Roberts, *Theory Construction in Nursing: An Adaptation Model*. Englewood Cliffs, N. J.: Prentice-Hall, Inc., 1981, pp. 63–66.

Waterman, Talbot H. "Systems Theory and Biology—View of a Biologist," in *Systems Theory and Biology*, D. Mesarovic, ed. New York: Springer-Verlag, 1968, pp. 1–37.

ADDITIONAL READINGS

Galbreath, J. S. "Sister Callista Roy," in Nursing Theories Conference Group, *Nursing Theories: The Base for Professional Nursing Practice*. Englewood Cliffs, N. J.: Prentice-Hall, Inc., 1980.

Galligan, A. C. "Using Roy's Concept of Adaptation to Care for Young Children," *The American Journal of Maternal–Child Nursing*, vol. 4, 1979, pp. 24–28.

Porth, C. M. "Physiological Coping: A Model for Teaching Pathophysiology," *Nursing Outlook*, vol. 25, 1977, pp. 781–784.

Randell, Brooke, Mary Poush Tedrow, and Joyce Van Landingham. *Adaptation Nursing: The Roy Conceptual Model Applied*. St. Louis: The C. V. Mosby Company, 1982.

Roy, Sister Callista. "Adaptation: A Conceptual Framework for Nursing," *Nursing Outlook*, vol. 18, no. 3, March 1970, pp. 43–45.

Roy, Sister Callista. "Adaptation: A Basis for Nursing Practice," *Nursing Outlook*, vol. 19, no. 4, April 1971, pp. 254–257.

Chapter 3

The Roy Model Nursing Process

Sister Callista Roy

BEHAVIORAL OBJECTIVES:

After studying this chapter, the reader will be able to:

1. Define the key concepts of the chapter.
2. Illustrate reasons for using a problem-solving-based nursing process.
3. Describe three ways to make a nursing diagnosis.
4. Distinguish between all human behavior and the behavior the nurse assesses.
5. Specify methods of assessing behavior.
6. Differentiate focal, contextual, and residual stimuli.
7. Identify a nursing goal that is stated as a behavioral outcome for the person.
8. Apply the nursing judgment model to an ordinary decision in life.

KEY CONCEPTS DEFINED

Nursing Process: a problem-solving procedure used by the nurse to gather data, identify problems, select and implement approaches, and evaluate the results of care aimed at promoting health, quality of life, and dying with dignity.

Human Behavior: actions or reactions under specified circumstances.

Behavior Assessed by the Nurse: the person's responses to environmental changes that require further adaptive responses. These responses can be observed or measured or are subjectively reported.

First-Level Assessment: gathering data about behavior in each adaptive mode by skillful observation, accurate measurement of responses, and communicative interviewing.

Nursing Interview: structured interaction with the person to obtain subjective data about individual responses to changes in health and illness.

Norm: a standard of behavior to guide judgment about what promotes integrity.

Second-Level Assessment: identification of the focal, contextual, and residual factors that influence the person.

Focal Stimulus: the degree of change or stimulus most immediately confronting the person and the one to which the person must make an adaptive response, that is, the factor that precipitates the behavior.

Contextual Stimuli: all other stimuli present that contribute to the behavior caused or precipitated by the focal stimulus.

Residual Stimuli: factors that may be affecting behavior but whose effects are not validated.

Nursing Diagnosis: the nurse's interpretation of assessment data stated as a summary label for one mode, as a statement of the behaviors within one mode, with the most relevant influencing factors, or as a label that summarizes a behavioral pattern with more than one mode being affected by the same stimuli.

Setting Priorities: a procedure inherent throughout the nursing process by which the nurse determines the hierarchy of importance of nursing actions.

Goal Setting: establishing clear statements of the behavioral outcomes of nursing care for the person.

Intervention: selection and carrying out of an approach to change or stabilize adaptation by managing stimuli.

Evaluation: judging the effectiveness of the nursing intervention by looking at the effect it had on the adaptive behavior.

The *nursing process* has been identified as a particular format for nursing activities. In many nursing service departments, some steps of this process are written out in a formal *nursing care plan*. The various nurse theorists, some of whom were discussed in Chapter 1, have their own way of describing the steps of the nursing process. Each specific description identifies the theorist's unique perspective of the developing science of nursing.

In their broadest outlines, however, all these particular approaches to the nursing process follow steps similar to those used by other health professionals. This stepwise procedure is the problem-solving process. In using this process, the person first gathers data, then identifies the problem. An approach to the problem is selected from among possible alternatives, and finally the results of the approach are evaluated. As we explore the Roy Adaptation Model nursing process in this chapter, this general outline will be apparent, but the specifics of nursing based on this model will also be clarified. The Roy Adaptation Model determines for nurses what data to collect, how to identify the problem and essential goals, what approach to use, and how to evaluate the effectiveness of the approach.

THE RATIONALE FOR THE NURSING PROCESS

There are two major reasons why nursing uses a problem-solving-based nursing process. The first reason is the person-centered goal of nursing. The second is the accountability of the profession as a scientific discipline which is practice oriented.

We have described nursing's goal, according to the Roy Model, as to promote adaptation in the adaptive modes, thus contributing to health, quality of life, and dying with dignity. Persons as individuals, members of families, or as members of the communities are the recipients of nursing care. Each person copes differently with changes in health status. Since nursing is to help persons adapt to these changes, the nurse must be able to identify clearly the person's level of adaptation and coping abilities to define any difficulties so that she may intervene to promote adaptation. Any nurse who gives nursing care can verify that no two persons are alike. Even given a common medical diagnosis, people present unique ways of coping with their situations. One person will be able to cope well with the pain following an appendectomy. Another will find the pain intolerable. Since the goal of nursing is to promote adaptation, the nurse must go through the process of assessing adaptation and planning accordingly for each individual. Only in this way can she fulfill the person-centered goal of nursing.

As a scientific discipline, nursing must be accountable for its practice within society. To maintain itself as a needed service, nursing must be able to verify that its practice makes a difference in terms of what is valued by society. The experience of fluctuation in health status is a universal phenomenon. Even the most robust of persons will at some time in life experience such fluctuations. It seems accurate to say that most people will also at some time experience difficulty in coping with these changes. According to the Roy Adaptation Model of nursing, nursing aims to promote this adaptation throughout life. It is a basic assumption of the model that this service is valued by society. Nursing must then validate that it can, in fact, affect a person's adaptation. It can do this only if it can demonstrate by using a scientific approach that nursing activities can change a situation of ineffective behavior into a situation of adaptation. To do this the nurse must assess adaptation, plan care, and evaluate the effectiveness of her approach.

Thus the problem-solving nursing process is required by the person-centered goal of nursing and by the need to verify the service that the nurse provides. The rest of this chapter shows how this process is developed according to the Roy Adaptation Model of nursing.

STEP ONE: ASSESSMENT OF BEHAVIORS

The first step of the problem-solving-based nursing process is data collection. The Roy Adaptation Model outlines the data the nurse collects. Since the nurse's goal is to promote adaptation, she must first evaluate the current level of adaptation. We described in Chapter 2 that the person, as an adaptive system, manifests adaptation through behavior that is adaptive or ineffective. Furthermore, Roy's concept of how this behavior comes about was outlined.

The person receives input from the internal and external environment. Part of the person's internal environment is an individual adaptation level relative to the situation. This level is like the setting on a thermostat and indicates a range within which the person can easily cope with the new input. For example, some persons have a low setting for tolerance of pain while others may have a higher setting. As one adventurer stated after skydiving over the North Pole, "I've been doing a lot of things that people think are exceptional, but I don't think they are. You see, people make their own limits." (McCann, 1983, p. 110). As stimuli enter the person-system, the control processes of regulator and cognator coping mechanisms are activated. These processes involve chemical–neural–endocrine and cognitive–emotional pathways. Based on the person's own development of regulator and cognator coping mechanisms, coping behavior is manifested.

Observations of a large number of persons in many health care situations (Roy, 1971) resulted in classifying observable behavior into four categories: physiologic, self-concept, role function, and interdependence. Roy has proposed (Roy and Roberts, 1981) that these four categories represent modes of adaptive behavior. That is, physiologic, self-concept, role function, and interdependence are the broad categories within which the cognator and regulator function to meet human needs. The output of the person system that can be observed, then, is behavior in each of the adaptive modes. This behavior is the nurse's first unit of observation in the assessment process.

Behavior Assessed by the Nurse

Human behavior is defined generally as actions or reactions under specified circumstances. Thus, if a psychologist is testing a person's learning of nonsense syllables, the measured behavior is the response of repeating the syllables under the conditions specified, for example, in a dark room with no sensory input. At the same time, the person will have internal responses, which the psychologist can also monitor. The psychologist may also have leads attached to the subject to measure any increase in heart rate. Since this increase is also a response to the situation, it is also called a behavior. Behaviors, then, may be internal or external. Some internal behaviors, at the present stage of sophistication of behavioral science, can only be subjectively reported. If the subject who is repeating the nonsense syllables knows that the performance has been poor, that person may feel disappointed. For the psychologist to be aware of this internal response, the subject must give some report of feelings, either verbally or in some clearly manifested, nonverbal communication.

We can now describe generally the object of the nurse's first level of assessment. The nurse looks at the person's responses, internal or external, that can be observed or measured, or which are subjectively reported.

Our definition of human behavior stated that it comprised reactions under specified circumstances. The nursing model must point out what those circumstances are. The Roy Adaptation Model of nursing states that changes in internal and external environmental input trigger the coping mechanisms. At times the environmental changes are outside the person's zone of positive adaptation. The specific circumstance under which the nurse observes human behavior, then, is change in internal and external stimuli that places stress on the person's regulator and cognator coping abilities.

Our general description of *behavior assessed by the nurse* can be summarized as *the person's responses to environmental changes that require further adaptive responses. These responses can be observed or measured or subjectively reported.*

If the nurse is to look at behavior resulting from environmental changes that strain a person's coping mechanisms, she must know what behavior manifests this strain. An ongoing part of developing the science of nursing is generating an outline, or assessment guide, of what responses to observe. Nursing texts, nursing instructors, and nurses in clinical practice help clarify what observations will provide data about a person's current level of adaptation.

At the present time we may define a person's heart rate, or pulse, or respiration as measurements indicating responses to changes affecting oxygenation. The nurse will thus observe these measurements. Subjective reports regarding self-worth may be indicators of responses to changes affecting self-esteem. Thus the nurse will be aware that these are some of the behaviors she assesses. Specifying behaviors to observe in each of the adaptive modes is one objective of the remaining chapters of this book. Each chapter should be read with the purpose of outlining clearly what behavior to assess.

Methods of Assessing Behavior

How the nurse assesses behavior is basically the same process for all nurses, but how the process unfolds is largely a function of the circumstances in which she meets the person. When the student nurse is learning to assess behavior she may look at only one adaptive mode or one response at a time. Thus she may describe only one set of behaviors relative to that mode. When the independent nurse practitioner[1] is describing the total adaptation problems of a person, she may systematically gather data regarding each adaptive mode. Similarly, the clinical specialist or primary care nurse in the hospital setting may make a total assessment of the person on admission to initiate the plan for nursing care. The team leader or associate nurse may update that plan by quickly assessing presenting behavior in each mode for a group of persons. The nurse in an acute situation, such as an emergency room or critical care unit, may be summoned by one presenting behavior, such as a change in cardiac rhythm. Assessment of this behavior takes precedence over a total adaptation assessment. Although such variations in use of the assessment process are recognized, the basic process of assessment will be discussed.

In assessing behaviors—that is, making *first-level assessment*—the nurse systematically looks at behavior in each adaptive mode. She does this by means of her observation skills, her ability to measure internal and external responses, and her interviewing skills to obtain subjective data.

In the skill of observing the nurse uses all of her senses to obtain data about responses to changes in need states. She may see cyanotic skin color, hear a trembling voice, feel a weakened pulse, or smell foul excreta. When she is making an initial assessment, she goes through a systematic process of gathering data through her senses regarding each adaptive mode. The specific data to be gathered are discussed in the chapters on the adaptive modes. When she makes contact with the person later, she quickly turns her attention to each known area of importance. The data enter the nurse's perception and are quickly processed as behavior indicative of responses in regard to given adaptive modes. There are times when a behavior may be

---

[1] The terms used here for various roles of the nurse can be found described in texts that deal with issues in the profession. See, for example, Kelly (1981).

indicative of responses in more than one mode. For example, if the nurse observes hard, dry stools, this may be a response to the body's need to adapt to changes in food and fluid intake, for example, after surgery. On the other hand, this behavior could be indicative of slowing peristalsis due to self-concept changes taking place following a loss. Behaviors that the nurse observes through her senses are classified as clearly as possible according to the adaptive mode about which they speak. Sometimes more than one mode is identified so that interrelated modes may be analyzed together.

At the present time, the nurse's ability to measure internal and external responses is limited in some areas. Certain measurements, for example, determining arterial and venous pressures of the blood, are well established and defined. Each nurse learns these in basic nursing education, and techniques can be found in any basic textbook of nursing skills. Other measures are only in the early stages of testing. Some nurses have experimented with paper-and-pencil tests to measure certain aspects of adaptation (see, for example, Idle, 1977).

For other responses to environmental changes in health and illness, there are as yet no known nursing tests. We do not know how to measure the body's response to the increased need for rest during convalescent stages. Nor do we know how to measure the adequacy of expressive role responses when there is a role change in health and illness.[2] At this point we can say that the nurse systematically utilizes the known tools for measuring internal and external responses to changes during health and illness. At the same time the nurse is alert to developing and testing new methods of measuring adaptive behavior.

The *interview* is one generalized tool the nurse uses to assess behavior. It is potentially her most important tool. Adaptive responses to situations of health and illness have a largely subjective element. When the body is adjusting to a decrease in oxygen, only the person can feel the subjective state of anxiety and panic. The feeling of loneliness in the absence of a loved one is perceived only by the person. Thus the nurse must be able to structure her interaction with the individual in such a way as to obtain these subjective data. The term *interview* is used to describe this process, whether it involves a structured set of questions asked at one time or the purposeful listening with little comment spaced throughout the nurse–patient relationship.

The person and his or her subjective experience of responses to changes in health and illness are the subject of the nursing interview. To obtain these data, the nurse must maintain open lines of communication with the person. The process of communication involves a sender, a message, and a receiver. Communication has been successfully accomplished when a message is understood by the receiver in the appropriate manner in which the sender intended. Since the nurse is trying, in the assessment phase of the

---

[2]A tool for measuring adequacy of instrumental role behaviors of the mother of the hospitalized child has been developed. See Roy (1967).

nursing process, to receive a message, she encourages the person's participation.[3] The nurse does this by using open-ended questions, paraphrasing, reflection of perceived meaning, and gesturing such as nodding and leaning forward. The nurse must also be skillful in nonstructured interviewing and in the purposeful use of silence within the trusting nurse–patient relationship to get the maximum benefit of the person's subjective perception of his or her own adaptive status.

Thus as any nurse begins the process of assessment, whether her client be a person in a critical care unit or a pregnant woman in a prenatal clinic, or whether her client be a family or the community at large, the nurse notes behavior in each adaptive mode by means of skillful observation, accurate measurement of responses, and communicative interviewing. This is the process of first-level nursing assessment.

Judgment about Behaviors of Concern

The first step in the nursing process, assessment of behavior, culminates in a nursing judgment about whether or not the behavior is of concern to the nurse and/or to the person. In general, the nurse determines, in collaboration with the person, whether the behavior is adaptive or ineffective. As noted in Chapter 2, *adaptive* responses are those that promote the integrity of the person in terms of the goals of the person-system: survival, growth, reproduction, and mastery. *Ineffective* responses are those that do not contribute to these goals.

For certain responses, we have *norms* to guide our judgments about what promotes integrity. For example, there is a range of pulse rates, blood pressures, and temperature readings for various age groups which are considered indicators of physiologic integrity for that group. For other behaviors such norms do not exist. We do not know what level of expression of grief about a loss is actually helpful to promote psychic integrity. In all areas, norms are merely guidelines. They are not applied rigidly and to the same extent in all instances. For example, pulse varies by age groups, and expression of grief varies by culture. In addition, the process of the evolving capabilities of the human species seems to indicate that norms will continue to change. Examples frequently cited include the height and weight charts for the growth in childhood and the sleep and activity cycles of both the young and the old. In some instances, however, it is possible to identify an area of concern by recognizing that, by some standard or norm, a response either promotes or interferes with the integrity of the individual or group. Thus when a person with a specified fluid deficit drinks water, this behavior is adaptive, since it will promote physiologic integrity. On the other hand, if

---

[3]The use of communication as a therapeutic tool of intervention by the nurse is discussed in other texts. See, for example, Hein (1980).

this person refuses to drink, the behavior can be considered ineffective in meeting the goal of physiologic survival.

To judge adaptability in areas where norms are not available, the nurse applies some general criteria hypothesized by the Roy Adaptation Model of nursing to the specific circumstances. The general signs of adaptation difficulty are identified as pronounced regulator activity with cognator ineffectiveness (Roy, 1970). Some observations indicative of pronounced regulator activity are: increase in heart rate or blood pressure, tension, excitement, or loss of appetite. Responses that demonstrate cognator ineffectiveness include (1) faulty perceptual/information processing, (2) ineffective learning, (3) poor judgment, and (4) inappropriate affect. In general, the nurse asks herself whether the behavior she observes is a useless spending of energy that does not leave the person free to respond to other stimuli; or, she asks whether the behavior effectively frees energy for promoting health.

Thus if the nurse observes excessive bleeding, she knows that pronounced regulator activity will be present and that bodily energies are drained from the getting-well process to the process of coping with the emergency of hemorrhage. In this case, the behavior can be labeled as quite clearly ineffective. In the realm of the cognator, if a mother whose newborn infant died several days previously continues to repeat misperceptions about the cause of the baby's death, the nurse can recognize cognator ineffectiveness. The mother's energies are being bound up with responding needlessly to inaccurate perceptions and are not free for other activities, such as relating to those closest to her. The mother's ineffective perceptual processing may interfere with the emotional attachments she needs at this time.

As the nurse makes judgments about the adaptability of behavior, she must be continually aware that the person will be involved in this judgment process. The person is often the best judge of whether or not behavior is effective in coping with a given stimuli. (Recall the example noted earlier of the North Pole adventurer who makes his own limits.) For example, a patient may tell the nurse that the hospital bedtime routines do not result in a good night's sleep for him. Or the son of an elderly patient may share with the nurse the fact that he is having a very difficult time making a decision about how to provide convalescent care for his father. The nurse should always take the person's observations of his or her own behavior into account in making a judgment about whether the behavior is adaptive or ineffective. The range of adaptive responses is wide. Norms are broad and circumstances change the judgment about whether a behavior is adaptive or ineffective.

The nurse is concerned about any behaviors that are obviously ineffective in relation to the immediate integrity of individuals or those about them. She is also concerned about adaptive behaviors that could become ineffective as environmental conditions continue to change, or that might become ineffective if they are prolonged beyond their usefulness. An example of the latter might be prolonged denial in the grief process, which eventually interferes with resolution of the loss. When the person identifies that his or her own responses are not promoting personal goals, this behavior is also one of concern.

Summary of First-Level Assessment

In the first step of the nursing process, the nurse gathers data about behavior in each of the adaptive modes. The behaviors she assesses are the person's responses to environmental changes. These changes require a further adaptive response. The resulting response can be observed or measured or it can be subjectively reported. The behaviors to be observed in each mode are further identified throughout this book. The nurse uses skillful observation, known tools of measurement, and interview to gather data about behavior. First-level assessment is completed with a tentative judgment about whether the behavior is adaptive or ineffective. Criteria used in making this judgment include: whether or not the behavior promotes integrity of the individual, whether or not there is regulator and cognator effectiveness, and whether or not the person perceives the behavior as adaptive.

STEP TWO: ASSESSMENT OF INFLUENCING FACTORS

Once the nurse has tentatively identified behaviors of concern, she can proceed to the next step of the assessment process, called *second-level assessment*. This step involves the assessment of the factors that influence the behaviors of concern. She is interested in ineffective behaviors because she wants to change them to adaptive behaviors. And she is interested in adaptive behaviors because she wants to maintain or enhance these behaviors, particularly if the person's coping abilities are threatened by changing influencing factors.[4] With the realities of time constraints and other limitations of the nursing situation, the nurse cannot consider all behaviors equally important to assess further. At this point she will have to begin setting priorities about what behaviors are most important for her consideration. Principles for setting priorities are discussed below. When she has set priorities and identified the most significant behaviors, she then identifies the focal, contextual, and residual stimuli influencing or contributing to these behaviors.

[4]In situations where all presenting behaviors appear adaptive, it may be necessary to carry out second-level assessment to identify potential threats to that adaptation. This observation was suggested to the author by a graduate student at the University of Connecticut, Karen Des Rosiers.

Identifying Focal Stimuli

The *focal stimulus* has been described as the degree of change that precipitated the behavior being observed. This stimulus is the one most immediately confronting the person and the one to which the person must make an adaptive response. It may be an environmental change, such as the occupancy of a single bed in a double hospital room instead of occupancy of a double bed in a private bedroom. Or it may be a change in a relationship, such as increased presence and solicitude of in-laws after the birth of a baby. Possible focal stimuli for given behaviors are identified throughout the chapters on the specific adaptive modes. The nurse uses the same method in assessing the focal stimuli that she used in assessing behaviors. That is, she makes skillful observations, collects measurements for which she has appropriate tools, and interviews the persons involved. When she has made a hypothesis about with what stimulus the person is having difficulty coping, she shares this hunch with the person, if possible, to obtain validation of her assessment. Ida Jean Orlando (1961) emphasized the importance of sharing such observations with the person. With the current awareness of patient rights and with the Roy Adaptation Model value of the individual person, it is important that the person be involved in every phase of the plan for care. This involvement has already begun in the step of first-level assessment and is continued in the second-level assessment—assessment of influencing factors.

We should point out that what is behavior observed in one adaptive mode may become the focal stimulus for another mode. Thus grieving behavior, when loss is the focal stimulus affecting self-concept, may itself be focal to causing behavior indicative of role function. For example, the nurse may notice that a mother is unable at a given time to fulfill the role of consoler in the family. Her own grief behavior of crying and talking about a child she has lost is the stimulus causing her to fail to respond to a sibling's questions and concerns about the loss.

At the same time, one focal stimulus can affect more than one adaptive mode. Hemorrhage is an immediate threat to the need for oxygen, but at the same time, the patient may feel self-consistency threatened by the fear of death. In any case, in assessing the focal stimulus, the nurse is looking for the most immediate cause of the observed behavior.

Identifying Contextual Stimuli

Contextual stimuli are those contributing to the behavior caused or precipitated by the focal stimulus. They are all other stimuli present that affect the behavior being observed. Again, the stimulus may be external, such as surrounding conditions, or internal, such as factors within the person.

For example, a hospitalized school-age boy has the ineffective role behavior of not studying. The focal stimulus has been identified as the fact that his usual schedule is missing. However, contributing to the effect of this stimulus is the internal factor that until yesterday he felt "sick" and the external factors of being in isolation and of the usual rewards of school and home being missing. These are considered contextual stimuli. Contextual stimuli are identified by the same process of observation, measurement, interview, and validation.

Nurses sometimes ask whether stimuli can be both positive and negative. That is, does the nurse identify factors that make the behavior more adaptive at the same time that she searches for those that contribute to making it ineffective? The answer is that at times it may be important to know stimuli which are tugging in a direction opposite to the focal stimulus because these can be capitalized on to change the effect of the focal stimulus. For example, if a supportive mother is contributing to promoting a young woman's adaptation to her new mothering role, she should be identified as a positive contextual stimulus. In the intervention phase, to be discussed later, the nurse may be able to make this stimulus more focal.

In summarizing earlier work on the Roy Adaptation Model, Martinez (1976) identified the following contextual factors as influencing all adaptive modes: genetic makeup, sex, developmental stage, drugs, alcohol, tobacco, self-concept, role functions, interdependence, social interaction patterns, coping mechanisms and styles, physical and emotional stress, cultural orientation, religion, and physical environment. Throughout this text, significant contextual stimuli are discussed in relation to each of the adaptive modes. Chapter 4 provides a more thorough consideration of the major influencing stimuli that are often contextual. These include cultural factors such as socioeconomic standing, religion, and ethnicity; family influence, including structures and tasks; and growth and development, particularly stages of development.

As the nurse assesses stimuli affecting a person's behavior, she is mindful that changing circumstances can change the significance of the stimuli. What is contextual at one moment may become focal at another. For example, the presence or absence of a loved one may be taken for granted as the backdrop or a contextual stimulus for other more focal concerns. However, if a sudden change occurs, such as death or separation from the person, the absence of the person becomes focal and the other concerns become contextual. The image of a kaleidoscope[5] can be used to portray this rearrangement of parts in relation to each other and to the whole. (See Fig. 3.1.) A careful assessment of all relevant contextual stimuli is important for the ongoing process of assessment and for making nursing diagnoses and planning nursing intervention.

[5]The image of the kaleidoscope in connection with the Roy Adaptation Model of nursing was first suggested by Patricia Whalen, a graduate student at the University of San Diego.

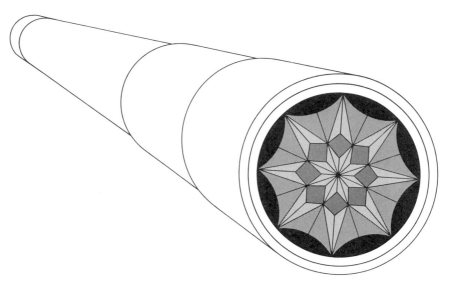

Figure 3.1   The kaleidoscope as an image of the Roy Adaptation Model of nursing.

Identifying Residual Stimuli

The third category of influencing factors that the nurse assesses is called *residual stimuli.* In a study of adaptation levels by Helson (1964), he noted the influence of past experiences on present behavior. In experiments of persons lifting successive sets of weights, the judgments of heaviness of each weight were systematically affected by whether heavier or lighter weights had been lifted before. The notion that Helson is describing is that many factors from past experience are relevant in determining how we experience the present situation. However, we cannot always systematically measure this effect as we can in the case of the sets of weights. Helson considered that attitudes, traits, and cultural determinants were all residual stimuli having an immeasurable effect on the current situation. These factors acted as an unknown, or x, factor in mathematical calculations of adaptation level.

As nurses have used the notion of residual stimuli proposed by Roy (1970), a working description of the concept has emerged. Residual stimuli are factors that may be affecting behavior but whose effects are not validated. The nurse can presume, from theoretical knowledge, that a certain factor may be influencing a person's behavior. For example, she considers that religious beliefs affect how a person responds to the awareness that he or she is dying. However, it is not always feasible, or possible, to clarify in what way this is so for a given person. In her nursing assessment, the nurse notes this factor as a residual stimulus to be investigated further as warranted. In addition to possibilities from theoretical knowledge, the nurse may identify residual stimuli from her own intuitive hunches in a given situation. For example, the nurse in the emergency room may pick up subtle cues from a person that the presenting injuries were not the result of an accident, as claimed. As an unvalidated major influencing factor, she would label the possibility of a cause other than an accident such as some form of violence, as a residual stimulus.

Residual stimuli become contextual or focal stimuli when the nurse is able to validate in some way what effect the stimulus is having on the current situation. That is, the nurse identifies that the stimulus is present to the person as the initiator of the behavior (focal) or as part of the internal or external context that contributes to the behavioral response. Validation of the stimuli takes place: (1) by the person confirming that this factor is affecting him or her, and/or (2) by the nurse having enough knowledge to establish the confirmation.

It should be noted that fine-line distinctions about what a stimulus is called are less important than the understanding of the configuration of factors that are affecting the person. Factors that often are assessed as residual stimuli are discussed in the later chapters on the adaptive modes.

STEP THREE: NURSING DIAGNOSIS

After the process of nursing assessment has been carried out, whether completely and painstakingly as by a clinical specialist, or in isolated areas in haste by a critical care nurse, the nurse makes a *nursing diagnosis*. A nursing diagnosis is the nurse's interpretation of the assessment data that have been compiled (Gordon, 1982). Roy (1979) has described three ways of interpreting the data gathered by the nurse in the first- and second-level assessments.

A beginning typology of adaptation problems was identified by Roy in early writings (1973, 1976). One method of making a nursing diagnosis, then, is to cluster the assessment information by behaviors within each of the four adaptive modes and to name each cluster with one of the labels from the suggested typology. A nursing assessment might show that a young mother is blaming herself for the death of her infant, and has misperceived the explanations that have been given for the death. As the nurse scans the related behaviors and stimuli, she categorizes them under the part of the self-concept mode called the moral–ethical self (see Chapter 14). The corresponding diagnostic label is that of *guilt* (see Chapter 21).

A revision of the initial typology of adaptation problems is listed in Table 3.1. These labels represent adaptation problems currently identified

TABLE 3.1
Working Typology of Common Adaptation Problems (Revised)

A. Physiologic Mode	*B. Self-Concept*
1. *Oxygenation* Hypoxia Shock Overload	1. *Physical self* Decreased sexual self-concept Aggressive sexual behavior Loss
2. *Nutrition* Malnutrition Nausea Vomiting	2. *Personal self* Anxiety Powerlessness Guilt Low self-esteem
3. *Elimination* Constipation Diarrhea Flatulence Incontinence Urinary retention	*C. Role Function* Role transition Role distance Role conflict Role failure
4. *Activity and rest* Inadequate physical activity Potential disuse consequences Inadequate rest Insomnia Sleep deprivation Excessive rest	*D. Interdependence* Separation anxiety Loneliness
5. *Skin integrity* Itching Dry skin Pressure sores	

as commonly recurring according to the Roy Adaptation Model. They have been useful in identifying relevant content for nurses to study and thus have been used in organizing some chapters of this book.

In a second approach to nursing diagnosis, behavior and stimuli related to each mode are clustered as they were in the first method. In this approach, however, the diagnosis is made by simply stating the behavior with the most relevant influencing factors. This method allows for the incompleteness of the typology of problems, and, as will be described below, it provides more specific indications for nursing intervention. In the example used above, the nurse might state the diagnosis as "making statements of self-blame for the death of her infant related to misperception of information."

A final method of nursing diagnosis is to summarize behaviors in more than one adaptive mode being affected by the same stimuli. This approach recognizes the holistic functioning of the person and the interrelatedness of the adaptive modes. For the young mother whose infant has died, a diagnosis that crosses the modes may be stated as "depressive behavior pattern related to the death of the infant." Behaviors include the self-blaming behaviors in the self-concept mode and the ineffective mothering behaviors in the role function mode. Taken together, all these behaviors are reflective of the recognizable behavior pattern of depression (see Chapter 26). This type of nursing diagnosis is explored further in the discussion of adaptation across the adaptive modes in Part V.

It should be noted that any of the three approaches to nursing diagnosis may be used to describe an adaptive situation that the nurse would want to maintain and enhance. We could describe a positive diagnosis for the mother who has lost a child as follows: (1) adaptive loss; or (2) grieving behaviors appropriate to loss; or (3) integrating loss and grieving into self-concept and role function.

In the nursing profession as a whole, there has been increasing interest in the past ten years in developing the area of nursing diagnosis. The National Conference on the Classification of Nursing Diagnoses has been meeting every two years since 1973, under the sponsorship of St. Louis University School of Nursing, in St. Louis, Missouri (see Kim, McLane, and McFarland, 1984). The committed energies of hundreds of nurses from practice, education, and research have been put to this total effort to develop a taxonomy that expresses the focus of nursing in an organized and scientific language. This group has recently been renamed, under new bylaws, the North American Nursing Diagnoses Association. Since Roy has worked closely with this group, we can expect mutual influence from this project and her own work in clarifying nursing diagnoses according to the Roy Adaptation Model. In later chapters, Gordon's (1982) groupings of the labels approved by the conference group are indicated as they relate to developments within the adaptive modes of the Roy model.

Criteria for Setting Priorities

Setting priorities is viewed not as a separate step of the nursing process, but rather as a procedure inherent throughout the process. As behaviors are identified, the nurse selects behaviors on which to focus in doing a second-level assessment, that is, identifying influencing factors. Once both first- and second-level assessment is complete, nursing diagnoses are made. These diagnoses are then placed in a hierarchy of importance. Setting of goals is influenced by the relative importance of the diagnosis. The nature and timing of interventions will also depend on the priorities set. Even the time and effort given to the evaluation process are relative to the priority of the situation. Thus it is important for the nurse to have principles or criteria on which to base setting of priorities.

Priority is defined as precedence, especially established by order of importance or urgency. Other authors have identified criteria for determining a hierarchy of importance among types of nursing diagnoses or patient problems (see, for example, Bower, 1977). Within the nursing process of the Roy Adaptation Model, the goals of adaptive systems can be used to determine the relative significance of the assessment, diagnosis, goals, interventions, and evaluations.

The goals of the adaptive system have been identified as: survival, growth, reproduction, and mastery. In general, the process of adaptation is to promote integrity. Within each step of the nursing process, then, the nurse uses the following hierarchy of importance of the situation:

1. Those that threaten the survival of the individual, family, group, or community
2. Those that affect the growth of the individual, family, group, or community
3. Those that affect the continuation of the human race or of society
4. Those that affect the attainment of full potential for the individual or group

Thus the nurse will always give top priority to diagnoses in the first category, then move on down the list. At times the nurse can plan to meet needs in more than one category with one nursing intervention. While teaching a new mother to nurse her baby, the nurse has the child's need for life-giving nourishment as one priority, but the potential effect of the mother–child relationship on the infant's growth and development is also being considered. In planning with an individual, the person's view of the priority of the situation is also used as data in establishing a hierarchy of importance.

When the nurse is setting priorities for groups of persons, the priority factors may interact to clarify what has highest priority. For example, in a disaster area, the nurse finds that many lives are threatened. The further criterion of continuity of the race and society helps the nurse to decide where to concentrate the most energies. Persons with the greatest potential for recovery and less risk of genetic damage may be cared for first.[6]

Setting of priorities is also influenced by pragmatic factors of the availability of resources. Resources include nursing personnel, equipment, time, and money. The availability of resources is considered in relation to the significance of the situation. For example, when a problem reaches the point of greater threat to integrity, greater costs may be tolerated. Thus with the continuing illegal drug usage problem in society, with its potential for destroying the integrity of the community, the government and private

---

[6]The issue of setting priorities raises many moral-ethical questions. The reader is encouraged to explore these questions in other readings. See, for example, Silva (1974).

funding sources are willing to undertake the high cost of preventive drug abuse programs.

The nurse uses these criteria for setting priorities throughout each phase of the nursing process.

STEP FOUR: GOAL SETTING

The nurse makes a clear behavioral description of the person's situation in the assessment and diagnosis. The *goal* for nursing care is established from this description. In general, the goal of nursing intervention is to maintain and enhance adaptive behavior and to change ineffective behavior to adaptive. Thus the goal is stated in terms of the resulting behavior expected of the person. A goal may be stated in such a way that a change within a short span of time is expected. This would be a short-term goal. In other situations the nature of the nursing diagnosis indicates that a long-term goal that is oriented toward the future is indicated.

An example of a nursing goal related to skin integrity might read: The client's open skin area on the sacrum will decrease in size within two weeks as measured by observation. This is a relatively short-term goal that is based on the specific assessment of skin integrity. A goal may be even more immediate, such as: The patient will experience relief from pain within 1 hour as indicated by statements about being more comfortable and by a decrease in behaviors manifesting tension.

A long-term goal for a mother being seen in her home after the birth of a baby might read: The mother will exhibit increasing instrumental and expressive mothering behaviors over the next six weeks and will express confidence in her role before terminating nursing services. Another person receiving counseling in a clinic by a nurse may set up the goal that he will assess his abilities and limitations realistically and experience increasing acceptance and self-esteem as shown by his statements in conversations with the nurse over the next 2 months.

Goals, then, are clear statements of the behavioral outcomes of nursing care for the client. Examples of this step of the nursing process are included throughout this text.

STEP FIVE: INTERVENTION: SELECTION OF APPROACHES

The next step of the nursing process, *intervention* or selection of approaches, is based directly on the way the Roy Adaptation Model views the process of adaptation. We have pointed out that the ability to respond positively, or to adapt, depends on the degree of change taking place and the state of the person coping with the change; that is, adaptation depends on the focal stimulus and on adaptation level. If the nurse wants to effect change or to stabilize adaptation, the focal stimulus can be altered or the adaptation level broadened by changing the other stimuli present. In either case, the nurse acts to manage the stimuli affecting adaptation. In selecting which stimuli to change, Roy points out that the nurse uses the nursing judgment method outlined by McDonald and Harms (1966). This method is a way of listing possible approaches, then selecting the approach with the highest probability of achieving the valued goal. Combining this method with the Roy Adaptation Model, we can say that the various stimuli affecting patient behaviors are listed. Then the consequences of dealing with each stimuli are outlined. The probability of each consequence is determined. In addition, the values of the outcomes of the approach are judged. The approach with the highest probability of reaching the valued goal can then be selected.

For example, a problem of elimination might be that the person after surgery has hard, dry stools due to decreased fluid intake and limited mobility. Analyzing two possible approaches in this situation would provide the outline listed in Table 3.2. In this example, the first approach, altering the focal stimulus of decreased fluid intake, has a fairly high probability of

TABLE 3.2
Nursing Judgment Method Combined with the Roy Adaptation Nursing School

Alternative Approach	Consequences	Probability	Value
Alter stimuli of decreased fluid intake	Improve bowel function	0.70	Desirable
	Do not improve bowel function	0.30	Undesirable
	Cause circulatory overload	0.05	Undesirable
Alter the stimuli of limited mobility	Improve bowel function	0.70	Desirable
	Do not improve bowel function	0.30	Undesirable
	Cause disturbance of spinal fusion site	0.90	Undesirable

achieving a desirable consequence, which is the goal of the intervention. At the same time the undesirable consequences of this approach, not improving bowel function and causing circulatory overload, have a low probability. On the other hand, one undesirable outcome of the second approach, causing disturbance of spinal fusion site, has a very high probability. Thus the first approach, altering the stimuli of decreased fluid intake, is selected for nursing action. It should be pointed out that whenever possible the focal stimulus should be the target of nursing intervention since it is seen as the primary initiator of the behavior being considered.

STEP SIX: EVALUATION

The final step of the nursing process is the *evaluation* of the effectiveness of nursing intervention. This effectiveness is judged by the result that the nursing approach had regarding the person's adaptive behavior. The nurse simply asks whether or not the desired goal was attained. Did the person manifest the behavior stated in the goal? In gathering data to answer this question the nurse uses the same methods as in gathering data in the first and second steps of the nursing process — she makes skillful observations, uses tools of measurement, and interviews the person. As in some examples cited earlier, the nurse would simply measure current behavior against the behavior stated in the goal: Did the client's open skin area on the sacrum decrease in size? Or, did the person show relief from pain? Or, is the mother acting and feeling confident in her mothering role? Or, does this person's conversation manifest greater self-acceptance and self-esteem?

When the nurse determines the effects of intervention, she returns to the first step of the nursing process. The nurse looks more closely at behaviors that continue to be ineffective and reassesses the factors influencing these. For behaviors that have become adaptive, with no threat of returning to ineffective, the nurse may delete this behavior as a priority of nursing concern. For behaviors that are still ineffective, influencing stimuli are reassessed to see if the nursing approach should be modified by managing another stimulus. Evaluation, then, is a crucial tool in updating the plan for nursing care.

SUMMARY

In this chapter we have considered the nursing process as specified by the Roy Adaptation Model of nursing. This process is built on the problem-solving process used by other professionals in giving health care service. However, the nursing model has been used to determine the specific data to collect, that is, assessment of behavior in each adaptive mode and focal, contextual, and residual factors influencing those behaviors. To gather the data, the nurse uses skillful observation, the known tools of measurement, and interview. Three methods of making nursing diagnoses were described. The nursing model was also used to describe the step of stating goals in terms of expected behaviors. The discussion of selecting approaches to meet the goal focused on management of stimuli. The Roy Model emphasis on adaptation being a function of adaptation level was combined with the nursing judgment model proposed by McDonald and Harms. The final step of evaluation came as a logical conclusion of the earlier discussion. Behavior is reassessed to decide whether or not the nursing approach has achieved the stated goal. Modifications are made or new priorities are set based on this evaluation. This process is illustrated in Fig. 3.2.

STUDENT LEARNING ACTIVITY

Using the nursing process flowchart in Fig. 3.2, apply the six steps of the nursing process to your observations of the nutritional status of a friend. Please check the appendices for several examples of use of the nursing process according to the Roy Adaptation Model.

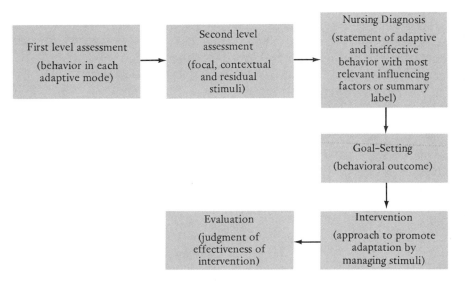

Figure 3.2   Flowchart illustrating the nursing process based on the Roy Adaptation Model of nursing.

REFERENCES

Bower, Fay Louise. *The Process of Planning Nursing Care*, 2nd ed. St. Louis: The C. V. Mosby Company, 1977.

Gordon, Marjory. *Nursing Diagnosis: Process and Application.* New York: McGraw-Hill Book Company, 1982.

Hein, Eleanor C. *Communication in Nursing Practice*, 2nd ed. Boston: Little, Brown and Company, 1980.

Helson, Harry. *Adaptation Level Theory*. New York: Harper & Row, Publishers, 1964.

Idle, Betty A. "SPAL: A Tool for Measuring Self-Perceived Adaptation Level Appropriate for an Elderly Population." In Sigma Theta Tau, *Clinical Nursing*

Research: Its Strategies and Findings. Monograph Series 78-Two. University of Arizona, September 15 and 16, 1977.

Kelly, Lucy. *Dimensions of Professional Nursing*, 4th ed. New York: Macmillan Publishing Co., Inc., 1981.

Kim, M. J., G. McFarland, and A. McLane, *eds. Proceedings of Fifth National Conference on Classification of Nursing Diagnoses*. St. Louis: Mosby, 1984.

Martinez, Cecilia. "Nursing Assessment Based on Roy Adaptation Model," in Sister Callista Roy, *Introduction to Nursing: An Adaptation Model*. Englewood Cliffs, N.J.: Prentice-Hall, Inc., 1976, pp. 379–385.

McCann, Hugh. "In Search of Adventure," *American Way*. May 1983, pp. 106–110.

McDonald, F. J., and Mary Harms. "Theoretical Model for an Experimental Curriculum," *Nursing Outlook*, vol. 14, no. 8, August 1966, pp. 48–51.

Orlando, Ida Jean. *Dynamic Nurse–Patient Relationship*. New York: G. P. Putnam's Sons, 1961.

Roy, Sister Callista. "Role Cues and Mothers of Hospitalized Children," *Nursing Research*, Spring 1967, pp. 178–182.

Roy, Sister Callista. "Adaptation: A Conceptual Framework for Nursing," *Nursing Outlook*, vol. 18, no. 3, March 1970, pp. 43–45.

Roy, Sister Callista. "Adaptation: A Basis for Nursing Practice," *Nursing Outlook*, vol. 19, no. 4, April 1971, pp. 254–257.

Roy, Sister Callista. "Adaptation: Implications for Curriculum Change," *Nursing Outlook*, vol. 21, no. 3, April 1973, pp. 163–168.

Roy, Sister Callista. *Introduction to Nursing: An Adaptation Model*. Englewood Cliffs, N. J.: Prentice-Hall, Inc., 1976.

Roy, Sister Callista. "Nursing Diagnosis from the Perspective of a Nursing Model," *Nursing Diagnoses Newsletter*, St. Louis University School of Nursing, vol. 6, December 1979.

Roy, Sister Callista, and Sharon Roberts. *Theory Construction in Nursing: An Adaptation Model*. Englewood Cliffs, N. J.: Prentice-Hall, Inc., 1981.

Silva, Mary. "Science, Ethics, and Nursing," *American Journal of Nursing*, vol. 74, no. 11, 1974, pp. 2004–2007.

Chapter 4

Major Factors Influencing Adaptation

Marsha Keiko Sato

BEHAVIORAL OBJECTIVES

After studying this chapter, the reader will be able to:

1. Define the key concepts of the chapter.
2. Identify the influence of culture, family, and growth and development on a person's behavior.
3. Demonstrate sensitivity in caring for persons from a different cultural background.
4. Define the concept of family and identify tasks of the family.
5. Apply Duvall's developmental framework as a basis for studying the family.
6. Discuss the relationship between the developmental tasks and expected behaviors utilizing Erikson's eight stages of development.

KEY CONCEPTS DEFINED

Culture: group's design for living, a shared set of socially transmitted assumptions about the nature of the physical and social world, the goals of life, and the approximate means of achieving them (Paul, 1975).

Ethnocentrism: belief that one's way of life is superior.

Ethnic Peoples of Color: a term used to describe unassimilated groups who have remained distinct from the larger, dominant society. Often factors that influence assimilation include ethnic differences and obvious skin color differences.

Family: traditionally defined as a group of persons united through marriage, blood, or adoption. More broadly defined as members who relate to one another through specified patterns, regardless of ties, including individuals living in communes, close-friend living groups, and so forth.

Growth: increase in body size and/or changed structure, function, and regulatory processes until optimal maturity.

Development: orderly changes in behavior occurring over a lifetime due to the processes of maturation.

Developmental Task: growth responsibility during a period of development where successful achievement leads to success with later tasks. Failure results in unhappiness, societal disapproval, and difficulty with later developmental tasks (Duvall, 1971).

The assessment of a person as a whole reveals the influence of many factors on adaptive behavior. The Roy Adaptation Model categorizes these factors as focal, contextual, and residual stimuli. General stimuli that appear to have a lifelong and permeating effect on behaviors include: culture, family, and growth and development.

The cultural background of a person affects perceptions of health, illness, and attitudes toward utilization of health services. Consideration of culture as an influencing stimulus enables nurses to respond more adequately to a person's total health needs. It is significant to be aware that there are variations within each cultural group depending on time and location, and the information in this chapter is to be used only as a broad guide within which the nurse looks at the specific influences on the individual's life experience.

The family unit is an important factor affecting behavior in all four adaptive modes outlined by the Roy Adaptation Model. The assessment of the family utilizing an appropriate framework provides the nurse with a tool for evaluating the level of family functioning and the resulting effect on the person's behavior. The symbolic interaction theory is introduced in this chapter, with major emphasis on Duvall's developmental frame of reference for the family.

The process of growth and development occurs throughout life and is characterized by behaviors expected in each stage. Expected behaviors based on age provide knowledge of a key stimulus affecting the use of the nursing process with persons of varying age levels.

Culture, family, and growth and development are viewed as important stimuli influencing the person's adaptive behavior, and some major concepts and theories that describe and explain these factors are presented in this chapter. The reader may refer to the references cited for further study in these areas.

CULTURE

Definition of Culture

For the purpose of this text, *culture* is defined as a group's design for living and includes shared assumptions which are socially transmitted about the physical and social world (Paul, 1975). The group can be any collection of people having some unifying relationship. Within each group there are cultural components that dictate the style of living. These components are: rules, knowledge, art, music, language, beliefs, religion, customs, and philosophy of life.

General Nursing Assessment

The assessment of a person's cultural background is significant, as it affects perceptions of wellness and attitudes toward health care. This assessment is especially crucial when the nurse's cultural background differs from that of the person seeking care. When interviewing any person to make a nursing assessment, the nurse seeks data about the specific beliefs and about the person's particular culture. Suggested questions that could be used in such an interview are presented in the following paragraphs. In addition, the nurse is alert to use her observational skills, sensitivity to nonverbal behaviors, and other means of assessing cultural influences.

Identify the problem. What is the client's perception of the problem, and how does the person define "wellness" and "illness?" This definition may be a major factor influencing how the person will adjust to the changes in health status and to seeking health care. It will influence the behavior the nurse sees as the person responds to these changes.

Identify the person's beliefs and practices regarding the assessed problem. What does the person believe to be the focal stimulus, or precipitating event, for the situation that brought him or her for health care, or for other identified problems? What types of interventions are viewed as helpful and needed by the person? Does the person practice self-medication and/or receive treatment from family members or a folk practitioner?

Assess the person's previous experiences with the dominant health care system. Was the person satisfied with the treatment received? Did the prescribed treatment conflict with the person's cultural beliefs?

Assess the cultural background of the client. What are the person's beliefs and values regarding childbirth, allocation of resources, male–female roles, death, religion–spirituality, and so forth? Does the person have a cultural preference regarding music, food, art, spiritual expression, and recreation? What occupations are valued by the culture? (This becomes an important stimulus when assessing the person's secondary role—see Chapter 15.) What types of behaviors are valued by the culture? Cultural values provide one norm for evaluating the person's behavior as adaptive or ineffective. Are there any taboos dictated by the group? If so, what is the person's degree of belief and adherence?

Broad Adaptation Problems

The person from a cultural group different from the dominant society is presented with problems stemming from a divergent value system. The differing ways of life can become a source of conflict and affect the person's ability to adapt or cope with life situations, including health care. Examples of problem areas include language barriers to communication and the ethnocentric attitudes of others.

A *language barrier* potentially exists between persons of a different cultural group and the dominant larger system. The person's inability to communicate with ease may hinder the tendency to ask questions or acknowledge a lack of understanding. The health care worker from the dominant group may accept the silence as comprehension by the person. The result is failure of communication, and the person is seen exiting from the health care scene dissatisfied with the care received.

The language barrier to effective communication can be alleviated through the utilization of appropriate interventions. This may be done by employing bilingual personnel as auxiliary staff and as health professionals or by instituting language classes for staff development. The use of technical terms should be clarified into lay terminology and health practices demonstrated through the use of visual aids. Knowledge of proper communication styles for the particular cultural group is helpful. For example, some cultural groups, including Mexican–Americans, use the proper form of address when talking to a stranger, such as "Mr. Garcia" instead of "Tony."

The adaptation problem caused by the cultural imposition of beliefs, practices, and values upon the cultural group by the dominant system reflects the latter's *ethnocentric* attitude. The larger group is convinced that its practices are best and that it possesses knowledge which others need. The result is often a conflict of values between the dominant system and the cultural group seeking care. The person's traditional beliefs and customs are questioned with a resulting sense of confusion. The person may resolve the problem by leaving the dominant health care system, or certain cultural values may be relinquished. If the latter alternative is selected, the person is exposed to family and/or group discord and sometimes ridicule.

The degree of imposition of beliefs on the smaller cultural group may be reduced through education and increasing awareness of all health professionals concerning different cultural values and folk-health practices. Nurses working with persons from diverse heritages strive to provide care within that particular cultural context. In the next sections, examples of cultural variations by way of socioeconomic status, religion, and ethnicity are discussed.

Poverty as a Culture

One's socioeconomic status is an important component influencing behavior. In particular, persons in a state of chronic poverty are viewed as a cultural group since poverty is a way of life that is passed from generation to generation (Lewis, 1969) in the same way that economic privilege may be inherited. Poverty as a culture will be discussed here because large numbers of persons with whom nurses deal are affected by this culture, and these persons have relatively fewer resources to handle their problems of health and illness than the privileged classes. However, the nurse will be mindful of the impact of each person's socioeconomic status, including the particular effects of middle-class status and the more subtle needs of the economically privileged.

The poor are a group characterized by a low level of political power and a time orientation focused on the present. The culture of poverty is described further by using the framework of the Roy Adaptation Model of nursing.

Physiologic Mode.   For persons with poverty as a cultural background, there is an increased incidence of death due to contagious diseases. The life span is shorter, which accounts for the lower rate of cardiovascular diseases and neoplasms. The maternal and infant mortality rates are higher than those of the general population because of the influencing factors of poor nutrition and inadequate prenatal care. Malnutrition is a common problem identified in assessing the nutritional needs of the poor client.

Self-Concept Mode.   In this cultural group, the low marriage rate and the high rate of births outside a stable home reflect the culture's particular beliefs that become part of the self-concept. Feelings of fatalism and inferiority can be a disruption of the person's self-ideal with the corresponding adaptation problem of powerlessness (see Chapters 14 and 20). The sense of fatalism is expressed by the feeling that one is unable to control the direction of life. This feeling greatly affects the person's sense of self-worth or esteem.

Role Function Mode.   Later in this text (Chapter 15), secondary roles are discussed. There are general roles that influence behavior in a variety of settings. The secondary role of spouse is less frequent in this cultural group, and there are a large number of families with a single parent. Occupation as a secondary role is unstable with a high rate of unemployment.

Interdependence Mode.   The tendency to underutilize health services for prevention or treatment is characteristic of the culture of poverty. This behavior reflects the inability to seek out adequate support systems when needed as described in the interdependence mode (see Chapter 16). The probable focal stimulus is the feeling of hopelessness for the future and the accompanying sensation of powerlessness. In addition, the availability of adequate, affordable services can be another influencing factor.

Stimuli.   The culture of poverty is perpetuated from generation to generation and reflects a method of coping with the environment. The feelings of powerlessness and hopelessness associated with low socioeconomic status are probably the focal stimuli for the ongoing cycle. The number of children, unemployment, and inadequate education are additional influencing factors. Other contextual stimuli for poverty as a culture include: living in a poor geographic location, development of technology without consideration of human resources, and advancing age.

Religion as a Culture

Religion is one broad category of the cultural components. This category includes the major organized religions of the world. In addition, for some persons, this cultural component involves spiritual beliefs, practices, and philosophies that are not necessarily attached to institutional forms of religion. One distinct religious group, the Jewish faith, is presented as an example of a cultural group whose religion exerts an influence on total life experiences as well as on health attitudes and practices.

The Jewish religion is considered a cultural group with rules encompassing a separate body of knowledge, a language form, and customs unique to the group.

There are three major groups in the Jewish faith: reform, conservative, and orthodox. All of the groups trace their ethnic origin to Abraham, Isaac, and Jacob and accept the first five books of the *Old Testament*. The groups differ on the degree of acceptance of the remaining books of the *Old Testament* and the later writings which are found in the *Talmud*. The *Talmud* describes human and social behavior in 613 commandments, of which 213 pertain to areas of health and are respected by the orthodox Jew (Zussman, 1970). The adherence to the *Talmud* by the orthodox Jew is described according to the most relevant parts of the Roy Adaptation Model of nursing.

Physiological Mode.   Nutrition needs are influenced by the dietary laws, which state that only animals with cloven hooves who chew their cud may be eaten. This includes sheep, cattle, goats, and deer, plus the 24 birds listed, including chicken, turkey, geese, ducks, and doves (Donin, 1972). Camels, pigs, and hare were not included in the *Talmud*. The animal must be slaughtered according to ritual and cause the least pain to the animal. The meat is koshered to remove the blood through the process of salting and soaking the meat. Meat is not usually koshered in the hospital, and in this case, it is preferable to order fish or eggs for the person who is an orthodox Jew. Acceptable seafood must have fins and scales, which omits lobsters, oysters, shrimps, clams, and crabs. Meat and dairy products should not be served at the same meal for, "You shall not boil a kid in its mother's milk."

Behaviors related to endocrine function and sexuality include forbidding sexual intercourse beginning with the onset of the menstrual period and extending to 7 "clean" days afterward for an average of 12 days abstinence. The use of birth control pills is not prohibited; however, large families are looked upon favorably.

The expression of pain is behavior noted in the physiological mode (see Chapter 10), and persons of Jewish background are often more expressive verbally and nonverbally about their pain experience than are persons of other groups. The pain experience may seem to be exaggerated, with demands for pain relief, and the phrases "Oy" or "Oy vei" are heard as a response to pain (Chapman, 1944; Zborowski, 1952). Nursing interventions are focused on talking to the person, providing reassurance, and on the assessment of the pain behavior so that appropriate additional relief measures are used.

Self-Concept Mode.   The orthodox Jew's religious beliefs have a significant influence on the moral-ethical-spiritual component of the self-concept mode (see Chapter 14). This component represents the person's belief system, morals, and the evaluator of who one is. For the Jew, the Sabbath begins at sunset on Fridays with the lighting of two candles, which may be substituted by electrical fixtures while in the hospital. During the Sabbath, the person will not handle money or travel by means other than foot. A wheelchair or guerney is unacceptable. Some persons will refrain from using the telephone, light fixtures, call buttons, and television. However, if life is in jeopardy, it is a duty to cooperate with any life-saving measures.

A strong value of Jewish society is the importance of the family and, therefore, abortion for convenience is prohibited unless the mother's life is at risk. On the eighth day after birth, every male child is to be circumcised and enters a covenant with God. A qualified rabbi may perform the circumcision.

Euthanasia is strictly prohibited and is condemned as murder. If the person is expected to die within 3 days, it is permissible to withdraw the life-supporting apparatus. When a Jewish person is deceased, *hevra kadish* (pious Jews) care for the body and prepare for the burial. Autopsies are unacceptable and are viewed as a desecration of the dead.

Ethnic Peoples of Color

Ethnic peoples of color represent a particular cultural grouping since they are unassimilated groups who are distinct from the larger, dominant group. They are members of a society who have often been excluded from the services and benefits enjoyed by the majority. Asians, blacks, Latinos, and American Indians are ethnic peoples of color many of whom did not assimilate within American society because (1) they are physically distinct, (2) their introduction to America differs from that of other immigrants, and (3) enclaves were formed and their own cultural values and norms were retained. Three groups of ethnic peoples of color, significant in American society, are further described according to the Roy Adaptation Model, focusing on the adaptive modes that seem most relevant for planning nursing care.

Black American Culture.   The black American's introduction to the United States as a slave resulted in the forced disruption of tribal ties, forbiddance of speaking in the native African language, and the outlawing of religious and social customs by the dominant group in an attempt to decrease the possibility of slave uprisings (Branch and Paxton, 1976). During this period, blacks treated themselves for illnesses and based this treatment on trial and error, knowledge from Africa, and the observation of white families. After the Civil War, blacks were often unable to receive medical care due to discrimination, cost, and inaccessibility of services, and thus continued to use home remedies.

The black American culture as it developed and adapted within the United States is discussed utilizing the Roy Adaptation Model as a framework.

Physiological Mode. The physiological behaviors exhibited by a black person are influenced by genetic background. Certain behaviors are considered adaptive and are expected within the black population and are characteristic of that group. Where a particular nursing assessment and/or intervention is appropriate, this is listed. Some of these behaviors are:

1. *Mongolian spots.* These are benign pigmented areas usually found in infancy on the lumbar-sacral area and which may persist throughout life. Such spots also are found on other ethnic peoples of color.
2. *Hyperpigmented oral mucous membranes.* The mucous membranes in the oral cavity may be hyperpigmented, with 50 to 90 percent of the population affected by age 40.
3. *Sclera.* Deposits of melanin appear in the sclera as the individual ages and are noticeable in the third or fourth decade of life. These deposits are benign and do not interfere with vision in blacks but are considered to be malignant in whites.
4. *Nevi (moles).* These raised, discolored lesions are asymptomatic and commonly appear during the second and third decades and grow in size and number during the fifth and sixth decades.
5. *Keloids (hypertrophic scars).* Keloids are benign tumors composed of dense fibrous tissue. The focal stimulus may be infection, insect bites, surgical incision, or injuries. During the second stage of wound healing, fibroplasia appears to be overreactive. Commonly affected are the face, neck, and sternal areas. The growth of keloids seems to be age related, as it occurs more often in young blacks than in the elderly and is, therefore, possibly influenced by hormonal circulation.
6. *Scar hyper/hypopigmentation.* The hyper/hypopigmentation of a scar is in response to the inflammatory process, which is more intense in blacks. Usually, the scab formation is hypopigmented and later becomes hyperpigmented. Many blacks believe that cocoa butter will return the skin to its original color and retard keloid formation.
7. *Pseudofolliculitis.* In this condition, hair pierces a follicular papule in the region of the moustache and beard and is commonly seen in blacks. Contextual stimuli include shaving, ingrown hairs, and curly hair. Nursing intervention is focused on the application of warm soaks prior to shaving to open the pores.

8. *Disruptions in skin color.* A person's skin color may be the first clue to a systemic problem, and the ability to assess dark skins is vital. A guide to the assessment of disruptions in skin color in blacks is provided below.

   (a) *Pallor.* Depending on the person's degree of pigmentation, the skin may appear pale to yellowish to brown to ashen gray. Changes in color are also evident in the nail beds and the oral mucous membranes and can be tested by blanching the skin to observe the speed with which color returns.

   (b) *Cyanosis.* Continuous observation of skin color is important when assessing for cyanosis in the dark-skinned person. The usual sites of observation are mucous membranes in the mouth, the nares, the vagina, and the conjunctiva nearest the eyelids. The color in these areas will be varying shades of blue with dark brown undertones if the patient is cyanotic. Other areas to assess for changes in skin color are the soles of the feet, palms, and nail beds. It is helpful to question members of the family as to the normal skin coloring of the person. The clinical symptoms of restlessness, level of consciousness, flaring of the nostrils, and changes in personal behavior provide the nurse with additional data regarding the need for oxygen.

   (c) *Erythema.* The identification of erythema requires good lighting to examine the skin texture for rash and the skin color "red as a beet."

   (d) *Jaundice.* Jaundice is noticeable in the sclera and, depending on the level of pigmentation, it is observable on the body surface.

Interdependence Mode.   Assessment within the interdependence mode reveals the importance of the family as a support system. For centuries in Africa, the family has been considered a major unit, economically, politically, and religiously (Billingsley, 1968). The family in American society continues to be an important concept, as members depend on the group for nurturing and positive reinforcement. The extended family is preferable over the nuclear family, which is demonstrated by the desire of young couples to live with their families (Clark, 1978).

An adaptation problem of interdependence among the black culture, as in the culture of poverty, is the underutilization of health services as a support system. There is the belief that health and illness are to be treated on a crisis basis, and care is obtained only when function is impaired. This relates to the black culture's concept of wellness, which is the ability to labor productively, versus sickness, which is conceived as a state of incapacitation

(Branch, 1976). Once the immediate problem is alleviated, appointments for follow-up care are broken for other important needs.

A contextual stimulus influencing the problem of underutilization of health services is the lack of compensation for illness in the lower-paying jobs, which all too often are disproportionately held by blacks. Quite often, temporary or seasonal employment does not provide "sick days," which is significant when the income is vital to one's livelihood. The problem of finances is related to the inability to pay for health services and limited access to these services. When the person attends a public health agency, it becomes difficult to establish a relationship with a primary caregiver. It becomes easier to discontinue follow-up care when the person providing health care changes from appointment to appointment.

Nursing interventions aimed at increasing the use of health services as a support system are the inclusion of the client in the planning and provision of care and the scheduling of a primary health worker. This incorporates the necessary teaching to inform the client of the importance and meaning of therapy and its effect on health while taking into consideration the establishing of rapport.

Self-Concept Mode.   The black cultural belief that aging is the natural process of attaining grace and that the elderly should be respected reflects the moral-ethical component of the self-concept mode. The culture places value on its aging members and believes they should be taken care of. This philosophy partially explains the continued viability of the extended family structure within the black community.

The need for privacy when dressing and during a physical examination is a behavior of the physical self/body image. Providing the client with privacy and allowing for modest behavior are nursing interventions to implement.

Latino/Chicano Culture.   The Latino/Chicano group includes Hispanics, Spanish Americans, Latin Americans, Mexican Americans, and Mexicans. Cultural differences exist between these Spanish-speaking groups of America, and each may have diverse values, beliefs, and morals. The description presented in this text discusses some of the common traditions that may be shared among these Spanish-speaking groups.

Interdependence Mode.   The utilization of health services as a support system is dependent on several influencing factors. The person's degree of acculturation to the dominant culture influences the use of clinics. The less acculturated, who are usually members of the lower class, rely more heavily on folk medicine and traditional healers. The acculturated Latino/Chicano may seek medical care as a status symbol and ridicule folk medicine. The degree of acculturation is dictated by the family unit, and the health practices reflect the family's belief.

The age of the client affects cultural beliefs. Older members tend to cling to the ways of tradition, whereas the younger members may be influenced by the dominant culture. However, the Chicano movement has stressed the rediscovery of ethnicity, and the number of people utilizing both traditional and modern practices may increase.

The concept of God-given health wherein illness is viewed as a punishment from God (*castigo de Dios*), as discussed below, lends feelings of powerlessness in controlling the affliction by the ill person. Persons who believe in this concept will turn to a priest for blessing instead of a health care worker. The priest will call upon the patron saint on behalf of the ill person, and family members pray for the recovery of the sick through rituals.

Role Function Mode.   Regarding the sick role, some Latino/Chicano people divide illnesses into two categories: supernatural and natural diseases. The supernatural diseases are further subdivided into three causative areas: (1) disease sent by God or a saint as punishment for evil behavior (this may be manifested as congenital disruptions in children for punishment of parental sins); (2) fright sickness (*espanto*), caused by seeking ghosts or spirits; and (3) diseases caused by witchcraft or the *evil eye*. In the case of witchcraft, potions, herbs, and voodoo practices are used to bring evil to the victim. Evil eye (*mal de ojo*) is an illness of the victim caused by an outsider desiring or envying a physical trait of the victim. Children and women are more susceptible, and the disease can be prevented by the admirer touching the desired object.

Susto, empacho, and *caida de la mollera* are examples of natural diseases. *Susto* (fright sickness) differs from *espanto* in that it is caused by being frightened by a natural phenomenon, such as witnessing an accident or seeing a snake. Symptoms of *susto* include anxiety, insomnia, indigestion, palpitation, and anorexia. The frightening experience is believed to cause the soul to leave the body. Herbs, rituals, and prayers are used to cure the disease. *Empacho* can be caused by eating bad foods, eating against one's will, or experiencing emotional trauma during a meal. The treatment requires the manipulation of the abdomen and back with sacred oils. Children are usually susceptible to *empacho*. *Caida de la mollera* (fall of the fontanel) is a common ailment of infancy, with symptoms resembling dehydration. It is thought to be caused by a fall, or the child having been dropped, and carries the implication of parental neglect.

The supernatural and natural diseases can only be cured by a *bruja(o)* or *curandera(o)*. The *bruja(o)* is similar to a witch doctor and receives curative powers from the devil, unlike the *curandera(o)*, who receives curative powers from God. The curandra(o) uses herbs, prayers, and rituals in conjunction with these powers to treat a variety of illnesses.

The demonstration of adaptive sick role behaviors is affected by several important stimuli. One is the belief that men are healthier than women or children, and that good health is part of being a man. Another factor is the belief that health is freedom from pain, and the ability to perform the activities of daily living. The denial of the sick role is enhanced by this belief, for as long as one is able to work without pain, one is not sick. A last major influencing factor or stimulus is the feeling that hospitals are places to die, and admission indicates the seriousness of the disease or impending death.

American Indian Culture.   There are approximately 300 American Indian tribes in the United States scattered on 24 reservation states, with the largest numbers clustered in Oklahoma, Arizona, California, and New Mexico (Backrup, 1979). Evidence of human-made tools among the inhabitants of North America dates back at least 15,000 years, and well-established cultures based on various ecologic conditions were found by the Europeans who arrived on this continent in the fifteenth century. Many of the current tribes do not share the same language or culture; however, among Indians, there is great respect for each other's different ways of life.

Physiological Mode.   Significant behaviors in the physiological mode are the health problems common to the American Indian population, which affect the group's level of wellness. A problem of major importance is the infant mortality rate, which is twice as high as that of the white population. The maternal mortality rate is also two to three times higher for the American Indian woman than for a white woman.

The incidence of communicable diseases among children continues together with poor dental care. Accidents, alcoholism, and the resulting mental health problems affecting all modes completes the list of major health problems within the physiological mode.

Stimuli contributing to these problems vary; however, poor nutrition, unsanitary living conditions, and a low income are important influencing factors.

Interdependence Mode.   The extended family is an integral part of the American Indian's life-style, with the children and the grandparents being the most important members. Children are seen as valuable assets to the family, and the elderly are highly respected and loved. It is the aging members who are looked to for advice and who pass down traditions and customs through story telling.

Role Function Mode.   Each member of the family has a distinct role to fulfill. The man is considered to be the head of the house, and the woman is the one who holds the family together.

The sick role is believed to be caused by an imbalance between the person and the natural or supernatural forces. To prevent illness from occurring, Indians participate regularly in ceremonies (spring dance, winter chants) to ward off evil. The wearing of charms, drinking herbal teas, and the rubbing of the body with evergreens are thought to be helpful practices (Backrup, 1979).

If a person is ill, a medicine man (shaman) is called to intervene. The role of the medicine man is similar to the combined practices of the minister, physician, and psychiatrist in the white culture. The shaman has supernatural powers and is an important and respected member of the tribe. The shaman's treatment is focused on curing the whole person through the religious rituals of chanting and dancing, which take from 20 minutes to 4 days. The medicine man receives cooperation in his role from the family members, who assist with the ceremony and rituals (Backrup, 1979).

Self-Concept Mode.   An important moral–ethical behavior is the belief that God is the primary giver and cause of life. Also, there is the belief that a spiritual relationship exists between human persons and nature. This belief gives the American Indian a holistic view of life.

The suicide rate for American Indian teenagers is five times higher than the national average. A postulated precipitating cause is the transition from a tribal life-style to an industrialized society whose values are different.

Culture, then, in its many facets is a major influencing factor that the nurse will consider in each person for whom she cares. We turn now to another major influencing factor for all persons — the family.

FAMILY

Definition of the Family

A *family* is traditionally described as a group of persons united through marriage, blood, or adoption. They reside in a single household, interact through social roles, and maintain a common culture (Torbett, 1973).

A broader definition of family states that, regardless of the tie, the members relate to one another through specified patterns of behavior. This definition allows other structures, such as communes and close-friend living groups, to be considered as a family unit.

Various theories and frameworks have been developed for studying the family. Some of these will be discussed in Chapter 29, for example, Tapia's approach to family development. For now we can point out that the family viewed as a unit is growing and changing. It is theorized that families have critical tasks to meet at certain stages of the family's development. Successful fulfillment of the task enables the family to grow as a unit. For example, the family with a preschool child strives to adapt to the critical needs and interests of preschool children in stimulating, growth-promoting ways. At the same time, the parents have to cope successfully with energy depletion and their own lack of privacy.

Family Structures

The structural unit of a family varies in its composition of members and the way in which the members relate to one another. Family structures have been categorized as traditional and experimental.

Traditional family structures are those which have been accepted by society and viewed as legitimate living arrangements. The nuclear family, nuclear dyad, single parent, single adult, and the extended family are common, traditional family structures. The nuclear family consists of a husband, wife, and children living together in a common household. This structure has largely replaced the once popular extended family, which included relatives outside the nuclear unit. The nuclear dyad comprises a husband and wife living alone. The single-parent family has only one parent—as a result of death, divorce, abandonment, or separation—together with a child or children.

Examples of alternative or experimental family structures are communes or community living arrangements. These groups vary in the type of membership, organizational structure, and general purpose. Some units focus on agriculture and are seeking closeness to the land. Others are organized for religious reasons or focus on common interests, such as crafts or a unifying goal. There may be a sharing of resources, expenses, household chores, and child care.

Tasks of the Family

The adaptive functioning of a family unit depends on the fulfillment of certain critical ongoing tasks. A nursing assessment of the family takes into consideration whether these tasks are being met or their degree of fulfillment.

Reproduction and providing economic security are tasks of the family unit. The physical maintenance of members, such as the availability of clothing, shelter, and food, is considered. The family is also responsible for the socialization of its members through role modeling and the establishment of the interaction process. This encompasses the motivation of behavior, which includes values and beliefs. An environment allowing for personal happiness and growth opportunities is expected within the family. A final task of the family is releasing its members through marriage, death, or for other reasons.

A beginning family is faced with new roles and different expected behaviors which may require a period of adjustment. In addition to the tasks mentioned previously, a new family has other obligations to fulfill.

The duties and responsibilities of marriage provide the family with a major task, developing satisfactory relationships with relatives and in-laws. Learning to cooperate with one's partner becomes a crucial aspect in building a harmonious family unit. Cooperation may be demonstrated, for example, by the method in which the household duties are divided. When there is disagreement, the ability to express differences and to find ways of accommodation are vital to the relationship.

Inherent in building a family unit is the making of decisions that are satisfactory to each partner. An example is the resolving of the matter of finances; that is, how will the family income be obtained and spent?

Other major tasks to assess are the achievement of a satisfactory sexual relationship and the desire for parenthood. These are some basic tasks that confront a new family which require the development of effective coping behaviors.

Family as an Influencing Stimulus for the Adaptive Person

The family has a lifelong effect on a person's behavior in varying degrees. A person's nutritional habits are learned in the family as well as hygiene practices. The occupational role is sometimes influenced by role models present in the environment. The level of self-esteem is also related to the self-concept of the family. Other behaviors influenced by the family are presented according to the modes of adaptation.

Physiological Mode.   The overall health status and physical history are affected by the family. This pertains to nutritional habits, the practice of preventive health care, and the physical environment. The person's attitude toward health care is dependent on familial beliefs regarding the cause and cure of illness. These beliefs ultimately affect the type of care selected, if any, which has physiologic effects.

Self-Concept Mode.   The family's influence is readily observed in a person's moral-ethical-spiritual component of self. Beliefs, values, and religious affiliation are a direct result of the group's philosophy of life. The overall self-concept mode is affected, as perceptions of self, body image, and level of self-esteem are reflections of the response of significant others, as discussed in Chapter 14. The family, for most persons, provides this vital input during crucial developing years.

Role Function Mode.   The ability of the person to display adaptive role behaviors originates within the family unit through the process of social learning. In this way the person learns basic role expectations and the feelings associated with particular roles. The family is also responsible for the transmission of the basic skills of living. The person's potential to fulfill the age-related developmental tasks is a function of the family's ability to foster individual growth.

Interdependence Mode.   The family provides the foundation by which the person establishes interaction with others. This is accomplished through the teaching of effective communication skills and the give and take of love, respect, and value within the family. A person's awareness of self in relation to others is developed and cultivated in this primary support group. The tendency to utilize other support systems, such as the church, community, or health centers, is determined through the past pattern of behavior.

Having considered the two major external factors influencing a person's behavior, culture, and family, we turn now to a significant internal factor — the person's growth and development.

GROWTH AND DEVELOPMENT

Growth and development affect every stage of the life cycle, and characteristic behaviors are expected within each age level. It is important for the nurse to understand the process of normal growth and development to use as a reference point for assessment and intervention. The appearance of certain conditions and illnesses in the various age groups can be anticipated based on the stage of development. Knowledge of growth and development also provides a basis for the evaluation of behavior as adaptive or ineffective.

Growth is the increase in body size and/or changed structure, function, and regulatory processes until optimal maturity. The term also refers to the different rate of growth changes at different periods during the life span (Klauger, 1974). The body does not grow as a total unit: instead, the various structures develop at different times throughout the life cycle. The body experiences age-related changes in which structural deterioration usually precedes functional decline. The result is a decreased capacity for adaptation in later life. *Development* is the orderly change in behavior occurring over a lifetime due to the processes of maturation. The process of development is a predictable and sequential pattern of overlapping stages.

Principles of Growth and Development

Some basic principles of growth and development that are applicable to the use of the nursing process according to the Roy Adaptation Model can be summarized as follows:

1. *Growth* refers to increase in size; *development* implies an improvement in skill and functioning.
2. *Normal development* is the term used when the person performs behaviors expected at a certain age.
3. Within each *stage* of development there is a *range of time* for achieving given behaviors. For example, a child may begin to walk anywhere from 9 to 18 months of age and still be considered to be developing normally.
4. The *cephalocaudal trend* marks a person's mastery of body and environment. That is, control proceeds from the head downward; for example, the child lifts the head before sitting up.
5. There is also a *proximal-to-distal trend* to development. The parts closer to the center of the body develop before peripheral parts. Thus control of the arms comes before control of the fingers.
6. Behaviors develop in a *sequence* with one behavior building on the accomplishment of another. For example, development of the pincer grasp (thumb to forefinger) allows for feeding behavior.
7. *Genetic and environmental factors* influence growth and development.
8. The *family* is an important environmental factor influencing growth and development.
9. *Specific tasks* accompany each stage of development.
10. Successful *mastery of tasks* in one period provides the foundation for mastery of the succeeding developmental period.

Stages of Development

Stages of development are important to the Roy Adaptation Model for nursing since an understanding of human development provides a basis for assessing and promoting the adaptive potential of the person. The approaches of several theorists to stages of development are discussed in Chapters 14, 15, and 16 in relation to the theory and development of self-concept, role function, and interdependence. The work of Erik Erikson (1963) has been particularly useful to nurses applying the Roy Adaptation

Model to nursing practice. The following paragraphs present an overview of Erikson's stages of development.

Erikson (1963) stressed the relationship of the individual to family, community, and the world. According to Erikson, there are eight stages of development categorized according to their major *task* of the period. These are trust versus mistrust, autonomy versus shame and doubt, initiative versus guilt, industry versus inferiority, identity versus role confusion, intimacy versus isolation, generativity versus stagnation, and ego integrity versus despair.

Stage one, *trust versus mistrust*, focuses on the period from birth to 1 year of age. The major task is to acquire a sense of basic trust in the environment as well as with self while overcoming a sense of mistrust. The acquisition of trust requires a feeling of confidence that one's needs will be met and the feeling of being physically secure. The infant is totally dependent on others to meet basic needs for food, warmth, hygiene, and love. The primary factor influencing the infant's ability to master the task is the responsiveness of the significant other.

The significant other for this stage is the constant caretaker, usually the maternal parent. Support systems usually include the remaining parent, family members, a consistent child caregiver or babysitter, and grandparents. If these persons provide care that is consistent and in response to the infant's cues, a sense of trust will be developed by the infant.

Behaviors indicating trust that are expected include ease of feeding, depth of sleep, ease of bowel movements, and allowing the nurturing person to be out of sight without showing great distress.

Mistrust is demonstrated by uncertainty and anxiety about the environment and whether or not the environment will be positive. Behaviors that are expected if mistrust is developed include irritability, difficulty feeding, loose or constipated stools, and extreme difficulty in allowing the mothering person out of sight. However, these behaviors can indicate something other than simple mistrust, for example, a physiological disruption. Thus, in using the nursing process, a thorough second-level assessment must be done prior to making a judgment that the infant is failing to develop trust during this stage.

Erikson believes the development of trust is the basic cornerstone of the person's future development. It provides the basis for trusting others, of trusting one's self, of being "all right," of being oneself and relying on oneself, and of becoming what other people trust one will become—facets of the developing self-concept. It is the basis of the person's learning to use one's own resources to meet personal needs and depend on others. It involves a balance between trust of self and trust of others.

Acquiring a sense of *autonomy* while *overcoming* a sense of *doubt* and *shame* is the task of the child during stage two, from about age 1 to 3 years. The infant who acquires a sense of trust has experienced the predictable behaviors of caretakers and the environment, and realized that one's behavior has an effect on others. The focus of this stage is to establish oneself as a separate entity from others and to gain control over one's body and environment. As the child's ability to move around, speak, feed oneself, and gain bladder and bowel control emerge, a sense of self as a separate entity forms.

Behaviors indicating autonomy include saying no, recognition of self in a mirror by saying "me" or "I," exploration of the environment, and holding-on and letting-go actions, such as repeatedly dropping an object.

The desire to exert autonomy conflicts with the enjoyed dependence on others. If the infant exerts his or her will, negative consequences will follow; however, dependent behavior is usually rewarded with affection and approval. Continued dependency on others creates a sense of doubt in the toddler regarding the ability to control actions. The toddler experiences doubt and shame for wanting to rebel against others. This doubt is evidenced by behaviors of lack of activity in general, hesitance in exploring the surroundings, and extreme self-consciousness.

Specific tasks of this stage, according to another developmental theorist, Havighurst (1972), include learning to walk, talk, take solid foods, control elimination, and differentiate between right and wrong. Increasing verbal ability strongly influences development of interdependent relationships. Interactional patterns are solidified, and much of later nurturing ability is developed.

Stage three focuses on the child aged 3 to 6 years, whose major psychosocial crisis is acquiring a *sense of initiative versus guilt*. This is the stage of energetic learning in which the preschooler plays, works, and lives to the fullest. The child experiences a sense of accomplishment and satisfaction in the completion of activities. The conflict arises when one's ability is overestimated, with resulting feelings of guilt for behaving inappropriately. Tasks of this stage also include: learning appropriate male–female roles, developing a moral–ethical–spiritual self through awareness of the family's sociocultural mores, and achieving personal independence. Parents continue to be a strong influence and model for the accomplishment of these tasks. The child incorporates qualities and attitudes of significant others— parents, peers, and other adults—into his or her developing self-concept.

Children working to master the task of initiative exhibit characteristic behaviors: asking many questions—about birth and death, right and wrong, religion and sex differences—they are ashamed when caught doing something "wrong" or that is against the moral code, and they play creatively— dressing up and taking roles of significant others in dramatics. Preschoolers attack "a task for the sake of being active and on the move" (Erikson, 1963, p. 255).

With the development of initiative, a beginning conscience emerges and guilt becomes possible. Behaviors indicating unrealistic levels of guilt include fear of bodily harm—especially genital harm—rigid and excessive self-control, and inability to compromise or to initiate action freely: A healthy child will feel guilty for harming others. Development in the interdependent mode continues to occur as skills are developed that stimulate others to respond to the child as a person.

Successful mastery of the first three stages of psychosocial development, in which the child develops trust, autonomy, and initiative, provides a firm foundation for learning and competition associated with stage four, *industry versus inferiority*. The school-age child, 6 to 13 years, who has mastered the first three stages is confident within an environment of loving relationships and is ready to engage in experiences beyond the intimate group. The child identifies the self by "I am what I learn or do." This stage is characterized by an eagerness to produce meaningful and socially useful work through diligence. Expected behaviors of the school-age child working on mastery of industry include imitation of attitudes, dress, and behavior of heroines, heroes, and peers; having an adult hero or heroine; and expression of interest in a realistic future occupation. They follow rules, even though they may protest them; the feelings of others are understood; and they make decisions based on family belief systems.

Problems arise when situations are imposed on the child, resulting in a sense of inferiority. This sense of inadequacy is caused by unsuccessful achievement in the previous stages or an inability to assume responsibility. All children, to some degree, experience inferiority related to specific skills which they have not mastered. The feelings of inferiority are derived from the child or the social environment and are reflected in the following behaviors: fatalistic attitudes about one's race or social heritage, and statements such as "I'll never be able to do that well." The child will achieve a sense of industry (accomplishment) when a task is completed successfully despite individual differences and when there is an appropriate reward.

School-age tasks, according to Havighurst, include: learning how to share and divide; developing fundamental skills in reading, writing, and calculating; learning an appropriate masculine or feminine role; achieving personal independence; and developing attitudes toward social groups and institutions. The young person is looking outside the home to school experiences, peers, and adult models in completing the tasks of stage four.

Stage five, *identity versus role confusion*, centers on the age period from 13 to 19 years of age, a period of intense feelings and uncertainty. The adolescent seeks to develop a sense of identity as a distinct individual. The youth strives to achieve autonomy from the family, thereby developing a sense of personal identity instead of experiencing role diffusion. Role diffusion occurs when the adolescent is unable to form a satisfactory identity from the multiplicity of aspirations, roles, and identifications. This is usually shown by an inability to settle on an occupational identity. The peer group becomes an important support system for it offers identity to the adolescent and suggests appropriate age-role behavior. Adolescents may place less value on relationships with their parents, and best friend(s) will probably be described as the significant other. Most interdependence needs will be met by these people.

Developmental tasks facing the adolescent, according to Havighurst, are the achievement of mature relations with both sexes, a masculine or feminine social role, socially responsible behavior, and emotional independence from one's parents. Other tasks are: defining and preparing for a future vocation, accepting one's physical characteristics, preparing for marriage and family life, and acquiring a set of values.

The young adult emerging from the search for identity is ready for intimacy and commitment to a partnership in stage six, *intimacy versus isolation.* The young adult, age 20 to 35 years, is faced with the tasks of: establishing oneself as an independent adult among family and friends, building a strong affectional relationship with a significant other, and being able to nurture one's spouse and offspring. The positive end result of this stage is the development of affiliation and love. The danger of this stage is isolation, where the young adult avoids intimacy and responsibility due to a fear of ego loss. This individual's behaviors show a withdrawal from relationships, and a defending of self from persons seen as different and threatening.

The generative adult, age 35 to 60 years, is in stage seven, *generativity versus stagnation.* The previous developmental stages prepare the person of this age to teach and guide the younger generation to their place in society. Other tasks invovle: learning to be interdependent with people other than spouse, developing leisure-time activities, maintaining a satisfying marital relationship, managing a home, learning to accept the physiological changes associated with middle age, maintaining an economic standard of living, and fulfilling the needs of one's own aging parents. Successful mastery of this stage results in productivity, caring, and accepting responsibility with affection. Without feelings of generativity, stagnation and a sense of personal impoverishment occur. The person experiences self-indulgence and is unable to respond to others or the work situation.

The last stage, in which all the previous phases of the life cycle come together, is known as *ego integrity versus despair,* stage eight. The mature adult with integrity, age 60 years plus, accepts one's own life and defends the dignity of the life-style led. The feeling of satisfaction with the life that one has led is certainly influenced by one's self-concept and by the number and quality of relationships one has had. Without ego integrity, there is a feeling of despair and disgust, with the hope of reliving one's life. Life is viewed as too short to start over, and death becomes feared. Tasks facing the mature adult include: accepting help from others as the body ages, facing loss of spouse or significant others, finding or maintaining satisfying relationships beside one's partner, learning new affectional roles with one's children and grandchildren, adjusting to retirement and a reduced income, establishing living arrangements, and beginning to anticipate death.

The process of growth and development determines behaviors expected of persons based on chronological age. Knowledge of this process enables nurses to assess persons for critical behaviors characteristic of the age period. It provides a norm for the evaluation of a behavior as adaptive or ineffective and suggests ways of intervening. Specific application of these general processes will be discussed throughout this text, particularly in Part III, which focuses on the theory and development of the psychosocial adaptive modes.

SUMMARY

Culture, family, and growth and development were presented as major factors influencing a person's adaptation throughout life. Guides to assessing behaviors as influenced by these factors were outlined in this chapter. With an understanding of the concepts and theories discussed, the reader will be able to apply this knowledge in using the nursing process with persons for whom they provide care. Throughout the nursing process, the nurse will be aware that each person has a unique experience of culture, family, and growth and development that is influencing the person's adaptation.

STUDENT LEARNING ACTIVITY

Consider your own behavior in one situation during the past week and list examples of how your culture, family, and growth and development may have been factors influencing what you did.

REFERENCES

Backrup, Ruth. "Implementing Quality Health Care for the American Indian Patient," in *Implementing Quality Health Care for Ethnic People of Color. Washington State Journal of Nursing*, Special Supplement, 1979.

"Becoming Aware of Cultural Differences in Nursing," speeches presented during the 48th Convention, American Nurses' Association, 1973, Kansas City.

Billingsley, A. *Black Families in White America*. Englewood Cliffs, N. J.: Prentice-Hall, Inc., 1968.

Branch, Marie Foster, and Phyllis Perry Paxton. *Providing Safe Nursing Care for Ethnic People of Color*. New York: Appleton-Century-Crofts, 1976, Chapter 9.

Chapman, William P. "Measurements of Pain Sensitivity in Normal Subjects and in Psychoneurotic Patients," *Psychosomatic Medicine*, July 1944.

Clark, Ann. *Culture, Childbearing, Health Professionals*. Philadelphia: F. A. Davis Company, 1978.

Donin, Rabbi Haim Halevy. *To Be a Jew*. New York: Basic Books, Inc., Publishers, 1972.

Duvall, Evelyn. *Family Development*. Philadelphia: J. B. Lippincott Company, 1971.

Erikson, Erik. *Childhood and Society*. New York: W. W. Norton & Company, Inc., 1963.

Havighurst, R. *Developmental Tasks and Education*. New York: David McKay Company, Inc., 1972.

Implementing Quality Health Care for Ethnic People of Color. Washington State Journal of Nursing, Special Supplement, 1979.

Klauger, George, and M. Klauger. *Human Development: The Span of Life*. St. Louis: The C. V. Mosby Company, 1974.

Lewis, Oscar. "The Culture of Poverty," in *On Understanding Poverty*, David Monyneham, ed. New York: Basic Books, Inc., Publishers, 1969.

Murray, Ruth Beckmann, and Judith Proctor Zentner. *Nursing Assessment and Health Promotion through the Life Span*. Englewood Cliffs, N. J.: Prentice-Hall, Inc., 1979.

Paul, B. D. "Anthropological Perspectives on Medicine and Public Health," in *Social Interaction and Patient Care*, U. Skipper and R. Leonard, eds. Philadelphia: J. B. Lippincott Company, 1975, pp. 199–200.

Rotkovitch, Rachel. "Ethnicity and Health Care—The Jewish Heritage," *Ethnicity and Health Care*. New York: NLN Publication 14-1625, 1976.

Torbett, D. "The Single Parent Family," in *Maternity Nursing Today*, J. P. Clausen et al., eds. New York: McGraw-Hill Book Company, 1973.

Zborowski, Mark. "Cultural Components in Responses to Pain, " *Journal of Social Issues*, vol. 8, no. 4, August 1952, pp. 16–30.

Zussman, Muntner. "The Jewish Contribution to Medicine," *Medica Judaica*, vol. 1, no. 1, July 1970.

Part II

Adaptation
in the Physiological Mode

The preceding chapters dealt with Roy's descriptions of the person as an adaptive system and of nursing as a process of promoting adaptation. Nurses support and enhance persons' abilities to respond positively, or to adapt, to internal and external environmental changes. In this way, nurses contribute to health and quality of life for members of society. According to the Roy Adaptation Model, the two basic coping mechanisms—the regulator and the cognator—act in relation to four effector modes. Nurses observe and deal with people's adaptive responses as they are manifested by physiological function, self-concept, role function, and interdependence.

Part II focuses on adaptation in the physiological mode. Chapters 5 through 9 cover the basic needs for oxygenation, nutrition, elimination, activity and rest, and skin integrity. Each need is looked at in relation to the major steps of the nursing process, including behaviors and stimuli to assess, as well as common adaptation problems and nursing diagnosis in each need area, with basic nursing interventions related to these problems.

Chapters 10 through 13 approach adaptation in the physiological mode from the perspective of the role played by other physiological components in the adaptation of the total system. The senses, fluid and electrolytes, and neurological and endocrine function are discussed as integral to the regulator adaptive processes. Again, an overview of first- and second-level assessment of each of these components and common adaptation problems and interventions is provided.

It can be noted at this point that the distinction being made between adaptation problems and nursing diagnosis is based on the developing work in both of these fields. At this point, adaptation problems are seen *not* as nursing diagnosis but as areas of concern for the nurse related to the adapting person or group. These areas of concern are helpful in organizing content relevant to nursing and have been used to select major topics to be dealt with in this section on the physiological mode of adaptation, as well as in the rest of the text. Nursing diagnosis, on the other hand, involves the process of judgment and the terminology used in labeling specific instances within these broad areas of concern. Wherever relevant, the work of the North American Nursing Diagnoses Association has been identified as related to the adaptation problems described within the chapters.

Chapter 5

Oxygenation

Sharon A. Vairo

BEHAVIORAL OBJECTIVES

After studying this chapter, the reader will be able to:

1. Define the key concepts of the chapter.
2. Identify the person's basic need for supply of oxygen to all body tissues.
3. Identify and assess behaviors and common stimuli related to oxygen and circulation.
4. Discuss the primary adaptation problem related to oxygen need.
5. Specify nursing interventions to be used in managing hypoxia.

KEY CONCEPTS DEFINED

Respiration: a combination of cardiovascular and pulmonary processes by which a sufficient amount of oxygenated blood to meet metabolic requirements is provided and the end products of metabolism are removed.

Systemic Circulation: the major circulation by which blood is pumped from the left ventricle of the heart through the arteries and arterioles to the capillaries and returned to the right side of the heart.

Pulmonary Circulation: the lesser circulation by which blood is pumped from the right heart through the pulmonary vessels, is equilibrated with the oxygen and carbon dioxide in the alveolar air and transported to the left side of the heart.

Respiratory Center: the respiratory neurons located in the medulla oblongata and lower pons.

Hypoxia: various degrees of oxygen deficiency.

Dyspnea: difficult or painful breathing.

Orthopnea: difficult or painful breathing while lying down.

Paroxysmal Nocturnal Dyspnea: dyspnea at night.

Cough: a response to clear the airway.

Hemoptysis: coughing up of blood.

Cyanosis: bluish or purplish color of skin and/or mucous membranes.

Hyperventilation: increase in rate and depth of respiration. (A decrease in rate and depth of respiration is termed *hypoventilation.*)

Pulse: the fluid wave through the arteries which results from the left ventricle of the heart contracting and forcing blood into the aorta.

Bradycardia: slow heartbeat. Generally defined as fewer than 60 beats per minute.

Tachycardia: rapid heartbeat. Generally defined as more than 100 beats per minute.

Shock: inadequate tissue perfusion.

Hypercarbia: buildup of carbon dioxide.

Respiratory Failure: the respiratory system is unable to maintain adequate oxygenation of the blood.

Cardiovascular Failure: the cardiovascular system is unable to provide a sufficient amount of oxygenated blood to meet the needs of the various body tissues.

The need for oxygen is a priority factor in the person's physiological adaptation. This chapter considers oxygen need and the related process of circulation. The structure, function, and regulation of the cardiovascular and pulmonary systems are described. Nursing assessment of behaviors related to oxygen need and factors influencing this need are discussed. The major nursing concern of hypoxia is noted, and appropriate nursing interventions are listed and then demonstrated in a sample Adaptation Nursing Process Care Plan in the Appendix.

STRUCTURES AND FUNCTIONS RELATED TO OXYGEN NEED

The cardiovascular and pulmonary systems are responsible for providing to all body tissues, under all conditions, a sufficient amount of oxygenated blood to meet the metabolic requirements of each tissue and to remove the end products of metabolism that have accumulated. This entire combination of processes is referred to as *respiration*.

Human respiration is comprised of three parts. The first is external respiration, which involves taking in oxygen from the air and excreting carbon dioxide. This process is controlled by neural and mechanical devices. Second, respiration includes the transport of oxygen and carbon dioxide. This is the chemical and physical process of gas exchange between blood and cells in the tissues. Third, internal respiration is the term used to cover the physiochemical and biochemical processes of cellular metabolism in which oxygen and carbon dioxide are produced.

The pulmonary system by itself is concerned primarily with the intake and exchange of respiratory gases. The system is basically composed of the lungs; the air passages to and from the lungs; the thoracic and abdominal muscles, which do the actual work involved in breathing; and the pleural spaces, which allow the movements of breathing. The actual exchange of the respiratory gases takes place in the numerous small alveoli of the lungs. This exchange is controlled by the laws governing the diffusion of gases, which are discussed in detail in any of the available medical-physics texts.

The cardiovascular or circulatory system is the transport system of the body. It is responsible for carrying the oxygen absorbed from the alveolar surfaces of the lungs to the tissues of the body and returning carbon dioxide to the lungs to be removed. The vehicle for this movement is the blood. The blood is able to carry large amounts of oxygen because of the hemoglobin contained in the red blood cells. Oxygen combines reversibly with hemoglobin and is transported in this form to the individual tissues of the body. This oxyhemoglobin combination is influenced by the partial pressure of oxygen in the surrounding environment. Carbon dioxide is transported mainly in the form of bicarbonate ions in the blood plasma and in the red blood cells.

The blood, which is carrying these respiratory gases, is propelled through the system of blood vessels by the heart, which functions as a pump. In reality, the heart is two pumps joined together. From the left ventricle of the heart, blood is pumped through the arteries and arterioles to the capillaries, where the substances carried are transferred to the interstitial fluid and from there to the individual cells. The waste products of cell metabolism are picked up by the blood at this time and transported back to the right atrium of the heart through the venules and veins. This is called the major, or *systemic circulation*. From the right atrium, blood travels to the right ventricle, which pumps it through the pulmonary blood vessels to the left atrium and then on to the left ventricle. Circulation through the pulmonary vessels is known as the lesser, or *pulmonary circulation*. It is in the pulmonary capillaries that the blood equilibrates with the oxygen and carbon dioxide in the alveolar air. This entire circulation is controlled by a multiplicity of regulatory systems whose general function is to maintain adequate blood flow and thus adequate oxygenation of body tissues.

REGULATION RELATED TO OXYGEN NEED

Respiration is controlled and regulated by a neural and chemical balance within the body. The principal integration and regulation of breathing are achieved by respiratory neurons located in the medulla oblongata and lower pons.[1] This *respiratory center* is influenced by structures at higher levels of the nervous system as well as by changes in the chemical environment. For example, the cerebral cortical center provides for sufficient voluntary control of breathing to allow talking, laughing, and holding of breath. The major chemical factor affecting breathing is considered to be the blood carbon dioxide concentration. An increase in arterial pCO_2 results in an increased pCO_2 in tissue fluids, and thus decreased pH within the chemosensitive neurons of the respiratory center. These changes result in an increase in ventilation. This increased activity will then cause a decreased pCO_2, and ventilation will correspondingly decrease. This feedback control system maintains the arterial pCO_2 within narrow limits unless there is a disturbance of the respiratory center or the cardiovascular-pulmonary structure itself.

The circulatory system is capable of adjusting to varying demands of body tissues. Blood supply to active tissues is increased and heat loss can be increased or decreased. Flow of blood of vital organs such as the brain and the heart will be maintained at the expense of other less vital body tissues. These circulatory adjustments are brought about by neural and chemical mechanisms that change the caliber of the arterioles and other resistance vessels, increase or decrease blood storage in venous reservoirs, and vary the rate and stroke output of the heart.

FIRST-LEVEL ASSESSMENT

First-level assessment of oxygenation involves the nurse's description of behaviors related to oxygen need. Behaviors indicative of deficits in oxygen are a prime concern. Disruptions anywhere in the cardiovascular and pulmonary systems that cause an interference with oxygen supply to the tissues cause *hypoxia*. The term *anoxia* is also often used; however, *hypoxia* is the more accurate term, in that it implies various degrees of oxygen deficiency, whereas anoxia means an absence of any oxygen.

Nursing assessments are directed toward the early recognition of the signs and symptoms of hypoxia. It may be either acute or chronic. The signs and symptoms of acute hypoxia are similar to those of acute alcoholic intoxication. Indeed, acute alcoholic intoxication is an example of one type of

---

[1]These are structures of the brain stem, which, together with other references to anatomy and physiology, will be found described in a basic text on this subject.

hypoxia. The behaviors indicative of chronic hypoxia resemble those of fatigue.

Early objective changes in the vital signs resulting from cardiovascular response to hypoxia include an increased pulse rate indicative of tachycardia. Respirations may increase in depth (hyperpnea) and rate (tachypnea). Systolic blood pressure rises slightly as cardiac output increases. The general norms for pulse, respirations, and blood pressure are given in Table 5.1.[2] When the hypoxic state becomes more advanced and the body's compensatory efforts fail, the pulse rate and blood pressure will fall.

TABLE 5.1
General Norms for Pulse, Respirations, and Blood Pressure of a Healthy Adult

Pulse:	60–100 beats per minute
Respirations:	12–20 per minute
Blood pressure:	100–140/60–90 mm Hg

Temperature changes are seen whenever the system disruptions change body metabolic requirements. For example, a moderately elevated central temperature is very common in the early stages of an acute mycardial infarction (heart attack). If the person's temperature is elevated at the same time the skin temperature is normal or subnormal, it would indicate a cutaneous vasoconstriction resulting from decreased cardiac output.

Dyspnea, cough, and hemoptysis are three common behavioral signs indicative of disruptions in the pulmonary and/or cardiovascular systems. *Dyspnea* is a subjective sensation and is defined as difficult or painful breathing. The degree to which this sensation is felt varies greatly with the individual. Dyspnea that develops when the person lies down is called *orthopnea.* When it occurs at night it is called *paroxysmal nocturnal dyspnea. Cough* occurs when there is a need to clear the airway. It is always considered abnormal since it has no role in the normal respiratory cycle. It may result from disturbances in the pulmonary system itself or in the cardiovascular system. *Hemoptysis,* or coughing up blood, occurs when there is bleeding into the respiratory tract. It, too, may result from direct disturbances in the pulmonary system or as a result of cardiovascular disturbance.[3]

Skin color may or may not indicate the presence of hypoxia. It is inaccurate to assume that the patient who is not cyanotic (bluish tinged) is not hypoxic. Very severe degrees of hypoxia can exist in the absence of *cyanosis.* For the bluish or purplish color of cyanosis to be seen in the skin

[2]Methods for measuring these parameters and others and further discussion of variations in measurement can be found in texts on nursing skills.

[3]A comprehensive discussion of dyspnea, cough, hemoptysis, and other medically related bodily responses referred to in this text can be found in references on signs and symptoms, such as Mitchell and Pierce (1970).

and mucous membranes, the capillary blood must contain approximately 5 grams (g) per 100 ml or more of unoxygenated hemoglobin, and the surface capillaries must be dilated and must have blood circulating through them. Persons with carbon monoxide poisoning have a very characteristic cherry pink color to their skin resulting from the combination of carbon monoxide and hemoglobin (carboxyhemoglobin), which is a cherry-red-colored compound. These patients are very hypoxic because the hemoglobin which is combined with carbon monoxide is not free to combine with oxygen, thereby depriving body tissues of an adequate oxygen supply.

Hypoxia is also accompanied by changes in the gastrointestinal and renal systems. These changes may occur as a direct result of the hypoxia on the involved tissues or indirectly through the effects of hypoxia on the nervous system. For example, anorexia, nausea, and vomiting frequently occur when oxygen tension falls.

Hypoxia of renal tissue results in oliguria (infrequent voiding) and, unless corrected, eventually anuria (a lack of urine production). The kidney is very sensitive to hypoxia; for this reason frequent measurement of urine output is a very important part of the assessment of the patient with acute hypoxia.

The first signs and symptoms of hypoxia result from the effects of oxygen deficit on the central nervous system. Since the most oxygen-sensitive tissue in the body is the retina, the earliest symptoms may involve vision. However, this is usually unnoticed, as the first change is a decrease in dark adaptation (night vision). As hypoxia increases, a wide variety of central nervous system signs and symptoms may appear: headache, depression, apathy, dizziness, slowness of thought, euphoria, irritability, defective judgment and memory loss, diminished visual acuity, emotional disturbances, poor muscular coordination, fatigue, stupor, and finally unconsciousness. As can be seen by this partial list of behaviors, it is the cerebral cortex that suffers disturbances very early in the development of hypoxia. Three to five minutes is generally considered the approximate time period that the cerebral cortex can tolerate oxygen deprivation without irreversible damage. For this reason, the need for oxygen is considered the first-priority physiological need.

Although fluid retention may not often be thought of in connection with hypoxia, it is a common occurrence in pulmonary and cardiovascular disturbances that result in circulatory congestion.

The emotional and psychological responses of the patient who is unable to get his or her breath are very evident. Any emotional stress has a marked effect on respiration, and these patients are very apprehensive and anxious. Frequently, this will result in *hyperventilation*, thus compounding the problem. Persons who are having difficult breathing will try to sit bolt upright if possible, and if an oxygen mask is being used may frequently try to push it away because of the sensation that it is stifling them. Respirations become increasingly gasping and rapid. Breath to be used in speaking is very limited. As fears increase, so does energy requirement, which places an even greater load on the already overburdened respiratory system, and thus increases the hypoxia.

Behavioral assessment of oxygenation also involves the nurse's specific observations related to ventilation and circulation. The following section is a guide to this further first-level assessment.

Ventilation

Chest Appearance.   Indicate the bilateral appearance of the chest during both inspiration and expiration. Include any change in the contour or expansion of the chest.

Normally, the chest cage is bilaterally symmetrical and the rib cage expands and relaxes equally on both sides. There is no apparent effort with normal breathing at rest. The respiratory rate is regular and the respirations themselves are quiet. In the healthy adult one can expect the respiratory rate to range from 12 to 20 depending on age, activity, and general health.

Usually, the ratio of respiratory rate to pulse rate is 1:4. In fever, the respiratory rate increases with the pulse rate on an average of four additional respiratory cycles per minute for each 1 degree of elevation in temperature above normal (Sana and Judge, 1975).

The activity of respiratory cycles should be rhythmic and the interval between cycles should be equal. Normal respirations are usually two parts inspiration to three parts expiration. However, in emphysema the expiratory time is often prolonged. Amplitude of respirations should also be assessed. A decrease in amplitude will usually be noted in situations where pain is intensified by inspiratory effort, such as that occurring with fractured ribs, sprained muscles, or painful skin conditions.

The major muscle used in normal respiratory effort by both men and women is the diaphragm. However, since it is sometimes difficult to assess respiratory rate and quality accurately without the person being aware that you are doing so, it is helpful to know that you will generally see more costal movement in women and more diaphragmatic movement in men.

Use of the intercostal muscles and the accessory muscles in the neck during the respiratory process indicate increased respiratory effort. Any asymmetry of the chest during the respiratory cycle is abnormal and should be carefully described.

Breath Sounds.   Breath sounds are produced by turbulent air flowing through the airways. When listening to lung sounds symmetrical areas of the lungs should be assessed. Develop a consistent pattern of listening and in that way you will not miss or skip over areas of the lungs. Ask the person to breathe through the mouth more deeply than normal and listen to at least one full breath in each location (Bates, 1979, p. 127). A complete description of the types of normal breath sounds and their characteristics can be reviewed in any physical assessment text. In general, however, normal breath sounds are clear without any indication of wheezing or crackling sounds, and they are present throughout the lung fields.

If normal airflow is obstructed, breath sounds will be decreased or absent. An example of a condition causing decreased breath sounds is emphysema.

Two of the more common abnormal breath sounds you might hear are *rales*, and *rhonchi* or *wheezes*. Rales are discrete, noncontinuous, crackling sounds which are usually heard more on inspiration. This is probably secondary to delayed reopening of previously deflated airways (Bates, 1979, p. 134). Conditions or situations that can cause rales to be heard include congestive heart failure, pneumonia, and prolonged periods of recumbency when restoration excursion is limited. The classic example of the last is the person who lies quietly in bed after surgery and does not do frequent coughing and deep-breathing exercises. Rales may or may not clear after coughing, depending on what has caused them. For example, the rales of congestive heart failure tend to remain until the heart failure itself can be corrected, whereas the rales secondary to prolonged recumbency will generally clear with vigorous coughing and deep breathing. The terms *rhonchi* and *wheezes* are often used interchangeably. They last longer than rales and may be inspiratory, expiratory, or both (Bates, 1979). Their presence indicates that the air passages have been narrowed by the causative pathology. You will hear them, for example, in asthma or bronchitis.

Laboratory Values.   The primary laboratory test for assessment of the effectiveness of ventilation and gas exchange is the blood-gas test. In caring for persons with compromised respiratory function this test provides vital information as to how well body oxygen needs are being met and must be included in any nursing assessment of a person's respiratory and circulatory status. The pH, PaO_2, $PaCO_2$ percent oxygen saturation, base excess, and HCO_3, if done, are very specific indicators of respiratory and circulatory status. Often the nurse is the first person to see test results and is responsible for recognizing and identifying deviations from the normal, communicating them to the physician, and applying interpretations of the results to her further assessment of the condition of the patient.

Circulation

Peripheral Circulation.   When assessing the effectiveness of circulation, the first thing to look at is the appearance of the extremities. The nails should have a pink appearance and have a smooth look. They should be convex in shape. If you compress the nail and then release the pressure, the refill of blood into the underlying tissues should be immediate. This is called the *capillary refill*. Always compare one side of the body to the other. Skin color and general appearance should be consistent from one side to the other. The temperature of the skin should be warm over all the extremities. However, this is dependent to a considerable extent on environmental factors. A behavior that is often overlooked is the presence or absence of hair growth. If normal circulation is present, there will be a pattern of hair growth consistent with the rest of the body.

Normal skin appearance in the extremities, then, is warm, has the same color as the rest of the body, has normal-appearing nail growth, immediate capillary refill to the nail beds, presence of usual hair growth patterns, and good skin elasticity (turgor). The comparison of a normal extremity to one that has poor circulation is striking. The extremity with poor circulation is cooler to touch, has little or no hair present, presents a shiny taut appearance to the skin, and has poor turgor. Often the skin will give an appearance ranging from pallor to varying degrees of cyanosis. The nail beds tend more toward a cyanotic blue color and the capillary refilling time is quite slow. Depending on the pathology involved, the texture of the nail may be rough and the shape of the nail and finger/toe tip may be blunted. Nail growth is very slow. The person is often not aware of it, but when asked they will comment that it has been quite some time since their nails have required trimming. If circulation is not improved, eventually there will be atrophy of muscle and soft tissue and eventually ulcerations will occur.

Again, depending on the pathology involved, you may also note edema present in the dependent portions of the body. Since the lower extremities are the part of the body that is usually dependent, this is where the edema is usually seen. However, if the person has been lying in bed for any period of time, it is the sacral area that is dependent and it should be assessed for the degree of edema present. Dependent edema is also seen in the hands and fingers.

Edema that is caused by cardiac dysfunction is bilaterally present and usually dependent in nature. You will hear it referred to as *pitting edema*, which means that if you press on the edematous area, it will temporarily leave a pit, or depression, in the skin. Pitting edema is measured on a rather subjective scale of $1+$ to $4+$, with 4 being the most advanced. $1+$ is generally described as being a slight skin depression from pressing on the skin surface which disappears fairly quickly when the pressure is released. On the other hand, $4+$ is a deep depression which resolves very slowly. The only way to develop a good feel for the differences on the scale is to get into the practice of doing this assessment with anyone who has some dependent edema and then comparing your assessment with that of someone who has more experience.

Edema that results from a peripheral cause such as the blockage of a deep vein by an embolus will be unilateral in nature and tends to be nonpitting. The term *brawny* is sometimes used to describe it. The best way to assess the degree of this edema is to measure the circumference of the extremity and compare it to the opposite side. It is important to mark the area measured and be consistent from one side to the other. Always use the same site each time. Normally, one measures distance from a bony prominence, such as the bottom of the patella, to the area being evaluated. Record the distance and the point used as a marker so that the next person doing the measurement will do so in the same part of the extremity.

Finally, when doing an assessment of general circulation status, it is important to note when the person indicates the presence of pain. This may be verbally, by facial expression, or through body actions. If tissue is deprived of adequate circulation, pain will occur as long as the nerve supply to the areas is intact. It may be continually present or it may be felt intermittently when the tissue demand exceeds the available supply. The latter is called *intermittent claudication* and can be measured quite accurately. The person can usually tell you exactly how much activity can be done before pain occurs. For example, it may be that one flight of stairs can be climbed, or one block walked before the pain begins. The amount of activity that can be tolerated before pain occurs is one indication of the severity of the disease process.

Pulses. Peripheral pulses are an important indicator of circulatory status. When assessing general circulatory status, you are interested primarily in whether or not the pulse is present in the extremity, and if so, what its quality is. In the person who has normal circulation, the pulse should have the same feel or quality at all points where it is palpable. It is therefore again essential that one side of the body be compared to the other and the lower extremities compared to each other. Quality is usually described in terms of absent, thready, or weak (sometimes both terms are used), normal, or bounding (Sana and Judge, 1975, p. 186). Again, developing the feel for the differences is a matter of practice.

Pulse rate is a reflection of left ventricular contraction of the heart and is part of the assessment of cardiac function. The normal adult resting pulse rate is 60 to 100 beats per minute. A rate below 60 is arbitrarily referred to as *bradycardia* and above 100 is called *tachycardia*. These may or may not reflect pathology. For example, an athlete in good condition often has a normal resting pulse less than 60, and it is normal for most people who have been exercising or are frightened or anxious to have a rate temporarily over 100. The rate should be regular, although it is very common for most people to notice an occasional skipped beat. However, any persistence or frequency of these skips, which are correctly called *premature contractions* or extra systoles, requires a medical evaluation.

Blood Pressure.   This is a measure of the pressure exerted by the blood flow against the arterial walls. It varies with the cardiac cycle and is affected by the amount of blood pumped out by the left ventricle, the elasticity of the large arteries, the amount and viscosity of blood in the system, and finally, the peripheral resistance, which depends primarily on the caliber of the arterioles. The *systolic pressure* is the pressure present during the time the left ventricle is contracting and ejecting blood into the aorta. *Diastolic pressure* is the pressure in the arterial system during the resting phase between cardiac contractions and depends primarily on peripheral resistance. It is normal to find a difference of 5 to 10 mm Hg pressure between the readings taken in different arms. If possible, take subsequent measurements in the arm with the higher pressure (Bates, 1979, p. 179). A pressure difference of over 10 mm Hg suggests arterial compression or obstruction on the side with the lower pressure. If you measure blood pressure in supine, sitting, and standing positions, normally the systolic blood pressure will slightly decrease and the diastolic slightly increase as the person rises from the supine to the standing position. The usual upper normal limit for blood pressure that is listed in texts is 140/90. However, this varies greatly depending on many factors. In the young adult this would be considered a rather high reading.

Heart Sounds   Skill in recognizing and interpreting the various heart sounds requires much practice. However, in developing skills in beginning assessment, one can learn to recognize the normal heart sounds and the locations where they are best heard. There are five locations which are normally auscultated (listened to with a stethoscope) (Bates, 1979, p. 153):

1. *Aortic area*: second interspace right of the sternum
2. *Pulmonic area*: second interspace left of the sternum
3. *Erb's point*: third left interspace close to the sternum
4. *Tricuspid area*: fifth left interspace close to the sternum
5. *Mitral area (apical)*: fifth left interspace medial to the midclavicular line

In the normal heart one hears two heart sounds, simply called the first and second heart sounds, and usually written as S_1 and S_2. S_1 indicates the onset of ventricular systole and abrupt closure of the atrioventricular valves. This sounds like "lubb." S_2 signals the onset of diastole and the closure of the semilunar valves. It has a snapping quality, and sounds like "dubb." These are relatively high-pitched sounds and are best heard using the diaphragm of the stethoscope. There are other normal sounds, but we will consider only the two main ones. In the aortic and pulmonic areas, S_2 is normally louder than S_1. In the apical area S_1 is often, but not always, louder than S_2 (Bates, 1979, p. 161). You should be able to identify the two sounds and determine their rate and if they are regular in occurrence. If the rate is irregular, determine if there is a pattern to the irregularity.

When doing basic assessment, the apical pulse is very important. The heart rate of a person with cardiovascular dysfunctions should be measured using the apical rate rather than any of the peripheral pulse rates since the apical will provide a more accurate reading. Also, if the rate is irregular, you must count the number of pulsations for a full minute in order to obtain a correct reading. People sometimes have difficulty finding the apical pulse, particularly in an obese person or a woman with large, pendulous breasts. Repositioning the person to a forward leaning position or turned toward the left side may help. Normally, the location where the apical pulse is found is in the fifth interspace (sometimes the fourth) and 7 to 9 cm from the midsternal line. If the person has an enlarged heart, you can expect to find the apical pulse more lateral in the direction of the midaxillary line. The point where you can best hear (and often see and feel) the pulsation is called the *point of maximal impulse*. This is almost always recorded as the "PMI" and can be found on the physical examination form. Looking up the information before you go in to listen to try and find the apical pulse gives you an advantage in locating the correct area.

Laboratory Data.   There are many tests done to assist in evaluating cardiovascular status. These are discussed in some detail in medical-surgical texts. However, two of the most common ones encountered early in the evaluation process are the complete blood count (CBC) and the electrocardiogram (ECG or EKG). The CBC is important because it gives an indication of the capability of the blood to carry oxygen to the body tissues. The ECG is also an important tool because it provides a visual picture of the electrical impulses generated by the heart. Imagine a camera taking a photograph of the heart's electrical impulses from 12 different directions. This is exactly what is done when an ECG is run. The directions are called *leads* and the term you will hear is "12-lead ECG." Each lead has its own name or number and they are always done in the same order, beginning with Lead I. You will also hear the terms *monitor* or *monitoring* used. This means that a single lead is connected to a visual screen so that one has a constant visual picture to "monitor" for heart rate and rhythm. That is all that a monitor does. Many people have been needlessly frightened when their monitors have been removed because they had somehow erroneously received the impression that in some way the monitor was helping their heart to beat. Most important of all—if you notice something on the monitor that seems abnormal, do not jump to the conclusion that it is the person. It may be a malfunction in the monitoring system. Go in to see the person and do a good assessment. He or she may have developed a cardiac irregularity or may not have. The monitor is an early warning system and is to be treated accordingly.

SECOND-LEVEL ASSESSMENT

In second-level assessment the nurse assesses for the factors that are responsible for, or which affect, the identified behaviors. These include a wide range of coping mechanisms, environmental conditions, emotional and psychological changes, disease states, and failure of either the respiratory or cardiovascular component of the total system.

The individual with healthy cardiovascular and respiratory systems is able to compensate for, and physically tolerate very well, a wide variety of the environmental, physical, emotional, and psychological stresses encountered, unless the stresses are very severe or prolonged. However, the individual with a disease state causing function impairment of either or both systems has a tolerance that is reduced in direct proportion to the severity and extent of the disease state.

Changes in the External Temperature.   The cardiovascular and respiratory systems are responsive to changes in the environment. When the body is exposed to a hot environment, as, for example, in summer sunshine, vasodilatation occurs, which results in a great increase in blood flow to the skin. This increases the amount of heat lost from the body surface. Because this vasodilating effect results in a large decrease in vascular resistance, there is also a compensating increase in cardiac output to maintain blood pressure. The respiratory system responds with hyperventilation. When exposed to cold in the natural environment, or artificially, as when working in refrigerated areas such as the meat-packing industry, there is a general vasoconstriction, with the blood pressure rising and the cardiac output decreasing. Sudden exposure to cold results in a quick inspiration followed by hyperventilation. In a state of hypothermia, ventilation will decrease and the heart will slow. However, if the central body temperature falls below 30°C, ventricular fibrillation may occur.

Altitude Changes.   Changes in altitude also result in cardiovascular and respiratory changes. The higher one goes, as, for example, in mountain climbing, the lower the pO_2 of the air being breathed and therefore the pO_2 of the arterial blood. This results in an increase in respiratory rate and depth and in cardiac rate. Usually, these changes are minimal until one reaches approximately the 10,000-foot level, unless added stress is encountered. Many people who normally live at sea level have had the experience of going to the mountains and quickly discovering that their exercise tolerance is markedly decreased.

Any acclimatization to high altitude depends on the length of time exposed. Over a period of time pulmonary ventilation becomes increased, especially with exercise, and the arterial pCO_2 is reduced. The red blood cell count increases, as does the hemoglobin concentration of the blood. The arterial blood thus is able to carry larger amounts of blood and meet the oxygen needs of body cells even though pCO_2 is reduced.

Exercise.   Increased activity is one of the most common causes for increased metabolic demands. Physical activity as a means of maintaining fitness and health is an established trend in today's North American culture. Respiratory rate and depth quickly increase with exercise. Systolic blood pressure greatly increases and diastolic pressure usually rises a little. There is redistribution of blood flow, with the exercising muscles receiving a large increase. This response to exercise is primarily under the control of neural mechanisms and occurs very rapidly.

Emotional and Psychological Changes.   Emotional and psychological changes will bring about a response in the cardiovascular and respiratory systems. Numerous examples can be cited, from the rapid pulse one feels when entering a classroom to take an examination to an acute attack of hyperventilation following a near-accident while driving. These responses appear to be mediated through either the sympathetic nervous system or the parasympathetic nervous system. During feelings of anxiety and fear, sympathetic activity increases, which results in increased respiratory and cardiac rates and increased force of cardiac contractions. All of these actions result in increased cardiac output. Conversely, it appears that when sudden fright, extreme dejection, or hopelessness occurs, the parasympathetic nervous system is stimulated. This brings about vagal stimulation and results in bradycardia (slow heartbeat), decreased blood flow to skin and viscera, and increased arterial pressure.

Blood Loss.   A short-term adaptation to stress is illustrated by the effects of a sudden acute blood loss of 1 to 2 liters. This stimuli is commonly identified for the patient who has had major surgery. Peripheral vasoconstriction occurs; heart rate increases; sweating occurs, with the skin becoming cold, pale, and moist; renal blood flow decreases, with a resultant decrease in urine output; blood becomes diluted by interstitial fluid in an effort to restore volume; and an antidiuretic hormone is secreted. Respirations also increase in rate and depth. All of these compensatory changes are for the purpose of maintaining adequate tissue oxygenation by restoring blood volume and maintaining adequate arterial and venous pressure. Continued blood loss or other additional stresses will eventually exceed compensatory efforts.

Oxygen Deprivation.   Deprivation of oxygen will result in varying degrees of hypoxia. Oxygen deprivation can occur in situations such as smoke inhalation and in disease conditions such as emphysema. Although moderate hypoxia can be compensated for over a prolonged period of time, this is not true of acute hypoxia. People have essentially no oxygen reserve and when exposed to an acute interruption of oxygen quickly demonstrate the signs and symptoms of hypoxia.

These vary widely with individuals and their differing abilities to adjust physiologically. However, in general, the higher levels of the brain will show the effects of oxygen deficit very early. Intellectual function is impaired quickly, and because of this the person is usually unaware of what is happening. Behavioral manifestations of hypoxia have been discussed on pages 94 through 97.

A specific example of oxygen deprivation is the phenomenon of *shock*. The shock syndrome can occur from a wide variety of causes, such as a simple fainting response at the sight of an accident scene or as a complex medical emergency for the accident victim with internal bleeding. Detailed definitions of types of this condition can be found in medical texts. A common feature of all types of shock is that of inadequate tissue perfusion, that is, lack of oxygen permeation. The circulation becomes progressively inadequate, and the behaviors exhibited by the person reflect this inadequacy. The person in shock appears very pale, and the skin is cool and moist. Early in the chain of events one may be quite restless and agitated, but this progresses to apathy and confusion. Thirst is a common symptom, but usually little water can be tolerated because of nausea. Urinary output is progressively decreased. Breathing is rapid and shallow, and as shock becomes more severe the pulmonary function progressively deteriorates. Pulse rate is rapid but thready. Arterial blood pressure, particularly systolic pressure, rises early in shock for a brief period and then falls. The pulse pressure also tends to be narrow. These behaviors are all indicative of very severe stress and unless the cause of the shock can be corrected and supportive measures instituted, the prognosis is very poor.

Excessive Carbon Dioxide and Oxygen Intake. An overload of either carbon dioxide or oxygen constitutes stress on the cardiovascular and respiratory systems. A buildup of carbon dioxide can occur from excessive oxygen therapy or from sedation. The effects of this *hypercarbia* occur more slowly than do the effects of hypoxia. Effects are seen on the central nervous system, and the person may appear anywhere on a continuum from somnolence to coma. The usual early signs are drowsiness, inability to concentrate, confusion and irritability. Patients with carbon dioxide narcosis will often complain of a headache and being unable to sleep.

It is not really known why oxygen when present in excess will cause convulsions and other nervous aberrations. The first signs, which will occur within 24 hours, are substernal distress due to tracheal irritation plus irritation of other mucous membranes. Respiratory depression will occur, as will hypotension. As the oxygen overload continues, neurological signs will become more evident, and eventually bronchopneumonia and death may occur.

Failure of the Respiratory System.   When this system fails there is an inability to provide for the necessary gas exchange in the lungs. Many diseases and injuries can cause respiratory failure. Obstruction of the airway, emphysema, pulmonary tumors, and trauma to the chest are but a few examples.

Failure of the Cardiovascular System.   Failure of the cardiovascular system may occur even if the arterial blood is adequately oxygenated. Here the cardiovascular system is unable to provide a sufficient amount of oxygenated blood to meet the needs of various body tissues (hypoxia). This failure may result from a dysfunction of the heart pump itself or it may occur from damage in the vascular system resulting in an impairment of circulation. Examples include heart damage such as myocardial infarction, or obstructions such as thrombosis.

ADAPTATION PROBLEMS RELATED TO OXYGENATION

The most pressing category of concern, or adaptation problem, which the nurse encounters in providing for the need for oxygen is hypoxia. The behavioral assessment of hypoxia and the factors influencing it have been described. Specific plans for nursing care will be based on careful individual assessment. However, general interventions can be outlined here.

The most important measure in treating hypoxia is oxygen administration. It is important to monitor the patient closely to prevent the administration of too much oxygen. Essential components of oxygen therapy include: careful observation of respiratory status, vital signs, and reaction to therapy; use of aseptic technique to assist in preventing infections; thorough explanation to the person of the procedures being used; and understanding and correct usage of the equipment being utilized.

The fact that the person is receiving oxygen therapy should not cause other needs to be ignored. Positioning for comfort and correct body alignment is one area of continued importance. These nursing measures are discussed in Chapter 8. In addition, the person with respiratory difficulty will usually assume the position whereby he or she can get maximum ventilation. This is usually an upright position, sometimes leaning slightly forward. Postural drainage[4] is often of assistance in facilitating drainage of pulmonary secretions and thus improving ventilation.

[4]Discussions of the techniques of postural drainage can be found in text and journal articles related specifically to this topic.

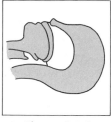

Airway closed

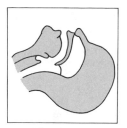

Airway open
(head hyperextended)

Figure 5.1   Position to maintain an open airway.

The importance of maintaining an open airway cannot be overemphasized. If an open airway is not maintained, no other therapeutic measures can be effective. Care in giving oral fluids and food, positioning to prevent accumulation of material in the airway, and suctioning of the airway when needed are means of achieving the goal of maintaining an open airway. Figure 5.1 demonstrates how hyperextension of the head facilitates opening of an airway. It is also essential to minimize metabolic demands to avoid excessive work by the cardiovascular and respiratory systems.

The deleterious effects of both physical and emotional stress on persons with cardiovascular and pulmonary dysfunctions were discussed earlier. Careful explanation by the nurse of any care being given; a calm, confident, and supportive manner on the part of the nurse; and as calm a physical environment as possible go a long way toward alleviating much of the stress encountered.

SUMMARY

In this chapter we have focused on nursing assessment of the basic need for oxygen. Behaviors to observe in assessing this need, and how these change with various influencing factors, have been identified. Some general interventions to meet the need for oxygen have been discussed. We thus have guidelines for carrying out the nursing process according to the Roy Adaptation Model to meet these needs. For each plan for care, specific nursing diagnoses will be formulated. Gordon (1982) lists the following diagnostic labels, related to oxygenation under the functional health pattern of activity-exercise as currently accepted by the North American Nursing Diagnoses Association:

Airway clearance: ineffective
Gas exchange: impaired
Breathing pattern: ineffective
Tissue perfusion: alteration in (cerebral, cardiopulmonary, renal, gastrointestinal, peripheral)
Cardiac output, alterations in: decreased

These labels may be helpful in stating nursing diagnoses related to oxygen need. They will continue to be refined as the North American Nursing Diagnoses Association and other nurse groups respond to the challenge to clarify nursing's taxonomy and develop a system of labels that can reflect various levels of problems that nurses legally treat, from the holistic-person level to the level of cell disruptions.

Nurses prepared to use the Roy Adaptation Model of nursing will state diagnoses in one of the three ways outlined in Chapter 3, that is, as summary labels, as specific behaviors with relevant stimuli, or as varying levels of regulator and cognator effectiveness.

Given thorough assessment and diagnoses of needs for oxygenation, the nurse sets outcome goals with the patient and plans interventions to manage the stimuli so as to promote physiological integrity. The outcome of nursing intervention is then evaluated by reassessment of the behaviors. Either the goal has been reached, and the need for oxygen met, or the behaviors do not reflect this, and thus the interventions will be modified.

STUDENT LEARNING ACTIVITY

Read the following case study about a middle-aged man brought to the hospital with chest pain and shortness of breath. Develop an adaptation nursing process care plan related to this person's oxygen need, stating: behaviors; stimuli or influencing factors as focal, contextual, and residual; nursing diagnosis; goal; interventions; and evaluation. See the Appendix for a sample care plan.

Case Study: Oxygen Need

Mr. A. is a 50-year-old man who was brought to the hospital because of shortness of breath and an aching pain in the substernal area radiating to his left jaw and neck. He is somewhat diaphoretic and short of breath. His heart rate is rapid and irregular.

Mr. A. has no family history of heart problems and except for the time he had his tonsils out at age 5, he has never been in a hospital. He owns his own business and habitually works long hours, although his work is rather sedentary. Mr. A. is about 30 pounds overweight and has smoked two packs of cigarettes a day for at least 20 years. He does not participate regularly in any exercise, although he does enjoy going fishing when he can get away from the office. Mr. A. is married and has three children. All family members are in good health.

This morning Mr. A. went out to cut the grass. He had planned on having his children do it, but they had left home early and gone on a picnic with neighborhood friends. Mr. A. had finished about half of the yard when he started to get some aching in his chest. He sat down and rested but the symptoms did not improve and he became a little frightened. He got his wife's attention and she decided to call the paramedics, who, after assessing his condition, contacted the hospital and brought Mr. A. in to be seen. Treatment was initiated enroute, so Mr. A. was feeling slightly better when he arrived at the hospital.

On arrival at the emergency room, Mr. A.'s blood pressure was 90/40; pulse was 130 and thready; respirations were 30. His skin was pale, cool, and moist. His facial expression is anxious as hospital personnel begin cardiac monitoring—that shows an irregular rhythm, taking x-rays, and starting an intravenous infusion of an antiarrhythmic medication.

Mr. A. insists he needs to be elevated on two pillows because, "I can't get my breath and being up on two pillows will help me get more air." Medicated with morphine, Mr. A. states the pain in his left chest has diminished.

Mr. A. continues to ask nurses of the whereabouts of his wife who is in the waiting room and has not seen him since he was taken to the hospital in the ambulance.

REFERENCES

Bates, Barbara. *A Guide to Physical Examination*, 2nd ed. Philadelphia: J. B. Lippincott Company, 1979.

Gordon, Marjory. *Nursing Diagnosis: Process and Application.* New York: McGraw-Hill Book Company, 1982.

Helming, Mary G., ed. "Nursing in Respiratory Disease," *Nursing Clinics of North America*, vol. 3, no. 3, 1968, pp. 381–487.

Luckmann, Joan, and Karen Sorenson. *Medical-Surgical Nursing: A Psychophysiologic Approach*, 2nd ed. Philadelphia: W. B. Saunders Company, 1980.

Mitchell, R. I., and J. A. Pierce. "Cough." In *Signs and Symptoms: Applied Pathologic Physiology and Clinical Interpretation*, 5th ed., Cyril MacBryde and Robert Blacklow, eds. Philadelphia: J. B. Lippincott Company, 1970, pp. 324–336.

Nursing Skillbook. "Assessing Vital Functions Accurately," *Nursing 77.* Springhouse, Pa.: Intermed Communications, Inc., 1977.

Sana, Josephine M., and Richard D. Judge, eds. *Physical Appraisal Methods in Nursing Practice.* Boston: Little, Brown and Company, 1975.

Chapter 6

Nutrition

Jane Servonsky

BEHAVIORAL OBJECTIVES

After studying this chapter, the reader will be able to:

1. Define the key concepts of the chapter.
2. Identify the person's basic need for nutrition.
3. Identify and assess behaviors and common stimuli related to nutrition.
4. Define common adaptation problems of the nutrition component.
5. Assess a person's nutritional patterns and apply the adaptation nursing process in planning care for the person.

KEY CONCEPTS DEFINED

Nutrition: the series of processes by which the person takes in and assimilates food necessary for maintaining human functioning, promoting growth, and replacing worn or injured tissues.

Ingestion: a person's act of eating and drinking.

Nutrients: substances that provide nourishment to the body. They include protein, fat, carbohydrate, vitamins, minerals, and water.

Appetite: the desire for and anticipation of eating, which may be stimulated by the sight, smell, or thought of food.

Satiety: a condition of satisfaction or a lack of desire for food after the ingestion of food.

Anorexia: the loss or lack of appetite for food.

Hunger: a strong desire to eat which is physiologically aroused by the body's need for food.

Digestion: the body's process of converting ingested foods into chemical substances that can be absorbed and utilized by the body.

Malnutrition: poor nutrition due to improper diet, resulting in an inadequate intake of nutrients, or to a defect in metabolism that prevents the body from utilizing food properly.

Obesity: the excessive accumulation of fat in the body, which increases the weight beyond the recommended measures with regard to bone structure, height, and age.

Nausea: an unpleasant sensation reported as a feeling of sickness with the urge to vomit.

Vomiting: the forceful ejection of stomach contents through the mouth.

This chapter is intended to provide an assessment guideline that each nurse needs to ascertain a person's state of nutrition and to aid the nurse in promoting the person's optimal nutritional level. It is not intended to teach the science of nutrition. The reader is encouraged to refer to one of the many nutrition textbooks for readings on the basic principles and science of nutrition.

Nutrition is a basic need, second only to the need for oxygen. The term *nutrition* refers to the series of processes by which the person takes in and assimilates food necessary for maintaining human functioning, promoting growth, and replacing injured tissues. *Ingestion* is the person's act of eating and drinking. Good nutritional habits play a major role in maintaining a person's integrity and health, since nutrition is fundamental for promotion of wellness and the prevention of illness. A nursing role is that of nutrition counselor, in which the nurse educates and collaborates with the person regarding nutritional needs. In recent years, there have been increased awareness of and interest in nutrition on the part of the general public. To respond to this interest effectively, the nurse needs basic knowledge and a framework in which to assess a person's dietary patterns and identify health implications.

The desirable characteristics to be considered when planning a diet for optimal nutrition are described by Suitor and Hunter (1980, pp. 12–13). To promote health, the diet should provide all *essential nutrients*, as discussed below, in adequate amounts for the daily needs of the body. The Recommended Dietary Allowances is the established nutrient guide that lists the amount of nutrients that allow healthy persons to achieve their full growth and health potential. The optimal diet should also provide a *caloric level* that will meet the energy needs of the body. Foods containing *fiber* should be ingested since the fiber provides bulk which stimulates intestinal elimination. The food eaten should *promote health* and provide a *measure of prevention* in protecting the person from illness throughout all stages of the life cycle. The established dietary pattern must be acceptable to the person or family. Acceptability includes establishing a diet that includes culturally defined differences as noted in Chapter 4 and later in this chapter. Taking account of such differences can be accomplished without much difficulty since there are many kinds and combinations of foods that constitute a well-balanced diet. Finally, the diet chosen should promote a good supply of *energy* for optimum performance of the person's activities of daily living and total human functioning.

Ingestion of *nutrients* is essential for the body's normal growth, and levels of growth and development are major factors influencing adaptation and health. Nutrient categories include protein, fat, carbohydrate, vitamins, minerals, and water. The U. S. Department of Agriculture has developed a *Daily Food Guide* for the purpose of promoting good nutrition. This guide provides a flexible framework to help a person achieve his or her nutrient needs as outlined in the Recommended Daily Dietary Allowances. The Daily Food Guide combines food with similar nutritional values into four main groups. They are the milk group, meat group, vegetable and fruit group, and grain group, commonly referred to as the Basic Four. In planning a diet the person should choose from each group a variety of foods that they like and can afford. The reader is referred to Fig. 6.1 for a general guideline, and to nutritional textbooks for a complete study of nutritional planning.

FIRST-LEVEL ASSESSMENT

When assessing nutritional needs, the nurse observes the following behaviors:

Appetite and Thirst.   *Appetite* is a pleasant sensation involving the person's desire for and anticipation of food or drink. The appetite is frequently affected by such specific stimuli as the sight, smell, and thought of food. It is psychological and is dependent on memory and associations. *Hunger*, however, is physiologically aroused by the body's need for food. The hypothalamus is the principal organ involved in the physiological regulation of eating. A functioning hypothalamus is responsible for sending *internal* cues that signal the person to eat in order to supply the body with needed energy. This process is one example of the regulator activity outlined in Chapter 2. The hypothalamus again signals through the *satiety* center, telling the person to stop eating. A healthy individual who responds to these internal cues that regulate energy balance is able to maintain a normal weight and control one's appetite. An example of an adaptive appetite behavior would be the statement: "I have a good appetite in the morning and eat a well-balanced breakfast," whereas an ineffective appetite behavior would be: "Although I had eaten a large lunch, the smell of a freshly baked cake tempted me into eating a big slice. I now feel very uncomfortable." A loss or lack of appetite for food is called *anorexia.*

Thirst is a desire for fluid or the dry sensation resulting from a lack of, or need for, water. This sensation of dryness is often felt in the mouth and back part of the throat. The hypothalamus contains the mechanisms for stimulating thirst and is activated by an increase in the solute concentration in body fluids. Thirst is usually a reliable guide to the body's need for water. The normal adult should consume an average of 1 or 1½ liters of water or other liquids daily in order to provide a sufficient amount of water needed for all physiological processes.

Water is also available to the body through other sources, such as beverages, solid foods, and a small amount through the oxidation of essential nutrients.

Height and Weight.   In a behavioral assessment of nutrition as a need, the nurse states the measured height of the person in feet and inches or centimeters, and the weight in pounds or kilograms. Height measurements are taken without shoes and the weight preferably is taken without clothing.

Two important measures of a person's nutritional status are their height and weight. A daily weight is also useful when assessing a person's fluid balance, as discussed in Chapter 11. In this case it is particularly important that the weight be taken at the same time of day and on the same scale. When a person is underweight or overweight, measurements taken over a period of time are more useful than a single measurement. Tables specifying appropriate height and weight for male and female adults have been established and serve as a guideline when making judgments regarding adaptive weight behaviors according to a person's height, sex, and body build. These tables may be found in textbooks on nutrition. In general, the nurse may use the following measure. The person should weigh 100 pounds for 5 feet, then add 5 pounds for each additional inch of height. For males, allow an extra 5 pounds per inch. Standard and reference growth charts for infants, children, and youth have also been established, and these guidelines are found in any growth and development book or pediatric textbook.

Eating Patterns.   The nurse obtains a diet history listing the quantities of all food and fluid ingested during the past 24 hours. The Recommended Dietary Allowances and Daily Food Guide can be used as a measure of judgment in determining if the quantity quality of the nutrients ingested are adaptive or ineffective.

Guide to Good Eating...

A Recommended Daily Pattern

The recommended daily pattern provides the foundation for a nutritious, healthful diet.

The recommended servings from the Four Food Groups for adults supply about 1200 Calories. The chart below gives recommendations for the number and size of servings for several categories of people.

Food Group	Recommended Number of Servings				
	Child	Teenager	Adult	Pregnant Woman	Lactating Woman

Milk
1 cup milk, yogurt, OR
Calcium Equivalent:
  1½ slices (1½ oz) cheddar cheese*
  1 cup pudding
  1¾ cups ice cream
  2 cups cottage cheese*
	3	4	2	4	4

Meat
2 ounces cooked, lean meat, fish, poultry, OR
Protein Equivalent:
  2 eggs
  2 slices (2 oz) cheddar cheese*
  ½ cup cottage cheese*
  1 cup dried beans, peas
  4 tbsp peanut butter
	2	2	2	3	2

Fruit-Vegetable ½ cup cooked or juice 1 cup raw Portion commonly served such as a medium-size apple or banana	4	4	4	4	4

Grain, whole grain, fortified, enriched
  1 slice bread
  1 cup ready-to-eat cereal
  ½ cup cooked cereal, pasta, grits
	4	4	4	4	4

*Count cheese as serving of milk OR meat, not both simultaneously

"**Others**" complement but do not replace foods from the Four Food Groups. Amounts should be determined by individual caloric needs.

Nutrients for Health

Nutrient	Important Sources of Nutrient
Protein	Meat, Poultry, Fish Dried Beans and Peas Egg Cheese Milk
Carbohydrate	Cereal Potatoes Dried Beans Corn Bread Sugar
Fat	Shortening, Oil Butter, Margarine Salad Dressing Sausages
Vitamin A (Retinol)	Liver Carrots Sweet Potatoes Greens Butter, Margarine
Vitamin C (Ascorbic Acid)	Broccoli Orange Grapefruit Papaya Mango Strawberries
Thiamin (B_1)	Lean Pork Nuts Fortified Cereal Products
Riboflavin (B_2)	Liver Milk Yogurt Cottage Cheese
Niacin	Liver Meat, Poultry, Fish Peanuts Fortified Cereal Products
Calcium	Milk, Yogurt Cheese Sardines and Salmon with Bones Collard, Kale, Mustard, and Turnip Greens
Iron	Enriched Farina Prune Juice Liver Dried Beans and Peas Red Meat

Figure 6.1   Example of the use of the four basic food groups

Nutrients are chemical substances obtained from foods during digestion. They are needed to build and maintain body cells, regulate body processes, and supply energy.

About 50 nutrients, including water, are needed daily for optimum health. If one obtains the proper amount of the 10 "leader" nutrients in the daily diet, the other 40 or so nutrients will likely be consumed in amounts sufficient to meet body needs.

One's diet should include a variety of foods because no *single* food supplies all the 50 nutrients, and because many nutrients work together.

When a nutrient is added or a nutritional claim is made, nutrition labeling regulations require listing the 10 leader nutrients on food packages. These nutrients appear in the chart below with food sources and some major physiological functions.

Some major physiological functions

Provide energy	Build and maintain body cells	Regulate body processes
Supplies 4 Calories per gram.	Constitutes part of the structure of every cell, such as muscle, blood, and bone; supports growth and maintains healthy body cells.	Constitutes part of enzymes, some hormones and body fluids, and antibodies that increase resistance to infection.
Supplies 4 Calories per gram. Major source of energy for central nervous system.	Supplies energy so protein can be used for growth and maintenance of body cells.	Unrefined products supply fiber — complex carbohydrates in fruits, vegetables, and whole grains — for regular elimination. Assists in fat utilization.
Supplies 9 Calories per gram.	Constitutes part of the structure of every cell. Supplies essential fatty acids.	Provides and carries fat-soluble vitamins (A, D, E, and K).
	Assists formation and maintenance of skin and mucous membranes that line body cavities and tracts, such as nasal passages and intestinal tract, thus increasing resistance to infection.	Functions in visual processes and forms visual purple, thus promoting healthy eye tissues and eye adaptation in dim light.
	Forms cementing substances, such as collagen, that hold body cells together, thus strengthening blood vessels, hastening healing of wounds and bones, and increasing resistance to infection.	Aids utilization of iron.
Aids in utilization of energy.		Functions as part of a coenzyme to promote the utilization of carbohydrate. Promotes normal appetite. Contributes to normal functioning of nervous system.
Aids in utilization of energy.		Functions as part of a coenzyme in the production of energy within body cells. Promotes healthy skin, eyes, and clear vision.
Aids in utilization of energy.		Functions as part of a coenzyme in fat synthesis, tissue respiration, and utilization of carbohydrate. Promotes healthy skin, nerves, and digestive tract. Aids digestion and fosters normal appetite.
	Combines with other minerals within a protein framework to give structure and strength to bones and teeth.	Assists in blood clotting. Functions in normal muscle contraction and relaxation, and normal nerve transmission.
Aids in utilization of energy.	Combines with protein to form hemoglobin, the red substance in blood that carries oxygen to and carbon dioxide from the cells. Prevents nutritional anemia and its accompanying fatigue. Increases resistance to infection.	Functions as part of enzymes involved in tissue respiration.

115

Food Allergies.   The nurse assesses whether or not the person has a known food allergy or sensitivity. An allergic reaction to a certain food or food group is the result of an inappropriate antibody-antigen reaction in the body. Identify which foods are avoided, and what behaviors such as skin rash, swelling of the face or mouth, or gastrointestinal reaction occur if the food is ingested.

Condition of the Oral Cavity.   Appraisal of the oral cavity, that is, the lips, teeth, gums, and tongue, is useful in determining the person's nutritional health and for identifying behaviors of deficiency. The lips of the healthy adult are smooth and free from lesions. The skin is thin with many vascular structures which give the lips their reddish appearance. The oral mucosa is normally smooth, moist, and pinkish red in color, with expected variations based on ethnic differences. The adult has 32 permanent teeth. They are examined for conditions that decrease their grinding action, such as loose or missing teeth, cavities, or wear. If dentures are used, they are removed to allow complete inspection of the mouth. Normal gums are solid in turgor and free of inflammation or bleeding. The tongue is pinkish in color. The dorsal surface is rough and the ventral surface is smooth.

Pain.   The nurse assesses for any pain related to the ingestion of food or fluids. Pain may be noted as a behavior by listing the person's statements regarding discomfort and pain following ingestion of food. For example, persons may state that they experience a burning sensation which they refer to as heartburn after the ingestion of foods such as onions. Assess all verbal and nonverbal behaviors and include severity, duration, and onset of the pain. A more thorough guide for assessing pain is included in Chapter 10.

Altered Means of ingestion.   If the person is unable to eat and drink normally, the altered means of nutritional intake should be assessed. This includes the person who is nourished through a nasogastric or gastrostomy tube. The amount and substance given should be noted. If the person is receiving intravenous fluids and electrolytes or a hyperalimentation solution, the solutions and rate of delivery will need to be assessed. The nurse keeps current her knowledge and skills related to these particular altered conditions by reading, clinical practice, and continuing education.

Sense of Taste and Smell.   The normal person will be able to determine taste on the anterior two-thirds of the tongue. Four basic substances will be experienced: sweet, sour, bitter, and salt. The sensory receptors for taste are the glossopharyngeal nerve (cranial nerve IX) and the facial nerve (cranial nerve VII). A person's sense of smell is controlled by the olfactory nerve (cranial nerve I). Nasal passages should be patent. Testing each nostril separately, the person should be able to identify such odors as coffee or tobacco.

SECOND-LEVEL ASSESSMENT

In second-level assessment, the nurse considers stimuli related to the ingestion and assimilation of nutrients. The nurse assesses for the factors influencing the identified behaviors. This assessment of stimuli includes the body's adaptive ability to maintain structure, function, and regulation of the digestive system, as well as coping strategies the person uses to maintain or change behaviors.

Homeostasis.   The nurse knows the normal homeostatic responses of the digestive system that function to receive and transfer nutrients from the external to the internal environment of the body. Through these responses, the body maintains a constancy of the internal environment. The alimentary canal consists of the upper, middle, and lower regions and is responsible for the *digestion* and absorption of nutrients. When food is ingested, a series of physical and chemical changes occurs which prepare the nutrients for absorption and utilization by the cells. The alimentary canal is regulated by the neural–chemical–endocrine processes that Roy describes as the regulator subsystem. Residue remaining after digestion and absorption is then excreted from the body.

Illness or Disease Process.   The nurse identifies whether or not a disease state is present that affects the normal structure, function, and regulation of the digestive system. Examples would include such conditions as obstructive lesions of the esophagus and malabsorption, which are explained in general textbooks of pathology. Also, the nurse assesses if a condition exists that prohibits the person from eating, such as recent surgery, or if the person is on a restricted or special diet, such as that for a person with a medical diagnosis of diabetes.

Knowledge, Perceptions, and Beliefs.   The person's level of knowledge regarding nutrition and perception of what constitutes a diet that promotes a healthy state and that fulfills nutritional needs is a major stimulus. The nurse assesses this knowledge and perception since it greatly influences what the person is presently ingesting, or what he or she desires to eat. This relationship exists for both adaptive and ineffective patterns of nutrition. Based on the *level of knowledge* about sound nutrition that the nurse assesses, she may give positive reinforcement or promote change through diet counseling. The nurse is also aware of the person's beliefs regarding the types of food he or she eats. Many people eat only vegetarian diets out of certain beliefs that fall into such categories as religious, economic, health, and ethical ecological reasons (Suitor and Hunter, 1980, pp. 24–25). Such beliefs are taken into account in diet counseling.

Medication.   The nurse identifies whether or not the person takes any medication that may influence his or her intake of food or the digestive process. For example, drugs that may decrease the appetite may be taken if the person is attempting to lose weight. Ascertain whether supplemental vitamins and minerals are used.

Caloric Requirements.   Factors affecting *caloric requirements* to consider are age, sex, size, activity, temperature, diet, race, climate, pregnancy, and endocrine hormones (Ruch and Patton, 1965, p. 1043). For example, an infant, because of a high rate of metabolism and relatively large body surface area, will require more calories per kilogram of body weight than will an adult. A person exposed to severe cold weather will expend additional calories to maintain body temperature. In periods of rapid growth during infancy and adolescence, and during pregnancy, there is an increased caloric need. Males, who usually have a greater body size and greater proportion of lean body tissue, will have a greater caloric requirement than will females. There is a steady decline in caloric need, starting with the early adulthood years. Inactive people require fewer calories than are needed by those with increased activity (Beland and Passos, 1975, p. 741). Exercise patterns of the person are also assessed, as they will influence caloric requirements.

Condition of the Oral Cavity.   In addition to manifesting nutritional status, the condition of the oral cavity influences the ingestion of food. Any mouth lesions, gum disease, teeth in need of dental repair, or improperly fitted dentures should be assessed. The nurse identifies whether or not there is dental pain and if it affects the ability of the person to chew or swallow food, or to ingest hot or cold liquids. Determine what coping strategies the person uses to deal with these difficulties, and if they are effective or ineffective.

Availability of Food.   The nurse considers the *availability of food* to the person and monetary and other resources. For example, an elderly person with a limited or fixed income may find it difficult to travel to the store and may have limited funds to purchase food.

Conditions of Eating.   The nurse determines who purchases and prepares the food the person eats. In the family setting, the health beliefs of this person regarding nutrition will greatly influence the ingestion behaviors of all members. One looks at whether or not the family meal planning provides a well-balanced diet. The nurse also notes what social and moral values are placed on eating. For example, is eating a highly social event, and is food used as a punishment or reward? The nurse further identifies the level of family or peer group influences regarding eating. The nurse considers if the person or family sets aside a special time for mealtime. Are the meals taken alone, with a group, at home, at fast-food services, or in a restaurant? Another condition of eating to explore is the person's familiarity with different types of food.

Culture.   The nurse determines the person's cultural, social, and religious patterns that influence eating and drinking. The person's food habits and preferences based on cultural experience begin early in life. Some general examples are cited here (Mitchell et al., 1976). *Seventh Day Adventists* do not eat meat, fish, or poultry, but allow cheese, milk, and eggs as a source of animal protein, with nuts and legumes as other sources of protein. As discussed earlier, *Orthodox Jewish* dietary habits prohibit pork in any form. They do allow goats, sheep, deer, and cows, which are classified as quadrupeds that have a cloven hoof and chew a cud. The poultry allowed includes chicken, duck, goose, pheasant, and turkey. All meats and poultry must be prepared by the process known as koshering or clean. This is the prescribed ritual of soaking the meat in salted water to remove all traces of blood. All fish eaten must have fins and scales; therefore, shellfish are not allowed. Combining milk and meat in the same meal is prohibited. The Jewish Sabbath and religious holidays also have dietary laws. On the Sabbath no food is allowed to be cooked. No leavened bread may be taken during Passover week. Yom Kippur is a fast day, and no food or drink is taken for a 24-hour period. The *Roman Catholic* dietary restrictions and fast days have been liberalized in recent years. Therefore, customs, days of abstaining from meat, and fasting may vary in different locations.

Other cultural and regional food patterns include the following. The *black American* living in the South consumes a diet that is described as "soul food." This term conveys special feelings of happiness and enjoyment. Their diet consists of the use of hot breads, not made with yeast, such as cornbread and biscuits. They use a wide variety of greens (turnip, collard) cooked in liquid using some form of pork. Grits, corn, and rice are popular sources of carbohydrates, with dried beans as a source of protein. Meats that are high in bone and connective tissue, such as spareribs, pigsfeet, and chitterlings (intestines) are favored. Meats are frequently prepared by stewing, barbecuing, and frying. Sweets are eaten in large quantities and milk products and cheese are used less frequently.

In the diet of the *Mexican American*, the use of a variety of dried beans, especially the pinto bean, chili peppers, rice, corn, and some vegetables is favored. Little meat is used in the diet. Corn tortillas are eaten as bread. Popular dishes include chili con carne, tamales, tacos, and enchiladas. Coffee is consumed in large amounts and is sometimes given to children.

The dietary habits of the *Chinese* include the use of meat, fish, eggs, cereals, and a variety of vegetables. Rice is used instead of bread. Meat is eaten in small amounts and is usually served with vegetables. Food is cut or chopped into small pieces and cooked quickly in small amounts of liquids or fats.

The *Japanese* diet has changed during the last 20 years due to the influence of Western culture. Their diet had consisted primarily of the use of rice, beans, curd, vegetables, fruit, raw or cooked fish, and pickles, but now includes eggs, meat, milk, and cheese. A whole meal may consist of noodles cooked in broth seasoned with bits of vegetables and fish. Tea has been the traditional favored drink.

With *Italian Americans*, bread and pasta served with a variety of sauces and cheeses are eaten. Foods are highly seasoned with spices and many dishes use a lot of eggs, tomatoes, green vegetables, and fruit. Italian foods are usually cooked or simmered in oil or in liquids such as broth or tomato sauce.

Starchy vegetables and tropical fruits are common in the *Puerto Rican* diet. Rice and beans are other staples. The favorite meats include beef, pork, and chicken. A typical dish would include dried beans cooked with tomatoes, onions, peppers, salt pork, and seasonings. Milk is used on a limited basis.

People with *Middle East* cultures, such as the Lebanese, Armenians, and Greeks, receive their major source of energy from the use of grains. The favorite meat is lamb. Bread is the center of every meal, and they favor cheeses and yogurt. Vegetables are generally the main dish. Their food is rich in fat and not highly spiced.

Cues for Eating.   When assessing factors influencing the person's amount of intake of food, it is important to *identify* the *internal and external cues* to which the individual responds. As mentioned earlier, a healthy, functioning hypothalamus sends the person internal cues to signal that enough food has been ingested. In cases of overeating, the nurse helps the person identify what external cues they are responding to when eating if the person is failing to respond to internal cues relating to appetite and hunger control. For example, some people might overeat as a means of coping with the stresses of daily living. The nurse identifies if the person's eating and drinking behaviors are influenced by emotions, social pressures, habits, or the good taste and palatability of food rather than the internal cues that control appetite. Cues from the external environment, such as a pleasant environment and freedom from pain or stress, also influence ingestion.

Weight Consciousness. Finally, the nurse identifies the person's desire to gain, lose, or maintain body weight. The consciousness and desire influence the person's present and future eating patterns.

ADAPTATON PROBLEMS RELATED TO NUTRITION

The general term *malnutrition* refers to poor nutrition due to improper diet, resulting in an inadequate intake of nutrients or to a defect in metabolism that prevents the body from utilizing food properly. Nursing interventions for malnutrition using the Roy Adaptation Model of nursing will depend on the stimuli identified as the nurse either promotes or reinforces the stimuli or takes action to change or delete them. However, there are adaptation problems with general interventions to meet nutritional needs. Some of the major ones are discussed next, together with their accompanying interventions.

Obesity

One of the most common adaptation problems related to nutritional need in contemporary North America is that of obesity. Obesity is the excessive accumulation of fat in the body, which increases the weight beyond the recommended measures with regard to bone structure, height, and age. The male is termed obese when his weight exceeds 20 percent of the average weight found in the standard height/weight tables, and the female is termed obese when her weight is 25 percent above the listed standard. The stimuli and interventions for obesity are many and varied; therefore, prevention and treatment are individualized.

It is important to rule out metabolic and endocrine factors that may have contributed to the development of obesity. If these physiologically based factors do not exist, other stimuli should be explored. A major influencing factor or stimulus of obesity is caloric imbalance. That is, more calories are taken in than are needed by the body. Daily activity level plays an important role in a person's caloric needs.

Other factors significant in the development of obesity are classified as cultural, behavioral, and psychological. The nurse helps the person identify the specific *external cues* to which he or she is responding when overeating. Some of these cues have been described in the previous stimuli section. If a person decides that he or she is overweight and wants to do something about it, it is important to establish the *motivation* for the desired weight-losing regimen. Some reasons for wanting to lose weight may include an improved health status in order to avoid many of the chronic disorders linked with obesity. Other motivations may be a desire for improvement in personal appearance and avoidance of pressures from family and friends to lose weight.

An intervention that has been used successfully for changing a person's response pattern of eating because of external cues is *behavior modification* (Stuart and Davis, 1972). It is often helpful for the person to write down on a piece of paper what he or she is feeling before eating in order to help identify if he or she is eating in response to emotions such as anxiety, boredom, or loneliness. The person is then instructed to try to substitute other activities in place of eating at these times. Other techniques within this approach include:

1. *Slowing down* and making the act of eating a conscious acknowledged action. A meal should last at least 20 minutes so that the hypothalamus can send out satiation signals.
2. In the process of slowing down, doing only one activity at a time: that is, preparing each bite of food separately, putting the eating utensils down between bites, taking a sip of beverage between bites, and using the napkin frequently while concentrating on slowing down all actions.
3. Cutting the food into smaller pieces, cutting only one bite at a time, and chewing each piece of food longer.
4. Pausing in the middle of the meal and noting the level of appetite. If a feeling of satisfaction is felt, stop eating.
5. Always leaving some food on the plate.
6. When eating with others, always being the last to finish.

In the weight-loss program, it is realistic and healthy to lose only 1 to 2 pounds per week. The loss of 1 pound of adipose tissue is equal to 3500 calories. Therefore, to lose a pound in a week the person would need to reduce the daily caloric intake by 500 calories. For example, a person requiring 1800 calories per day would lose 1 pound in a week by reducing the caloric intake to 1300 calories per day.

Nausea and Vomiting

Nausea and *vomiting* are other adaptation problems related to nutritional needs. These problems are frequently associated with each other, but may be experienced separately. Nausea is an unpleasant sensation reported as a feeling of sickness with the urge to vomit. Vomiting is the forceful ejection of stomach contents through the mouth. The vomiting reflex can be stimulated by a number of intrinsic and extrinsic factors, namely, unpleasant odors, tastes, sights, and sensations such as severe pain, as well as chemical agents used in the treatment of disease, or x-ray therapy. It is important to identify the cause or factors that may predispose the person to vomit.

General interventions for nausea and vomiting include:

1. Limiting the person's food and fluid intake until nausea and vomiting subside. Use of intravenous fluids may be necessary to prevent fluid and electrolyte imbalance.
2. If fluids are tolerated, offering carbonated beverages, which may be comforting. Ice chips may also be tolerated and oral hygiene is refreshing.
3. Decreasing any pain that is experienced.
4. Keeping the person's environment quiet and preventing sudden movements.
5. Eliminating unpleasant strong odors in the environment.
6. Relieving distention of the stomach and removing any irritating substances.
7. Giving antiemetic drugs as ordered by the physician when necessary.
8. Positioning the person with head raised and turned to the side.
9. When the diet is resumed, offering foods that are bland, especially dry toast or soda crackers.

SUMMARY

This chapter has provided basic guidelines for the nurse to use in helping a person maintain integrity by meeting nutritional needs. Assessment factors of behaviors and stimuli are used to make a nursing judgment of diagnoses that the nurse treats by planning goals and interventions as prescribed according to the Roy Adaptation Model of nursing. Some general adaptation problems related to nutritional needs were discussed. Gordon (1982) identifies the following specific diagnoses, accepted by the North American Nursing Diagnoses Association as being within the nutritional-metabolic functional health pattern area:

Nutrition, alterations in: less than body requirements
Nutrition, alterations in: more than body requirements
Nutrition, alterations in: potential for more than body requirements

Nursing care is planned to manage the internal and external environment that is fostering behaviors indicative of patterns that do not promote the adaptive integrity of persons. When specific behavioral goals are outlined together with the person receiving nursing care, mastery of these goals is used as the criterion for evaluating the effectiveness of the specific nursing interventions related to nutrition.

STUDENT LEARNING ACTIVITY

Interview a person with a different cultural background from yours. Obtain a diet history and relate cultural and family influences affecting the identified behaviors.

REFERENCES

Beland, Irene L., and Joyce Y. Passos. *Clinical Nursing: Pathophysiological and Psychosocial Approaches*, 3rd ed. New York: Macmillan Publishing Co., Inc., 1975.

Gordon, Marjory. *Nursing Diagnosis: Process and Application.* New York: McGraw-Hill Book Company, 1982.

Mitchell, Helen S., Henderiks J. Rymbergen, Linea Anderson, and Marjorie V. Dibble. *Nutrition in Health and Disease*, 16th ed. Philadelphia: J. B. Lippincott Company, 1976, pp. 201–207.

Ruch, Theodore C., and Harry D. Howell-Fulton Patton. *Physiology and Biophysics*, 19th ed. Philadelphia: W. B. Saunders Company, 1965.

Stuart, Richard, and Barbara Davis. *Slim Chance in a Fat World: Behavioral Control of Obesity*. Champaign, Ill.: Research Press, 1972.

Suitor, Carol, and Merrily Hunter. *Nutrition: Principles and Application in Health Promotion*. Philadelphia: J. B. Lippincott Company, 1980.

ADDITIONAL READINGS

Caly, Joan C. "Assessing Adults' Nutrition," *American Journal of Nursing*, vol. 77, no. 10, 1977, pp. 1605–1609.

Pipes, Peggy L. *Nutrition in Infancy and Childhood*, 2nd ed. St. Louis: The C. V. Mosby Company, 1981.

Slattery, Jill S., Gayle A. Pearson, and Carolyn T. Tane. *Maternal and Child Nutrition: Assessment and Counseling*. New York: Appleton-Century-Crofts, 1979.

Williams, Sue Rodwell. *Mowry's Basic Nutrition and Diet Therapy*, 6th ed. St. Louis: The C. V. Mosby Company, 1980.

Chapter 7

Elimination

Jane Servonsky

BEHAVIORAL OBJECTIVES:

After studying this chapter, the reader will be able to:

1. Define the key concepts of the chapter.
2. Identify the person's basic need for elimination.
3. Identify and assess behaviors and common stimuli of elimination.
4. Define common adaptation problems of the elimination component.
5. Assess a person's elimination patterns and apply the adaptation nursing process in planning care for the person.

KEY CONCEPTS DEFINED

Stool: the fecal material discharged from the bowels.

Defecation: the process of passage of stool from the intestinal tract.

Homeostasis: the steady physiological states which enable persons to counteract changes in external conditions and in internal bodily functions.

Urine: the fluid secreted by the kidneys, containing water and waste products.

Constipation: a condition in which the fecal matter in the bowel is too hard to pass with ease, or a state in which the bowel movements are so infrequent that uncomfortable symptoms occur.

Diarrhea: rapid movement of the fecal material through the intestines, resulting in poor absorption of water, essential nutrients, and electrolytes, and in an abnormally frequent passage of watery stools.

Tenesmus: ineffectual and painful straining during stool or urination.

Flatus: gas or air in the gastrointestinal tract which may result in pain or feelings of abdominal fullness.

Anal Incontinence: inability to control fecal excretory function.

Urinary Retention: the inability to void, with the resultant accumulation of urine within the bladder.

Anuria: complete suppression of urine formation by the kidneys.

Oliguria: diminished urine secretion in relation to fluid intake.

Urinary Incontinence: inability to control the release of urine from the bladder.

As necessary as nutrients and the process of digestion and absorption are to a person to maintain the physiological balance of the body, so is the basic need for elimination of metabolic waste products. These waste materials must be expelled in order that homeostasis be maintained. Wastes are excreted from the intestines, by the kidneys, and by the skin and lungs. This chapter will deal with the excretory functions of the bowels and kidneys. Excretion through the lungs is dealt with in Chapter 5 and by the skin in Chapter 9.

The formation of a positive nurse–client relationship is essential in order to collect data about a person's elimination patterns. Since the topic of bodily secretions is considered personal by many, the nurse is aware of the privacy needs of the person, and her own reaction when inquiring about another's elimination pattern. In making a nursing assessment, the nurse establishes privacy and an intrusion-free environment. The nurse's data collection considers the person's language level and communication skills as influenced by his or her cultural and educational background.

INTESTINAL ELIMINATION: FIRST-LEVEL ASSESSMENT

When assessing intestinal elimination, the nurse observes the following behaviors:

Stool.   State the amount, color, consistency, frequency, odor, and effort. Normally, the *stool* that is evacuated is soft, formed, and brown in color for adults. The frequency of a bowel movement varies with each individual, although one bowel movement a day is average. In healthy persons, variations may range from a stool evacuated twice a day to a stool evacuated every 2 to 3 days. When making a judgment as to whether the frequency is adaptive or ineffective, the nurse should assess if the observed behavior represents a *change* from the person's normal pattern. The stool should be passed with ease without straining or discomfort when the *defecation* reflex is first felt.

Stool containing any unusual matter should also be noted, such as the presence of blood, mucus, pus, or intestinal worms. A careful, exact description of the stool is essential when blood is present. Observe whether the blood appears on the surface of the stool, or if it is mixed throughout. If the client is menstruating, this may be the source of bright-red blood on the surface of stool.

Normal stool has a characteristic odor caused by bacterial action on the foods that are eaten. Any *unusual* odor should be noted, for it may have clinical significance.

Bowel Sounds.   Note the presence, frequency, or absence of bowel sounds. The abdomen is auscultated in all four quadrants proceeding in a clockwise fashion. Using the diaphragm part of the stethoscope, listen in each quadrant, changing the auscultatory site 2 or 3 inches with each move. It is important to remove the stethoscope completely from the abdomen when changing locations, for pulling the stethoscope across the abdomen will produce interfering sound, may cause involuntary muscle spasms, and may be uncomfortable for the person.

Normal bowel sounds heard will be high-pitched, gurgling noises usually occurring five or more times a minute. Ineffective bowel sounds include extremely weak or infrequent sounds, or a complete absence of sounds, which may indicate bowel hypomobility or immobility. Before a determination of bowel sounds can be made, the abdomen should be auscultated for at least 3 minutes. Bowel sounds indicating possible hypermotility of the bowel will be auscultated as frequent rushes of loud, high-pitched sounds (Burns and Johnson, 1980, p. 206). Passage of gas is a good indication that peristaltic movement is occurring.

Pain.   Assess for any pain related to defecation. Pain may be included as a first-level nursing assessment behavior by listing the person's statements regarding discomfort and pain upon evacuation of the bowel or the excessive accumulation of flatus or gas in the intestines. Assess all verbal and nonverbal behaviors and include location, severity, duration, and onset of the pain.

Laboratory Values of the Stool.   Note the results of laboratory findings for stool if these are available. Specimens of the feces may be tested for occult blood when intestinal bleeding is suspected, but gross blood is not visible upon inspection.[1]

---

[1]Laboratory values and procedures for assisting with laboratory tests are readily available in resource texts such as Byrne et al., (1981).

INTESTINAL ELIMINATION: SECOND-LEVEL ASSESSMENT

In second-level assessment, the nurse gathers data about factors influencing the behaviors identified in the first-level assessment. This includes the important factor of the body's adaptive ability to maintain structure, function, and regulation of the eliminative component, as well as the coping strategies the person uses to maintain or change behaviors.

Homeostasis.   *Homeostasis* comprises the steady physiological states which enable persons to counteract changes both in external conditions and in internal bodily functions. The homeostatic process in the bowel is largely responsible for adaptive stool behaviors. The digestion of food is completed in the small intestine as it absorbs nutrients from the ingested substances. Peristaltic waves push the substance through the ileocecal valve into the large intestine, which absorbs a high percentage of the liquid from the wastes as well as salts. Intestinal contents are then propelled toward the rectum for evacuation.

Disease Process.   Identify if a disease state is present which affects the normal structure, function, and regulation of the gastrointestinal system. Examples would include such conditions as ulcerative colitis and intestinal obstruction, which are explained in general textbooks on pathology.

Type and Amount of Diet.   State the person's present daily nutritional intake. Evaluate whether or not these foods:

1. Provide roughage and bulk, such as high-residue foods of fresh fruits and vegetables.
2. Contain natural laxative effects that promote normal stool consistency, such as prunes and brans.
3. Influence the production of excessive intestinal gas, such as cabbage and beans.
4. Influence the color or consistency of stool: for example, the high milk intake of an infant may cause light-colored stool, and intolerance to certain foods may promote diarrhea.

Fluid Intake.   Note the amount of fluid the person is taking, both orally and intravenously. Decreased fluid intake may promote stool that is dry and hard.

Presence or Absence of Peristalsis.   Assess for factors that maintain or increase peristalsis, such as the person's daily activity level or pattern of exercise. Factors that decrease peristalsis include bed rest, immobility, or recent anesthesia.

Normal Pattern of Bowel Habits.   Identify the person's coping strategies used to maintain his or her pattern of elimination. These could include the use of laxatives, mineral oil, enemas, or suppositories. Assess if the person has a routine schedule or time set aside each day for evacuation. Assess for special coping strategies used, such as drinking a hot liquid or fruit juice. Have the person evaluate if the strategies used are effective or ineffective.

Family or Cultural Beliefs.   Detemine any relevant information regarding the cultural or family beliefs concerning the need and schedule to eliminate wastes from the bowel. Such beliefs and their relationship to health often begin early in childhood and are discussed in Chapter 4.

Stress.   Be aware of signs of physical and psychological stress, such as illness or anxiety. These factors frequently influence stool behaviors. Stress is discussed in detail in Chapter 13.

Immediate Environment.   Observe the environment. This would include if the person has maintenance or lack of privacy for evacuation. Assess the availability of the toilet to the person, or if the use of a bedpan is required, as well as the temperature and comfort of the room. The position the person is required to be in may also influence defecation. For example, a person immobilized in traction who uses a bedpan while in the reclining position may have difficulty adapting usual bowel evacuation to this changed environment.

Age.   Note the age of the person, since this will influence intestinal elimination. For example, the older person may show a decline in the motility of the gastrointestinal tract which occurs with advancing years, or the young child may have difficulties with toilet training.

Medications.   Assess for medications that may influence stool behaviors. For example, iron may cause dark, hard stools; codeine may cause behavior indicative of constipation; and sensitivities to certain other drugs may cause behaviors of diarrhea.

Treatments or Tests.   List any treatments or tests that may influence bowel elimination behaviors, such as barium enemas, gastrointestinal x-ray series, or soapsuds enemas.

Pain.   Validate with the person the cause of pain related to bowel elimination. Possible causes would include the presence of disruptive processes, such as hemorrhoids, anal fissure, or abdominal cramping due to excessive intestinal gas. Assess the coping strategies the person uses for the pain. For example, with hemorrhoids, the person may use sitz baths, ointments, or special skin care for the irritated skin around the anus.

Altered Means of Elimination.   Note if the person has an altered means of elimination, such as an ileostomy or a colostomy.

URINARY ELIMINATION: FIRST-LEVEL ASSESSMENT

When assessing urinary elimination, the nurse observes the following behaviors:

Urine.   State the amount of urine per voiding and the total for 24 hours. Assess its color and transparency, odor, frequency, any urgency felt, and effort.

Normally, the amount of urine voided by the average adult will vary from 1000 to 2000 cc in a 24-hour period. Urine is normally pale yellow or amber in color, due to the presence of the yellow pigment urochrome. In healthy individuals, urine that is pale and almost colorless is probably very dilute with a low specific gravity, while urine that is darker in color may have a higher specific gravity. Freshly voided urine has a clear transparency; cloudy urine or urine containing a sediment may represent a disease state. This change in transparency could be due to a reactional change of the urine if left standing for a period of time, as the pH changes from acidic to alkaline. The odor of fresh-voided urine is aromatic. When left standing, urine may develop an ammonia smell due to decomposition of urea by bacteria.

The frequency of urination, urgency felt, and effort in starting and stopping the flow of urine may depend on many factors. In general, the musculature of the bladder is capable of distending to the approximate capacity of 300 cc before the urge to void is felt. When the stretch receptors in the bladder are stimulated, the internal sphincter located at the opening of the bladder into the urethra relaxes to permit the flow of urine.

Pain.   Assess any pain related to urinary elimination. This would include pain or burning sensations prior to, during, or after urination. Normally, the person will void with ease, without pain or discomfort.

Laboratory Data.   Note findings in a routine urinalysis and compare these findings and those of other specific tests with normal values.

URINARY ELIMINATION: SECOND-LEVEL ASSESSMENT

Stimuli that influence urinary elimination and are assessed by the nurse include the following:

Homeostasis.   Know the adaptive response of the urinary system, which plays a major role in homeostasis or physiological steady states. Structures included are the kidneys, ureters, bladder, and urethra. The functions of the urinary system are to remove waste products from the bloodstream, and to regulate fluid and electrolyte balance, acid-base balance, and osmotic pressures within the body. The end product of this process is the production of urine. As the kidneys produce the urine, it is transported through the ureters and stored in the bladder. When the bladder fills with urine, the micturition (or voiding) reflex is stimulated by the stretch receptors in the bladder wall. The internal sphincter relaxes, allowing urine to flow to the outside of the body.

Disease Process.   Identify if a disease state or condition, a surgical procedure, or trauma has taken place which affects the normal structure, function, or regulation of the urinary system. Examples include urinary tract infections; disturbances of the central nervous system pathways, causing loss of voluntary control; tissue damage to the sphincters; relaxation of the perineal structures from childbirth; pressure on the bladder during pregnancy; poorly regulated diabetes mellitus; and chronic renal failure.

Fluid Intake.   Note the amount of fluids taken in both orally and intravenously for the previous 24 hours and presently. This will influence the amount of urine excreted. Insensible loss of water through the skin and lungs must be considered in relation to urinary output. Basically, when evaluating intake and output per 24 hours, these values should be approximately equal, allowing for some margin of difference. In instances that are critical to the person's maintenance of health, a basic measurement of fluid loss or gain is daily weights, taken at the same time each day.

Fluid and Electrolyte Balance.   Assess for conditions that may affect the fluid and electrolyte balance of the body: for example, losses of fluids via other routes, such as liquid stools, nasogastric tube drainage, emesis, or insensible loss occurring with high-body temperature. Fluid and electrolytes are discussed further in Chapter 11.

Usual Daily Urinary Elimination Pattern.   Note the usual pattern and if the present pattern is a change from the person's normal pattern.

Family and Cultural Beliefs.   Identify any factors regarding cultural or family beliefs concerning the need and schedule for emptying the bladder. Culture and family as common influencing factors are discussed in Chapter 4.

Stress.   Assess for physical or psychological states that may stimulate or hinder urination. For example, frequently with anxiety or stressful situations, the person may notice a feeling or urgency to void, although he or she has just emptied the bladder. Or the person who has experienced a painful urination may develop muscular tension resulting in an inability to relax the perineal muscles that promote urination for fear of a repeat of the painful situation. (See Chapter 13 for further discussion of the stress response.)

Environmental Stimuli. Observe for factors that may influence the person's ability to void, such as the maintenance or lack of privacy to void; temperature and comfort of the room; availability of the toilet, bedpan, or urinal; and the position the person is required to be in to void. For example, the male who is unable to stand to void may have difficulty adapting his usual pattern within this environmental change.

Altered Means of Elimination. Note if the person has an altered means of elimination, such as a urinary catheter or ureterostomy.

Age. List the age of the person since it is an important influencing factor affecting urinary elimination. For example, the young child may lack sphincter control or not yet be toilet trained.

With the natural aging process, there are generalized circulatory changes, and blood flow to the kidneys may be diminished due to a decrease in cardiac output. Therefore, renal function may decrease.

With aging, the pelvic floor muscles become weakened and the supporting connective tissue alters, causing the bladder to become funnel shaped. This change may result in bladder wall irritability. There may also be decreased bladder capacity due to its inability to elongate. Therefore, the aging person may present behaviors of frequency, incontinence, retention, and dysuria (Pinell, 1975).

Another example would be an elderly male who has frequency of voiding accompanied by problems in initiating and ending the stream of urine. This may be due to prostatic enlargement with resultant urinary retention. Also, consider the elderly female who has relaxation of the perineal muscles, who may present with behaviors of stress incontinence.

Medications. Consider medications the person may be taking that may influence the color or amount of urine. For example, certain vitamins and Pyridium may cause dark orange urine, and diuretics increase the amount of urine excreted.

Factors That Influence Pain with Urination. Assess, for example, whether the person has mucosal irritation due to recent removal of a urinary catheter or a cystoscopy examination, or whether there is a urinary tract infection present.

Coping Strategies.   Assess the person's ability to cope with ineffective behaviors such as burning or pain with urination. Assess how these behaviors have affected the voiding pattern and how they are coped with. For example, the person may use sitz baths, or avoid voiding.

For behaviors indicating retention, incontinence, difficulty starting or stopping the stream of urine, or dribbling, describe how these alterations have affected the person's activities of daily living. Assess if there are predisposing factors that make the behaviors better or worse. For example, urinary incontinence may be precipitated by laughing, coughing, stress, activity, and so forth. Assess what coping strategies are presently being used and if the person feels they are effective or ineffective.

ADAPTATION PROBLEMS RELATED TO ELIMINATION

The intervention step of the nursing process according to the Roy Adaptation Model depends on the identified stimuli as the nurse either promotes or reinforces the stimuli or takes action to change or delete them. There are, however, adaptation problems with general interventions that can be identified for intestinal and urinary elimination. Some of the major problems are discussed next together with their accompanying interventions.

Constipation

One of the most common adaptation problems of elimination is that of constipation. Simple constipation may present with the behaviors of excessive hardness of stool, without regard to the frequency of bowel movements, or an infrequent passage of dry, hard stools with accompanying excessive straining. General interventions include: increasing fluid intake to ensure adequate hydration; exercise; providing a diet that is adequate in residue, including increasing the intake of fruits, juices, bulk-producing vegetables, and bran cereals; responding to the urge to defecate to prevent additional reabsorption of water from the stool, thus avoiding hard, dry stools; and setting time aside to evacuate the bowel (for example, 30 minutes after the morning meal), or drinking a warm beverage or water early in the morning, may help to initiate a movement for some people. In learning healthy habits, chronic laxative use is avoided, for this abuse may lead to atonic bowel syndrome. However, if other conservative measures fail, the occasional use of a laxative to stimulate peristalsis and bowel evacuation may be indicated.

Diarrhea

When the person presents with behaviors of diarrhea, abdominal cramping and *tenesmus*, ineffectual and painful straining, may also occur. Frequently, diagnostic procedures or laboratory tests may be necessary to determine the exact cause of this symptom. Interventions should be directed toward those identified causes.

Other interventions include avoidance or elimination of allergic dietary substances or drugs that promote loose, watery stools. Many person are aware of the foods that often cause diarrhea, such as alcoholic beverages, highly caffeinated liquids such as coffee, or rich pastries high in sugar content.

With mild cases of diarrhea, nothing but clear liquids, such as water, tea, carbonated beverages, bouillon broth, and sweet fruit juices, are taken during the first 12 hours. Citrus juices are avoided. Cold liquids and concentrated sweets are poorly tolerated and thus are avoided.

During the next 12 hours, more foods, such as toast, soda crackers, and uncreamed soups may be added. After the stool begins to firm, other bland foods can be added, with gradual advancement to the person's regular diet.

With more severe cases of diarrhea, fluid and electrolyte replacement may be necessary, and/or the person may need administration of medication to decrease peristalsis and relieve abdominal cramping. Medical treatment of diarrhea is discussed in texts concerned with pathology.

The person with diarrhea is provided with an atmosphere conducive to relaxation and rest. The anal region is cleansed with mild soap and water after each movement to reduce local irritation and discomfort.

Flatulence

Excessive gas in the stomach and intestines is termed *flatulence* and may be accompanied by abdominal distension. Certain foods contribute to the formation of excessive gas and should be reduced or eliminated from the diet. These include beans, cabbage, cauliflower, onions, and highly seasoned foods. Milk products may produce excessive gas in some adults. If abdominal distension is also present, the person will avoid those activities that might promote air swallowing, such as using a drinking straw or chewing gum. Carbonated beverages are avoided. It may be helpful to eat more slowly and to increase the activity level to facilitate the passage of the gas.

Anal Incontinence

When *anal incontinence* (the inability of the anal sphincter to control the passage of feces) is present, a bowel training program may be initiated. It is important to set aside a consistent time for evacuation. Hot fluids may be given, followed by a glycerine suppository, or for some, the insertion of a gloved finger into the rectum will provide enough stimulation. The person should then attempt evacuation and allow adequate time.

The person should be encouraged to follow many of the interventions outlined in the constipation section, such as adequate fluid intake, a diet high in roughage, the intake of fruit juices, and so forth.

Incontinent persons may be embarrassed and have emotional distress. Special nursing care includes support and understanding, as well as measures to reduce possible skin irritation, odor, and the soiling of clothing and linen.[2]

Urinary Retention

The inability to void, with resultant accumulation of urine within the bladder, is termed *urinary retention*. Possible causes include obstruction at or below the bladder outlet, spinal or general anesthesia, muscular tension, emotional anxiety, and medications such as sedatives, opiates, psychotropic drugs, and antispasmodics, which interfere with the normal neurologic function of the voiding reflex. Besides the absence of voided urine, which may be confused with *anuria*, complete suppression of urine formation by the kidneys, or *oliguria*, diminished urine secretion in relation to fluid intake, in retention, the nurse may assess a distended bladder. As the bladder fills with urine, it rises above the level of the symphysis pubis, and may be displaced to either side of the midline.

Interventions include early ambulation following surgery, acquiring a sitting position or a standing posture in the male, providing the person with privacy, listening to the sound of running water, dangling the hands in warm water, pouring warm water over the perineum or sitting in a warm bath to promote perineal muscle relaxation, or any other measure that

---

[2]The reader is encouraged to seek additional references for more details about problems of incontinence, for example, Luckmann and Sorensen (1980).

might promote relaxation. If these measures fail, medications may be employed to promote the ease of voiding, or bladder catheterization may be used.

Urinary Incontinence

Urinary incontinence is the inability of the urinary sphincters to control the release of urine from the bladder. Causes may be both psychological and physiological. Common causes of sphincter damage or loss of control include weak abdominal perineal musculature, obstetrical trauma, complications from pelvic surgery, use of medications such as narcotics or sedatives, and use of alcohol.

A complete diagnostic workup is done to identify the causative and contributing stimuli for the incontinence. If stress incontinence is present, the person tries to avoid excessive straining or conditions such as chronic coughing. Weight reduction and pelvic exercises are helpful in regaining bladder control. Kegel exercises increase the tone of the perineal muscles. Instruct the person to contract the perineal muscles as though trying to stop the flow of urine. This should be done 10 to 15 times per session at least four times a day. Also, the person should try to start and stop the stream of urine when voiding.

A bladder training program may be required which includes an adequate intake of fluids, strengthening exercises for the perineal muscles, and a definite schedule set aside for voiding. The intake of fluids should be carefully spaced throughout the day and limited before sleep to promote adequate rest. The person is encouraged to void every 30 minutes to 2 hours, and as the program progresses, the urine is held for longer periods of time. As with anal incontinence, nursing care should include supportive measures to decrease emotional stress and possible skin irritation.[3]

SUMMARY

In this chapter we have focused on nursing assessment of the basic need for intestinal and urinary elimination. Some common problems that occur in these need areas were discussed. In relating this content to the Roy Adaptation Model nursing process outlined in Chapter 3, we note that specific guidelines are given for first- and second-level assessment in these areas. A nursing diagnosis, or interpretation of assessment data, might involve one of the problem areas discussed. When Gordon (1982) lists the diagnostic labels related to functional patterns of elimination that are cur-

[3]See the footnote on page 135.

rently accepted by the North American Nursing Diagnoses Association, she includes the following:

Urinary elimination, alterations in patterns of
Bowel elimination, alterations in: constipation
Bowel elimination, alterations in: diarrhea
Bowel elimination, alterations in: incontinence

The nurse prepared to use the Roy Adaptation Model of nursing can also state diagnoses as specific behaviors with the stimuli that are most relevant.

Based on thorough assessment and understanding of adaptation problems related to elimination, the nurse sets goals in terms of outcomes for the person. Then interventions are planned to change the stimuli so as to promote adaptation. Finally, the outcome of nursing intervention is evaluated by reassessing the behaviors to see if these reflect the behavior stated in the goal.

STUDENT LEARNING ACTIVITY

Complete a first- and second-level assessment of bowel and urinary elimination for two people of different age groups. The elderly person and the young adult or adolescent are suggested. Compare and contrast the behaviors and stimuli identified.

REFERENCES

Burns, Kenneth R., and Patricia J. Johnson. *Health Assessment in Clinical Practice.* Englewood Cliffs, N. J.: Prentice-Hall, Inc., 1980.

Byrne, C. Judith, Dolores F. Saxton, Phillis K. Pelikan, and Patricia M. Nugent. *Laboratory Tests: Implications for Nurses and Allied Health Professionals.* Reading, Mass.: Addison-Wesley Publishing Company, Inc., 1981.

Gordon, M. *Nursing Diagnosis: Process and Application.* New York: McGraw-Hill Book Company, 1982.

Luckmann, Joan, and Karen Sorensen. *Medical–Surgical Nursing: A Psychophysiologic Approach*, 2nd ed. Philadelphia: W. B. Saunders Company, 1980.

Pinell, C. "Disorders of Micturition in the Elderly," *Nursing Times*, vol. 71, December 18, 1975, p. 2019.

Chapter 8

Activity and Rest

Joan Seo Cho

BEHAVIORAL OBJECTIVES

After studying this chapter, the reader will be able to:

1. Define the key concepts of the chapter.
2. Discuss some of the basic theories underlying one's activity and rest need.
3. List the behaviors that are to be assessed in relation to activity and rest needs.
4. Discuss some of the common influencing factors for disruption in activity and rest need.
5. List common problems related to activity and rest needs, and discuss appropriate nursing interventions.

KEY CONCEPTS DEFINED

Activity/Rest Balance: ratio of activity to rest being in the state in which one's energy required for activity is balanced with energy production capability.

Mobility: state or quality of being mobile. Facility of movement or activity.

Immobility: a relative inactivity beyond the necessary rest period.

Disuse Consequences: physical or psychological phenomena that occur as consequences of a decrease in or absence of adequate physical activity.

Good Body Alignment: a natural or anatomically correct posture in which the body parts are arranged in an anatomically functional position.

Range of Motion (ROM) Exercise: movements of joints according to the range of motion of the particular joint; may be active, passive, or assisted.

Muscle Conditioning: maintenance of muscle tones by regular and deliberate use of muscles, such as in isotonic, isometric, and resistive muscle exercises.

Rest: a relative cessation of activity in which energy requirements are minimal.

Sleep: a state of rest in which the person has a decreased ability to interact with external stimuli.

Sleep Deprivation: a disruption in one's rest need in which one has not had adequate sleep in quality or length, due to various stimuli.

Insomnia: an ineffective state related to sleep need, in which one is having difficulty falling asleep or staying asleep, unplanned early awakening, or a combination of these.

Activity provides the needed physical stresses for normal cell growth and development; however, too much stress will cause exhaustion and consequent dysfunction. Maintenance of physiological integrity requires both activity and rest periods. Rest provides the body with periods of restoration and repair. There is, then, a basic human need for activity and rest. Nursing's concern for the person's activity and rest need is for the proper *balance between activity and rest.* The Roy Adaptation Model of nursing looks at the human need for physical activity and rest as a way of promoting the physiological and total integrity of the person.

One's activity and rest status depends on motor function, which provides mobility. *Mobility,* or facility of movement, depends primarily on adequate functioning of muscles, bones, and the governing nervous system. Therefore, any disruption in these body structures and their function will have a direct and immediate effect on one's mobility and thus on the person's activity and rest need. However, the focus of this chapter is not on dealing with pathological conditions of the musculoskeletal system. Any pathological conditions of musculoskeletal structure and its function are viewed as influencing factors causing changes in rest and activity need. This chapter focuses specifically on rest and activity need. Discussed are the theoretical basis for this need, assessment of behaviors and influencing factors, related adaptation problems, and appropriate nursing interventions.

ACTIVITY NEED

The importance of physical activity to one's physical and psychological integrity has been studied in numerous research projects beginning in the 1940s (Dietrich et al., 1948). Some basic concepts about activity were validated through projects in which a group of healthy individuals were subjected to physical *immobility* and researchers measured the consequences on the subjects' physiological and psychological functions. Interest in this area stemmed from observations of World War II soldiers. The common complications occurring among postoperative and postpartum patients were not common among those soldiers who were recovering from injuries but could not afford a long bed rest. It was hypothesized that perhaps the lack of prolonged bed rest might have been the influencing factor for the difference in complications. Studies indicate that a period of physical inactivity is inevitably followed by certain physiological as well as psychological changes. These changes are called *disuse consequences*. They are predictable and pathological.

As more of our institutionalized patient population is made up of elderly or seriously ill groups of people, the concept of immobility and its effect becomes one of the most important concepts in nursing. It is reasonable to say that the management of the institutionalized patient's activity need is entirely in the hands of the nursing staff. The common disuse consequences and preventive nursing interventions are listed in Table 8.1 and discussed later in this chapter. The extent and number of disuse consequences experienced by the individual person depend on the duration and degree of physical inactivity. However, it is important for the nurse to understand these predictable consequences and the underlying physiological changes so that they will be taken into consideration in planning total nursing care.

First-Level Assessment

Management of a person's activity need begins with assessment of behaviors related to motor activity. The primary purpose of assessment is to judge adequacy of the person's activity level and to identify any existing disuse consequences. Two major categories of assessment factors are considered: (1) the type and amount of physical activity carried out by the person, and (2) the person's motor function status, which includes assessment of muscle and joint mobility, posture and gait, and coordination.

Type and Amount of Physical Activity.   By observing and recording the type and frequency of activity, the nurse can judge the adequacy of activity level in relation to the person's total physical condition. Such simple

TABLE 8.1
Consequences of Physical Inactivity

Body Function	Underlying Changes	Disuse Consequences	Preventive Interventions
Musculoskeletal	*Muscles*: autolysis of unused muscles	Muscular atrophy with decreased strength and endurance	Muscle conditioning exercises: isometric, isotonic, and resistive exercises
	Bones: increased osteoclastic process due to lack of physical stresses of weight bearing on the bones leads to increased urinary excretion of calcium	Osteoporosis and vulnerability to pathological fracture	Physical activities which would produce the stresses of weight bearing—standing and walking, pushing and pulling
	Joints: decreased pliability and increased density of the collagen mesh work leads to fibrous formation and shortening of the muscle fibers	Joint contractures with permanent loss of joint mobility	ROM (range of motion) exercises: active, assisted, or passive ROM exercises
	Nerves: denervation due to prolonged compression on nerve fibers and decreased circulation	Paralysis, foot drop, and wrist drop	Frequent change of position; use of foot board
Circulatory	Cardiac overload due to central pooling of the circulatory volume	Deconditioning leads to poor exercise tolerance	Frequent change of position, including sitting up and standing positions, if possible
	Loss of regulatory mechanism to maintain central BP (normally with position change to sitting up, the splenic and peripheral vessels constrict to maintain the central blood volume)	Postural hypotension, dizziness, and fainting in upright position	
	Sluggish venous return due to lack of pumping mechanism generated by muscular contractions of physical activity	Dependent (local) edema, especially of the lower extremities	Muscle exercises to stimulate the circulation

TABLE 8.1 *Continued*
Consequences of Physical Inactivity

Body Function	Underlying Changes	Disuse Consequences	Preventive Interventions
	Hypercoagulability of blood (due to injury or surgery) combined with physical inactivity (see above)	Thrombus formation leads to pulmonary embolism	Well-fitting antiembolic stockings
Pulmonary	Increased intraesophageal pressure and decreased expansion of thoracic cavity in recumbent position; stasis of respiratory tract secretion	Hypoventilation	Positions of maximum chest expansion
		Hypostatic pneumonia	Frequent change of positions, and deep-breathing and cough exercises
Metabolic	Increased catabolic processes leads to increased excretion of nitrogen via gastrointestinal and urinary tract combined with poor protein intake due to poor appetite	Negative nitrogen balance leads to poor tissue healing	Ensure adequate intake of dietary protein
Eliminative	Urinary stagnation due to lack of natural position of gravity in recumbent position and loss of proprioception	Urinary retention	Frequent encouragement to void, providing adequate toilet facility and position of comfort; ideal position for male client is standing up, while sitting up is for female client
	Increased calcium content in the urine	Nephrolithiasis	Ensure adequate fluid intake with cranberry juice to acidify the urine pH level

System	Contributing Factors	Problem	Intervention
	Decreased gastrointestinal mobility combined with dependency on others to obtain toilet facility, lack of privacy, lack of bulk in the diet, and poor abdominal and pelvic muscle tones	Constipation or fecal impaction	Avoid unnecessary use of CNS depressants; muscle toning exercise for abdominal and pelvic muscles; ensure adequate fluid and bulk intake
Integumentary	Inability to carry out daily personal hygiene measures and prolonged compression on tissues (decreased circulation)	Pressure sores and decubiti ulceration formation with secondary infection	Frequent change of position; use of protective devices (pillow, padding); frequent massaging of all bony prominences
Sensory-perceptual	Decreased environmental stimuli lead to decreased sensory stimulation; changed perceptual axis with recumbent position; inability to manipulate own environment	Anxiety, disorientation, loss of proprioception – change in body image; boredom; egocentricity	Environmental structuring to provide meaningful stimuli; use of calendar, radio, TV, and wall clock can be helpful. Provide opportunity to carry out meaningful conversations with others. Visits from family and friends are very important

143

activity as participating in bathing and grooming while sitting up in bed allows the pulling and weight bearing of active movement, which is effective in promoting stimulation of general circulation, muscle conditioning of the involved body part, and mobility of the joints.

Motor Function.   Since motor function is essential in meeting one's activity need, assessment of motor status is important. Through this assessment, the nurse is able to determine the type of physical activity the person is capable of performing, and to identify the disuse consequences that exist. Assessment of motor function includes assessment of the *muscle masses* for their size, firmness, and strength, the *joints* for their mobility, *the posture and gait* for proper alignment and stability, and *neuromuscular coordination* for its effectiveness.

Muscle masses are grasped to check their size and firmness. The strength is assessed by the person's ability to contract the particular muscle group. All active movements, such as lifting, pushing, and pulling, require muscle contractions. A deficit in the muscle mass related to size, firmness, or strength indicates muscular atrophy and is the first and most common sign of disuse consequence.

Joint mobility is assessed by an active or passive demonstration of the particular joint's range of motion. A limitation in, or absence of, mobility indicates contracture of the joint. Joint contracture is one of the most common, and irreversible, disuse consequences. Flexion contractures of hips, knees, and elbows are common occurrences among semiconscious or unconscious patients due to their physical inactivity.

Posture is an anatomical arrangement of body parts in a given position (see Fig. 8.1). Posture is a key point in good body mechanics; thus it becomes a factor in one's physical safety. Good posture is a body alignment that permits optimal weight balance and operation of the motor function. It provides physical stability. Prolonged or frequent poor posture will result in permanent deformity due to contracture of the involved ligaments and surrounding muscles. While poor posture will not allow optimal motor function, poor posture itself is a disuse consequence.

Gait is a manner of walking. Walking provides the basic means of physical mobility to move around from place to place. An improper gait may impose undue stress on certain musculoskeletal parts and in time can lead to a permanent deformity. For example, when a patient is using a "swing through" gait on crutches, the movement does not simulate normal walking and will eventually result in weakening of the lower extremities due to atrophy of the leg muscles. A proper gait with good posture will allow a safe and optimal level of mobility.

Good motor *coordination* requires both intact neurological and musculoskeletal function. Any injury or pathological changes in these structures and functions will cause disruption in normal coordination (see Chapter

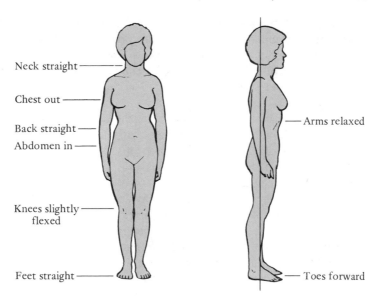

Neck straight

Chest out

Back straight

Abdomen in

Knees slightly
flexed

Feet straight

Arms relaxed

Toes forward

Figure 8.1   Correct standing position.

12). However, the primary purpose of assessment is not assessment of the pathological condition itself; it is to determine the extent of its affect on one's physical activity. Poor motor coordination could be the result of prolonged physical inactivity itself.

Second-Level Assessment

When a first-level behavioral assessment indicates that a person's activity need is not being adequtely met, the nurse proceeds to determine the underlying causative factors. Following are some of the most common causative and contributing factors underlying disruptions in activity need: (1) disruption in the structure and function of musculoskeletal system, (2) disease or illness requiring bed rest or limited physical activity, (3) psychological attitude, and (4) environment.

Disruption in the Musculoskeletal System.   Disruption in the musculoskeletal structure and function can occur by either direct physical injuries to muscles and bones or by central nervous system disorders. Regardless of the underlying causative factor, a dysfunctioning musculoskeletal system will cause a direct and immediate effect on one's motor function. A condition such as a fractured femur will inevitably necessitate a limitation of one's physical activity due not only to the loss of function, but also to the discomfort and pain one may experience. In the case of a fractured bone, a period of immobility may be medically prescribed for a therapeutic purpose. Immobility preoperatively prevents further damage to the fractured bone or the surrounding soft tissue. Postoperatively, it assures proper healing of the repaired part.

Disease or Illness in General. Depending on its nature and severity, a person with illness or disease will limit physical activity either voluntarily or because of medically imposed restrictions. "Bed rest" is often imposed as an integral part of the therapeutic measures because rest provides a period of restoration and repair.

In the case of a patient who is suffering acute cardiac insufficiency, "absolute bed rest" is one of the most important aspects of the therapeutic regimen. This measure is to conserve the O_2 expenditure that is required by nonessential physical activity, thus minimizing the cardiac load for the damaged heart muscles. The same principle applies when the nurse places a patient with fever on "bed rest." An elevation of 1°F in body temperature will require a 7 percent increase in basic metabolic rate, which, in turn, will require increased O_2 consumption and cardiac work load.

Psychological Attitude. One's psychological makeup at a given time and in a given situation has an effect on one's physical activity level. A person who is constantly sedated with medications, or consuming a large amount of alcoholic beverages, will not be ready, either physically or psychologically, to be involved in physical activity. Psychologically depressed persons tend to reduce their physical activity to a bare minimum. The catatonic state of a psychotic individual exemplifies this case. In a catatonic state, the individual is not able to initiate body movements, even though no demonstrable physiological or physical dysfunction exists.

One's previously learned knowledge about activity in a given situation also has an effect. A mother in the postpartum unit can be labeled as "lazy" when, unlike the other mothers, she does not get out of bed to take a shower. With further assessment, the nurse might learn that the mother's cultural upbringing taught her not to move out of bed for several days following giving birth to a baby.

Immediate Environmental Factors. The immediate environmental factors include the suitability of the environment, availability of the space, and availability of adequate physical and personal assistance. Unsuitable environmental factors, such as unpleasant environmental temperature, surroundings, and lack of privacy, will discourage normal physical activity. A limited space will restrict the range of physical activities. A child placed in a playpen all the time will have a restricted range of physical activity, and in time this restriction will have an effect on the child's normal growth and development.

Availability of physical and personal assistance is another important factor. Those persons who are acutely ill or confused are totally dependent on others for meeting their activity needs. Lack of adequate supervision and physical asistance may be one of the major causative factors for the disuse consequences experienced by institutionalized elderly clients.

Adaptation Problems Related to Activity

Adaptation problems related to one's activity need can be classified into two major categories: (1) inadequate physical activity, and (2) prevention of disuse consequences.

Inadequate Physical Activity.   This condition is diagnosed if a person's behavioral assessment indicates a lack in quantity and quality of physical activity when there are no medically imposed restrictions on physical activity. The underlying influencing factors involve stimuli other than disruptions in the motor function itself, and the person's physical condition does not require bed rest or limitation in physical activity.

Prevention of Disuse Consequence.   This situation is diagnosed if a person's physical activity is curtailed because of medically imposed restrictions. Medical restriction is usually imposed to immobilize certain body parts to allow a healing period without disturbing the therapeutic alignment, or to conserve the oxygen and energy consumption required by nonpriority physical activity so that the already stressed body is spared further exhaustion. Some specific areas of disuse consequence are listed in Table 8.1. The chart is organized by major body functions and the underlying changes that result from physical inactivity. Preventive interventions for each disuse consequence are listed in the last column.

Nursing Intervention

Nursing intervention for the problem of *inadequate physical activity* begins with management of the specific causative factors. The general goal of nursing care is to increase the person's physical activity to a level adequate to meet the activity need. The "adequate" level is to be determined according to the individual's physical and psychological conditions at the given time. For example, competitive sports activities that require both vigorous physical as well as psychological stresses may not be suitable for a patient who is recovering from a major heart attack. Preventive nursing intervention for disuse consequence has general and specific aspects. The general aspect includes those preventive measures that promote maintenance of normal motor functions. By promoting a person's motor activity, the nurse facilitates accomplishment of daily living tasks, and also helps provide the body with the physical stresses that are essential in maintaining the internal physiological functions.

Planning of preventive nursing interventions takes into consideration the nature and extent of medically imposed restrictions. As we have noted, at times a period of complete bed rest is medically imposed to allow the healing process to take place in certain parts of the body. However, without proper preventive nursing interventions, the entire body can be predisposed to the consequences of physical inactivity. With well-planned preventive nursing interventions, one can avoid or minimize the disuse consequences without sacrificing the purpose of needed temporary immobilization or limited activity.

The general preventive nursing interventions include following four major concepts: (1) maintenance of good body alignment, (2) frequent change of positions, (3) maintenance of joint mobility, and (4) conditioning of the muscles. Specific aspects of preventive interventions are summarized in the last column of Table 8.1.

Good Body Alignment.   *Good body alignment* is a body posture in which the body parts are arranged in an anatomically functional position and the weight distribution is well balanced in a stable manner. The normal functional standing alignment is having the center of gravity just over the instep and the knees slightly flexed. Good body alignment should be assumed in all body positions. For example, in supine position, one's body should be in full extension, resembling the upright position (see Fig. 8.1). Incorrect body alignment or posture will impose undue stresses on muscles, ligaments, and joints. Frequent or prolonged use of poor body alignment will leave a permanent defect, such as flexion contracture of neck and foot drop, which are not uncommon among bedridden patients.

Frequent Change of Position.   Changing the patient's position serves many important purposes, since many of the disuse consequences are in part a direct result of static body positions for prolonged periods of time. The recumbent, or lying-down position, is the most common position assumed by ill individuals. Prolonged use of the static recumbent position without spontaneous body movements is the major stimulus for many disuse consequences. A frequent change of position with proper body alignment should be carried out with consideration of the following points: prevention of nerve damage in the pressure areas, joint contractures, pressure sores, and loss of the postural adjustment mechanism for the maintenance of central blood pressure in the upright position. Within the medically imposed restrictions, the patient's body position should include many different positions. Frequent changes of position not only relieve the pressure of body weight, thus promoting general circulation, but they also facilitate dislodging of bodily discharges, such as mucus secretions of the respiratory tract. An active change of position to a sitting-up position is effective in maintenance of the postural adjustment mechanism and, consequently, prevents the symptoms of postural hypotension or lowered blood pressure upon standing.

At times it is easy for the nurse to think that "sitting up in the chair" is too big a task for a particular patient. However, the nurse keeps in mind that although the process of struggling to get out of the bed and moving to a chair to sit down for a few minutes takes a lot of effort on the part of both the patient and the nurse, the benefits of such motor activity are paramount. This activity provides almost all of the physical exercises that are effective in prevention of the disuse consequences.

Maintenance of Joint Mobility. Joint mobility exercising can be done either actively or passively. In active *range of motion (ROM) exercise*, the person initiates and completes the full range of motion. For a person who is too weak or is partially paralyzed, assisted or passive ROM exercising may be done. In assisted ROM exercise, the person initiates the movement, but the nurse may have to complete the full range of motion. In passive ROM exercise, used if the person is paralyzed or unconscious, the nurse initiates and completes the full range of motion. The nurse supports a limb at the joints and moves the limb according to the normal range of the joint motion. Figure 8.2 shows the basic range of motion movements.

Passive limb movement does not require muscle contractions as in active motion. Therefore, it is not effective for muscle conditioning, but it is effective in preventing joint contractures. Joint motion exercise should never be carried out beyond the point of pain or resistance.

Muscle Conditioning. There are several types of exercises that contribute to *muscle conditioning*. The primary purpose of muscle conditioning exercise is to prevent muscular atrophy and weakening. However, because of their physical stress on the bones, all types of muscular exercise also aid to some extent in promotion of general circulation and prevention of osteoporosis.

All active body movements, such as lifting and moving objects, induce isotonic exercise. In *isotonic exercise*, the muscle fibers shorten during the muscle contraction. *Isometric exercise* occurs without actual shortening of the muscle fibers. A "setting" exercise is an example of an isometric exercise. *Muscle setting* is accomplished simply by contracting or hardening of a group of muscles for 10 seconds by intension, and releasing to relax. This type of exercise is effective in conditioning the abdominal, gluteal, and quadriceps muscles. However, institution of this type of exercise requires a certain degree of caution. During the muscle-setting period, one's intrathoracic pressure increases due to the trapping of the air against the closed

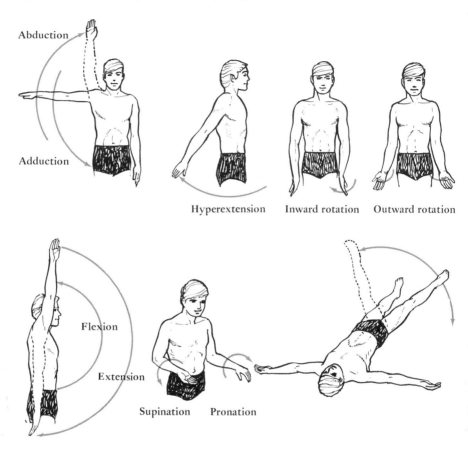

Figure 8.2   Range of Motion Movements.

epiglottis, a phenomenon called the *Valsalva maneuver*. The Valsalva maneuver may precipitate cardiac arrest in persons who have a damaged heart. This untoward reaction occurs because the increased intrathoracic pressure prevents normal cardiac input and subsequently decreases cardiac output and the coronary circulation. In any case, if this type of exercise is instituted, the person should be taught to exhale during the muscle-setting period.

Resistive exercise is another form of muscular conditioning exercise. This exercise is done by pulling or pushing against a stationary object. Because of its pumping effect on the venous system, this type of exercise is effective not only for muscle conditioning, but also in stimulating venous returns. Simple activity, such as pushing the feet against the foot board, is effective in conditioning the gastrocnemius and quadriceps muscles. Pulling on the trapeze bar is effective in conditioning upper arms and shoulder muscles.

REST AND SLEEP

While physical activity is essential for normal growth, development and maintenance of body structures and functions, rest and sleep provide us with periods of restoration and repair. During rest and sleep, most of our physiological processes are slowed down to allow renewal of energy for future activity. We could say that the body's "battery is being recharged" during our rest and sleep. A lack of sleep and rest, like a lack of physical activity, will cause predictable consequences to one's physiological as well as psychological integrity.

Rest cannot be defined as mere physical inactivity or the absence of physical activity. Rest includes the quality of relaxation that comes with freedom from physical discomfort and psychological stresses, such as anxiety.

Rest becomes *sleep* when one's ability to respond to minute environmental stimuli is diminished. Studies indicate that all living organisms need sleep periods for their survival. Human beings spend an average of one-third of their lifetime in sleeping. As individual's sleep need depends on his or her physical and psychological conditions at a given time, a definite, positive correlation exists between the amount of sleep one needs and the level of physical and psychological stresses the individual experiences.

Generally, the younger one is, the longer the time spent for sleep, until the individual reaches young adulthood. The average time spent for sleep in different age groups can be summarized as follows: 22 hours for the neonate, 14 to 16 hours for infants, 10 to 12 hours for toddlers and pre-schoolers, and 8 to 10 hours for school children. Young adults and elderly individuals spend an average of 7 to 8 hours daily for sleep.

It is indicated that during sleep there is an increased release of growth hormone and a decreased concentration of corticosteroids. These changes seem to promote protein synthesis, which assists in restoration and repair of biological structures and functions (Oswald, 1976).

The effects of sleep on physiological and psychological integrity have been studied by observing and recording behavioral changes that occur following a period of *sleep deprivation* (Pasnau et al., 1968; Sassin, 1970; Opstad et al., 1978). These studies indicate that loss of sleep brings changes in brain function and causes alteration in biochemical processes in the body. Sleep loss causes not only physical fatigue and poor neuromuscular coordination, but also signs of psychological dysfunction which manifests itself as general irritability, inability to concentrate, disorientation, and confusion. The severity of these effects depends on the degree and length of deprivation and the individual's predeprivation condition.

The Nature of Sleep

Recordings of brain electric potentials (EEG) and other observations of persons during sleep enable sleep researchers to understand some of the nature and characteristics of sleep. During a typical night sleep of 7 to 8 hours, one goes through several cycles of sleep in an orderly sequence. Each cycle takes an average of 90 minutes, more or less, and consists of five stages. Stages 1 through 4 are called the NREM (no rapid eye movement) phase, and stage 5 is called the REM phase because of the rapid eye movements characteristic of this stage.

Sleep always begins with stage 1, the NREM phase. During this stage one's muscle tone and ability to respond to internal as well as external stimuli are somewhat decreased, but not lost. One may stay only 10 minutes in this stage.

The second stage begins with increased muscular relaxation and decreased cerebral activity. During this stage, one's ability to respond spontaneously to stimuli is further diminished.

Deep sleep begins with the third stage. During deep sleep, one's basic metabolic rate is decreased by 10 to 20 percent, and this is demonstrated by a drop in body temperature, heart rate, and blood pressure. Muscle tone becomes completely atonic. The skin may become flushed and warm, with mild diaphoresis.

The fourth stage of sleep is actually deep, deep sleep. Within 30 minutes of sleep onset, one may reach the fourth stage of sleep. Bedwetting in children usually takes place during this stage due to the lost ability to respond to internal stimuli as well as external stimuli. One may be able to respond only to strong stimuli. It is believed that during this stage, growth hormone is released in an increased amount and synthesis of new protein takes place.

Sleep researchers postulate that NREM sleep is an anabolic state and responsible primarily for one's physiological restoration. This possibility is supported by the fact that NREM sleep takes precedence over REM sleep when one is recovering from sleep deprivation.

Following the fourth stage, the cycle reverses, retracing back to stage 2 before it enters the fifth stage, the REM phase of sleep. REM sleep is characterized by the presence of rapid eye movement. During this stage there is an overall, but transient increase in physiological activities in the body. The body temperature, heart rate, and blood pressure are all increased, sometimes even to above the level of a waking period. An increase in cerebral activity is indicated by increased cerebral flow. The cerebral activity during this stage is similar to that of the first stage. When awakened during this stage, many persons report a vivid dream. Nocturnal attacks of such conditions as anginal pain, gastric pain of duodenal ulcer, and asthma are believed to occur during this stage. Although the skeletal muscles are completely relaxed and the knee-jerk reflex is absent, some integrated motor activity or jerky movements are present.

It is believed that REM sleep is responsible for sorting out and consolidating information received in our daily lives. REM deprivation may occur among individuals whose night sleep is interrupted frequently at an interval shorter than 90 minutes, or whose night sleep period lasts only 4 to 5 hours. This is because REM sleep takes place only at the end of each cycle, and mostly during the last half of the nightly sleep. When sleep is interrupted, sleep has to begin again with the first stage. Some substances, such as barbiturates, tranquilizers, and alcohol, also seem to induce REM sleep deprivation. The clinical manifestation of REM sleep deprivation includes increased appetite, anxiety, irritability, and difficulty in concentration. Consequently, individuals with REM deprivation experience difficulty in coping with stressful life situations (Dement, 1960; Sassin, 1970). Some of the behavioral manifestations of a prolonged or frequent total sleep deprivation include general irritability, fatigue, difficulty in carrying out cognitive processes, and episodes of disorientation with misperception. In severe cases, hallucination and feelings of persecution are not uncommon (Zelechowski, 1977).

In planning total patient care, the nurse should keep in mind our developing knowledge about sleep. The physical and psychological stresses commonly experienced by hospitalized patients augment the importance of providing a suitable environment for meeting rest and sleep needs.

First-Level Assessment

First-level assessment related to a person's rest need involves the observation of behaviors related to the adequacy of meeting this need. The assessment factors include: (1) quantity and quality of daily rest, (2) sleep pattern, and (3) signs of sleep deprivation.

Quantity and Quality of Daily Rest. These factors are assessed simply by observing and recording rest periods throughout the day. The need for daily rest periods other than nightly sleep depends on one's physical and psychological condition in a given situation. However, for most hospitalized patients, deliberately planned rest periods may be a necessary part of total care. Continuous "turning and tossing" while resting in bed or fidgeting of hands may indicate restlessness. The mere absence of physical activity may not provide effective rest for a person who is under mental stress. Some

form of mild physical exercise, such as walking or manual tasks that provide temporary diversion, may be more effective in achieving good-quality
rest.

Sleep Pattern.   A person's sleep pattern is assessed by observing and
recording the frequency of duration of sleep periods and number of
arousals during each sleep period. Some persons may have adequate total
sleep hours but a lack of REM sleep due to too many interruptions at short
intervals.

Signs of Sleep Deprivation.   These are observed to diagnose problems already existing. In addition to those behaviors of sleep deprivation
discussed previously, the nurse should recognize reddened conjunctiva,
puffy eyelids, dark circles around the eyes, and frequent yawning as signs of
sleep deprivation.

Second-Level Assessment

The following are major factors affecting one's rest and sleep need: (1)
physical condition, (2) current psychological condition, and (3) personal
sleep habits and environment.

Physical Condition.   One's rest and sleep need increases with increased physical stress. Individuals with disease or illness will spend more
time resting and sleeping. Since restoration and repair take place during rest
and sleep, most hospitalized patients need rest and sleep periods beyond the
usual level.

Physical activity during the day tends to increase deep sleep (Shapiro
et al., 1975), whereas extreme fatigue or vigorous exercise near bedtime affects sleep negatively (Matsumoto et al., 1968).

As discussed earlier, frequent consumption of alcoholic beverages,
and drugs such as barbiturates, amphetamines, and opiate derivatives, may
be effective for temporary relief of sleep difficulties, but in the long run
they actually induce sleep deprivation, due to their tendency to suppress
REM sleep. These substances are habit-forming and, as a person develops
tolerance, become ineffective with prolonged use. Pain and discomfort are
other common physical causes that reduce the level of satisfactory rest and
sleep (see Chapter 10).

Psychological Condition.   Any psychological stress will stimulate
the individual's cerebral cortical activity and, since sorting and consolida-
tion of information of our daily living are done by the brain during sleep, a
person who is under psychological stress will have increased need for rest
and sleep. Often, psychologically stressed persons wake up with dreams and

complaints of unsatisfactory rest and sleep even after spending many hours in bed trying to sleep.

Change in Sleep Habits and Environment.   As human beings require an average of one-third of their total lifetime for sleeping, each individual develops his or her unique ritualistic habits through the years. It is not uncommon for an individual to experience difficulties in falling asleep, or staying asleep, if the usual sleep habits cannot be followed.

Unfamiliar or unsuitable environment also disrupts one's rest and sleep needs. Such things as unpleasant noise, light, odor, and room temperature can be disturbing factors.

Adaptation Problems Related to Rest and Sleep

The major adaptation problems related to one's rest and sleep needs are: (1) inadequate rest, (2) insomnia, (3) sleep deprivation, and (4) excessive rest and sleep.

Inadequate Rest.   Inadequate rest is diagnosed when and if the person's sleep needs are adequately met, but the individual's ongoing physical activity level is beyond the available energy level, resulting in a negative energy balance. Complaints of physical weakness and a feeling of exhaustion are common following rest periods lacking in quantity as well as quality.

Insomnia.   Difficulty in falling asleep or in staying asleep are classified as *insomnia*. Insomnia is not a case of total lack of sleep, but a subjective feeling of having not slept well. The problem is almost universal: victims of insomnia are found among all sociocultural and economic groups. Undue psychological stress seems to be the most common influencing factor. In some individuals there are no identifiable stimuli. Prolonged dependency on drugs and alcohol may be responsible in some cases. Often, this problem accompanies a condition of depression (see Chapter 26).

Sleep Deprivation.   Total absence or lack of daily sleep periods is considered a problem of sleep deprivation when it is accompanied by the behaviors indicative of sleep deprivation that were discussed earlier. REM sleep deprivation may occur when an individual goes to bed later than his or her usual bedtime, gets up at an earlier hour than the usual wake-up time, or has sleep interrupted frequently throughout the night.

Excessive Sleep.   This is not a common problem among hospitalized patients because their sleep needs are usually increased due to their physiological and psychological stresses. Although individual sleep needs among individuals vary greatly, there seems to be a rather narrow range for an optimal sleep period for a given individual. Individuals who make up their sleep losses by a longer than usual sleep period often complain of a "worn-out" feeling.

Nursing Intervention

The nursing intervention for a specific diagnosis should be planned according to the alterable stimuli underlying the specific disruption. However, the following are some of the general nursing measures that are basic to promoting quality rest and sleep: (1) provision of physical comfort, (2) alleviation of psychological stresses, (3) structuring a daily activity schedule, and (4) structuring a restful environment.

Provision of Physical Comfort. Physical pain and discomfort are among the most common causes for disruption in rest and sleep. Appropriate choice and timing of analgesic administration are important aids to promotion of rest and sleep. The choice of drug should be carefully made so that the person does not develop a long-term dependency and the consequences of REM sleep deprivation. Good personal hygiene aids physical comfort and thus improves the quality of one's rest and sleep. Soothing backrubs can be comforting and effective in inducing sleep. Comfort measures are discussed further in Chapter 10.

Alleviation of Psychological Stress. As discussed earlier, mere physical inactivity does not provide good-quality rest. The person should be provided with opportunities to ventilate feelings of fear, anxiety, and frustration. Lack of knowledge breeds fear of the unknown and feelings of powerlessness. Misperception or incorrect understanding can cause unnecessary anxiety. The nurse must be sensitive to a person's subtle, as well as obvious, behaviors that are indicative of psychological stresses and deal with them appropriately. (See Chapter 19 for a discussion of anxiety.)

Structuring a Daily Activity Schedule. Since physical activity induces NREM sleep, adequate amounts of physical activity, within the individual's activity restrictions, should be worked into the daily schedule. Any vigorous physical activity or events of emotional excitement are avoided near bedtime.

Every effort is made to ensure that the sleep cycles can take their full course so that the person will not suffer from REM sleep deprivation. Treatment procedures and other activities should be grouped together in such a way that the number of interruptions is kept to a minimum. Each sleep cycle takes 60 to 120 minutes. Therefore, scheduling the interruptions at longer than 2-hour intervals will allow each sleep cycle to take its full course. A large amount of food and fluid taken in the late evening will require unnecessarily frequent arousals due to increased gastrointestinal and bladder stimulations. Any drugs that have a diuretic effect are not to be administered at bedtime.

Structuring a Restful Environment.   In structuring the environment, the nurse takes into consideration the individual's personal habits. The environment should be free from all kinds of obnoxious stimuli. Room temperature, light, noise, and odor should be checked out for suitability. Any unavoidable, but unpleasant noise could be disguised by pleasant music.

The person can be told that the usual effects on one's sleep of changed surroundings do not last more than 3 or 4 days. The environment can instill a sense of security, so that the person is free of the fear of physical injury.

SUMMARY

This chapter has focused on assessment of the basic need for activity and rest. Some common problems in adapting to changes affecting this need were discussed. These problems are similar to some of the accepted diagnostic labels related to the functional health pattern areas of activity, exercise, and sleep-rest that Gordon (1982) lists from the North American Nursing Diagnoses Association. These include:

Mobility: impaired physical
Self-care deficits: level and type specified
Diversional activity: deficit
Sleep pattern disturbance

The nurse using the Roy Adaptation Model of nursing uses one of the suggested diagnostic labels from this text or from the Nursing Diagnoses Association to summarize her assessment in recording her plan for care. Or she may use a summary of the specific patient behaviors with the most relevant stimuli from her assessment. Based on a careful assessment and a clear diagnostic statement, the nurse sets goals with the patient based on outcomes that they both expect. Interventions are then planned, as discussed in this chapter, to manage internal and external stimuli in such a way as to promote adaptive responses to the need for activity and rest. Reassessment is then used to evaluate the outcome of nursing intervention.

STUDENT LEARNING ACTIVITY

Mrs. L. is a 73-year-old widow with a social history of no known relatives or close friends who can visit her during her hospital stay. Following a major surgical procedure for a fractured left femur, she is placed on an activity restriction of *complete bed rest*. Indicate some of the nursing problems that are likely to develop due to her limited physical activity, and plan appropriate preventive nursing interventions for each problem. (See the Appendix for a list of problems and preventive nursing interventions.)

REFERENCES

Deitrich, John, G. D. Whedon, and G. Schorr. "Effects of Immobilization upon Various Metabolic and Physiological Functions of Normal Men," *American Journal of Nursing*, vol. 4, 1948, pp. 3–36.

Dement, W. "The Effect of Dream Deprivation," *Science*, vol. 131, June 10, 1960, pp. 1705–1707.

Department of Health, Education and Welfare. "Update on Sedative Hypnotics," *Food and Drug Administration Bulletin*, vol. 9, 1979, pp. 16–17.

Downs, Florence S. "Bedrest and Sensory Disturbance," *American Journal of Nursing*, vol. 74, pp. 434–438.

Gordon, Marjory. *Nursing Diagnosis: Process and Application*. New York: McGraw-Hill Book Company, 1982.

Griffen, Susan J., and John Trinder. "Phsycial Fitness, Exercise and Human Sleep," *Psychology 1978*, vol. 15, 447–450.

Kottke, F. J. "The Effects of Limitation of Activity upon Human Body," *Journal of American Medical Association*, vol. 196, 1966, pp. 117–122.

Matsumoto, J., et al. "Influence of Fatigue on Sleep," *Nature*, vol. 218, 1968, pp. 177–178.

Opstad, Per Kristian, et al. "Performance, Mood and Clinical Symptoms in Men Exposed to Prolonged, Severe Physical Work and Sleep Deprivation," *Aviation, Space and Environmental Medicine*, vol. 49, 1978, pp. 1065–1073.

Oswald, Ian. "Why Do We Sleep?" *Nursing Mirror*, vol. 138, 1976, p. 71.

Pasnau, Robert V., et al. "The Psychological Effects of 205 Hours of Sleep Deprivation," *Archives of General Psychiatry*, vol. 18, 1968, pp. 496–505.

Ryback, Ralph, F. Lewis Oliver, and Charles S. Lessard. "Psychologic Effects of Prolonged Bed Rest in Young, Healthy Volunteers (Study II)," *Aerospace Medicine*, vol. 42, 1971, pp. 529–535.

Sassin, John F. "Neurological Findings Following Short-Term Sleep Deprivation," *Archives of Neurology*, vol. 39, 1970, pp. 187–190.

Shapiro, Colin M., et al. "Sleep Pattern after Graded Exercise," *Journal of Applied Physiology*, vol. 35, 1975, pp. 620–625.

Williams, Robert L., and Ismet Karacan, eds. *Sleep Disorder: Diagnosis and Treatment*. New York: John Wiley & Sons, Inc., 1978.

Zelechowski, Gina Publiese. "Helping Your Patient Sleep: Planning Instead of Pill," *Nursing '77*, vol. 7, no. 5, pp. 62–65.

Chapter 9

Skin Integrity

Marsha Keiko Sato

BEHAVIORAL OBJECTIVES

After studying this chapter, the reader will be able to:

1. Define the key concepts of the chapter.
2. Describe the structure and function of the skin, hair, and nails.
3. Assess behaviors related to skin integrity and identify the major stimuli that influence this physiological need component.
4. Intervene in some common adaptation problems stemming from changes in skin integrity.

KEY CONCEPTS DEFINED

Keratin: protein compound present in the epidermis, hair, and nails.

Melanin: skin pigment deposited in the epidermis which determines the skin color.

Skin Turgor: resiliency of the skin after being pinched.

Edema: an excess of fluid in the interstitial spaces, which may be localized or general.

Cyanosis: dusky blue or gray coloring for Caucasians and blue or dark brown coloring for dark-skinned people, due to a lack of oxygen.

Jaundice: yellow coloring of the skin caused by the breakdown of bile pigment.

Alopecia: continuous loss of hair in large amounts.

Pruritis: severe itching.

Ulcer: open crater on the skin or mucous membrane, characterized by the disintegration of the tissue.

The body systems perform many protective functions to maintain a person's physical integrity. The neurological and reticuloendothelial systems carry out complex activities that promote integrity and defend against harmful internal and external stimuli. Although the processes involved are less complex, protection is a major function of the skin. This chapter focuses on skin integrity as a basic physiological need that provides a protective function. The skin, hair, and nails function as protective mechanisms for the human body by providing a physical barrier against infection, trauma, and temperature changes. Adaptive behaviors related to skin integrity contribute to a person's level of wellness and are vital to emotional and physical health. As the reader studies the chapters related to the self-concept, the integration of the person as a whole and the effect of physical integrity on the total person will be made more explicit. Skin care and the maintenance of its integrity are important aspects of the nursing goal to promote adaption and total integrity. Problem areas related to skin integrity are identified through nursing assessment, and an appropriate plan for care may be implemented as illustrated in this chapter.

STRUCTURE AND FUNCTION OF THE SKIN, HAIR, AND NAILS

The skin is composed of three layers: epidermis, dermis, and subcutaneous tissues.

The *epidermis* is the outer, thinner layer of squamous epithelial cells and is further divided into two layers. The outer layer is composed of dead keratinized cells and the inner layer is where *keratin*, a protein compound, and *melanin*, skin pigment, are formed.

The *dermis* lies beneath the epidermis and contains connective tissue, sebaceous glands, and part of the hair follicles. This layer is supplied with numerous blood vessels.

The *subcutaneous tissues* are located below the dermis and consist of fat, sweat glands, and the remainder of the hair follicles. Eccrine sweat glands are located in all areas of the skin with only a few exceptions, such as the nail beds and ear drums. The largest of these glands are located in the axillae and groin, with the greatest number per square inch located on the palms of the hands and soles of the feet. The sweat glands have a minor excretory function and secrete perspiration containing water, sodium chloride, potassium ions, urea, and lactic acid. Perspiration maintains body temperature at a constant level by evaporative cooling. The sweat glands are activated by the heat-regulating center and are under sympathetic control.

The main functions of the skin are:

1. To provide protection from microorganisms and injury to underlying tissues
2. To help to maintain fluid and electrolyte balance and normal body temperature
3. To assist in the excretion of water and waste products
4. To serve as a receptor organ for touch and pain
5. To facilitate the activation of vitamin D on exposure to ultraviolet light

A single hair contains four parts: shaft, root, hair follicle, and hair bulb. The shaft is the visible portion of the hair and the root is the part embedded in the dermis. Surrounding the root is the hair follicle and at the expanded end of the follicle is the hair bulb, which has live, germinating cells. These cells multiply and are the focal stimulus for the shafts of the hair to rise upward.

The functions of hair are: retention of body heat, to increase the sensation of touch, and protection of the eyes, ears, and nose.

Nails are epidermal cells that have been converted to keratin. They function as a protective mechanism for the fingers and toes and help in the manipulation of small objects.

FIRST-LEVEL ASSESSMENT

A first-level assessment of skin integrity behaviors is completed for every person under the nurse's care. The purpose of this assessment is to identify ineffective behaviors that may lead to adaptation problems. For the most part, the assessment process does not require special instruments. The techniques of inspection and palpation, adequate lighting, and a transparent, flexible ruler for the measurement of lesions are sufficient tools. The following section describes the behavioral manifestations of skin integrity that the nurse assesses and includes criteria for judging the effectiveness of these behaviors.

Condition of the Skin.   The nurse assesses a person's skin temperature with the backs of the fingers. The normal adaptive behavior is a skin warm to touch. Increased warmth, in general, is caused by an increase in blood flow as a result of the body's response to inflammation. Increased coolness is frequently the result of reduced blood flow in order to supply the vital organs when in shock. Local coolness is commonly found in the extremities and is again due to a decreased flow of blood and/or the effects of a peripheral vascular disease.

The nurse needs to assess for the presence of skin lesions, which are manifested in a myriad of forms. The principal responsibility of the observer is to describe the lesions accurately according to distribution, location, size, contour, and consistency. The adaptive behavior is a skin free of excoriations or lesions.

Skin Turgor.   The nurse notes the *turgor* of the skin by pinching a small section and observing the speed with which it returns into place. The expected response is a skin that is resilient and quickly resumes a smooth surface after being lifted. The skin may feel thin, inelastic, and dry, due to a lack of moisture within the skin, or it may be characterized by pitting upon pressure, when the water content of the skin is excessive (edema).

Skin Character and Pigmentation.   The person's color in general is described and any deviations, such as pallor, *cyanosis* (a change in skin coloring due to lack of oxygen), or *jaundice* (yellowing of the skin due to the breakdown of bile pigment), are noted. In areas of increased or decreased pigmentation, further assessment involves questions regarding the duration of the condition. The adaptive behavior is a skin even in pigmentation with an underlying tone of pink, or expected variations based on ethnicity (see Chapter 4).

Scalp.   The nurse observes the condition of the scalp while combing or washing the person's hair. The scalp should be smooth, moist, and clean.

Hair.   The distribution of the client's hair is assessed, but the nurse bears in mind that there are many normal variations. Variations that warrant further assessment are unexpected general or local hair loss (*alopecia*), a noticeable change in the character of the hair, excessive hair growth in women, and the disappearance of body hair from an area where it is normally present. Also, observations are made about the cleanliness of the hair. The expected adaptive behavior is the presence of clean hair in normal distribution and consistency on the head, extremities, trunk, pubic area, and face.

Nails and Nail Beds.   The nurse observes the color of the nail beds. The nail beds should be pink or reflect norms for the particular ethnic groups, for an adequate level of oxygenation. The condition of the nails is noted, together with color and the presence of any lesions. The nails should be firm, smooth, and clear in color.

Prespiration.   The nurse assesses for the quantity, odor, and location of perspiration on the body.

Insensible perspiration comprises water and electrolytes lost by diffusion through the skin. Since it is invisible, evaporates immediately, and is not produced by the sweat glands, the person is usually unaware of insensible perspiration. *Sensible* perspiration is noticeable on the skin's surface. Under normal conditions, the healthy adult will present with a very slight moisture in the axillae and groin. With emotional stress, the palms of the hands will become moist.

The odor of perspiration is caused by the breakdown of bacterial products found on the skin. The nurse assessing normal perspiration will find that it smells musty, salty, or sour. It is termed *malodorous* if it is particularly offensive.

Sensitivity to Pain and Temperature.   Assessment of a person's level of sensitivity to pain and temperature is important to persons who lack this protective function, as it adversely affects their defense mechanism of withdrawal from danger. This behavior may be elicited by applying warmth to the area or by pricking the person with a pin and asking if the sensation was experienced. The expected behavior is a skin that is sensitive to pain and temperature.

Pain and Skin Condition Related to the Operative Incision.   The nurse carefully assesses the postoperative pain and skin condition. Persons having surgery are expected to experience pain following an operation. The duration of pain depends on the nature of the surgery and on the person's tolerance for pain. The presence of pain is identified through the observation of activities such as crying, tense positioning, and a clenched face, and also through client statements. In describing the pain experience, note the type, duration, and location. A more thorough assessment guide for pain is given in Chapter 10.

The nurse assesses skin integrity at the operative site by observing color of skin, whether sutures or Steri-Strips are intact, and the presence or absence of drainage. If drainage is present, the nurse notes the color, amount, and odor present.

SECOND-LEVEL ASSESSMENT

Second-level assessment involves the identification of stimuli that influence a person's behavior. Common stimuli affecting skin integrity behaviors are presented below.

Age.   Infants are more prone to skin disorders because the skin structures are functionally immature. The infant dehydrates easily because the epidermis is very permeable. Milia and cradle cap are common protective behaviors due to the increased activity of the sebaceous glands during late fetal life and early infancy. Temperature regulation is more labile in the neonate since the skin has an immature ability to shiver in response to cold or to perspire in response to heat. During the adolescent period the sebaceous glands become extremely active and increase in size. The condition of the skin often is disrupted by the development of acne. The skin integrity behavioral manifestations of an elderly person are affected by the aging process. Skin pigmentation becomes uneven due to the clustering of melanocytes. The elasticity of the skin is decreased and the skin is more delicate as a result of decreased hydration and vascularity of the dermis. Lines and wrinkles appear from the loss of subcutaneous fat. The hair becomes thicker in the nose and ears while the scalp hair grays and thins. The nails become hard and brittle.

External Irritants.   External irritants may be influencing stimuli for the skin integrity need. These factors include: temperature, poison ivy, radiation, medications, urine, feces, and soap. Environmental stimuli that influence perspiration include room temperature, amount of circulating air, and humidity. Cold weather as an environmental stimulus contributes to dry skin, whereas exposure to the sun may burn the skin. Poison ivy, urine, feces, soap, and some medications irritate the skin, and this may lead to the development of a rash. The stimulus of radiation has the potential to cause severe disruptions to the integrity of the skin.

Factors influencing perspiration include the thickness of clothing worn and personal hygiene measures used, such as frequency of bathing and the use of soaps and deodorants. Increased exercise or activity and stress or anxiety situations in which the person is fearful also contribute to increased perspiration.

Internal Conditions.   There are a variety of internal conditions that affect the manifestation of behaviors related to skin integrity. The degree of hydration is an influencing factor for skin turgor, as demonstrated by the dehydrated client with nonresilient skin. Fluid overload in the tissue is reflected through the observation of edema. The cardiopulmonary status of a person is a stimulus for the color of skin. Cyanosis reflects hypoxia caused by either heart or lung disease. Hormonal disorders may be responsible for loss of hair. The pathological condition of diabetes is an influencing factor for decreased sensation experienced in the feet.

The process of infection/inflammation alters the surface of the skin by the presence of exudate and necrosis. Thickening of the nails may be caused by infection. Certain disease or infectious states may cause an elevation in body temperature and influence the amount of perspiration.

The person's nutritional status affects the overall condition of the skin, hair, and nails. Skin appearing pale may be due to a diet low in iron, leading to anemia. Hair loss is evident in those suffering from a nutritional disturbance. Psychological disorders are sometimes manifested through skin disruptions such as rashes, itching, and acne. Nail biting may indicate a problem of an emotional nature.

ADAPTATION PROBLEMS

Adaptation problems, or broad areas of concern within the component of skin integrity, that are commonly experienced include itching (*pruritis*) and dry skin. Pressure sores (*decubitus ulcers*) occur frequently in the elderly and those who are immobilized. These problems are discussed further below, together with the relevant stimuli and suggested nursing interventions.

Itching.   The focal stimulus for itching may be a skin disorder from a systemic disease or pregnancy. An allergic reaction, local lesion, dry skin, and emotional upset are other influencing factors. The time of day is a contextual stimulus since itching is often worse at night, when there are fewer things on which to focus. A warm environment also increases the desire to itch.

Nursing interventions focus on changing the focal stimulus when possible, that is, removing the most immediate cause of the disorder. General interventions to control the itching include soothing baths, trimming the nails, and the use of firm pressure instead of scratching. For localized itching, the application of cool, wet compresses may be used. Temperature control and the use of diversionary activities such as watching television are suggested interventions.

Dry Skin.   Dry skin may be a result of overbathing, swimming, prolonged exposure to low humidity, or overuse of a strong soap. Excess water loss, ultraviolet lighting, advancing age, and a fair complexion summarize the other possible influencing factors.

Interventions for a dry skin concentrate on dealing with the stimuli noted above. Subsequently, it is preferable to have a daily partial bath to the face, axilla, and perineum, with a weekly bath during the winter months, and a bath twice a week during the summer months. Superfatted soaps are used for bathing and lotion is applied to moisten the skin. Air-conditioned areas should be avoided because air conditioning dehumidifies the air.

Pressure Sores.   This problem of skin integrity is characterized by a disruption within the integrity of the skin. The focal stimulus is probably a combination of prolonged pressure over the bony areas, anoxia, ischemia, and immobility. Poor nutrition, anemia, extreme debilitation, and edema are contributing factors. Moisture, such as soiled or wet bed clothes, and heat increase the likelihood of developing a pressure sore. The pulling up of clients in bed creates friction and a shearing force on the skin, which is a stimulus affecting the breakdown. Elderly persons are prone to the development of pressure sores because their skin is thin and fragile.

An important nursing intervention is frequent changing of the person's body position, at least every 2 hours. Ambulating the person as soon as possible helps to decrease the incidence of pressure sores. However, if the person is fairly immobilized, the nurse can give backrubs and massage over the bony prominences at every shift. Foot cradles, heel protectors, and egg crate mattresses are useful aids to reduce pressure on the skin.

The nurse observes the skin color of the person and notes localized areas of red, blue, or mottled skin, which indicates decreased circulation. Rubbing around these areas helps to restore circulation.

To decrease the stimulus of moisture on the skin, the client and bed need to be clean and dry. Lifting persons instead of pulling, and keeping the bed wrinkle-free, decrease the problem of friction. A diet high in protein and vitamins is essential to the repair of tissue, and the application of lotion helps keep the skin soft and intact.

SUMMARY

This chapter has focused on the assessment of behaviors related to the need for skin integrity, and the major stimuli influencing these behaviors were discussed. Common adaptation problems and corresponding nursing interventions were presented. The specific nursing diagnoses in this area that Gordon (1982) lists as accepted by the North American Nursing Diagnoses Association and within the nutritional-metabolic functional pattern area are:

Skin integrity, impairment of: actual
Skin integrity, impairment of: potential

In using the nursing process based on the Roy Adaptation Model to plan care for a person with a nursing diagnosis related to skin integrity, the nurse sets specific behavioral goals, and uses these goals in evaluating the effectiveness of nursing interventions. In this way, providing for the person's need for skin integrity as a protective function of the body can contribute to the overall integrity of the person.

STUDENT LEARNING ACTIVITY

The following case study focuses on the skin integrity need of the physiological mode. As a learning activity, the reader is asked to perform a first- and second-level assessment by identifying behaviors and relevant stimuli. Then select a problem and utilize the adaptation nursing process in devising a nursing care plan by stating the diagnosis, goal, interventions, and evaluation.

Case Study

Mr. Thomas is 76 years old, and is recovering from a cerebral vascular accident. He has been hospitalized in a stroke rehabilitation unit for 3 months.

Mr. Thomas has a pressure sore approximately 1 cm in diameter on his sacrum. He prefers to lie on his back because he is able to watch television from that position.

The bulk of his diet consists of carbohydrates. Mr. Thomas comments: "I really like potatoes, noodles, and bread. Meats are too difficult to chew."

His skin is dry and thin in appearance, with uneven pigmentation of brown spots noted on his face and upper extremities. Skin turgor is nonresilient. Mr. Thomas's scalp is smooth and clean, although his hair is thinning and gray. His nails are brittle. (An example of an Adaptation Nursing Process Care Plan, based on these data, and some appropriate assumptions about the situation, is presented in the Appendix.)

REFERENCES

Bates, Barbara. *A Guide to Physical Examination.* Philadelphia: J. B. Lippincott Company, 1979, pp. 43–51.

Cloherty, J. P. and Stark, A. R., eds. *Manual of Neonatal Care.* Boston: Little, Brown and Company, 1980, pp. 307–314, 349–353.

Gordon, M. *Nursing Diagnosis: Process and Application.* New York: McGraw-Hill Book Company, 1982.

Sherman, Jacques, and Sylvia Kleiman Fields. *Guide to Patient Evaluation.* Garden City, N. Y.: Medical Examination Publishing Company, Inc., 1974, pp. 52–61.

ADDITIONAL READINGS

Michelsen, Dana. "How to Give a Good Back Rub," *American Journal of Nursing,* vol. 78, no. 7, 1978, pp. 1197–1199.

Mikulic, Mary Ann. "Treatment of Pressure Ulcers," *American Journal of Nursing,* vol. 80, no. 6, 1980, pp. 1125–1128.

Chapter 10

The Senses

*Sheila Driscoll**

BEHAVIORAL OBJECTIVES

After studying this chapter, the reader will be able to:

1. Define the key concepts of the chapter.
2. Identify and assess behaviors and common stimuli related to the senses.
3. Apply the nursing process in identifying and intervening in adaptation problems involving the senses, including those evolving from sensory deprivation or overload.
4. Discuss the significance of the pain phenomenon as a major component in effective adaptation.
5. Assess the behaviors of persons experiencing pain and specify nursing interventions to be used to assist these persons in using the nursing process.

KEY CONCEPTS DEFINED

Primary Senses: special faculties of sight, hearing, touch, taste, and smell by which conditions inside and outside the body are perceived.

Sensory Deprivation: enforced absence of common and accustomed sensory stimuli.

*This chapter is a revision of the chapter in the first edition written by Jeanine R. Dunn, "Regulation of the Senses," pp. 133–150.

Sensory Overload: excessive sensory stimuli which cause a person to feel threatened or overwhelmed.

Acute Pain: discomfort which is intense but relatively short-lived and reversible — usually measured in minutes to hours.

Chronic Pain: discomfort which is of a long duration (measured in weeks and years), and which may or may not be reversible.

Pain Levels: intensity or degree of discomfort which can be experienced by an individual.

Pain Threshold: point of stimulus intensity at which majority of individuals report that discomfort is felt.

Pain Tolerance: individual reaction to discomfort.

Analgesic: drug utilized to relieve pain — divided into two groups: opiate and related drugs, which bind to opiate receptors, and nonopiates, which have no affinity for opiate receptors.

Addiction: condition of being habituated to a substance such as alcohol or a drug.

Placebo: relatively inactive substance given to an individual in lieu of a drug.

Positive Placebo Response: response to a placebo resulting in a decrease in the level of discomfort.

Pain Control Centers: inpatient or outpatient facilities in which persons experiencing chronic, incapacitating pain learn improved methods for coping with their pain phenomenon.

The senses play an important role in the adaptive process, since they are a person's channels for the input necessary to interact with the changing environment. In any clinical situation, then, the nurse assesses the intactness of sensory function and the effect of temporary or permanent problems related to sensation. This chapter provides basic guidelines for the assessment of the primary senses of seeing, hearing, and feeling. Taste and smell are also considered special or primary senses, and recent scientific work deals with the additional channels of input for extrasensory perceptions. However, our focus is on the basic physiologic senses and interventions related to problems of altered sensation. The sensory experience of pain, which nurses encounter frequently in clinical practice, is discussed in some detail, together with implications for planning nursing care.

FUNCTIONING OF THE SENSES

Our senses play an important role in the way we perceive the world we live in, and the people with whom we relate. Nurses who are aware of this fact can more competently assess the sense abilities of persons for whom they care. It is also vital for nurses to understand that loss of a functioning sense will change the way in which others, including health professionals, view a person. This is illustrated by the common complaint of legally blind people that store clerks, waiters, and others rarely address them directly when they are accompanied by a sighted person. Another illustration of how people change their views of those with sensory loss is the frequent hospital situation in which a hard-of-hearing or partially sighted person becomes labeled as confused when they do not give what are considered appropriate responses to the queries of hospital staff. Many confused patients have been "cured" when the nursing staff recognized the person's sense limitations and made efforts to compensate for the loss.

Our *primary senses* of seeing, hearing, and touching are channels, then, by which we receive and exchange information needed for life's activities, including relating to others. Limited functioning of any of these senses will seriously affect a person. However, as the Roy Adaptation Model clearly emphasizes, people have great capacities to adapt to changed circumstances. A loss, partial or complete, of a sense need not mean that the person's independence is also lost. Nursing's role, as in all aspects of human functioning, is to assist persons to achieve and maintain the highest level of adaptation of which they are capable.

ASSESSMENT OF THE PRIMARY SENSES

The following section discusses the assessment of the senses in a limited manner. Although it is true that nurses conduct baseline assessments of senses, as in the example of a nurse performing eye screening tests for school children, this basic assessment of senses is generally not a prime focus of nursing practice. For this reason, and also because of the scope of this chapter, the reader is referred to medical-surgical textbooks for detailed information regarding assessment, pathology, and treatment of conditions causing loss of function in eyes, ears, and touch receptors. Our focus will be on the nurse recognizing the degree of function present, and assessing the effects of altered sensation. The nurse is also concerned with implementing approaches to the person which will aid in adaptation. It is possible to combine some guidelines for assessment of eye, ear, and touch abilities and generalize about what is of concern to the nurse.

Guidelines for assessment can be summarized by six basic questions (see Table 10.1). The nurse will want these questions answered before the assessment is complete. In examining each question, the Roy Adaptation Model process of assessment can be followed in identifying the person's behaviors and the stimuli affecting those behaviors. However, the following discussion is simplified by focusing on the major questions of concern.

The first question is: "Is the person's impairment temporary or perma-

TABLE 10.1
Questions for Nursing Assessment of Sensory Impairment

1. Is sense impairment temporary or permanent?

2. Is impairment recent or of long standing?

3. Is more than one impairment present?

4. How does person view the loss of function?

5. How is person affected in the current environment?

6. What health teaching is indicated?

nent, or is this an unanswerable question at the current time?" An example may involve the nurse's encounter with three persons newly admitted to a hospital neurological unit. They all have paralysis and loss of sensation in their right arms and hands. In reviewing the medical reports and in interviewing these people, the nurse determines by first- and second-level assessment (see Chapter 3) that one of them has a probably correctable situation. He has been admitted for workup before brain tumor surgery, which is thought to have good possibilities for correcting the loss of arm sensation. The second person sustained the loss of sensation in a sky-diving accident 5 years ago, and the loss appears permanent. The third person had a cerebral vascular accident 3 days ago, and it is uncertain at this time whether or not sensation will return to the right limb. It is clear that without incorporating this kind of information in assessment data, it would be difficult to complete the remaining steps of the nursing process with these persons.

The second question closely follows the first, as it is fundamental to assessment: "Is the impairment recent or of long standing?" When an 80-year-old man casually comments that he has not been able to hear anything with his left ear since he was young, the nurse may register this information with a sense of significance different from her response to another person's complaint of sudden loss of hearing after a period of unconsciousness caused by a malfunction of scuba-diving equipment.

The third question raises the concern: "Is more than one impairment present?" Perhaps a person with diabetes is learning to adjust to paresthesia (or loss of feeling) affecting both feet, but is also experiencing retinal degeneration causing pronounced loss of vision.

Throughout the assessment, the nurse is incorporating information regarding the fourth question: "How does the person view the loss of function?" There is a wide range of reactions regarding both old and new problems involving the major senses, and these reactions are based on all the contextual and residual factors that make the person unique. For example, the slightest danger of a potential loss of hearing could be very threatening to a musician, whereas a person who works around jet aircraft might take it in stride as an expected component of the job. Nurses assess how persons feel about newly developed losses, and also try to understand how persons are coping with long-standing incapacities. Does the blind person confront the loss of vision with continued anger, forced resignation, or matter-of-factness? Some people, for example, may still require a great deal of help in reaching a level of adaptation even many years after becoming blind, while others may be at a stage of knowing they have met such a challenge with the best possible adaptation.

The nurse deals with the fifth question and considers it of immediate relevance in all nursing encounters: "How is the person affected in the current environment of home, work, school, clinic, or hospital?" The person's comfort in these settings is very important, but even more fundamental are safety factors. The nurse is very careful to assess the sense with a view to potential safety problems. To what degree does the person not see, hear, or feel, and what hazards does this present? Can the school child with retinitis pigmentosa safely play sports in the bright sunlight, or would school gym sports such as tumbling and swimming be better choices? Does the hard-of-hearing hospitalized person tend to smile and nod even when addressed by a name other than his own? Does the patient with cataracts see well enough to ambulate safely around obstacles in the hospital corridor? The nurse learns quickly that nursing according to the Roy Adaptation Model fosters and encourages physical independence. However, responsibility in assessing the senses is rooted in a sharp awareness of potential situations that could result in harm to the person. In particular, the combination of a new environment, as when a person is admitted to the hospital, and the stress of illness may change the context so as to reduce the safety level for a usually adapted person.

The sixth assessment question follows naturally from the other five, and helps the nurse finalize the assessment: "What health teaching is indicated and desirable at this time?" Do we need to teach for long-range purposes, as, for example, the proper method for inserting contact lenses, or how the newly diagnosed glaucoma patient will instill daily eyedrops? Is the concern short-term specific bits of information, such as safety precautions while one eye is bandaged? Is it appropriate for one nurse to conduct all the teaching, or do notes need to be made on charts, care plans, or home care flowcharts so that more than one nurse can contribute to teaching information and reinforcing the learning that has been accomplished? Are persons significant to the patient also to be involved in health teaching? How much can the person be expected to absorb, and on which senses can one rely? The nearly blind person will learn little from a teaching film, and the person who is in the process of adapting to a hearing aid will profit little from a small-group discussion.

NURSING DIAGNOSIS OF ADAPTATION PROBLEMS

After the initial assessment, data are summarized to formulate the appropriate nursing diagnoses. This is the time for the nurse to ask: "What are the situations for this person that warrant nursing attention?" Common examples in the area of the primary senses could be: inability to perform activities of daily living without assistance, inadequate information regarding physical condition, probable sensory deprivation, potential for distorted communication, or sensory overload. It is a good idea to ask a person at this time if there is anything special regarding the sight, hearing, or touch impairment with which he or she would like nursing's assistance. A mutual sharing of what each sees as concerns can be very helpful and can assist a person to understand better what is within the realm of nursing services. When the nursing diagnoses are made, each adaptation problem should be delineated clearly. That is, it is better to have several separate diagnoses rather than to attempt to combine too many factors in one problem.

NURSING INTERVENTION AND EVALUATION

The following example of a child with a partial vision loss illustrates the ongoing nursing process, highlighting nursing intervention and evaluation for one problem of altered sensation. Chris, a 9-year-old, is being seen in the outpatient clinic of a medical center for care, following the acute hospital treatment of an eye injury sustained during a softball game. Chris has lost vision permanently in the affected eye. The discharge planning nurse of the hospital has worked with the nurses who cared for Chris and prepared a summary of the adaptation problems identified during hospitalization, and the progress made in solving these problems. The summary states that Chris has experienced the grieving process for the loss of sight in one eye in a very appropriate manner for a 9-year-old. This problem is considered temporarily resolved, but there is a note to the clinic nurse to reevaluate it at a later time, since it is too soon after the loss experience to assume that it is permanently resolved. Problems relating to Chris's roles as schoolchild and peer have been identified and still need nursing intervention. In regard to the senses, the discharge planning nurse provides the clinic nurse with a working care plan as exemplified by Table 10.2.

Based on this report, the clinic nurse plans that Chris's visit will be spent evaluating the outcome of the short-term goals set by the hospital nurses, modifying approaches as necessary, and breaking down the long-term goals into manageable segments with appropriate interventions. Specifically in regard to the problem of potential for injury, the nurse will

TABLE 10.2
Nursing Care Plan for Chris's Problem of Potential for Injury

Behaviors	Stimuli		
	Focal	Contextual	Residual
No vision left eye for 4 weeks Left eye suture and close-covered with patch States unexpectedly bumps into objects	Baseball struck left eye 6/25/82, causing retinal damage and permanent blindness	Sudden injury Good vision right eye Well coordinated for age Supportive family Accident occurred during summer, so no school time lost	Age: 9 years

Nursing Diagnosis	Goals	Interventions
Potential for injury while traveling to and from school	Short term: Chris will be able to travel to and from school safely. Long term: Chris will be able to participate in classroom and school activities safely and effectively.	1. Provide Chris and parents with booklet on safety for the partially sighted. 2. Determine distance and terrain to be covered on way to school. 3. Spend 10 minutes each day with Chris practicing walking in an area with obstacles. 4. Enlist sibling to accompany on first few walks. 5. Refer Chris to Junior Blind Club.

evaluate whether or not Chris has been able to travel to and from school safely. Based on the success with this task, the nurse will plan with Chris and family members those goals involving other specific activities, and will carry out specific approaches to meet them.

INTERVENTION IN SENSORY DEPRIVATION AND SENSORY OVERLOAD

In considering interventions for adaptation problems involving the senses, special comment should be made regarding nursing concerns evolving from sensory deprivation or overload. These interventions usually involve an especially tangible and immediate changing or managing of stimuli. When a person is deprived of adequate sensory input, as could happen when blind or deaf or both, in an isolation room, confined in traction or by a respirator, the nurse may make direct use of personal contact on a scheduled basis; television, radio, and tapes, and judicious choice of roommates and room location are some interventions designed to increase stimulation. If the adaptation problem evolves from an overdose of stimulation, as can occur with hospital admission days, prolonged outpatient testing procedures, noisy roommates, and intensive care unit situations, the nurse will again intervene. This time the plan may provide for uninterrupted rest periods, a move to a quieter location, rescheduling of tests so that they occur over a period of days, and similar measures designed to reduce the amount of new experiences with which the person is confronted in a given time period.

PAIN

The phenomenon of persons experiencing pain is one of the most significant areas of nursing practice. Varying degrees of discomfort usually accompany the conditions for which people seek nursing and medical services. The nurse constantly encounters persons in pain, and all the advances of health science have not, to date, eliminated the phenomenon of pain. This fact is distressing, but the nursing student quickly realizes that the ability of the nurse to provide comfort and alleviate suffering is a fundamental component of nursing responsibility. The experienced nurse who is competent never forgets this ability and strives to improve comfort-giving measures throughout his or her career. There is extensive recent literature dealing with the phenomenon of pain. In various publications, including McCaffery's *Nursing Management of the Patient with Pain* (1979), the reader finds evidence of research which is opening a new perspective on the experience of pain. The student will want to peruse various sources for indepth discussion of challenging topics related to pain which can be dealt with only in a limited manner in this text. We are considering pain as an experience of the sense of feeling.

It is an unpleasant truth that pain can be a frightening and at times an overwhelming experience, not only for the afflicted person, but also for the health worker witnessing it. For this reason it is suggested that nurses gain some insight into their own feelings regarding pain so that they can acquire a level of personal comfort when coping with the pain experiences of patients. The nurse appreciates that, difficult as it may be to witness suffering, people in pain cannot be helped when they are avoided. Feeling confident regarding what is effective nursing activity for people experiencing pain will help alleviate some of the nurse's own apprehensions. Because pain has many facets, no single approach can be used to help the uncomfortable person, but the following section offers guidelines for the nurse who wants to employ the nursing process effectively, according to the Roy Adaptation Model, to ease pain.

There are undeniably various categories of pain, but our focus is on pain felt on a physiological level, that is, as a sense experience. This focus is appropriate at this time even though it is acknowledged that mental and emotional pain is interwoven with physical discomfort. Pain can be acute or chronic, and the assessment and interventions can be quite different, as the literature increasingly reveals. *Acute pain*, as described by Sheridan et al. (1982), is relatively short-lived, intense, and reversible. It may have a useful component, as when it alerts a person to an illness or injury, and the symptom of pain may aid health workers in determining the nature of the problem. Short-term acute pain can also accompany many therapies and diagnostic procedures. Perhaps the most common example of this is post-operative surgical incision pain, which at least serves as a reminder to a person that the problem requiring surgery has received attention. *Chronic pain*, which does not offer hope of a predictable time limit, serves no useful purpose, and so creates situations frustrating to patients and nurses alike.

In looking for a *definition of pain*, whether chronic or acute, perhaps the one most practical and comprehensive is McCaffery's (1979) statement that "pain is whatever the experiencing person says it is, existing whenever he says it does." This definition establishes an openness so that the nurse meets with the person in an atmosphere not clouded by apology or defensiveness. There are other, more technical definitions of pain that focus on the transmission of neurological impulses, and how these impulses are recorded in the brain. However, in reality, the mechanism of pain is only beginning to be understood. The research has established theories, and currently they remain only theories, as to how pain is perceived, transmitted, recorded in one's present consciousness, and recorded in one's memory.

Levels, Threshold, and Tolerance

It is known that there are *levels of pain* that can be experienced by an individual. This simply means that various stimuli provoke varying amounts or degrees of pain. For example, a small area of burned tissue does not hurt as much as a more extensive burn trauma, and although a surgical incision can always be uncomfortable, a high abdominal incision that is aggravated by deep breathing and coughing may produce a more intense level of pain. There are also *thresholds of pain*, which means that the beginning level of the experience of pain varies from person to person. Finally, there is *tolerance for pain*, which has to do with how much pain a person is willing to endure at a given time. Two persons may experience pain at the same threshold, but the higher-pain-tolerant person may more readily incorporate the pain into overall sensations at the time without allowing it to become a major focus of attention.

Understanding these terms of pain levels, threshold, and tolerance can be helpful to the practitioner, but it is important that they not be used to pass a negative judgment on any person's situation. Health workers may make comments such as "He doesn't tolerate much pain" or "She is exaggerating the discomfort from that simple procedure." The suffering person does not derive any constructive benefits from these statements. The experts in pain research emphasize over and over that discomfort, from any given cause, is a very individual, personal experience. The nurse who compares the pain experience of various people or clouds pain assessments with a personal standard of what pain levels it is acceptable to respond to does patients an injustice, and reveals an ignorance of the complex and highly individualized challenge that pain represents.

First- and Second-Level Assessment

It is reassuring for the nurse to know that even though the phenomenon of pain is complex and presents itself in a multitude of forms, there are basic assessment guidelines to be followed. Whether the school nurse encounters a 5-year-old child complaining of a stomach ache, the hospital nurse answers the call light of a terminally ill cancer patient, or the home care nurse visits a person afflicted with chronic rheumatoid arthritis, certain information must be obtained to promote adaptation. First- and second-level assessment of pain involves a behavioral description of the person's pain experience and the factors influencing it. Basically, one wants to know: the location of pain, if more than one source is involved, the onset and duration, if it is constant or intermittent, the intensity and type of pain, what the person thinks is causing the pain, and what the person thinks will give relief (see Table 10.3).

Location. A logical place to begin an assessment is with the location of the pain. Sometimes part or all of someone's pain is derived from an ob-

TABLE 10.3
Questions for Nursing Assessment of Pain Experience

1. Location of pain: obvious or concealed cause?

2. Is more than one source of pain involved?

3. Onset and duration?

4. Constant or intermittent?

5. Intensity and type, including acute versus chronic aspects?

6. What does person think is causing pain?

7. What does person believe will give relief?

vious problem, such as a fracture or deep cut. However, the fact is that nurses sometimes erroneously assume that they know the source of a person's pain complaint. For example, a 65-year-old man recovering from laminectomy surgery complained of being uncomfortable. The nurse assumed that he was experiencing surgical-incision-site pain and administered the potent intramuscular analgesic that was prescribed. After the injection, the patient commented: "At home I just take a couple of aspirin when I have a headache like this." It is also common for a person to have pain in more than one location at the same time, so it behooves the nurse to confirm the source of the person's pain each time she is assessing the situation.

Whenever possible, ask to have indicated exactly where each pain is. The person who complains of stomach pain may point to the left lower quadrant, or the headache may be cervical neck pain when the site is demonstrated. In addition, pain in an expected location may be derived from a newly developing problem, as when a person with an uncomfortable cast in place comments regarding increased pain in the cast area. The alert nurse may discover, by her careful questioning regarding the exact location of pain, that a newly developing infection under the cast has become a concern.

Onset and Duration.   It is also important to assess the duration and onset of pain. This is especially important during initial assessments to determine the acuteness or chronicity of the pain, but can also elicit helpful information whenever a complaint of discomfort is voiced. The simple question "When did you start noticing the pain?" may prompt the person to relate a certain position in bed or the ingestion of a particular food or medication to the discomfort they are feeling.

An aspect that is related to onset and duration is the constancy of the pain, and the individual is certainly the best judge of this. One person being treated for severe gastroenteritis complained of pain around the site of an intravenous infusion. There was no problem apparent to the nurse, but when the question of whether it hurt all the time was asked, the puzzle was solved. It was related that the discomfort started when the most recent intravenous-feeding bottle was hung, but was not present when the arm was held in a slightly bent position. The nurse realized that the higher dose of potassium in the most recent bottle was causing the pain, and it was relieved when the person bent his arm and so slowed down the rate of infusion. Rather than subjecting the person to the stress of an unnecessary intravenous restart, communication showed that a slower infusion rate, which the physician approved, kept the person comfortable.

Intensity and Type.   Intensity and type of pain are further areas to explore. Let people tell you, in their own descriptive words, how strong the pain experience is and also give information about the type of pain. They may choose terms such as burning, stabbing, sharp, dull, aching, feels like a boil, or feels like a lot of pressure. Try to avoid labeling the pain yourself, as the person may latch onto your terminology. If they don't come forth with a term, always give a choice of terms: "Would you describe it as a sharp pain or a dull pain?" Be alert to references or comparisons to past episodes of illness or pain: "It's a lot like the last time I came to the emergency room," or "Once I had distress like this after a big Italian meal," or "Of course, I've had stomach problems all my life, but this time it's pretty bad." These kinds of comments can be followed through to obtain a thorough assessment and can help establish whether the individual's pain experience is acute or chronic in nature.

Usually, people with acute pain show some visible signs of distress even when they may be trying to mask it. Anxiety is almost always present, and they will wince with certain movements, tense muscles, moan, register increased blood pressure and pulse rates, or show other individualized behavioral manifestations of their discomfort. People who have long endured chronic pain, even when it is severe, may have accommodated themselves to the feeling of pain and demonstrate little outward response. Also, depression often accompanies chronic pain, and this may serve to drain energy and cause the person to avoid both displays of pain and speaking of it due to feelings of helplessness or an "Oh, what's the use" attitude (see Chapter 26). Sometimes there may not even be any visible body part that looks affected. For example, the pain connected with some disorders of the pancreas is of such a chronic nature that a person may be observed watching television or talking casually on the phone even while experiencing severe pain.

Another point in assessing the type of pain is that persons with acute or chronic pain may not volunteer information about pain, as they assume the nursing staff knows their situations and needs. It may, in fact, be puzzling to patients that some nurses will quiz them about pain and others never mention it. One person, admitted for a kidney stone, thought that he was expected to have pain only in the late afternoon and evening hours, as the evening-shift nurses were the only ones who frequently checked his level of comfort. Other people will not rely on the solicitude of the nursing staff, and will readily share their response when they are hurting. The nurse must incorporate into her assessment this understanding not only of the individualized experience of pain, but also the very individualized methods of expressing it. She is also aware that her own behavior affects that expression.

The nurse should try to accumulate information without initially referring directly to pain. "How are you doing today?" and "Tell me how you're feeling this morning" types of comments accompanied by an interested and direct look at the person (as opposed to the tubes, bedside flowers, or the nurses' notebook) are quite successful in eliciting information regarding discomfort.

Sharing of Opinions. The final part of the assessment is a double check with the person to see if both of you have the same idea as to what is causing the pain. This has been discussed earlier in this text as validating the focal stimulus. An example of this process might be as follows. The nurse says to the patient: "It seems to me that you're a little more uncomfortable today. Is it because you didn't rest well last night?" "Well, that is partly it, but I was out of the back traction most of yesterday having x-rays and I can sure tell the difference today." This is also the time to check what the person thinks will give relief. Recalling that pain is a subjective experience, the nurse recognizes that the person is the only authority about the pain that he or she experiences. There is a tendency for health workers to think they are the best judge not only of the existence, but also the degree of pain. This attitude interferes with the ability to assess and relieve pain. McCaffery (1979) states that the pain phenomenon is one of the few times the patient makes his own diagnosis, just as he is the only one to tell whether or not techniques intended to bring comfort have been effective.

The nurse puts the assessment data she has collected together with the medical data available and so completes the first- and second-level assessment process, that is, a description of behaviors and related stimuli.

Adaptation Problems Related to Pain

Since pain can affect any part of the body, the possible nursing problems resulting are numerous. When people are hurting, many aspects of normal physiology involving communication, eating, walking, sleeping, moving, and sexual activity may become less effective. Common examples of nursing diganoses could be: the pain itself [Gordon (1982) lists this as comfort, alterations in: going under the cognitive–perceptual functional health pattern area], inability to perform activities of daily living, depression, potential for injury, inability to obtain adequate rest, inability to maintain adequate nourishment, inadequate exercise, or anxiety. Usually, nurses must focus on relief of the pain itself while not forgetting the additional problems, which are reminders of the complexity of the pain phenomenon.

One further observation pertinent to establishing nursing diagnoses is that health workers are generally more comfortable when involved with people who have a clearly defined cause for their complaint of pain. Burns, fractures, surgery, obvious wounds or swellings, and medical diagnoses of cancer are tangible evidence of causes for pain. Back pain, angina, arthritis, migraines, unlocated tumors, or premenstrual discomfort could be examples of conditions not so readily apparent. When these less definable pains are accompanied by nervousness or obvious fear of recurring pain episodes, it is possible for the health workers to begin to look to psychological distress as the main cause of pain. In this regard, the emphasis of recent years on psychosocial components of our life experiences may lead to a too rapid movement away from investigation of physical causes for pain. This is not to say that physical and emotional factors are not intertwined in the phenomenon of pain, as the presentation on the interrelatedness of the regulator and cognator in Chapter 2 clearly indicates. In fact, pure organic (somatogenic) pain that is totally physical or pure functional, (psychogenic) caused by mental processes, would be an unusual occurrence. The main point for nursing's concern is that just because the source of pain is not obvious, we should respond to the person's complaints with respect and thorough planning of care rather than precluding with our nursing diagnoses that there is no physical basis for the pain complaint.

Nursing Interventions for Pain

There are many options available when elimination of discomfort is the goal. Some of nursing's most satisfying moments can evolve from successful pain relief interventions.

Selecting an Intervention.   Based on the cause of pain the nurse selects one or more interventions. The common pain-relieving activities listed in Table 10.4 are particular ways of managing the focal and contextual factors contributing to the pain experience. It should be emphasized that the importance of more than one intervention is often overlooked. The

TABLE 10.4
Common Pain-Relieving Activities

1. Repositioning person, bed, wheelchair

2. Realignment of pillows, covers

3. Warm or cool baths or showers

4. Ambulation

5. Analgesic administration

6. Other drug therapies

7. Backrubs

8. Reassurance

9. Distraction, including the use of humor

10. Dressing changes

11. Local heat or ice applications

12. Staying with person in close physical proximity — touching arms, hands, shoulders

person with cholecystectomy incision site pain may require an intramuscular analgesic, but a short ambulation to relieve gas accumulation may also be in order. A refreshing bath, a lotion backrub, and some local heat application may be the correct combination for a person experiencing a flare-up of spinal osteoarthritis.

Attitudes.   The nurse should always suggest interventions to the patient in a positive manner, conveying the idea that they are being done for specific purposes. People want relief, and it is very helpful when the nurse shows, by empathy and a positive manner, that pain relief is the goal. Even when persons have to be denied what they see as a relief measure, a positive approach can help, as in the following example. A person was admitted at 2:00 A.M. to a surgical unit with the medical diagnosis of rule-out appendicitis. The emergency room physician wrote orders for close observation, admitting lab studies, intravenous fluids, and "no pain medication until seen in A.M. by surgeon." The person asked the nurse for a shot for pain. The nurse did not respond flatly that no medication could be given, but indicated that potent medications could mask symptoms and complicate the process of the medical diagnosis. The nurse did stay with the person for several minutes and incorporated the following comments into their conversation: "You'll be able to rest better now that you have actually been admitted to your room. I'll check on you frequently throughout the night, but I feel you'll be able to sleep now. You were dehydrated and the intravenous fluid will eliminate that problem." The person was able to relax enough to sleep for 3 hours and had to be awakened when the surgeon arrived.

Another example of the importance of attitude in pain situations is seen by a woman who was experiencing severe pain after a mastectomy. When her biopsy was reported as negative for node involvement, she no longer requested pain medications as frequently. "I can cope with anything now that I know they removed all the cancer." The change in knowledge was a change in contextual stimulus that affected her attitude and thus her level of ability to deal with the pain experience.

Health Teaching.   Whatever intervention is employed, the nurse accompanies her approach with health teaching. Many people are not familiar with the physiologic effects of various medications, heat and cold treatments, or benefits to be derived from ambulation. Explanations of these effects are available in texts on nursing skills. Simple health teaching can help establish a needed knowledge base for the person. This is illustrated by the frequently encountered lack of information regarding drug therapy. The physician may prescribe analgesics, muscle relaxants, antacids, vasodilators, anti-inflammatory drugs, and others, all intended to keep people comfortable. The nurse can ask the person: "Do you know why you're receiving this medication or treatment?" She then documents for other nurses the level of patient understanding. For example, it may be noted, "Receiving Valium for severe back strain — needs reinforcement of understanding of drug's muscle relaxant properties."

Oral and Injectable Analgesics.   *Analgesics* are common drugs of choice when pain relief is the goal, even though they treat only the symptom of pain and not the cause. Although more complete information can be found in other sources, a brief discussion is appropriate here. Analgesics accomplish their mission by two methods. Some drugs interfere with the transmission of painful stimuli from body sites, whereas others alter perception, and consequently responses, to pain on a cerebral level.

The oral and intramuscular agents are classified as narcotics and non-narcotics. The narcotics, such as morphine, are the more potent category, and the non-narcotics, such as aspirin, are considered less strong, although very effective, for certain pain situations such as arthritis. Some authorities categorize analgesics according to their ability to interact with opiate receptors in the body, since narcotics do bind with opiate receptors, whereas non-narcotics do not have this affinity.

The oral analgesics can be very helpful for a wide range of mild to moderate pain experiences when used alone, and they can be used to supplement injectable drugs. This last use of oral analgesics can be an aid when the person has had many injections and is getting decreased absorption of intramuscular doses due to scar tissue formation. It is beyond our scope to discuss all the various drugs, but it is important not to underestimate the usefulness of oral pain medications. The person often may obtain very satisfactory relief, particularly if the health teaching being done with the medication corrects the prevalent attitude that "It's just a pill."

The injectable medications are generally employed for a period of days to weeks for acute bouts of pain. They can also be beneficial when pain is persistent over a longer period of time, as may occur with cancer, multiple injuries as from a car accident, or extensive burns. Since intramuscular or subcutaneous injections are used for more intense levels of pain, it is important for the nurse to remember that preventing severe pain can be easier than relieving intense pain. This implies that injectable narcotics should not be used as a last resort type of intervention, but rather should be employed in amounts and frequencies that prevent pain from reaching such significant levels that the person feels that it is out of control.

The reader is referred to the current nursing literature, including McCaffery (1979), Miller and Pelczynski (1982), and Sheridan et al. (1982), for comprehensive practical information regarding the use of oral and injectable analgesics.

Drug Therapies Other than Analgesics.   We can mention here briefly drug therapies other than analgesics. The nurse is aware that many drugs that treat a particular physiologic disorder also effectively contribute to pain relief. Examples of these medications are: coronary vessel dilators for angina; antirheumatics for gouty arthritis; tranquilizers and muscle relaxants for muscle spasms; antihistamines for nasal swelling; drugs such as Tagamet, which reduce the amount of gastric secretions; and numerous others. The beginning practitioner will want to develop habits of awareness of all medications prescribed for the individual, including those prescribed to be taken on an "as needed" basis.

Use of Narcotics.   Persons experiencing pain that requires narcotic administration may worry that they will become addicted to the drug. Some people have negative feelings about the use of any pain medication. Nurses may also feel concern that by frequently administering potent drugs, they are contributing to eventual *addiction*. These concerns are not unwarranted and certainly no nurse wants to be even partly responsible for helping someone along the agonizing path of drug addiction. However, research reveals that most patients, sometimes reported as 97 to 99 percent (McCaffery, 1979, p. 222), do not become addicted and will stop taking pain relief medications when they are free of pain. Perhaps the key notion here is that when people take drugs for the purpose of pain relief, they are far less likely to become addicted than when people take drugs to escape problems, experience a high, or for other such nontherapeutic reasons. The authorities tell us not to withhold narcotics because we fear causing addiction.

The question of drug dependence is rooted in reality, but nurses are in the position, by reason of their knowledge, to make sound judgments in this matter. Certainly the nurse will communicate to the physician observations made regarding signs of inappropriate drug use. The nurse should also rely on her own experience and assessment of each person to suggest to the physician that the time has come to reduce the amount or frequency of administration of pain medication, or to change from injectable to oral doses. Often a person will welcome alternating injectable and oral doses or saving intramuscular doses for more acute bouts with pain. An alert nurse can do much to keep analgesics within the range of therapeutic use.

A special note of precaution must be inserted for both beginning and experienced dispensers of controlled substances. It is essential at all times to follow strictly the prescribed protocols for narcotics. It is an unfortunate truth that health workers are not themselves immune to the danger of drug misuse.

Nursing Judgment Involving Medication.   Deciding which medication to give, especially when several may be prescribed, requires nursing judgment of a high order. The physician may order options for control of the expected pain situation with oral and intramuscular preparations — several different drugs and various doses for the same drug. For example, a 34-

year-old man was admitted to an orthopedic unit after sustaining several fractures and various lacerations during a motorcycle accident. After surgery to insert a pin and cast application, his pain relief medications were as follows: Demerol 75 — 100 mg IM every 3 to 4 hours for severe pain; Demerol 50 — 75 mg IM every 3 to 4 hours for moderate pain; Vistaril — 50 mg IM may be added to Demerol doses prn; Tylenol grains — 10 p.o. every 4 hours prn; Mylanta — 30 cc p.o. every 4 hours prn. The physician in this, and many such situations, relies on the nursing staff to differentiate between moderate and severe pain, decide if Vistaril will be of help to this person, administer Tylenol and Mylanta where the need is seen, and decide how long an interval between Demerol injections is appropriate. The nurse will want to know what kinds of discomfort the person is experiencing at a given time, the exact hour and amount of the last pain medication and how it affected him, how the person perceives the pain, and his size and weight.

Another important area for nursing judgment occurs when the nurse believes that the person has the potential for increased discomfort and judiciously uses medication as prophylaxis. Examples could be situations when someone is ambulating after surgery, involved in physical therapy exercises, or is having burn or surgical dressings changed or diagnostic tests.

Placebos.   Space permits only a brief mention of the use of *placebos.* Placebos are relatively inactive substances such as water, saline, or sugar granules given to a person in lieu of a drug. The word means "I shall please," which is interesting in the light of placebo studies of recent years. Researchers are finding that it is possible for an idea to influence the body to produce its own pain killers in some situations. These pain relievers, such as endorphin, may explain the phenomenon of pain relief from placebos. The function of naturally released analgesic substances by the body and the action of placebos are areas worthy of study (see, for example, Perry and Heidrich, 1981; West, 1981; and Wilson and Elmassian, 1981). Too often in current practice a person who shows a *positive placebo response* is labeled as a malingerer, overly dependent or anxious, or other such negative terms, implying that real pain does not exist. This is unfortunate, as placebo reactors may actually be very efficiently combining their physiology and their mental processes to combat pain in a way that might be predicted from the Roy Adaptation Model's general approach to regulator–cognator relatedness.

Pain Control Centers.   Hopefully, all nurses will seek exposure to the innovative help being given by *pain control centers* to people troubled by chronic, incapacitating pain. These centers emphasize the proper uses of nutrition, medication, exercise, relaxation techniques, and insight therapy in a combined effort to make changes in the person's attitude and life-style. The goal is to change the situation so that pain is no longer the main focus of their lives. The end result is often a compatible life-style more satisfying to the person, and yet realistic about the physical pain which cannot be totally eliminated. This approach could be considered an example of enhancing contextual stimuli while the focal stimulus remains constant.

Team involvement is a fundamental aspect of the pain center's approach. The person learns not only due to the expertise of many disciplines, but also from the shared experiences of the other members of the group.

Evaluation of Interventions for Pain.   The main criterion for evaluation of any intervention for pain is to determine if the pain was relieved. Sometimes the person may state that the situation was partially improved, and this is significant. Perhaps the intervention is partly effective but needs to be modified in some way. For example, the person may require a larger dose of analgesic, increased ambulation, more frequent position changes, reinforcement of relaxation techniques, or a combination of interventions to obtain more complete relief.

It is especially important in acute pain situations for the evaluation to follow the interventions in a relatively short span of time. A person who has no appreciable relief within 20 to 30 minutes probably requires additional assistance. In chronic pain experiences, the time span for expected improvement may be enlarged to days or weeks. The main point remains that the health team must anticipate some appropriate time frame for improvement and incorporate this into the nursing care plan.

Another area to evaluate is whether or not the person is experiencing any negative effects from the intervention. It is possible for people to have dangerously decreased respirations from analgesics, strained muscles from overzealous physical therapy, allergic responses to various substances, and other unwelcome reactions to treatments intended to be beneficial. The person and family can often give information helpful in the evaluation process, but the nurse must also rely on skilled powers of evaluation to decide how effective the interventions have been. This involves observing the person closely for decreased anxiety, greater ease of movement, ability to rest or sleep, and interest in eating, reading, or other activities. The nurse will also use objective evaluation tools, such as vital signs or ability to raise an inflamed elbow joint to a higher level after a heat treatment, as aids to determine the level of comfort achieved.

SUMMARY

This chapter has discussed assessment of the primary senses, nursing diagnosis, and intervention for adaptation problems related to the senses. Particular attention was given to the phenomenon of pain and nursing assessment, diagnosis, intervention, and evaluation in the frequently encountered clinical experience of interacting with a person in pain. Knowledge from tested clinical practice has been incorporated with an understanding of the Roy Adaptation Model to provide a specific approach to caring for persons with alterations related to the senses.

STUDENT LEARNING ACTIVITIES

1. List three practical interventions that nurses can employ to help patients compensate for both hearing and vision losses.
2. Give examples of observed behaviors that might lead the nurse to establish diagnoses of sensory deprivation and sensory overload.
3. Discuss how the interventions listed in this chapter for both sensory deprivation and sensory overload might be instigated and carried out in a practical way.
4. How might the nurse alter nursing interventions when the impairment of vision of the diabetic patient, as noted in this chapter, becomes apparent along with a problem of adjustment to paresthesia?
5. Role-play the three patient comments on page 179 to determine how the nurse can use these comments as a basis for obtaining additional pain assessment information.
6. Identify possible medical conditions and kinds of pain that could be the focal stimuli for the nursing problems listed on page 180.
7. Discuss the comments made by the nurse caring for the person with possible appendicitis on page 182. What was the intent behind the remarks? Do you feel that these comments enhanced or interfered with the nurse–patient rapport?

REFERENCES

Falconer, Mary W., Eleanor Sheridan, H. Robert Patterson, and Edward A. Patterson. *The Drug, The Nurse, The Patient*, 7th ed. Philadelphia: W. B. Saunders Company, 1982.

Gordon, Marjorie. *Nursing Diagnosis: Process and Application*. New York: McGraw-Hill Book Company, 1982.

McCaffery, Margo. *Nursing Management of the Patient with Pain*, 2nd ed. Philadelphia: J. B. Lippincott Company, 1979.

Miller, Ruth, and Linda Pelczynski. "You Can Control Cancer Pain with Drugs," *Nursing '82*, June, pp. 50–57.

Perry, Samuel, and George Heidrich. "Placebo Response: Myth and Matter," *American Journal of Nursing*, no. 4, 1981, pp. 720–725.

West, B. Anne. "Understanding Endorphins: Our Natural Pain Relief System," *Nursing '81*, February, pp. 50–53.

Wilson, Ronald, and Bonnie Elmassian. "Endorphins," *American Journal of Nursing*, no. 4, 1981, pp. 722–725.

ADDITIONAL READINGS

Beyerman, Kristine. "Flawed Perceptions about Pain," *American Journal of Nursing*, no. 2, 1982, pp. 302–304.

Booker, Jack. "Pain, It's All in Your Patient's Head (or Is It?)," *Nursing '82*, March, pp. 47–51.

Cummings, Dana. "Stopping Chronic Pain Before It Starts," *Nursing '81*, January, pp. 60–62.

McGuire, Lora, and Shayne Dizard. "Managing Pain in the Young Patient," *Nursing '82*, August, pp. 52–55.

"Pain and Suffering," (Special Eight-Article Supplement), *American Journal of Nursing*, no. 3, 1974, pp. 489–520.

Panayotoff, Karen. "Managing Pain in the Elderly Patient," *Nursing '82*, August, pp. 53–57.

Chapter 11

Fluid and Electrolytes

*Nancy Zewen Perley**

BEHAVIORAL OBJECTIVES

After studying this chapter, the reader will be able to:

1. Define the key concepts of the chapter.
2. Discuss the person's basic need for fluid and electrolyte balance.
3. Identify and assess behaviors and common stimuli related to fluid and electrolyte balance.
4. Describe behaviors that indicate more common fluid and electrolyte imbalances.
5. Specify nursing interventions to be used in problems of fluid deficit, edema, and common electrolyte alterations.

KEY CONCEPTS DEFINED

Tissue Turgor: fullness and resiliency of tissue demonstrated by springing back of skin when it is pinched.

Edema: excessive fluid stored in body tissue spaces.

Levels of Consciousness: the state of awareness of the person.

　　Alert and oriented: knows time and place.

*Edited for the second edition by Sally Valentine.

Stuporous: partial unconsciousness; can be aroused with difficulty.

Comatose: profound unconsciousness; cannot be aroused.

Tetany: excitability of the nervous system, resulting in carpopedal spasm, larygnospasm, and convulsions.

Osmotic Equilibrium: balance established by movement of water across cellular membranes from an area of lower concentration to an area of higher concentration.

Dehydration: fluid volume deficit — decreased extracellular water volume.

Overhydration: fluid volume overload — increased extracellular water volume.

Hyponatremia: sodium deficit of extracellular fluid.

Hypernatremia: sodium excess of extracellular fluid.

Hypokalemia: potassium deficit of extracellular fluid.

Hyperkalemia: potassium excess of extracellular fluid.

Hypocalcemia: calcium deficit of extracellular fluid.

Hypercalcemia: calcium excess of extracellular fluid.

pH: a measurement of the hydrogen ion concentration, and thus of acidity.

Metabolic Acidosis: base bicarbonate deficit of extracellular fluid.

Metabolic Alkalosis: base bicarbonate excess of extracellular fluid.

Respiratory Acidosis: carbonic acid excess of extracellular fluid.

Respiratory Alkalosis: carbonic acid deficit of extracellular fluid.

Many systems within the body play important parts in the maintenance of fluid and electrolyte balance at adaptive levels both in the physiological mode and for the individual as a whole. Ineffective functioning or failure of the respiratory, circulatory, renal, endocrine, gastrointestinal, or nervous systems leads to fluid and electrolyte imbalances. The receptors and neural–chemical–endocrine channels of the regulator system, as described in Chapter 2, respond to the imbalances by making adjustments to restore homeostasis.

The nurse caring for a person must have an understanding of behavioral norms indicating fluid and electrolyte balance and be a skilled observer. This nurse is in an excellent position, due to frequent contact with the person, to assess both subtle and overt behaviors and changes in these behaviors that indicate ineffective body responses. It is easier to prevent imbalances if the nurse has knowledge of stimuli that influence balance. The nurse then uses this knowledge to predict and monitor the person for potential imbalances.

The purpose of this chapter is first to provide basic guidelines for assessment of fluid and electrolyte status. The focus is on those behaviors altered by imbalance—the norms having been presented in previous chapters. Second, stimuli that influence the delicate balance are identified. Finally, a few common adaptation problems are presented with appropriate nursing interventions described.

FIRST-LEVEL ASSESSMENT

Maintaining bodily fluid and electrolytes in delicate, balanced proportions is vital for effective adaptation of the individual. Cellular, extracellular, and systemic function will be disrupted and ultimately fail without the activity of fluid and electrolytes. Disruption of balance can occur on any of the three levels, and therefore the person with a fluid or electrolyte imbalance may exhibit any one or more of a wide range of clinical behaviors. Some behaviors, such as poor tissue turgor or dry mucous membranes, are obviously quickly associated with specific imbalances. Other subtle behaviors may indicate imbalance, but the specific disorder cannot be diagnosed readily because the behavior is vague, inconclusive, and may be the symptom of more than one disorder. A decreased level of consciousness or weakness are examples of subtle behaviors that may indicate imbalance. Further assessment and validation of the symptom are essential in preventing misdiagnosis.

In obtaining a first-level fluid and electrolyte assessment, the nurse considers both subjective and objective data as discussed in Chapter 3. Subjective data come from the person or his or her family and may be in the form of a statement which cues the nurse as to the possibility of fluid or electrolyte imbalance. "I feel like I sleep all the time and I used to get by with only six hours a night" or "Yesterday Grandpa recognized me and he doesn't today; he really seems confused" are examples of subjective statements useful to the nurse doing first-level assessment. Subjective data must be supported by objective data which can be obtained by observation or clinical measurement.

Validation of initial impressions is usually achieved by clinical measurement. Laboratory tests may be the only concrete evidence that an imbalance is present.

Using components of the physiological mode as a guide, the nurse systematically assesses the person for behaviors indicating fluid and electrolyte status. The following list guides the nurse in collection of these data.

1. *Oxygenation.* Observe respirations for dyspnea (difficulty breathing) and unexplained increases or decreases in rate. Check apical or radial pulses and note deviations from normal rate, strength, and rhythm. An electrocardiogram may deviate from normal.
2. *Nutrition.* Assess appetite. Note fluctuations in weight which may

be acute or chronic. Gather information on nausea and vomiting. Assess fluid intake considering age, weight, output and disease process. Note extreme thirst. Record parenteral fluid intake, both volume and type of solution.

3. *Elimination*. Note urinary output, taking into consideration age, intake, and disease process. Assess bowel elimination patterns, looking for diarrhea or excess laxative use.

4. *Activity and rest*. Observe for appropriate balance of action and rest. Note signs of fatigue, restlessness or agitation, and muscular weakness.

5. *Skin integrity*. Look for open, draining wounds, burns, or fistulas. Assess *tissue turgor* (when pinched, skin will spring back to normal position immediately with good turgor). Mucous membranes should be moist. Tongue should not be red, rough, and dry. Evaluate *edema* (excessive fluid stored in body tissue spaces) and identify location—lower extremities, hands, face, and eyelids are most common locations.

6. *The senses*. Evaluate pain or cramping, voice changes, and tinnitus (ringing ears).

7. *Fluid and electrolytes*. Review laboratory test values.

8. *Neurological function*. Assess *level of consciousness* (alert and oriented, stuporous, or comatose). Evaluate numbness or tingling of extremities, muscle spasms, and paralysis. Hallucinations and delusions should be noted. Observe for *tetany* [excitability of the nervous system resulting in carpopedal spasm (feet turn down with toes flexed), laryngospasm (spasm of vocal cords), and convulsions] (see Chapter 12).

SECOND-LEVEL ASSESSMENT

Fluid and electrolyte disturbances may be caused by a single factor or by many factors, depending on the situation. The nurse must be aware of the situations that commonly cause imbalances so that appropriate interventions can be initiated before serious consequences develop. The nurse is often in a position to help the person to maintain or regain normal balance. Table 11.1 illustrates the major categories of stimuli (focal, contextual, and residual) that influence and/or contribute directly to the development of these imbalances.

ASSESSMENT OF COMMON ADAPTATION PROBLEMS

The preceding sections have identified behaviors associated with fluid and electrolyte status, and several potentially related stimuli were identified. To make an accurate nursing diagnosis, the nurse needs specific informa-

TABLE 11.1
Major Categories of Stimuli Likely to Cause Fluid and Electrolyte Disturbances

Category	Examples
Imbalances occurring in clinical conditions[a]	
Acute illnesses	Adrenal insufficiency (deficient aldosterone production results in loss of sodium, conservation of potassium)
Chronic illnesses	Renal disease (inefficient kidney has limited or no ability to excrete hydrogen ions, potassium, and water)
Injuries	Massive crushing injuries (result in loss of extracellular fluid and release of cellular potassium)
Imbalances caused by medical therapy	Administration of potent diuretics (causes loss of fluid, potassium, and sodium)
Imbalances resulting from loss of specific body fluids (gastric juice, intestinal juice, sensible and insensible fluid, bile wound exudates, pancreatic juice)	May occur due to the following: vomiting, diarrhea, gastrointestinal suctioning, fistulas, drainage, infants on radiant warming beds
Additional factors that may contribute to imbalances	Age (infant or elder) Poor nutritional status Climate (intense heat causes excessive perspiration, leading to fluid and sodium loss)

[a]This is not designed to be an all-inclusive list. Basic pathophysiology texts will give a more complete list of disease processes that influence fluid and electrolyte status.

tion about the more commonly occurring imbalances. Of the 16 disturbances possible (Metheny and Snively, 1983), only the most common are presented.

Fluid Imbalances

Bodily fluid constitutes approximately 60 percent of the total adult body weight and is divided between two compartments, intracellular (45 percent) and extracellular (15 percent). For the infant, 80 percent of the total body weight is in a fluid state. For metabolic processes to take place in the body, a transport system is needed. Fluid serves as a transport medium in which vital exchanges of electrolytes and other important substances occur. In addition, fluid functions to maintain *osmotic equilibrium* by allowing free movement of water across the cellular membranes and capillaries. Movement occurs from an area of lower concentration to an area of higher concentration until equilibrium or balance is established.

Imbalances can occur when there are significant gains or losses of body fluid. Due to the two major functions of fluid just described, these imbalances may also be accompanied by an abnormal concentration of various electrolytes, creating further disequilibrium for the person. The following list categorically illustrates the numerous behaviors and stimuli that are associated with fluid imbalances.

Fluid Volume Deficit   (Synonym: *dehydration*—decreased extracellular water volume)

Behaviors

1. *Clinical observations*
    a. *Poor tissue turgor:* when pinched, skin remains raised for many seconds, depending on degree of fluid loss.
    b. Dry, sticky mucous membrances.
    c. *Decrease in weight:* may occur on either an acute or chronic basis.
    d. *Decreased intraocular tensions:* loss of fluid in the eyeball decreases the intraocular tension. The result is a "sunken eyes" appearance.
    e. Sunken facial appearance.
    f. *Oliguria or anuria:* significant fluid loss results in decreased cardiac output. As a compensatory mechanism, the blood is shunted away from the kidney to provide oxygen to the more immediately vital tissues. As a consequence, there is decreased urine production.
    g. *Tachycardia:* the heart also attempts to compensate for the decreased cardiac output by accelerating its rate.
    h. *Impaired sensorium:* exhibited in the person by confusion, disorientation, stupor, and coma, and is due to cerebral cellular dehydration (see Chapter 12).
2. *Laboratory data:* fluid loss is reflected in laboratory data by the following reports: increased hemoglobin, increased hematocrit, and increase in number of red blood cells per milliliter.

Influencing Factors

1. Specific illnesses or injuries, for example, gastritis or pyloric obstruction.
2. *Decreased water intake:* major contributory factor in fluid volume loss that is especially observed in elderly or extremely ill persons.
3. *Fever:* causes significant water loss through the mechanism of perspiration.
4. *Diarrhea:* any pathological state that results in diarrhea may contribute to significant water loss. Examples are ulcerative colitis and parasitic disease.

5. Drainage from tubes or fistula.
6. *Diuresis:* examples are the administration of potent diuretics and diabetic acidosis.
7. Excessive perspiration due to increased environmental temperature.

Fluid Volume Overload (Synonyms: edema, *overhydration* — increased extracellular water volume)

Behaviors

1. Clinical observations
   a. *Puffy eyelids:* due to edema around the eyes.
   b. Round, puffy facial appearance.
   c. *Edema:* may be observed in the extremities (especially ankles and fingers), face, or abdomen (ascites).
   d. *Tachypnea and moist rales:* these behaviors occur when the fluid volume overload results in pulmonary congestion.
   e. *Increase in weight:* as in fluid volume deficit, this ineffective behavior may be acute or chronic in onset.
2. *Laboratory data:* although there is usually no change in the hematocrit, there may be a significant drop in the serum sodium concentration [below 125 milliequivalents (mEq)/ml].

Influencing Factors

1. Administration of excessive quantities of intravenous injection (IV) fluid.
2. *Inappropriate antidiuretic hormone (ADH) syndrome:* oversecretion of this pituitary hormone results in excessive water retention by the kidney tubules.
3. *Congestive heart failure:* since the heart is an inefficient pump, excessive fluid retention may result.
4. *Renal disease:* the kidney in the uremic state has limited capacity to produce urine; therefore, fluid intake may exceed fluid output.

Sodium Imbalances

Sodium, a cation that is chiefly found in extracellular fluid, functions primarily to control the distribution of water throughout the body. This is accomplished by maintaining osmotic equilibrium between the intracellular and extracellular compartments. The excretion of sodium is controlled principally by the kidney, which acts as a highly efficient organ (in the absence of pathology) to both conserve and excrete this electrolyte, depending on the serum concentration. This task is aided by two hormones, aldosterone (inhibits renal sodium excretion) and ADH (promotes water reabsorption by the kidney tubules). Excretion of sodium from the skin is minimal under normal conditions. However, this loss may be accelerated considerably due to perspiration from muscular exercise, fever, or increased environmental temperature.

The major sodium imbalance that the nurse will encounter in clinical practice will be that of sodium deficit of extracellular fluid. Since this electrolyte has such a close relationship with water, the stimuli for a deficit imbalance should be grouped into three major categories: *depletional hyponatremia* (loss of sodium without a proportionate loss of water), *dilutional hyponatremia* (water replacement or retention without concomitant sodium replacement), and conditions with unclear etiology.

Hypernatremia occurs when either water intake is inadequate or the loss of water is greater than the loss of sodium. Rarely is hypernatremia reflective of sodium gain (Nursing Skillbook, 1978). Most often it occurs with both cellular and extracellular fluid deficit or dehydration. The nurse should consider potential hypernatremia in any patient who cannot obtain water as he or she wishes. Severely dehydrated infants are at risk for hypernatremia. The list that follows identifies behaviors and stimuli for sodium imbalances.

Sodium Deficit of Extracellular Fluid   (Synonyms: hyponatremia, low-sodium syndrome)

Behaviors

1. Clinical observations
   a. Muscular weakness and fatigue.
   b. *Apprehension and apathy, possibly progressing to delusions and hallucinations:* this ineffective behavior is due to the automatic shift of fluid into the cerebral cells in an attempt to restore extracellular isotonicity.
   c. Convulsions, coma, and death in severe cases.
2. *Laboratory data:* a serum sodium concentration below 137 mEq indicates a sodium deficit of extracellular fluid. However, clinical symptoms usually are not apparent until the concentration drops to approximately 120 mEq/ml, with severe symptoms occurring at a level of 110 mEq/ml.

Influencing Factors

1. Depletion hyponatremia
   a. Administration of potent diuretics.
   b. *Loss of sodium-rich bodily fluids (wound exudates, bile and gastric, intestinal, and pancreatic juices):* usually occurs in conjunc-

tion with diarrhea, drainage, fistulas, and gastrointestinal suctioning.

   c. *Adrenal insufficiency:* decreased aldosterone production causes decreased renal conservation of sodium.

   d. *Renal disease:* damaged renal tubules cannot reabsorb sodium ion.

  2. Dilutional hyponatremia

   a. *Excessive perspiration plus drinking plain water:* water is replaced, but not sodium.

   b. Inhalation of fresh water (drowning).

   c. Excessive plain water enemas.

   d. Administration of electrolyte free parenteral fluids.

   e. *Psychogenic polydipsia:* a neurotic condition in which the individual drinks large quantities of plain water.

  3. Conditions with unclear etiology

   a. *Inappropriate ADH syndrome:* this syndrome is a pathological state in which the production of the antidiuretic hormone is increased. The result is an excessive conservation of water by the kidney tubules, thus diluting the serum sodium level.

   b. Congestive heart failure.

   c. Cirrhosis of the liver.

    Sodium Excess of Extracellular Fluid   (Synonyms: hypernatremia, salt excess)

Behaviors

1. *Clinical observations:* the person may be asymptomatic. However, in symptomatic people, there is usually an associated dehydration with the clinical observations due to that particular condition.
2. *Laboratory data:* a serum sodium concentration above 147 mEq/ml is indicative of a sodium excess of extracellular fluid.

Influencing Factors

1. *Diabetes insipidus:* in this case, ADH is deficient due to a tumor or surgical removal of the pituitary. The result is excessive water loss without a proportionate sodium loss.
2. Inhalation of salt water (drowning).
3. Decreased water intake.

Potassium Imbalances

Potassium is the major intracellular cation, with only 2 percent of total body potassium being found in the extracellular fluid. In addition to affecting intracellular integrity and osmolarity, this ion also participates in various metabolic processes and influences the conduction of nerve impulses and skeletal muscle function. In contrast to sodium, potassium is poorly conserved, thus depending heavily on adequate daily intake. In renal pathology, however, abnormal retention can occur.

Due to the factors mentioned above, potassium imbalances are frequently encountered in clinical practice, thus necessitating close nursing observation. The following categorically lists behaviors and stimuli related to these imbalances.

Potassium Deficit of Extracellular Fluid   (Synonym: *hypokalemia*)

Behaviors

1. Clinical observations
   a. *Weakness and fatigue:* although these behaviors are very vague and easily misdiagnosed, they may be the only early signs of this imbalance.
   b. *Muscular system involvement:* as the imbalance becomes more severe, the muscular system is affected. Manifestations are: constipation progressing to paralytic ileus, shallow breathing (secondary to weakness or paralysis of the respiratory muscles) progressing to apnea and respiratory arrest, and cardiac arrhythmias.
2. *Laboratory data:* the following data would support the diagnosis of potassium deficit of extracellular fluid: serum potassium level below 3.5 mEq/ml and an electrocardiogram exhibiting a depression of the T wave, elevation of the U wave, and sagging of the ST segment.

Influencing Factors

1. *Hyperaldosteronism:* an oversecretion of this hormone results in excessive renal loss of potassium.
2. *Chronic administration of adrenal cortical hormones:* the mechanism involved is similar to the above.
3. *Administration of potent diuretics:* in this case, potassium is lost in conjunction with water and sodium.
4. *Loss of gastric juices:* since gastric juice is rich with potassium, its depletion may result in a hypokalemic condition. This may be due to gastric suctioning and any state that induces vomiting.
5. *Loss of intestinal juices:* since these juices also have a high concentration of potassium, the following conditions may induce a hypokalemic state: suctioning, fistulas, excessive water enemas, and diarrhea.

6. Decreased dietary intake.
7. *Stress:* may contribute to loss of potassium due to the increased cortisol.

Potassium Excess of Extracellular Fluid   (Synonym: *hyperkalemia*)

Behavior

1. Clinical observations
   a. No clinical observations in mild cases.
   b. *Muscular system involvement:* in severe cases, the person will exhibit behaviors similar to those associated with a hypokalemic state. These include: flaccid paralysis resulting in difficulty in speaking and shallow breathing, and depression of the myocardium with cardiac arrhythmias and death.
2. *Laboratory data:* in potassium excess of extracellular fluid, there is a serum potassium above 5.6 mEq/ml, and an abnormal electrocardiogram (high T wave with depressed ST segment and loss of P wave).

Influencing Factors

1. *Adrenal insufficiency:* a deficient or absent production of aldosterone will result in an excessive conservation of potassium.
2. Excessive parenteral administration of potassium.
3. Oral intake of potassium exceeding renal tolerance.
4. *Acidosis:* this pathological state causes intracellular potassium to be released into the extracellular fluid.
5. *Renal pathology:* the diseased kidney has a decreased or absent capacity to excrete potassium.

Calcium Imbalances

Calcium, the most abundant electrolyte in the body, has a 99 percent concentration in the bony skeleton, with the remainder being found in the skin and extracellular fluid. The only chemically active form of calcium in the extracellular fluid is in the ionized form, with the rest being complexed or bound to protein. The functions of this electrolyte are numerous. In addition to its contribution to the bony skeleton, the calcium ion has several other important capacities: (1) it is necessary for normal blood coagulation; (2) it has a regulatory control over nerve impulses, perhaps by decreasing cell permeability; and (3) it appears to influence contractility and excitation of the skeletal muscle.

Calcium imbalances can occur when the ionized form of this electrolyte is not maintained in the appropriate concentration in the extracellular fluid. The following list illustrates the behaviors and stimuli that are related to these imbalances:

Calcium Deficit of Extracellular Fluid   (Synonym: *hypocalcemia*)

Behaviors

1. Clinical observations
   a. Muscle rigidity.
   b. Carpopedal spasm.
   c. Tingling sensation around lips.
   d. Numbness of extremities.
   e. Tetany.
   f. *In severe cases:* respiratory stridor and death.
2. *Laboratory data:* a hypocalcemic client may be diagnosed with a serum calcium level below 4.5 mEq/ml, or 8 to 9 mg%. However, these data reflect the total serum concentration and do not distinguish between the two major forms of serum calcium, ionized and protein-bound. Since ionized calcium is the only chemically active form, it is necessary also to consider the serum albumin (protein) level to arrive at an accurate diagnosis.

Influencing Factors

1. *Hypoparathyroidism:* since parathormone (a hormone secreted by the parathyroid glands) regulates the serum calcium level, an undersecretion will result in a hypocalcemic state. This condition is caused by primary failure or surgical removal.
2. *Acute pancreatitis:* lipase is liberated from the pancreas during an inflammatory process and acts on fat tissues in the abdominal cavity to cause a release of fatty acids. Since fatty acids can combine with the calcium ion and render it chemically inactive, the serum calcium level decreases as a result.
3. *Renal failure:* the serum phosphorus level increases in the presence of renal failure due to the inability of the kidney to excrete it. Phosphorus and calcium have an inverse relationship to each other in the extracellular fluid. Therefore, since the serum phosphorus level is increased, the serum calcium level will decrease as a consequence.
4. *Excessive administration of citrated blood:* citrate, a preservative used in transfused blood, can combine with the calcium ion, thus rendering it chemically inactive. Although this condition is rarely a focal stimulus for the development of a hypocalcemic state, it certainly can be an important contributory factor.
5. *Alkalosis:* this metabolic state results in decreased ionization of

serum calcium. As above, this condition may not be focal, but rather contextual to the development of the extracellular calcium deficit.
6. Decreased dietary intake.

Calcium Excess of Extracellular Fluid   (Synonym: *hypercalcemia*)

Behaviors

1. Clinical observations
   a. Flank pain due to kidney stones.
   b. Muscle flaccidity.
   c. Anorexia.
   d. *Hypercalcemic crises:* observed only in severe conditions and characterized by the following: nausea, vomiting, constipation, dehydration, thirst, stupor, coma due to central nervous system (CNS) depression, and possibly cardiac arrest.
2. *Laboratory data:* a serum calcium level about 5.5 mEq/ml, or 11 mg%, may be diagnostic of calcium excess of extracellular fluid. As mentioned previously, these data must be interpreted in conjunction with the serum albumin level.

Influencing Factors

1. *Hyperparathyroidism:* may be due to an adenoma or malignant tumor; causes excessive amounts of calcium to be released from the bone. As a consequence, the serum calcium level increases.
2. *Vitamin D intoxication:* increased intake of vitamin D through food or tablets may cause a hypercalcemic state by increasing the absorption of calcium from the intestines.
3. *Metastatic cancer of the bone:* a breakdown of bone causing excessive amounts of calcium to be released into the bloodstream.
4. *Prolonged immobilization*: can also cause bony breakdown. Specific cases include osteoporosis and Paget's disease.
5. *Acidosis:* an acidotic state may contribute to the development of hypercalcemia due to the fact that acidosis causes increased ionization of serum calcium.

Hydrogen Ion Imbalances

The pH of extracellular fluid must be maintained between 7.35 and 7.45 to preserve adaptive matabolic processes. If the pH falls below 6.8 or rises above 7.8, death will eventually follow. Since acids and alkalis are constantly being introduced into the bloodstream (in normal conditions, cellular metabolism, exercise, and ingestion; in abnormal conditions, disease process), the body must enforce certain regulating mechanisms to uphold this intricate balance. These mechanisms, appropriately termed "the three lines of defense," include: the buffer system (primarily base bicarbonate and carbonic acid in a 20:1 ratio), the lungs (blow off or retain carbon dioxide), and the kidneys (excrete or conserve hydrogen and bicarbonate ions).

Hydrogen ion imbalances will evolve when the concentration of this ion in the extracellular fluid increases as in acidosis or decreases as in alkalosis, and may be respiratory or metabolic in nature. The following list outlines the behaviors and stimuli associated with these imbalances.

Metabolic Acidosis   (Synonym: base bicarbonate deficit of extracellular fluid)

Behaviors

1. Clinical observations
    a. Lethargy, headache.
    b. *Deep, rapid breathing (Kussmaul respirations):* illustrates the compensatory effort of the lungs to excrete excessive acid in the form of carbon dioxide.
    c. With improper fat metabolism, breath smells fruity.
    d. Stupor.
    e. In severe cases, coma and death.
2. *Laboratory data:* a serum pH below 7.35 and serum bicarbonate below 20 mEq/ml are diagnostic of metabolic acidosis. However, this condition is usually considered to be moderately severe when the base bicarbonate level drops to 15 mEq/ml, and very severe at 8 mEq/ml.

Influencing Factors

1. *Diabetic acidosis:* in uncontrolled diabetes, carbohydrates are not utilized for metabolism due to lack of insulin. Body fat is metabolized instead, with keto acids produced as a by-product. This increased amount of acid is in excess of the body's buffering capacity, with a fall in pH as a result.
2. *Decreased food intake (especially carbohydrates) or ketogenic diet (deficient in carbohydrate):* a depletion of the carbohydrate reserve will eventually result in body fat metabolism similar to that stated above.
3. *Diarrhea:* loss of the bicarbonate ion in intestinal juice may be greater than loss of the hydrogen ion, resulting in a decreased pH.

4. *Renal disease:* diseased kidney is unable to excrete the hydrogen ion.
5. Salicylate intoxication.

Metabolic Alkalosis   (Synonym: base bicarbonate excess of extracellular fluid)

Behaviors

1. Clinical observations
   a. *Decreased rate and depth of respiration:* due to a compensatory attempt of the lungs to conserve carbon dioxide (carbonic acid).
   b. *Tingling of the fingers and toes:* alkalosis causes a decreased ionized calcium concentration.
   c. Confusion, irritability, agitation.
   d. In severe cases, tetany, convulsions, coma, and death.
2. *Laboratory data:* a definite indication of metabolic alkalosis is a serum pH above 7.45 and a serum bicarbonate above 32 mEq/liter (Stroot et al., 1977).

Influencing Factors

1. Excessive alkali intake.
2. *Loss of gastric contents:* since gastric contents contain a significant amount of hydrochloric acid, loss of these juices through suctioning or vomiting may result in a rise in pH.
3. *Hypokalemia:* a potassium deficiency due to administration of potent diuretics or loss of gastrointestinal juices, for instance, may cause a rise in pH.

Respiratory Acidosis   (Synonym: carbonic acid excess of extracellular fluid)

Behaviors

1. Clinical observations
   a. Decreased ventilation, increased pulse.
   b. Weakness.
   c. Dyspnea or cyanosis (a late sign).
   d. Disorientation and confusion (common).
   e. In severe cases, coma and death.
2. *Laboratory data:* diagnostic of respiratory acidosis is: pH below 7.35, serum bicarbonate above 30 mEq/liter, and a pCO_2 (carbon dioxide pressure) over 40 mm Hg (Stroot et al., 1977).

Influencing Factors

1. *Pneumonia, emphysema, asthma, and occlusion of breathing passages:* these respiratory conditions may prevent the efficient elimination of carbon dioxide, thus resulting in decreased pH.
2. *Barbiturate, morphine, and meperidine poisoning:* these drugs depress the respiratory center with the result that carbon dioxide is inefficiently eliminated.
3. Breathing excessive amounts of carbon dioxide.
4. CNS disturbances of the respiratory center.
5. Inaccurate regulation of a mechanical respirator.

Respiratory Alkalosis (carbonic acid deficit of extracellular fluid)

Behaviors

1. Clinical observations.
   a. Rapid respirations.
   b. Tetany observations.
   c. Convulsions.
   d. In severe cases, coma and death.
2. *Laboratory data:* the following may be indicative of respiratory alkalosis: a serum pH above 7.45, a serum bicarbonate below 20 mEq/ml, and a pCO_2 below 40 mm Hg (Stroot et al., 1977).

Influencing Factors

1. Intentional overbreathing.
2. *Oxygen lack:* in this condition, the respirations increase with an excessive amount of carbon dioxide being eliminated as a consequence.
3. *Anxiety reaction:* may induce hyperventilation, which will cause an excessive elimination of carbon dioxide.
4. CNS disturbances of the respiratory center.
5. Inaccurate regulation of a mechanical respirator.

NURSING INTERVENTIONS FOR FLUID AND ELECTROLYTE BALANCE

After behaviors and influencing factors or stimuli have been carefully assessed, the nurse makes a nursing diagnosis reflective of the identified problem. Common problems include: dehydration, edema, and electrolyte imbalance. Goals for the patient are formulated and a plan of care is organized. Ideally, the plan will be designed to manage stimuli for the purpose of restoring homeostasis. Changing the offending stimuli, however, may not be feasible in some conditions (for example, renal failure or diabetic acidosis). Changes of the condition may not provide the most effective means for reestablishing the adaptive state. Supportive measures are instituted to modify the behavior until actual alteration of the stimulus is possible.

The nurse has an essential role in the reestablishment of fluid and electrolyte imbalances to an adaptive state. Many of the interventions are medical or pharmacological in nature and are dependent on physician orders; however, the nurse also has unique and independent functions. These include devising goals and a plan of care for the person based upon total assessment within the Roy Adaptation Model, and providing constant reevaluation of the plan to enable the person to meet the goal of fluid and electrolyte balance. Education is essential in certain chronic disease processes in which fluid and electrolyte imbalances readily occur — for example, the client with renal failure must be fully informed of dietary restrictions necessary to prevent frequent electrolyte imbalance and to promote a relatively healthy life style.

The following list illustrates by categories specific interventions associated with previously discussed imbalances.

1. Fluid volume deficit
   a. Treat underlying cause (manage stimuli — for example, control fever).
   b. Continuous intake and output.
   c. Daily weights.
   d. Replacement of lost fluid to restore the normal composition of the extracellular fluid (may be accomplished either orally by pushing fluids or intravenously).
2. Fluid volume overload
   a. Treat underlying cause (manage stimuli — for example, monitor IV closely).
   b. Continuous intake and output.
   c. Daily weights.
   d. Restriction of fluids so that normal fluid concentration is restored without altering the electrolyte composition of the extracellular fluid.
3. Sodium deficit of extracellular fluid
   a. Treat underlying cause (manage stimuli — for example, control diarrhea).
   b. Replacement of sodium deficit so that sodium level of the extracellular fluid is restored without causing a fluid volume overload.
   c. Restrict fluids.

4. Sodium excess of extracellular fluid
   a. Treat underlying cause (manage stimuli — for example, increase water intake).
   b. Administration of hypotonic fluid either orally or intravenously to dilute increased sodium concentration.
5. Potassium deficit of extracellular fluid
   a. Treat underlying cause (manage stimuli — for example, increase dietary intake).
   b. Administration of potassium either orally or intravenously to restore this electrolyte to its normal concentration in the extracellular fluid.
6. Potassium excess of extracellular fluid
   a. Treat underlying cause (manage stimuli — for example, monitor parenteral administration).
   b. Restriction of potassium in the diet.
   c. Administration of kayexalate (induces potassium excretion through feces).
   d. Give fresh blood when transfusing.
   e. In renal disease:
      (1) Administration of dextrose and insulin (glucose causes potassium to be deposited within the cells; insulin accelerates this action).
      (2) Administration of alkali (causes shift of potassium to intracellular space).
      (3) Peritoneal or hemodialysis (mechanically rids body of potassium).
      (4) Kidney transplantation.
7. Calcium deficit of extracellular fluid
   a. Treatment of underlying cause (manage stimuli — for example, increase intake).
   b. Administration of calcium either orally or intravenously in such amounts necessary to restore normal calcium concentration.
   c. Administration of vitamin D (increases intestinal absorption of calcium).
8. Calcium excess of extracellular fluid
   a. Treatment of underlying cause (manage stimuli — for example, provide exercises for those on bed rest).
   b. Hydration (push fluids to dilute the excessive concentration of calcium in the extracellular fluid).
   c. Administration of phosphate (results in calcium deposition in the bones).
   d. Administration of lasix (causes calcium excretion in the urine).
   e. Administration of calcitonin (suppresses calcium release from the bone, used experimentally).

  f. Dietary restriction of calcium.
 9. Metabolic acidosis
   a. Treatment of underlying cause (manage stimuli — for example, increase carbohydrate intake).
   b. Administration of bicarbonate intravenously (buffers excessive hydrogen ions).
   c. Administration of intravenous fluids (promotes renal excretion of the hydrogen ion).
 10. Metabolic alkalosis
   a. Treatment of underlying cause (manage stimuli — for example, limit gastric suctioning).
   b. Administration of saline (exchange bicarbonate ions with chloride ions).
   c. Correction of associated hypokalemia if present.
 11. Respiratory acidosis
   a. Treatment of underlying cause (manage stimuli — for example, regulate respirators carefully).
   b. Mechanical ventilators (promotes blowing off of carbon dioxide and may be used continuously or intermittently).
 12. Respiratory alkalosis
   a. Treatment of underlying cause (manage stimuli — for example, decrease anxiety).

SUMMARY

This chapter has focused on nursing assessment of fluid and electrolyte status. Behaviors to observe and influencing stimuli to assess were identified in relation to several specific adaptation problems of imbalance. Specific nursing interventions were listed for the imbalances cited. These, then, are the guidelines for carrying out the nursing process according to the Roy Adaptation Model in meeting the body's homeostatic needs for fluid and electrolyte balance.

The nurse devises specific nursing diagnoses for each plan of care. Gordon (1982) lists the following diagnostic labels related to fluid balance, under the functional health pattern of nutritional-metabolic, as currently accepted by the North American Nursing Diagnoses Association:

Fluid volume deficit: actual
Fluid volume deficit: potential

After assessment and diagnosis, goals for the plan of care are established. Nursing interventions implemented to meet the established goals are evaluated by reassessment of behaviors and influencing stimuli. Either the

TABLE 11.2
Adaptation Nursing Process Care Plan Related to Fluid and Electrolyte Needs for an Infant Admitted to the Hospital with Diarrhea and Vomiting

Behaviors	Stimuli		
	Focal	*Contextual*	*Residual*
Poor tissue turgor	Fluid loss through diarrhea and vomiting	Inexperienced mother who increased sugar intake with initial symptoms	6 weeks old (greater proportion of body weight is water)
Dry, sticky mucous membranes	Potassium loss by vomiting	No potassium supplement	Fluid balance labile because of age
6-oz weight loss		Crying due to discomfort	
Sunken eyes		In isolation room	
Decreased urinary output			
Weakness and fatigue			
Lab report: potassium below 3.5 mEq/ml			
Receiving IV fluids			

Nursing Diagnoses	Goals	Interventions	Evaluations
Dehydration related to fluid loss through diarrhea and vomiting	Infant will have improved hydration as shown by: 1. Good tissue turgor 2. Moist mucous membranes 3. Weight regained 4. Urine output normal 5. Eyes not sunken	Maintain intravenous fluids. Give fluids by mouth when tolerated. Record accurate intake and output, daily weight.	Weight regained in 2 days. Mucous membranes are pink and moist. Urinary output within normal range for age and weight.

Hypokalemia related to loss of potassium by vomiting	Infant will have increased serum potassium and increased activity and energy level.	Maintain intravenous fluids. Give fluids and food by mouth when tolerated—especially those high in potassium (bananas). Instruct mother in infant diet adjustments and relationship between sugar and diarrhea.	Serum potassium 4.5 mEq/ml. Mother explained the relationship between sugar and diarrhea to the nurse in a return demonstration.
Potential fluid volume overload[a]	Infant will not have signs of overload.	Maintain IV potassium intake. Control vomiting by limiting oral intake. Keep infant comfortable. Regulate flow of IV at least hourly. Maintain an accurate intake and output record. Carefully observe for signs of fluid overload.	IV intake administered as ordered. Infant sleeping between feedings. Accurate intake and output maintained.

[a]When a person has an increased risk of developing a problem, it is stated as a potential problem.

goal has been met and the fluid and electrolyte balance has been restored or the goal has not been met and the interventions will be modified.

STUDENT LEARNING ACTIVITY

Read the nursing process care plan given in Table 11.2 related to fluid and electrolyte needs for an infant admitted to the hospital with diarrhea and vomiting. Assume that the infant develops fluid volume overload. From your knowledge of other content on the physiological adaptive mode, describe how this problem can act as a focal stimulus to change behaviors in the other physiological components.

REFERENCES

Burgess, A. *The Nurse's Guide to Fluid and Electrolyte Balance*, 2nd ed. New York: McGraw-Hill Book Company, 1979.

Burke, S. R. *The Composition and Function of Body Fluids*. St. Louis: The C. V. Mosby Company, 1972.

Carroll, H. J., and M. S. Oh. *Water, Electrolyte and Acid–Base Metabolism*. Philadelphia: J. B. Lippincott Company, 1978.

Gordon, Marjory. *Nursing Diagnosis: Process and Application*. New York: McGraw-Hill Book Company, 1982.

Guyton, A. *Textbook of Medical Physiology*. Philadelphia: W. B. Saunders Company, 1976.

Heath, J. K. "A Conceptual Basis for Assessing Body Water Status," *Nursing Clinics of North America*, vol. 6, no. 1, March 1971, pp. 189–198.

Kee, J. L. *Fluids and Electrolytes with Clinical Applications*, 2nd ed. New York: John Wiley & Sons, Inc., 1978.

Metheny, N. M., and W. D. Snively, Jr. *Nurses' Handbook of Fluid Balance*, 4th ed. Philadelphia: J. B. Lippincott Company, 1983.

Nursing Skillbook. "Monitoring Fluid and Electrolytes Precisely," *Nursing '78*. Springhouse, Pa.: Intermed Communications, Inc., 1978.

Snively, W. D., and D. R. Beshear. "Water and Electrolytes in Health and Diseases," in *Advanced Concepts in Clinical Nursing*, Kay C. Kintzel, ed. Philadelphia: J. B. Lippincott Company, 1971.

Stroot, V. R., C. A. Lee, and C. A. Shaper. *Fluids and Electrolytes: A Practical Approach*, 2nd ed. Philadelphia: F. A. Davis Company, 1977.

Urrows, S., ed. "Symposium on Fluid, Electrolyte and Acid–Base Balance," *Nursing Clinics of North America*, vol. 15, no. 3, September 1980, pp. 535–646.

Weldy, N. J. *Body Fluids and Electrolytes*. St. Louis: The C. V. Mosby Company, 1972.

Chapter 12

Neurological Function

Marsha Milton Roberson

BEHAVIORAL OBJECTIVES

After studying this chapter, the reader will be able to:

1. Define the key concepts of the chapter.
2. Recall the basic structure and function of the nervous system.
3. Identify and assess behaviors and common stimuli of neurological function.
4. Differentiate between level of consciousness and level of orientation.
5. Describe basic adaptation problems related to neurological function.
6. Name nursing interventions appropriate to given adaptation problems.
7. Apply the nursing process according to the Roy Adaptation Model in developing a nursing care plan for a person with deficits in neurological functioning, as described in a case study.

KEY CONCEPTS DEFINED

Level of Consciousness (LOC): one's level of wakefulness. This is sometimes globally interpreted to mean level of orientation as well.

Level of Orientation: level of intellectual functioning in terms of awareness of time, place, person, purpose.

Coma: a condition of deep stupor or sleep from which the person cannot be aroused. Few to absent neurological responses are seen.

Paralysis: loss of movement in a group of muscles, extremity, or combination of extremities.

Aphasia: the inability to interpret and implement the signs and symbols of the language.

Increased Intracranial Pressure (IICP): an above-normal pressure of cerebrospinal fluid in the subarachnoid space of the brain and spinal cord. The increased pressure results from almost any neurological disturbance and can eventually cause death.

Tremor: a shaking or quivering movement.

Seizure: a behavioral response seen in several disorders in which there is a loss of consciousness and any one or a combination of the following: jerking movements, erratic behavior, unusual sensory perceptions.

A person's neurological functioning is a complex and fascinating process. Understanding of the role of neurological function in a person's adaptation, and applying problem-solving skills in promoting this adaptation, offer a challenge to the nurse. In Chapter 2 we noted that the regulator coping mechanism involves processing changes in internal and external stimuli through neural–chemical–endocrine channels. The neurological channels are significant for such diverse functions as controlling and coordinating all bodily movements and mediating intellectual activity, including reason.

Various threats to neurological functioning, such as trauma, infection, and vascular disturbances, result in both physical and cognitive limitations that change the person's adaptive potential. This chapter focuses on the nurse's assessment of neurological status and of factors that contribute to changes in that status. Setting goals to promote adaptive behavior and minimize neurological handicaps is discussed in general. Adaptation problems commonly arising from altered neurological function are identified with the related nursing interventions.

NEUROLOGICAL STRUCTURE AND FUNCTION

The anatomical and functional unit of the nervous system is the neuron. Each operates in conjunction with other neurons in a chainlike fashion to send impulses throughout the body. Impulses carrying information to and from the skin, muscles, and other areas are sent from the brain and spinal cord by these neurons.

Various structures and cells comprise what is known as the central nervous system (CNS) and the peripheral nervous system. The former includes the brain and spinal cord. The function of the brain and spinal cord is multifaceted. The major structures and their specific functions are outlined in Fig. 12.1.

The skull, as well as three membranes, the dura mater, arachnoid, and pia mater, has a protective function. Beneath the arachnoid membrane is the subarachnoid space where an important fluid, cerebrospinal fluid (CSF) circulates. This fluid has a cushioning effect against trauma and utilizes an

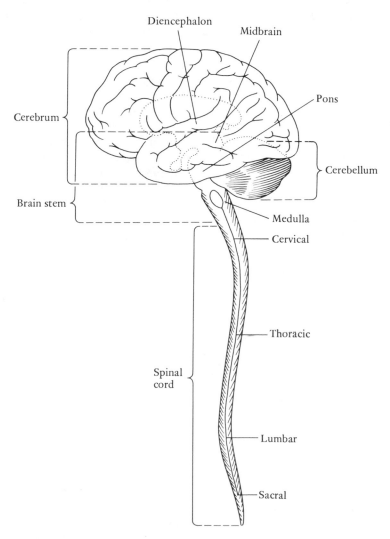

Figure 12.1   Lateral view of the central nervous system structures with major functions listed. Reprinted from L.L. Langhley and Ira K. Telford. *Dynamic Anatomy and Physiology.* New York: McGraw-Hill, ©1974, p. 228.

autoregulatory mechanism which can slightly modify increasing intracranial pressure (see Fig. 12.2).

The spinal cord contains three types of functional pathways, the sensory, motor and reflex. The sensory pathway contains afferent neurons which transmit neurological impulses from the body through the spinal cord to the brain. The motor pathway contains efferent neurons which transmit impulses from the brain through the spinal cord to nerves supplying muscles or glands. The third pathway of the spinal cord is the reflex arc, which bypasses the brain in impulse transmission. The various body reflexes take place at this level in the following manner:

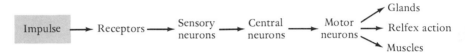

In terms of structural classification, the second major portion of the nervous system is the peripheral nervous system. This system contains the following: (1) spinal nerves, which carry sensory impulses to the spinal cord (efferent); and (2) cranial nerves, which carry special sense impulses (visual, auditory, and so forth) to and from the brain. The various functional subsystems of the peripheral nervous system are shown in Table 12.1. The reader can readily identify that basic understanding of neurological structures and function is significant for future explorations of the regulator subsystem of adaptation proposed by the Roy Adaptation Model of nursing.

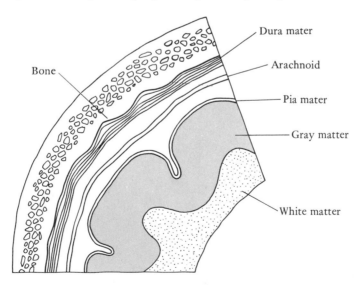

Figure 12.2 Vertical section of the meninges.

TABLE 12.1
Peripheral Nervous System: Functional Classification

Somatic Nervous System	*Autonomic Nervous System*
Initiation of motor action	Regulation of internal glands
Innervation of skeletal muscle	Initiation of involuntary actions
Excitation of effector organs	Innervation of smooth muscle, cardiac muscle, glands
	Excitation or inhibition of effector organs

FIRST-LEVEL ASSESSMENT

First-level assessment of neurological function involves observing and eliciting behaviors indicative of the person's level of functioning and/or impairment. Ongoing assessment of behaviors that evidence major neurological change often is an important nursing function in both hospital and home care. The detail of the initial neurological assessment varies according to the person's condition and the particular role of the nurse and physician within the setting. For example, an emergency room admitting nurse may make a quick initial assessment of an accident victim with head trauma that results in an immediate decision to summon a neurosurgeon. A more detailed neurological assessment is the responsibility of the physician. More often the nurse assesses neurological function over time and is alert to changes that can alter the medical or nursing diagnosis and plan of care. Major areas for assessment of behaviors include: history of onset of behaviors; level of consciousness/level of orientation; cranial nerve functioning; sensory and motor evaluation; and other indicators, such as reflexes, vital signs, laboratory values, and diagnostic measures.

Level of Consciousness and Level of Orientation

Nurses often focus on pupil checks to determine neurological status, however, it is the level of consciousness that is unequivocally the major assessment factor. Slight changes in level of consciousness often are significant. Increasing forgetfulness or slight lethargy may be the first behavioral indicators of increasing intracranial pressure.

History

On initial presentation, a careful history is done. This is largely the responsibility of the physician, but the nurse can be instrumental in contributing meaningful data from the patient, family, and/or witnesses to the onset of behaviors. In the case of an automobile accident, did the person lose consciousness first and then collide with another car? Did a painter simply fall from the ladder or did he clutch at his chest first? Was the person taking drugs or alcohol? Was he or she recently having dizzy spells or losing consciousness? Such behavioral history is particularly useful in medical evaluation of neurological function.

There are a number of systems used to classify level of consciousness. Often these sources differ in their definitions of the varying levels described. Therefore, for more accurate communication, the nurse will describe the actual behaviors related to level of consciousness. The following categorization, modified from Rudy (1977), discriminates between *level of consciousness*, or wakefulness, and *level of orientation*, or intellectual activity. The terms used here and their behavioral descriptions can serve as a guideline for nursing assessment.

1. Level of consciousness
   a. *Alert:* responds to stimuli in the environment
   b. *Lethargic:* inactive, indifferent; responds slowly or incompletely to stimuli; capable of verbal responses
   c. *Obtunded:* very drowsy; very indifferent; capable of remaining awake, but may appear asleep
   d. *Stuporous or semicomatose:* aroused only by continuous painful stimuli
   e. *Comatose:* response to intense stimuli is rudimentary or reflex; response absent (deep coma)
2. Level of orientation
   a. *Oriented:* responds appropriately to auditory, visual, and somatosensory stimuli; knows the time, place, person, and purpose, that is, what day it is, where he or she is, his or her name, and why he or she is here
   b. *Confused:* appears dazed; disoriented to varying degrees (time, place, person, purpose), either continuously or intermittently

Nursing observations related to level of consciousness include noting the person's mood, expressions, grooming, mannerisms, and speech. Persistency of unexpected behaviors may indicate the need for a more thorough mental status examination. Such an exam might be conducted by an advanced practitioner in psychiatric nursing, or by a person from another discipline, such as psychology or psychiatry. The nurse is aware of the overlap of behavioral manifestations of neurological functioning and of mental status.

Although the previously mentioned terms related to level of consciousness and orientation are currently the most universally used, a more reliable tool is gaining increasing popularity. This is the Glasgow Coma or Responsiveness Scale (Jennett and Teasdale, 1977). It allows for the monitoring of a comatose patient with less ambiguity than other tools and terminology. *Coma* is described as the inability to obey commands, to speak, or to open the eyes. Therefore, each of these behaviors is categorized and graded according to the level of response elicited by a stimulus. For example, the response of opening the eyes spontaneously is scored 4 points, whereas no eye opening is scored 1 point, a more comatose state. The best

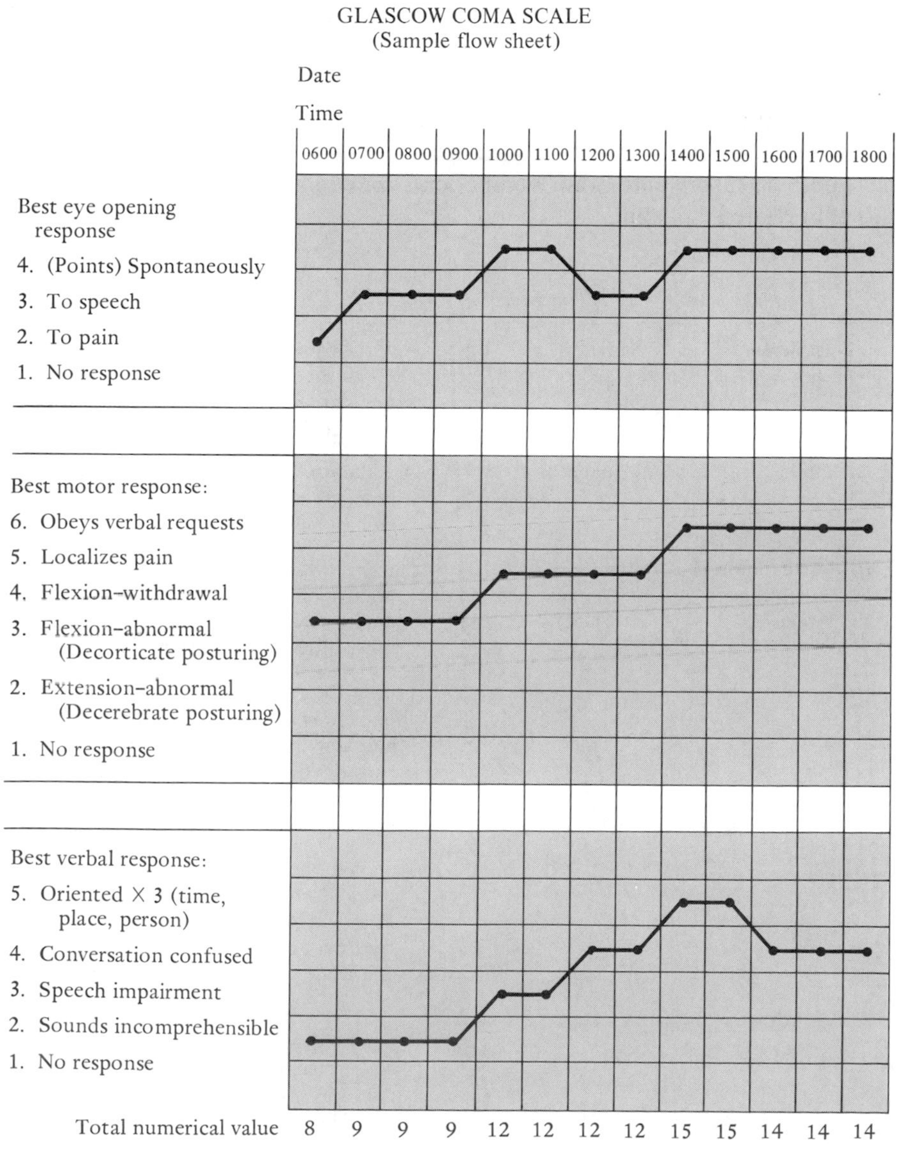

GLASCOW COMA SCALE
(Sample flow sheet)

Date

Time

	0600	0700	0800	0900	1000	1100	1200	1300	1400	1500	1600	1700	1800

Best eye opening response
4. (Points) Spontaneously
3. To speech
2. To pain
1. No response

Best motor response:
6. Obeys verbal requests
5. Localizes pain
4. Flexion–withdrawal
3. Flexion–abnormal
(Decorticate posturing)
2. Extension–abnormal
(Decerebrate posturing)
1. No response

Best verbal response:
5. Oriented × 3 (time, place, person)
4. Conversation confused
3. Speech impairment
2. Sounds incomprehensible
1. No response

Total numerical value	8	9	9	9	12	12	12	12	15	15	14	14	14

Figure 12.3   Glasgow Coma Scale. Reprinted from B. Jennett and G. Teasdale. "Aspects of Coma After Severe Head Injury", *Lancet*, 1977, i:878–81.

motor response and verbal response are scored similarly (see Fig. 12.3). The best response elicited from the patient in each of these three categories is noted and scored. The highest cumulative score, 15, reflects a fully oriented, alert person, whereas a score of 3 to 5 is considered low. By noting a person's score on a flow sheet, his or her level of progress can be more objectively and expediently determined and evaluated over time.

Cranial Nerves

A modified assessment of the cranial nerves is especially important on initial observation. Although omitted here, cranial nerves V, VII, IX, and X have both a sensory and motor component; only one component is given in this abbreviated guideline.[1]

Cranial Nerve[a]	Function	Assessment
I. Olfactory	Sense of smell	Ask the person to close his or her eyes. He or she should be able to identify familiar and easily recognized odors (e.g., coffee, tobacco, cloves).
II. Optic	Visual acuity	Ask the person to cover one eye at a time and read something out loud (e.g., a newspaper).
III. Oculomotor IV. Trochlear VI. Abducens	Pupils/Extraocular eye movement (EOM)	Nurse is aware of history. 25% of population have slightly unequal pupils. Are persons using atropine or other drugs? Test—use dark room.
		To test for direct response, flash light in one eye at a time. Note size of pupils and how they respond. They should constrict to light. For a more thorough assessment, measure pupils in millimeters. Note shape of each.
		To test for accommodation, ask persons to focus on an object. Hold the object close and far away. The pupils should constrict as the object is brought close and dilate as it is taken farther away.
		An expected pupil response would be: pupils equal, round, reactive to light, and accommodating [commonly referred to by the acronym PERRLA;

[1] A more detailed explanation can be found in textbooks related to neurological physical assessment.

Cranial Nerve[a]	Function	Assessment
		often abbreviated PERL (pupils equal, reactive to light)].
		Ask the person to follow your finger with his or her eyes as you move your finger up, down, medially, or laterally. Failure of the eye to move in all directions of gaze indicates nerve dysfunction to cranial nerve III, IV, and/or VI.
V. Trigeminal	Facial sensation and jaw movement	Touch the person's face with a wisp of cotton on the forehead, cheeks, jaw, and chin while his or her eyes are closed. The person should be able to state when he or she is being touched.
	Corneal reflex (used more frequently in assessing the comatose patient)	A person should blink when the *cornea* is lightly touched with a wisp of cotton.
VII. Facial	Facial movement and taste sensation (anterior two-thirds of tongue)	Ask the person to show his or her teeth, puff out cheeks, frown, smile, and raise eyebrows. Any asymmetry indicates nerve impairment.
VIII. Acoustic	Gross hearing	With the person's eyes closed, move a ticking watch toward one ear at a time. A person tells the examiner when he or she first hears the ticking. This response should occur at a similar distance from each ear.
IX. Glossopharyngeal X. Vagus	Gag reflex and ability to swallow	Stimulate the back of the throat with a tongue depressor; this should produce a mild gagging response. Have the person take several short swallows of air.
XI. Spinal accessory	Head movements	Note the strength of the trapezius muscles while the shoulders are shrugged against gentle resistance. Note the strength of the sternocleidomastoids (lateral neck area) as the head is turned to the side against your hand. Assess for equality.
XII. Hypoglossal	Tongue	Ask the person to protrude the tongue and assess for deviation to one side. Or listen to speech for slurring (indicating nerve dysfunction).

[a]Nerves III, IV, and VI were tested together, as were nerves IX and X.

Sensory Evaluation

Two basic tests are suggested to determine sensory function: pain and light touch. If behaviors other than those expected are noted, a more thorough assessment is made. When testing for a particular bodily response, always assess while the person's eyes are closed. Test bilaterally (both sides), distally (far from center), and proximally (close to center) where possible. Assess for pain by using the sharp and dull end of a safety pin. Ask the person to state whether the stimulus is sharp or dull. Test for light touch with a fine wisp of cotton. Ask the person to state when you are touching him or her.

If consciousness is impaired, determine the quality of the response to pain. The response to pain can be evaluated during a painful procedure such as drawing a blood sample or endotracheal suctioning. If these procedures are not being done, test the response to pain by applying pressure to the Achilles tendon, the trapezius or gastrocnemius muscle, or the fingernail. The following possible responses to pain are listed in order of behavioral responses of increasingly disrupted neurological functioning.

1. *Purposeful movement.* Movement is made away from the pain stimulus.
2. *Nonpurposeful movement.* A random movement is made in response to pain.
3. *Decorticate rigidity.* The legs extend and rotate internally with the feet plantar flexed. The arms *adduct* and are pulled into the chest with the wrist and fingers flexed. Indicates interruption of cortical motor fibers but intact pathways through the brain stem.
4. *Decerebrate rigidity.* As in decorticate posturing, the legs extend, the arms extend, the wrists and fingers are flexed. Indicates disruption of motor fibers in the midbrain and brain stem.

Decerebrate and decorticate posturing may at first be unilateral and then become bilateral, the former being less serious. The posturing may occur first only with noxious stimulation (such as endotracheal suctioning, pain). As the dysfunction increases, the posturing is continual.

With severe neurological dysfunction, there is no response to pain. This is usually a grave sign.

Motor Evaluation

Test basic motor functioning by asking persons to squeeze your two hands simultaneously. Ask them to push their feet against your hands (if in bed), and assess for equality of strength. Note the general equality of all movements, as decreased muscle strength is a frequent behavioral response noted in neurological disruptions. If persons are ambulatory, assess gait. Again note the equality of movements, balance, swinging of the arms, posture, and any other particular characteristics. The gait may be waddling (resembling that of a duck), propulsive (increasing speed), steppage (as though one were climbing stairs), spastic (stiff, with spasms), or ataxic (uncoordinated). If persons are ambulatory, assess for cerebellar functioning by asking them to hop in place with one foot at a time.

Other Indicators of Neurological Function

In the first-level assessment of neurological function, the nurse is aware of other behavioral indicators, such as reflexes, vital signs, and any laboratory and diagnostic reports that might be relevant. Vital signs can give important indications of a person's neurological status, but in the case of increased intracranial pressure, for example, these changes occur very late. Blood pressure is particularly important to monitor in the acute cerebral vascular accident (stroke) patient. If there has been a cerebral hemorrhage (resulting in a cerebral vascular accident), the blood pressure must be high enough to ensure adequate cerebral perfusion, yet low enough to prevent further bleeding. Temperature regulation is of major concern because central nervous system function is impaired with as little as 4°C (9°F) above or below the normal range (Luckmann and Sorensen, 1980, p. 548). Reflex responses such as the knee-jerk and plantar response may be tested as part of a preliminary assessment. Descriptions of these tests and their meaning may be found in texts on physical assessment.

The electroencephalogram (EEG) is a frequently used screening procedure in which the electrical activity of the brain is recorded. The lumbar puncture is another basic and frequently used test in which cerebral spinal fluid is analyzed for such findings as blood, protein, and sugar. Intracranial pressure (ICP) monitoring is a fairly new technique by which changes in ICP can be continually followed with relative reliability.

SECOND-LEVEL ASSESSMENT

Once the nurse has completed the first-level assessment of neurological function, she proceeds to identification of related stimuli. In this second-level assessment, factors that contribute to changes in neurological status are identified. Major factors that the nurse considers are listed in Table 12.2. These include the medical-related factors of neurological disruptions, treatment modalities, and laboratory values, as well as the person-related factors within the four modes of adaptation. Examples of these various categories of stimuli are discussed briefly below.

TABLE 12.2
Factors Affecting Neurological Function

I. Medical-related stimuli
    A. Neurological disruptions
        1. Trauma
        2. Infection
        3. Neuromuscular disease
        4. Vascular disturbances
        5. Developmental disturbances

    B. Treatment modalities
        1. Medication
        2. Surgery

    C. Laboratory values

II. Person-related stimuli
    A. Physiological
        1. Nutrition
        2. Fluid and electrolyte balance
        3. Activity
        4. Position
        5. Stress

    B. Self-concept
        1. Body image
        2. Self-expectancy

    C. Role function
        1. Age
        2. Environment

    D. Interdependence
        1. Family
        2. Significant others

Medical-Related Stimuli

In any clinical situation, medical-related stimuli may have a great effect on the person's neurological functioning. A given *neurological disruption* is often the focal influencing factor for behavior the nurse observes. For example, a tumor located near the cerebellum will affect the person's ability to stand on one foot. The various kinds of disruption, trauma, infection, neuromuscular disease, vascular disturbances, and developmental disturbances result in varying degrees of changes in neurological functioning. A vascular spasm may cause a brief and temporary headache that has little effect on the person's adaptive potential. On the other hand, conditions such as cerebrovascular accidents (strokes) and multiple sclerosis can result in extensive changes that require great and prolonged efforts to maximize adaptive potential.

Similarly, the nurse recognizes that various *treatment modalities*, including medication and surgery, affect neurological functioning. For example, drugs categorized as anticonvulsants, cerebral vasodilators, and narcotic analgesics all affect behaviors indicating level of alertness and the vital signs.

Drugs may result in a dramatic behavioral change such as with the use of induced barbiturate coma. This procedure is being used in carefully monitored patients to decrease cerebral metabolism, with the goal of preventing further ischemia or the effects of decreased blood supply. The nurse is particularly aware of the person's use of alcohol and smoking habits as they affect neurological functioning. Mild alcohol intake may help to decrease the tremors of Parkinson's disease. The use of alcohol is, however, contraindicated if the individual is taking the medication L-dopa, as alcohol decreases the medication's efficacy. Excessive alcohol intake is a causative factor in particular neurological diseases, such as polyneuritis. Smoking causes vasoconstriction and therefore will reduce cerebral circulation and increase hypoxia. It is also a factor in increasing the risk of cerebrovascular accident. The nurse often observes the effect of surgery on identified neurological deficits, such as a person's increased level of orientation following repair of a cerebral aneurysm.

Finally, in the category of medical-related stimuli, the nurse notes *laboratory values* that affect neurological status. In Chapter 5 the *laboratory values* of arterial blood gases and hemoglobin levels were considered behavioral indicators of oxygen need, that is, as first-level assessment factors. As we examine neurological functioning, these same values can be viewed as indicators of conditions affecting this functioning; that is, laboratory values can be considered a stimulus or second-level-assessment factors. A good illustration of this is shown in the following schematic presentation of the impact of the partial pressure of the CO_2 in the arterial blood (expressed as $PaCO_2$) and PaO_2 on cerebral blood flow and thus on the level of consciousness.

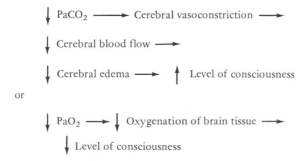

Similarly, if the hemoglobin is low, the oxygen-combining capacity of the blood is reduced and cerebral hypoxia is exacerbated. If the hemoglobin is above normal, there is a greater tendency for clot formation, resulting in vascular obstruction and therefore ischemia.

Person-Related Stimuli

All of the factors affecting neurological function that have been discussed above are related to the person and his or her adaptive potential. However, they can be categorized as medical-related stimuli since they involve the pathophysiology and treatments that principally are the concern of the medical profession. In addition, we may categorize stimuli that affect neurological function that are basic to the Roy Adaptation Model of nursing's view of the person as an adaptive system. Major stimuli in the areas of physiological needs, self-concept, role function, and interdependence will be highlighted. In this discussion we see further examples of the kaleidoscopic aspect of the model referred to above and discussed in Chapter 3, by which behaviors can become stimuli and one stimulus affects another.

Nutritional behaviors can affect neurological functioning. For example, the nurse considers that obesity increases one's risk of having a cerebrovascular accident. Similarly, certain nutritional deficits affect one's neurological status. For example, thiamine deficiency results in disturbances in the metabolism of nerve tissue. The tissue is then unable to utilize carbohydrates, resulting in the neurological effects of weakness, muscle pain, and tenderness.

Fluid intake may affect neurological status in such ways as decreased fluid intake reducing intracranial pressure, and increased intake hastening recovery in certain neurological infections. The effect of electrolytes on neuromuscular functioning is discussed in Chapter 11.

In neuromuscular disruptions, *activity* may either exacerbate or relieve particular behavioral manifestations of the condition. For example, tremors in Parkinson's disease decrease with activity and increase with rest. The distressing behavior of increased muscular fatigability in myasthenia gravis increases with activity and decreases with rest. Although an important activity after many surgeries, coughing is inadvisable in many cranial surgeries, as well as head injuries, because it increases intracranial pressure. Deep breathing and turning instead can promote adaptive ventilation.

The nurse can use knowledgeable *positioning* to enhance neurological and adaptive functioning. For example, after a thrombotic or embolic cerebrovascular accident, keeping the patient in a side-lying position decreases the risk of aspiration, and keeping the head of the bed low for the first few days may promote cerebral circulation. Keeping the head of the bed slightly elevated and the head in alignment with the body are important for the patient with increased intracranial pressure. If the head is out of alignment with the body (that is, the body is flat and the head turned to the side), venous return from the brain is impaired and pressure increased further.

Stress Factors

The neurohormonal response to stress is discussed in Chapter 13. Stress may take the form of painful procedures, emotional trauma, or a lowered body resistance from fatigue and malnutrition. Such stress factors serve as a stimulus for aggravating neurological behavior. For example, the noxious stimulation of suctioning or a venipuncture can cause intracranial pressure to increase. As this pressure increases we see neurological behavioral manifestations worsening, such as lethargy progressing to a stupor. In a neuromuscular disruption, such as multiple sclerosis and myasthenia gravis, the stress factors of fatigue, malnutrition, cold, damp weather, and even pregnancy exacerbate the behavioral manifestations of those diseases, that is, neuromuscular weakness.

One's expectations of a neurological disruption may be inappropriately negative. If so, anxiety, fear, depression, and hopelessness may be the result. Expectancies are related to knowledge level. For example, brain tumor erroneously signifies death to many, although death occurs only in some cases. Paralysis may signify sterility, which is not usually the case in the female. It is therefore essential that the nurse have knowledge about the particular disruption and that she understands the specifics of the individual case and medical prognosis. The exchange of information between doctor and nurse can be a key factor in the patient developing realistic self-expectations.

For all disruptions, the nurse must assess the patient's and family's understanding. Assessing this stimulus is important for the intervention phase of planning care. Information is given according to the level of comprehension. Teaching is initiated when the acute period has subsided and learning readiness is evident: for example, lack of denial of medical facts, lack of excessive anxiety, pain in control, and so forth.

Teaching measures include a discussion of what one should expect in terms of physiological changes as well as modifications in one's self-concept, interdependence, and role function. To prevent complications or possible recurrence, the nurse informs the family and the individual of behaviors to report to the physician. Adjustments to changes in neurological functioning can be made more successfully, with less stress, when one can distinguish between expected changes and indications of complications in what one experiences in one's body. The nurse helps clarify these expectations.

Self-Concept

An adaptive self-concept is of utmost importance in dealing with chronic neurological impairments. Once the individual has been able to grieve the loss in function, integration of a new *body image* is essential.

With the self-concept bruised but not destroyed, one can go about the tasks of rehabilitating to the extent possible. An adapted body image can make the difference between one's relearning to walk, speak, and generally live up to one's potential or being prone to progressive debilitation.

Role Function

Within the role function mode, we consider developmental level as the determinant of primary role. In the context of this chapter, we can note that specific neurological disruptions are more common at certain *ages* than others. For example, multiple sclerosis occurs most frequently in the young adult, whereas Parkinson's disease and cerebrovascular accident occur more frequently in the elderly adult. Disorientation is more prevalent in the elderly due in part to sensory impairments and vascular degeneration.

Role changes often involve changes in *environment*. The environment may positively or negatively affect one's adaptation. In the case of a disoriented person, the hospital environment itself can greatly accentuate ineffective behavior. Artificial lighting, the noise of foreign machinery, and altered time schedules all contribute to a person's confusion. Once such persons are medically stable, returning them to the familiar surroundings of their homes can promote adaptation. Noise is an important stimulus, as it can further increase intracranial pressure. Even the lack of clutter in the environment serves as a stimulus. In the case of a person who has had a cardiovascular accident, uncluttered surroundings in the home or hospital promote the behavior of orientation.

Interdependence

The interdependence adaptive mode highlights the importance of significant others and support systems in the life of an individual. For the person with difficulties in neurological functioning, *family members* hold unusual prominence in the person's ability to cope with these changes. Many of the behaviors associated with changes in neurologic function are chronic. Situations of altered communication ability, muscular weakness, and disorientation require a great deal of patience to be contended with. If the family and/or significant others offer support and understanding, this can act as a stimulus to help the person's ability to cope. In some instances the family may not be able to change a particular behavioral manifestation of neurological dysfunction (such as progressive muscular weakness in Duchenne's dystrophy), but their support can help prevent complications in all four adaptive modes. With the encouragement of the family the patient may be better motivated to strengthen new muscle groups as other muscles are affected. This action not only affects the physiological mode in helping prevent the complications of inactivity, but the person's self-concept is better maintained. Similarly, feelings of independence are encouraged as one is better able to carry out some of the responsibilities of previous roles by the simple fact of being more physically mobile.

Whenever possible, the nurse assists the neurologically impaired person to maintain his or her role in the family. In the paralyzed individual, cognitive processes such as contributing to family decision making are promoted. The nurse assists the family in identifying the remaining adaptive behaviors and promoting these. If neurological impairments are irreversible, the nurse assists the family in preventing complications.

The nurse who is assessing stimuli affecting a person's neurological functioning, then, considers carefully the family and significant-other relationships that are primary factors influencing how the person will be able to deal with changes in neurological function.

ADAPTATION PROBLEMS

In the area of neurological function, certain behaviors and stimuli that have been discussed as assessment factors can cluster to create frequently occurring areas of concern for nursing care. These concerns are considered under the common topic of adaptation problems. In this section these problems are described, together with the appropriate nursing interventions in common use. Given this general level of knowledge, the nurse who uses the Roy Adaptation Model of nursing will be able to assess an individual clinical situation and plan care based on the assessment, diagnoses, and goals determined for that situation.

Loss

I feel so sad when I think of how I am, I could cry. I think of all the things I could do before. Then I look around me and see all the healthy people my age, and get jealous, and begin to hate them. But then I get to feeling guilty because they've never done any harm to me, and I'm overwhelmed by a blue feeling.
(From a young adult woman with myasthenia gravis; Perez, 1970)[2]

The person experiencing a loss of the physical self through neurological changes, be it loss of strength, movement, or a particular bodily function, goes through a type of grief response for that loss.[3] In the above-

[2]David Perez, "Reaction to Loss" eds. Schoenberg, Bernard, Carr, and Arthur, *Loss and Grief: Psychological Management in Medical Practice* (New York: Columbia University Press, © 1970).

[3]Loss as an adaptation problem is discussed in Chapter 18, but its particular relevance during changes in neurological function are noted here.

quoted thoughts we see a progression from grief to depression—from an initial sadness over her illness and the loss of her usual functioning to an unacceptable rage and jealousy. The angry feelings are then turned upon herself.

The nurse's role here focuses on interventions related to those used for any person responding to a loss (see Chapter 18). Expression of feelings— anger, helplessness, frustration, and anxiety—is encouraged and movement through the various phases or stages of the grief process is facilitated.

As the grief process reaches a close, the individuals need to see how they can learn to live with the impairment; adaptation, integrity, and health are severely threatened if one cannot. This process involves establishing alternative methods to meet particular needs. For example, if speech is unintelligible, long-term speech therapy is helpful. In the short term, assist the individual and family to establish an alternative method of communicating, such as different sounds to mean certain standard words, or the use of writing or gestures. By at least partially restoring a particular body function, the integrity of one's self-concept is to some degree maintained. Persons often need to be reminded of what they *can* do. In the above-mentioned situation of impaired speech, all other functions are intact. The nurse needs to promote a realization of this to the patient and family and in some cases assist in the further development of those skills. The loss can be *partially* compensated by the enhancement of other skills, although that loss can never be fully replaced.

This threat to one's self-concept, specifically the physical self, becomes a cross-modal problem (as discussed further in Part V). It involves interdependence problems in that when there is a loss of control over the particular dysfunctional body part, there is some resulting degree of dependency on others for physical help and greater acceptance and support. Role function is threatened to varying degrees, as persons have limitations on how fully they will be able to carry out various responsibilities or the instrumental behaviors of their various roles. The loss of given role functions compounds the personal sense of loss.

Paralysis

Paralysis is a condition which is frequently irreversible and is exhibited in various forms. It is caused by trauma, vascular changes, or neuromuscular disorders. *Monoplegia* refers to the paralysis of a single limb or single group of muscles. *Hemiplegia* refers to paralysis of one side of the body. *Quadriplegia* is the paralysis of the lower extremities, trunk, and varying degrees of weakness of the upper extremities. The latter two conditions will be the focus of this discussion.

Nursing care of the paralyzed person is comprehensive and challenging in all four modes described by the Roy Adaptaton Model of nursing. The basic goal of care is to prevent complications and maximize the activity level for the individual.

In the physiological mode, airway patency is of first priority. Another concern is preventing the hazards of bed rest and/or inactivity (see Chapter 8). Turning (a technique called *log rolling* is used in trauma and many postoperative conditions), coughing, and deep breathing help to prevent respiratory infections, a frequent complication in the paralyzed individual. Once the acute period of trauma has subsided, range of motion exercises prevent contractures, foot and wrist drop, and maximize one's rehabilitative capacity.

Decubitus ulcers are a constant threat for the bedridden as well as the person in a wheelchair. Immaculate skin care, changes in position, adequate diet and fluid intake, and skin massage are all essential interventions.

The paralyzed person is particularly susceptible to urinary tract infections. Luckmann and Sorensen (1980, p. 548) report that urinary tract infections are the most frequent cause of death for persons with lower-extremity paralysis. Adequate fluid intake, maintenance of a closed drainage system for indwelling catheters, routine catheter care, checking and correcting bladder distention, and assessing for urinary tract infections must all be incorporated into the nursing plan of care.

By the very nature of paralysis, one's interdependence, role function, and self-concept modes of adaptation are threatened. For the person with paraplegia, the relationship to significant others and support systems is modified by initial physical dependence. To promote the person's total integrity, this dependency is progressively minimized. This goal is achieved initially by showing the person how to turn in bed, later to transfer to a wheelchair, and eventually to ambulate with a brace. Restoring one's ability to perform activities of daily living can be initiated early. The nurse and rehabilitation team incorporate as many self-care activities as possible. Activity is therapeutic physically. It also demonstrates to the individual a relative independence, and thus strengthens a threatened self-concept.

Role distance and failure are almost inevitable adaptation problems for the person with paralysis. Essentially all roles are affected — work, position in the family, and relationship with the sexual partner. The nurse is often the first and most constant contact the paralyzed person has to help deal with these changes. Support and guidance are essential. Employment can often be found, although career plans may be radically modified. One must also keep in mind that the handicapped continue to be discriminated against in the job market.

The threat to sexuality that paralysis brings is a sensitive but often a very important issue to the individual. A detailed discussion is not possible here, but a few guidelines can be kept in mind. Impotence is a frequent problem in the male quadriplegic, but much depends on the type of injury, and individual differences cannot be predicted. For the male, sterility often is a problem due to degeneration that occurs after the initial paralysis. Women do not generally have sterility problems.

The goal in addressing one's sexual role is that concerns will be expressed and that the individual will continue to view himself or herself as a sexual person. Again, a major loss has occurred and the person needs an opportunity to discuss it. The individual also needs to be reminded that there are alternative ways of seeking sexual and affectional gratification. The individual may be helped by a sexual counselor, who is often available in a rehabilitation or medical center.

Change in Level of Consciousness/Level of Orientation

In dealing with the problem of change in level of consciousness/level of orientation, the nurse performs neurological checks (a modified neurological assessment) every 2 to 4 hours. Any decrease in responses is reported to the physician. The nurse keeps in mind that slight forgetfulness or lethargy may be the first indication of increased intracranial pressure (IICP) and thus reports this type of change at once if IICP is suspected. The goal in caring for a person with an altered level of consciousness or orientation is that the highest level of functioning possible will be seen. The nurse explains all procedures regardless of the level of consciousness and reorients the patient when necessary. Orientation is enhanced by the following: open curtains so that natural sunlight is visible; keeping a clock and calendar with each day marked off near the bedside; having photos of the patient with family members visible; occasionally utilizing the television or radio for news programs; and allowing quiet for periods of rest and sleep. The nurse uses a flashlight at night whenever possible for nursing activities to avoid waking patients needlessly. It is advisable to allow for at least two uninterrupted rest periods during the day. Periodically, the nurse can discuss the patient's condition, why he or she is in the hospital, and include brief remarks about current events.

Memory Deficit

Adaptation problems related to memory may occur transiently, as in concussion, or for a prolonged period as with a stroke. The nurse assesses the quality of the deficit. Is the memory deficit continual or intermittent? Does it involve recent or past events? For long-term memory problems, a notebook with important information that the person has difficulty remembering may be helpful. Such items as the person's address and phone number might be included. An appointment book and various checklists may also be helpful.

The deficit may involve a short retention span, that is, difficulty remembering a number of items of information. An appropriate intervention in this case is to give short, concise messages; allow the individual to act on the request before further information is given. For example, asking the patient to get out of bed, brush his teeth and hair, bathe, and get dressed and put on his brace may be more than he can remember at one time. The nurse divides such messages into smaller components.

The individual may have difficulty associating old learning with new. For example, he may not be able to remember his room number on the rehabilitation unit. Writing this in his notebook and placing personal items in the room or a photo of himself next to the room number can be helpful.

Change in Behavioral Style

Some degree of personality change is a frequent component of illness. Simply making the transformation to the sick role, however minor it may be, does often alter one's behavior. When the disorder is chronic and involves major handicaps such as paralysis, the change in personality may be greater.

Changes in personality that are organically based can also occur. Again, after a stroke an emotional lability may occur in which the individual will begin crying for no particular reason. An intervention to share with the family is first asking the person to discuss what's upsetting him. It may be the role function or self-concept disturbances noted above that need to be discussed. If the person does not know what it is that is troubling him or her, one can try distraction techniques. In an organic deficit, the person will become easily distracted in another activity.

In some changes of neurological functioning, social judgment may be impaired. Social judgment means the ability to do the right thing at the right time. For example, the previously cautious person may become impulsive and act in ways that are unsafe to self or others. The previously withdrawn individual may become quite loud, aggressive, and use vulgar language. The nursing intervention here requires first identifying the change in behavior, and then helping the family understand the organic nature of the disturbance, if applicable. The patient will then need appropriate, frequent, and firm but supportive feedback to move the patient toward more adaptive behavior, that is, control of responses that promote his or her own integrity and that of the group.

Aphasia

Aphasia refers to the inability to interpret and implement the signs and symbols of language. It is categorized in various ways, but basically can be organized into three types: receptive, expressive, and global. In most cases there is a combination of receptive and expressive aphasia. The general goal for aphasia is that the person's needs will be met and some type of communication will be implemented. In *receptive aphasia* the individual has difficulty comprehending the written or spoken word, depending on which area of the brain is affected. The person may instead have difficulty understanding gestures. If receptive aphasia has been established, words will probably sound like static to the person. In this situation an effort is made to use pantomime or pictures to communicate. If the person has established some means of communicating, those who deal with this person will need to know what this is and utilize it. In time, relearning to implement standard language may be possible, but in the meantime the person needs to be able to communicate. For some reason we wrongly assume that someone who does not understand our language is deaf or childlike. Aphasia does not necessarily go hand in hand with intellectual dysfunction. Give simple, concise messages in a normal tone of voice. Check for discrepancies in the person's replies and avoid overestimating the level of understanding.

Expressive aphasia is the inability to speak, write, or possibly use gestures effectively for communication. It is due to damage in various areas of the brain. Specifically, motor speech dysfunction is due to damage at Broca's speech center. It may take the form of word substitution in which the person says *bed* for *tired* or *fork* for *hungry*. There may be a memory defect, in which case the person can say a familiar phrase such as "how are you?" or sing a familiar song, but cannot speak in a conversation. A general principle is to allow the person to express himself or herself in the best way possible. Allow *time* to do this; avoid jumping to conclusions regarding what is trying to be expressed. As noted earlier, patience on the part of all concerned is imperative.

Global aphasia is severe brain dysfunction in which the individual cannot understand or express himself or herself in any fashion. In all types of aphasia, particularly in the acute period, anticipate the person's needs so that the need for the person to communicate is minimized.

Increased Intracranial Pressure

Increased intracranial pressure (IICP) is a condition that can be seen in almost any neurological disruption. To understand this mechanism, recall that the brain is enclosed in an unexpandable box, the skull. If pressure in the brain increases, there is little room to accommodate the change. IICP refers to an increase in pressure in the subarachnoid space, where cerebrospinal fluid (CSF) circulates in the surface area of the brain, spinal cord, and special chambers called ventricles. Pressure may increase for three general reasons: (1) increase in tissue mass, such as a tumor or cerebral edema, that is, increased water content of the brain; (2) increased CSF due to increased production or an obstruction to its circulation; and (3) hemorrhage (excessive bleeding into the area), although this is a less frequent cause of IICP. There are few bodily adaptive mechanisms available to compensate for the stress of increased pressure. Some types of brain herniation temporarily reduce pressure, but the compensation is usually short lived and can soon thereafter be life threatening. Brain herniation is a result of IICP and consists of the brain protruding into another compartment or area. There are a few major types of brain herniation: the behavioral responses of two of these, central and uncal, are outlined in Fig. 12.4. *Central* (transten-

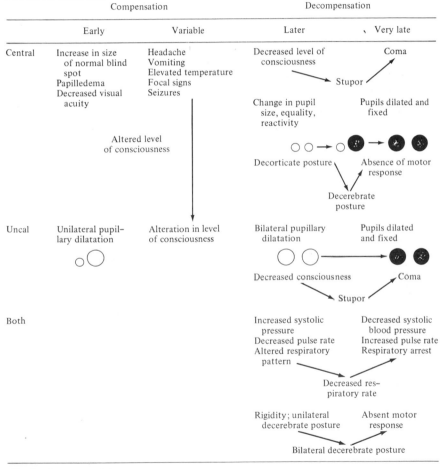

	Compensation		Decompensation	
	Early	Variable	Later	، Very late
Central	Increase in size of normal blind spot Papilledema Decreased visual acuity	Headache Vomiting Elevated temperature Focal signs Seizures	Decreased level of consciousness → Stupor	Coma
		Altered level of consciousness	Change in pupil size, equality, reactivity	Pupils dilated and fixed
			Decorticate posture Decerebrate posture	Absence of motor response
Uncal	Unilateral pupillary dilatation	Alteration in level of consciousness	Bilateral pupillary dilatation	Pupils dilated and fixed
			Decreased consciousness Stupor	Coma
Both			Increased systolic pressure Decreased pulse rate Altered respiratory pattern Decreased respiratory rate	Decreased systolic blood pressure Increased pulse rate Respiratory arrest
			Rigidity; unilateral decerebrate posture Bilateral decerebrate posture	Absent motor response

○ Pupil reactive to light.

● Pupil nonreative to light.

Figure 12.4 Behavioral responses of supratentorial IICP; classified by stage of appearance and herniation syndrome. Reprinted from Harriet Moidel. *Nursing Care of the Patient with Medical Surgical Disorders.* New York: McGraw-Hill, ©1976, p. 868.

torial) *herniation* occurs when there are expanding hematomas or other types of lesions in the occipital, frontal, or parietal lobes of the brain. *Uncal herniation* is a lateral movement from lesions in the temporal lobe. Uncal herniation exhibits the same general progression of behaviors, with two exceptions. Uncal herniation usually progresses quite rapidly, and the first indication of the syndrome is a pupillary change. The various types of behavioral responses will be recalled from the earlier discussion of first-level assessment of neurological functioning.

The goal of care is to minimize intracranial pressure and prevent complications. Nursing interventions that help modify intracranial pressure include the following:

1. First priority—maintain an open airway.
2. Observe and report slight neurological changes, especially change in level of consciousness.
3. Maintain a quiet environment.
4. Elevate the head of the bed 30° with the head in alignment with the body (turning the head alone can result in constriction of vessels in the neck and decrease venous blood return from the brain).
5. Prevent sudden increases in pressure (from vigorous coughing, isometric exercises—contraction and relaxation of a muscle without mechanical work—straining during defecation, which can bring on the Valsalva maneuver).
6. Minimize emotional and physical trauma (brief family visits with instructions given to avoid emotional upsets).
7. Turn gently every 2 hours only.

Coma

Varying degrees of coma require attenton to all physical nursing measures. It is the nurse's responsibility to prevent complications of the comatose state, such as decubiti, stomatitis, and atelectasis. The patient is turned and repositioned every 2 hours and given back massage. Turning alternates the pressure to different areas of the skin as well as enhancing respiratory ventilation. Various devices, such as gel pads, egg crates, sheepskin, alternating pressure pads, and waterbeds, help prevent decubiti. An alternating pressure mattress is particularly effective because pressure in various areas is frequently altered. A rubber doughnut placed around a decubitus actually serves one function, to create further decubiti. This is caused by the increased pressure on the skin beneath the doughnut. The nurse uses foot supports or a foot board to prevent foot drop, that is, falling of the foot due to flexor paralysis of the ankle.

If the eyes are open and blinking is absent, artificial tears may be used but patching protects the eyes better. A usual approach is to wet eye patches in a sterile water or saline solution and gently cover the eyes with the lids closed. The nurse removes the patches to do pupil checks and allow for possible sensory input for short periods. In cases of coma, a neurological assessment is done every 2 to 4 hours. For cranial nerves, checks are done on III (pupils), V (corneal reflex), and IX and X (swallow and gag). Any voluntary movements and responses to pain are noted. A check is made for the plantar reflex. As in all other conditions, an open airway is a top-priority concern. The patient's trachea is suctioned if breath sounds are congested and/or the airway obstructed. The nurse assesses for incontinence and abdominal or bladder distention. Mouth care is provided every 2 hours to prevent infection, such as stomatitis, respiratory tract infection, and aspiration. The nurse explains to the patient what she is going to do, and never discusses a negative prognosis at the patient's bedside. The sense of hearing is often present although no other neurological faculties appear intact.

Tremor

An involuntary quivering of muscles is a frequent occurrence in particular neuromuscular disruptions. There are various types of *tremor*, including intention tremor, which occurs when voluntary movement is attempted; rest or static tremor, present at rest, seen in Parkinson's disease; and intermittent tremor, present when voluntary movement is attempted in affected hemiplegic muscles.

Nursing interventions are related to the cause, and medications are effective for many types of tremors. In rest or static tremor, encouraging activity of the involved muscles is helpful, as the tremor decreases with activity. For example, the nurse can try having the person work a small rubber ball in the hands, or sift change through the fingers.

Seizures

Seizures can be defined as "irritative phenomena characterized by abnormal synchronous activation of groups of cerebral neurons" (Davis and Mason, 1979, p. 216). Seizures are caused by a variety of conditions, including neurosurgery, head trauma, and hyperthermia. They take a variety of forms, from temporary loss of consciousness to violent attacks of involuntary contractions, sensory changes, and behavioral abnormalities.

Goals in caring for persons with seizures include protecting them from harm during an attack and minimizing the frequency of seizures. The latter goal is usually achieved by medications, but sometimes with surgery. During a seizure, one does not attempt to restrain or move the person. Any objects that may result in harm, such as pieces of furniture, are moved away.

The first priority is to establish an airway, which may be difficult. Any restrictive clothing is loosened and the person's head is turned to the side if possible to allow secretions to drain. If a plastic oral airway is available, it is gently placed in the mouth unless the teeth are tightly clenched. For the hospitalized patient, airway and suction equipment is kept at the bedside for those with seizure disorders. The side rails are padded, and if the patient is not protected during a seizure, the nurse can place pillows around him or her.

Once protection is ensured, the nurse notes the presenting behaviors. Did the individual experience any sensory change prior to the seizure (for example, the smell of burning hair)? What was the body position at the onset of the seizure, and the area first involved? What was the progression of activity (for example, turning of head to arm spasms to leg spasms)? The specific type of movement is described together with changes in the eyes, such as deviation to one side or pupillary reaction to light. The nurse notes the level of consciousness prior to and during the seizure. Skin color, respirations, and evidence of incontinence are also observed. The length of the seizure is timed. After the episode, the nurse asks the person how he or she feels, that is, are they weak, dazed, or feeling a headache, and records the findings and vital signs.

SUMMARY

Neurological function has been discussed as an integral component of the adaptation process. Basic structures and functions involved in neurological assessment were reviewed. Various components of first- and second-level neurological assessment were covered. Frequently occurring adaptation problems related to change in neurological functioning were discussed together with general goals and the nursing interventions in common use.

STUDENT LEARNING ACTIVITY

Based on this patient situation, and your knowledge of neurological function, state the major behaviors to be noted and the related stimuli, goals, and interventions. An example of an Adaptation Nursing Process Care Plan for this person is provided in the Appendix.

Case Study

Marilyn B. is a 26-year-old airline stewardess from New York who flew into Los Angeles 3 days ago. At that time she was in a car accident in which she received a head injury; this was later diagnosed to be a mild brain contusion (bruising). She has been lethargic and occasionally disoriented to time, place, and purpose. There are no other neurological deficits. You are concerned with the possible problem of increased intracranial pressure (IICP).

REFERENCES

Bates, Barbara. *A Guide to Physical Examination.* Philadelphia: J. B. Lippincott Company, 1979.

"The Battered Brain," *Emergency Medicine*, March 15, 1970, pp. 15–30.

Davis, Joan E., and Celestine B. Mason. *Neurologic Intensive Care.* New York: Van Nostrand Reinhold Company, 1979.

Fischbach, Frances Talaska. "Easing Adjustment to Parkinson's Disease," *American Journal of Nursing*, vol. 78, no. 1, 1978, pp. 66–69.

Fowler, Roy S., and W. E. Fordyce. "Stroke: Why Do They Behave That Way?" *Washington State Heart Association*, 1974.

Guyton, Arthur. *Textbook of Medical Physiology*, 5th ed. Philadelphia: W. B. Saunders Company, 1976.

Isselbacher, Kurt J. et al., eds. *Harrison's Principles of Internal Medicine*, 9th ed. New York: McGraw-Hill Book Company, 1980.

Jennett, B., and G. Teasdale. "Aspects of Coma after Severe Head Injury," *Lancet*, I (8017), April 23, 1977, pp. 878–881.

Langhley, L. L., and Ira K. Telford. *Dynamic Anatomy and Physiology.* New York: McGraw-Hill Book Company, 1974, p. 228.

Luckmann, Joan, and Karen Creason Sorensen. *Medical–Surgical Nursing*, 2nd ed. Philadelphia: W. B. Saunders Company, 1980.

Merritt, Hiram H. *Textbook of Neurology.* Philadelphia: Lea & Febiger, 1979.

Moidel, Harriett. *Nursing Care of the Patient with Medical–Surgical Disorders*, 2nd ed. New York: McGraw-Hill Book Company, 1976, p. 868.

O'Brien, Mary T., and Phyllis J. Pallet. *Total Care of the Stroke Patient.* Boston: Little, Brown and Company, 1978.

Perez, David. "Reaction to Loss," in *Loss and Grief: Pyschological Management in Medical Practice*, Bernard Schoenberg, Arthur Carr, David Perez, and Austin H. Kutscher, eds. New York: Columbia University Press, 1970.

Rudy, E. "Early Omens of Cerebral Disaster," *Nursing '77*, February, pp. 58–62.

Schmidt, Lee, and Corrine Hatton. "The Concept of Loss," unpublished article through the School of Nursing, University of California at Los Angeles.

Chapter 13

Endocrine Function

*Mary Howard and Sally Valentine**

BEHAVIORAL OBJECTIVES

After studying this chapter, the reader will be able to:

1. Define the key concepts of the chapter.
2. List behaviors indicating structural or functional disruption of the endocrine system.
3. Delineate contextual and residual factors that may influence endocrine function.
4. Describe the general adaptation syndrome and relate this to stress as a focal stimulus.
5. Specify nursing interventions to be used in problems related to endocrine function.

KEY CONCEPTS DEFINED

Hormone: chemical substance from a gland carried by the bloodstream, which assists in the control of involuntary and self-regulating processes.

Metabolic Processes: chemical and physical changes going on in the cells.

---

*This chapter is a revision and expansion of the chapter "Regulation of the Endocrine System," by Edda Coughran and Sonja Liggett, in the first edition, pp. 151–165.

Feedback Mechanism: the process by which the hormones act as messengers to regulate their own production.

Master Gland: a term used for the pituitary gland since it directly controls the secretions of all the endocrine glands except the adrenal glands.

Hypersecretion: increased production of a hormone.

Hyposecretion: decreased production of a hormone.

General Adaptation Syndrome (GAS): a generalized response to stress involving stimulation of endocrine function and phases of alarm, resistance, and exhaustion.

The maintenance of adaptive processes involving the endocrine system is like the functioning of an intricate piece of machinery. When all interrelated parts are running smoothly, adaptive behaviors can be observed. But let one part become disrupted, and other parts of the endocrine system and the body and person as a whole may be affected. As part of the regulator mechanism, adaptive endocrine behaviors involve the blending of many different processes all aimed at one major goal or need — to maintain a life-sustaining environment for the cells.

This chapter reviews briefly the normal structure and function of the endocrine system as a basis for assessing the adaptive regulation controlled by this system. The assessment of significant behaviors and influencing factors is outlined. The stress response is related to endocrine functioning and general nursing interventions are discussed.

NORMAL STRUCTURE AND FUNCTION

Because of the importance of the structure and function of the endocrine system for the nurse's assessment of the person's adaptation, this aspect of the regulatory physiological process will be discussed.

The endocrine system is composed of the hypothalamus, pituitary, thyroid, parathyroids, islets of Langerhans, the adrenals, and the sex glands. These glands perform the intricate functions of coordination and integration of body functions. The endocrine system assists the autonomic nervous system in the control of involuntary and self-regulating processes by secreting chemical substances called *hormones* from the glands directly into the bloodstream en route to specific physiological and anatomical structures.

Ineffective behaviors may be caused by basic types of pathological conditions and can be observed clinically by behaviors indicating hyperactive or hypoactive hormone secretion. Ineffective behaviors are seen when the originating hormone site or target issues are dysfunctional.

The endocrine system is concerned primarily with *metabolic processes*, that is, the chemical and physical changes going on in the cells. The action of each hormone is specific. The entire systemic metabolic process may be affected by one hormone, such as thyroxin, while another hormone, such as parathormone, may have only a regional effect. The endocrine system, as a part of the regulator process, also has a *feedback mechanism* whereby the hormones act as messengers to regulate their own production. For example, the thyroid gland may secrete an excessive amount of thyroxin if the blood level of this substance is low. When the serum thyroxin level is within normal limits, thyroxin secretion is decreased. This reciprocal feedback mechanism is essential if an adaptive state is to be maintained.

The pituitary gland is commonly referred to as the *master gland*, in that it may, to some extent, directly control the secretions of all the endocrine glands except the adrenal glands. The pituitary gland is composed of two lobes, anterior and posterior, and is located in the cavity of the sphenoid bone just below the brain center.

The anterior pituitary secretes six hormones essential for adaptation. Obviously, ineffective behaviors can be observed when the rate of secretion is disturbed. These disturbances may be *hypersecretion* (increased production) or *hyposecretion* (decreased production). The six hormones are:

1. *Somatotropic hormone* (STH), also known as growth hormone (GH). This hormone affects nutritive metabolism and growth of the skeletal system. The ineffective behaviors exhibited by the dysfunctional secretion regulation depend on the age of the person. If hypersecretion occurs before maturity, the person exhibits behaviors of gigantism. However, if hyposecretion occurs before maturity, dwarfism is manifested. After maturity an increased secretion of growth hormone results in excessive growth of flat and terminal bones. This disease process is termed *acromegaly*.
2. *Adrenocorticotropic hormone* (ACTH). Stimulates the adrenal cortex, which in turn secretes the adrenal steroids necessary to maintain life.
3. *Thyrotropic hormone* (TSH). This hormone is often referred to as thyroid-stimulating hormone. It is necessary for the thyroid function of maintaining an adequate metabolic rate.
4. *Follicle-stimulating hormone* (FSH). Stimulates the development of ovarian follicles, and in combination with the luteinizing hormone it stimulates the growth and development of male testes and spermatogenises.
5. *Luteinizing hormone* (LH). Functions primarily in conjunction with FSH to stimulate growth and development of male testes and spermatogenises. It also has a role in ovulation and development of the corpus luteum during the menstrual cycle.

6. *Luteotropic hormone* (LTH), also referred to as *prolactin*. Stimulates the mammary glands for the production of milk. During the menstrual cycle it initiates and maintains the secretion of progesterone from the corpus luteum.

Two hormones are secreted by the posterior lobe of the pituitary: *oxytocin* and *antidiuretic hormone* (ADH). Oxytocin is noted primarily for its ability to contract uterine muscles and is thought to enhance milk secretion by the lactating mammary gland. ADH, also referred to as *vasopressin*, affects the renal reabsorption of water. With hyperactivity of the pituitary, ADH is decreased in blood concentration and persons have been observed to void 20 liters of urine per day. With hypersecretion of ADH, the individual may exhibit water retention.

As one can readily see, the anterior and posterior pituitary hormones are essential for adaptive processes of the body. For example, dysfunctions of ACTH may cause Cushing's disease (marked by rapidly developing obesity), diabetic tendencies, and problems in essential nutrients metabolism.

In some cases a hypophysectomy, the excision or obliteration of the pituitary, may be indicated. Therefore, it is essential for the nurse to know which body functions are affected by each hormone. Also, it is important to know which hormone will be supplemented by medication.

The thyroid gland is composed of a left and right lobe connected by a narrow isthmus located anterior to the trachea and inferior to the larynx. This gland has an abundant supply of arterial flow. Two hormones secreted by the thyroid gland are *thyroxine* (T_4) and *triodothyronine* (T_3).

Although triodothyronine is more potent than thyroxin, its action is less sustained in blood concentration. Thyroxin is more important physiologically. It is formed in the thyroid by the synthesis of iodine, which has been absorbed from the bloodstream. The thyroxin in the blood combines with a protein, globulin, and becomes protein binding. Thyroxin is the principal circulating hormone of the thyroid gland.

The thyroid hormones are essential for metabolism in most cells by regulating oxidating processes. As stated, the anterior pituitary secretes TSH, which stimulates the release of the thyroid hormones. Therefore, ineffective activity of the thyroid gland can be caused by dysfunctions of the anterior pituitary or the thyroid gland itself. Diseases of hyposecretion are cretinism and myxedema. Grave's disease, or exopthalmic goiter, are hypersecretion functions.

The parathyroid glands, numbering from four to eight, are located around the thyroid gland. The hormone of the parathyroids, *parathormone*, controls the blood concentration of calcium and phosphorus. Parathormone also affects calcium metabolism in the body. Hypofunctioning of the parathyroids produces increased neuromuscular irritability due to the decrease of serum calcium and phosphorus. This dysfunction is termed *tetany.* Hyperfunctioning of the parathyroids increases the serum calcium and decreases the serum phosphorus levels. This deprives the bone of calcium and makes it very susceptible to fractures.

The pancreas is an organ located posterior to the stomach and anterior to the first and second lumbar vertebrae. The pancreas, from its islets of Langerhans, secretes two endocrine hormones necessary for cell metabolism: *insulin* and *glucagon.* Insulin is secreted from the beta cells, glucagon from the alpha cells.

The primary function of insulin is to assist glucose in its entry into the cell for cell metabolism. Insulin also assists in carbohydrate metabolism. Carbohydrates, fats, and protein are broken down into the end product of glucose, which is the primary form of carbohydrate that can be utilized by the cells for energy. Insulin lowers the blood glucose level and enables the glucose to pass through the cell membrane for metabolism. The primary disease of the beta cells is the hyposecretion of insulin, known as diabetes mellitus.

The primary function of glucagon is to increase the breakdown of glycogen into glucose to be used by the cells for energy. Therefore, its action is the opposite of insulin, in that it increases the blood glucose level.

The adrenal glands are located superior to the kidneys, with one on the left kidney and the other on the right. Each gland is divided into the outer tissue, called *cortex,* and the inner tissue, called *medulla.* The adrenal glands are the only glands not directly stimulated by the pituitary.

The adrenal cortex secretes chemical substances known as *steroids,* which affect the synthesis of protein, carbohydrates, and fats. There are three major categories of these essential steroids:

1. Glucocorticoids, which primarily affect carbohydrate metabolism
2. Mineral corticoids, which affect the metabolism of minerals
3. Adrenosterones, which stimulate growth of sex-related tissue

Hyperfunction of the adrenal cortices causes Cushing's disease. Hypofunction results in Addison's disease, marked by a bronzelike skin pigmentation and progressive anemia.

The adrenal medulla secretes the hormones epinephrine and norepinephrine. Not necessary for maintenance of life, they are helpful in enabling man to adapt to stressful situations. Epinephrine is less potent than norepinephrine but has a longer-lasting effect. It is the primary circulating hormone of the adrenal medulla. Epinephrine increases blood pressure by increasing myocardial contraction and increasing cardiac output. Norepinephrine constricts the arterioles, resulting in an increased peripheral resistance that increases the systolic and diastolic blood pressure.

Since these two hormones are not essential for life, hypofunctioning of the adrenal medulla is insignificant. However, hyperfunctioning results in the disease called pheochromocytoma, a tumor which secretes hormones that result in increased blood pressure.

The last glands of the endocrine system are the *sex glands*, referring to all structures that secrete the sex hormones. They are discussed in Chapter 17.

FIRST-LEVEL ASSESSMENT

Based on knowledge of the normal structure and function of the endocrine system, the nurse will observe and record adaptive versus ineffective behaviors. Specific manifestations of dysfunction can be summarized as follows:

1. Structural dysfunction
    (a) Observe for dysfunction of soft tissue development, for example, thickening of the facial tissue (acromegaly) or changes in skin pigmentation (Addison's disease).
    (b) Observe for increase in adipose tissue (hypothyroidism) and enlargement of glandular tissue (hyperthyroidism).
    (c) Observe for dysfunctions of skeletal system development, for example, enlargement of flat bones (acromegaly), skeletal decalcification (hypersecretion of parathormone), and hypertrophy, or increased size of the arms and legs (gigantism).
2. Functional dysfunction
    (a) Observe for changes of the blood pressure, pulse, respiration, and temperature. Increase in the blood pressure may denote an adrenal medulla tumor; increased heart rate may denote hyperthyroidism. Respiratory changes may signal a decrease in the rate of insulin secretions. Temperature changes may denote dysfunction in the hypothalamus or thyroid gland.
    (b) Observe neuromuscular responses. Restlessness and tremors might be indicative of hyperthyroidism or pheochromocytoma. Lassitude and drowsiness may be indicative of diabetic coma or hypothyroidism. Fatigue is a vague complaint that may be observed in many endocrine dysfunctions.
    (c) Observe for hyper- or hyporenal responses; they may indicate pituitary, pancreatic, or adrenal dysfunctions.
    (d) Observe for lack of control of emotional responses, which may indicate adrenal or pituitary problems.
    (e) Observe for changes in the menstrual cycle or in sexual development. Such changes may be indicative of pituitary dysfunction or of hypogonadism (decreased secretion of sex hormones).

The nurse uses the skills of observation, the measurement of internal and external responses, and interviewing to gather data about endocrine function in first-level assessment. Often the information is used in referring the person for appropriate further diagnosis.

SECOND-LEVEL ASSESSMENT

The nurse must further assess the person to identify an influencing factor or factors that affect optimal functioning of the endocrine system. Behaviors in modes other than the physiological mode are assessed, as endocrine malfunction affects the person as a whole.

The ineffective endocrine behaviors mentioned in the earlier section are most directly influenced by the focal stimulus of glandular dysfunction, such as hypoplasia (decrease in cell multiplication), hyperplasia (increase in cell multiplication), atrophy, infection, trauma, inflammation, and hypertrophy. Specific discussion of glandular pathologies can be found in medical science textbooks.

In assessing the factors influencing the endocrine system, the nurse also searches the internal and external environments for focal, contextual and residual stimuli, that are contributing to the behavior. Thus temperature changes noted in dysfunction of the hypothalamus or thyroid gland may be increased by changes in environmental temperature and humidity. Similarly, the lassitude that is evidence of hypothyroidism may be augmented by a socially impoverished milieu.

Environmental and emotional stress may also be factors affecting endocrine function in the individual. Since each individual is constantly adapting to stressors, an understanding of stress responses will enhance nursing efforts in assisting persons to cope more effectively in health or illness.

Hans Selye (1956, 1963) has documented the effects of stress on the functioning of the endocrine glands. He noticed that certain behavioral responses were common to several illnesses: for example, watery eyes and flushed skin. His later research on rats documented that various physiological and psychological stresses had common effects on the body.

STRESSORS AND THE STRESS RESPONSE

In this section we focus on stressors and two particular forms of the stress response. Stressors can be viewed as influencing stimuli, and the stress response may be looked at in terms of its behavioral manifestations or resulting problems. In any case, a basic understanding of what is known about stress from the physiological sciences is crucial for the nurse using an adaptation model.

Insofar as certain stressors can be isolated and studied, it has been shown that a stressor can elicit two responses: (1) the general adaptation stressor is causing a local adaptation syndrome; and (2) there are other times when we have some suspicions of what the stressors may be but no real evidence of a particular stressor causing the local adaptation syndrome (LAS). For instance, in looking at carcinogens, we believe that certain chemicals, viruses, radiation, hormones—perhaps even physical irritation and genetic coding—are among the stressors that cause malignant neoplasms to develop. However, in any one person who is being treated for neoplasia, the precise carcinogen is never really identified. Another good example of a local adaptation syndrome response to a stressor is the immune response. This is a local reaction to many different kinds of injury. If the stressor is an allergen, the immune response is a specific antibody reaction. If the stressor is surgical trauma, we are concerned with wound healing. The local changes that occur in an inflammatory or immune response are, however, one and the same.

In the relationship between the two syndromes, any local adaptation syndrome that is in process will stimulate, prolong, and maintain the *general adaptation syndrome* (GAS). If it does so, the adrenals will continue to secrete an increased amount of corticosteroids into the circulation. Chief among these are proinflammatory corticosteroids, and anti-inflammatory corticosteroids. Because of these chemicals, it may be that many diseases that have been looked at as stress-associated diseases are so because a local adaptation syndrome has maintained a general adaptation syndrome. Or the disease may occur because the stressor has caused a general adaptation syndrome that the person has been unable to cope with effectively. It is speculative that such diseases as nephrosclerosis, atherosclerosis, and multiple sclerosis could easily be stress related, on the basis of adrenal function which has activated proinflammatory hormones to the point of causing residual scar tissue formation.

The major stress response, or GAS, is also triphasic. It is first manifest as an alarm reaction, then may continue to go through a stage of resistance during which this general adaptation syndrome is attempting to help the body resist the stressor. This not being possible, the body responses continue to be prolonged to the point of exhaustion. If the stress response reaches the point of exhaustion, the question becomes whether or not the stage of exhaustion is reversible or irreversible. It is probably in the phases of resistance and exhaustion that nurses encounter most patients. As a nurse looks at the stage of alarm, any particular stressor may cause only a fleeting alarm reaction that is so minor as to be imperceptible. A stress response may go unrecognized because it was so fleeting and gave no perceptible evidence of the presence of a stressor. For example, a nurse may simply deliver a message that a person's spouse called and not recognize that the message can be producing a stress response.

In times past it seemed that the majority of efforts in adaptation nursing were concerned with the local adaptation responses, whether or not we have recognized this fact. In today's world, we are becoming more and more aware that one's real defense against illness and the ability to promote health may rest in being able to cope effectively with the general adaptation syndrome. Some of the local adaptation responses that we have become accustomed to coping with are things such as immune responses, neoplasia, hyperplasia, and teratogenic effects.

The stressors for this localized syndrome, then, include such things as teratogens, carcinogens, antigens, chemicals, trauma, microorganisms, and drugs. As we look at these various things that are stressors, it becomes clear that other stressors are unknown. There are instances in which we know the syndrome and also the local adaptation syndrome. Every time a person is stimulated by a stressor, the GAS will be initiated. In addition to this, a more localized response or LAS may be initiated — a syndrome that may affect only one component, and is frequently the stress response that is more obvious and amenable to specific treatment. These localized responses occur in target tissues. The general adaptation syndrome as it has been studied thus far is a response that is not specific to any particular stressor, but is present with any stressor. Although all modes of one's existence respond to stressors, only changes occurring within the physiological mode are discussed in this chapter. Changes in each physiological component are measurable to a degree and are the result of alterations of neurological and endocrine regulation of the entire body. Both general adaptation and local adaptation are involved in the physiological stress response and have a relationship to each other.

In looking at the general adaptation syndrome, it has been noted that a stressor, any particular stressor, first stimulates the stomach and the pituitary. Once the pituitary is stimulated, it produces an increase of ACTH, which stimulates the adrenal glands into increased activity. When the adrenal glands are stimulated, their secretions circulate out into the system and stimulate the central nervous system, all the endocrine system, and the stomach. This is an interesting aspect of the syndrome, in that a stressor stimulates the stomach directly to increase its secretions and motility, then again indirectly stimulates the stomach through its effect on the pituitary and adrenals. In the course of this particular part of the stress response, it is easy to see that every organ and every chemical in the body are affected. The responses to the stressor are physical, chemical, and mental.

Indeed, a look at the inflammatory response, all by itself, shows that inflammation is not always protective and does not always form a function such as engulfing microorganisms and protecting the person against them. Rather, in some instances the inflammatory response actually creates scarring and manifests another disease of its own. Drugs, too, may be used to combat a particular local adaptation syndrome. But at the same time that they are doing this, they are also a stressor, and either by themselves or through their local response are initiating, continuing, and probably increasing the general adaptation syndrome. This effect could be restorative or could be disease producing.

Since local adaptation syndromes vary in location and vary in their outcome, these responses are best understood as the responses of illness or of the components of the physiological mode. Thus we need not examine them further here. However, the general adaptation syndrome is always a factor whenever a stressor has stimulated the body in any way, whether it be an allergen, a teratogen, a carcinogen, a microorganism, a drug, a frightening event, or a distressing situation. No matter what the stressor, there will always be a general adaptation syndrome initiated and maintained as long as the stressor is operating or as long as a local adaptation syndrome is occurring.

In studying the components of the physiological mode of the Roy Adaptation Model of nursing, it is instructive to look at the effect of the general adaptation syndrome on each of the physiological components. First, in looking at oxygenation, the GAS would probably initiate more rapid, shallow, and irregular respirations—either briefly or over an extended period of time, depending on the relative strength and veracity of the stressor. Also depending on the strength of the stressor, there may or may not be increased secretions, painful breathing, and wheezing. These are the types of changes in respiration that will occur as part of the general adaptation syndrome whether or not the stress response proceeds to the point of resistance and exhaustion and the manifestations of a LAS. The GAS aspect of the stress response will manifest itself further in relation to oxygen need by stimulating tachycardia, increasing blood pressure, causing edema, and increasing levels of serum enzymes.

As one looks at the components of nutrition and elimination, the variable responses occurring with the general adaptation syndrome appear in different ways with different people. In fact, responses are a little different in each person at any given time. There almost seems to be a choice of opposing responses in both the nutrition and the eliminative components. For instance, the stress response in one instance may initiate anorexia, nausea, and increased motility of the gastrointestinal tract. In other instances, the GAS may cause decreased motility of the gastrointestinal tract and sometimes hunger. Similarly, in elimination, perspiration may be increased or decreased. Motility of the colon may be increased or decreased. However, urine production seems always to be increased in connection with the GAS. The activity and rest needs are affected by an increase in muscle tonus and pain and a reduced tolerance to exercise. Neurological function may be affected and manifested in altered orientation and judgment, and an increase in temperature and pain. The senses may be affected with impaired sensation and increased sensitivity to stimuli such as sound, sight, and touch. Skin integrity is affected by a change in skin turgor and increased sensitivity, flushed color, and pain.

As noted earlier, the general adaptation syndrome is a triphasic response. The phases vary in duration and intensity in relation to the veracity of the stressor that initiated the syndrome. For example, a sudden, brief, unexpected loud noise may stimulate only the alarm phase and not necessitate the stress response to continue into the phases of resistance and exhaustion. Because of this noise, the following changes might occur: increased pulse; increased respiration; increased mucous secretions; heightened gastrointestinal motility; an increase in urine production; greater sensitivity to sight, sound, and touch; and increased muscle tone. However, these behaviors may not be great enough or be sustained long enough to be measured with the tools currently available. It is possible that the only perceptible change would be a feeling of motility in the abdomen which we commonly refer to as "butterflies in the stomach." The noise, as a stressor, stimulated the stomach and the adrenal cortex so that the hormonal and neurological regulation of the entire body was affected. However, no noticeable alterations of behaviors were maintained that a person looking on could observe.

An example of a stressor that would influence the general adaptation syndrome of many persons on into the second phase — that of resistance — is taking an examination. In this instance, at least some of the behaviors enumerated above would be changed enough to be measurable. In addition, one might note anorexia, urinary frequency, preoccupation, tremors, and other signs that taking the exam is a significant stressor which has caused a greater general adaptation syndrome than in the preceding example. For some persons, this event would cause little, if any, perceptible response, whereas in a few, the changes might progress to loss of sleep, impaired judgment, nausea, vomiting, and diarrhea. At this point the stress response would be increased to the phase of exhaustion, the third phase of the GAS.

The two examples given above were events that could be termed mental stressors, and yet the changes discussed were all within the components of the physiological mode. Similarly, stressors that are physical or chemical in nature would also be stimuli influencing these behaviors. In viewing a microorganism as a stressor, the behaviors indicative of the GAS can be readily observed. If the body fails in the resistance phase to fight the organism and rid itself of the stressor, that microbe will thrive and a local adaptation syndrome will begin to operate together with the general adaptation syndrome. The generalized response can progress into the exhaustion phase. For instance, when a person has a bacterial nasopharyngitis, one of the stressors is the invading organism, which continues and exacerbates the GAS at the same time that it triggers the onset and proliferation of a local adaptation syndrome in the throat. Observations relative to the throat reveal an inflammatory or immune response. The prime stressor is an antigen and the inflammation is an active adaptive immune reaction to the invading organism. This reaction or LAS also functions to maintain the GAS and to regulate its intensity and duration. These two adaptive syndromes are thus interrelated.

Ideally, medical and nursing measures are designed to support and enhance a person's coping effectiveness. However, too often, interventions contribute more stressors. For example, one group of stressors that are commonly added to the situation is drugs. It is not unusual to use an antibiotic, an antipyretic, a corticosteroid, or an analgesic as interventions for the throat condition. Each of these medications has some effect on the original stressor and the stress responses, that is, the GAS and the LAS. For example, adrenal corticosteroids will produce changes in the behaviors recognized as a part of both the GAS and LAS. It can be noted in a more general way that anyone with adrenal insufficiency cannot cope physiologically with stressors as another person can. This basic deficiency produces a situation that can mean fatal results if not recognized and treated adequately and promptly.

Thus we see that making efforts to support and *not inhibit* natural bodily defenses is an important role for any health care worker. For nurses who are prepared to use the Roy Adaptation Model, promoting adaptation is a basic premise for all their nursing practice. Research is discovering that much of what is known about pathophysiology is related to immunity or can focus on the local adaptation syndrome. At this point we can conjecture that it is possible that morbidity rates can be curtailed if people learn to cope more effectively with stressors and reduce the intensity of the stress responses. Much work is being accomplished by studying stress management, and early research efforts are attaining gratifying results. Adaptation nursing, as a specific scientific approach, holds great potential for the field of health in general.

NURSING INTERVENTION

In any form of endocrine imbalance, the nurse has two types of intervention: dependent functions, which are carried out under prescribed orders by a physician; and independent functions, which, although often accomplished in conjunction with the medical regime, are initiated independently by the nurse.

Medically dependent interventions include the following:

1. Assistance in medical diagnosis
    (a) Physical preparation for diagnostic tests such as basal metabolic rate (BMR) or thyroid scans
    (b) Physical preparation for laboratory tests such as catecholamine testing of urine or serum tests for thyroxin
    (c) Reporting of signs and symptoms as noted above in assessment of structural and functional ineffectiveness
2. Administration of specific therapeutic measures
    (a) Administering prescribed hormones and other indicated drugs

    to supplement deficiencies and administering antagonists that control excess excretion

    (b) Assisting at surgical procedures as indicated

    (c) Providing prescribed diets such as low-carbohydrate, low-calorie, or low-protein diets for diabetic or hypothyroid clients

3. Evaluation of physiologic responses to therapy by recording all behaviors and responses to therapeutic measures

Further discussion of these functions may be found in medical textbooks. What are viewed here as independent nursing interventions in relation to endocrine imbalance can be classified into six basic approaches:

1. *To promote normal functioning of the body, especially the skin, renal, and gastrointestinal systems.* When any one endocrine gland is affected, physiologic effects can be observed within other body functions. Thus increased perspiration with hyperthyroidism will necessitate that the nurse plan for frequent cleansing of the skin. Similarly, nursing measures to promote bowel elimination (see Chapter 7) will be initiated with the patient whose hypothyroidism causes sluggish peristalsis.

2. *To teach the patient and his or her family about anatomical and physiological changes that are occurring.* Research has shown that most persons will have a less traumatic illness experience if they are aware of the progress of their bodily functions. The information should be on a level that the person is able to understand. Also, time should be allowed for the patient to ask questions. Emotional support is essential for the patient who witnesses daily changes in body appearance and function. Disruption in body image is a major concern of persons with endocrine imbalance. Obesity, coarse features, hirsutism, and deepened voice are just a few body image disruptions that may occur. The health teaching carried out at the time of menarche and menopause are examples of the type of intervention used frequently by nurses in the problem of disturbed physical self-image (see Chapter 18).

3. *To teach the patient and family about the diagnostic tests and procedures, laboratory examinations, and medications.* The patient must know why these therapeutic measures are necessary, how they affect body functions, and the procedures necessary for the successful completion of the therapeutic measures. This is especially important for medications, diet, and activity levels. The patient will usually be responsible for self-administration of drugs and diet; therefore, thorough knowledge and understanding are very important. Also, physical limitations should be stressed, with emphasis on the positive aspects of activity. The patient should be aware of

possible behaviors or complications, such as diabetic coma or insulin shock, if medication, diet, or activity levels are neglected. Education to specify therapeutic measures will prevent the possibility of complications and maintain optimum adaptive behaviors.

4. *To promote role mastery in the areas frequently disrupted in endocrine imbalance.* Problems in completing the patient's role as mother, father, wife, husband, or employee often become real threats. Some endocrine problems may cause mood swings that may threaten a wife–husband relationship. Other endocrine problems may induce impotence, which may affect sex relations and prospective mother or father roles. These role problems may be caused by increased dependency needs. For example, if a person is unable to work for a period of time due to fatigue, the spouse or a relative or friend may be required to supply more manual, financial, or emotional support. See Chapter 23 for interventions in problems of role function.

5. *To evaluate and promote a positive emotional response to therapy and the acceptance of the limitations of the sick role.* Effective physiological treatment is dependent to a great extent on the person's response to therapy. The nurse observes this response and the factors influencing it. She changes the factors influencing that response until a positive or adaptive response is made. The nursing process is completed, as always, with an evaluation of whether or not the nursing interventions have been successful in promoting adaptation. Modification of approaches is planned and carried out as needed.

6. *To help persons develop stress reduction techniques for their lives in general and for specific circumstances* (see the Additional Readings at the end of this chapter).

SUMMARY

Endocrine function, an integral component of the individual's adaptation process, has been discussed. First- and second-level behavioral assessment was described. The general adaptation syndrome, a nonspecific stress response, was described in detail. The nurse may use this theory in intervening with persons in both health and illness.

STUDENT LEARNING ACTIVITY

Think back to the last major exam you took and list behaviors you exhibited that would show the effect of the general adaptation syndrome on your physiologic mode. Using the References at the end of this chapter, identify at least two methods you can use to reduce stress before your next major examination.

REFERENCES

Selye, Hans. *The Stress of Life*. New York: McGraw-Hill Book Company, 1956.

Selye, Hans. "Perspectives in Stress Research," in *Life and Disease: New Perspectives in Biology and Medicine*, Dwight J. Ingle, ed. New York: Basic Books, Inc., Publishers, 1963.

ADDITIONAL READINGS

Antonovsky, Aaron. *Health Stress and Coping*. San Francisco: Jossey-Bass, Inc., Publishers, 1979.

Beeson, P. G., and W. McDermott, eds. *Cecil-Loeb Textbook of Medicine*, 13th ed. Philadelphia: W. B. Saunders Company, 1971, p. 1718.

Garfield, Charles A., ed. *Stress and Survival: The Emotional Realities of Life-Threatening Illness*. St. Louis: The C. V. Mosby Company, 1979.

Groer, Marueen E., and Maureen E. Shekleton. *Basic Pathophysiology: A Conceptual Approach*. St. Louis: The C. V. Mosby Company, 1979.

Guyton, A. C. *Textbook of Medical Physiology*, 4th ed. Philadelphia: W. B. Saunders Company, 1971, Chapters 75–79.

Jasmin, Sylvia A., Lyda Hill, and Nancy Smith. "Keeping Your Delicate Balance: The Art of Managing Stress," *Nursing '81*, vol. 11, June, pp. 53–57.

Morris, Carolyn L. "Relaxation Therapy in a Clinic," *American Journal of Nursing*, vol. 79, no. 11, 1979, pp. 1958–1959.

Neher, F. H. *Endocrine System and Selected Metabolic Conditions*. The Ciba Collection of Medical Illustrations, vol. 4. Summit, N. J.: Ciba Pharmaceutical Company, 1965.

Richter, Judith M., and Rebecca Sloan. "A Relaxation Technique," *American Journal of Nursing*, vol. 79, no. 11, 1979, pp. 1960–1964.

Smith, Marcy J. T., and Hans Selye. "Reducing the Negative Effects of Stress," *American Journal of Nursing*, vol. 79, no. 11, 1979, pp. 1953–1955.

"Symposium on Endocrine Disorders," *Nursing Clinics of North America*, vol. 15, September 1980.

Williams, Robert H., ed. *Textbook of Endocrinology*, 4th ed. Philadelphia: W. B. Saunders Company, 1968.

Part III

Theory and Development of the Psychosocial Adaptive Modes

This section focuses on the basic theories that have been useful in describing the psychosocial adaptive modes and the development of each one within the person. Chapter 14 deals with the self-concept mode, Chapter 15 with role function, and Chapter 16 with interdependence. Each chapter includes guidelines for nursing assessment of the given adaptive mode. Case study material is used to illustrate the concepts presented and to facilitate beginning skill in viewing the person as an adaptive system that manifests him or herself in large part through self-concept, role function, and interdependence behaviors.

Chapter 14

Self-Concept: Theory and Development

*Marjorie H. Buck**

BEHAVIORAL OBJECTIVES

After studying this chapter, the reader will be able to:

1. Define the key concepts of the chapter.
2. Explain the importance of self-concept to adaptation nursing.
3. List and define the components of the self-concept mode.
4. Discuss the theories from which the Roy Adaptation Model self-concept mode was derived.
5. List common nursing approaches for promoting mastery of each developmental stage.
6. Discuss the nursing process in the self-concept mode.
7. Identify self-concept behaviors and influencing factors in the case study.
8. Apply the nursing process in the self-concept mode to an ordinary life experience.

KEY CONCEPTS DEFINED

Self-Concept: the composite of beliefs and feelings that one holds about oneself at a given time, formed from internal perceptions and perceptions of other's reactions, and directing one's behavior.

*This chapter is a revision and expansion of two chapters written by Marie J. Driever in the first edition: "Theory of Self-Concept," pp. 169–179, and "Development of Self-Concept," pp. 180–191.

Psychic Integrity: the basic need of the self-concept mode: it means that one needs to know who one is so that one can be, or exist with a sense of unity.

Physical Self: the person's appraisal of one's own physical being, including physical attributes, functioning, sexuality, health–illness states, and appearance.

Personal Self: the individual's appraisal of one's own characteristics, expectations, values, and worth.

Self-Consistency: the part of the personal self component which strives to maintain a consistent self-organization, and thus to avoid disequilibrium.

Self-Ideal/Self-Expectancy: that aspect of the personal self component which relates to what the person expects to be and do.

Moral–Ethical–Spiritual Self: that aspect of the personal self which functions as observer, standard-setter, dreamer, comparer, and most of all evaluator of who this person says that he or she is.

Learning: behavioral change that is dependent on processes involving rewards, imitation, and insight.

Inner Cell of the Self-Concept: those perceptions about self which seem most vital; fundamental important aspects of the individual.

Self-Esteem: the individual's perception of self-worth.

The nurse views each person as a whole and is concerned about the person's psychological, spiritual, and social well-being as well as physical well-being. Each individual is an integrated whole with all aspects in constant interaction. To facilitate learning and planning nursing interventions, the Roy Adaptation Model looks at the person as having four major adaptive modes. Part II considered the physiologic mode, which deals with physiological needs and functions of the person. This chapter introduces the self-concept mode which focuses more specifically on the psychological and spiritual aspects of the individual. Psychic integrity is the underlying need of this mode. One needs psychic integrity to know who one is so that one can be, or exist with a sense of unity.

Satir (1972) talks about the individual's concept of self in her book *People Making.* The following poem by Satir (1970, 1975) is quoted to provide an overview of the self-concept.

Take a moment and reflect on your reaction to reading the quotation. What thoughts came to mind? What feelings did you have about yourself?

Although all of us—theorists, scholars, you, and I—have difficulty defining exactly who we are, our concept of self plays a major part in everything we do. How we feel about ourselves at a given time influences what we choose to eat (physiologic mode), what we wear (self-concept mode), what

I AM ME[1]

In all the world there is no one else exactly like me.

There are persons who have some parts like me,
but no one adds up exactly like anyone else.

Therefore, eveything I present can only come from me.

I own everything about me —
my body, including all its thoughts and ideas;
my eyes, including the image of all my eyes behold;
my feelings, whatever they may be —
anger, joy, frustration, love, disappointment, excitement;
my mouth and all that comes out of it —
words — polite, sweet or rough, correct and incorrect;
my voice — loud or soft;
and all my actions, whether they be to others or to myself.

I own all my triumphs and successes,
all my failures and mistakes.
I own my fantasies, my dreams, my hopes, my fears.
Because I own all of me,
I can become intimately acquainted with me,
I can love me and be friendly with me in all my parts.

I know that there are aspects about myself I do not know,
and there are parts of me that puzzle me.

As long as I am friendly and loving to myself,
I can courageously look for the solution to the puzzles
and continually look for ways to find out more about me —
how I look and sound, what I say and do,
and how I think and feel.

No one else looks and sounds, says and does,
and thinks and feels exactly like me.

In being well acquainted with myself,
loving myself, and being friendly with myself,
I can then make it possible for all of me
to work in my best interests.

However I look and sound, whatever I say and do,
and whatever I think and feel at a given moment is me;
it is authentic and represents where I am
at that moment in time.

---

[1]From the book *Self Esteem*, © 1970, 1975 by Virginia Satir, published by Celestial Arts, Milbrae, Ca. Reprinted with permission.

When I review later how I looked and sounded,
what I said and did, and how I thought and felt,
parts may turn out to be unfitting,
and I can discard that which proved unfitting
and keep that which proved fitting
and invent something new for that which I discarded.

I own me and therefore I can engineer me.

I can learn all the new things that I need
and discard all the things that no longer fit.

I can see, hear, feel, think, say, and do.

I have then the tools to survive and grow,
to be close to others and to be productive,
and to make sense and order out of the world
of people and things outside of me.

I am me and I am okay.

choose to eat (physiologic mode), what we wear (self-concept mode), what career we choose (role function mode), and who we choose for our friends (interdependence mode). The person who feels good about himself or herself is more likely to live healthfully than the person who feels of little value.

Think about yourself again for a moment. You probably know a great deal about what things lead to health—nutrition, exercise, rest, and so forth. How do you behave in terms of those things when you are feeling good about yourself? How do you behave when you are not feeling very good about yourself?

As a nurse, you will often find that the person you care for knows the information about a particular health subject, but is still having great difficulty using it. For example, a 15-year-old young woman may know that eating chocolate contributes to skin blemishes. She states she would like to have a clear complexion, yet she continues to eat chocolate. It could be that she is feeling bad about herself, how she looks with a broken-out face, how she feels unattractive, how she was not included in an activity that all her friends attended. Because she feels bad, she eats chocolate and hopes to feel better. Before she can stop eating chocolate she may have to deal with her feelings of being unattractive and left out. The nurse often finds that a low sense of self-worth on the part of the person interferes with the person's ability to heal and maintain health. In the example above, any approaches aimed at helping the young woman obtain a clear complexion which did not deal with her feelings about herself would be unsuccessful in the long run.

This chapter presents a description of the self-concept mode, including the behaviors and common influencing factors for each component of the mode. Following a discussion of relevant theories of self-concept, the last sections of this chapter cover application of these theories through use of the nursing process.

DESCRIPTION OF THE SELF-CONCEPT MODE

Self-concept is defined as "the composite of beliefs and feelings that one holds about oneself at a given time, formed from perceptions particularly of others' reactions, and directing one's behavior" (Driever, p. 169). The underlying need of the self-concept mode is to maintain *psychic integrity*. Self-concept is the mediator between the external and the internal worlds of the person. With a sense of oneself as a unity, the person can be as an individual. To understand self-concept is to understand the meaning of the question "Who am I?"

Self-concept is a complex and deeply personal aspect of an individual. To understand and apply the nursing process, the self-concept mode is divided into two major subareas: the physical self and the personal self.[2] The *physical self* includes two components. The first component is body sensation—how one's body feels personally. It includes the *body sensations* we use as input to allow us to experience ourselves as physical beings. Examples of behaviors for body sensation include such statements as "I feel _____" (limp, strong, sexually responsive, faint, pained). *Body image*, the second component of physical self, is how one's body looks to oneself and how one feels about how one's body looks. Behaviors in this area include such statements as "I feel I'm _____" (fat, too thin, attractive, ugly, healthy, coordinated).

The second subarea is the personal self which is divided into three components:

1. *Self-consistency* is one's actual performance, one's response to a situation, and one's "personality traits." Examples of behaviors include direct observation of the person's response to a situation—manner, facial expression, tone of voice; and such statements as "I'm _____" (calm, happy, sad, self-confident, timid, frightened).
2. *Self-ideal/self-expectancy* is what one would like to be, related to what one is capable of being. Examples of self-ideal behaviors include statements as, "I would like to be _____" (stronger, less jumpy, calm in all settings, a plumber).
3. *Moral-ethical-spiritual self* is the person's belief system, morals, and the evaluator of who one is. Examples of behaviors include

[2]The original literature review, including the development of this classification and the theory underlying the self-concept mode, was done by Marie J. Driever at Mount St. Mary's College under USPHS Grant No. 5T02MH06442 1969-70.

such statements as "I believe in _____" (being honest at all costs, taking care of me first, a just and kind God) and "I believe I am _____" (doing the best I can, a lousy person, never going to achieve what I want to be).

DEVELOPMENT OF THE SELF-CONCEPT

The newborn infant comes into the world with genetic material unique to that individual. Despite such differences, each new person has the potential to be an example of the "model human being" (Jackins, 1974) or the "potential human being" (Huxley, 1978). Characteristics of this person include a sense of aliveness, love for life and other humans, ability to think clearly and creatively, ability to overcome emotional hurts in a rational way, and a sense of connectedness with all others which leads to responsible behavior.

You probably look very much like this model human being at times. At other times you may look quite different. How do we come to act as we do? The self-concept of each individual is a strong influencing factor for all of one's behavior. How, then, do we come to hold a certain view of ourselves? Various social scientists have developed theories to explain the development of the self-concept. The Roy Adaptation Model of nursing has drawn from the works of several such theorists. Understanding the theories and principles of development of the self-concept allows the nurse to look at behaviors and factors influencing the person's behavior and to plan interventions in an organized, systematic manner.

The theories and principles discussed in this section provide the nurse with specific categories of behaviors and influencing factors to assess and manage in the self-concept mode.

Principles of Learning

Theories of self-concept utilize principles of learning and of growth and development. *Learning* is a change of behavior through processes of reinforcement, imitation, and insight. Through the process of learning a person comes to hold certain thoughts, feelings, and beliefs about self. The nurse can use an understanding of learning principles as a guide to looking at how certain events influence the person's current behaviors and to plan and carry out nursing approaches. The following list includes principles that are important in the learning process.

1. *Generalization* is the process that occurs during learning whereby

the person responds in a specific way to a nonspecific stimulus. For example, if a mother repeatedly uses the word *bad* with a child, that child is likely to feel that the word relates to his or her total person.

2. *Discrimination* is the process by which the person makes a more specific response. Following the same example, the mother may be able to help the child understand that the word *bad* relates only to the action of hitting baby sister and not to the child as a person.

3. *Spaced trials* over a period of time are generally more effective than one concentrated session of learning. For example, a mother's consistent response to the child is more important than one pleasant afternoon spent together.

4. *Active participation* facilitates learning. The person who is able to do something to show competence is more likely to incorporate a competent attitude into self-concept.

5. *Meaningful material* is learned more quickly than material without meaning. If a person has identified a certain characteristic — for example, dependability — as being personally important, the person can acquire this trait more readily than a trait personally considered irrelevant, for example, a sense of humor.

These principles of learning act together with the principles of growth and development, discussed in Chapter 4, in the development of the self-concept mode.

Coombs and Snygg.   The work of Coombs and Snygg is used as part of the basis for the Roy Adaptation Model's definition of self-concept, the self-consistency component. Furthermore, it identifies major influencing factors for self-concept.

In the self-concept theory developed by Coombs and Snygg (1959), what one thinks and how one behaves are determined largely by the concepts one holds about oneself and one's abilities. The pivotal point of this theory is on perception. These authors believe that each person continually attempts to achieve an adequate concept of self in order to preserve psychic integrity. Because of this fundamental need, perceptions of self have a tremendous influence in determining behavior. How a person acts in any given situation depends on how the individual perceives self.

Coombs and Snygg postulate that the perceptions a person has at a particular time are dependent on the concepts that this individual holds about self and one's abilities. Thus, for these theorists, the self-concept is a basic variable affecting and controlling perceptions, which eventually affects the behavior of the person. In turn, behavior and perceptions affect one's concept of self in an ongoing circle. This process is further illustrated and explained in Fig. 14.1.

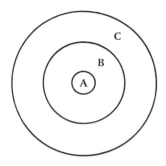

Figure 14.1 Coombs and Snygg perceptual theory of self-concept.

Circle A.   This central portion or *inner cell of the self-concept* includes those perceptions about self which seem the most vital, fundamental, important aspects of the individual. Examples include: "I am a capable mother," "I am fat," or "I am stupid."

Circle B.   This encompasses the inner circle and in addition includes all the perceptions that an individual holds about self, regardless of their importance. This partciular concept has been termed the *phenomenal self* or the perceived self. Examples of perceptions about self that are not vital include: "I can cook well," "I am always punctual," or "I have a good sense of humor."

Circle C.   The final circle illustrates the total *perceptual field of the self-concept* by including all the perceptions that one has about self (circles A and B) plus those perceptions that are outside the self (not the self). The not self may be exemplified by the following statements: "The United States is a wonderful place in which to live," and "People who are kind to others are usually happier."

In addition to describing their hypothesis of the nature of the self-concept as being derived from the phenomenal self (circles A and B) and the perceptual field (circle C), Coombs and Snygg postulate the following characteristics of the phenomenal self:

1. *Perceptions of the phenomenal self have the feeling of being very real to the individual.* On the other hand, this individual is probably never able to perceive the total organization of self-perceptions clearly at any one moment. Instead, the person perceives those concepts of self that emerge from time to time as the person attempts to satisfy needs.

2. *Perceptions of self vary in sharpness for the individual.* These perceptions may be cloudy and vague in nature or clear and sharply defined. An example is a man who identifies himself as "Teddy's father," as contrasted with one who sees himself as "a good father." The first example is sharply defined; "a good father" is unclear and may mean many different things. Another example is an adolescent who wavers between perceiving herself as a woman or girl, thus contributing to a vague concept of self. This

vague concept of self may cause an individual great difficulty. Coombs and Snygg believe that the self-concept continually develops with greater and greater clarity throughout one's life. This clarity assists the person in discovering who and what one is.

3. *Some self-perceptions appear to be more basic to a person than others, as illustrated in circle A.* Because the perceptions are central to the person's self-concept, the person will probably resist attempts to change these core perceptions.

4. *Another characteristic of the phenomenal self is consistency.* Once the phenomenal self is established, it serves as a fundamental frame of reference and has a high degree of stability. Even an unsatisfactory self-organization is likely to prove highly consistent and resistant to change.

In summary, Coombs and Snygg's theory views the self-concept as a map that each individual consults in order to understand self, especially during moments of crisis and/or decision. It also may be seen as a shorthand approach by which people symbolize and reduce their own vast complexity to workable, usable terms so that they can perceive and respond effectively.

Cooley, Mead, and Sullivan.   The social interaction theories provide further theoretical basis for the Roy Adaptation Model's approach to self-concept. It also highlights the reactions of others as a major influencing factor. As the nurse works with people, he or she will apply ideas from the following discussion of theories as a basis for identifying self-concept behaviors and influencing factors, planning and carrying out nursing interventions, and evaluating the results of the nursing actions. Interaction theorists, notably Cooley, Mead, and Sullivan, assume that interaction with others, especially significant others, control and alter the individual's appraisal of self or concept of self.

Cooley (Epstein, 1973) introduced the concept of the "looking-glass self"—the person's perception of self results from the way one perceives the responses of others. Thus if one thinks of oneself as slow-moving, it is because one perceives that others react as if one *were* slow-moving.

Mead (1934) expanded Cooley's concept and saw self-concept as an outgrowth of the individual's concern about how others react to one. He postulated that the way the self achieves an appraisal of itself is to take the role of the "generalized other." Thus a person puts self in the shoes of the others in interactions and takes on their attitudes toward him or her. The motivation to take on the attitudes of others comes from concern about what others think.

In a similar way, Sullivan (1953) sees the self as arising out of social interaction. He emphasizes the interaction with significant others as the key to formulating the self-concept. He identifies *significant others* as those who provide rewards and punishments in a person's life. Based on these

well-being. The nurse who has these understandings possesses the ability to communicate purposefully. Working with others, the nurse continues to grow in understanding of theory and communication skills.

Self-concept is expressed in the verbalization of thoughts and feelings as well as in actions. An individual's view of self cannot be inferred from observing a few behaviors. A thorough assessment is done before a nursing diagnosis can be made. To obtain a thorough assessment, the nurse creates an atmosphere in which the person feels safe to express feelings. The attitude of the nurse does much to set the tone of safety or lack thereof. Since feelings are the subjective response of the individual, there are no good, bad, right, or wrong feelings. Laughing, crying, raging, shaking, and talking are expressions of feelings, not feelings themselves. You know it is possible to feel very angry, for example, without raging or even talking about it. Such suppression of feeling, however, ties up psychic energy and interferes with the ability to do other things, such as thinking clearly and healing. The nurse who conveys an accepting, nonjudgmental attitude can facilitate the expression of feelings, thus intervening while assessing. The nurse who shows disapproval or states "You shouldn't feel that way" will block expression of feelings. The nurse must be in touch with his or her own feelings on a personal level and be able to listen to the expression of feelings by the other person without imposing those personal feelings.

Another important aspect in creating a safe environment for the person is the ability to state clearly and directly the purpose of an interaction or interview. For example, the nurse might say, "I'm going to spend some time talking with you about your thoughts and feelings about yourself. Since each person is different and responds differently to _____ (giving birth, surgery, cancer, and so on), it is important for me to understand how you are feeling now. That way I can plan care based on your needs and wishes." The actual wording will be varied for the individual situation.

The time and place of an interview will be appropriately planned. The person who is in pain, for example, cannot attend to questions relating to the self-concept. The person whose room is filled with other people also may be unable to attend to questions relating to self-concept. The immediate physiological needs and the need for privacy will be met prior to beginning a self-concept assessment.

USE OF THE NURSING PROCESS IN THE SELF-CONCEPT MODE

The nurse draws from an understanding of growth and development, learning theory, and the theories of Coombs and Snygg, Cooley, Mead, and Sullivan, Gardner, and Erikson as a basis for each stage of the nursing process as it focuses specifically on the self-concept mode.

Assessment of Self-Concept

Once the nurse has established an optimal situation for assessment by explaining her or his purpose, providing privacy, and meeting the person's immediate needs, the nurse is ready to proceed with an in-depth assessment of the person's self-concept. As discussed in Chapter 3, the first-level assessment is the observation and recording of behaviors in each of the adaptive mode components. Table 14.1 gives a brief description of each component in the first column. Refer to the beginning of this chapter for a review of the discussion of each component. The table is meant to serve as a guide. You will need to work with the ways of eliciting the behaviors suggested in the second column until you develop phrases and questions that fit your communication style. Do not try to use these questions verbatim. Be sure to ask your questions in the context of the individual's current situation. For example, you might ask, "Now that you are pregnant, how do you feel about your body?" The person's behaviors will be the actual statements made as well as the tone of voice, facial expression, body posture, grooming, and dress. Record the person's responses verbatim whenever possible. Column three in Table 14.1 lists examples of behaviors in each component.

After you have assessed the person's self-concept behaviors, you will do the second-level assessment, which identifies the influencing factors or stimuli. As you are learning to work with this mode, you will probably carry out the first- and second-level assessments separately. As you become more accomplished, you will be able to collect the data for both levels in one process. The theories related to self-concept discussed earlier in the chapter provide the categories or compartments to be covered in the second-level assessment. Table 14.2 lists the general categories of influencing factors and gives a brief discussion of each and examples of how to collect data in each category.

The first category, perception, is based primarily on the theory of Coombs and Snygg. The nurse can use other theories which focus on a person's perception of self here as it seems fitting. Such theorists include Carl Rogers, Selma Freiberg, Frieda Fromm-Reichman, and Rollo May. The essence of this category is the individual's perception of self and not-self, and how that perception influences the person's formation and maintenance of a concept of self. For example, if a person perceives of self as weak-willed and easily controlled, the person's self-concept may be one of low self-worth. Gaining an understanding of the person's internal perceptions of self gives the nurse information upon which to plan nursing approaches in the self-concept mode. One approach, perception alteration, will be discussed in the nursing intervention section of this chapter. Data in this category are obtained by interviewing the person (see Table 14.2).

The second category of influencing factors is growth and development.

TABLE 14.1
First Level Assessment of the Self-Concept Mode

Components and Characteristics	How to Elicit Behavior	How the Behavior Is Manifested
Physical Self		
Body sensation: how one's own body feels to self; sensations allow one to experience own body	How do you feel physically? What physical sensations are you experiencing now? Describe yourself physically.	"I feel _____" [cold, warm, pained, sick, well, tired, sexy, etc.] Facial expression Muscular tension or relaxation
Body image: body traits— how one feels about own body; how one's own body looks to self	How do you feel about your appearance?	"I am _____" [tall, small, pretty, ugly, fat, thin, etc.] Body posture, grooming
Personal Self		
Self-consistency: personality traits; how one views self in relation to actual performance or response to situation	Describe yourself as a person. Describe your personal characteristics.	"I am _____" [a weak person, a strong person, a person of willpower, incapable, like a child, not worthwhile, etc.]
Self-ideal: what one would like to be or to do— related to what one is capable of being or one's goal	What are your aspirations in your life? What would you change about yourself if you could?	"I would like to be _____" [rich, famous, a strong person, leader, etc.]
Moral–ethical–spiritual self: one's spiritual, ethical view of self; related to one's value system, belief about "rightness" or "wrongness," evaluation of "who I am"	Describe your beliefs about life's standards. How do you meet your spiritual needs? How do you feel you measure up to your own expectations?	"I believe in _____" "I should _____" "I shouldn't _____" "I believe that one should _____" "I believe that I am _____" "I am _____" [good, bad, dishonest, etc.]

Source: Based on the unpublished work of Joan Cho, Department of Nursing, Mount Saint Mary's College, Los Angeles, 1979–80.

Here the adaptation nurse uses the first-level physiological mode assessment viewed in terms of the person's age and degree of physical development as influencing factors for the person's self-concept. For example, the physiological behavior of inability to control excretion of urine will have a different effect on the self-concept of a 1-year-old person than on that of a 16-year-old person. The nurse also applies known standards of growth and development, for example, height and weight charts, in this category. Data in this category are obtained from interviewing the person, reviewing the physiological assessment and written records, and from knowledge of growth and development charts.

The third category of influencing factors to consider in the second-level assessment is learning. The concept of the model or potential human being was presented earlier in this chapter. Each new person has to some degree a sense of self as all-powerful, very intelligent, loving, and joyful. As time goes by the individual notices that certain characteristics are rewarded by significant others and society whereas others are not. Race, sex, class, religious, and other societal discriminations affect the individual's concept of self. By assessing what the significant people in an individual's life expect, what an individual has learned is expected of her or him, and what the social values are, the nurse will discover how the person has been led to compromise that original sense of self. Data in this category are obtained by interviewing the person and significant others and by reviewing the literature on social discrimination (see Chapter 4 on culture).

The fourth category of influencing factors, reactions of others, incorporates the work of the interactionists. Review the summary of the theories of Cooley, Mead, and Sullivan presented earlier. The essence of these theories is that the individual starts to think of self in the ways in which he or she perceives others' views of him or her. For example, the student who is repeatedly told, "You are very slow in your written work," will incorporate a sense of being too slow or even no good at writing. When the nurse discovers the source of such a self-concept belief, the door for planning an approach to change the belief has been opened.

The family members of an individual are very significant people in terms of formation of one's self-concept. The nurse assesses the influence of the family on the person's self-concept in this category. Who are the family members? What is the family's value of the individual members? Who does the person receiving care feel particularly close to in the family? Does the individual feel valued and respected in the family? What are the levels of self-esteem of the various members? All of these data will give the nurse ideas for how to plan approaches in the self-concept mode. Data in this category are obtained through interviewing the person, significant others, and family members as well as through direct observation of interactions between the person receiving care and others.

Next the nurse considers the person's stage of development according to Erikson (see Chapter 4). By knowing the tasks on which the person is working, the nurse can see what challenges are facing the person. Major threats to the self-concept, be they physical, emotional, or social, may cause the person to regress to an earlier stage of development. The nurse compares the stage of development in which the person is exhibiting behaviors and that defined by the person's age. The nurse then plans approaches to

TABLE 14.2
Second-Level Assessment of the Self-Concept Mode[a]

General Categories of Influencing Factors (Stimuli)	How to Obtain Information on the Influencing Factors
1. *Perception* (Coombs and Snygg) How the person generally sees self Inner cell: the most vital, fundamental, and important views one holds about self Phenomenal self: all perceptions of self regardless of their importance Perceptual field: all perceptions of self and nonself	1. *Perception* Inner cell: "When faced with big changes in your life (e.g., surgery, graduation, etc.) what particular personal qualities do you use to help you maintain a sense of stability?" Phenomenal self: all statements the person makes about self during the interview; look at those statements that relate to the person's current situation in particular
2. *Growth and development* (Gardner and Havighurst) Age, physical abilities, ability to use tools, ability to control bodily functions	2. *Growth and development* Collect these data from direct observation, the written records, the first level physiological mode assessment, and growth and development charts
3. *Learning* Past experiences, presence or absence of rewards for having certain characteristics—e.g., U.S. society rewards females who are dainty, graceful and quiet; see pages 260–261	3. *Learning* With a child, collect data from the parents and the child. To the parents: "What characteristics do you particularly like to see in your child? How do you try to bring out those characteristics?" To the person receiving care: "What personal characteristics do you feel you are supposed to have? What specific pressures do you feel to be that way?" To the child: "What kind of person do your parents want you to be? What is it like when you are that way? What happens when you are not that way?"
4. *Reactions of others* (Cooley, Mead, and Sullivan) The response of significant others Looking-glass self—how the person perceives the responses of others to self	4. *Reactions of others* "What kind of person do you think _____ (a specific significant other) sees you as? When you are with that person, how do you feel about yourself?"

270

5. *Maturational crisis* (Erikson)
Stage of life according to Erikson
Tasks of current stage; how well the person mastered the tasks of the previous stages

6. *Coping Mechanisms*
How the person habitually responds to maintain a state of adaptation

7. *Other*

5. *Maturational crisis*
List the tasks according to Erikson for the person's stage of development; compare the person's current functioning (role, interdependence, and self-concept behaviors) to the tasks for that stage of development; ask questions based on the tasks to collect further data as necessary

6. *Coping mechanisms*
"What things do you do to feel good about yourself? In the past when faced with a situation similar to this one, how have you handled it?"

7. *Other*

aTable 14.2 lists the general categories of factors that might affect the self-concept mode based on the theories presented earlier in this chapter. Any one of the categories of stimuli can be focal, contextual, or residual. The categories are designed to help the nurse be inclusive in assessing influencing factors. The nurse may find that a number of important factors do not seem to fit into any of the first six categories. In that case, use category 7.

Data for the second-level assessment are obtained through direct interview, from the chart, report from other health care professionals, interview of the person's family members, and from theory. Remember that all focal and contextual stimuli will be validated with the person or by theory.

Moderate self-esteem is indicated by ready compliance with norms, dependence on social acceptance, active seeking of social approval, and uncertainty of one's own capabilities and worth.

Low self-esteem is indicated by a pattern of discouragement and depression, feelings of isolation and unworthiness, extreme difficulty in expressing or defending oneself, feelings of helplessness and lack of ability to change, asserting self over others to prove or elevate one's self, fear of anger of others, fear of self-exposure, and a persistent pattern of listening as opposed to participating. The problem of low self-esteem is discussed in Chapter 22 and other problems occurring in the self-concept mode are also explored in Part IV. Part V covers diagnoses affecting more than one adaptive mode, including problems that have the greatest effect on self-concept.

Goal Setting for the Self-Concept Mode

Following formulation of the nursing diagnosis, the nurse sets goals for how the person's behavior(s) will change. Mutual goal-setting with the person is important. The individual's agreement with the goal is vital to the success of the nursing approaches. The goal states a specific behavior, how it will change, and a time frame. The goal must be measurable. Stating "The person will have an improved sense of personal self" is not sufficient. "The person will be able to verbally identify some area of satisfaction with her or his self-consistency by noon today" is a more clearly stated goal. As discussed in Chapter 3, goals are stated as realistic and attainable.

Nursing Intervention

Once the goals are set, the nurse plans and carries out the nursing approaches. The interventions manage the identified influencing factors so as to allow the person to make an adaptive response. Stimuli, or influencing factors, having a positive effect will be reinforced. Factors having a negative effect will be altered, eliminated, or countered whenever possible. The following discussion will cover some possible ways of managing the categories of influencing factors identified in Table 14.2.

When the individual is experiencing a problem in the self-concept mode resulting primarily from the influence of perceptions of self, the nurse may use perception alteration as an approach.[4] To carry out this approach the nurse interviews the person seeking details about the events surrounding the perceptions which are having a negative effect on the person's self-

---

[4] This discussion of perception changes is based on the unpublished work of Betty Dambacker, School of Nursing, University of California at Los Angeles, 1972.

concept. As the individual recalls more and more details, he or she will frequently come to see that current thoughts and feelings about self are based on misunderstood past events, incomplete information, and stereotypes. Through such realizations and ventilation of accompanying feelings the person may be able to relinquish certain negative perceptions of self, thus clearing the way for a more positive self-view.

The following is an example of using perception alteration as an approach. A young man states that he feels fat and therefore ugly (body image behavior). He relates that he was 50 to 60 pounds overweight from the ages of 19 to 26 (growth and development factor). At that time he lost the extra weight and has maintained his current weight, which is within the normal range, for the past 6 years (growth and development influencing factor). He tells you that he knows that he is not overweight but that he sees himself as fat in his mind's eye (perception influencing factor). He holds a perception of his body that is incongruent with the present reality. By exploring in detail the events around the inclusion of his perception of self as fat, and the events of his losing weight, he may come to be able to let go of the old perception and incorporate his actual body appearance into his body image.

Approaches that manage growth and development, the second category of influencing factors, include providing the individual with materials and instructions for use of needed tools and control of bodily functions. An individual may be exhibiting self-consistency behaviors of feeling incompetent and incapable. The factors influencing these behaviors are the need to give self insulin injections to control diabetes, lack of information about how to give injections, and feelings that it will be too difficult a skill to learn (growth and development factors—inability to use needed tools). The goal of having the person feel competent and capable can be met by providing the person with the necessary tools, instructions, and learning trials to master the skill of giving self insulin injections.

When a person's self-concept is affected by the influencing factor of loss of control of bodily function, for example, loss of ability to speak resulting from a laryngectomy, a nursing approach for reestablishing the person's self-concept would be taking steps that lead to the person's regaining control over the lost function.[5]

One nursing approach that manages the third category of influencing factors, learning, is interviewing the person to allow him or her to reexamine past experiences in terms of presence or absence of rewards or models for certain personal characteristics and to devise current means for obtaining rewards for personally valued characteristics. The current rewards may be obtained either internally or externally. For example, a woman may feel weak and physically unfit (physical-self behaviors). The second-level assessment reveals her growth and development to be normal. She is in good

[5]See Luckmann and Sorensen (1974, pp. 1599–1601) for specific steps to take.

health. The data under learning factors include: her mother was chronically ill and by this person's description, "very feminine." In spite of the changing norms, the mainstream of U. S. culture views women as more often sick and relatively weak as compared to men. The client was taught that physical activity was unfeminine. The mutually set goal is to feel strong and healthy. The nurse would interview this woman to see what rewards and punishments she received in the past for being physically active and feeling well. The next step would be to have her devise a way of obtaining rewards for being physically active and feeling well. The plan should include an exercise routine so she will obtain the rewards of an increased sense of physical well-being that follows physical conditioning. Identifying women she knows who are feminine, active, strong, and healthy could be another way for her to gain reinforcement for being active.

Since the individual's self-concept is also greatly affected by the stereotypes held by society, the nurse needs to direct approaches toward changing the limiting stereotypes held by groups and society. For example, a school nurse could work with groups of students to help them understand how the oppression of racism works and how to relate to each other outside the stereotypes of racism. Another example would be to work for legislation that guarantees access to health care for all regardless of sex, age, or income level.

Approaches that manage reactions of others as an influencing factor include working with significant others to change how they react to the person receiving care and by using perception correction with the person to bring about changes in how the individual perceives the responses of others. Refer to the discussion above of perception correction as an approach. An example of the first approach can be seen in working with the responses of people to an individual with a condition that changes his or her appearance greatly. The individual may be struggling to maintain a sense of physical and personal worth (behaviors) in the face of the condition and the reactions of others who look disgusted and repulsed, or who simply do not visit (influencing factors). Sitting down with the others, allowing them to ventilate their feelings about the client's appearance and then giving them information about what kind of response the person with the condition needs manages this category of influencing factors.

Nursing approaches that promote mastery of Erikson's stages of development must be specific for the task to be mastered. In the next several paragraphs, nursing approaches for each developmental stage will be discussed.

To help promote mastery of the task of *developing trust* in the infant, the nurse can provide classes to give parents information and support. The parenting people must have a sense of conviction on which to base their actions. Organized religion has often served that purpose. Child development theories and books are also serving the purpose. A popular phrase is "Dr.

Spock says _____." In the hospital setting, open visiting hours, rooming-in, and consistent staff assignments will help promote a sense of trust in the infant.

The nurse can help promote *mastery of autonomy* in the toddler years by telling parents that the child needs firm, reassuring outer controls, respect for his or her "no" whenever possible, and freedom to explore the environment safely. The child is more likely to achieve a sense of autonomy if shaming is not used for punishment and training. It is also helpful to make statements whenever there is no choice. "It is bedtime" as opposed to "Are you ready for bed?" The nurse can also provide anticipatory guidance for and listen to feelings of "I'm losing my baby" on the part of the nurturing person. Parents need a great deal of support during this stage of their child's life. The nurse should be aware of community resources available to parents and to make appropriate referrals.

Since the parenting figures continue to play such a primary role when the child is a preschooler, the nurse can help promote *mastery of initiative* by supporting the parenting efforts through providing information and referrals. When interacting with the child the nurse can promote initiative by answering the child's questions, being a moral and work role model, making sure that words and actions are congruent, setting reasonable limits, providing for vigorous activities, and making it clear that thoughts and wishes do not cause serious harm to others. Again, it is of great importance to avoid the use of shaming and guilt-inducing approaches when working with a child in this stage of development.

The nurse can support normal self-concept development of the school-age child and *mastery of the task of industry* by facilitating the child's adjustment to school, providing preventive health measures (for example, immunizations and vision and dental screenings); supporting parents to set firm, reasonable limits while providing opportunities to gain recognition; allowing the child to assume responsibility; and allowing adequate time with peers. The parents may also need support to be able to listen to the child expound on what the hero or heroine does and says. The parents may feel that their authority and influence over the child is being threatened by that "other" person.

The hospitalized child 6 to 12 years old needs to maintain as much control over bodily functions as possible, be able to make decisions, do some self-care, and maintain contact with peers.

To help the adolescent *master the task of identity* as it relates to the self-concept, the nurse can provide accurate information about how the body works (that is, health, nutrition, sexuality); provide a warm, nonjudgmental attitude; and set age-appropriate limits and model direct communication. The nurse shoud be aware that adolescents frequently set up situations that lead adults to argue and disagree. An adolescent young man may tell his mother, "Dad said I could buy a new suit." The mother may angrily ask the father why he said such a thing when the son has a new suit on layaway. Perhaps the father never made the statement. Perhaps he did not know about the suit on layaway. Depending on how the father responds, there may be a large family argument. The best way to avoid such pitfalls is to listen and reserve judgment until all the information can be obtained. Another approach when working with adolescents is the use of peer pressure. The young person is more likely to respond positively to a sanction given by peers than one given by parents.

The parents of adolescents need support during this stormy time. The nurse can provide nonjudgmental listening as well as information by way of support. At the community level, the nurse needs to be aware of various programs and activities available to adolescents and their families so that needed referrals can be made.

The two primary nursing approaches to facilitate *mastery of the tasks of intimacy for* the young adult are nonjudgmental listening and information sharing. The young adult needs accurate information on family planning, pregnancy, birthing, and parenting. The young adult also needs a nonjudgmental environment in which to ventilate frustrations and rewards of vocational, social, and family situations. Some people at this stage need assistance finding meaning in the choice to remain single and/or childless. Again, the nurse must be familiar with the community agencies that provide services for this age group and be able to make needed referrals.

Nursing actions that support meaningful family interactions, give accurate information about the aging process, and provide anticipatory guidance for dealing with losses of all kinds will facilitate *mastery of generativity* for the adult.

Finally, the nurse can assist the mature adult's *mastery of the developmental tasks of ego-integrity* by providing anticipatory guidance for dealing with retirement, the possible need to move from one's lifelong home, and decreasing physical abilities; supporting the person through the grief process (see Chapter 18 on loss for details); providing for the maintenance of the person's daily activities as much as possible; consulting with agencies to work with mature adults; and making appropriate community referrals.

Approaches that manage coping mechanisms, the sixth category of influencing factors, are problem solving and crisis intervention. Much has been written on both of these approaches. The nursing process is an example of the problem-solving approach. Refer to the References at the end of the chapter for other sources of information on these approaches. Briefly, once the person has identified past ways of coping with similar situations, the nurse helps the person see how to apply those ways of coping to the present situation or how to develop new ways of coping to meet the present need.

The discussion above briefly illustrates how the nurse can use various theories, principles, and approaches within the Roy Adaptation Model to bring about adaptation in the self-concept mode. The nurse using this model considers all of the first- and second-level assessment data and carries out approaches designed to alter the person's behavior by managing the influencing factors specific to that person. The nurse often uses a combination of approaches, managing several influencing factors to reach a specific goal. As you can see, interventions in the self-concept mode frequently involve working through and with family members, other hospital staff, and community agencies, as well as with the individual directly.

Evaluation

The final step of the nursing process is evaluation of the approaches to see if the goals were met and doing further planning and revision as needed. The nurse reassesses the behavior defined in the goal to see if it is present. If the behavior is present, the goal has been met and the nurse and the person receiving care can decide if a new goal should be set and the process continued. If the behavior is not present, the nurse reworks the entire process to discover what went wrong. The nurse asks the following questions. Was the goal realistic and acceptable to the person? Were the approaches carried out properly? Were the first- and second-level assessment data accurate and complete? Based on the answers to these questions, the nursing process is reworked.

SUMMARY

This chapter has defined and discussed the self-concept mode of the Roy Adaptation Model of nursing. The importance of the person's self-concept to maintaining a high level of health was pointed out. The organization of self-concept into components and categories of common influencing factors was presented. The social theories used as the basis for the development of self-concept were outlined. Self-concept development was discussed, and common nursing approaches were identified to promote mastery of each developmental crisis. Finally, the application of the nursing process to the self-concept mode was outlined.

STUDENT LEARNING ACTIVITIES

1. Read the case study.[6] List Mr. H.'s self-concept behaviors according to components. List and categorize the influencing factors for his behaviors. Mark each stimulus as (+) if it has a positive effect on his ability to adapt or as (−) if it has a negative effect on his

ability to adapt. Write diagnoses, goals, and interventions. An example analysis of this case is given in the Appendix.
2. Interview a well person to assess the self-concept mode. List the behaviors and influencing factors. Write diagnoses and goals.

Case Study

Mr. H. is 75 years old. He was born in Russia and came to the United States when he was 18 years old. He works as a waiter and must work 3 more months to be eligible for a pension. He lives alone in the small house where he and his wife lived until her death a year ago. They had been married for 52 years.

The following interview took place in Mr. H.'s home. SN stands for student nurse; H stands for Mr. H.

SN: Hello, Mr. H. I'm a student nurse at MSMC. I'd like to talk to you for a few minutes about your life, your thoughts, and your feelings about yourself.

H: OK. I can tell you I am very tired today. My feet are burning with arthritis. I worked until 9:00 last night.

SN: How do you usually feel after a night of work?

H: I'm usually tired these days. I'm starting to feel old. Especially since my wife died. It's just not the same coming home to an empty house.

SN: You're starting to feel your age more since her death?

H: Yes, I guess you could say so. I've always been strong and a hard worker. I thought we would live forever. Having arthritis also makes me feel old.

SN: Tell me more about what feeling old is like for you.

H: Oh, I guess it's realizing I've done most of what I'm going to do. I always wanted to get my high school diploma. Now it looks like I won't do it.

SN: How does that realization affect how you feel about yourself?

H: I really wanted a diploma. It's important to be educated in this country. I'm disappointed.

SN: What things are going well for you that make you feel good about yourself?

[6]The dialogue in this case study is stilted and overstructured for the purpose of providing particular data for analysis. The nurse recognizes that good interviewing techniques include following the person's cues and timing questions within the flow of the nurse–patient relationship.

H: I know I've lived my life well. I was very happy living here with my wife. I have many good memories. Now, I work day to day to get my pension.

SN: Looking at your life now, are there any things you would like to change?

H: I'd like to have young feet again so I could work without being in pain.

SN: Mr. H., you've talked about being a hardworking man all your life. Now you are dealing with the loss of your wife and pain in your feet. What beliefs do you have to help you deal with such things?

H: Oh, I believe in a just God. I'm Jewish. All my life I believed that if I did my best, God would be with me. I've lost many friends and family through the years. Somehow I keep on going.

SN: You've experienced many losses, but your belief in God has somehow helped you.

H: Yes, that's right.

SN: Thank you for sharing your time and thoughts. I've enjoyed hearing about your life.

REFERENCES

Coombs, Arthur, and Donald Syngg. *Individual Behavior—A Perceptual Approach to Behavior.* New York: Harper Brothers, 1959.

Driever, Marie J. "Theory of Self Concept," in Sister Callista Roy, *Introduction to Nursing: An Adaptation Model,* 1st ed. Englewood Cliffs, N.J.: Prentice-Hall, Inc., 1976.

Epstein, Seymour. "The Self-Concept Revisited or a Theory of a Theory," *American Psychologist,* vol. 28, no. 5, May 1973, pp. 404–416.

Erikson, Erik H. *Childhood and Society,* 2nd ed. New York: W. W. Norton & Company, Inc., 1963/London: Hogarth Press Ltd.

Gardner, Bruce D. *Development in Early Childhood.* New York: Harper & Row, Publishers, 1964.

Hall, Calvin S., and Gardner Lindzey. *Theories of Personality.* New York: John Wiley & Sons, Inc., 1970.

Havighurst, Robert J. *Developmental Tasks and Education.* New York: David McKay Company, Inc., 1952.

Huxley, Laura. Oral presentation made at the inaugural conference of Our Ultimate Investment, a non-profit organization for the nurturing of the possible human, Los Angeles, April 1978.

Jackins, Harvey. *The Human Side of Human Beings.* Seattle: Rational Island Publishers, 1974.

Lecky, Prescott. *Self-Consistency: A Theory of Personality*. New York: Doubleday & Company, Inc., 1969.

Luckmann, Joan, and Karen Creason Sorensen. *Medical–Surgical Nursing*. Philadelphia: W. B. Saunders Company, 1974.

Mead, George Herbert. *Mind, Self, and Society*. Chicago: University of Chicago Press, 1934.

Rubin, Reva. "Body Image and Self-Esteem," *Nursing Outlook*, June 1968, pp. 10–23.

Satir, Virginia. *Peoplemaking*. Palo Alto, Calif.: Science & Behavior Books, Inc., 1972.

Satir, Virginia. *Self Esteem*. Milbrae, California: Celestial Arts, 1975.

Sullivan, Harry Stack. *The Interpersonal Theory of Psychiatry*. New York: W. W. Norton & Company, Inc., 1953.

ADDITIONAL READINGS

Aguilera, Donna C., et al. *Crisis Intervention*. St. Louis: The C. V. Mosby Company, 1970.

Allerhand, Melvin E., et al. *Adaptation and Adaptability*. New York: Child Welfare League of America, Inc., 1961.

Fink, Stephen. "Crisis and Motivation: A Theoretical Model," *Archives of Physical Medicine and Rehabilitation*, November 1967, pp. 592–597.

Fitts, William, et al. *The Self Concept and Self Actualization*. Monograph III. Nashville, Tenn.: Dede Wallace Center, July 1971.

Freiberg, Selma H. *The Magic Years*. New York: Charles Scribner's Sons, 1959.

Fromm-Reichmann, Frieda. *Principles of Intensive Psychotherapy*. Chicago: University of Chicago Press, 1964.

Gould, Roger. "The Phases of Adult Life: A Study of Developmental Psychology," *American Journal of Psychiatry*, vol. 129, no. 5, November 1972, pp. 521–531.

Holderby, R. A., and Elizabeth McNulty. "Feelings...Feelings: How to Make a Rational Response to Emotional Behavior," *Nursing '79*, October, pp. 39–43.

Jungman, L. B. "When Your Feelings Get in the Way," *American Journal of Nursing*, no. 6, 1979, pp. 1074–1075.

May, Rollo. *Man's Search for Himself*. New York: The New American Library, Inc., 1953.

Norris, Catherine M. "The Professinal Nurse and Body Image," in *Behavioral Concepts and Nursing Intervention*, Carolyn Carlson, ed. Philadelphia: J. B. Lippincott Company, 1970, pp. 39–66.

Perez, Joseph F., and Alvin I. Cohen. *Mom and Dad Are Me*. Monterey, Calif.: Brooks/Cole Publishing Company, 1969.

Rogers, Carl R. *On Becoming a Person*. Boston: Houghton Mifflin Company, 1961.

Tiedt, Eileen. "The Adolescent in the Hospital: An Identity-Resolution Approach," *Nursing Forum*, vol. 40, no. 2, 1972, pp. 120–140.

Wu, Ruth. "Child Development: A Basis for Nursing Care," in *Current Concepts in Clinical Nursing*, vol. 1, Bergerson, Betty S., et al., eds. St. Louis: The C. V. Mosby Company, 1967, pp. 269–283.

Ziller, Robert, et al. "Self-Esteem: A Social Construct," *Journal of Consulting and Clinical Psychology*, vol. 33, no. 1, 1969, pp. 84–95.

Chapter 15

Role Function: Theory and Development

Kathleen Anschutz Nuwayhid *

BEHAVIORAL OBJECTIVES

After studying this chapter, the reader will be able to:

1. Define the key concepts of the chapter.
2. State the rationale for assessing the role function mode.
3. Explain the significance of the partitions in the assessment of the role function mode.
4. Identify three approaches for data collection in the role function mode.
5. Identify primary, secondary, and tertiary roles for a given person.
6. Perform a first- and second-level assessment of the role function mode for a client.
7. Apply the nursing process to the role function mode for a given situation.
8. Label behaviors in the role function mode as either adaptive or ineffective.
9. List stimuli other than the partitions that influence role performance.
10. Describe the nursing diagnosis of role mastery and give examples of role mastery from everyday life situations.

*This chapter is a revision of the chapter "Theory of Role Function," pp. 245–255, by Nancy Malaznik, and the chapter "Development of Role Function," pp. 256–264, by Brooke Randell, in the first edition.

KEY CONCEPTS DEFINED:

Role: the functioning unit of our society: it is a defined set of expectations about how the person occupying one position behaves toward a person occupying another position. Thus it is a special kind of norm: a shared rule about behavior.

Position: the place in society that a person occupies for the tasks or behaviors of a role to be performed.

Role performance: defines the actions taken in relation to expected behaviors of a particular role.

Role Mastery: indicates that a person demonstrates both expressive and instrumental behaviors that meet social expectations associated with the assigned roles.

Social Integrity: the basic need of the role function mode: it means that one needs to know who one is in relation to others so that one can act.

Primary Role: an ascribed role based on age, sex, and developmental stage. It determines the majority of behaviors engaged in by a person during a particular growth period of life.

Secondary Role: a role that a person assumes to complete the tasks associated with a developmental stage and primary role. There are usually several secondary roles that influence a person's life and behavior in a variety of social settings. Secondary roles are achieved positions usually requiring specific role performance rather than qualities.

Tertiary Role: a role that is freely chosen by a person, temporary in nature, and often associated with the accomplishment of a minor task in a person's current development.

Instrumental Behavior: the actual physical performance of a behavior to achieve the goal of role mastery. Long-term goal-oriented behavior.

Expressive Behavior: the feelings, attitudes, likes, or dislikes that a person has about a role or about the performance of a role. Short-term goal-oriented behavior.

This chapter presents the role function mode. The theoretical basis for the role function mode comes from a variety of theories in social psychology. The works of Banton, Parsons and Shils, and selected others are used as the basis of this description of the role function mode. The purpose of this chapter is to present these theories and to describe their contribution to an understanding of the role function adaptive mode. The nursing process is applied as specified by the Roy Adaptation Model. The role theories discussed are used to identify content relevant to the nursing process. The focus of this chapter is on adaptive role development, adaptive role behaviors, role assessment, and the nursing diagnosis of role mastery.

RELEVANCE OF THE ROLE FUNCTION MODE

The rationale for assessing role function lies in the Roy Adaptation Model's beliefs about the person as an integrated whole. Because of this belief, complex relationships among the biological, psychological, and social aspects are recognized. A person continually strives to achieve integrity in all aspects of his or her life. A disturbance or disruption in one adaptive mode often affects the other adaptive modes. Nursing's goal, according to the Roy Adaptation Model, is to promote a person's adaptation in health and in illness. Roles that people hold are a part of one's life in health or illness. Therefore, knowledge of role theory and the ability to assess role performance are essential to the practice of nursing.

A person needs to know who he or she is in relation to others and what the expectations of society are for the positions that are held so that one can act appropriately. The person must also know the roles that the others in the environment occupy if one wants to know and interact with other persons. These are the needs of the role mode. The function of the role mode is to meet these needs as optimally as possible. The goal of the role mode is social integrity. A person does not act as an isolated unit in society. The person constantly interacts with others in the environment in meeting the needs and goals of the role mode. However, changing circumstances of life or in society and the environment may require that the person: (1) take on a temporary role such as the sick role, or role of a student; (2) acquire a new and sometimes permanent role, such as mother, breadwinner, or diabetic patient; or (3) alter an existing role that one already occupies such as wife or employee. Disruptions in the role function mode may lead to role failure and have adverse effects on one or all three of the other modes.

ROLE THEORIES

In the study of the role function mode, the term of major significance is *role*. Goffman (1961, p. 85) describes role as consisting of "the activity the encumbent would engage in if he (she) were to act solely in terms of the normative demands upon someone in this position." *Position*, as described by Parsons and Shils (1951), is the smallest element of society organized to reach certain goals—specifically, it is the individual's title. In the role function mode we have combined the definition of Goffman and Parsons so that the term *role* will be used to mean the title given to the individual—mother, son, student, teacher—as well as the behaviors that society expects an individual to perform in order to maintain the title.

Role performance, then, is the collection of behaviors observed when an individual with a particular title undertakes those actions that society attributes to a person with that title. Roles are the functional units of society, and by our description, the functional unit of the role function mode.

Assumptions

Turner (1966, p. 151) states that "the first essential characteristic of the ideal framework that guides the role-taking process is the view that every role is a way of relating to other roles in a situation." This point of view gives rise to the two basic assumptions on which roles operate. They are:

1. Roles exist only in relationship to each other.
2. Roles are filled by individuals.

Very simply, the first assumption states that to fill a role an individual is dependent on a complementary role (in order to be a student, there must be a teacher), and the second says that to occupy a role, an individual must exist (the individual must have a self-perception as an individual so as to achieve role mastery). For example, if Mary Smith has a perception of herself as a pleasant, bright person, she will be able to choose appropriate role behaviors when confronted with the complementary role of a teacher, and she will achieve *role mastery*. However, if Mary has an uncertain perception of herself as indicated by behaviors that reflect ambivalence about herself or her intelligence and/or her value to others, she will have difficulty achieving role mastery. In that case, Mary will probably demonstrate a role problem. Stated simply, then, Mary must have a self-concept compatible with the role, and her environment must provide her with a person occupying a complementary role.

These two assumptions provide our formulation of the basic need underlying the role function mode. That need is the need for *social integrity*: one needs to know who one is in relation to others so that one can act.

Identification of Role

In order to be able to identify and then assess the possible roles that a person may occupy at a particular moment in time, we rely upon the work of three theorists, Banton (1965) and Parsons and Shils (1951).

A classification system based on work by Banton divides roles into primary, secondary, and tertiary headings and explains their relation as analogous to a tree with trunk and branches. Generally, Banton's system appears to be based on developmental theory and therefore allows us to draw relationships between self-concept and role function modes of adaptation.

Banton defines a basic role which we call *primary* as one that determines most of the way of life assumed by the person. His example of a basic role may be a married woman. The general or *secondary* role is a branch of the basic and is defined as a role that influences the individual's behavior in a variety of social settings. General roles might include such things as boy's mother and/or minister's wife. Independent roles or *tertiary* roles are frequently related to general roles. They are defined as roles that are freely chosen and have little or only temporary influence on other roles. These might include such roles as golf club member or PTA president.

For the adaptation approach to Banton's role tree, we have made some minor alterations in applied definitions. Using one of our basic premises—that an individual must exist in order to occupy a role—we have pulled from the self-concept mode a means of identifying an individual's primary role. As we know from Chapter 14, the self-concept mode gives an indication of the person's perception of self, and this perception is in part based on the person's success and/or failure in completing the developmental tasks as defined by Erikson. Therefore, we have chosen to equate developmental stages with the concept of primary role. For example, Elaine T. is a 25-year-old, married woman and the mother of two children; Banton would identify Elaine's primary role as married woman. The role mode would identify Elaine's primary role as that of a 25-year-old young adult female. It is important to include chronological age when stating the primary role because it enables us to expect more specific role behaviors in relationship to the developmental stage and will assist the assessment portion of the nursing process later. Other primary roles might include: 15-year-old adolescent female, 35-year-old generative adult male, 65-year-old mature female, or 6-year-old school-age female. Returning to Banton's definition and our basic premise, the primary role is an ascribed role based on age, sex, and developmental stage. It determines the majority of behaviors engaged in by a person during a particular growth period of life (Malaznik, 1976).

If primary roles are determined by age, sex, and developmental stage, then secondary roles become those roles which accomplish the goals of each developmental stage. The developmental tasks of the young adult are to separate one's self from family and to establish a family of one's own, and to take on adult roles. Possible secondary roles of the young adult primary role would be wife, mother, an occupation or profession, coworker, or peer. A person usually assumes many secondary roles which influence one's life and behavior in a variety of social settings. Secondary roles are achieved positions usually requiring specific role performance rather than qualities. Secondary roles also imply a sense of stability in that they develop and are mastered over time and are not easily relinquished.

Tertiary roles are usually temporary in nature. They are related primarily to a person's secondary roles, but may be related to the primary role as well. These roles represent ways in which individuals choose to meet their obligations associated with the primary and secondary roles (Malaznik, 1976). These roles might include hobbies or club or civic activities. An individual occupying a primary role of adolescent male might have the tertiary role of football player associated with his secondary role of student. A generative adult female (primary role) might have a tertiary role of PTA president associated with her secondary role of mother, and a tertiary role of women's rights activist associated with her primary role. By definition, then, a tertiary role is a role that is freely chosen by a person, temporary in nature, and usually associated with the accomplishment of some minor task in a person's current development.

It is important to keep in mind that our definition of the three types of roles occupied by individuals during their lives need to be altered to take into account certain special circumstances of role changes. An example of this is the sick role. Sick role, because of its usually temporary nature, is labeled a tertiary role. By definition, tertiary roles are chosen, yet few people have an actual choice as to whether to be sick or well. Instead, the person has the choice to adopt the sick role, perform adaptive sick-role behaviors, and become well, or to deny illness. However, when an illness becomes chronic, the sick role moves into the position of a secondary role.

Identification of Role Behaviors

Now that we know how to identify the three types of roles, it is important to be able to identify the appropriate behaviors associated with each respective role. The work of Parsons and Shils facilitates the process of behavioral identification. In their discussion of the content of roles, these theorists describe three sets of problems: (1) instrumental interaction, (2) expressive interaction, and (3) integrative problems (1951, p. 209). In early theoretical work on the role function mode, it was found useful to label role performance as having instrumental and expressive components. These components are not enacted in a mutually exclusive manner, but can be described independently for classification and evaluation. Each of the three types of roles has both an expressive and an instrumental component.

Instrumental behaviors are those performed to accomplish a certain goal. Since immediate gratification is not the focus, these behaviors tend to have a long-term orientation and often require disciplined activity. They are usually physical actions performed by the individual or the person's description of the activities engaged in during performance of the role.

Expressive role performance is similar to the instrumental component, but the goal is for direct or immediate feedback. The behaviors are emotional in nature rather than physical, action-oriented behaviors. They include the feelings, attitudes, likes, or dislikes that a person has about a role or about the performance of a role. These behaviors result from interactions that permit the person to express feelings related to role performance in appropriate ways.

For both the expressive and instrumental role content, Parsons and Shils (1951, p. 210) describe categories of requirements within the social structure for the person's enactment of the role. For example, they note that given the division of labor, other persons must be the beneficiaries of the person's goal-directed behavior. Similarly, one needs to find responsive social objects for expressive role behavior.

The role performance requirements outlined by Parsons and Shils have been condensed for use with the Roy Adaptation Model into four partitions that affect both instrumental and expressive role behavior. These partitions are as follows:

1. Consumer
2. Reward
3. Access to facilities or set of circumstances
4. Cooperation/collaboration

These four role partitions are viewed as major stimuli for role behavior. Identifying the presence or absence of these stimuli enables the nurse to identify expected behaviors for a particular role. By way of example, let us look at the secondary role of nurse using the partitions as a framework for analysis. If asked to describe the instrumental behaviors that a nurse might perform, possible expected behaviors would be seeking employment as a nurse, going to work in a health care setting, giving nursing care to people, and working with other health care professionals. Yet it is difficult, if not impossible, to perform instrumental nursing role behaviors unless there is a consumer of nursing care, that is, a person or groups of people. The reward that the nurse receives is that persons achieve a higher level of wellness because of the nurse's work, and she also receives a salary for her time and services. Any action-oriented behavior that enables the nurse to maintain a nurse–patient relationship would also be considered an instrumental behavior.

When a nurse uses a thermometer to take a temperature or attends continuing education courses to increase her knowledge of a particular condition, she is demonstrating instrumental behaviors that indicate that she has access to facilities. Other examples might be a public health nurse utilizing transportation to reach patients, a clinical specialist teaching a newly diagnosed diabetic patient how to prepare and inject insulin, or a staff nurse reading a procedure manual to validate her knowledge of a particular procedure.

Cooperation or collaboration would be the degree to which the nurse is free or allowed to perform her role behaviors. For example, a nurse may be a mother or a father with young children at home who needs the cooperation of a babysitter to watch the children while he or she is working. The nurse may also need the cooperation of an employer who schedules work times that make it easier for the nurse to go to work.

By partitioning the instrumental behaviors into categories of the stimuli that affect them, we are better able to identify all possible instrumental behaviors. In this way, the nurse performs a more complete and thorough assessment of primary, secondary, and tertiary roles. If a significant number of instrumental behaviors are identified during the assessment process, the nursing diagnoses that are formulated and the interventions that are undertaken will be more effective because they are based on accurate and sufficient data.

Similarly, the significance of the expressive partition is that one can more clearly define categories of expected behaviors for the expressive component of a role. In our example of the nurse, she needs an appropriate and receptive person to relate to for immediate feedback. Her behavior would be directed at maintaining this relationship. This would be appropriate expressive role behavior related to a consumer. For example, a nurse joining with her peers to discuss staffing problems on her unit with her supervisor, or asking her supervisor for a conference to discuss job dissatisfaction, would be appropriate expressive role behaviors.

When the nurse asks questions of her peers or supervisor about her role performance, she elicits feedback. At the same time she is establishing a network that will provide for feedback on her role performance in the future. This in turn will lead to other sources of gratification. All of these behaviors serve to meet the gratification needs of the self involved in role performance. These needs include satisfaction, power, prestige, love, affection, reward, and similar types of feelings. These behaviors relate again to the rewards in the environment. We can see how the expressive role behavior needs and expressive role performance are closely related in the self-concept mode and the interdependence mode. We can also see how a disruption in the role function mode would have the potential for disrupting the other two modes as well.

The third partition refers to access to facilities or a set of circumstances; that is, one must feel that one has what one needs to accomplish the task at hand. Finally, the listing of cooperation and collaboration indicates that expressive role performance presupposes a generally positive emotional tone and belief in the mutuality of the system where one carries out the role. In performing her role within a hospital setting, the nurse needs to feel that this place provides both the circumstances and the climate she needs to fulfill her role as a nurse.

Table 15.1 summarizes some of the theoretical understandings of role development. This table is meant to be a short form of reference and in no way replaces study in greater depth of theories on the development of roles. However, it can be a useful tool for the nurse when carrying out the assessment phase of the nursing process in the role function mode.

TABLE 15.1
Summary of Theoretical Basis of Role Development

Age	Develop- mental Stage	Focus of Tasks or Crises	Adaptive Outcome
0-1½ yrs	Infant: Trust vs. Mistrust	To develop confidence in having needs met To feel physically safe	Optimism about world
1½-3½ years	Toddler: Autonomy vs. Shame	When needs are consistent- ly met, anticipation of satisfaction occurs "I am what I imagine I can be." Fantasy play precedes each effort	Autonomy
3½-6 yrs	Preschool: Initiative vs. Guilt	"I am what I do."	Initiative
6-11 years	School age: Industry vs. Inferiority	Skills and values expand to include those of the school and neighborhood	Industry
11-18 years	Adolescence Identify vs. Role con- fusion	To know "who I am" Values become those of the peer group and of leaders To develop the ability to love in terms of intimacy Values are those of fideli- ty, friendship and cooperation Sexual behavior and com- petition approach the adult type	Identity
18-35 years	Young Adult Intimacy vs. Isolation	Establishment as indepen- dent individual Building a strong, mutual affectional bond with (possible) marriage part- ner and family of spouse To be able to nurture, sup- port and provide for spouse and off-spring	Intimacy

Ineffective Outcome	Social Goal	Social Process
Pessimism about world	Social development of the individual	Society contributes to the individual
Shame Doubt Sense of uselessness	Social development of the individual	Society contributes to the individual
Guilt	Social development of the individual	Society contributes to the individual
Inferiority	Social development of the individual	Individual begins to contribute to society
Identity diffusion	Social development of the individual	Individual relates to society through peer groups
Alienation		
Isolation	Social development of the individual	Individual becomes an independent member of society and begins to contribute toward the continuance of society by starting a new family

TABLE 15.1 *Continued*
Summary of Theoretical Basis of Role Development

Age	Developmental Stage	Focus of Tasks or Crises	Adaptive Outcome
35-60 years	Generative Adult Generativity vs. Stagnation	Learning to be interdependent with others other than spouse, leaning on another person as well as to succor in time of need and developing leisure-time activities Maintaining a strong and mutually satisfying marriage relationship Assisting in the establishment and guidance of the next generation Meeting the new needs of affection of one's own aging parents and parents of spouse	Generativity
60 years and on	Mature Adult Ego integrity vs. Despair	Accepting the help needed from others as dependency needs increase Facing loss of spouse and developing sources to meet affectional needs. Learning new roles with one's own children and grandchildren as their roles change Finding or preserving satisfying relationships outside of the family	Ego integrity

ASSESSMENT OF ROLE FUNCTION

There are certain demographic data that are pertinent to all four of the adaptive modes. Factors such as age, sex, culture, and others should be identified before attempting to use the nursing process as specified by the Roy Adaptation Model. This information may be obtained from the person, the family, friends, or a hospital chart or records of some kind. Role data are gathered in much the same fashion, with the exception that some of the information, especially expressive role behaviors, must come from the person himself or herself.

Ineffective Outcome	Social Goal	Social Process
Stagnation	Implementing and maintaining norms of society	Individual becomes involved with the survival of society through own efforts and the guidance of the next generation
Despair	Maintaining society	Individual becomes able to incorporate becoming a follower, again, sometimes in the sense of being a consultant, as well as to continue to lead

In first-level assessment, determine the person's primary role by identifying age, sex, and developmental stage as noted in Table 15.1. Using the same chart, project in your own mind some of the secondary and tertiary roles that this individual may occupy. For example, if your client is a 25-year-old female, her developmental stage is young adult. You would expect her to occupy roles that would help her achieve her goal of intimacy. These might include a student, a professional, a spouse, a mother, a nonprofessional tennis player, a good friend, or a book club member.

Except for the infant and toddler, most persons will be able to give information concerning their various roles. Generally, the more mature and educated the individual is, the greater the depth of information he or she can give. Ask the person what he or she does during the week. Ask which things take more of the person's time. Which things are more important to the person? This will enable you to formulate a hierarchy of roles in their importance to the person. Once you have identified as many of the individual's roles as you can, rank them in order of their importance to the person based on the information given.

For each primary, secondary, and tertiary role, ask the person such questions as, "What do you do for this job (role or task)?" This will define the instrumental behaviors. Then ask, "What feelings do you get while performing this job?" This will identify the expressive behaviors. Other information about behaviors is noted when examining the role partitions; for example:

1. Instrumental behaviors
   (a) Consumer: "Who or what benefits when you perform this job?"
   (b) Rewards: "What rewards do you get from this job/role?"
   (c) Access to facilities: "What things do you need to perform your job?"
   (d) Cooperation: "With whom do you work in this job, or who helps you with these responsibilities?"

Questions about expressive behaviors would be similar in their approach. When you have identified all of the person's roles with their instrumental and expressive behaviors, you will have begun the nursing process and be halfway through the first-level assessment in the role function mode. The remainder of the first-level assessment of role function is the direct observation of behaviors related to the roles that have been identified.

As noted earlier, the partitions of instrumental and expressive role components are used for second-level assessment as well as for identifying the role behaviors. For each role, the nurse determines one set of partitions: that is, the consumer, rewards, access to facilities, and cooperation for that role. An example might be that the salary offered by the job is a major factor or stimulus influencing the instrumental role behavior. In second-level assessment, then, the partitions are examined again for the identification of focal, contextual, and residual stimuli. Often it is the absence of a necessary contributor to role performance, that is, the partition, that is responsible for ineffective role performance.

In addition to the four partitions for both instrumental and expressive components of role, second-level assessment includes other factors influencing role behaviors. Additional major influencing stimuli have been identified and are assessed in the given situation. These include:

1. *Social norms.* Society determines the standards of behavior or prescription for a role. These standards are usually general for society as a whole, but they become very specific at the cultural level. Role prescriptions may vary greatly from culture to culture. For example, mothering behaviors for a mother in West Africa may differ greatly from the mothering behaviors of a mother in India.

2. *The physical makeup of the individual and/or the chronological age.* It is very difficult to be a jockey for racing horses if you are 6 feet, 4 inches tall and weigh 250 pounds, or if you are 82 years old.

3. *The individual's self-concept.* See Chapter 14.

4. *The number, quality, and responses of the role models to the individual.* Role models can be ideals to live up to or they can be the cause of ineffective role behaviors.

5. *The individual's knowledge of the expected role performance behaviors.*

6. *The individual's ability or capacity to fill the role* as influenced by emotional makeup and well-being.

7. *Role performance of other roles occupied by the individual.* For example, a mother cannot go to work and perform her secondary role of secretary because she has a sick child at home and must perform mother-role behaviors.

Based on the assessment of role behaviors and stimuli, the nurse makes a nursing diagnosis and plans care related to the social integrity of the person. To illustrate the nursing assessment and the remaining steps of the nursing process, we will use a specific case study.

Use of the Nursing Process in the Role Function Mode: A Case Study

The following case study is about a fictitious person named Susan A. Susan is the only informant in the case study, but in actual practice, data can be gathered not only from the person, but also from significant others as well. This approach would broaden the person's perceptions of events and situations, thus increasing the validity of the data. For demonstration purposes we will identify all of Susan's roles, the first-level assessment, and then carry out a complete second-level assessment on her role of teacher, utilizing the nursing process.

Case Study.   My name is Susan A. I am 30 years old. I have been married 8 years to a terrific man named Dale. I have two children, Anthony, age 7, and Maria, age 5. Probably the most important part of my life right now is my family. I love my job as a teacher, but my family is really important to me. I enjoy being a wife and mother and doing things for my family.

I work full time, and sometimes it's tough taking care of the kids and working. Both kids are in school now and I have found a very responsible older woman to take care of them after school. She picks them up and takes care of them until I get home. My husband, Dale, takes the kids to school in the morning. He is very helpful and shares the household chores with me. He is very supportive of my working.

In my job I do the usual things that any high school teacher does. I lecture, counsel students, give tests, grade papers, and so forth. Most of all, I enjoy watching my students learn and seeing them grow as individuals.

Last year I went back to school and earned an M.A. in education so that I might be more effective as a teacher. I certainly wouldn't try to kid you; it also increased my salary. Having the advanced degree has also helped to give me job security. The increase in salary gives us some extra money to spend on the kids and the house.

The school where I teach is private and well funded. We have a beautiful language lab and an excellent library. My fellow teachers are easy people to work with. We share teaching problems and try to help each other. Our principal has instituted weekly teacher forums to vent feelings and share ideas. It has helped the faculty to grow as a group. My best friend teaches in another department at school and she is a tremendous sounding board. When it is all said and done though, I have Dale to go home to. I try to support him emotionally and he does the same for me.

My evaluations at school are good. Last year when I went back to college, my principal was very cooperative in helping me with my teaching responsibilities until I finished my course work.

Please don't misunderstand the things that I am telling you. Our life is not perfect—we have arguments, the kids fight with each other, and sometimes our house is dirty. However, I feel that when it comes to the important things in life, Dale and I are in agreement.

We are both of Italian descent and are Catholic. We both love and want our kids to have the extended families that we had. Our families both live in town and we see our parents at least once a week, usually on Sundays. Dale has two brothers and I have one brother and two sisters. They are all married. It's quite an event when we all go home to visit "Mama." Our families get along well together, and that helps tremendously.

I do have a little spare time. Dale and I each have one night a week when we go and do something for ourselves. Dale enjoys music, so he's taking an extension course at the university. I am an avid camera bug and I have a darkroom set up in the house. Right now I am taking a course in developing color negatives, and I love it.

Once a week after school I volunteer at the local community center in a remedial reading program for elementary school children. I also knit, and once a month I am an assistant leader for Anthony's cub scout group.

I feel that I am a good wife and mother. My husband tells me how proud he is of me and the children. Both of my parents quit school after the eighth grade, so they are very proud of my college education and profession. My mother, a confirmed homemaker, was upset at first because she didn't think I could be a wife, mother, and a full-time teacher. She has changed her opinion now, and admits that we are doing well. She also acknowledges the fact that Dale is a very supportive husband.

Adaptation Nursing Process Care Plan of Susan A.   Based on the information that Susan has given us and the chart for identification of primary role, we determine Susan's primary role to be:

1. 30 years old
2. Female
3. Young adult developmental stage

Susan has identified her secondary and tertiary roles very clearly for us. She has even given us clues as to the importance that she affords each role. This enables us to determine her secondary roles and to identify them in an order of importance based on her perceptions. Because our data are not complete, the ranking is not absolute. Susan herself would have to rank them for us in order for them to be complete. Her secondary roles include:

1. Wife
2. Mother
3. Teacher
4. Daughter
5. Sister
6. Friend
7. Peer

The purpose for determining the importance of roles is that it will enhance the formulation of a nursing diagnosis in the event that a disruption is identified, or indicate the potential for a disruption to occur between two roles. For example, there may come a time when Susan may have to choose between her role as mother and her role as a wife, or between her roles as wife and as teacher.

Tertiary roles are usually less important and do not compete with secondary roles. The one exception to this would be the sick role. Susan's tertiary roles include:

1. Camera bug
2. Volunteer
3. Assistant cub scout leader

For the purpose of demonstration we have taken the secondary role of teacher and will continue on to the second-level assessment. However, all the roles that we have identified could be assessed in the same manner. The partitions for instrumental role behaviors and for expressive role behaviors tell us what a person needs to have present in the environment in order to achieve role mastery. These are the initial contextual stimuli that the nurse should identify in the assessment process. Role mastery cannot be achieved without the presence of these stimuli.

Although role mastery cannot be achieved without the presence of the partitions, the presence of all of the partitions does not ensure a diagnosis of role mastery. There are at least seven other major influencing factors or stimuli that are to be assessed after completing the role partitions. These were described earlier. Based on the data gathered from Susan, the following is a first- and second-level assessment of Susan's secondary role of teacher.

As you read the adaptation nursing process care plan outlined in Table 15.2, there are several key points to keep in mind:

1. As behaviors are recorded a decision is made as to whether the behavior is adaptive or ineffective. You will notice that the symbols (A/I) follow the instrumental behaviors. This means that the behavior is adaptive, that is, behavior that maintains the social integrity of the individual, and that it is an instrumental behavior. Ineffective behavior would be labeled (I/I), ineffective/instrumental behavior. Expressive behaviors or labels similarly.
2. The focal stimulus identified is general in order to show the relationship between theory and the taking on of roles. In actual practice a more specific focal stimulus is desired.
3. The goals stated in the assessment are assumed to be mutual goals agreed upon by the nurse and the person. All goals for care will be mutual goals.
4. There is a time limit generally given for completing a goal. However, because this diagnosis is role mastery, a stated limited time frame is not appropriate.
5. The concept of a secondary role implies retention of the role by the individual over time. Evaluation of nursing interventions and modification of these interventions occurs over time, perhaps even as long a period as one year. There are today an increasing number of settings where nurses work with the same persons over longer periods of time or on a recurring basis. It is therefore more possible to make a contribution to these persons' overall role mastery and thus social integrity.

SUMMARY

In this chapter various theories related to role have been presented to establish a theoretical basis for the role function mode. Methods of identifying roles and adaptive role behaviors were explored. The partitions, or major contextual stimuli affecting role performance, have been discussed, compared, and contrasted. Their significance for role performance was examined. Other influencing factors, or stimuli, also to be identified when assessing role behaviors have been identified and examples given. A case study was presented which applies the theory presented by using the nursing process as specified by the Roy Adaptation Model. Complete first- and second-level assessments utilizing the case study were carried out. The case study was structured so that the diagnosis for the role behaviors would be role mastery. A developmental approach to roles correlated the relationship between the mastery of secondary and tertiary roles and the completion of developmental tasks for a particular stage. The achievement of the developmental tasks in a particular stage meets the need of the role function mode—social integrity.

STUDENT LEARNING ACTIVITIES

1. Identify primary roles utilizing Table 15.1.
   a. Yourself
   b. A close friend
   c. Your mother and father
   d. One of your teachers
   e. One of your siblings, if you have one
   f. A person with whom you are in frequent contact
2. Utilizing Table 15.1, perform a complete assessment of your student role. The case study of Susan A. should serve as a helpful guide.
3. Utilizing the case study about Susan A., complete the second-level assessment of her wife role, mother role, and/or daughter role.
4. Outline a role tree for a good friend. Outline first- and second-level assessments for the secondary role of one of your friends. Has your friend achieved role mastery?

REFERENCES

Banton, Michael. *Roles: An Introduction of the Study of Social Relations.* New York: Basic Books, Inc., Publishers, 1965.

TABLE 15.2
Role Mastery Adaptation Nursing Process Care Plan

Secondary Role	Behaviors	Focal	Contextual	Residual
			Stimuli	
Teacher		Developmental task of becoming an individual and being able to support and nurture self and offspring (validated by Erikson's theory of developmental stages).		
		The individual has a choice: we will not all be teachers. We can choose other appropriate professions or other secondary roles to meet these tasks.		
		A more specific focal stimulus might be the person's desire to be a teacher, but the focal stimulus behind this desire would be the achievement of the developmental tasks of the young adult.		
	Instrumental Teaches high school. Lectures, counsels, gives tests. (A/I) Makes a good salary. (A/I) Earned advanced degree and increased salary. (A/I)	In general, as above, but specific stimuli may be identified for each particular behavior.	Consumer – students Reward – good salary, satisfaction	Health, intelligence Role models (once validated, these stimuli could become contextual stimuli for role behaviors)

Teaches in a well-funded, private school. (A/I)

Utilizes library and language laboratory when teaching. (A/I)

Teaches full time. (A/I)

Expressive

"My principal was very cooperative in helping me with my teaching responsibilities while I finished my course work." (A/E)

"I love teaching." "My husband is proud of me." "My parents are proud of me." "My personal evaluations at school are good." (A/E)

"Our principal has instituted weekly teacher forums to vent feelings." (A/E)

"My fellow teachers are easy to work with." "We share teaching problems and try to help each other." "My best friend teaches . . . is tremendous sounding board." "I have Dale to go home to." (A/E)

Access to facilities — school, library, and language lab

Cooperation or collaboration — husband helps with housework, takes children to school; babysitter cares for children after school.

Consumer — principal.

Reward — personal satisfaction, praise of significant others.

Appropriate circumstances — access to principal in an appropriate setting.

Cooperation or collaboration — other teachers, good friend, and husband.

Religion

Culture

(Although we know that Susan is of Italian descent, and Catholic, we do not know what effect these facts have had on Susan. We need more data for these to become contextual stimuli.)

TABLE 15.2 *Continued*
Role Mastery Adaptation Nursing Process Care Plan

Behaviors	Contextual Stimuli	Nursing Diagnosis	Goals	Interventions
"My mother was upset about my working at first." "Now she admits I am doing well." (A/E)	Other: Mother's perception of Susan's role as a teacher	(Includes all instrumental and expressive behaviors)	Client will continue to exhibit role mastery behaviors in her teacher role.	1. Nurse will discuss potential conflicts that might arise between the client's other roles.
"Probably the most important part of my life right now is my family." "I love my job as a teacher, but my family is really important to me." (A/E)	Susan's performance of the role of mother	Role mastery, teacher role, as evidenced by the presence of all partitions for instrumental and expressive role behaviors.	Client will continue to have positive relationships with others in her role as teacher.	2. Nurse and client will identify potential areas in which conflict might occur. 3. Nurse will assess the client's present coping styles. 4. Nurse will give anticipatory guidance regarding the resolution of potential conflicts. 5. Based upon client's present coping mechanisms, nurse will teach appropriate mechanisms if needed. 6. Nurse will reassess the client's role function mode at 1 year intervals or if client identifies a problem.

304

Goffman, Erving. *Encounters*. Indianapolis: The Bobbs-Merrill Company, Inc., 1961.

Hardy, Margaret E., and Mary E. Conway. *Role Theory: Perspectives for Health Professionals*. New York: Appleton-Century-Crofts, 1978.

Malaznik, Nancy. "Theory of Role Function," in Sister Callista Roy, *Introduction to Nursing: An Adaptation Model*. Englewood Cliffs, N.J.: Prentice-Hall, Inc., 1976, pp. 245–255.

Parsons, Talcott, and Edward Shils, eds. *Toward a General Theory of Action*. Cambridge, Mass.: Harvard University Press, 1951.

Roy, Sister Callista, and Sharon L. Roberts. *Theory Construction in Nursing: An Adaptation Model*. Englewood Cliffs, N.J.: Prentice-Hall, Inc., 1981.

Turner, Ralph H. "Role-Taking, Role Standpoint and Reference Group Behavior," in *Role Theory: Concepts and Research*, Bruce Biddle and Edwin Thomas, eds. New York: John Wiley & Sons, Inc., 1966.

Wu, Ruth. *Behavior and Illness*. Scientific Foundations of Nursing Practice Series. Englewood Cliffs, N.J.: Prentice-Hall, Inc., 1973.

ADDITIONAL READINGS

Gross, Neal, Alexander McEachern, and Ward Mason. "Role Conflict and Its Resolution," in *Role Theory: Concepts and Research*, Bruce Biddle and Edwin Thomas, eds. New York: John Wiley & Sons, Inc., 1966.

Parsons, Talcott. *The Social System*. New York: The Free Press, 1964.

Parsons, Talcott. "Role Conflict and the Genesis of Deviance," in *Role Theory: Concepts and Research*, Bruce Biddle and Edwin Thomas, eds. New York: John Wiley & Sons, Inc., 1966.

Robischon, Paulette, and Diane Scott. "Role Theory and Its Application to Family Nursing," *Nursing Outlook*, July 1969, pp. 52–57.

Ruddock, Ralph. *Roles and Relationships*. Altantic Highlands, N.J.: Humanities Press, Inc., 1969.

Winton, Ralph. *The Study of Man*. New York: Appleton-Century-Crofts, 1936.

Chapter 16

Interdependence: Theory and Development

Mary Poush Tedrow *

BEHAVIORAL OBJECTIVES

After studying this chapter, the reader will be able to:

1. Define the key concepts of the chapter.
2. Describe an example of the stages of developing a nurturing relationship.
3. List five stimuli that are associated with developing interdependence behaviors.
4. Apply the nursing process in the interdependence adaptive mode to a written case study or clinical situation.

KEY CONCEPTS DEFINED

Interdependence: the close relationships of people that involve the willingness and ability to love, respect, and value others, and to accept and respond to love, respect, and value given by others.

*The interdependence mode has evolved in a way unlike the other adaptive modes. Initially, in the early 1970s, the interdependence mode was described and operationalized with dependent and independent behaviors. By 1975, theoretical and clinical application of the content revealed that there was redundancy of this content in the self-concept and role modes. Joyce Van Landingham, Dorothy Clough, and Mary Tedrow worked to clarify the interdependence mode. Further empirical findings led to a major revision of the mode in 1977 by Joyce Van Landingham, Mary Hicks, and Mary Tedrow. This revision was further developed in teaching and practice by the author. She acknowledges the clarifications by Brooke Randell.

Affectional Adequacy: the feeling of security in nurturing relationships with others. Basic need of the interdependence mode.

Nurturing: providing growth-producing care and attention.

Significant Other: the individual to whom the most meaning or importance is given. It is a person who is loved, respected, and valued, and who in turn loves, respects, and values the other to a degree greater than in all other relationships.

Support Systems: all persons, groups, or animals that contribute to meeting the interdependence needs of the person.

Receptive Behaviors: the person's receiving, taking in, or assimilating nurturing behaviors from the significant other or support systems.

Contributive Behaviors: giving or supplying nurturing as initiated by the person toward the significant other and/or support systems.

The final adaptive mode to be introduced is the interdependence mode. This mode, like the role function mode, involves interaction with others. The relationships of this mode, however, involve closer relationships than those implied in roles or positions in society. The interdependence mode is the one in which affectional needs are met. Each person strives for adequacy. In the interdependence mode, that sense of adequacy is experienced through satisfying relationships with other people. These relationships often involve the same persons that one interacts with in role performance. However, they differ from the relationships of role function because the purpose of these relationships is to achieve affectional adequacy. Affectional adequacy is the feeling of security in nurturing relationships. Through such nurturing relationships, one continues to grow as a person and as a contributing member of society.

This chapter presents the interdependence mode from a theoretical perspective and then proceeds to explore how close relationships develop. Finally, the nursing process according to the Roy Adaptation Model will be used to illustrate the application of the theory to clinical situations.

RELEVANCE OF THE INTERDEPENDENCE MODE

The nurse is concerned about the interdependence mode of her clients as well as herself. With the heritage of nursing as a caring discipline and the particular humanistic philosophy of the Roy Adaptation Model, close relationships, and their meaning and development, become a significant topic of concern.

Nurses frequently meet persons who are experiencing disrupted wellness or illness. People who are ill or in a state of change usually experience an increased need for love, respect, and affirmation. The person who has a

DEVELOPMENT OF THE INTERDEPENDENCE MODE

In Chapter 14 Buck writes that

> The newborn infant comes into the world with genetic material unique to that individual. Despite such differences, each new person has the potential to be an example of the "model human being" or the "potential human being." . . . Characteristics of this person include a sense of aliveness, love for life and other humans, ability to think clearly and creatively, ability to overcome emotional hurts in a rational way, and a sense of connectedness with all others which leads to responsible behavior.

Notice that the characteristics of the person include love for life and other human beings, and a sense of connectedness with all others. Both of these characteristics reflect the interdependence mode of acting.

This author believes that when a baby is born, two modes are operational, the physiological mode and the interdependence mode. Many studies document the infant's need for touch and physical contact, the bonding process and love. Out of the interactions that are primarily affectional or nurturing in nature arises the beginning self-concept, and finally roles are learned. The author further believes that with the living out of one's life, the modes are given up in reverse sequence. For example, people who are admitted to convalescent centers in their final years give up many of their previously held roles and sometimes even the identity of their self-concept. If the person moves to senility or a comatose state, a form of the interdependence mode, the receptive part of interaction, and the physiological mode remain operational. According to this view, one begins and ends this life as a physiological and interdependent being. There are exceptions to this continuum, such as sudden death or a long productive life with minimal deterioration of functioning. However, we may illustrate a general picture of the development and relinquishing of the four adaptive modes as shown in Fig. 16.1.

Many studies have been done and articles written elaborating on the quality and length of life (see Roy, 1981). Often, the factors identified with both the length of life and the "good" life are relationships with others. For

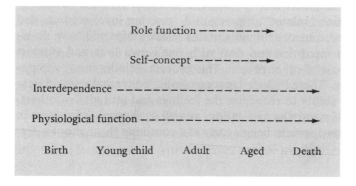

Figure 16.1   Four Adaptive Modes from birth to death.

years, it has been known that married people live longer and are healthier and often happier than unmarried people. The "social contact index" (Berkman, 1978) often used in these studies takes into account whether the individual is married, has close contacts with friends or relatives, belongs to a religious group, or has organizational links. People who have contacts in only one of these categories appear to have a greater risk of dying than those who have contacts in more than one category. The classic study of Spitz (1945) showed that infants who were deprived of touch or affection simply wasted away and died. Maslow places love, belonging, and closeness needs as fourth in his hierarchy of needs. Figure 16.2 compares Maslow's hierarchy of needs with the four adaptive modes.

We have been discussing the recognized human need for giving and receiving love, respect, and value through social interaction. Interaction patterns are learned, and are in turn a means of learning. The infant and child learn interaction patterns in the family unit. The child then moves to the secondary group of extended family, school, clubs, and peers to modify or enhance the learned patterns of interaction. At the same time, through these interactions, the child learns about him or herself, about relationships with others, and the ways of response and expression that are acceptable or unacceptable, that are effective or ineffective in giving and receiving love, respect, and value.

As two people interact, each has demands, needs, and expectations related to interdependence. When these demands, needs, and expectations are parallel, both parties in the relationship can experience satisfaction in the relationship. If, however, the demands, needs, and expectations of the two persons are not parallel, the relationship is likely to be unsatisfying for one or both persons.

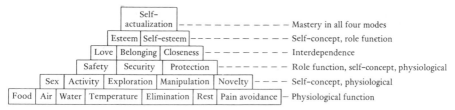

Figure 16.2 Maslow's hierarchy of needs compared with adaptive modes. Based on Kalish, R.A., The Psychology of Human Behavior. Copyright © 1966 by Wadsworth Publishing Co., Inc., Reprinted by permission of the publisher, Brooks/Cole Publishing Co., Monterey, Ca.

Development of Two Types of Close Relationships

To explore further the development of significant interactional relationships, we will discuss friendship and love relationships. Work by Selman (1980) provides a description of five stages of friendship that can be helpful in learning about this type of relationship. The stages and their characteristics are listed below.

Stage 0 (Ages 3–7): Monetary Playmate. The child has difficulty distinguishing between a physical action, such as grabbing a toy, and the psychological intention behind this action. Children this young cannot distinguish between their viewpoint and those of others. Friends are valued for their material and physical attributes, and defined by proximity. As one child stated, "He is my friend." Why? "He has a giant Superman doll and a real swing set."

Stage 1 (Ages 4–9): One-Way Assistance. At this stage, the child can differentiate between one's own perspective and those of others. However, the child does not yet understand that dealing with others involves give-and-take between people. In a "good" friendship, one party does what the other party wants one to do. At this stage, the child's assessment of friendship deals with the viewpoint, needs, or satisfaction of only one party. Said one child, "She is not my friend anymore." Why? "She wouldn't go with me when I wanted her to."

Stage 2 (Ages 6–12): Two-Way Fair Weather Cooperation. The child has the ability to see that interpersonal perspectives are reciprocal, each person taking into account the other's perspective. Conceptions of friendship include a concern for what each person thinks about the other; it is much more a two-way street. Friendship is seen as not working unless both friends participate. However, the limitation of this stage is that the child still sees the basic purpose of friendship as serving many separate self-interests, rather than mutual interests. "We are friends," said one youngster. "She likes me and I like her. We do things for each other."

Stage 3 (Ages 9–15): Intimate, Mutually Shared Relationships. Not only can the child take the other's point of view, but by now he or she can also step outside the friendship and take a generalized third-person perspective on it. With the ability to take a third-person perspective, the child can move from viewing friendship as a reciprocal cooperation for each person's self-interests to seeing it as a collaboration with others for mutual and common interests. Friends share more than secrets, agreements, or plans. Friends share feelings, help each other to resolve personal and interpersonal conflicts, and help each other solve personal problems. The reasoning at this stage can also limit young people's thinking, because close friendship is viewed as an exclusive, intimate, and rather possessive connection. An example: "He is my best friend. We can tell each other things we can't tell anyone else; we understand each other's feelings. We can help each other when we need it."

Stage 4 (Age 12 and Older): Autonomous Interdependent Friendships.
The individual sees relationships as complex and often overlapping systems.
In a friendship, the adolescent or adult is aware that people have many
needs and that in a good friendship each partner gives strong emotional and
psychological support to the other, but also allows the friend to develop
independent relationships. Respecting needs for both dependency and
autonomy is seen as being essential to friendship. According to one child,
"One thing about a good friendship is that it's a real commitment, a risk you
have to take. You have to be able to support and trust and give, but you
have to be able to let go, too."

A friendship builds out of some commonly held beliefs, values, and
interests. Some people experience the growth of a friendship out of working
together. It is at this final stage of friendship that an adult love relationship
can develop. Fromm (1956) talks about love being a feeling and an action.
Love has the characteristics of knowing, caring about, respecting, and feeling responsibility toward the receiver of love. Each of us has a need to be
loved and supported and to love and support. The love relationship is an intense interaction with close identification with the loved one. As such, the
joy and pain as well as stresses and happiness of the other are experienced
by both people in the relationship. The love relationship includes a friendship with the other person. Love is expressed by certain behaviors that communicate a positive feeling. These behaviors are reciprocal and may be
initiated by either person. Some behaviors that usually indicate a deep
friendship and/or a love relationship are physical closeness; eye-to-eye contact that is held for long periods; smiling; statements of affection; and
various forms of touching, such as hugging, kissing, and caressing.

The capacity to love is enhanced when: the level of self-esteem is high;
the definition of self as a separate and adequate person is clear; there is acceptance and love of oneself; one's own love needs are met; interpersonal
skills are highly developed; one holds realistic and accurate perceptions of
the other's and one's own needs; each person has the ability to disclose one's
inner self; and finally, the couple has allowed for and learned how to
resolve stress/anger in a nondestructive way.

Factors Influencing the Development of Interdependence Behaviors

The interdependence mode, then, reflects the reciprocal relationship
implied in the word interdependence. There is a circular relationship that involves giving and receiving between the person and at least one other in the
external environment. There are many factors that contribute to the development of giving and receiving interdependence behaviors. The influencing

factors that will be discussed here are: (1) expectations of the relationship and awareness of needs, (2) nurturing ability of both persons, (3) level of self-esteem, (4) level and kinds of interactional skills, (5) presence in the physical environment, (6) knowledge about friendships, and (7) developmental age and tasks.

The expectations of the person and the other affect the quality of the relationship. If the person expects that affection is expressed by physical proximity, by spending time together, by physical contact, and by remembering birthdays, it is important that the other in the relationship be aware of and respond to these expectations. When two people in a relationship can define their expectations clearly and communicate them, the relationship is enhanced. Once each person is aware of expectations and needs of the self and the other, it is also essential that both act on this information in a consistent fashion.

The nurturing ability of each person in the relationship also contributes to the quality of the relationship. Nurturing involves providing growth-producing care and attention. A person who experienced early bonding[1] as an infant and tactile and verbal loving as a child will usually be able to move into adult love relationships with ease. He or she has experienced a high-quality love relationship and knows what it feels like and what the characteristics are. An adult who experienced delayed bonding or minimal bonding and a parent–child relationship that was characterized by distance, separation, and verbal negating will probably need help in learning how to build a friendship or love relationship.

The level of self-esteem is discussed in Chapter 22 and is an influencing factor for interdependence relationships. People tend to choose friendships and love relationships with persons who have a similar level of self-esteem; that is, people who have low self-esteem choose as friends people with low self-esteem. They are then reinforced in the feelings of negative self-worth and the circular process continues. Similarly, when two people, both of whom experience high self-esteem, develop a caring relationship, the reinforcement from the other serves to enhance the already high level of self-esteem.

The level and type of interactional skills are closely related to the level of self-esteem. If the person has open communication, is flexible, can articulate clearly, and is sensitive to the other's verbal and nonverbal behavior, the relationship is facilitated. If one of the partners does not have the interactional skills at the level desired, those skills can be learned with help.

The presence of the other in the physical environment influences the relationship. If friends or a couple are separated often and for long periods, it is more difficult to maintain the relationship. An area of relationships that is being studied regarding presence is maternal bonding. Attachment

[1]For a discussion of the process of bonding, see Klaus and Kennell (1981).

occurs more readily when mother and baby have frequent and early access to each other. Any relationship is maintained more easily when proximity is possible.

Knowledge about friendship and how to build or maintain a friendship is an important influencing factor. There are many theoretical discussions of friendship available. McGinnis (1980) describes five activities that can deepen a friendship. These activities are: (1) to put friendships or relationships first or give them top priority; (2) to talk about and express your affection for the other person; (3) to create space in the friendship so that both people can maintain their identity and autonomy; (4) to cultivate the art of affirmation, making sure that the other person knows what you value about him or her as a person; and (5) to accept your own and the other person's anger on a temporary basis. When a person has developed his or her nurturing ability and has significant knowledge regarding the dynamics of friendship, there is a greater possibility of an in-depth relationship.

The final influencing factor is developmental age or developmental tasks or crises. In Chapter 4 the developmental stages described by Erikson (1963) are discussed in detail as they relate to all the adaptive modes. Table 15.1 in an earlier chapter summarizes the social focus of each developmental stage as it affects role development. The interdependence mode, dealing further with social integrity, is also influenced by the outcome of each task or crisis. In addition to those factors discussed earlier, the developmental stage thus affects whether or not affectional adequacy is experienced by the person.

USE OF THE NURSING PROCESS IN THE INTERDEPENDENCE MODE

The nurse will use her understanding of interdependence needs and her knowledge of how close relationships develop as a basis for implementing the nursing process in the interdependence mode.

The interdependence mode is a social mode; therefore, assessment and intervention will tend to be verbal and nonverbal social interaction. Many behaviors and stimuli will be observed as the nurse sees the person interacting with others. Refer to Chapter 14 for a review of how the milieu for the nursing process is created.

Assessment of Interdependence

The nurse begins assessing in the interdependence mode when meeting the client. The nurse is keenly tuned to listen for behaviors that the person might reveal spontaneously. After creating a comfortable milieu, the nurse may proceed with an in-depth assessment of behaviors and stimuli. The nurse should first assess in the two major areas of behavior under significant other and support systems (Randell et al., 1982). The first group of behaviors describe the person as a *recipient* of love, respect, and value. The second group of behaviors describes the person as the *contributor* of love, respect, and value. By definition, a recipient is one who receives, takes, or assimilates; a contributor is one who gives or supplies.

Observations in these two categories include nurturing behaviors that occur between the person and other significant persons in the environment. The significant other and/or the support system(s) gives nurturing, that is, care and attention, protection, recognition, offers of help, and other signs of love, respect, and value. Recipient behaviors include the person's response to this nurturing.

Contributive behaviors include the person's reaching-out behaviors to nurture another person(s). These behaviors include physically touching; caring, such as feeding; sitting nearby; and/or talking about life experiences (Randell et al., 1982). Table 16.1 illustrates first-level assessment of the interdependence mode. The two major components of significant others and support systems are listed in the first column, with the major areas of contributive and receptive behaviors for each. Questions that might be used to elicit behaviors are shown in the second column, and behavioral examples for each component are given. Table 16.1 is meant to serve as a guide. It is expected that each practitioner develops an individual approach to assessment of the interdependence mode.

For the first-level assessment, the data are organized as illustrated in the final column in Table 16.1. The advanced practitioner will usually begin the second-level assessment during the time she is doing the behavioral assessment. The second-level factors that are usually assessed are those that were discussed earlier. Table 16.2 lists these general factors. The focal stimulus in the interdependence mode will usually be the need to give and receive love, respect, and value. The contextual stimuli are other relevant factors that are influencing this situation right now.

Once the nurse has completed the assessment step of the nursing process, she is ready to move to nursing diagnoses and planning for nursing care.

Diagnosis

The next step in the nursing process is to make judgments about the data collected. The judgment will reflect whether or not the behaviors indicate that the need underlying the mode is being met. In the interdependence mode, that means: Is the person experiencing affectional adequacy? Are the needs for love, respect, and value being met? If so, the diagnosis might be

TABLE 16.1
First-Level Assessment of the Interdependence Mode

Components and Characteristics	How to Elicit Behavior	How the Behavior is Manifested
Significant other(s)	Who is the most important person in your life?	*Significant other* (Sophia)
The most important person in my life	How do you express your caring to that person?	*Contributive:*
Contributive: nurturing behaviors that I initiate	Nonverbal behaviors to observe for are: physical contact, giving of gifts, making phone calls to	"I tell her that I love her." "I plan activities for us to do."
Receptive: my response to nurturing behaviors from another	How do you know when _____ (significant other) is expressing affection?	"I hug her and share things that happen with her."
	How do you feel about those expressions of affection?	*Receptive:*
	Nonverbal behaviors to observe for are: physical contact, displaying of cards and gifts, and general affect	"I love the way she rubs my back." "I express appreciation when she does things for me."
Support systems	Who else are you close to?	"I try to be open and listen to her."
Other people, groups, or animals in my life that contribute to meeting my needs	What groups (clubs) do you belong to that you really enjoy?	*Support system* (Arthur)
Contributive: same as above	With whom do you spend your leisure time?	*Contributive:*
Receptive: same as above	Contributive and receptive behaviors (as above)	"I critique his work, if he asks." "I help him solve a tough problem." "I treat him to lunch on Friday."
		Receptive:
		"I like it when he listens to my problems." "He covers for me sometimes." "I appreciate his taking me to lunch on Mondays."

TABLE 16.2
Second-Level Assessment of the Interdependence Mode

General Categories of Stimuli

1. Expectations of the relationship and the awareness of needs
2. Nurturing ability of the self and the other
3. The level of self-esteem of the self and the other
4. Interactional skills of the self and the other
5. Presence, proximity
6. Knowledge about friendships
7. Developmental task or stage

stated: _____ is experiencing affectional adequacy due to (focal and contextual stimuli), her significant others' presence and nurturing ability, and mastery of the developmental task of maintaining a strong and mutually satisfying relationship with another. If the person is not experiencing affectional adequacy, the diagnosis might be stated: _____ is not experiencing affectional adequacy due to, for example, the absence of a significant other, not having learned how to communicate effectively, and/or not having learned how to nurture others. Diagnoses in the interdependence mode may be written globally for the mode or specifically for the components of significant other and support systems, depending on the situation.

Goals, Intervention, and Evaluation

The next steps in the nursing process include the settings of goals, nursing interventions, and evaluation of the nursing interventions to see if the goals were met.

Goals in the interdependence mode might be general or specific. An example of goals in the interdependence mode might be: _____ will state that she feels loved and supported; or _____ will discuss with _____, her significant other, what her nurturing needs are; or _____ will join a club and develop one friendship within the next month. Goals in the interdependence mode may be either short term or long term, as described in Chapter 3.

Nursing interventions are implemented after the goals have been mutually set with the person. Interventions manage the stimuli to allow the person to maintain or make an adaptive response. Stimuli frequently worked with in this mode are the seven influencing factors discussed on page 314. The nurse generally uses herself purposefully to explore with the person, and possibly the significant other, their understanding of nurturing needs, communication skills, and knowledge about the self and others in close relationships. The nurse, in initiating, maintaining, and terminating a relationship with a person, has rich opportunities to provide a model of the process of developing a relationship. The nurse can also use herself therapeutically in the area of physical touch. A good backrub or sitting and holding a person's hand while the person is in pain are both nurturing activities. The ultimate goal of intervention is to help the person learn how to elicit from others the nurturing they need and to reciprocate love and caring.

The final step in the nursing process is to evaluate the effectiveness of intervention. This means that behaviors are again assessed and the behaviors are compared with the goals, which are behavioral statements. Depending on the evaluation, the process either ends here or revision and further planning are instituted as needed.

Interdependence Case Study

The following case study demonstrates the nursing process—assessment, diagnosis, goals, intervention, and evaluation—as applied to the interdependence adaptive mode.

Joe Russell is a 32-year-old man. He has been married to Sophia Lopez for three years. He works as an accountant for the telephone company. Joe is active in his church, belongs to a theology study group, and is a counselor for the senior high youth group. An interview with Joe reveals that his best friend is Sophia. His other friends are the six people in the theology class, the minister of education at the church, and the accountant, Arthur, with whom he shares an office. His parents live about 2 hours' time away and he likes them. He has no siblings. Sophia's mom lives an hour's time away, and Joe thinks "she's a crazy but neat lady." The actual interview is not reflected here, but data collected are organized in the care plan in Table 16.3 to illustrate an adaptive interdependence assessment and care plan.

Diagnosis.   Joe has a mutually satisfying relationship with his significant other and has multiple support systems that meet his interdependence needs.

Goals.   Joe will continue to explore ways to give and receive nurturing from Sophia. Joe will continue to maintain his relationships with his support systems.

Interventions.   Joe is experiencing an adaptive situation and will probably continue to do so even with a major stressor. The nurse could explore the young adult developmental tasks, talk about the direct, open communication she experiences with him, and affirm him for building several support systems, which will probably have the effect of strengthening his relationship with his wife, Sophia, since he will not need her to meet all his nurturing needs. The nursing interventions would be supportive in nature.

TABLE 16.3

Interdependence Case Study: Adaptation Nursing Process Care Plan

Behaviors	Stimuli
Significant Other (Sophia)	
Contributive	*Focal:* Need to give and receive love, respect, and value
"I tell her that I love her."	
"I plan activities for us to do."	
"I hug her and share things that happen with her."	*Contextual:* Developmental task: achieving intimacy. To build a strong mutual affectional bond with another; live together, spend 3 to 4 hours a day together
Receptive	Able to state expectations of relationship; communication with Sophia is open and direct
"I love the way she rubs my back."	
"I express appreciation when she does things for me."	Client, moderate self-esteem
"I try to be open and listen to her."	Sophia, moderate self-esteem
Support Systems	
Theology Class	
Contributive	*Focal:* Need to give and receive love, respect, and value
"I always share what I got from the class."	
"I greet everyone at the Peace."	*Contextual:* Group has an emphasis on longitudinal caring relationships
	Wife belongs to group
Receptive	Group meets for 3 hours once a week
"I feel such a sense of community and belonging every Tuesday night."	Group members see each other on Sunday morning also
"I'm learning a lot about the ebb and flow of life from these people."	Developmental task: to continue establishing oneself as a separate person
Arthur	
Contributive	*Focal:* Need to give and receive love, respect, and value
"I critique his work if he asks."	
"I help him solve a tough problem."	
"I treat him to lunch on Friday."	*Contextual:* Developmental task: to continue establishing oneself as a separate person
Receptive	
"I like it when he listens to my problems."	Proximity, spends 9 hours per day in same office
"He covers for me sometimes."	
"I appreciate his taking me to lunch on Mondays."	
Church Youth Group	
Contributive	*Focal:* Need to give and receive love, respect, and value
"I think it's really important to have Christian adults available to our high school youth."	
"I make myself available to them by phone."	Developmental task: assisting in the guidance of the next generation
"Friday evenings I'm 'at home' to them."	Not a parent, but meets with youth every Friday night
	Uses direct, open communication
	Moderate-level self-esteem

TABLE 16.3 *Continued*
Interdependence Case Study: Adaptation Nursing Process Care Plan

Behaviors	*Stimuli*
Receptive	
"I'm gratified by the kinds of concerns they share with me."	
"I really feel good when we play hard together."	
Parents	
Contributive	*Focal:* Need to give and receive love,
"I call them every Saturday."	respect, and value
"I talk through major decisions with	
them."	Developmental task: to continue to establish
	oneself as an independent individual
Receptive	Lives 2 hours away
"I find it difficult to see their powers	Moderate self-esteem: values maintaining
fail."	family relationships
"I enjoy seeing them on holidays."	

Evaluation. At the stated time or the next interaction, the nurse would review the goals and then assess behaviors that would indicate whether or not the goal is being met.

SUMMARY

This chapter has defined and discussed the interdependence mode of the Roy Adaptation Model of nursing. The mode is social in nature and has as its goal affectional adequacy. This is accomplished through relationships with significant others and support systems. Examples of the development of this mode in friendship and love relationships were discussed. Seven commonly occurring stimuli affecting interdependence behaviors were explored. This content was applied to the nursing process in general and in a specific case study of a person whose interdependence behaviors are adaptive.

STUDENT LEARNING ACTIVITIES

1. Define and relate the key concepts listed.
    (a) Interdependence
    (b) Affectional adequacy
    (c) Nurturing
    (d) Significant other
    (e) Support systems
    (f) Receptive behaviors
    (g) Contributive behaviors

2. List and discuss five stimuli affecting interdependence behaviors.
3. Identify your own affectional needs and how you meet them.

REFERENCES

Berkman, B. Mental Health and the Aging. "A Review of the Literature for Clinical Social Workers," *Clinical Social Work Journal*, vol. 6, 1978, pp. 230–245.

Erikson, Erik H. *Childhood and Society*. New York: W. W. Norton & Company, Inc., 1963.

Freed, Alvyn. *Transactional Analysis for Tots*. Sacramento, Calif.: Jalmar Press, Inc., 1973.

Fromm, Eric. *The Art of Loving*. New York: Harper & Row, Publishers, 1956.

Havighurst, R. J. *Human Development and Education*. New York: Longman, Inc., 1953.

Kalish, R. A. *The Psychology of Human Behavior*. Belmont, Calif.: Wadsworth Publishing Company, Inc., 1966.

Klaus, Marshall and John Kennell. *Parent-Infant Bonding*, 2nd ed. St. Louis: The C. V. Mosby Company, 1981.

McGinnis, L. *The Friendship Factor: How to Get Closer to the People You Care For*. Minneapolis: Augsburg Publishing House, 1980.

Mahler, M. S., F. Pine, and A. Bergman. *The Psychological Birth of the Human Infant*. New York: Basic Books, Inc., Publishers, 1975.

Randell, B., M. Tedrow, and J. Van Landingham. *Adaptation Nursing: The Roy Conceptual Model Applied*. St. Louis: The C. V. Mosby Company, 1982.

Roy, Sister Callista, "A Systems Model of Nursing Care and Its Effect on Quality of Human Life," in G. E. Lakser, ed. *Applied Systems and Cybernetics*, vol. IV, New York: Pergamon Press, 1981, pp. 1705–1714.

Selman, R. C. *The Growth of Interpersonal Understanding: Developmental and Clinical Analyses*. New York: Academic Press, Inc., 1980.

Spitz, R. "Hospitalism: An Inqury into the Genesis of Psychiatric Conditions in Early Childhood," in *The Psychoanalytic Study of the Child*, vol. 1, O. Feinichel et al., eds. New York: International Universities Pess, 1945.

Waldo, A. L. *Sacajawea*. New York: Avon Books, 1978.

Part IV

Adaptation
Within the Psychosocial
Adaptive Modes

This section focuses on selected adaptation problems, that is, general areas of concern for nurses using the Roy Adaptation Model of nursing. The problems considered here are those that tend to occur most commonly and can be most easily ascribed to one mode, that is, can be understood by relying on the theoretical understanding and development of self-concept, role function, and interdependence. Chapters 17 through 22, which discuss sexuality, loss, anxiety, powerlessness, guilt, and self-esteem, relate most directly to our understanding of the self-concept; Chapter 23, which describes role transition, distance, and conflict, is clearly focused on role problems; and Chapters 24 and 25, on separation anxiety and loneliness, are based on an understanding of the Interdependence Mode. However, in each chapter the author(s) have also noted the interrelatedness of the three psychosocial modes. The nursing process and planning nursing care based on assessment according to the Roy Adaptation Model is emphasized throughout this section.

This chapter discusses sexuality as an area of adaptation within the psychosocial modes. A brief overview is presented on the structure, function, and regulation of the reproductive system with the major focus on behaviors, stimuli, common adaptation problems, and nursing interventions. The reader is referred to a maternity textbook for guidance on the behavioral assessment of a pregnant woman.

A biopsychosocial–spiritual assessment takes into consideration the reproductive health of the person since sexual behavior is a basic need of human beings. Disruptions in the area of sexuality may affect the total wellbeing of the person and are manifested by ineffective behaviors in the modes of self-concept, role function, and interdependence. Nurses have a background in the physical, social, and behavioral sciences which provides an excellent foundation for the skills of assessment and counseling in the area of reproduction. Client-centered care is made possible with the nurse's knowledge of the social, emotional, and interactional factors that influence a person's behaviors.

STRUCTURE, FUNCTION, AND REGULATION
OF THE REPRODUCTIVE SYSTEM

The major function of the reproductive system is the preservation of human life and essential to this process are the gonads, the testes and ovaries. The testes are the source for the male sperm and the ovaries are the source for the female egg. The gonads produce hormones which affect the sexual development of the body and whose function is regulated by the pituitary gland. The pituitary gland and the gonads operate on a feedback system where the pituitary produces gonadotropins which stimulate testicular and ovarian function. These hormones, the gonadotropins, relay signals back to the pituitary gland when gonadotropin production should be inhibited.

Contained within the scrotum are the testes, which consist of seminiferous tubules and interstitial cells (of Leydig). The function of the seminiferous tubules is the production of sperm, which are collected within the central cavities of the testes. Mature sperm travel through the tubules and enter one of the ducts of the epididymis and continue to the urethra via the vas deferens duct. The function of the interstitial cells is the production of the sex hormone, testosterone, which is released into the capillary network. The accessory glands (seminal vesicles, prostate, bulbourethral glands) contribute their secretions to form the semen, which is released during an orgasm.

During each ovarian cycle, several eggs grow and develop within the graafian follicles. However, only one follicle usually matures. The mature follicle is drawn close to the surface of the ovary, where it ruptures and expels the egg into the pelvic cavity. The ovum is then conveyed from the fallopian tube to the uterus, where the fertilized egg will implant. The uterus leads to the vagina, which is the passageway for the birth of the infant. The glandular secretions from the uterus, vagina, and glands of Bartholin are discharged through the vulva.

The ovary is responsible for producing, and releasing into the circulatory system, the hormones, estrogen and progesterone. These hormones control the functioning of the accessory sex structures.

Reproduction is essential to the continuation of life and requires specialized organs whose activities are regulated by the endocrine and nervous systems.

CONDUCTING A SEXUAL HEALTH INTERVIEW

As part of a person's total assessment, the nurse will conduct a sexual health interview. The ability to conduct a sexual health interview depends on several factors. The proper environment is important for promoting the person's comfort while also taking into consideration the manner in which the interview is handled. The effective use of communication skills and techniques is crucial, especially during the initial stage of the interview, when trust and rapport are being developed. Perhaps the most significant factor affecting the assessment is the interviewer, the nurse.

A major stimulus or influencing factor affecting the interview process on reproductive health is the nurse's comfort level with his or her own sexuality. Being at ease with one's sexuality may be demonstrated by having a positive body image which involves accepting and liking one's physical characteristics. It is also evidenced by the nurse's overall sexual adjustment and is manifested by having a healthy and open attitude toward sex. This characteristic is tested when the nurse is exposed to persons whose sexual preferences and activities are different and requires the nurse to display a nonjudgmental attitude.

The nurse's beliefs, attitudes, and values toward sexuality will determine how the professional interacts with the person. Nurses are entitled to possess their individual attitudes and beliefs in relation to sexuality, but it is important to remain objective, thereby setting up a positive climate. Nurses who are uncomfortable discussing the topic of sexuality or recognize biases in their attitudes may choose to have other professionals interact with the person; however, being aware of one's biases is the first step in overcoming the feelings of discomfort.

The interviewer should possess current and accurate knowledge regarding sexual development and expression, reproduction, and the sociocultural–spiritual aspects of sex, marriage, and the family. This knowledge base should include content related to sexual dysfunction and disease.

The second stimulus to consider is the setting of the interview. Providing a nonthreatening environment with a warm, objective, and frank approach helps to facilitate the expression of sexual concerns. Establishing the proper climate, which includes privacy and confidentiality, is important when trying to place the client at ease. Avoidance of note taking and a nonmoralistic attitude increase the person's comfort level.

The process and technique of communication is the last major stimulus to consider when conducting an interview on sexual health. The nurse may begin the assessment by preparing the person at the start of the interview by indicating that some personal questions will be asked. The questions can be structured in an order where the topic progresses from a less personal nature to areas of increased sensitivity.

The nurse should convey a matter-of-fact approach and use accurate terminology while understanding the words used by the other person (Hogan, 1980). It is important to validate the meaning of words to make certain that you are both talking about the same thing. Persons begin to question the professional's level of competence when they use "street" expressions and are shocked if the professional talks in slang. Slang terminology holds a highly emotional connotation for some persons receiving care and the use of such words by nurses adds to the emotional value.

Open-ended questions may be asked to provide leads for possible areas of the person's concern, such as: "Many persons are worried about their sexual activity following a heart attack. What concerns might you have?" The questions are prefaced with the normality of the topic and acceptable behaviors are emphasized. If the client hesitates in answering, allow time for reflection and the use of silence. Be aware of nonverbal cues indicating feelings of discomfort and offer to ask the question later in the interview.

FIRST-LEVEL ASSESSMENT

The assessment of behaviors related to sexuality involves a psychological and physiological aspect. The order and degree in which the assessment is completed depend on the needs of the person. The purpose of the physical examination is to identify ineffective behaviors and the questions on sexuality are used to determine the client's level of adaptation. The following paragraphs provide guidelines in the conducting of a sexual health assessment.

The physical assessment portion requires good lighting, warm hands, and gloves in case of infection. It is important to explain to the person, in advance, each step of the exam and to drape the person adequately. The assessment of the female and male are described separately because of the anatomic variations betweeen the sexes.

Examination of the female.   Observe the mons pubis, labia majora, and perineum for lesions, reddening, or edema. Separate the labia majora and inspect the labia minora, clitoris, urethral orifice, and vaginal opening. Note any areas of inflammation, ulceration, discharge, swelling, nodules, or varicosities. The expected adaptive behavior is a labia free of swellings and lesions. The urethra should be flesh-colored, without swelling or discharge. The perineum is intact and without scars.

The inspection of the breasts provides an ideal time to teach women the procedure of a self-breast exam. Observe the breasts in a sitting position with the woman's arms at her sides. Note the size and symmetry of the breasts while taking into consideration that differences in size are common and usually normal. Inspect the appearance of the skin for color, edema, and venous pattern. To bring out *dimpling* or skin retraction, have the woman raise her arms over her head and then press her hands against her hips. With dimpling, there is an abnormal traction on the suspensory ligament caused by the disease process infiltrating the tissue, which pulls a portion of the skin overlying the lesion.

Observe the size and shape of the nipples and note the direction in which they point. The nipples should be erect and point straight forward; however, simple nipple inversion of long-standing is common and usually normal. Note the presence of rashes, ulcerations, pigmentary changes, edema, and discharge. To elicit discharge, compress the nipple between your thumb and index finger and note the color, amount, and consistency.

Inspect the axillae for retractions, bulging, discoloration, or edema.

Have the woman lie down with a small pillow under her shoulder on the side to be palpated for masses. With a circular motion, use the pads of three fingers to palpate the breast tissue for the presence of masses. Describe the location of the mass by the clock method and the number of centimeters from the nipple. State the size and the mass in centimeters, shape (round or irregular), consistency (soft or firm), and whether it is well circumscribed, movable, or tender.

The expected adaptive behaviors are symmetrical breasts without dimpling, nipple discharge, masses, or tenderness. The breasts should be flesh-toned and free of inflammation.

Assess the woman's menstrual pattern. What is her length of cycle and duration of flow? The length of cycle usually ranges from 20 to 36 days, the average being 28 days. A normal period lasts 2 to 8 days, with 4 to 6 days being the average. Each woman has her own cycle, which is more important when considering her normal pattern of menstruation.

Does she experience *dysmenorrhea* (pain associated with menstruation), which is a common problem? Typical behaviors include cramps, water retention, backaches, breast pains, irritability, depression, and lethargy.

Examination of the male.   Inspect the skin of the penis and the urethral meatus. Retract the foreskin if present. Note ulcers, scars, nodules, discharge, or any areas of inflammation. The expected adaptive behaviors are a retractable foreskin (on the uncircumsized male), and a penis free of ulcers, scars, nodules, or inflammation. The urethral meatus is located ventrally in the shaft of the penis, is patent, and is void of discharge.

Observe the skin of the scrotum and identify the presence of nodules, swelling, or ulcers. Using the index and middle fingers of the right hand in a scissorslike fashion, palpate the scrotum and separate the two testes. The right testicle should be in your right hand and, with gentle pressure by your left fingers, the bimanual palpation of the left testicle is accomplished. The expected adaptive behaviors are a scrotum without nodules, inflammation, or ulcers. The testicles have descended and are symmetrical and free of masses.

Inspect the nipple and areola for nodules, swelling, ulceration, discharge, and tenderness. Note breasts that appear to be enlarged and discern whether they are soft and fatty due to obesity or are the firm disks of glandular enlargement. Observe the axillae for rash, infection, or unusual pigmentation. The expected adaptive behaviors are symmetrical breasts without nipple discharge, masses, or tenderness with no breast tissue present.

The questions asked in a sexual health assessment provide the nurse with information that may point out areas of concern for the person. Again, the order and need of the questions should be determined on an individualized basis.

Number of biological children.   Determine the number of *biological children* in terms of those living and dead (include miscarriages). The expected adaptive behavior is an intact reproductive and neuroendocrine system, capable of conception.

Family planning.   Assess the person's use of a birth control method and the suitability of the method for the particular life-style chosen. The expected adaptive behavior varies depending on the particular person. Generally speaking, any form of birth control is adaptive for the client as long as it meets the person's needs.

Present illness or surgery.   Determine the person's perceptions and feelings regarding the effects of the illness or surgery upon body image and sexuality. Correct any misperceptions as needed. Certain treatment procedures and diseases have an adverse effect on a person's usual pattern of behavior, which is to be expected. However, it is considered to be an ineffective behavior if it detracts from the person's attaining a high level of wellness.

Sexual activity.   Determine if the person is sexually active and the feelings regarding the sexual relationship. Assess for the presence of pain with intercourse or problems associated with erections. Encourage the person to ask any questions about reproduction and sexuality. There is no expected adaptive behavior, as sexual norms will vary within cultures and between individuals. What is important is that the nurse not impose his or her own values on the other person. According to Chez (1967): "Whatever is pleasurable and gratifying for both participants is normal for that couple as long as there is communication and mutual participation without coercion." Within certain religious or ethnic groups, particular norms may limit this definition, as described below.

SECOND-LEVEL ASSESSMENT

The factors influencing reproduction and sexuality are based on a composite of biological, psychological, spiritual, and social stimuli which shape the individual's sexual behavior. A high level of self-esteem is necessary for a good sexual relationship, since the person needs to be comfortable seeking pleasure and asking another to help satisfy one's sexual needs.

Sociocultural factors such as social-class level and educational background affect sexual behaviors. Each social group is convinced that its sexual style is the best of all patterns. Some social groups base their sexual behavior on issues of morality, while others explain their activities on the basis of what is natural. Education appears to have a liberalizing effect on sexual behavior and beliefs.

Any major life event, such as loss of employment, a change in socioeconomic level, or a change in the usual role of the sexual partners, affects sexual functioning. The quality of the relationship with the *significant other* influences the degree of impact caused by the life-event change and experienced by the client. The significant other may be supportive, negative, or punitive.

Religion has a profound influence on sexual behavior. The Old Testament Jewish patterns and the teachings of the early Christian fathers provided a basic standard for sexual behavior. The attitudes and values of the Judeo-Christian were brought to America by the Puritans. Their highly regulated and antisexual pattern became the official and accepted structure.

According to Katchadourian and Lunde (1975), the puritanical influence on sexual behavior cannot be denied.

Each religion has different teachings regarding the constitution of sexual morality. Orthodox Jews, traditional Catholics, and traditional Protestants forbid masturbation, abortion, and homosexuality. Intercourse is reserved only for marriage. The liberal branches may sanction any activity or behavior that is necessary for the maintenance of health.

The familial environment in which the client was raised affects the development of attitudes. The degree of openness or reserve toward sexual behavior expressed by the parents and attitudes regarding nudity are reflected in the family's values.

The presence of health problems, past and anticipated surgery, and medication therapy may result in physiological changes causing *sexual dysfunction*. The perceived change in body image is a source of anxiety for a person and can lead to functional problems. Intact nervous, hormonal, and vascular systems are needed for optimal sexual response.

ADAPTATION PROBLEMS

The sexual health problems frequently experienced by hospitalized persons and thus most often encountered by nurses are: (1) the feelings of a decreased sexual self-concept due to the illness, and (2) aggressive sexual behavior while hospitalized. The behaviors of these problems and the possible influencing factors are described in the following paragraphs. Suggested nursing interventions are provided in an effort to promote the person's adaptation through the expression of feelings.

Decreased Sexual Self-Concept.

The disease process facing the hospitalized person may directly compromise the physiological response to sexual stimulation. The pain and discomfort associated with an illness or surgery has the effect of limiting the sexual response. The role of the nurse is to maintain the person's sexual integrity when threatened by hospitalization. The maintenance of sexual integrity is important because it contributes to the person's concept of self.

Feelings of anxiety, depression, guilt, resentment, and hostility may be a sign of a decreased sexual self-concept accompanied by statements indicating decreased self-worth. Persistent questioning about the bodily effects caused by the illness, medication, or treatment alerts the nurse to an area of sensitivity. Aggressive sexual behavior may be initiated when the individual's usual sexual activity is compromised. A loss of interest in sex and the lack of concern about the decreased responsiveness are other behaviors indicating an altered sexual self-concept.

The sociocultural belief that sexual activity should be suspended in the hospital setting contributes to the adaptation problem of a decreased sexual self-concept. Substitution by an asexual hospital gown designed to fit all sexes and sizes for a person's everyday clothing is a further stimulus. Persons whose sexual identity is based on money, jewelry, or other valuables are asked to leave those items at home for safekeeping. Hospital routines and procedures are invasive and are considered to be an assault on sexual privacy. While hospitalized, the person is unable to carry out his or her occupation and hobbies, which are a symbol of sexual identity.

The disease or surgical procedure aggravates the problem of a decreased sexual self-concept. Any pathology related to the skin, face, breast, genitalia, or internal sex organs poses a threat to a person's sexual integrity.

Once the problem of decreased sexual self-concept is identified, the goal is focused on the promotion of the person's sexual integrity by increasing feelings of worth and value. A long-term goal is aimed at restoring the person's usual sexual role activities.

This adaptation problem can be alleviated through anticipatory teaching prior to surgery or therapy to decrease the threat to sexual self-esteem caused by misconceptions. Possible effects on sexual functioning as a result of therapy should be explained to the person ahead of time. The nurse allows persons to express their feelings about what they expect to happen in relation to their sexuality or what has happened to them.

Assisting persons in maintaining their usual personal appearance through grooming and personal clothing helps individuals retain their sexual identity. Staff and significant others are encouraged to make positive and realistic comments about the hospitalized person's appearance. Explain to the significant others the importance of being attentive and demonstrating feelings of love toward the person.

As soon as possible, clients should resume their previous role functions of work and continue their accustomed hobbies and interests. If this is not possible, new interests and roles should be explored with the person, with the assistance of a social worker or occupational therapist.

Aggressive Sexual Behavior while Hospitalized

Aggressive sexual behavior is a clue indicating a possible problem in coping with hospitalization and illness. These ineffective behaviors are a reflection of a larger adaptation problem, which is a decreased sexual self-concept.

Asking for the nurse's first name, address, and telephone number is considered to be an aggressive sexual behavior. The person may inquire as to whether the nurse is seeing someone special and may follow it with a proposal for a date. Flirtatious compliments and attempts to hold, fondle, or kiss parts of the nurse's body may be experienced. Hospitalized persons may deliberately expose their genitals while being bathed or when lying in bed. Other persons will make seductive comments and jokes with sexual connotations.

The basic stimulus affecting the presentation of aggressive sexual behavior is generally the person's fear regarding the outcome of illness. The person perceives a threat to their sexual identity, causing a sensation of anxiety, with the resultant response of aggressive sexual behavior as a coping mechanism. Flirting is used to decrease the person's feelings of helplessness in the control of their lives and is a means of denying the severity of the illness.

The nurse's response to aggressive sexual behavior is to address the subject promptly when the overt sexual advances continue. The approach used should be firm but not hostile or presented in a manner to degrade the person. The relationship between a professional and the hospitalized person can be defined to the sexually aggressive person. Explain to the person that it is common to experience sexual frustrations when hospitalized. These frustrations may cause them to react in various ways. Assist the person in identifying the meaning behind the sexually aggressive behavior. Listen to the person's complaints and concerns related to dependency and fear of outcome. Assess the situation and determine if the staff might have contributed to the behavioral pattern. The use of role playing between staff members is a helpful way in learning how to therapeutically manage sexually aggressive behavior.

SUMMARY

A biopsychosocial–spiritual approach to nursing assessment includes sexuality, for a person's level of adaptation is affected by feelings of sexual adequacy. This chapter presented a guideline for first- and second-level assessments of sexuality. Some common problems of adaptation experienced in regard to the sexuality of the hospitalized person were discussed, together with general interventions the nurse might use in dealing with these problems. Related diagnoses from the North American Nursing Diagnoses Association include sexual dysfunction and rape-trauma syndrome.

STUDENT LEARNING ACTIVITY

The case study presented focuses on behaviors related to sexuality and the application of the adaptation nursing process. After reading the case study, identify the presenting behaviors and pertinent stimuli. Select a problem and carry it through the nursing process by stating the diagnosis, goal, interventions, and evaluation. The sample key for this case study is given in the Appendix.

Case Study

Ann is a 27-year-old female who receives routine care at the Women's Health Center. Ann is married to John, age 26. Both are Mexican American and were raised in Tucson, Arizona.

They have one child, Ricky, age 2 years. Ann was raised in a large family and had nine siblings. Both Ann and John would like to have a large family; however, Ann is interested in furthering her education as an architect. John is supportive of her occupational goals. They have decided to continue using a diaphragm and condoms as a method of birth control.

Ann's physical assessment revealed that her right breast was slightly larger (her dominant side is the right), and both breasts were symmetrical. No dimpling or retraction was noted. The nipples are slightly inverted. Ann comments that she has always had nipple inversion, which made breast feeding a greater challenge. The breasts and nipples are free of rash and ulcerations. No discharge or nodules are present. She examines her breasts on a monthly basis.

The genital area is free of lesions, nodules, and inflammation. Ann states, "I occasionally have a small amount of cloudy discharge from my vagina. It doesn't itch or have an unpleasant odor."

The client's last menstrual period was 12 days ago. Her menstrual period occurs every 26 to 28 days, with a usual duration of 4 to 5 days. Ann describes the flow as light to moderate and she changes tampons every 3 to 4 hours. She denies any bleeding between menstrual periods. Ann's concern is the back pain that she experiences from the menstrual cramps. Her mother has advised the drinking of cinnamon and camomile tea and to rest as much as possible. Upon questioning, the client admits that she has not been able to exercise but would like to. Ann would like to know if her dietary intake could be an influencing factor for menstrual cramps and if there is anything else that she can try.

Ann enjoys her sexual relationship with John and feels that her needs are being met.

REFERENCES

Bates, Barbara. *A Guide to Physical Examination.* Philadelphia: J. B. Lippincott Company, 1979, pp. 186–199, 221–248.

Chez, R. "The Female Patient's Sexual History," in *Sexual Problems: Diagnosis and Treatment in Medical Practice*, C. W. Wahl, ed. New York: The Free Press, 1967, pp. 1–12.

Hogan, Rosemarie. *Human Sexuality: A Nursing Perspective.* New York: Appleton-Century-Crofts, 1980.

Katchadourian, H. A., and D. T. Lunde. *Fundamentals of Human Sexuality.* New York: Holt, Rinehart and Winston, 1975.

Krozy, Ronna. "Becoming Comfortable with Sexual Assessment," *American Journal of Nursing,* no. 6, 1978, pp. 1036–1038.

Luckmann, Joan, and Karen Creason Sorensen. *Medical–Surgical Nursing: A Psychophysiologic Approach.* Philadelphia: W. B. Saunders Company, 1980, pp. 1809–1903.

Ujhely, G. B. "Two Types of Problem Patients and How to Handle Them," *Nursing '76,* vol. 16, p. 66.

Watts, Rosalyn Jones. "Dimensions of Sexual Health," *American Journal of Nursing,* no. 9, 1979, pp. 1568–1572.

Chapter 18

Loss

Marjorie H. Buck*

BEHAVIORAL OBJECTIVES

After studying this chapter, the reader will be able to:

1. Define the key concepts of the chapter.
2. Describe the behaviors, influencing factors, and common nursing approaches in each stage of grieving a loss.
3. Discuss the events of surgery, pregnancy, and aging in terms of loss theory.
4. Apply the nursing process to a problem of loss in a case study.

KEY CONCEPTS DEFINED

Loss: any situation, either actual or potential, in which a valued object is rendered inaccessible to an individual or is altered in such a way that it no longer has qualities that render it valuable.

Significant or Valued Object: any object that is essential for psychic functioning.

Object: includes people, possessions, job, status, home, ideals, parts or processes of the body.

*This chapter is a revision and expansion of a chapter in the first edition written by Barbara J. Gruendemann, "Problems of Physical Self: Loss," pp. 192–201.

Grief: the series of emotional responses that occur following the perception of or anticipation of a loss of one or more valued objects.

Stages of Grieving a Loss: categorizations of behaviors of those experiencing a loss into (1) shock and disbelief, (2) apprehending the loss, (3) attempting to deal with the loss, and (4) final restitution and resolution.

Denial: refusal to accept or comprehend the perceived data.

Throughout one's lifetime, each person is faced with many losses. Some are predictable and can be planned for; others are totally unpredictable. *Loss* is defined as a situation, either actual or potential, in which a valued object is rendered inaccessible to an individual or is altered in such a way that it no longer has qualities that render it valuable. A *valued object* is any object that is essential for psychic functioning. *Object,* in its broadest sense, includes people, possessions, an individual's job, status, home, ideals, and parts and processes of the body. Any loss interrupts one's psychic functioning and is experienced as a threat to self. Thus loss of any type is *ultimately* experienced as a loss of self. The study of loss is included in the self concept mode for that reason, although the effects of loss on the individual actually affect the person in all four adaptive modes.

Some losses are brought on by normal growth and development. At birth the infant loses the security of the womb. The first born loses the sense of being the only one with the birth of a sibling. The young adult experiences the loss of childhood by taking on adult responsibilities such as work, marriage, and parenting. The generative adult experiences the loss of one's own parents. The mature adult loses a job upon retirement. You can think of many other examples of losses that occur as part of normal growth and development.

Other losses are the result of unplanned events. The infant experiences a sense of loss when mother leaves the room. The infant's response is called *separation anxiety* and is covered in Chapter 24. A person may experience the change in control of bodily functions during illness as a loss. Birth of a defective child may be experienced as a loss. Death of a loved one is experienced as a major loss. Many other experiences, less obvious to the observer, may be experienced as a loss by the individual. As nurses, our responsibility is not to judge whether a situation merits being experienced as a loss or not, but to be aware of the behaviors indicating that a person is experiencing a loss and to carry out appropriate interventions.

The series of emotional responses that occur following the perception of or anticipation of a loss of one or more valued objects is called *grief.* Investigators have identified behaviors that are characteristic of the grief response. The *grief response* has been categorized into four *stages*: (1) shock and disbelief (including *denial*), (2) apprehending the loss, (3) attempting to deal with the loss, and (4) final restitution and resolution of the loss. Table 18.1 lists expected behaviors, common stimuli, and common nursing approaches for each phase of the grief process. The phases and behaviors are based primarily on the work of Engel (1964) and Lindemann (1979), who found that people go through a process with predictable phases when faced with the loss of a loved one. Of course, there will be individual differences. An example of such differences might be one person sitting motionless and silent in phase 1, while another person, showing intellectual acceptance of the loss, starts making plans for the funeral. No one will demonstrate all of the behaviors listed, but each grieving person will show some of the behaviors in each phase.

The common stimuli listed in Table 18.1 focus on the importance of the lost object to the person, the person's ability to tolerate and express painful emotions, and the response of others. Cultural prescriptions of how to grieve strongly influence what outward manifestation the grief process will take. Some cultural norms call for loud crying and wailing, while other cultural norms call for no outward show of emotions. Past experiences with losses also shape the current grief process. Any past unresolved losses will resurface at the time of a new loss. Thus an individual may be grieving more than one loss.

The nursing approaches in Table 18.1 are based on the therapeutic use of self and therapeutic communication techniques. A prerequisite for working with a grieving person is to work through personal feelings about death and loss. The process of grieving a loss takes time and calls for patience on the part of the nurse.

Death is the most commonly thought of cause for the grief response. The work of theorists Engel (1964), Lindemann (1979), Shneidman (1973), Kubler-Ross (1975), and others has helped to bring the subject of death and grief back into the realm of everyday thought. Loss due to death is discussed in detail in Chapter 28. The remainder of this chapter will focus on three specific life events that may elicit a grief response: surgery, pregnancy, and old age. The grief responses elicited by these three events will follow the same general sequence as the grief response elicited by the death of a loved one. The responses in these instances may also show many qualitative and quantitative differences. The theory of loss and grief will be used as a framework for discussing the threats to the self-concept that these three events pose. Each event will be discussed according to the Roy Adaptation Model's format of identifying expected behaviors and common influencing factors, making nursing diagnoses, and outlining goals and interventions. The interventions change the stimuli to enhance the person's ability to make an adaptive response to the event.

TABLE 18.1
Stages of Loss

Expected Behaviors	Common Stimuli[a]	Common Nursing Approaches
I. *Shock and disbelief*—lasts minutes to days Refusal to accept the fact of the loss: "Oh no, it can't be true" Stunned numb feeling Blank expression Sitting motionless and dazed No attention to the surroundings Automatic carrying out of routine Intellectual acceptance and making plans for dealing with the loss	Need to protect self from being overwhelmed by painful feelings—F Suddenness of the news of the loss—C Other circumstances surrounding the loss—physical illness, need to support others affected by the loss—R	Be present—use touch to communicate caring and presence Let the person know you are there to help Refrain from making judgments Provide for privacy Allow denial—don't agree or refute it Ask the person to talk about how it feels right now Provide for contact with significant others Provide for basic physiological needs
II. *Apprehending the loss* Sighing Slight sense of unreality Intense subjective distress Loss of strength Emptiness in chest or epigastium Tightness in throat Loss of appetite Inability to sleep Sense of emotional distance from others Anger at circumstances Crying Tendency to respond with anger and desire not to be bothered Restlessness Inability to engage in organized activity Beginning ability to talk about the reality of the loss: "I guess it's really happen-	Mention of the lost object—F Presence of other people—C Importance of the lost object—C Degrees of ambivalence towards the lost object—C Ability to experience and express painful feelings—C Response of significant others—C Cultural norms of how to grieve—C	Be present and listen Gently remind the person of reality Provide for privacy Tell the person that the responses of this stage are normal and expected Reflect, paraphrase, and use silence to encourage expression of feelings Use all of the above approaches with significant others to support them Notify clergy of the person's choice

III. *Attempting to deal with the loss*—the main work occurs intrapsychically and takes months to years to complete Preoccupation with the lost object Talks about the lost object and experiences with that object Feelings of loss of intactness and wholeness of self Altered body sensations—may have physical sensations the lost object suffered prior to death Development of asthma, colitis, or rheumatoid arthritis Idealization of the lost object—repression of all hostile and negative feelings toward the lost object Forming a distinct mental picture of the lost object Taking on of certain attributes and qualities of the lost object	Importance of the lost object—F Degree of ambivalence toward the lost object—C Spiritual beliefs—C Age of the person—children have more difficulty resolving grief—C Degree of preparation for the loss—C Cultural prescription of how to grieve—C Number and nature of other relationships—C Physical and psychological health of the person—C Amount of guilt felt—C Ability to experience and express painful feelings—C	Be present and listen Tell person it is normal and expected to feel sorrow, guilt, anger, and helplessness Use open-ended questions to elicit feelings Refrain from making judgments Ask the person to talk about the meaning of the lost object Ask the person to talk about past losses—how it felt, what helped, how it was resolved Remind the person that it takes time to go through the process of grieving Use touch to communicate presence and caring Ask the person about spiritual beliefs Involve clergy as requested to do so Support significant others by applying the above approaches to them
IV. *Final restitution and resolution* Interest in new relationships or alternatives for the lost object Renewed interest in matters not related to the lost object	Successful completion of the previous stages of grief—F All the stimuli listed above	Active listening techniques Help person problem-solve how to form new patterns of interaction Refrain from judging Point out the person's strengths and gains Refer the person to appropriate agencies for needed socialization and/or physical rehabilitation

aF, focal stimulus; C, contextual stimulus; R, residual stimulus.

SURGERY AS A THREAT TO THE SELF-CONCEPT

Physical self is an important aspect of one's self-concept. In the Roy Adaptation Model, physical self constitutes one of two major subdivisions of the self-concept mode. Through his extensive work with body experiences, Fisher (1978) has come to view the body as a vital sensory source for defining one's self and one's identity. Due to the fact that body image plays such a vital part in one's sense of self, the individual goes to great length to maximize its bodily consistency. Rubin (1968) views the loss of, or threat of loss of, a complex, coordinated, and controlled functional activity which has been achieved and integrated into the personal system as a loss of or threat of loss of self. The threat of loss of self is ultimately translated into a fear of death. Since the threat of loss of self brings on such strong responses, the nurse must be aware of common situations that pose such a threat.

The experience of surgery is one such situation. Individuals react differently to the prospect of surgery. To some people surgery holds hope of relief from chronic pain and/or disability. To others it is a necessary inconvenience. To others it means loss of control of body function. Others fear the pain and question their ability to handle it. Some fear the possible outcome of an unfavorable diagnosis. Others fear that they will die during or as the result of surgery. Every surgery involves a change in the actual physical body and necessitates an accompanying alteration in body image, the picture one has of one's body, the thoughts and feelings one holds about one's body. As the person works to reconcile the differences between the body image and the actual body structure and function, the person will go through the grief process. One must face the loss of the old body image and incorporate the changes that occur as a result of surgery. The surgical patient will go through the phases of grief outlined in Table 18.1. Behaviors observed in surgical patients will resemble those outlined in the first column.

By reviewing the work of theorists who have studied the responses of people undergoing surgery, specific factors which influence the individual's ability to integrate the changes that result can be identified. The importance of the surgery to the person influences the ability to cope with the results. The person who seeks plastic surgery will probably focus on the expected positive change and ignore the physical discomforts immediately following the surgery. Some people undergoing plastic surgery, however, are not able to incorporate the change in their physical appearances and still feel unattractive. These people will show a variety of behaviors indicating anger, hostility, and disappointment. The woman who has had severe bleeding, pain, and fatigue may welcome the surgical removal of her uterus. A woman who wishes to have children may have great difficulty integrating the changes brought on by a hysterectomy.

The response of significant others is a strong influencing factor for the person's ability to cope with the threats of surgery. Fujita (1972) views the quality of the relationship between child and parent as perhaps the most important factor in how a child handles the body-image threat of surgery. The sex, age, and developmental stage of the person play an important part in the individual's response to surgery. For the child under 3 years of age, the separation from the mothering person(s) is the primary threat, for example. The child's ability to test and master reality verbally or through acting out in play are other important influencing factors. Another important factor is whether the surgery is planned and therefore prepared for, as opposed to an emergency situation.

Lindemann (1979) found that the site of surgery and the woman's presurgical psychiatric history influenced her ability to cope after surgery. In his study group, women with a history of depression who had pelvic surgeries had postoperative depression more frequently than other females undergoing surgery. Perhaps the most influential factor of all is the person's perception of the event and its outcome as opposed to the actual event and its outcome.

When working with the person undergoing surgery, the nurse needs to be aware of the possible responses individuals may have and assess behaviors indicating that the person is involved in the grieving process. (See Table 18.1 for a list of expected behaviors.) Knowledge of the common influencing factors will provide a framework for doing the second-level assessment and planning goals and interventions. A complete self-concept assessment should be carried out pre- and postoperatively. The goals for the person experiencing a loss — whether it is loss of a body part, body function, physical appearance or sense of wholeness — will be to complete successfully the process of grieving, establish a new body image based on the alterations caused by surgery in the actual body, and resume former interests and activities.

Common nursing approaches for helping a person complete the grieving process include: providing an environment in which the person feels free to express feelings of shock, disbelief, anger, rage, and grief. The nurse must convey an attitude of understanding and acceptance. She should let the person know that the grief response is the expected response to any loss and that grieving is the way to heal oneself of the loss. She must let the person know that crying is a natural and powerfully healing action. Many people will feel embarrassed by their crying and may try not to cry. The nurse can help promote crying by providing privacy. If the person is unable to make necessary decisions, the nurse will take steps to have a significant other take over temporarily or delay the need for making a decision until the person is able to do so.

Dealing with a person who is grieving will probably bring up certain feelings in the nurse. It is imperative that the nurse have dealt with her feelings about losses and grief before she tries to intervene with a grieving person. Clinical conferences and seminars on loss and grief should be provided for students and professional nurses.

Another important common nursing approach is to help the person mobilize a support system. The nurse may call a clergy person, requested counselor, family or friends to serve this purpose. The person who has had surgery will need help regaining control of bodily functions lost or interrupted by surgery. Viewing the wound and talking about it will facilitate acceptance of the altered body. The nurse must remember and also tell the individual that grieving is a process that takes time. Patience is called for on the part of the nurse. The nurse will assess the person continually, determine what stage of grief the person is in, and alter her approaches to meet the changing demands of each stage.

PREGNANCY AS A COMMON INFLUENCING FACTOR FOR THE GRIEF RESPONSE

Most people view pregnancy as a time of happiness and joy. In many respects, it is a time of great hope and cause for rejoicing. Theorists have found, however, that even in the best of circumstances pregnancy also brings forth feelings of uncertainty, fear, and grief. At the beginning of pregnancy, the woman must deal with the task of accepting it as real. Rubin (1970) and Caplan (1959) both observed women to be dismayed by finding themselves actually pregnant. Although the idea of being pregnant is often appealing and perhaps proof of femininity, the actual event elicits not only joy but also a sense of "not now" (Rubin, 1970, p. 502). Common influencing factors for the expected behavior of "not now" include one's financial situation, relationship to the father of the baby, attitudes toward pregnancy and motherhood, relationship with one's own mother, desire to continue working outside the home, or desire to stay home when one's income is necessary, past experiences with pregnancy and child rearing, financial and emotional support available, and the response of significant others. As the woman begins to grasp the reality of her pregnancy, she will also recognize the fact that she is no longer separate and independent. She may demonstrate behaviors which indicate that she is experiencing a sense of loss of her independence. She may make such statements as, "I guess I won't be spending money on myself after the baby comes" or "From now on when you see me, it will be me and the baby." The couple may express a sense of never being alone even during sexual intercourse. The couple will need to grieve the loss of their exclusive relationship as the birth of their first child approaches.

The nurse can facilitate the accomplishment of the task of accepting the pregnancy as real by listening to all of the responses of the couple or individual to the news of the confirmation of the pregnancy. The expression of great joy and "Oh, isn't that wonderful!" on the part of the nurse will block the expression of any negative feelings on the part of the parents-to-be. The pregnant couple needs to know that a sense of dismay and "not now" is normal and acceptable. Nonjudgmental listening is the key to helping the person do any grief work necessary during the early phase of pregnancy. As the pregnant person moves through the grief response, she will become able to accept the pregnancy as real. Different people will have differing degrees of grieving to do. Some people may show very little or no sense of loss at becoming pregnant, whereas others may show a marked grief response. In the latter case, the nurse must do an in-depth assessment of the influencing factors and decide whether referral for further counseling is indicated. Some sense of loss is normal and expected.

As the couple or individual is dealing with the reality of the pregnancy, the woman begins to feel changes within her body. Body sensation and body image changes during pregnancy are extreme and frequently bring forth a sense of loss. Early in the pregnancy the woman may experience physical discomforts of nausea, vomiting, fatigue, and/or urinary frequency. Such sensations cause the person to confront her uncontrollable biological state. Rubin (1968) talks about the need to coordinate functional competence and achievement with situational time and place. Any loss of that control poses a serious threat to the self-concept of the individual. The pregnant woman feels out of control of her body and thus a sense of loss of self to some degree. She learned to control elimination to appropriate time and place long ago. Now she has to rush to the bathroom when struck by nausea or urinary urgency regardless of where she is or what is going on around her.

As the pregnancy progresses, the woman's body begins to change shape. She must give up her usual clothes, which are a part of her body image. She may now express the expected behaviors of questioning her beauty, her attractiveness to men, her desirability to her partner. The cultural stereotype of defining a woman in terms of the man she is attached to is still very strong. Any perceived threat to one's definition of self calls forth a sense of potential loss and accompanying panic. Society's high value on a slim female figure is probably the focal stimulus for the expected behaviors listed above. A review of popular magazines and television will provide a clear picture of the ideal stereotyped female body size and proportion. The pregnant body definitely does not match that stereotype.

Slade (1977) found that pregnant women at their fourth month tend to overestimate their physical dimensions in an absolute sense and in comparison to nonpregnant women. In a study of 38 married couples who came for Lamaze classes, Shane and Linn (1977) found that the husbands were more satisfied with the pregnant body than were the wives. They also found that the wives were unable to predict how satisfied their husbands were with the pregnant body. The husbands in the study adjusted to body changes in their wives more quickly than did the wives. The husband's actual attitude is a strong influencing factor as is the wife's perception of his reaction. The study by Shane and Linn showed that those husbands had positive attitudes toward their wives' body changes, but the wives were not able to perceive their attitudes accurately. The depth of ingraining of the cultural stereotype of thinness for women may be the primary influencing factor for the wife's inability to predict her husband's response accurately.

During the last part of pregnancy, the woman may have an intensified feeling of being out of control of her body. The fetus is growing larger and moving around. The woman may have expected behaviors of difficulty sleeping, heartburn, urinary frequency and urgency, and back pain. All of these sensations contribute to her sense of lack of control of her body.

Her body size is becoming cumbersome to her, and the nurse may hear such statements as "I feel like an elephant" and "Will my body ever be the same again?" Some women are concerned about being big enough to deliver the baby. In the past and still today, a primary influencing factor for these expected behaviors is lack of information. Again the stereotype of what the female body should look like is a strong influencing factor. The woman's coping mechanisms influence her ability to handle all the dramatic changes in her body image. Body image is so central to one's sense of self that one will do all she can to maintain a consistent body image. Most women are able to handle the gross body changes of body size and sensation without significant disturbances to their sense of self. However, some women may spend a great deal of psychic energy trying to maintain an adequate sense of self in the face of the dramatic changes brought on by pregnancy.

The nurse can intervene to help the person achieve the goals of acceptance of body changes and maintenance of a positive body image during pregnancy by allowing the woman to express freely all of her varied emotional responses to what she is experiencing. Chapter 14 outlined the steps for establishing trust and promoting expression of feelings. By being aware of the theory of loss and grief, the nurse can assess for behaviors indicating loss, identify the stage of grief, and provide appropriate interventions to promote the completion of the grief process. The process of grief will be essentially the same in all cases, but the events (influencing factors) will be unique to each individual. The nurse must do a thorough second-level assessment before planning specific interventions. The changes of pregnancy are profound in the entire family. Much joy, hope, and anticipation are felt. The nurse must remember that feelings of loss of control, loss of privacy, loss of physical attractiveness, loss of independence, and loss of career opportunity may also be elicited by the pregnancy. The person experiencing such feelings needs to be able to talk about them in a nonjudgmental environment so as to be able to gain a sense of control and hope. The pregnant woman who feels that she must keep such feelings to herself ties up psychic energy that is much needed to deal with the challenges of preparing for parenting.

AGING AND LOSS

The experiences of surgery and pregnancy are generally associated with the hope of positive outcome and are in-and-of themselves time-limited. The process of aging, on the other hand, is generally viewed as a negative process, its scope of time unknown, and its end marked by death. Therefore, the behaviors of loss manifested during aging may be somewhat less obvious as grief responses than those manifested during pregnancy and surgical experiences. Simply by virtue of living to a certain stage, one faces many circumstances of loss.

As people age, they face acute losses, such as the death of parents, friends, spouse, possibly of children, and more subtle ongoing losses, such as decreasing sensory acuity, decreasing stamina, changes in appearance, loss of physical beauty, loss of position and influence in the work world, decreased income, and so forth. Expected behaviors for acute losses are listed in Table 18.1. Expected behaviors for the subtle ongoing losses may be any of the expected behaviors listed in Table 18.1, but the syndrome of loss will be less obvious. Aging individuals may not be consciously aware that what they are experiencing is a sense of loss. The behaviors may be the somatic ones of the second stage: loss of strength, loss of appetite, inability to sleep, tightness in the throat, emptiness in the chest or epigastrium; the tendency to respond with irritability and the desire not to be bothered; or a sense of emotional distance from others. Crying is less likely to occur if the person is unaware on a conscious level of the losses being experienced. The reminiscing of the mature adult can be viewed as an expected behavior for the sense of loss of the past life.

The maturational crisis for the mature adult, according to Erikson (1963), is ego integrity versus despair. Many mature adults master this crisis very well. Lee (1976) found the subjects in her study to vary greatly from individual to individual more than according to age groups. Many of the mature adults showed a high level of ego integrity. Linn and Hunter (1979) studied the perception of age in the elderly and found those subjects with an age perception younger than their actual chronological age to have better overall psychological functioning. Mature adults have been stereotyped as lonely, unhappy, preoccupied with themselves and their aches and pains, and uninterested in the world around them. The studies quoted indicate that these stereotypes are not true and are limiting to individuals and to society as a whole. Many significant contributions have been made by people in their later years. Consider the examples of Albert Schweitzer, Grandma Moses, Winston Churchill, Golda Mier, Eugene Ormandy, and George Burns.

While the nurse avoids stereotypes and assesses each individual, the nurse is also aware of the various factors that may be influencing the behavior of the individual. Common influencing factors for the mature adult's ability to handle changes of aging include society's value of mature adults and attitudes toward aging, one's level of mastery of past maturational crises, one's coping mechanisms, one's relationship to significant others, the timing of important life events in relationship to work and family changes, one's financial situation, one's physical and psychological well-being, past experiences with loss and the success of grieving those losses, one's spiritual belief system, one's lifelong sense of worth, and one's cultural and ethnic background. The person who has suffered under social stereotypes (as a black or Hispanic person, for example) all of his or her life and then faces the stereotypes of being older lives with double threats to the self-concept (Kimmel, 1974).

Awareness of the theory of loss and grief will give the adaptation nurse a framework in which to organize assessment and interventions in the psychosocial modes. The nurse will be aware that a mature adult may be experiencing subtle losses and will assess for expected behaviors of loss and common influencing factors. The nurse will be aware that older people may not be consciously aware of the losses they are experiencing. As the practitioner works with the mature adult, the nurse will validate hunches with the individual and set mutual goals with the person. Goals for mature adults experiencing subtle losses might be to maintain a sense of ego integrity, to complete the grief process successfully, to establish new ways of obtaining a sense of self worth, and to establish new relationships and renew old ones.

Specific nursing approaches will be based on the actual stimuli influencing the actual loss behaviors. Common approaches to consider when planning interventions include conveying a sense of respect for the person through verbal and nonverbal expressions. The nurse needs to examine in a safe setting the stereotypes personally held of aging and older people. Nurses need to examine the feelings they have about their own aging and eventual death. By becoming consciously aware of personal thoughts and feelings held, the nurse can make the decision not to impose these attitudes on mature adults. To do so is no small task and demands continuing self-surveillance and work. Part of conveying an attitude of respect involves including people in planning their care, listening openly to the other's thoughts and requests, providing for privacy, and using a normal tone of voice as opposed to the condescending tone sometimes inappropriately used with younger or older people.

Another common approach is to provide a safe environment in which the people can freely express whatever feelings or thoughts they are having. The nurse can use the therapeutic communication techniques of reflecting and paraphrasing feelings to help people clarify exactly what they are feeling. The nurse must accept all feelings — joy, grief, anger, and fear — and encourage people to express fully whatever they need to express. Once the person has clarified and expressed feelings, the person will be ready to problem-solve with the nurse and come up with alternative ways of handling seemingly difficult situations.

The nurse needs to make sure that the mature adult is obtaining good health care, including physical examinations. Some behaviors that could be attributed to a grief response could be the result of some physiological abnormality, malnutrition, or medication reaction.

Action can be taken at the community level to make services available to mature adults. Senior citizen centers with activities, meal programs, and the opportunity to make new friends are serving a much needed function. The nurse needs to be aware of all the various programs and activities available and make referrals when indicated.

When working with an individual with sensory losses, there are approaches that do much to decrease the effects of those losses. The nurse can stimulate more than one mode of sensory input at a time. For example, when working with a person with a hearing loss, the nurse can make sure that the person can see the nurse's face whenever the nurse is speaking.

The use of thoughtful, purposeful touch, for example, hand holding or neck or back rubbing, can convey a sense of caring and provide needed comfort and relaxation. As the mature adults' social world narrows, they may not be getting the warmth of human touch that all human beings need.

SUMMARY

This chapter has dealt with the concept of loss and the accompanying grief response. Theorists have identified the stages of grief that one must go through to recover from a loss. The problem of loss due to death is covered in Chapter 28. The common situations of surgery, pregnancy, and aging have been discussed as events that may elicit a grief response. Expected behaviors, common influencing factors, goals, and common nursing approaches have been identified. Related nursing diagnoses from the work of the North American Nursing Diagnoses Association include:

Grieving: anticipatory
Grieving: dysfunctional
Self-concept: disturbance in (body image)

Gordon (1982) lists the first two as within the role-relationship functional health pattern area and the last within the self-perception/self-concept pattern. The theories of loss and grief provide the nurse using the Roy Adaptation Model with a framework for working with the self-concept mode of the person experiencing a loss.

STUDENT LEARNING ACTIVITY

Read the following case study. List behaviors that indicate Mr. H. is experiencing a loss. Identify the stimuli and write a diagnosis, goals, and nursing interventions. See the Appendix for a sample Adaptation Nursing Process Care Plan.

Case Study

Mr. H. is 75 years old. He was born in Russia and came to the United States when he was 18 years old. He works as a waiter and must work 3 more months to be eligible for pension. He lives alone in the small house where he and his wife lived until her death a year ago. They had been married for 52 years. He is now receiving weekly home visits from the student nurse. The first interaction was reported in the case study at the end of Chapter 14. This is the dialogue from the next visit. SN stands for student nurse; H stands for Mr. H.

SN: Hello, Mr. H. When we talked a week ago, you told me you were feeling tired and old. How are you doing today?

H: Oh, about the same, I'd say. It's very hard working at the restaurant. Most of the other waiters are young, and I feel so slow compared to them.

SN: When you compare yourself to the younger waiters, you feel that you are not fast enough?

H: Yes. You know, I have arthritis and sometimes it is so painful to walk. My wife used to make me soak my feet at night, and then she'd rub them. That seemed to help.

SN: It sounds like you miss that attention from your wife.

H: I guess I still miss her. Here's a picture of us when we were young. Wasn't she beautiful?

SN: Yes, she was.

H: I think of her often. She was like a part of me. We went through so much together. My son tells me, "Look around, there are other people in the world." I'm just not ready. I used to cry when I thought of her. Now I just feel lonely.

SN: Sounds like your wife was very important to you and you don't feel ready to meet new people even though you feel lonely.

H: I guess that's it.

SN: How do you spend your time when you're not working?

H: I take care of the house and yard. I rest and watch TV.

SN: What about visiting other people?

H: My son comes over. I go to the Jewish Community Center sometimes. Mostly I feel too tired to go out.

SN: From what you've told me, it sounds like you spend your free time mostly alone, thinking about your wife and feeling lonely.

H: When you say it like that, it sounds very grim.

SN: How is it for you?

H: Grim a lot.

SN: Would you like it to be different?

H: Yes.

SN: Let's talk some more and see if we can figure out how to make it different.

REFERENCES

Caplan, Gerald. *Concepts of Mental Health and Consultation*. Washington, D.C.: Department of Health, Education and Welfare, 1959.

Engel, George. "Grief and Grieving," *American Journal of Nursing*, vol. 64, no. 9, 1964, pp. 93–98.

Erikson, Erik H. *Childhood and Society*, 2nd ed. New York: W. W. Norton & Company, Inc., 1963.

Fisher, Seymour. *The Female Orgasm*. New York: Basic Books, Inc., Publishers, 1973.

Fisher, Seymour. "Body Experience before and after Surgery," *Perceptual and Motor Skills*, vol. 46, 1978, pp. 699–702.

Fujita, Milton. "The Impact of Illness or Surgery on the Body Image of the Child," *Nursing Clinics of North America*, vol. 7, no. 4, 1972, pp. 641–649.

Gordon, M. *Nursing Diagnosis: Process and Application*. New York: McGraw-Hill Book Company, 1982.

Gruendemann, Barbara J. "Problems of Physical Self: Loss," in Sister Callista Roy, *Introduction to Nursing: An Adaptation Model*. Englewood Cliffs, N.J.: Prentice-Hall, Inc., 1976, pp. 192–201.

Kimmel, Douglas. *Adulthood and Aging: An Interdisciplinary, Developmental View*. New York: John Wiley & Sons, Inc., 1974

Kubler-Ross, Elisabeth. *Death: The Final Stage of Growth*. Englewood Cliffs, N.J.: Prentice-Hall, Inc., 1975.

Lee, Roberta. "Self Images of the Elderly," *Nursing Clinics of North America*, vol. 11, no. 1, 1976, pp. 119–124.

Lindemann, Erich. *Beyond Grief: Studies in Crisis Intervention*. New York: Jason Aronson, Inc., 1979.

Linn, Margaret, and Kathleen Hunter. "Perception of Age in the Elderly," *Journal of Gerontology*, vol. 34, no. 1, 1979, pp. 46–52.

Rubin, Reva. "Body Image and Self Esteem," *Nursing Outlook*, vol. 16, June 1968, pp. 2–23.

Rubin, Reva. "Cognitive Style in Pregnancy," *American Journal of Nursing*, vol. 70, no. 3, 1970, pp. 502–508.

Shane, Rachel, and Margaret Linn. "The Pregnant Couple," *International Journal of Gynecology and Obstetrics*, vol. 15, 1977, pp. 231–234.

Shneidman, Dewin S. *Deaths of Man*. New York: The New York Times Book Company, 1973.

Slade, P. "Awareness of Body Dimensions during Pregnancy: An Analogue Study," *Psychological Medicine*, vol. 7, 1977, pp. 245–252.

ADDITIONAL READINGS

Cath, Stanley H. "Some Dynamics of the Middle and Later Years," in *Chrisis Intervention: Selected Readings*, Howard J. Parad, ed. New York: Family Service Association of America, 1965, pp. 174–190.

Charitas, Sister Mary. "Body Image in Pregnancy: Its Relation to Nursing Functions," *Nursing Clinics of North America*, vol. 7, no. 4, 1972, pp. 631–639.

Colman, A., and L. Colman. *Pregnancy: The Psychological Experience*. New York: Herder and Herder, Inc., 1971.

Corbeil, Madelein. "Nursing Process for a Patient with Body Image Disturbances," *Nursing Clinics of North America*, vol. 6, no. 1, 1971, pp. 155–163.

Fawcett, Jacqueline. "The Relationship between Identification and Patterns of Change in Spouses Body Image during and after Pregnancy," *International Journal of Nursing Studies*, vol. 14, 1977, pp. 199–213.

Gruendemann, Barbara. "The Impact of Surgery on Body Image," *Nursing Clinics of North America*, vol. 10, no. 4, 1975, pp. 635–643.

Jessner, Lucie, Edith Wright, and James Foy. "The Development of Parental Attitudes during Pregnancy," in *Parenthood: Its Psychology and Psychopathology*, E. James Anthony and Therese Benedek, eds. Boston: Little, Brown and Company, 1970, pp. 210–244.

Norris, Catherine. "The Professional Nurse and Body Image," in *Behavioral Concepts and Nursing Intervention*, Carolyn E. Carlson, coordinator. Philadelphia: J. B. Lippincott Company, 1970, pp. 39–65.

Chapter 19

Anxiety

*Nancy Zewen Perley**

BEHAVIORAL OBJECTIVES

After studying this chapter, the reader will be able to:

1. Define the key concepts of the chapter.
2. List and explain both internal and external behaviors associated with anxiety.
3. Describe the three underlying states of mind associated with an anxious state (isolation, insecurity, helplessness), and give an example of each.
4. Differentiate between real threat and imagined threat.
5. Differentiate between a primary diagnosis of anxiety and a secondary one.
6. Discuss nursing interventions appropriate to anxiety using the three-step approach, and give practical examples.

KEY CONCEPTS DEFINED

Anxiety: a painful uneasiness of mind due to an impending or anticipated threat.

Real Threat: present-oriented danger with the threat due to a definite, identifiable object or event.

*Edited for the second edition by Marjorie H. Buck and Sally Valentine.

Imagined Threat: future-oriented threat not specifically recognized or identified.

Primary Diagnosis: diagnosis in which behaviors and stimuli are chiefly
related to a problem within the given mode, with the overall goal being the reestablishment of the integrity related to the mode.

Secondary Diagnosis: diagnosis in which presenting behaviors have certain
mode components but the major disruption lies within one of the
other modes.

Self-consistency is the continuity of self over time. "I am who I am
because there is a relationship between the self that is me today and the self
that is me tomorrow." Anything that threatens this constancy of self causes
anxiety in a person. Thus anxiety is discussed here as a significant topic
related to the total integrity of the person.

Anxiety is a response that involves the total person. In this chapter,
then, the assessment of anxiety is related to manifestations in all the adaptive modes. Factors influencing anxiety are reviewed. Anxiety is discussed
both as a primary and a secondary diagnosis. Finally, nursing goals and
interventions for anxiety are pointed out.

THE CONCEPT OF ANXIETY

Anxiety is an emotion that pervades all peoples, irrespective of sex,
age, or socioeconomic background. Perhaps due to its complexities, this
term has many definitions, one of the most comprehensive being found in
Webster's dictionary. It states that anxiety is "a painful uneasiness of mind
due to an impending or anticipated ill; concern about some future or uncertain event; a pathological condition occurring in nervous or mental disease . . . synonyms: concern, fear, foreboding, misgiving, worry, solicitude, uneasiness, disquietude...." This very powerful emotion is also an
extremely personal one because its manifestations are as complex and particular as each individual. For instance, one person may exhibit anxious
behaviors by showing signs of restlessness, overeating, and demanding attention; another may laugh and joke while discussing an impending operation.

Because anxious behavior is so complex, individualistic, and diverse,
it often mimics other diagnoses and may therefore be mistreated. With careful validation, the nurse can implement the steps of the nursing process to
facilitate successful adaptation for an anxious person, and thus reestablish
one's sense of self-consistency. In addition, it is equally important that the
nurse be aware of anxiety responses in herself and her colleagues because,
for example, an angry, hostile reaction to a complaining, demanding person
will almost certainly cloud effective intervention. The nurse must face the
anxiety and threat to the self from which this behavior stems.

BEHAVIORAL MANIFESTATIONS OF ANXIETY

Internal Responses

As we know, anxious behavior is a response to a threat to the self. However, before the reaction to the provoking stimulus becomes apparent externally, the autonomic nervous system is activated, resulting in a number of physiological responses. The overall effect of this activation is to prepare the body to respond to the emergency situation by either fight or flight. The functioning of various bodily systems is altered to allow the individual to react to the perceived threat with greater strength and heightened mental activity. The different events that occur in a body during a fight-or-flight response may be enumerated as follows:

1. The brain perceives the threat and transmits the message down the sympathetic branch of the autonomic nervous system to the adrenal medulla.
2. Increased amounts of epinephrine are released from the adrenal medulla, resulting in deepened respiration, increased heart rate, increased arterial blood pressure, and increased blood glucose levels due to accelerated glycogenolysis and inhibition of insulin release from the pancreas.
3. The hypothalamus exerts its influence by activating the pituitary gland, which results in adrenocorticotropic hormone (ACTH) secretion, release of growth hormone, and decreased release of gonadotropins.
4. The increased ACTH secretion from the pituitary gland stimulates the adrenal cortices to produce cortisol, which in turn induces production of glucose.
5. Blood is shunted away from the systems of lesser importance (for example, digestive) to the areas of greater importance (brain and skeletal muscles).
6. The spleen contracts, discharging its supply of red blood cells.
7. In addition to the physiologic changes previously mentioned, the following occur: the skin blanches and becomes cool to touch, the mouth becomes dry, the hands and skin become clammy due to increased perspiration, there is an increased inclination to eliminate urine and excrete feces, the pupils dilate, the appetite is diminished, and thought processes are enhanced, resulting in increased ability to observe, focus attention, and learn.

Two points should be stressed when discussing the physiologic changes of a reaction to a threatening situation. The first point is that the brain cannot adequately distinguish between a physical threat and a psychological one. Therefore, whether the individual is faced with an oncoming automobile or with a verbal attack from someone, the bodily responses are the same. Second, it is also important to note that although frequent, inappropriate, and severe anxiety responses serve to hinder the individual from adapting to the environment, all anxiety responses are not detrimental. As long as the person is not impeded from moving ahead to constructive action, the tense, jittery, uneasy feelings that one experiences during an anxiety reaction are actually normal and frequently useful responses of the body. As a result of these responses, the individual is given greater fortitude and alertness, which heightens the ability to react to the threat and thus reestablish a sense of self-consistency (see Chapter 13 for discussion of stress responses).

External Responses

Eventually, the individual exhibits some type of behavior in attempting to cope with the threat that is faced. Because so many of the bodily systems participate in an anxiety syndrome, the nurse should expect in many cases to observe a syndrome of behaviors rather than just one. The behaviors that a person might demonstrate take one of two courses. First, the individual may react to the threat by actually facing up to it either adaptively or ineffectively. On the other hand, another person may respond by withdrawing from the disturbing situation, by physically or mentally removing oneself.

These two courses represent the fight-or-flight response. In addition, the nurse should consider that this syndrome may include behavior patterns for all four modes, thus making it imperative for her to exercise very careful validation with the person receiving care to avoid misdiagnoses. Following is a partial, categorial list of possible behavioral reactions that have been associated with anxiety.

Physiologic Mode

1. Oxygenation
   a. *Bronchial asthma*. There is considerable evidence that tension plays a part in inducing bronchial asthma attacks.
   b. *Hyperventilation*. Hyperventilation syndrome and other ventilation difficulties. Anxiety may have its effect on respiration in the following ways: breath holding, dyspnea ("I just can't seem to get enough air in"), deep sighing, and hyperventilation with a possible consequence of respiratory alkalosis.
   c. *Pale appearance*. This "white as a sheet" appearance is often associated with anxiety states, as the blood is shunted away from the less important superficial arteries.

d. *Tachycardia.* Due to the increased amounts of epinephrine being released in threatening situations, the nurse may commonly encounter a pulse rate of 100 or above in anxious individuals.

e. *Palpitations.* The nurse may often hear statements from anxious people such as the following: "I get so nervous every time I try to give myself a shot that I can feel my heart pound and pound" or "I get such a funny feeling every time that I have to care for that crotchety man in 312—it feels that my heart is going to burst out of my chest!"

f. *Heartburn.* Excessive acid production in the stomach during a tension state may account for the complaint of heartburn and may even be confused with chest pain.

g. *Premature ventricular contractions* (PVCs). This cardiac rhythm aberration has often been shown to be associated with anxiety reactions.

h. *Cardiac neurosis.* In severe anxiety states, the person may experience intense chest pain, which might lead the practitioner to suspect angina pectoris or a myocardial infarction. However, in these cases, the electrocardiogram would prove to be negative, with the chest pain probably due to muscle spasm.

2. Nutrition

a. *Polyphagia* (overeating). Many obese or borderline-normal-weight individuals crave the comfort of food during depressions that accompany tension. The nurse may often encounter an individual who has faithfully followed a diet until plagued by emotional or physical trauma or by feelings of disgust with the body image. At that time, the person may cast away plans for the diet and plunge into the security that food offers.

b. *Anorexia nervosa.* Contrary to the above, some individuals are repelled by the thought of food during anxiety responses and may state to the nurse: "Please take this awful food away—I just can't eat a thing." In extreme cases, such self-induced food aversion may serve as a solution for deeper psychic conflicts.

c. *Cravings.* Tension and stress have been known to be contributory factors to the development of excessive cravings, such as for food, alcohol, drugs, and smoking. (See Chapter 27 on substance abuse.)

d. *Nausea and vomiting.* During tension states, many individuals experience varying degrees of nausea, even to the point of vomiting. One theorist suggests that this may be due to the body trying to rid itself of a psychologically "poisonous" thought, as it would under actual physical conditions. This is consistent with the common statement: "I get sick just thinking that horrible thought!"

e. *Gastrointestinal disease conditions.* Conditions such as ulcerative colitis and peptic ulcers have been known to have anxiety as a precipitating factor (see Chapter 13).

3. Elimination
   a. *Polyuria.* A frequent desire to urinate may be a behavioral response to an anxiety-producing situation. The individual may even state: "I get so nervous—it seems that I'm always running to the bathroom, even when there's nothing really there!"
   b. *Diarrhea.* Due to increased peristalsis as a physiological response to a threatening state, the person may be having frequent loose stools. They may be explosive in nature and be accompanied by abdominal cramping.
   c. *Constipation.* The person's anxiety state may precipitate poor bowel habits, which could result in constipation.
   d. *Flatus and eructation.* Swallowing air in an anxiety reaction often produces gas, which is eliminated by belching and expelling flatus.

4. Activity and rest
   a. *Insomnia.* The person may express to the nurse an inability to fall asleep, stay asleep, or have a peaceful, undisturbed night's rest. He or she may also speak of being plagued by nightmares or a vague sense of uneasiness during the night.
   b. *Somnolence.* Contrary to the above, some people may sleep or appear to be asleep most of the day and evening as well as during the night. Furthermore, they may refuse care and treatments with statements such as: "Please leave me alone and let me sleep" or "I just can't seem to get enough sleep."
   c. *Hyperactivity.* Some people may exhibit signs of extreme restlessness and constant movement. They may continually fidget, walk around the room furiously, or state an inability to sit still.
   d. *Fatigue.* An individual may constantly complain of extreme fatigue. Whether it be in the hospital, clinic, doctor's office, or the home, the nurse may hear the person receiving care say, "I don't know what the matter is—I'm just tired all the time," or "I just can't seem to get myself out of bed in the morning."

5. Skin integrity
   a. *Cold, clammy skin.* This stress response has been noted to be due to blood being shunted away from superficial vessels. An increase in perspiration may be observed on the forehead, periphery, underarms, and chest.
   b. *Rashes and acne.* These disruptions in skin integrity have been associated with anxiety. The mechanism involved is not clearly understood.
   c. *Alopecia.* This condition—loss of hair on the body—has been known to occur during situations of great stress.

6. The senses
   a. *Pain.* Whether the pain be a headache, abdominal cramping, or generalized aches and pains, anxiety has been known to initiate, sustain, or increase the intensity of the painful experience.
7. Fluid and electrolytes
   a. *Pseudo-Cushing's disease.* As mentioned previously, cortisol is secreted from the adrenal cortices in increased amounts during an anxiety reaction. This phenomenon accounts for a pseudo-Cushing's disease, which is accompanied by sodium retention and potassium loss.
   b. *Psychogenic polydipsia.* Extreme thirst has been noted during anxiety responses.
8. Neurological function
   a. *Stuttering, tics, and muscle twitching.* These neurological manifestations have been noted to be contributory effects of an anxiety reaction.
   b. *Conversion reactions.* Unexplained blindness, paralysis, aphonia, and others have been associated with severe anxiety responses.
9. Endocrine function
   a. *Amenorrhea.* The female individual may experience amenorrhea as a resultant effect of an anxiety reaction. This is probably due to the increased release of gonadotropins during a stress response.
   b. *Pseudocyesis.* This is a phenomenon in which a woman falsely believes and insists that she is pregnant. It has been hypothesized to be the result of severe anxiety during the oral phase of childhood development.

Self-Concept Mode

1. Physical self
   (a) *Body sensation*
       Sexual difficulties. A lack or lessened ability to perform or achieve pleasure in the sexual realm is often related to anxiety. It has been theorized that these problems may be due to the past conditioning of the individual, in which fear and anxiety constrict him or her from attaining full performance and/or pleasure. Some of these problems are impotence and premature ejaculation (male) and frigidity and dyspareunia (female).
   (b) *Body image*
       (1) *Disgust with body.* An individual under stress may express disgust with his or her physical appearance or bodily functions. Statements of this nature would include: "I feel so

awful today and what's worse I can't do a thing with my hair or face!" or "I have enough trouble and now I have to worry about my bowels functioning properly!"

(2) *Self-mutilation.* An extremely anxious and depressed person may sometimes angrily try to cope with anxiety by mutilating himself or herself and may exhibit one or a combination of burns, bruises, cuts, or stab wounds.

2. Personal self

(a) *Anger.* Being a derivative of anxiety, anger serves as a coping mechanism in which the individual tries to fight the stress. One may do this in a direct manner ("I'm angry with you and I never want to see you again!") or because of the fear of retaliation may feel forced to express anger in a more covert, indirect way ("I'm a little unhappy with what you did today"). Anger is not always an ineffective response, for a mild form of it can activate the motivation for the individual to take constructive action.

(b) *Denial.* In this case, the anxious person copes with the tension-producing stimulus by taking flight. Until the level of anxiety reduces to the point where it can be dealt with realistically, the individual must physically or mentally withdraw from the trauma and perhaps even deny that it actually exists. Statements that illustrate denial may be: "Please leave me alone—I don't want to talk about it" or "Cancer? I don't know what you are talking about."

(c) *Pseudo-cheerfulness.* The individual who laughs and jokes while discussing stressful, tension-producing subjects may also be using a form of denial as a coping mechanism. In this manner, the person may be attempting to avert the painful reality of the situation. A typical statement that exemplifies this coping mechanism might be: "Oh, no, I don't mind going to surgery this morning—I like to have new experiences."

(d) *Intellectualism.* By intellectualizing, the person tries to cope with the stress by removing the painful emotional tones from the anxiety-producing situation. For example, an individual who has diabetes may talk quite knowledgeably about the pathology and clinical nature of the condition. However, when the nurse asks how he or she feels about the condition and what problems it may present, the person may uncomfortably try to change the subject.

(e) *Crying.* This is an emotional response that often accompanies an anxiety reaction. With the exception of crying for joy, it usually signifies a state of helplessness or grief on the part of the individual. This response can be either effective or ineffective, depending on the course of action the individual takes following the initial weeping. In an effective response, the crying behavior helps to dispel some of the frustrations associated with the stressful stimulus, and thus it permits the individual to proceed to constructive action. In ineffective crying, the person is frozen and cannot progress to solve the stress. If the individual cannot progress to a solution, the nurse should consider making a referral to a trained therapist.

(f) *Guilt.* It is not unusual in an anxiety reaction for the person to feel that he or she may in some way have caused a frustrating, tension-producing situation. For example, a pregnant unwed teenager is wringing her hands, pacing the floor, and crying. She states to the nurse, "If I hadn't done *that*, this never would have happened. It's all my fault and I don't know what to do!" (see Chapter 21 on guilt).

(g) *Depression.* Depression has been defined as a feeling of intense madness, dejection, or melancholy, and is often an accompaniment of anxiety. If the individual chooses to express a feeling of sadness to the nurse, a typical statement may be: "I feel so blue today—everything seems so hopeless." (See Chapter 26 on depression.)

Role Function Mode

1. *Role failure.* Anxiety may precipitate, contribute to, or be a resultant effect of role failure. Statements that exemplify this are: "I give up! I'm so nervous, I just know that I'll never be a good engineer" or "I've failed as a college student—I'll never be able to do anything now!"

Interdependence Mode

1. *Non-reciprocal relationship with the significant other.* The person experiencing anxiety may express frustration and irritability in such a manner that the significant other feels at fault. The individual may actually make such statements as "He does not understand me or support me anymore." On the other hand, the significant other may lose patience with the anxious person and view the relationship as not meeting his or her needs for nurturing.

2. *Ineffective use of support systems.* The person experiencing anxiety may be unable to identify and use available support systems. The individual may say: "I don't know where to turn for help; no one can help me now" or "I've worn out my welcome with all my friends."

This list of behaviors associated with anxiety shows various ways that the individual tries to cope with a threatening situation. The aim of these behaviors is to avoid, decrease, or relieve anxiety. They may help to lessen the threat temporarily so that the individual can eventually proceed to solve the problem, or they serve to obstruct and hinder, thus making a constructive solution much more difficult. In assessing anxiety, then, the nurse watches for these behaviors.

FACTORS INFLUENCING ANXIETY

Behavioral manifestations of individuals experiencing anxiety have been discussed at length. But the stimulus for the behaviors was mentioned simply as a threat. At this point of the assessment process, the nurse needs to delve more specifically into the actual cause of the behaviors.

To assess the influencing factors or stimuli, it is important for the nurse to understand that the threat of the self is usually associated with three underlying states of mind. These are a sense of helplessness, of isolation, or of insecurity. Many examples would illustrate these three states of mind. A few of them follow.

1. Sense of helplessness
   (a) A 68-year-old woman with abdominal pain submits to seemingly endless diagnostic tests which she neither understands nor feels that she personally controls.
   (b) A 57-year-old man who experienced a recent stroke is unable to perform previous functions with ease, such as walking, bathing, and feeding himself.
   (c) An 18-year-old young woman is trying to care for a new baby for the first time with no one to help or give direction.
2. Sense of isolation
   (a) A 36-year-old man with a recent heart attack is confined to a coronary care unit with minimal, scheduled visits from family and friends.
   (b) A 38-year-old man with diabetes feels that no one really understands what it is like to have a chronic illness.
   (c) A 15-year-old adolescent contracts a venereal disease and feels rejected by peers and family.
3. Sense of insecurity
   (a) A 32-year-old woman who has had a breast removed feels that she will no longer be sexually attractive to her husband.
   (b) A 28-year-old salesperson who recently had surgery for a bowel obstruction is concerned that there will not be enough money to pay the hospital bills and household expenses.

(c) A 42-year-old amputee is worried that he will never be able to earn a living again.

As the nurse gathers the information that is necessary to understand what is causing the anxious behaviors, she needs to classify them as to focal, contextual, or residual. Several points regarding this classification need to be stressed. First, there may be several anxiety-producing stimuli that are provoking the behaviors, not just one. For example:

> Mrs. Alice Forman, a 32-year-old woman who had a breast removed, was exhibiting the following behaviors: crying; frequent requests for the bedpan; refusal to have care and treatments; hostile, angry attacks on the nurses; and unwillingness to see her husband. After observing these behaviors and talking with Mrs. Forman, the nurse assessed these stimuli: focal—fear of loss of attractiveness; contextual—worry over inability to pay hospital bill, dread of recurrence of cancer, and suspicion that the nurses were making fun of her; and residual—expression of anger and hostilty seems to be the way she has always dealt with anxiety.

Second, an anxiety-producing stimulus or threat to the self may be only one of the causes of the behavior, with the other causes being of an entirely different nature. For instance, a person may be having sleepless nights in the hospital because she is afraid that she has an incurable disease, but this also may be due to pain, noise at the nurses' station, and an uncomfortable bed.

The third point to consider is that the nurse may not easily be able to assess the stimuli for the anxious behaviors. Occasionally, the threat is so painful that the individual will have difficulty accepting that he or she is anxious. At this time, the nurse can only make hypotheses of the disturbing stimuli and delay more definite assessment until the person's anxiety level decreases.

OTHER FACTORS TO CONSIDER IN THE ASSESSMENT OF ANXIETY

Before proceeding to diagnosis and intervention, there are several factors that the nurse needs to consider in the assessment process. It may be most helpful for the nurse to ask herself or himself the following questions regarding the compiled data.

1. Is the stress *real* or *imagined*? Although the term *anxiety* is used collectively throughout this section, in the literature a number of differentiations are employed. For simplification, these terms may be divided into categories.
   (a) *Real threat* (synonyms: fear, normal anxiety, actual threat). This term connotes a recognized, present-oriented danger, with

the threat being a definite identifiable object or event. Typical statements that illustrate this include: "The doctor just told me that I have cancer—I don't know what is going to happen to me now!" or "I am overdrawn at the bank and I have no insurance—how am I ever going to pay those hospital bills?"

(b) *Imagined threat* (synonyms: anxiety, neurotic anxiety, perceived threat). This term differs from the above in that the threat is future-oriented and not specifically recognized or identified. Although the individual usually feels in some way physiologically or psychically threatened, the person has only a general, vague awareness of the offending stimulus. Statements of this nature are: "The doctors try to tell me there is nothing wrong with me, but I just *know* there is!" or "I'm not going to let those doctors operate on me—I'm just sure that they'll make a mistake!"

2. Is the response adaptive or ineffective? The nurse can assess this by deciding whether or not the behavioral response leads the person to take constructive action to alleviate the threatening situation.

3. Is the response mild, moderate, or severe? The degree of severity of the anxiety does not correlate with whether it is normal or neurotic. It may be distinguished by assessing the person's ability to focus on what is actually happening in a given situation. For example:

(a) *Mild anxiety.* In this case, the person is able to focus on most of what is actually happening.

(b) *Moderate anxiety.* The person in this situation has limited ability to focus on what is actually happening.

(c) *Severe anxiety.* The degree of anxiety is so great that the individual cannot focus on what is actually happening and may be presumed to be in a panic state.

NURSING DIAGNOSIS

After gathering and assessing as many of the data as possible, the nurse is ready to establish a diagnosis. Since behavioral manifestations of anxiety occur in all four modes, the practitioner needs to decide which of the modes is the most disrupted in order to determine whether the diagnosis of anxiety is a primary or secondary one. For instance,

1. *Primary diagnosis.* If the behaviors and stimuli are chiefly related to the problem within the self-concept, with the overall goal being the reestablishment of the psychic integrity, the most appropriate diagnosis would be "Anxiety—self-concept mode." An example would be an individual who is so insecure that fear of failure in any

venture prevails. This feeling persists despite encouragement and assistance from family and friends.

2. *Secondary diagnosis.* Although the presenting behaviors have anxiety components, the major distribution may lie within one of the other three modes: physiologic function, role function, and interdependence. Since these other modes have therapeutic approaches different from those of the self-concept one, anxiety would be considered to be more suitable as a secondary diagnosis. An illustration of this in the role function mode would be a student nurse who is shaking considerably and almost on the verge of tears during the first day in the hospital. The instructor recognizes this and assists in promoting adaptive behaviors by giving role cues. The diagnosis in this instance would be "Role failure with anxiety." (See Chapter 23 on role function problems.)

It is also important to consider that due to vague and incomplete data, the nurse may not be able to formulate a definite diagnosis. In this situation, the nurse can establish a tentative diagnosis or hypothesis until new facts are introduced.

GOALS AND INTERVENTIONS

Once the behaviors and stimuli have been assessed and the nursing diagnosis has been established, the nurse is ready to develop goals for the individual receiving care. These goals will be to decrease the intensity of the anxious behavior or to alleviate it entirely. The interventions will be designed to manage the anxiety-producing stimuli.

Following is a three-step process of goals and interventions that will facilitate the promotion of adaptive behavior.

1. *The individual will be able to realize that he or she is anxious.* In order to enact this goal, the nurse needs to establish an environment that is conducive to a beneficial nurse–patient relationship. It is important that the person receiving care be able to sense an atmosphere of warmth, trust, concern, and reassurance from the nurse. Of equal importance, the nurse should also examine how she or he is reacting so that the anxiety of the individual receiving care does not elicit anxious behaviors from the nurse. It is obvious that the nurse is not exempt from feelings of insecurity, isolation, and helplessness. By keeping in mind the fact that the care receiver is ventilating feelings of isolation, insecurity, and helplessness, not personal attacks on the nurse, the nurse can avoid taking the outpouring of feelings personally.

The nurse can help the individual recognize his or her anxiety through a discussion which leads to the individual acknowledging the anxiety. This acknowledgment may need to be initiated by the nurse because the individual may feel awkward, hesitant, or embarrassed to do so. In general, the most helpful approach may be one in which the nurse directly confronts the person with observed behavior. Opening statements could be: "I've noticed that you've been pacing back and forth in your room today and refusing all meals. Is something bothering you?" or "You seem to be very angry today. Could there be something troubling you?" The level of conversation that ensues as a result of such an introductory statement often depends on the degree of anxiety that the person is experiencing. Although direct verbalization of the behavior and underlying feelings related to it would be most preferable, the person may not be able to relate on this level at the present time. If the individual's response is negative to open verbalization ("No! I'm not angry!" or "Leave me alone—I don't want to talk about it"), the nurse needs to respect this because further inducement to verbalize will only serve to increase the anxiety. However, the nurse should indicate either verbally or nonverbally the willingness to pursue the discussion at a time that is comfortable to the individual receiving care.

2.   *The individual receiving care will be able to gain insight into his or her anxiety.* After the person acknowledges that he or she is anxious and is able to discuss the underlying feelings related to this anxiety, the person needs to explore some of the causes (or stimuli) for the behavior. The nurse may be able to assist in this exploration by introducing into the discussion the assessed stimuli. These stimuli may be either previously validated or hypothesized. For example: "Mr. Jones, you seemed to be particularly upset when your doctor left the room this morning" or "Do you recall how disappointed you said you were when your brother did not visit you last night?" If the person can identify the source of the anxiety, a greater understanding of the limitations of the threat, a dispelling of some of the energy associated with it, and a more realistic view of the situation will be gained. If the person cannot pinpoint the offending stimulus at present, to pursue this line of discussion would only leave the person feeling that the situation cannot be resolved, thus resulting in an increase in the anxiety level. However, this person can still benefit by releasing this anxious energy more adaptively through verbalizations to the nurse.

3.   *The person will be able to cope with the anxiety in more constructive ways.* Once the person has gained greater insight into his or her anxiety, he or she will be able to cope with the threat in more constructive ways, thus promoting adaptive behavior. This may be accomplished by the person exploring with the nurse the following questions: "Have I overestimated this threat—is it really 'that bad'?" or "Can I remove or reduce the source of this threat from my life?" or "Have I considered all possible ways of dealing with this threat?" By carefully reflecting on these questions, the person may be able either to eliminate, modify, or reduce the anxiety-provoking stimulus, thus eliciting a change in behavior.

SUMMARY

In this section anxiety has been viewed as a natural phenomenon that is experienced by all individuals in a multitude of ways. With the application of the Roy Model nursing process coupled with the human elements of sincerity, empathy, and concern, the nurse can assist others in coping with anxiety in the most adaptive manner.

It can be noted that the diagnosis of anxiety has been studied repeatedly by the North American Nursing Diagnoses Association, but at this time is not on the accepted list. However, fear is listed as an accepted nursing diagnosis. This phenomenon merits further study as a problem area in nursing.

STUDENT LEARNING ACTIVITY

After assessing a person with behavioral manifestations of anxiety, determine if the anxiety is a primary or a secondary diagnosis. List a strategy that you would use in helping the person cope with the anxiety.

SUPPLEMENTARY READINGS

"Anxiety—Recognition and Intervention," *American Journal of Nursing*, vol. 64, no. 9, 1965, pp. 135–136.

Aspects of Anxiety. Philadelphia: J. B. Lippincott Company, 1965, pp. 10–11.

Goldman, Douglas, and George A. Wete. *Practical Psychiatry for the Internist*. St. Louis: The C. V. Mosby Company, 1968, p. 51.

Howells, John G. *Modern Perspectives in Psycho-Obstetrics*. New York: Brunner/Mazel, Inc., 1972. p. 64.

Kaplan, Helen Singer. *The New Sex Therapy*. New York: Brunner/Mazel, Inc., 1974, pp. 126–132.

Kodadek, Shirley, ed. *Continuing Education in Psychiatric Mental Health Nursing for Faculty in Associate Degree Programs*. Boulder: Western Institute for Higher Education, 1973, p. 13.

Leif, Harold, and Nina R. Leif, eds. *The Psychological Aspects of Medical Practice*. New York: Harper & Row, Publishers, 1963, p. 284.

McCaffery, Margo. *Nursing Management of the Patient in Pain*, 2nd ed. Philadelphia: J. B. Lippincott Company, 1979, pp. 141–142.

Schwartz, Lawrence H., and Jane Linker Schwartz. *The Psychodynamics of Patient Care*. Englewood Cliffs, N.J.: Prentice-Hall, Inc., 1972, p. 405.

Ujhely, Gertrude B. "When Adult Patients Cry," *Nursing Clinics of North America*, vol. 2, no. 4, December 1967, p. 726.

Chapter 20

Powerlessness

Sister Callista Roy*

BEHAVIORAL OBJECTIVES

After studying this chapter, the reader will be able to:

1. Define the key concepts of the chapter.
2. Differentiate between situational powerlessness and powerlessness as a life philosophy.
3. List and explain behavioral manifestations of powerlessness.
4. Describe the factors influencing powerlessness.
5. Identify a problem of powerlessness if given a case study illustrating this problem.
6. Specify nursing interventions to be used in the problem of powerlessness.

KEY CONCEPTS DEFINED

Powerlessness: the perception on the part of the individual of a lack of personal or internal control over events within a given situation.

Mass Society: a model of the human community which includes the elements of low control over one's fate, heavy reliance on specialized experts, bureaucratic authority, and loss of community ties.

*Edited for the second edition by Sally Valentine.

Social Displacement: being outside the social life of which one was formerly a part.

One component of the personal self is the self-ideal and expectancy. One is what one would like to be and what one expects oneself to be. To be what one intends means that one has some sense of power or control over one's being. To have a problem of self-ideal and expectancy is to feel powerless. This chapter discusses the problem of powerlessness as assessed and dealt with by a nurse using the Roy Adaptation Model of nursing.

THE CONCEPT OF POWERLESSNESS

One important author in the literature on powerlessness, Melvin Seeman, describes it as one of the variants of alienation. He defines *powerlessness* as "the expectancy or probability held by the individual that his own behavior cannot determine the occurrence of the outcomes, or reinforcements, he seeks" (1959). Seeman emphasizes the subjective element of alienation; that is, powerlessness is a perception of the person. Furthermore, there is no implication regarding an objective or subjective value placed on power. The individual simply does not feel power and may or may not desire power. Seeman intended to limit this meaning of alienation to a statement of man's relation to the larger social order. He seems to see it as a personality trait as indicated by one of the scales he utilized to measure the degree of powerlessness. Seeman and Evans (1962) selected items to represent a general life philosophy of low personal control.

Powerlessness may also represent a situational variable; that is, it may occur only within certain circumstances. Mothers of chronically ill children were studied by means of the Seeman scale of powerlessness and a scale determining feelings of control over health and illness. There was no relationship between the two scales (Grubbs, 1968). Thus mothers of chronically ill children can show a difference between feelings of powerlessness toward life in general and toward the health situation in particular.

The view of *powerlessness* most appropriate to application in nursing practice can be summarized as follows: *the perception on the part of the individual of a lack of personal or internal control over events within a given situation.*

FIRST-LEVEL ASSESSMENT

We begin an assessment of the problem of powerlessness by looking at the person's behavior. The behavior produced by various forms of alienation has been a subject of speculation and research. The individual who has a strong belief in the control of one's own destiny is likely to: (1) be more alert to those aspects of the environment that provide useful information for future behavior; (2) take steps to improve his or her environmental conditions; (3) place greater value on skill or achievement reinforcements and be generally more concerned with his ability, particularly failures; and (4) be resistive to subtle attempts to influence one (Rotter, 1966). The person who has a low sense of control may then be expected to have opposite behaviors, such as apathy, withdrawal, resignation, fatalism, and malleability.

Seeman pointed out in several studies that powerlessness is related to knowledge. In his study of tuberculosis patients in a hospital (Seeman and Evans, 1962) he found that those who were high in powerlessness showed significantly poorer knowlege concerning their health than did persons who were low in powerlessness. This lack of knowledge was shown both in a true–false test and in the client's behavior on the ward, as identified by staff members. Mothers of chronically ill children who scored high in powerlessness had lower scores on knowledge of illness than did mothers who scored lower in powerlessness (Grubbs, 1968). Thus another behavior a nurse may note in a situation of high powerlessness is a low knowledge of illness.

A nursing journal describes a nursing assessment of a 65-year-old woman who was hospitalized for removal of a polyp of the colon (Durand and Price, 1966). One nursing diagnosis is "feelings of powerlessness." The authors describe the facts obtained during the nursing investigation as follows:

1. The woman talked of coming into the hospital feeling well and now being sick. She said she expected the polyp could be removed by a proctoscope and "now all of this," (the woman's expectations regarding hospitalization and treatment have not been met.)
2. The woman stated, "I'm told it will take time to get well. But I don't know what they mean by time—a day, a week, a month," and "I don't know why I have to have intravenous tubes. The doctor probably knows best." (The woman does not feel she can plan what is to come or what she can do.)
3. The woman also stated, "All these tubes—I just want to get rid of them so I can be on my own" (she does not understand or feel in control of her environment).

Thus in observing behavior, the nurse may note a pattern of statements reflecting feelings of low control.

Another article describes some observations of person's reactions to their provisional existence in a tuberculosis sanitarium (Sorensen and Amis, 1967). Since these people are to a large extent powerless to control events of their situation and be what they want to be, their behaviors may be considered indicators of powerlessness.

The typical powerless person feels anxious and uneasy. They are restless and sleepless in bed and wander around endlessly. They feel frail, victimized, aimless, and powerless to determine the future. They may even feel depressed and that the hospitalization is unnecessary. Feelings of helplessness may lead them to leave the hospital against medical advice. Apathy makes them unable to see choices of existence that are available. They are without direction and lack decision. Thus the following behaviors can be added to the list of behavioral manifestations of powerlessness: anxiety, restlessness, sleeplessness, wandering, aimlessness, and lack of decision making.

SECOND-LEVEL ASSESSMENT

When nurses obtain a second-level assessment, they look for the stimulus most immediately confronting the person (focal stimulus), for all other factors in the environment which also may be affecting the behavior (contextual stimuli), and the values, attitudes, traits, and other past experiences that the person brings to the situation (residual stimuli), which have some undetermined effect.

Although the focal stimulus will change according to the individual, in general it may be assumed that the very fact of illness has an immediate effect on the development of feelings of powerlessness. Talcott Parsons (1958) has described one aspect of the sick role as: "This incapacity is beyond his powers to overcome by decision-making alone. . . . Some kind of therapeutic process, spontaneous or aided, is conceived to be necessary for recovery." In illness the person is not expected to fulfill normal role responsibilities, which give the individual some control over life and which help fulfill the self-ideal. Breadwinners of the family may feel that they can influence certain family decisions and may also live up to the ideal of being a good provider by fulfilling the work role. However, when ill, the breadwinner does not work. Thus illness itself may tend to be a focal cause of powerlessness.

Some of the contextual factors leading to powerlessness in the person include: the hospital setting, social displacement, and the gulf between persons and health personnel. Seeman and Evans (1962) pointed out the resemblance of the hospital to the *mass society* discussed by theorists in sociology.

> We took the view that hospitalization for treatment in a tuberculosis hospital, like the medical situation in general, represents a microcosm of the alienative features that are so often discussed in the literature. . . it contains important elements of the model called "mass society"—e.g., low control over one's fate, heavy reliance upon specialized experts; bureaucratic authority; and the loss of community ties. (p. 773).

The person in the hospital has been described as follows: "He becomes subject to rules, regulations, and jurisdictions that are strange to him. He loses prerogative and is forced into compliance" (Simmons and Wolff, 1956).

Some common expectations of the hospitalized person are dependency and compliance to the hospital rules and regulations, to daily routine, and to the decisions that are made by the physician and the nurse. The hospital involves a deemphasis on the internal power and prestige that the person had enjoyed outside the hospital.

Social displacement is another experience of the hospitalized person. This person was formerly a part of a certain social life, and is now outside of it. Whether family and friends will visit is controlled by them and by hospital rules. The person has low control over this aspect of social life. The realization of the self-ideal is built on the reactions of those around the person. Self-concept, then, may depend on the presence of those close and the freedom to interact with them. However, this freedom is often denied in the hospital.

Sometimes a gulf exists between the person and the hospital staff. The perspectives of each differ. Illness exaggerates feelings in the person, but the experience is not happening to the others. The staff thinks in terms of future wellness, but the person thinks only of the present. This gulf may be expected to deprive the person of the staff as a means of self-validation and thus increase feelings of self-estrangement. Residual factors influencing powerlessness and alienation include personality variables, age, religion, occupational prestige, education, income, and rural background.

It has been pointed out that Seeman's measure of powerlessness was related to a general life philosophy of low control. Thus powerlessness in the adult may represent a more or less permanent personality trait. A person who had a generalized low expectancy of control in life may be expected to feel even more powerless in illness.

There is a relationship between increasing age and increasing powerlessness. As a person becomes older, there is a gradual giving up of the rights and obligations of relationships. The sphere of influence and control becomes constricted. One author found in his empirical study a small but positive correlation between three components of alienation—powerlessness, normlessness, and social isolation—and advancing age (Dean, 1961). In the same study Dean also found that there was greater alienation among persons who were lower in occupational prestige, education, income, and rural background.

Another study related social and behavioral variables in the alienated Appalachian region (Zwerling, 1968, pp. 17–18). The author concluded that fatalism is associated with low social status and high religious fundamentalism. Social status and religion may thus influence degrees of alienation in a person.

Thus in assessing the factors influencing powerlessness in the person, the nurse has some guidelines as to focal, contextual, and residual influencing factors. The factors summarized in Table 20.1 can be used in the nursing assessment.

TABLE 20.1
Nursing Assessment Factors in Powerlessness

Behaviors	Influencing Factors		
	Focal	Contextual	Residual
Apathy	Illness	Hospital setting	Personality
Withdrawal		Social displacement	Age
Resignation		Gulf between person	Religion
Fatalism		and staff	Occupation
Malleability			Education
Low knowledge of illness			Income
Statements of low control			Rural background
Anxiety			
Restlessness			
Sleeplessness			
Wandering			
Aimlessness			
Lack of decision making			

NURSING INTERVENTIONS

According to the Roy Adaptation Model of nursing, nursing intervention aims at removing the focal stimuli or changing the influencing factors to promote adaptation. It has been stated that the situation of illness is an important focal factor leading to powerlessness. Thus one method for promoting adaptation is for the nurse to carry out all therapeutic measures which lead toward wellness so that the focal stimulus of illness will be removed from the person as soon as possible.

However, during the time of illness the nurse can aim to remove the specific aspects that lead to powerlessness, namely the low expectancy of control and the constant discrepancy between the person's condition and ideal self. She can do this by (1) helping the person recognize and learn to use control measures—for example, by letting the person know when he or she may have a say in the scheduling of visitors and/or other activities, and (2) helping the person set realistic goals and expectations, for example, sitting up 10 minutes longer each day.

In addition, the nurse may modify the hospital environment, which often contributes to powerlessness. The nurse does this by personalizing nursing care, for example, using the person's name when speaking to or about him, and by consulting the person as much as possible in planning and carrying out nursing care. One example of this is the trend in mental health agencies for the persons to share with the staff the responsibility for the conduct of the ward or hospital. The person should know that he or she has the right to participate in the decisions that affect ones life inside and outside the hospital.

To overcome the effects of the gulf between the person and the staff, the nurse must try to grasp, as fully as an outsider can, the individual's life experience and try to coexperience the existence of nonbeing and of being in the hospital world. When the person's feelings of helplessness are appreciated, greater efforts will be made to reduce dependency and the staff will use more carefully their power over hospitalized persons.

The nurse cannot directly influence the residual factors influencing powerlessness. Personality, age, religion, occupation, education, income, and rural background are all factors that the person brings to the situation. However, the nurse can recognize those who are most prone to powerlessness and can plan their care to minimize its occurrence.

SUMMARY

The nurse using the Roy Adaptation Model of nursing will be alert to intervene to decrease feelings of powerlessness in the person and to promote self-concept adaptation. The diagnosis of powerlessness is not specifically listed by Gordon (1982) as one of those accepted by the North American Nursing Diagnosis Association. However, this list of accepted nursing diagnoses is continually being developed and expanded.

The adaptation problem of powerlessness and the nursing process emphasized here are relevant to many situations in both health and illness. It should be recognized that more severe and prolonged forms of powerlessness may occur, especially when illness is the focal factor. Advanced nursing practitioners and additional nursing literature must be consulted to deal with the more complex situations.

STUDENT LEARNING ACTIVITY

In a hospital setting, assess an ill child's *parent* for powerlessness behaviors (or a family member of another patient). Identify influencing factors and appropriate nursing intervention that you would use to decrease feelings of powerlessness in that parent or family member. What criteria would you set so that you could evaluate the effect of your intervention?

REFERENCES

Dean, Dwight G. "Alienation: Its Meaning and Measurement," *American Sociological Review*, vol. 24, October 1961, pp. 753–758.

Durand, Mary, and Rosemary Price. "Nursing Diagnosis: Process and Decision," *Nursing Forum*, vol. 5, no. 4, 1966, pp. 50–64.

Gordon, Marjory. *Nursing Diagnosis: Process and Application.* New York: McGraw-Hill Book Company, 1982.

Grubbs, Judy. "Powerlessness among Mothers of Chronically-Ill Children," Master's thesis, University of California at Los Angeles, 1968, p. 31.

Kritek, Phyllis Beck. "Patient Power and Powerlessness," *Supervisor Nurse*, June 1981, pp. 26–34.

Parsons, Talcott. "Definitions of Health and Illness in the Light of American Values and Social Structures," in *Patients, Physicians and Illness*, Gartley Jaco, ed. Glencoe, Ill.: The Free Press of Glencoe, 1958, pp. 165–188.

Rotter, Julian B. "Generalized Expectancies for Internal versus External Control of Reinforcement," *Psychological Monographs: General and Applied*, vol. 80, no. 1, 1966, pp. 1–28.

Seeman, Melvin. "On the Meaning of Alienation," *American Sociological Review*, vol. 24, no. 6, December 1959, p. 784.

Seeman, Melvin, and John Evans. "Alienation and Learning in a Hospital Setting," *American Sociological Review*, vol. 27, December 1962, pp. 772–783.

Simmons, Leo W., and Harold G. Wolff. *Social Science in Medicine.* New York: Russell Sage Foundation, 1956.

Sorensen, Karen, and Dorothy Bruner Amis. "Understanding the World of the Chronically Ill," *American Journal of Nursing*, vol. 67, no. 4, 1967, pp. 811–817.

Travelbee, Joyce. *Interpersonal Aspects of Nursing.* Philadelphia: F. A. Davis Company, 1966, pp. 70–72.

Zwerling, Isreal. *Alienation and the Mental Health Professions.* Richmond, Va.: Virginia Commonwealth University, 1968.

ADDITIONAL READINGS

Johnson, Dorothy E. "Powerlessness: A Significant Determinant in Patient Behavior?" *Journal of Nursing Education*, vol. 6, no. 2, April 1967, pp. 39–44.

Pack, Rebecca Jeanne. "Needs and Concerns of Mothers with Infants in the Neonatal Intensive Care Unit," Master's thesis, University of California at Los Angeles, 1978.

Chapter 21

Guilt

Joyce Van Landingham*

BEHAVIORAL OBJECTIVES

After studying this chapter, the reader will be able to:

1. Define the key concepts of the chapter.
2. Describe the development of guilt and discuss its relationship to the superego or conscience.
3. List and describe the behavioral manifestations of guilt.
4. Describe and discuss the factors that influence the person's response to guilt.
5. Differentiate between the three types of guilt.
6. Identify and discuss the steps of the Roy Adaptation Model nursing process when it is used with persons experiencing guilt.
7. Discuss the nursing strategies designed to help persons cope with and resolve the experience of guilt.
8. Identify and discuss the behavioral manifestations of guilt in a client in an actual clinical situation.

*Special appreciation is extended to Nancy Zewen Perley for her original work on the "Problems of Moral-Ethical Self: Guilt" in the first edition, pp. 202–209.

KEY CONCEPTS DEFINED

Guilt: the judgment a person makes about his or her personal transgression of social, moral, or ethical codes, laws, or rules.

Choice: the person's careful selection of the best alternative in a given situation.

Decision: the person's conclusion about a needed course of action.

Conscience: the adaptive mechanism the person uses to evaluate the rightness or wrongness of his or her motives or conduct.

Realistic Guilt: a type of guilt that occurs when the person consciously violates a moral–ethical code.

Pseudo-Guilt: a type of guilt emerges when the person constantly violates his or her unrealistic strivings for perfect conduct.

Neurotic Guilt: a type of guilt that presents itself when the person is overwhelmed with a sense of responsibility for all the problems or ills in his or her world.

A person's response to guilt or to feelings of guilt can be a deciding factor in one's ability to cope effectively. When the person experiences guilt, his or her self-concept is threatened or disrupted, thereby lowering self-esteem and causing a reduction in coping energy. To regain this energy and return to a higher level of adaptation, the person needs information and control. By using the nursing process according to the Roy Adaptation Model in collaboration with an identified client, the nurse can help provide such information and support, thus facilitating the process through which the client can regain adaptive energy and resolve the guilt experience.

A person develops, changes, and redefines his or her concept of self in response to growth, challenge, and crisis. The adapting person is constantly confronted with needs, oughts, and possibilities. He or she is faced with a moral sense of what is and what could be; therefore, one must judge, decide, choose and act in multiple, complex situations. The cognator weighs this moral tension and either affirms or disaffirms the person's moral stance, choice, or decision. This cognator process is reflected in the adaptive function of the conscience, which attempts to resolve and integrate the inherent conflict between the person's perception of personal need and social responsibility. The moral–ethical self stems from this personal interpretation of one's own rightness or wrongness, goodness or badness. When conflict is unresolved or personal perceptions are transgressed, the person judges self as guilty and feels a sense of responsibility for some real or imagined offense or crime. This sense of guilt threatens the person's self-esteem and results in a loss of coping energy.

THEORETICAL OVERVIEW OF GUILT

Guilt is a common psychological phenomenon which evokes such a variety of images and perceptions that it is difficult to provide a commonly accepted interpretation. Guilt is perceived by many as the feeling of pain or discomfort experienced when a person believes that he or she has done something wrong or bad. Some equate guilt with a sense of shame and inferiority, while others view guilt as a feeling of anger or depression when one fails to meet one's own or other's expectations. Although guilt is interrelated with, and often accompanies, such emotions as anxiety, pain, loss, anger, depression, shame, and sadness, it has an important psychological difference that the nurse needs to keep in mind to help clients deal effectively with disrupted coping and lowered self-esteem.

For the purposes of this text, *guilt* is defined as the *judgment* a person makes about his or her personal transgressions or violations of social, moral, or ethical codes, laws, or rules. In this definition, guilt is distinct from the emotions and feelings that frequently result from and accompany it. Because guilt, in this definition, involves a judgment rather than the feelings that accompany it, it is the client's conflict of decision or choice that must be considered. This conflict assumes importance because it reflects the realm of possibilities; that is, the person could have chosen or decided on a different plan or course of action. This realm of possibility, whether real or imagined, becomes a distinct force for action and influences the cognator's choice of coping strategies engaged in for the purpose of coping with life situations. When conflict is unresolved, the person concludes that he or she has chosen a bad or wrong course of action and judges oneself culpable or guilty. Such a judgment forces the person to reexamine intentions and actions, and thus use valuable coping energy in reweighing the possibilities open. When the course cannot be altered or rectified, the person depletes the store of coping energy in vain regrets or "if only's". It is this treadmill effect of guilt which concerns nursing because it interferes with the person's adaptive response and depletes resources for coping with the physical and emotional assault of stress or illness. In other words, the person will not have the energy to initiate effective coping strategies when faced with new conflicts and situations of stress and disruption. The person will experience a lowered self-esteem, which in turn will influence the cognator process and limit the ability to choose or decide on new courses of action in the light of a now-confused world of possibilities.

Choice and decisions are important influencing stimuli for the phenomenon of guilt. *Choice* is the person's careful selection of the best alternative in a given situation. It occurs once the cognator, having effectively processed emotional or situational constraints, makes a precise assessment of the situation and provides the person with the opportunity for choosing the best alternative. *Decision*, on the other hand, is the person's conclusion about a *needed* course of action. It takes place when the cognator assesses the situation in the light of multiple situational and emotional constraints and persuades the person to draw a conclusion and take a stand on a course of action. Both are processes the person uses to effect his or her own lived reality. Either can precipitate a sense of satisfaction or a sense of guilt, depending on the person's judgment about the rightness or wrongness, goodness or badness of the final conclusion or action. When the final judgment is positive, the person's self-esteem is enhanced, and coping energy is increased. Conversely, if the final judgment proves a negative or guilty one, the person's self-esteem is lowered and adaptive energies are reduced. The nurse, using the Roy Adaptation Model, is called upon to help the person resolve the conflict and reverse the negative adaptive force which can accompany the experience of guilt.

DEVELOPMENT OF GUILT

Many authors agree that guilt emerges somewhere between the ages of 2 and 5 (Redlich and Freedman, 1966, p. 97, and Erikson, 1963), in his *Eight Ages of Man*, clearly defines the development of guilt in the young child. He postulates that guilt evolves during the child's third, or initiative versus guilt stage of development. Guilt arises out the child's need to explore, act, and function independently. The child's need for conquest inevitably leads him or her into conflict with parental expectations and control. Each conflict situation brings with it elements of disapproval, fear of punishment, and loss of love, and therefore the child accepts parental judgments and experiences a sense of badness or guilt. At this stage of development the child has no internal guidelines or restrictions about seeking pleasure and acting out impulses. In order to become a responsible person within a given society, it is necessary for the child to learn to control impulses and live within social boundaries. Therefore, parents or parental substitutes use love, reward, disapproval, and/or punishment to induce the child to develop a conscience. *Conscience* can be described in many ways, but here will be defined as the adaptive mechanism person's use to evaluate the rightness or wrongness of their motives or conduct. The person's conscience or superego is meant to serve as a guide or model as well as to provide an adaptive mechanism for analysis and self-direction. The child learns boundaries and begins to differentiate between what he or she should and should not do to remain within society's social and legal codes. During this exploration and superego development stage, the child needs to feel secure and adequate. This need fulfillment is dependent on parental love, affection, and affirmation; therefore, the child curbs wishes and controls impulses in order to conform to the parents' standards. This affords the parents a great deal of control over the child's immediate behavior and future moral and social self-judgments.

In the older child and adult, the conscience or superego assumes the role of parent and imposes a positive or negative judgment on conflicting choices or decisions. A negative judgment of guilt can be the product of a conscious or unconscious conflict. When the conflict is unconscious, it tends to stimulate abnormal behavior, whereas when it is a conscious one, the person experiences an accompanying sense of discomfort, pain, sorrow, or remorse. The maturing individual will need to reassess earlier-formed judgments in order to differentiate between realistic culpability and early childhood programming. This ability to reassess for distortion or misinterpretation is a cognitive–emotional skill that adults may lack, and consequently, may need help to master. On the other hand, many adults master this skill intuitively; still others need well-defined guidelines, while some may not have the insight or the opportunity for mastering such a skill. Mastery of this cognitive–emotional skill is also influenced by whether the conflict in a given situation proves to be conscious or unconscious.

TYPES OF GUILT

Although the response to guilt is considered to be highly individual, there seem to be three common expressions of this moral–ethical phenomenon: realistic guilt, pseudo-guilt, and neurotic guilt. Nurses encounter all three types in health care situations.

1. *Realistic guilt* arises when the person consciously violates a moral–ethical code. This person frequently experiences a sense of remorse, but he or she may or may not be willing to accept the consequences of the decisions or actions.
2. *Pseudo-guilt* is manifested in a person whose expectations exceed reality and who must, therefore, constantly strive to maintain a facade of perfection. Such an individual consistently violates unrealistic strivings for perfect conduct and ruthlessly judges the self as culpable. Such an individual, haunted by the belief that one ought to be able to conduct personal affairs without flaw or error, finds it difficult to reassess the realities of the situation and to reshape judgments by either lowering expectations to better match actual skills and abilities, or removing the self from the impossible situation demands.
3. *Neurotic guilt* is present when a person anticipates and dreads any form of behavior that may threaten loss of self-esteem. In reality, this person rarely does hurtful or wrong things; nevertheless, he or

she is constantly overwhelmed with a sense of responsibility for all the problems or ills in the world, even when they have their origin in other people.

In all cases of guilt, the person strives to redefine one's own actions or decisions in the light of perceived moral–ethical constraints. Guilt becomes a nursing concern when the person wastes valuable coping energy in trying to recreate the incident in order to reverse or obliterate the actions. This prevents the person from accepting the reality of the situation and attempting to cope with the consequences of the moral–ethical actions and decisions. The person experiencing pseudo or neurotic guilt has the most difficult time accepting an objective reappraisal of reality and, therefore, needlessly expends valuable coping energy.

GUILT AND THE ADAPTATION NURSING PROCESS

The nurse plays an important role in helping the client to cope with guilt and the consequent disruption of the moral–ethical self. By implementing the nursing process according to the Roy Adaptation Model, the nurse can establish a collaborative relationship with the client and facilitate (1) redefinition of guilt, (2) reestablishment of harmony between actual level of functioning and moral–ethical ideals, and (3) redirection of coping energy in order to adapt more effectively in the health–illness situation.

ASSESSMENT

To be effective as a collaborator and facilitator in handling client's concerns, the nurse evaluates the client's current level of adaptation. To do this, the nurse assesses the client's behaviors and influencing stimuli.

First-Level Assessment: Behaviors

The client's response to guilt is behaviorally expressed; therefore, the nurse must be aware of expected or predictable responses in order to help the client to adapt. Guilt reactions may be manifest in many ways. Some individuals overtly communicate their sense of guilt by such statements as: "I feel it is my fault that I got sick. I have so many things to do at home, and I feel guilty lying here in bed." Still others articulate their sense of guilt in a somewhat more covert manner, using expressions such as: "I know that my asthma is related to smoking, but I can't seem to cut down to one pack of cigarettes a day." Although there are many ways of expressing guilt, each response contains common elements, which can be identified and anticipated. Because any person who judges himself or herself to be guilty will experience feelings of sadness, anger, anxiety, shame, loss and/or remorse, it is possible to predict and categorize those behavioral responses associated with guilt. The following is a partial list of such clues:

Physical Behavioral Clues

Body carriage slumped, head bowed
Steps hesitant and indecisive
Sense of fullness with constipation
Epigastric distress, loss of appetite
Disruptive intestinal sensations — possible prelude to ulcerative colitis
Disrupted breathing with asthmalike respirations
Stammering
Blushing
Difficulty in sleeping — may lead to insomnia
Behaviors associated with loss, anxiety, and depression (see Chapters 18, 19, and 26)

Psychosocial Behavioral Clues

Expressions of sorrow and loss: "I feel sad." "I feel so unhappy." "I feel so discouraged."
Expressions of lowered self-esteem: "I never seem to do the right thing." "I hate myself." "I always fail, no matter what I do."
Expressions of culpability: "I feel so guilty." "I am fully responsible for this happening." "I know better; I am so disgusted with myself."
Statements of apology, remorse, amends: "I deserve to be punished." "I wish I had not done that." "I am sorry I hurt you." "I want to apologize; please forgive me." "What can I do to set this right?"
Rationalization: "If the doctor hadn't sprung that on me, this wouldn't have happened." "I know I overexerted myself, but the nurse told me to start exercising."
Crying or crying easily in unprovoked situations: "I cry more than I used to." "I cry all the time now and I can't seem to stop."
Behaviors associated with depression (see Chapter 26).
Avoidance behaviors: seeks to allay or avoid acknowledging guilt feelings by physical or emotional withdrawal.
Compulsive behavior such as handwashing: uses ritual to rid the self of the sense of guilt and responsibility.
Sexual disruption, such as impotence, retarded ejaculations, orgastic dysfunction, and denial of sexual pleasure: feels unworthy of rewards or pleasure, therefore avoids full participation in and pleasure from involvement.

Self-punishing behaviors: attempts to atone for bad actions by inviting mistreatment from others and by inviting adverse happenings such as accidents, illness, or loss of money, job, or friends.

Self-recriminating behaviors: keeps track of failures and guilty actions, establishes a litany of chronic and grandiose faults and failings, because the person blames self for all adverse happenings in his or her life experiences.

Self-blame behaviors: blames self for hurting another's feelings, being mean, being lazy, ill. "If only I had not said or done that." "If only I had gone to the doctor, I wouldn't be sick now." "I am worthless; I just hurt people all the time."

Hypersensitive behaviors: becomes defensive or angry if senses others are judging one's guilt, motives, or actions.

Angry behaviors: outbursts that result from an overwhelming sense of being out of control, being pressured or made to feel overly responsible for actions that are not in one's control, or being forced to act in unacceptable ways; therefore, attacks, yells, shouts, reproaches, or may even throw things.

Although this list of behaviors is not exhaustive, it provides a meaningful guideline for first-level assessment. Such behaviors are ones the nurse addresses when assessing for the presence of guilt. There is no single behavior that will pinpoint guilt. Rather, the client will manifest a variety of physical and psychosocial clues which will indicate that he or she is experiencing guilt, and has, therefore, a disruption in the self-concept mode. Having gathered behavioral data which clearly indicate that a client is experiencing guilt, the nurse needs to address the stimuli that precipitated and influenced such behaviors.

Second-Level Assessment: Influencing Stimuli

At one time or another, the majority of people experience some type of guilt. In the consciously adapting person, guilt frequently arises in situations in which the individual inadvertently transgresses one's own moral–ethical code, or when he or she acts before having had time to weigh decisions and actions. The responsible weighing of decisions involves the three-step process: In a clear and deliberate fashion, the person (1) evaluates the alternatives, (2) considers the costs or rewards the actions will bring, and (3) selects the actions to employ in carrying out the decision. This deliberation process has a marked influence on realistic guilt; however, its impact is less apparent in pseudo and neurotic guilt. Therefore, the following guideline for identifying influencing stimuli will address those factors that influence all three types of guilt as well as outline any stimuli that may be specific to one type or classification of guilt.

Residual Stimuli: Internal Influencing Factors.   Residual stimuli, like focal stimuli, are comprised of *internal* influencing factors. The following residual stimuli are potential contributing factors in the experience of any one of the three types of guilt:

1. The person's response to and internalization of parenting styles encountered in childhood, whether one was loved or rejected, whether one was valued for one's self or merely as an extension of the parent's self-worth.
2. The person's response to and internalization of any incongruence found between the family's moral–ethical code and that found in society at large; actual conflict that may have arisen and how well these two sets of expectations are assessed and evaluated.
3. The person's response to and internalization of parental expectations, how clearly they were defined, and how consistently they were rewarded and punished.
4. The person's response to and internalization of the concept of conscience; one's ability to see that a conscience can be a stimulus for growth and challenge as well as a force for controlling those actions one would rather not engage in.

NURSING DIAGNOSIS AND GOAL SETTING

Once the nurse using the adaptation model has validated the presence of given behaviors and influencing stimuli, she makes a judgment about the client's adaptive state and then defines a specific goal for the reestablishment of his or her coping level. A general diagnostic statement in this instance could read:

> The client is experiencing guilt and a consequent disruption in his self-concept mode related to specified influencing stimuli; focal, contextual, and residual.

Next, the nurse articulates a general client goal statement such as:

> The client will resolve his or her guilt experience and regain coping energy in order to reestablish conscious adaptive functioning and increase self-esteem.

Within this globally stated goal, specific goals can be set based on the unique first- and second-level assessment of the individual client situation.

EXAMPLES of Specific Client Situations

To demonstrate possible responses that individuals who are experiencing guilt and a disruption in their moral–ethical selves may exhibit, the following examples are included with a brief comment on the situation based on the theoretical understanding of the guilt experience presented in this chapter.

Example 1

A college student was ill two weeks before his final exam and was not able to prepare for it adequately. Because he was afraid that he would fail the exam, he prepared an information sheet to keep underneath his shirt sleeve, even though this was a definite transgression of his moral–ethical code. Although the sheet was not discovered during the exam, the student suffered considerable feelings of guilt for using it.

In this example, a basic ethical code—"Thou shalt not cheat"—is violated. In the individual with a basically adaptive self-concept, there is serious wish to make amends and refrain from committing the prohibitive behavior in the future. This is contrasted with the disturbed individual, who continually commits the transgression to obtain neurotic benefits from the painful guilt feelings.

Example 2

An elderly woman had been generally independent all of her life and was very proud of her independence. Following a stroke, she was hospitalized for an extended period of time and was fed, bathed, and dressed, thus removing most of her independent functions. Because dependence was a transgression for her, guilt feelings ensued.

This example illustrates guilt which results from a transgression that is forced upon the individual. This exemplifies the necessity for the nurse to assess carefully the client's moral–ethical self in order to assist the client in modifying, reducing, or eliminating the stimuli associated with forced transgressions.

Example 3

A mother gives birth to an infant with multiple severe anomalies. Since this child will require almost constant care for the rest of its life, the health team advises the parents to place the infant in an institution. Although the mother realizes that she has other children at home and that she cannot possibly care for her infant in the manner necessary, she feels overwhelming guilt in accepting the health team's advice.

In this case, the transgression that the mother feels she is committing is the abandonment of her child. However, if she does not consent to place the child in an institution, the resulting disruptions may cause an intolerable situation, leading to a breakdown in the family unit. Other examples of this may include the following: an unwed mother decides to place her infant for adoption; a middle-aged couple mutually consent to a divorce; an elderly, disoriented parent is placed in a long-term care facility rather than living with his children.

NURSING INTERVENTIONS

After identifying the nursing diagnosis and client goals within an understanding of the experience of guilt, the nurse, using the Roy Adaptation Model, plans intervention strategies that will most effectively manage the stimuli immediately impinging on the person and his or her experience of guilt. In guilt situations, two types of intervention strategies are deemed relevant: one type is designed to help the individual deal with the internal stimuli, and the other type is geared to changing and enhancing significant external stimuli.

Internal Stimuli Interventions

The strategies in this category are intended to help the person (1) *become aware* of the need to address one's guilt experience, (2) *realistically reassess* one's moral–ethical dilemma, (3) *correct any misperceptions or beliefs* about unrealistic expectations and/or responsibilities in the real world (4) *redefine one's criterion* for moral–ethical judgments in the light of actual constraints and conflicts, (5) *accept and deal with* the consequences or repercussions of one's actions, and (6) *redirect* one's energies toward more effective coping. Interactional skills are essential tools used in the interventions of this strategy. The following guideline provides a six-step procedure for carrying out these interventions with clients who are experiencing guilt:

Interactional Skill Guidelines for Internal Intervention

1. Establish a contract or agreement with the client. Clearly define your purpose (see the six purposes listed above). Provide time to develop a level of trust to promote the client's free discussion of his or her experience of guilt and consequent feelings.
2. Allow time and your presence for the client to articulate his or her own criteria for judgment.
3. Let the client explore alternative ways of making decisions and offer possible approaches or options.
4. Use guiding statements to help the client explore the irrational elements involved in the experience of guilt.
5. Guide the discussion to help the client explore more effective ways of managing the consequences of moral–ethical decisions and explore effective ways of managing future moral–ethical dilemmas.
6. Ask the client to rephrase his or her insights and intentions for regaining control of the guilt experience, stating those actions that he or she would like to use in future ethical–moral dilemmas or

situations. Together, reexamine the purposes and see if each aspect was understood and addressed by you and the client.

We will now consider interventions with external environmental stimuli. It can be noted, however, that although the two sets of intervention strategies used in guilt situations frequently are employed at the same time, they are presented separately for the purpose of clarity.

External Environmental Stimuli Interventions

The intervention strategies in this section are centered around supplying the person with (1) accurate information about the moral–ethical situation, the decision-making process, and valid criteria for moral–ethical judgments; (2) support and affirmation during the reassessment and future direction process; and (3) the opportunity of controlling present and future activities in order to cope more effectively with one's moral–ethical self and thereby enhance adaptive response in the self-concept mode.

As with internal stimuli strategies, interactional skills are used in this instance as well. However, in changing or enhancing external environmental stimuli, the nurse expands her skills to include advocacy, counseling, and teaching and learning principles. The following is a guideline for the use of these skills and principles:

Interactional Skills, Guidelines, and Related Principles
for External Interventions

Pre-interactional Steps

1. Organize the information you wish to share with the client to be used as a criterion for judgment: the theoretical concepts and processes involved in guilt situations, and the awareness that the person is not a victim but an active agent in deciding on his or her moral–ethical issues.
2. Make a pact with yourself that you are a facilitator, and therefore you are not in control of the client's resolution of guilt.
3. Clarify your own value system. Be sure, in instances when you also judge that the person's actions have violated a social code, that you can *value* the individual as a person. If you cannot do this, provide the client with another resource person who can offer this sense of caring.
4. Clarify and establish your own sense of empathy in order to respond to both the client's feelings and content statements with understanding and genuineness.

5. Take the time and thought to enter into the client's experience and try to understand his or her individual response to the guilt situation.

6. Recognize that neither self-disclosure nor self-exploration on the part of the client is a goal in itself. These processes are adequate and effective only if they lead to the kind of self-understanding that helps the person reevaluate moral–ethical conflicts, dilemmas, or decisions and act accordingly.

Interactional Steps

1. Establish with the client a clear understanding of the purpose of the interaction.

2. Provide a time, a place, and an atmosphere of quiet and privacy.

3. Communicate with the client without distorting his or her message; keep the conversation focused on the here-and-now experience.

4. Respond immediately to the person's feelings and stated needs; do not wait for the client to come up with "right" responses.

5. Help the client to articulate the restraining forces and his or her personal assets and skills perceived as present in this moral–ethical situation; then help the person to articulate ways in which he or she can control and direct such forces.

6. Assist the client to establish a realistic process for thinking through the conflicts experienced in moral–ethical situations.

7. Help the person become aware of the fact that one's own expansion of knowledge, understanding, and emotional awareness is the greatest mechanism for control in moral–ethical situations and that ignorance can be a tremendous weapon that others can use to make one feel unrealistically responsible and guilty.

8. Assist the client to realize that since guilt stems from a self-judgment of wrongdoing or failure, one must learn to accept and forgive oneself for his or her conduct and then attempt to deal with the consequences, if any, of such actions.

9. Offer possible alternative interpretations of the guilt experience so that the client can gain insight into his or her own behavior and potential for self-direction and control.

10. Help the individual to assess the consequences of personal decisions and actions in moral–ethical situations.

11. Summarize the essential elements the client has expressed in the reassessment process and ask if it accurately reflects his or her thinking; ask the person if he or she feels in control of and comfortable with the decisions and resolution process.

12. Offer your own and other resources if they are needed, then terminate the interaction.

Interactional Steps in Unusual Situations.   In situations in which the client is unable or incapable of verbally responding to an interaction, the nurse still uses interactional skills and principles listed above to offer meaningful support and affirmation. The nurse provides her presence and caring so that the individual can reassess his or her perceptions and actions in a nonarticulate fashion and begin to resolve the guilt experience.

1. Use nonverbal behaviors and body language to let clients know that you care and affirm them as valued persons.
2. Employ both verbal and nonverbal behaviors to help clients realize that you are sensitive to their sense of guilt and accompanying feelings, such as remorse, sadness, depression, loss, and/or anger.
3. Demonstrate the same behaviors to help clients concentrate on the pressing need to cope with the immediate crisis or critical care situation. Let them know that you are there and care.
4. Verbally share with clients that once the crisis is over, and they have the energy to attend, you will be there to support and facilitate them working through their guilt experiences.
5. Follow through with this statement and provide the time and privacy for such an encounter.

Post-interactional Steps

1. Take the time to clarify your own response to the interaction and remind yourself that clients are in control and can either choose or refuse to develop better mechanisms for coping with guilt and the consequent disruptions in self-esteem. You can only facilitate.
2. Remind yourself that you are not responsible for the final outcome of your facilitator process; ultimate responsibility resides in the client who is experiencing the moral–ethical disruption.

The intervention strategies for coping with guilt that have been proposed in this chapter are not intended to be exhaustive. Nurses using the Roy Adaptation Model will continue to explore and use as many effective mechanisms as are available for carrying out their role of facilitating adaptation. However, the strategies outlined here can be readily integrated into the nurse's experiential learning process and can prove meaningful in helping a client to cope with the experience of guilt and lowered self-esteem.

SUMMARY

In the process of adapting to a rapidly changing world, individuals will continue to develop and redefine their moral–ethical judgments and decisions. Conflicts between what is and what could or ought to be are bound to occur. These conflicts and tensions can prove to be either negative or positive influences. As a positive force, tensions and conflicts can provide an opportunity for the person to reassess judgments, more clearly define his or her moral–ethical code, and take active control over one's consequent decisions, choices, and actions. Conversely, as a negative force, conflicts and tensions can provoke a confused and unclear evaluation of the moral–ethical issues involved, and the person's consequent self-judgment will create a sense of guilt and lowered self-esteem. When clients experience this moral–ethical disruption, they may need help in regaining coping effectiveness. Gordon (1982) includes a value-belief pattern as a functional health pattern area and lists the accepted diagnosis of spiritual distress (distress of the human spirit) under this pattern. By using the nursing process based on the Roy Adaptation Model, the nurse can assess, diagnose, plan, and collaboratively intervene with the client in this distress to help him or her resolve the experience of guilt and achieve a more effective level of personal integrity.

STUDENT LEARNING ACTIVITY

What factors influence a person's response to guilt? How would you vary the nursing strategies you use to help a person cope with and resolve the guilt experience?

REFERENCES

Erikson, Erik H. *Childhood and Society*, 2nd ed. New York: W. W. Norton & Company, Inc., 1963, pp. 247–274.

Erikson, Erik H. "Eight Stages of Ego Development," in *Comprehensive Textbook of Psychiatry/II*, vol. 1, 2nd ed., Alfred Freedman, Harold Kaplan, and Benjamin Sadock, eds. Baltimore: The Williams & Wilkins Company, 1975, pp. 568–569.

Gordon, M. *Nursing Diagnosis: Process and Application.* New York: McGraw-Hill Book Company, 1982.

Redlich, Frederick C., and Daniel X. Freedman. *The Theory and Practice of Psychology.* New York: Basic Books, Inc., Publishers, 1966.

ADDITIONAL READINGS

Aspects of Anxiety. Philadelphia: J. B. Lippincott Company, 1965, p. 74.

Campbell, James E. "Shame and Guilt," *Arizona Medicine*, September 1979, pp. 665–666.

Carlson, Carolyn E., and Betty Blackwell. "Shame," in *Behavioral Concepts and Nursing Interventions*, 2nd ed., Carolyn E. Carlson and Betty Blackwell, eds. Philadelphia: J. B. Lippincott Company, 1978, pp. 51–70.

Dodson, Fitzhugh. *How to Parent*. New York: New American Book Company, 1970, pp. 41–97.

Gardner, Bruce D. *Development in Early Childhood*. New York: Harper & Row, Publishers, 1964, pp. 80–125.

Goldman, Douglas, and George A. Ulett. *Practical Psychiatry for the Internist*. St. Louis: The C. V. Mosby Company, 1968, p. 18.

Goulding, Mary M., and Robert L. Goulding. *Changing Lives through Redecision Therapy*. New York: Brunner/Mazel, Inc., 1979, pp. 160–173.

Horney, Karen. *New Ways in Psychoanalysis*. New York: W. W. Norton & Company, Inc., 1939, pp. 232–245.

Lidz, Theodore. *The Person*. New York: Basic Books, Inc., Publishers, 1968, p. 160.

McBride, Angela B. "The Anger–Depression–Guilt Go Round," *American Journal of Nursing*, no. 6, 1973, pp. 1045–1049.

Reeves, Clement. *The Psychology of Rollo May*. San Francisco: Jossey-Bass, Inc., Publishers, 1977, pp. 35–51, 136–140.

Tudor, Mary. *Child Development*. New York: McGraw-Hill Book Company, 1981, pp. 144–148.

Wu, Ruth. *Behavior and Illness*. Englewood Cliffs, N.J.: Prentice-Hall, Inc., 1973, pp. 164–166.

Chapter 22

Self-esteem

*Marie J. Driever**

BEHAVIORAL OBJECTIVES

After studying this chapter, the reader will be able to:

1. Define the key concepts of the chapter.
2. Explain how self-esteem is related to all aspects of the self-concept.
3. Describe two areas of response from significant others that are important in developing self-esteem.
4. Identify the behaviors of and factors influencing low self-esteem.
5. Specify nursing interventions to be used in the problem of low self-esteem.

KEY CONCEPTS DEFINED

Self-Esteem: that pervasive aspect of the personal self component which relates to the worth or value the person holds of the self.

Low Self-Esteem: a negative feeling of self-value or worth, which handicaps a person's ability to adapt to the environment.

Limit Setting: the defining and setting forth by a person of the kind of behavior acceptable in the self or others.

Self-Definers: the reinforcement or feedback a person receives from others.

*Edited for the second edition by Marjorie H. Buck.

At the core of a person's description of who and what she or he is is the value that the person places on the self. *Self-esteem* is that pervasive aspect of the self-concept which relates to the worth or value the person holds of the self. The person experiences self-esteem in the form of a feeling. It is a feeling that can be difficult to isolate and identify because the individual experiences it constantly. Self-esteem is part of every feeling and emotional response of the person. It is thus a significant concept in the analysis of self-concept adaptation.

THE CONCEPT AND DEVELOPMENT OF SELF-ESTEEM

Abraham H. Maslow (1954) postulates that all people have a need to esteem or value themselves. Whatever view of the self a person holds, the person seeks to value this concept of who and what he or she is. People need to be able to place high positive values on the concept of self they hold. This experience helps them to seek and deal with their environmental experiences. If a person has a low value of self, that person tends to perceive the environment as negative and threatening. The individual will perceive the world as giving negative feedback and threatening or attacking who and what one is. The person's ability to perceive environmental stimuli and deal with them is disrupted by the attempt to ward off further threat to an already low esteem.

The person will be able to deal more actively with the environment if feelings of self-value and security have been internalized. The secure individual will perceive fewer external events as threatening, and therefore will have less anxiety to deal with and will therefore find it easier to modify or change aspects of the concept of self. As various maturational and situational crises demand changes, the person will adapt successfully. On the other hand, if a person feels of little value, that person will have an impaired ability to adapt to the changing environment. On a day-to-day level, the person's value of self is challenged by maturational and situational crises. The heart of adaptation of self-concept for the person is to achieve and maintain a high positive value of self over time in the midst of ever-changing views or concepts of self. A person with *low self-esteem* therefore has difficulty or a problem because of impaired ability to adapt.

An examination of what constitutes a feeling of value and how the person achieves a level of self-value is necessary to understand the problem of low self-esteem. Self-esteem is closely related to all aspects of the self-concept—the physical self, moral–ethical–spiritual self, self-consistency, and self-ideal and expectancy. We have already seen the primary influence of perceptions of how others see one in the formation of the self-concept. This influence is particularly significant for the development of self-esteem.

The fact that feelings of loss and consequent depression can result from changes in the physical self-concept was discussed in Chapter 18. When one has suffered the loss of body parts or functions, the person may also question his or her value. The situation with the moral–ethical–spiritual self is similar. If one's behavior is consistent with the code of behavior one deems desirable, the person is able to see the self as a good, desirable, or valued individual. If some of one's behavior goes against a personal moral code, guilt is experienced. The experience of guilt causes the person to feel that he or she is "bad" and unlovable, and to have less self-value. The need for maintaining self-esteem within a changing self-concept points to the significance of self-consistency. Prolonged anxiety, which results from threats of self-consistency, can be a cause or effect of insults to self-esteem. In regard to self-ideal and expectancy, if people feel that they have power and control to perform what they expect of themselves, they feel valuable. This stabilizes or increases their degree of self-esteem. If a person fails, however, to meet personal ideals, the failure decreases the feeling of self-worth.

We know that feedback of significant others is incorporated into a person's view of the self. The kind and amount of reinforcment the person receives is particularly crucial in providing a basis for self-valuation. There are two areas of response from significant others that provide ways of communicating worth to the person. In terms of the person valuing the self by the degree of meeting self-expectations and those of others, the first area relates to the types of expectations and the ways in which these are derived from others. One type of expectation is how one learns to be aware of and handle one's feelings, especially feelings of anger and aggression. Every person learns from others a set of expectations or standards of behavior for handling the environment and expressing feelings.

Small children respond to the loss of valued objects, usually a significant person such as mother or father, by protesting and acting out angry feelings. Separation or loss, even temporary, threatens the child's feeling of personal and environmental security. The child attempts to deal with this loss/anxiety experience by angry, protesting behavior. (See Chapter 24 on separation anxiety.)

However, persons around the child usually respond to this acting out by trying to control the behavior. They usually tell the child directly or indirectly that the child is bad for being angry. Thereafter any time the child feels anger, and acts it out by screaming, yelling, temper tantrums, or other behaviors, significant others reprimand him or her. Both the unacceptable behaviors and the child's feelings of anger are condemned. Thus the child learns a pattern of not being able to act out angry feelings, let alone feel them. The child can transfer this pattern of awareness and expression to other feelings. Most commonly, the child attributes this pattern of any feelings of asserting or acting out one's own wishes, goals, ideas, and desires on the environment. So, throughout life when day-to-day situations provoke angry feelings, the person feels guilty for having these feelings, and angry and disappointed at the self for not meeting the expectations of others.

When the adult person experiences a loss of a valued object or person, the person struggles to deal with the loss of support and feedback. The adult person also has to deal with the response pattern of not showing anger. Such a response pattern makes it difficult to be aware of and deal with the feelings of sadness and anger that the loss provokes. Thus the person turns the anger and sadness inward and feels of less worth.

The second area of response from significant others from which the child learns some degree of self-value is the limits that the child experiences while growing up. Some generalizations drawn from the research of Stanley Coopersmith (1967, 1968) explain the role that limits have in helping people develop high levels of self-esteem. Limits, or *limit setting*, refers to the defining and setting forth by a person of the kind of behavior that he or she will allow in the self or others. A child who grows up with well-defined and enforced limits set on behavior learns many things, such as what reality is, by the fact that behavior results in consequences. The young person also learns to predict what these consequences will be. The child can then choose what behavior to use based on knowing what consequences can be expected. The individual not only learns decision making but also how to get reinforcement. The child learns that positive feedback will be gained if certain behavior is chosen. From this the child learns to trust the self based on the ability to choose behavior that will be successful (get positive reinforcement). The child learns to set internal limits and thus learns independence. When problems arise, the young person has these coping behaviors of looking at the consequences of behaviors and decision making to aid in the self-reliance to solve these problems. Thus, from the experience of having reasonable, strict, defined, and enforced limits set, the child experiences seeing the self as a competent person and one who achieves positive feedback from others. A child who does not have these limits set loses the opportunity to experience the competence and positive feedback from which a high level of self-esteem is achieved. As an adult, the person with positive childhood experience with limits is more easily able to set limits for personal behavior and that of others. Such an ability will enable the person to have control and direction in interpersonal situations. This will help the person to maintain high positive self-esteem.

Thus feedback from significant others in the form of limits and how one should handle feelings, the ability to control bodily functions, the ability to use behavior that brings satisfaction with self-expectancy, self-consistency, and the moral–ethical–spiritual self all provide the person with data. The data help to achieve a feeling of how competent and secure one is with oneself. Based on the degree of self-competence and security, the person derives a feeling of self-value or worth. How high or positive this feeling is for the person is the individual's feeling of self-esteem. If it is a low or negative feeling, the person has low self-esteem. A feeling of low self-esteem is a problem because it handicaps one's ability to adapt through the self-concept mode of adaptation.

ASSESSMENT OF LOW SELF-ESTEEM

Table 22.1 identifies the behaviors that a person with low self-esteem manifests. From these behaviors, one can conclude a picture of someone who perceives the self to be incompetent, unlovable, insecure, and unworthy. There are degrees to the feeling of low self-esteem, determined by the focal, contextual, and residual factors affecting a person's behavior. Depending on the quality, number, and degree of these factors, the person will experience varying degrees of feeling of low self-worth. The degree of feeling will determine the number and degree of behaviors exhibited.

Through observation of behavior and the use of communication techniques, the nurse can assess the degree of self-esteem that the person feels. The nurse completes the assessment by identifying the focal, contextual, and residual stimuli influencing the person. Table 22.1 also lists the focal, contextual, and residual factors influencing low self-esteem behaviors.

Generally speaking, these influencing factors can be grouped into three main themes. First, any situation or stimulus causing the person to question self-value is likely to be focal. This is particularly true for any perceived personal loss. Second, the kinds of feedback, reinforcement, and the person's awareness of these *definers of self and self-value*, as well as the pattern of dealing with feelings, provide the environmental or contextual stimuli. Third, any previous experience with loss, limits, and ability to cope with challenges to how one sees oneself provides the residual stimuli.

A person's projections of one's current level of esteem also becomes a contextual or residual factor in developing new levels of esteem. For example, a person with low self-esteem projects an image of being unlovable and worthless. This often determines the responses of others, which give additional messages of incompetence and worthlessness.

The nursing diagnoses that summarize assessment of self-esteem are stated in terms of behaviors and stimuli or as levels indicating level of self-esteem. See Chapter 14 on nursing diagnosis in the self-concept mode.

NURSING INTERVENTION IN LOW SELF-ESTEEM

The goal of nursing intervention with the problem of low self-esteem is to help the individual see the focal stimulus as having a positive valuing influence, rather than as being another negative devaluing experience. Nursing interventions can be grouped into actions directed toward managing contextual stimuli and those directed toward managing residual stimuli.

In working with contextual stimuli, the nurse uses communication techniques to help the person define what kind of reinforcement or feedback is received and from whom. The person needs to identify and answer the question: "What are my self-definers?" The person also needs to dis-

TABLE 22.1
Nursing Assessment of Low Self-Esteem

| Expected Behavior of Low Self-Esteem[a] | Influencing Factors | | |
	Focal	Contextual	Residual
1. Loss of appetite (often leading to weight loss)	1. Any experience or situation causing the person to question and/or decrease the value of self; loss experiences are particularly important	1. Any body changes the person is experiencing – growth or illness	1. Age and coping mechanisms person has developed
2. Overeating (leading to obesity)		2. The maturational crisis the person is experiencing and how well the person is mastering the developmental tasks of maturational crisis	2. Kinds and degree of threatening situations person has previously experienced and how well the person has coped with them
3. Constipation or diarrhea			
4. Difficulty in sleeping – difficulty in falling asleep, awakening during night or early morning, inability to return to sleep, no restful feeling after sleeping		3. Situational crisis caused by demands which exceed the person's ability to cope	3. Previous messages of value received from significant others
5. At times withdrawal to bed and/or oversleeping		4. Messages, feedback the person received from significant others as to one's worth and value	4. Previous developmental and situational crises person has experienced and how well the person has coped with them
6. Complaints of fatigue			
7. Poor posture			
8. Withdrawal from activities		5. How well the person meets self-expectations and those of significant others	5. Previous experience with powerlessness and hopelessness and how the person has coped with them
9. Difficulty in initiating new activities			
10. Decrease in sex drive		6. Feeling of control the person experiences over reinforcers in environment	6. Previous losses and ability to grieve and resolve the loss
11. Decrease in spontaneous behavior			
12. Appearance of sadness and/or anxiety, discouragement		7. The variety and kinds of self-definers the person has,	7. How many and degree of
13. Expression of feeling of isolation, being unlovable, unable to express or define oneself, and too weak to confront or overcome difficulties			
14. Fearful of angering others			

TABLE 22.1 Continued
Nursing Assessment of Low Self-Esteem

Expected Behavior of Low Self-Esteem[a]	Influencing Factors		
	Focal	Contextual	Residual
		how aware of them the person is, and how the person uses them to define self-value; present limits of self set	successes or failures experienced
15. Avoidance of situations of self-disclosure/notice in any way			8. Previous experience with meeting self-ideals, expectancies, and standards of behavior set for self
16. Tendency to stay in background, be listener rather than participant		8. Experiences of guilt, shame, powerlessness, and how the person copes with these feelings	9. Previous experience of control of self and environment
17. Sensitivity to criticism, self-conscious, preoccupied with inner problems			10. Previous experience with decision making and consequences of those decisions
18. Expression of feelings of helplessness/inability to do what one chooses		9. The kind and number of changes demanded in how the person sees and how these demanded changes are handled	11. Previous experience with limits as a child, whether limits were clear, defined, and enforced
19. Expression of being unable to do anything "good" or productive, feeling of badness, worthlessness, inadequacy		10. Awareness of what affects self-concept (e.g., feedback from others) and how the person deals with these stimuli	
20. Degrading talk, self-depreciating, self-dislike, unhappiness with self			
21. Denial of past successes/accomplishments, present possibility of success of activities			
22. Feeling that anything one does will fail, be meaningless			

400

11. How many failures the person allows without judging self to be valueless
12. How good the person feels about self, level of self-value, esteem, level of security with self
13. Limits in environment, awareness and use of those limits
14. The support from significant others and ability to accept and use the support
15. Ability to be aware, express and deal with anger, as well as other feelings
16. Person's current feeling of hope, comfort with self

23. Rumination about problems
24. Seeking reinforcement from others, making efforts to gain favors but failing to reciprocate such behavior
25. Seeing self as a burden to others
26. Alienation from others by clinging and self-preoccupation
27. Self-accusation
28. Demanding reassurance but not accepting it
29. Hostile behavior
30. Angry at self and others but unable to express these feelings directly
31. Decrease in ability to meet responsibilities, do simple tasks
32. Decrease in interest, motivation, concentration
33. Complaining of being "boxed in"
34. Taking longer to do tasks
35. Decrease in self-care, hygiene
36. Complains of aches, pains of various kinds

[a]Indicates that a person with low self-esteem may exhibit any number of these behaviors and to different degrees. The number and degree of behaviors are expressions of the degree of low esteem the person holds of self.

cover what feelings of sadness, loss, anger, unhappiness, joy, and gladness personally feel like. The individual needs to know what they mean personally, and what situations elicit these feelings. The nurse helps the individual identify and express feelings. The nurse also assists the individual in gaining an understanding of the relationship between unrecognized, unexpressed feelings and a low sense of self-worth. Gaining insight into that relationship allows the individual to begin to see feedback from others as separate from the self. The person can then make a conscious decision about what feedback to take seriously and how to handle feedback that is negative or incongruent with one's self-concept.

Through the use of communication techniques, the nurse can help the person understand the current maturational and/or situation crisis, the accompanying expections of others and the self. The nurse can also explore with the person how these expectations can be met and the crisis resolved. The individual needs to understand, define, accept, and try out control of the environment that is personally comfortable.

The person also needs to develop awareness of what experiences of loss, shame, guilt, powerlessness, and failure feel like, what situations bring these feelings on, and ways of coping with them without self-devaluation.

In managing the residual stimuli, the nurse uses communication techniques that will help the person gain a perspective of how the past influences the present. The individual needs to recognize that current ineffective patterns resulted from past experiences of being made to feel guilty for expressing angry feelings. Feelings, especially anger, are usually not directly expressed. The nurse helps the person identify patterns of behavior now used and resolve the way in which these patterns got started. With the anger example, the person needs to identify how the bad feeling came about and how to express those feelings so that a decision can be made regarding as to how to deal with angry feelings in the future.

Through intervention with therapeutic communication techniques, the nurse will help the person change her or his view of life. A person with low self-esteem feels that life is just a series of confirming self-degrading experiences. Everyone needs to see life as unfolding experiences with the potential for defining in a meaningful and self-valuing way who and what one is. Each person needs to find ways of perceiving the self as a joyful being. Helping the person gain the ability to differentiate past and present experiences will assist the individual in achieving a hopeful perception. Many times the way in which the nurse can do this is by telling the individual that experiences of self and environment can be satisfying and that it is all right to have both positive and negative feelings. Above all, through therapeutic response to the person, the nurse needs to help the individual be aware of personal feelings and way of dealing with these feelings constructively.

Through therapeutic communication, the nurse can aid the individual in feeling hope. Sister Madeleine Vaillot (1970) defines hope as the feeling of to be. To feel hope is to feel a positive level of value or self-esteem based on the belief that it is possible to truly be and to influence the environment and to have others respond positively. Thus the nurse needs to help the person gain a clear view of the self and self-expectations and make the decision to continue actively to choose life situations that will support these views of the self. If the choices are limited, the nurse needs to help the person understand how and why these experiences contribute to valueless feelings. In this way the nurse can assist the person to define the self in a competent, satisfying way and to achieve the feedback to continue that view. With this kind of positive picture of the self, the person will be able to change self-views, yet maintain esteem and thereby adapt through the self-concept.

SUMMARY

Self-concept is a core reality experienced by all persons in health and illness. Self-esteem, or value held of the self, is significant for adapting the self in a satisfying way to the world around us. Gordon (1982) lists the accepted nursing diagnoses — self-concept, disturbance in (self-esteem, personal identity) — as being within the functional health pattern area of self-perception/self-concept pattern. This chapter has looked at the way that levels of self-esteem are established. Every individual will have some level of self-esteem. Low levels of self-esteem often prolong rates of recovery, particularly in rehabilitation and psychiatric illnesses. Thus nursing assessment and intervention with manifestations of low self-esteem are an important part of nursing care.

STUDENT LEARNING ACTIVITY

You are talking to the mother of a 2-year-old child about well child care. What would you tell her about limit setting and its effects on self-esteem?

REFERENCES

Coopersmith, Stanley. *The Antecedents of Self Esteem*. San Francisco: W. H. Freeman and Company, Publishers, 1967.

Coopersmith, Stanley. "Studies in Self-Esteem," *Scientific American*, vol. 218, no. 2, February 1968, pp. 96–106.

Gordon, Marjorie. *Nursing Diagnosis: Process and Application*. New York: McGraw-Hill Book Company, 1982.

Maslow, Abraham H. *Motivation and Personality.* New York: Harper & Row, Publishers, 1954.

Vaillot, Sister Madeleine Clemence. "Hope: The Restoration of Being," *American Journal of Nursing*, vol. 70, no. 2, 1970, pp. 268–277.

ADDITIONAL READINGS

Carlson, Carolyn E. "Grief and Mourning," in *Behavioral Concepts and Nursing Intervention*, Carolyn Carlson, coordinator. Philadelphia: J. B. Lippincott Company, 1970, pp. 95–115.

Crary, William, and Gerald Crary. "Depression," *American Journal of Nursing*, vol. 73, no. 3, 1973, pp. 472–475.

Fraiburg, Selma H. *The Magic Years.* New York: Charles Scribner's Sons, 1959.

Jourard, Sidney. "Suicide, the Invitation to Die," *American Journal of Nursing*, vol. 70, no. 2, 1970, pp. 269–275.

Lange, Silvia. "Shame," in *Behavioral Concepts and Nursing Intervention*, Carolyn Carlson, coordinator. Philadelphia: J. B. Lippincott Company, 1970, pp. 67–94.

Lyon, Glee Gamble. "Limit Setting as a Therapeutic Tool," *Journal of Psychiatric and Mental Health Services*, November/December 1970, pp. 17–24.

Mendels, Joseph. *Concepts of Depression.* New York: John Wiley & Sons, Inc., 1970.

Neylan, Margaret P. "The Depressed Patient," *American Journal of Nursing*, vol. 61, no. 7, 1961, pp. 77–78.

Thaler, Otto. "Grief and Depression," *Nursing Forum*, vol. 5, no. 2, 1966, pp. 8–22.

Tiedt, Eileen. "The Adolescent in the Hospital: An Identity-Resolution Approach," *Nursing Forum*, vol. 11, no. 2, 1972, pp. 120–140.

Toffler, Alvin, ed. *Learning for Tomorrow: The Role of the Future in Education.* New York: Vintage Books, 1974.

Travelbee, Joyce. *Interpersonal Aspects of Nursing*, 2nd ed. Philadelphia: F. A. Davis Company, 1971.

Ujhely, Gertrude. "Grief and Depression: Implications for Preventive and Therapeutic Nursing Care," *Nursing Forum*, vol. 5, no. 2, 1966, pp. 23–35.

Ujhely, Gertrude. "What Is Realistic Emotional Support?" *American Journal of Nursing*, vol. 68, no. 4, 1969, pp. 758–762.

Chapter 23

Role Transition, Distance, and Conflict

Kathleen Anschutz Nuwayhid

BEHAVIORAL OBJECTIVES

After studying this chapter, the reader will be able to:

1. Define the key concepts of the chapter.
2. Identify and explain the difference between a nursing diagnosis of role mastery and a diagnosis of effective role transition.
3. Identify and explain the nursing diagnosis of ineffective role transition.
4. Identify and describe the major contextual stimuli involved in a nursing diagnosis of ineffective role transition.
5. Identify and explain the nursing diagnosis of role conflict.
6. Identify and describe the major contextual stimuli involved in a nursing diagnosis of role conflict.
7. Differentiate between a diagnosis of intrarole conflict and interrole conflict.
8. Describe and explain the difference between a diagnosis of role failure and ineffective role transition, role distance, and role conflict.

KEY CONCEPTS DEFINED

Role Prescription: the instrumental and expressive behaviors to be performed by an individual occupying a specific role. These may be determined by society, culture, education, or a combination of these variables.

Role Transition: the process of assuming and developing a new role. It is growth in a positive direction, and is compatible with the tasks of the primary role of the individual.

Effective Role Transition: the individual exhibits adaptive expressive behaviors, and a few adaptive instrumental behaviors, that partially meet with the social expectations associated with the assigned role. However, the number or quality of the behaviors is not sufficient to formulate a diagnosis of role mastery. The adaptive behaviors indicate positive movement toward the goal of role mastery. There may or may not be some instrumental behaviors.

Ineffective Role Transition: the individual exhibits adaptive expressive behaviors, but exhibits ineffective instrumental behaviors for a particular role. This is usually the result of an absence of role models, or lack of knowledge or education of the role.

Role Distance: the individual exhibits both instrumental and expressive behaviors appropriate to a particular role, but these behaviors differ significantly from prescribed behaviors for the role (Schofield, 1976).

Intrarole Conflict: the individual fails to demonstrate either instrumental or expressive behaviors or both, appropriate for a role, as a result of incompatible expectations from one or more persons in the environment concerning the individual's expected behavior (Schofield, 1976).

Interrole Conflict: the individual fails to demonstrate the instrumental and/or expressive behaviors appropriate to the individual's role as a result of the occupation of one or more roles that require prescribed behaviors that are incompatible with one another.

Role Failure: the individual has an absence of expressive behaviors or exhibits ineffective expressive behaviors, and/or has an absence of instrumental behaviors or exhibits ineffective instrumental behaviors for a particular role.

In the practice of professional nursing we interact with individuals, who occupy a wide variety of primary, secondary, and tertiary roles. In applying the nursing process within the framework of the Roy Adaptation Model with these individuals, we assess, diagnose, and intervene regarding problems. Initially, the sheer number of roles that the nurse could possibly identify in a person is staggering. Fortunately, all roles have certain basic elements in common, as described in Chapter 15. It does not matter what the role is: mother, lawyer, school-age child, chemist, or auto mechanic—it exists in relationship to another role, and it is occupied by an individual. All roles have instrumental (that is, goal-oriented) behaviors and expressive (that is, affective) behaviors, and are influenced by common major stimuli.

In the same context, there are certain disruptions or problems, that are shared by all roles. This chapter identifies these common role disruptions based on role theory. Each disruption is presented using the case study format to enable the reader to distinguish among the disruptions more easily. The maternal role has been chosen to illustrate common role disruptions, because of its universal reference, its documentation in the literature, and its relevance for nursing practice. As in previous chapters, emphasis is placed on the application of the nursing process within the framework of the Roy Adaptation Model. Particular attention is given to the relationship between stimuli and behaviors and to the common role disruptions. The nursing interventions that are presented are applicable to roles other than the maternal role.

THE MATERNAL ROLE

The maternal role will be presented as occurring in the young adult stage of development, for the purposes of illustration, although motherhood can occur anywhere from adolescence through the generative adult phase of development. The secondary role of mother is most compatible with meeting the developmental tasks of the young adult. The maternal role theory presented in this chapter is used for the purpose of illustration, and in no manner is intended to be an adequate presentation of maternal role theory. The taking on of the maternal role is complex and multiphasic in nature, and provides an example that will enhance the reader's ability to learn the common role disruptions.

The maternal role has three distinct phases: childbearing, childbirth, and child rearing. Childbearing takes place usually in 9-month increments, and is spread over a period of years in a woman's life. Childbirth usually occurs over a period of hours. The average woman experiences childbearing and childbirth only two to four times in her lifetime. Child rearing, however, takes place over the first 18 years of the child's life. Although the expressive maternal behaviors and the instrumental maternal behaviors change as the child grows older, the secondary role of mother is permanent and is relinquished only upon death.

The transition from nonmother to mother begins in pregnancy (Rubin, 1967). As with the assumption of any new role, the pregnant woman's beginning behaviors are primarily expressive behaviors (Randell, 1976). She verbalizes these feelings, and they become expressive behaviors. A positive self-concept is important during this phase in order for the woman to be able to think of herself as mother (Clausen, 1973). The woman begins to talk about her baby as another person, and to fantasize about herself as a mother. As the birth of the baby becomes imminent, she seeks out information pertaining to the role of mother from books, friends, and particularly, her own mother. She looks for role models to imitate in order to learn the instrumental behaviors of her new role (Rubin, 1967). Women experiencing their second pregnancies also exhibit similar behavior, because the role of mother is mastered over a number of years and changes with the birth of each child.

The literature tells us what expressive maternal behaviors and instrumental maternal behaviors to expect the mother to exhibit after the birth of her child. In the first 2 to 3 days after birth, the mother is passive and dependent. It is a period where the majority of maternal role behaviors are expressive, and this is adaptive. Naturally, second-time mothers would exhibit instrumental maternal behaviors much sooner than would a first-time mother. During the third to tenth days after birth, the mother begins to exhibit instrumental maternal behaviors. After the second week, and until several weeks thereafter, the mother experiences a period of grief work, wherein she mourns the loss of her role of nonmother, career woman, and so forth (Rubin, 1967). This grief work is resolved over time, and Rubin (1967) states that this usually occurs within four weeks if role transition is well in progress.

Research, and the descriptive literature, tell us how the maternal role is attained. Society, culture, the mother's self-concept, and her expectations of the maternal role tell a woman what the maternal role behaviors should be. That is, they provide *role prescriptions*, both expressive and instrumental. However, the mother's self-concept, and her expectations of the maternal role, must be compatible with society and culture's expectations, or the potential for disruption within the maternal role, and between other roles, will exist. Fortunately, there are wide variances of adaptive behaviors within the maternal role behaviors. These factors are presented later in the section discussing effective role transition.

ROLE TRANSITION

The process of assuming and developing a new role is called *role transition*. By definition, role transition indicates that it is growth in a positive direction. In the case of the maternal role, a secondary and permanent role, the new role is one of a series of roles that an individual assumes to meet the developmental tasks of her primary role. It is a continuous and ongoing process. As an individual ages chronologically, the primary role changes; new developmental tasks confront the individual, and new secondary and tertiary roles are assumed in order to meet these developmental tasks. It should be noted that the transition from one secondary role to another secondary role is a much more arduous and time-consuming process than moving from one tertiary role to another. Tertiary roles, by their nature, are usually temporary and require less emotional and physical involvement than secondary roles.

It should also be remembered that an individual does not always have a conscious choice about assuming a new role. Many secondary roles can be thrust upon the individual by circumstances and the environment. For example, a man who has worked all his life as a taxi driver may have an accident that leaves him unable to drive a taxi, but he may still be able to hold another kind of job. This man, then, has to seek a new job, and even, perhaps, retraining. He did not choose to seek a new secondary role, but his ability to adapt to his new role, and make an effective transition to a new secondary role, are threats to his social integrity. It is this threat, or potential disruption, that we, as nurses, are concerned with in assessment of the role function mode of adaptation.

In assessing the role function mode adaptation of various persons with whom the nurse comes in contact, you will identify many secondary and tertiary roles that are in transition. Based on the data gathered and the assessment made, the nurse will need to make a judgment about whether the role transition is effective (that is, adaptive) or ineffective before formulating a nursing diagnosis. In order to do this, there are certain factors to identify.

EFFECTIVE ROLE TRANSITION

In *effective role transition*, the individual exhibits adaptive expressive behaviors, and a few adaptive instrumental behaviors, that partially meet with the social expectations associated with the assigned role. However, the number or quality of the behaviors is not sufficient to formulate a diagnosis of role mastery. The adaptive behaviors indicate positive movement toward the goal of role mastery.

In the initial phase of effective role transition, the behaviors will primarily be expressive behaviors. However, this occurs for a very short period of time. Almost immediately, some instrumental behaviors are observable. If the transition is effective, the number and quality of instrumental behaviors will increase over time. As noted in the literature on role theory, for role transition to occur, certain factors must be present in the environment. These factors are the partitions described in Chapter 15. Also, the expressive and instrumental behaviors are usually affected by the seven major stimuli described in that chapter.

The following is a short case study designed to illustrate effective role transition from the role of nonmother to mother:

Case Study

Wendy S. is a 25-year-old primipara (a woman who has delivered her first child), who delivered a healthy 7 lb 11 oz baby boy 4 days ago. Her pregnancy was uneventful and uncomplicated. She and her husband attended Lamaze childbirth education classes and at the time of delivery she received no medication. Wendy is breast feeding her baby and plans to stay home with him, perhaps returning to work, when he is ready for nursery school. If their finances permit, Wendy would enjoy being at home with the baby full time.

Until one week before delivery, she worked as a hair stylist in a local beauty salon. She has been married for 3 years. She and her husband are both Catholic and of German descent. Wendy is close to her mother, but her mother lives far away and will not be able to come to help with the baby. Wendy also has a close relationship with her mother-in-law. Her mother-in-law will be staying with Wendy and the baby for the first 2 weeks after Wendy gets home. Wendy's husband will be taking a 2-week vacation after his mother leaves, so that Wendy will have at least a month of help at home. The husband is a truck driver, but he is seldom away from home for extended periods of time.

Wendy told the nurse that she took a Red Cross infant care course while she was pregnant because she wanted to have some formal preparation for baby care. Wendy says that she is thrilled and very excited to have a baby of her own. She says that it is even more thrilling seeing how excited her husband is about the baby. Wendy has helped care for friends' babies, and younger cousins, but realizes that having a baby of one's own is very different.

Wendy feels that having the baby in the room with her is a tremendous way to get to know the baby. She chose to breast-feed because she wanted to do everything that she could to help the baby be healthy. The nurse caring for Wendy has observed that Wendy holds the baby comfortably, asks many questions about breast-feeding, and is eager to dress and bathe him. Wendy also asks her roommate, a woman with three children, many questions about babies and what it is like when you are at home.

Assessment

Wendy's primary role is that of a 25-year-old young adult woman. Developmental tasks include establishment as an independent individual, with family and friends; building a strong, mutual, affectional bond with (possible) marriage partner and family of spouse; and being able to nurture, support, and provide for spouse and offspring.

Wendy is four days postpartum. The literature tells us that a woman who is in effective role transition will begin to exhibit beginning instrumental behaviors for the maternal role around the third day postpartum. Such instrumental behaviors as feeding, bathing, and changing the baby's diapers should be exhibited by this time (Rubin, 1961).

From the data given, we can identify Wendy's secondary roles as:

1. Wife
2. Mother
3. Daughter
4. Daughter-in-law
5. Hair stylist

These are tentatively ranked in order of importance. However, to be accurate, Wendy would have to rank them herself. For the purpose of learning, we will assume that Wendy has mastered all of her secondary roles, except for the maternal role. In actual practice a nurse would perform first- and second-level assessments on all roles occupied by the individual.

The following is a first-level assessment of Wendy S. based on the data collected. Behaviors are marked as E/A, expressive/adaptive; E/I, expressive/ineffective; I/A, instrumental/adaptive; or I/I, instrumental/ineffective. Keep in mind that effective role transition is a point on a continuum between nonmastery and mastery of a particular role. It is in constant motion, moving in a positive direction toward role mastery:

First-Level Assessment

Expressive Behaviors

1. Is thrilled with having a baby of her own.	E/A
2. Derives a great deal of joy and happiness from having produced such a healthy child.	E/A
3. Husband is thrilled that she gave him a child.	E/A
4. Wants to help baby be healthy by breast feeding him.	E/A
5. Likes having baby in the room with her.	E/A
6. Likes doing things for the baby.	E/A
7. Asks the nurse many questions about baby.	E/A
8. Asks roommate many questions about baby.	E/A
9. Tells nurse that she has a close relationship with her mother-in-law.	E/A

Instrumental Behaviors

1. Attended Lamaze childbirth classes.	I/A
2. Had prenatal care.	I/A
3. Actively participated in her labor and delivery.	I/A
4. Attended Red Cross infant care classes.	I/A
5. Giving physical care of baby during rooming-in.	I/A

6. Learning to care for baby in baby classes.   I/A
7. Breast-feeds baby.   I/A
8. Chose to deliver in hospital and remain in hospital for care.   I/A
9. Has planned for home care of baby and help at home.   I/A

All of the expressive maternal behaviors are adaptive. Notice that the expressive behaviors are numerous, and that even though there seem to be many instrumental behaviors present, the instrumental behaviors are primarily anticipatory in nature. The instrumental behaviors are aimed at learning the new role rather than actual role performance. This is adaptive and sequential in effective role transition. First, one feels the role; second, learns the instrumental role behavior; and finally, performs the instrumental role behaviors. In the second-level assessment, we determine if all the factors are present in the environment for this process to take place.

Second-Level Assessment and Interventions

Focal stimulus for all behaviors: pregnancy and delivery of a healthy 7 lb 11 oz baby boy.

All of the environmental stimuli or partitions are present for both the expressive and instrumental role behaviors. Although the instrumental behaviors are few in number, the stimuli are present that will allow these behaviors to occur and increase in number. We have been unable to identify any ineffective behaviors in the first-level assessment or any disruptions in our second-level assessment. We are ready to formulate the nursing diagnosis.

The nursing goal is a short-term goal because, as we said in the beginning of this chapter, mastery of the maternal role takes place over an extended period of time. It is better, then, to have short-term, attainable goals which will lead to the end goal of role mastery.

Because there are no disruptions, we search the assessment for possible weaknesses in the partitions or the potential for disruptions to occur. Again, we find none. All contextual stimuli are present and appear to be sound. Our nursing interventions, therefore, are aimed at supporting existing behaviors and increasing the number of adaptive behaviors. This is done by managing the contextual stimuli, especially role modeling, knowledge or education, the support system, rewards, and self-concept, as seen in our interventions.

In Wendy's case, she should be evaluated prior to discharge, and plans for her care at home should be formulated as well. It is important to realize that although Wendy has all the stimuli present that indicate effective role transition, the nurse's role is just as crucial as if there were a major disruption. The literature tells us that unless these behaviors are supported, and the stimuli maintained by nursing interventions, disruptions will occur.

Table 23.1 summarizes the second-level assessment and care plan.

ROLE PROBLEMS: INEFFECTIVE ROLE TRANSITION

A diagnosis of role mastery indicates that an individual demonstrates both expressive and instrumental behaviors that *meet* social expectations associated with the role. In *effective role transition*, the individual exhibits adaptive expressive behaviors, and a few adaptive instrumental behaviors, that *partially* meet the social expectations associated with the role. These are the two nursing diagnoses applicable to adaptive role behaviors. However, there are four possible nursing diagnoses for ineffective role behaviors: ineffective role transition, role distance, role conflict, and role failure. We will deal first with ineffective role transition.

In *ineffective role transition*, the individual exhibits adaptive expressive behavior but exhibits ineffective instrumental behaviors for a particular role. Unlike the other three disruptions, which usually arise from some sort of conflict, ineffective role transition is usually the result of a lack of knowledge, education, practice or role models.

Ineffective role transition resembles effective role transition in that all of the expressive behaviors are adaptive and all of the partitions or contextual stimuli for the expressive behaviors are present. The individual experiencing ineffective role transition—maternal role has the self-concept of mother, wants to be a mother, and may even know what a mother is expected to do, but she does not know how to accomplish the tasks.

Case Study

Gail G. is a 21-year-old woman, married for a year. She delivered a 6 lb 13 oz baby girl 3 days ago. Both she and baby are doing well.

Gail's husband is a business executive. They have recently moved to town, away from family and friends, because of a business transfer. They are both very pleased about the baby. Through a series of mishaps, Gail never took any childbirth preparation or baby care courses. She states that she has had very limited experience with babies, but feels that she can be a good mother. Up until two weeks prior to delivery, Gail worked as a dental technician. All of Gail's other secondary roles are in mastery.

TABLE 23.1
Second-Level Assessment of Wendy S. and Care Plan

Behaviors	Focal	Stimuli		
		Contextual	Residual	

Behaviors	Focal	Contextual	Residual
Expressive	Given		Religion
(1)		*Consumer*	Culture
		Baby	Intelligence (must be validated)
		Reward	
(2), (3), and (4)		Is able to think of self as mother; positive self-concept; praise of significant others	
(5) and (6)		Physical well-being of infant	
		Access to facilities	
(7), (8), and (9)		Has access to the baby in a supportive setting	
		Cooperation/collaboration	
		Husband, nurse, mother, mother-in-law, room-mate	
Instrumental		*Consumer*	Level of health
(1), (2), (3), and (4)		Baby and self	Physical structure
			Culture
		Reward	
(5), (6), and (7)		Healthy infant	
(8)		Self satisfaction	
		Access to facilities	
(9)		Physical environment of hospital; role models	

414

Experience with other children

Cooperation/collaboration
Mother-in-law and husband will be at home to help with the baby

Nursing Diagnosis	Goals	Interventions
(Includes all instrumental and expressive behaviors) Effective role transition, maternal role, as evidenced by: 1. Expressive behaviors which are compatible-expressive role behaviors of a woman 4 days after delivery (Rubin, 1961). 2. All partitions of the expressive and instrumental behaviors are present. 3. Beginning instrumental maternal role behaviors; client is learning and performing behaviors of the maternal role.	1. Client will continue to exhibit effective maternal role transition behaviors, as evidenced by an increase in the number of adaptive expressive and adaptive instrumental behaviors. 2. Client will continue to have a positive relationship with her husband, baby, and significant others.	1. Nurse will provide time for client to attend child care classes in the hospital. 2. Nurse will reinforce information and skills learned in child care classes, by demonstration to client, her husband and any interested significant other. 3. Nurse will support and praise all efforts made by client to care for infant. 4. Nurse and nursing staff will allow client to assume independence regarding child care at her own pace. 5. Nurse will recommend reference and reading materials concerning child care for client and husband. 6. Nurse will inform client of mother's support group, and community resources for new mothers. 7. Evaluate progress prior to discharge, and modify interventions as necessary.

First-Level Assesment

Gail G.'s primary role is as a 21-year-old young adult woman. Her secondary roles include:

1. Wife
2. Mother
3. Daughter
4. Dental assistant

Expressive Behaviors

1. I have always wanted a baby.	E/A
2. I believe that I can be a good mother.	E/A
3. I think I love my baby already.	E/A
4. I am so happy about my baby.	E/A
5. My husband is very pleased about my delivery.	E/A
6. I love holding my baby.	E/A
7. I want to do things for my baby; I just don't know how.	E/A
8. I do not know how to care for a small baby.	E/A
9. I have no family here. We just moved here.	E/A
10. My husband is a great help to me. He'll help me with the baby.	E/A
11. I speak to my family often by phone.	E/A

Instrumental Behaviors

1. Holds and cuddles baby whenever possible.	I/A
2. Touches baby and holds baby close to body.	I/A
3. Bottle-feeds baby only if nurse is present during feeding.	I/I
4. Requests nurse to change, bathe, and dress baby.	I/I

All of Gail's expressive behaviors are adaptive, and all partitions for the expressive behaviors are present. However, notice the scarcity of instrumental behaviors. Of the four observable instrumental behaviors, two are adaptive and two are ineffective. In our second-level assessment, we will focus on the ineffective instrumental behaviors and the absence or presence of contextual stimuli. Remember that the partitions must be present for effective role transition to take place.

Second-Level Assessment (Instrumental) and Intervention

Focal stimulus for all behaviors: pregnancy and delivery of a 6 lb 13 oz baby girl.

In the nursing interventions, we have supported the contextual stimuli that have a positive affect on Gail's instrumental behaviors. We have added teaching, education, and role models by attending infant care classes, and increased Gail's sources of praise. We have initiated a broadening of her co-operation and collaboration by referring Gail to mothers' groups in the community, obtaining help at home, and visits by the public health nurse. As in effective role transition, there should be an increase in instrumental behaviors on a daily basis, and Gail should be experiencing effective role transition within six weeks.

Table 23.2 summarizes the second-level assessment and care plan.

ROLE PROBLEMS: ROLE DISTANCE

The individual experiencing *role distance* at first appears to be experiencing ineffective role transition. However, a detailed assessment reveals that the individual's instrumental behaviors in role distance vary greatly in degree and in type of response from the individual experiencing ineffective role transition. For example, the individual has the knowledge and experience to perform the instrumental behaviors associated with a role, but does so only when absolutely necessary or when there is no one else around to perform the tasks. The individual functions at a point just short of role failure by performing the minimal number of prescribed instrumental behaviors for the role. By role distance we mean that the individual exhibits both instrumental and expressive behaviors appropriate to a particular role, but that these behaviors differ significantly from prescribed behaviors for the role (Schofield, 1976).

Perhaps the most significant difference between role distance and the other role mode nursing diagnoses is that the role is incompatible with the individual's self-concept. The individual feels uncomfortable because the role is undesirable, either in part or as a whole. This is important to consider because the individual may not reject an entire role, but rather certain behaviors associated with the role that the individual perceives as undesirable. The individual seeks to alleviate this discomfort by exhibiting expressive behaviors which make the role seem unimportant or unworthy. Individuals occupying complementary roles for the role are made to feel uncomfortable in their positions. The individual makes derogatory remarks about the role, jokes, belittles, and constantly speaks out about the role in negative terms, as if she is suited only for something better. It should be kept in mind that this occurs in degrees. The more undesirable the role, the more numerous, severe, and pronounced are the expressive behaviors exhibited.

TABLE 23.2
Second-Level Assessment of Gail G. and Care Plan

Behaviors	Stimuli	
	Focal	*Contextual*
	Given	
(1) and (2)		*Consumer*
		Baby and self
(3)		*Reward*
		Nurse's praise
(4)		*Access to facilities*
		Does not know how to care for baby
		No role models present in environment other than nurse
		No prenatal classes taken
		Limited experience with small children
		Cooperation/collaboration
		Husband is helpful, will help with baby; no family physically present; no close friends physically present

Nursing Diagnosis	Goals	Interventions
Ineffective role transition, maternal role, as evidenced by an almost total lack of instrumental behaviors. This is due to:	1. Client will progress from ineffective role transition to effective role transition within a period of 6 weeks. (long term)	1. Nurse will assess in depth, client's knowledge of infant care.
1. A lack of education or knowledge of infant care.	2. Client will maintain self-concept of mother, in order to lead to an eventual goal of role mastery. (long term)	2. Nurse will encourage client to perform any infant care task that she might know, and praise her appropriately for her performance.
2. The absence of appropriate role models		

in the environment.

3. At this time, the only support system that the client has is her husband.

3. Client will be able to feed, bathe, and change infant confidently prior to discharge in 4 days. (short term)

4. Client will be able to recognize and intervene appropriately for: infant choking, vomiting, temperature elevation, and changes in color, prior to discharge. (short term)

3. Client will attend infant care classes in the hospital.

4. Nurse will reinforce teaching from infant care classes, and act as a role model.

5. Nurse will encourage independence, but allows client to progress at her own pace.

6. Nurse will be present for client's first attempts at all infant care tasks.

7. Nurse will praise client appropriately for task performance.

8. Nurse will include client's husband as much as possible in teaching.

9. Nurse will encourage husband to praise client.

10. Nurse will encourage client and husband to obtain some kind of help at home, for the first few weeks, and explain the importance of this help.

11. Nurse will refer client to several mother's support groups in the community to enlarge her support system.

12. Nurse will evaluate client's progress daily.

13. Nurse will arrange for weekly follow-up in home visits by the public health nurse, for the first 6 weeks at home.

14. Client will be reevaluated in 6 weeks by the public health nurse.

First-level Assessment

Rebecca D., a 33-year-old young adult woman, delivered a baby boy, weighing 8 lb 10 oz, 4 days ago. Her secondary roles are:

1. Wife
2. Mother
3. Lawyer
4. Daughter

Ranking is not in order of importance. In speaking with Rebecca, one feels that the role of lawyer should be ranked first. This judgment must be validated with the client, however; it cannot be assumed.

Rebecca tells you that being a lawyer is the most important thing in her life.

Expressive Behaviors

1. I know how to care for my baby, but someone will do that for me when I get home.   E/I
2. I have more important things to do than feed and diaper the baby.   E/I
3. Thank goodness for bottles. Someone else can feed the baby for me.   E/I
4. I just couldn't imagine myself breast feeding.   E/I
5. I know that this sounds terrible, but I just can't wait to get back to work.   E/I
6. All of my friends are career women. None of them have babies.   E/I
7. You nurses seem much better suited to doing things for the baby.   E/I
8. My husband is thrilled with the baby. That's because he doesn't have to do anything for him.   E/I
9. I really want my baby, but being a mother doesn't mean changing dirty diapers.   E/A

Instrumental Behaviors

1. Feeds baby only if nurse is unable to do so.   I/I
2. Holds baby comfortably.   I/A
3. Talks to baby and kisses him.   I/A
4. Helps nurse bathe and dress baby only if requested to do so by nurse.   I/I
5. Attends baby care classes only if constantly reminded by nurse.   I/I
6. Is always the last one to arrive for class.   I/I

Second-Level Assessment

In role distance, usually all of the partitions are either present in the environment or readily available. Because Rebecca's behaviors are indicative of role distance, the nurse should look closely at Rebecca's self-concept and her reward system. Rebecca has not developed the self-concept of mother in that she is able to see herself as caretaker, and therefore does not see the performance of instrumental maternal role behaviors as a reward to herself or her self-esteem. Her perception at present is that instrumental maternal role behaviors are incompatible with being a career woman. She therefore has not developed satisfaction from her role of mother, although the elements of rewards are present for her to utilize. Rebecca views the maternal role as a threat to her self-concept of being an intellectual career woman. A positive *contextual* stimulus is that she is able to accept the responsibility of being a mother and seeing that her baby is adequately cared for by competent help.

Table 23.3 summarizes the second-level assessment and care plan.

Nursing Interventions

It is important to remember that the goals formulated by the nurse are mutual goals (that is, formulated by the nurse and the client). The nurse must discuss goals with the client and then plan interventions, or the whole process will be doomed to failure. In a diagnosis of role distance, the client is experiencing a threat to self-concept caused by a perception of the role being incompatible with self-concept. The nurse's primary focus is to decrease the threat or discomfort to the client's self-concept. It is highly unlikely that this can be done quickly, while the client is still in the hospital. Initially, the nurse should give the client information that shows the potential compatibility between the client's perception of herself and the role of performance behaviors. In the case of Rebecca, she indicated that intellectual stimulation rewards her as a person. The nurse needs to appeal to Rebecca's self-concept of an intellectual in her teaching of the maternal role. At the same time, all other stimuli that exert a positive influence on maternal instrumental behaviors should be supported.

Rebecca's reward system is adversely affected by her perception of the maternal role behaviors. The nurse can change this by teaching, role modeling, giving in-depth explanations for infant care, and offering scientific literature for Rebecca to read. Rebecca's husband should be included as much as possible for his praise is a potential reward for her maternal role. The supportive environment should be maintained, and Rebecca should be introduced to other successful career women who have mastered the maternal role. The long-term goal for Rebecca would be effective role transition, and then role mastery.

TABLE 23.3
Second-Level Assessment of Rebecca D. and Care Plan

Behaviors	Focal	Stimuli	
		Contextual	*Residual*
Expressive (1) and (9)	Delivery of an 8 lb 10 oz baby boy	*Consumer* Baby	Husband's relationship with client
(2), (3), (4), (5), and (8)	Accepts ultimate responsibility for the baby's welfare	*Reward* Minimal, does not have self-concept of mother; rewards blocked by client's perception of maternal role; caretaking responsibilities are available in the environment	
(6) and (7)	Loves baby and wants him	*Access to facilities* Has access to baby in a supportive setting.	
		Cooperation/collaboration Available	
Instrumental (1), (4), (5), and (6)	Accepts ultimate responsibility for the baby's welfare	Does not have self-concept of mother Perceives caretaker portion of maternal role, as being incompatible with being a career woman	Experiences with mothers and babies in the past Perceptions of other secondary roles
	Loves baby and wants him	*Reward* Health of infant Personal satisfaction is absent	
(2) and (3)		*Access to facilities* Tools, education, role models are all available in environment	

Nursing staff available in hospital
Financially able to have full-time help at home
Has flexibility in law practice

Nursing Diagnosis	Goals	Interventions
Role distance, maternal role, due to:	1. Client will develop an awareness of the psychological and sociological aspects of the instrumental behaviors of the maternal role.	1. Nurse will provide client with literature which describes the importance of primary caretaker, and the effect that stimulation has on infant growth and development.
1. Client has incomplete self-concept of mother, because she does not perceive caretaker portion of maternal role as being compatible with her self-concept.	2. Client will develop an awareness of the potential rewards to her self-concept, as a result of performing instrumental role behaviors.	2. Nurse will discuss this literature with client and her husband, to broaden their awareness of their parenting roles.
2. Rewards for maternal role are minimal due to client's perception of role.	3. Client will begin to develop expressive maternal role behaviors.	3. Nurse will introduce client to women with comparable careers, who have mastered the maternal role, and have the self-concept of mother.
3. Client has components of cooperation/collaboration available.	4. Client will maintain performance of adaptive instrumental behavior.	4. Nurse will praise all appropriate attempts at maternal instrumental behaviors, and explain psychological and sociological implications of the behavior for infant.
		5. Nurse will demonstrate appropriate instrumental behaviors, and explain their significance to infant growth and development.
		6. Nurse will include husband, and any significant others, in client teaching.
		7. Nurse will refer client to a professional mother's support group in the community, prior to discharge.
		8. Reevaluate prior to discharge.

ROLE PROBLEMS: ROLE CONFLICT AND ROLE FAILURE

Whenever an individual fails to perform the prescribed behaviors for a role, for whatever the reasons, a disruption exists. The focal stimulus or immediate cause for the behavior varies according to the disruption. In ineffective role transition, it was the absence of knowledge, lack of education, or scarcity of role models that caused the disruption. In role distance, the performance of prescribed role behaviors was a threat to the self-concept. However, in role conflict, the two major focal stimuli for the behaviors are so different in nature that they necessitate that role conflict be divided into two major disruptions: intrarole conflict and interrole conflict.

In *intrarole conflict*, the individual fails to demonstrate either instrumental or expressive behaviors, or both, appropriate for a role, as a result of incompatible expectations from one or more persons in the environment concerning the individual's expected behavior (Schofield, 1976). For example, Judy M. comes from a traditional Italian Catholic family. She maintains a very close relationship with her mother and is in mastery of her daughter role. Judy is now the mother of a 6-week-old baby girl. She has read and taken classes about baby care and is up to date on the current trends. Judy's mother, however, is old-fashioned, and still believes in dressing babies in three layers of clothing in the middle of summer. Judy's mother's praise and approval are very important to Judy. In peforming her role as mother, Judy finds herself performing behaviors that try to meet her own perceptions of the maternal role, and then trying to meet her mother's perceptions. As she vascillates back and forth, Judy applies all of her energy trying to accommodate two opposing views of the maternal role. Given this conflict, Judy will not achieve role mastery.

Interrole conflict occurs when an individual fails to demonstrate the instrumental and/or expressive behaviors appropriate to the individual's role as a result of the occupation of one or more roles that require prescribed behaviors that are incompatible with one another. In this situation the individual is occupying roles that are in competition with one another.

An example of interrole conflict would be the case of Louise B. Louise is an electrical engineer who was just promoted at work. She works 10 to 12 hours per day and is in role mastery. Louise delivered a baby boy eight weeks ago, and she now considers her life total chaos. She wants to be at work to maintain her position and control. At the same time, she wants to be with her baby and be involved with as much of his care as possible. As a result, she is torn between the two roles and is not experiencing mastery in either one.

Both intrarole conflict and interrole conflict are complex role problems. They require the nurse to work with multiple stimuli, from the environment and from the client. Similarly role failure is a complex problem.

Role failure differs from all the other role mode diagnoses in that the individual fails to exhibit adaptive expressive behaviors. In the beginning of the chapter we said that the individual must feel the role, or want to assume the role. In role failure the individual does not want to assume the role, and any expressive behaviors that are observed are usually ineffective because they are aimed at pleasing the consumers for the role. The individual has an absence of expressive behaviors, or exhibits ineffective expressive behaviors, and/or has an absence of instrumental behaviors, or exhibits ineffective instrumental behaviors for a particular role. The key element in role failure is the individual's desire. If the individual exhibits any adaptive expressive behaviors concerning a role, the individual cannot be in role failure.

This is important to remember because when expressive and instrumental behaviors are ineffective, nurses too often label the client as being in role failure when really, the behavior is indicative of ineffective role transition or role conflict. Role failure does occur, but it is doubtful that the nurse in clinical practice will be confronted frequently with role failure. Role failure is one of the most complex diagnoses in the role mode and usually involves one or more of the other modes of the Roy Adaptation Model. The more complex aspects of role problems are considered in Part V.

SUMMARY

The nurse is concerned with promoting the person's integrity in the role function adaptive mode in health as well as in illness. This chapter has identified the differences between role mastery and effective role transition, and has given an illustration using a case study. The simple role problems of ineffective role transition and role distance were presented with case study examples. Role theory from Chapter 15 was integrated throughout with nursing process. The complex role diagnoses of role conflict and role failure were introduced briefly. In Gordon's (1982) organization of the accepted diagnoses of the North American Nursing Diagnoses Association, roles are referred to in two places. First, role performance is considered a subconcept of the label disturbance in self-concept. Second, she lists six specific diagnoses under the title role-relationship pattern. Four of these are more closely related to other aspects of the Roy Adaptation Model; however, actual and potential alterations in parenting are labels that might be considered appropriate diagnoses within the role function adaptive mode.

STUDENT LEARNING ACTIVITIES

1. Utilizing people with whom you come in contact in your everyday life, identify and describe an example of:
   (a) Effective role transition

(b) Ineffective role transition
(c) Role distance
2. Identify the major contextual stimuli involved in each of the examples that you have described.
3. Describe your assessment of what you think would constitute student role failure. Do you know anyone like this?
4. Utilizing your student role, describe an example of intrarole conflict.
5. Utilizing your student role, describe an example of interrole conflict.
6. Perform a complete role assessment on someone whom you know. Try to choose someone whom you think might have a potential disruption in a secondary role. Formulate a nursing diagnosis for each of this person's secondary roles.

REFERENCES

Banton, Michael. *Roles: An Introduction to the Study of Social Relations.* New York: Basic Books, Inc., Publishers, 1965.

Clausen, Joy Princeton, et al. *Maternity Nursing Today.* New York: McGraw-Hill Book Company, 1973.

Goffman, Erving. "Role Distance," in *Encounters.* Indianapolis: The Bobbs-Merrill Company, Inc., 1961, pp. 85–152.

Gordon, Marjory. *Nursing diagnosis: Process and Application.* New York: McGraw-Hill Book Company, 1982.

Hardy, Margaret E., and Mary E. Conway. *Role Theory: Perspectives for Health Professionals.* New York: Appleton-Century-Crofts, 1978.

Malaznik, Nancy. "Theory of Role Function," in Sister Callista Roy, *Introduction to Nursing: An Adaptation Model.* Englewood Cliffs, N.J.: Prentice-Hall, Inc., 1976.

Randell, Brooke. "Development of Role Function," in Sister Callista Roy, *Introduction to Nursing: An Adaptation Model.* Englewood Cliffs, N.J.: Prentice-Hall, Inc., 1976.

Roy, Sister Callista, and Sharon L. Roberts. *Theory Construction in Nursing: An Adaptation Model.* Englewood Cliffs, N.J.: Prentice-Hall, Inc., 1981.

Rubin, Reva. "Basic Maternal Behavior," *Nursing Outlook,* vol. 9, no. 11, 1961, pp. 683–686.

Rubin, Reva. "Attainment of the Maternal Role: Part 1. Process," *Nursing Research,* vol. 16, no. 3, Summer 1967, pp. 237–245.

Schofield, Ann. "Problems of Role Function," in Sister Callista Roy, *Introduction to Nursing: An Adaptation Model.* Englewood Cliffs, N.J.: Prentice Hall, Inc., 1976, pp. 265–287.

ADDITIONAL READINGS

Gross, Neal, Alexander McEachern, and Ward Mason. "Role Conflict and Its Resolution," in *Role Theory: Concepts and Research*, Bruce Biddle and Edwin Thomas, eds. New York: John Wiley & Sons, Inc., 1966.

McFarland, M., and J. B. Reinhart. "The Development of Motherliness," *Children*, March/April 1959, pp. 48–52.

Parsons, Talcott. *The Social System*. New York: The Free Press, 1964.

Parsons, Talcott. "Role Conflict and the Genesis of Deviance," in *Role Theory: Concepts and Research*, Bruce Biddle and Edwin Thomas, eds. New York: John Wiley & Sons, Inc., 1966.

Reeder, Sharon. "Becoming a Mother—Nursing Implications in a Problem of Role Transition," in *ANA Regional Clinical Conferences*. New York: Appleton-Century-Crofts, 1967, p. 204.

Reeder, Sharon, et al. "The Family in a Changing World," in *Maternity Nursing*, 14th ed. Sharon J. Reeder, Luigi Mastroianni, and Leonide L. Martin, eds. Philadelphia: J. B. Lippincott Company, 1980, pp. 23–33.

Robischon, Paulette, and Diane Scott. "Role Theory and Its Application to Family Nursing," *Nursing Outlook*, July 1969, pp. 52–57.

Ruddock, Ralph. *Roles and Relationships*. Altantic Highlands, N.J.: Humanities Press, Inc., 1969.

Turner, Ralph H. "Role-Taking, Role Standpoint and Reference Group Behavior," in *Role Theory: Concepts and Research*, Bruce Biddle and Edwin Thomas, eds. New York: John Wiley & Sons, Inc., 1966.

Chapter 24

Separation Anxiety

Jane Servonsky and Mary Poush Tedrow

BEHAVIORAL OBJECTIVES

After studying this chapter, the reader will be able to:

1. Define the key concepts of the chapter.
2. Explain why separation anxiety is an interdependence problem.
3. Describe the process of attachment and separation as defined by the theorists Mahler, Bowlby, Robertson, and Erikson.
4. Identify and assess behaviors and common stimuli of separation anxiety.
5. Assess a person experiencing separation anxiety and apply the nursing process according to the Roy Adaptation Model in planning care for that person.

KEY CONCEPTS DEFINED

Separation Anxiety: a nursing diagnosis in the interdependence mode that describes the painful uneasiness of mind experienced by a person who is separated from a significant other. This condition is characterized by the three stages of protest, despair, and denial (detachment).

Significant Other: the individual to whom the most meaning or importance is given. It is a person who is loved, respected, and valued and who, in . turn, loves, respects, and values the person.

Bonding/Attachment: a reciprocal joining or uniting between two persons.

Separation–Individuation: the process by which the person is separated from the primary care giver and becomes an individual self.

The nurse using the Roy Adaptation Model of nursing views each person as a whole, integrated human being. When needs are not being met in one mode or component, a decreased level of adaptation is experienced. In responding to the needs of clients, the nurse anticipates stimuli that might decrease the level of adaptation or works with a person after they have experienced a decreased level of adequacy. The nurse's goal is to promote the highest level of adaptation and total integrity that the person can attain.

The interdependence mode is the mode in which affectional needs are met. Affectional needs represent the person's striving for relationships in life that provide the individual with a feeling of security in being nurtured, that is, in receiving growth-producing care and attention. The reciprocal nature of the mode is demonstrated by the person's willingness and ability both to give and to receive love, respect, and value within the relationship. Problems arise that stem from the interdependence mode when affectional needs are not met. Two such problems that occur frequently in North American society can be termed separation anxiety and loneliness. These two topics are explored in this chapter, and the next one, as they are relevant to nursing. This chapter provides a theoretical overview of separation anxiety and demonstrates how the nursing process based on the Roy Adaptation Model is used in meeting the needs of those who have this kind of unmet affectional need. In particular, we will show how the nurse, knowing that there are crisis periods for separation from the significant other, can reinforce or bring about a change in stimuli to decrease the intensity of the effect of the separation from a significant other.

THEORETICAL OVERVIEW

Separation anxiety is the painful uneasiness of mind due to separation from a significant other. Since the focal stimulus for this condition is the actual or threatened separation from a significant other, it is differentiated as a problem of interdependence from the earlier consideration of anxiety as a problem of the self-concept mode.

Separation anxiety is first experienced in infancy and the person then has the potential for experiencing it throughout the life span. There are developmental crises in the person's life that create a vulnerable period for anxiety related to separation. These developmental crises are explored in the following paragraphs. The works of Mahler (1979), Bowlby (1969, 1973), Robertson (1953), and Erikson (1963) will be used as the basis of this discussion.

The infant is separated at birth from the mother physiologically with the cutting of the umbilical cord. The beginning of emotional separation will occur during later stages of development. Before emotional separation can occur, emotional bonding or attachment (Klaus and Kennel, 1981) must occur with the significant other. *Bonding* is a term that describes a reciprocal joining or unity. It begins for the woman as she experiences pregnancy and proceeds through the tasks of pregnancy. Bonding probably begins for the fetus during this time, but is accelerated during and immediately following birth. By the time the child is ready to enter school, a process of *bonding and attachment* followed by a stage of separation and becoming a distinct separate individual has occurred. It is after the attachment phase and during the separation–individuation phase that separation anxiety first occurs and is most intense.

Margaret Mahler (1979) has done some of the definitive writing on the attachment–separation process. She describes three phases that are experienced in sequence. The first phase, *autism*, occurs during the first few weeks of life. The infant does not differentiate the self from the environment, but does learn to differentiate between pain and pleasure. The second phase, the *symbiotic phase*, refers to the attachment to the mother. At this time, about one month of age, the infant does not differentiate the self from the nonself but does attach to the mother. Mahler's third phase, the *separation–individuation* process, begins soon after the symbiotic or attachment phase.

There is a four-part progression that occurs during the separation-individuation process. *Separation* refers to separation from the constant care giver (usually the mother). *Individuation* refers to clearly becoming a self. The first subphase is termed *differentiation* and emerges as the infant becomes mobile by creeping, walking, climbing, and exploring the self and the environment. The infant stays near the mother and enjoys playing games with objects and people that repeatedly disappear and reappear, such as "where did it go?" and peek-a-boo. The next subphase is termed *practicing*, during which the child explores the environment near the mother and develops motor skills. The child in this stage accepts strangers readily as long as mother is near and the stranger does not approach. The next subphase, *rapprochement*, is one in which the child actively resists separation. It is manifested by the toddler using negative behavior, such as repeatedly saying no, or self-identity behavior such as saying "me" and "mine." There is an intense period of growth in the formation of the self-concept mode during the rapprochement phase. The separation from the mother is for longer periods, but the toddler continues to return to her frequently. The self-concept and interdependence modes are interconnected closely at this point of the toddler's life. The final subphase, *object constancy*, occurs from 18 to 36 months of age. The child develops intrapsychic symbols for the significant other. This development enables the child to begin separating without the overwhelming fear of abandonment.

Early work in separation anxiety was done by James Robertson (1953) and John Bowlby (1969). These authors describe the infant as recognizing the mother as an individual between 3 and 6 months of age. They go on to define the period of 18 to 24 months as a time of peak dependency on the care giver. The child at this time is possessively and passionately attached to the mother. The child is overwhelmed when the mother is separated from him or her. Bowlby and Robertson documented on film the behavior of children who were separated at the time of hospitalization. They defined three stages of separation anxiety through which the children proceed if their significant other is separated from them. The stages are protest, despair, and denial (detachment).

In the *protest* stage, children are acutely aware of their need for their mothers. They will do anything and do it vigorously to recapture their mothers. They do believe that their energetic protesting behaviors will in fact return their mothers to their sides.

The next stage of separation that children move to in a few hours or days is the stage of *despair*. During this stage, children are actively mourning the loss of the significant other and they withdraw. While mourning, each child remains preoccupied with the loss of the mother and remains vigilant for her return. It is the quiet phase of separation anxiety. The child is passive and will perform self-comforting activities, such as thumb sucking, clinging to a favorite toy or blanket from home, or masturbation.

The final phase of *denial* (*detachment*) is moved into slowly. At this point, children repress the need for their mothers and begin to be interested in the environment. Children begin to seek comfort in food and support from anyone who will give it to them. A stranger viewing a child at this stage would tend to remark on how well adjusted the child has become.

When the parents return, the child who has gone only as far as the stage of despair will usually reject the parents initially, and then respond to them slowly. The attachment is reestablished slowly as the child and significant other are reunited. Passing through these stages to a resolution hopefully will lead to a more comfortable separation another time. Although separation experiences are essential to the development of the individual, they should be minimized during periods of increased stress, such as hospitalization. This early work of Robertson and Bowlby has been helpful in the movement of extending visiting hours in pediatric hospitals and instituting policies of rooming-in for parents and families so that they may stay with the child at this time.

Erik Erikson (1963) has identified eight developmental crisis (stages) that are to be mastered sequentially through the life span. These tasks were described in Chapter 4. The tasks of infancy and early childhood relevant here are building trust and achieving autonomy. Thus another theorist describes the attachment and separation through which the child must proceed to attain a separation identity.

Ainsworth (1977) and Mead (1971) explored child behavior in other cultures. Ainsworth studied children and parents in Uganda and Mead in Samoa. Both cultures have extended family units with many adults in the child's environment. Both researchers documented that the infant did not attach as intensely to the mother and therefore did not experience the degree of separation anxiety that children do who are reared in a society without extended families.

Another crisis period for separation anxiety occurs for the school-age child with the beginning and the end of the school year. Phenomenon identified as school phobias are frequently separation anxiety. Ezor (1980) has studied the separation anxiety related to school. The adolescent experiences separation anxiety with high frequency. This chaotic period is not unlike the toddler period, with an emphasis on clarifying one's identity and again separating from one's parents. Separation from the peer group also causes anxiety.

The adult may also experience separation anxiety. Some examples of adult separation anxiety are the couple who are separating for a long period for a business or family commitment. During the process of saying goodbye the stages of protest, despair, and denial (detachment) may be experienced. Protest is manifested by such statements as: "I wish you weren't going" or "I'd like to be going with you." Feelings related to the protest stage are feelings of anxiety surrounding the actual separation and the projected time alone. The despair stage may be manifested by behaviors of listlessness and lack of interest in the environment or anger behaviors. Many couples experience feelings and behaviors of anger that are unexpected and disturbing to them as they separate. Most adults move into detachment quickly, maintain the relationship in whatever way is possible, and look forward to being reunited and the resolution stage.

When living in a highly mobile society, adults and children terminate from their support systems with some frequency. Stanford's (1977) work with groups, especially cohesive groups, reports on separation anxiety as a group comes to a closure. If a person has given importance to the group, he or she probably will demonstrate many of the behaviors identified by Stanford.

Although Stanford's work is with students, it appears that his observations may relate to individuals in the general population who are terminating with a group. Stanford's behaviors of termination anxiety are:

1. *Increased conflict.* Students may start bickering with one another for no apparent reason, or at least no significant reason. It is almost as though they were trying to prove to themselves that "I don't really like these people, else I wouldn't be fighting with them. And since I don't like them, it won't be painful for me to leave them."

2. *Breakdown of group skills.* Working together on a task, the group may suddenly exhibit what appears to be a complete lack of skills, and they may violate all the norms that were established previously. It is almost as though they were saying to themselves and the teacher, "You see, we really didn't change much this year. We're still like every other class. And since this is like every other class, it won't be so hard to leave."

3. *Lethargy.* Some students begin to show less and less interest in their work, as if to say, "What does it matter any more? If we're going to have to break up, what's the use of continuing to work?" Their lethargy may also be a symptom of depression indicating feelings of sadness about the imminent breakup of the group.

4. *Frantic attempts to work well.* Conversely, some groups may actually increase their productivity, taking on more and more projects and rushing to do everything they can before the term ends. They may display impeccable group skills, working far more effectively than ever before. Implicit in this behavior may be the message, "If we're a model class, maybe the teacher will like us so much we won't have to leave. Maybe our group can continue forever."

Thus separation anxiety can be demonstrated throughout the life span, all caused by a temporary separation from the significant other or a support system.

The nurse using the Roy Adaptation Model needs to understand clearly the developmental tasks of the life span as they relate to affectional integrity. As the nurse works with people on the health–illness continuum, the nurse will assess and intervene frequently in the interdependence mode. This is especially true with the newborn infant, the young child, and the significant others. The quality of the child's later life in the area of affectional needs is strongly related to what occurs in the infant and young child period. Through intervention, the nurse can help the child or adult reach higher levels of adaptation and integrity in the interdependence mode. Because of the particular vulnerability of the child to separation anxiety, and the more extensive knowledge available in this area, separation anxiety in the child is the example used to demonstrate use of the nursing process according to the Roy Adaptation Model in this problem.

FIRST-LEVEL ASSESSMENT

First-level assessment focuses on behavioral manifestations of separation anxiety. As stated earlier in this chapter, the child experiencing separation anxiety will present behaviors as identified by Robertson (1970) for the stages of protest, despair, and denial (detachment). The nurse remembers that each child is unique in his or her response to separation. Therefore, the discussion of behavioral manifestations of these stages serves only as general guidelines for the expected behaviors.

Protest

In the initial stage of protest, the child has a strong desire for the significant other and expects the significant other to respond to the protesting behavior. The child may present with restlessness, crying, screaming, and physical clinging as the significant other departs. The child will grieve and is inconsolable, constantly calling for the significant others and watching eagerly for their return. Since the child is unable to comprehend this experience, he or she will feel truly deserted by the significant other. Comforting and attention given to the child by another person at this time may be rejected. For example, Elizabeth was a 2-year-old. When she had to be hospitalized, her mother, a single parent, was unable to stay due to her work schedule. Elizabeth cried, screamed, and protested constantly for her mother during her 3-day stay in the hospital. She rejected all care and attention given to her by the nursing staff.

Despair

During despair, the second stage of separation anxiety, the child may present with behaviors of depression and withdrawal. The child will appear quiet, less active, and without sensation or feeling. The child mourns the loss of the significant other and feels increasing hopelessness. It is important during this stage not to mistake the behaviors of apathy as a sign of adaptation to the stress of separation. There may be disinterest in play or food. Behaviors demonstrating regression of developmental tasks previously mastered may be exhibited. These might include bed-wetting, loss of established vocabulary, and other learned skills. Self-comforting coping mechanisms may be initiated by the child, such as thumb sucking or clinging to a favorite toy or blanket. At the sight of the significant other, the child may again present protest behaviors. Care administered by the substitute care giver may no longer be resisted during this stage.

Denial

Denial, the third stage of the separation response, is also referred to as detachment. During this stage, superficially it appears that the child has adapted to the loss of the significant other. The child will show more interest in the surroundings, appear happy, and begin to play with others. The child detaches from the significant other, and the behaviors of this stage are a result of resignation because the child can no longer cope with the emotional distress of separation. The response of the child is not a sign of contentment, but rather is based on repression of feelings for the significant other. The child copes during this stage by establishing shallow relationships with substitute care givers, but avoids closeness with any one person. The child will become increasingly self-centered. The child may no longer react when the significant other comes or leaves. A typical pattern is that the child will not respond to the significant other at first, but then gradually reestablishes contact.

SECOND-LEVEL ASSESSMENT

The nurse assesses for the influencing factors affecting the identified behaviors related to separation anxiety.

The *focal* stimulus contributing to the separation behaviors is separation or absence of the significant other. The nurse identifies the length in time that the separation will or has occurred and assesses if the separation is only temporary or will continue for some time: for example, the mother who has to be away from a young child while she is giving birth to a new baby compared to the mother who will be hospitalized for many months due to a serious illness.

Other stimuli that the nurse assesses include the *degree of attachment or bonding to the significant other* that has occurred. This factor will depend, in large part, on the age of the child. The amount of usual separation and the extent of social contacts within and outside of the immediate family are further important influencing factors. For example, if the child has had an exclusive relationship with the significant other and has not been given the opportunity to deal with separation, the response may be more severe. Assess the child's *preparation for the separation*. Identify what the significant other has told the child about the separation. The child's *coping abilities* should be identified. These will depend on the child's cognitive and maturational levels.

One of the most important influencing factors to identify is the age and developmental level of the person. Separation anxiety is a major stress from middle infancy throughout the preschool years. The *age and developmental level* of the child greatly influence his or her emotional and physical response to the separation and the ability to adapt and cope with the stress. In general, infants by the end of the first six months are able to recognize their significant others and indeed are strongly attached to them. When separated from the significant other the *infant* will display displeasure with cries and screams, and reject the attention of strangers. Infants and toddlers are not yet able to comprehend that objects continue to exist even though they are out cf sight. *Toddlers* will present behaviors of protest, despair, and denial as outlined in the preceding section. *Preschoolers* can tolerate brief periods of separation from their significant other, and are able to establish trust in another significant person. If preschoolers are stressed with illness and are unable to cope, they will manifest the behavioral stages as described earlier. However, the protesting stage will be less aggressive and more passive in this age group. The *school-age child* will experience separation from the significant other as well as peers. However, as the child matures and coping abilities increase, the child will be better able to deal with the separation. When separation does occur, the school-age child may demonstrate behaviors of displaced anger, hostility, loneliness, boredom, frustration, depression, eating problems, or withdrawal. As the child becomes older and more verbal, his or her need to act-out feelings are decreased. The *adolescent* age group will experience separation especially from the peer group. The adolescent may manifest a response to separation through behaviors of depression, loneliness, withdrawal, or boredom.

The nurse also assesses if the person is *ill, hospitalized,* or *in pain,* for the separation response may be enhanced by these additional stimuli. For example, a 5-year-old child may present with behaviors of the protesting stage if he is separated from the significant other when ill and/or in pain.

Assessment of the *significant others' knowledge level* regarding the separation behavioral response is important since their participation in and understanding of the situation will enhance or delay the child's coping abilities.

The *environment* where the separation is taking place is important to identify. Strange surroundings with unfamiliar sights and sounds will create additional stress during the separation experience.

NURSING DIAGNOSIS

The nursing diagnosis reflects the stage of the separation response that has been assessed. An example of a diagnosis could be: The child is in the protest stage of separation anxiety related to absence of the mother because of prolonged illness: the child is 8 months old and is able to realize that he is a separate person from his mother, and has never had a separation experience before.

GOALS

The goals for the child experiencing separation anxiety will be dependent on the stage of response. The child who is protesting is allowed to protest. An example of a stated goal is: The child will remain in the protest stage of separation anxiety. The ultimate goal is for the child to accept love, support, care, and reestablishment of a trusting relationship with the significant other or substitute care giver.

INTERVENTIONS

It will be necessary for a substitute care giver to intervene to help the child cope with feelings of helplessness and anger when a separation has occurred. During the *protesting* stage, the substitute care giver stays with the child, has close contact, and allows the child to protest, even though this comforting and attention will be rejected. With the stage of *despair* the care giver shows by verbal and nonverbal communication that the child is worthwhile and loved. The child is encouraged to express feelings of despair and become more mobile in the environment. To promote a sense of security the care given can be as similar to that given by the significant other as possible. Familiar toys and special objects from home are left with the child at this time. The child's usual mealtime and bedtime rituals are incorporated into the plan of care. The child's most immediate need during the stage of *denial* is the establishment of a trusting relationship with one person. To accomplish this, a primary care giver is assigned to be responsible for establishing consistent routines. With the young child, frequent meaningful contacts are essential to accomplish the goal of forming a trusting relationship. Since the young child has not yet mastered the concept of time, the frequent contacts for short periods enable the child to deal with separation and increase a sense of trust that the primary care giver will return.

Significant others need education regarding the response of children during critical stages of development and during the stages of separation anxiety. They need to understand that these reactions are normal and acceptable, and the only way a child can express and cope with the situation. As an infant develops, he or she will learn how to cope with anxiety during the gradual separation process from the significant other. The infant is given opportunities to develop a sense of trust and deal with anxiety. To help the child master the concept that people and objects continue to exist even when out of sight, interventions such as peek-a-boo games are helpful for infants, and hide-and-seek for the toddler. The school-age child and adolescent may be helped to cope with separation by exploring new interests and finding comfort in peers. They are to be encouraged to verbalize their feelings regarding the separation experience.

When dealing with the young child it is best to expose the child first to separation in a familiar environment in which constant reminders of the significant other, such as pictures or possessions, can be seen. This helps to reassure the child that the significant other will return. When in an unfamiliar environment, it is ideal to bring in pictures of the significant other and family and objects from home. Separation can also be made to be less traumatic if the child can be left for short periods of time with another care giver who the child knows and enjoys.

When the significant other does leave, the child should be told in simple terms that she is leaving, when she will return, and who will be the substitute care giver while she is gone. Measures should be taken to reassure the child of the significant other's return. Since young children have no concept of time, it is best to relate the return to an event familiar to the child's routine. An example would be "I'll be back after your nap time," as opposed to "I'll be back at 3 P.M." The significant other should try to avoid leaving when the child is asleep, for this behavior would only reinforce that the child cannot trust the significant other.

If the child does have to be in a strange environment such as a hospital, it is best that the significant other make every effort to stay with the child, especially during painful or intrusive procedures. Since separation is stressful, progression to advanced developmental tasks, such as toilet training, should be avoided during this time.

SEPARATION ANXIETY CASE STUDY[1]

The purpose of this case study and nursing process care plan is to demonstrate how the nurse may prevent an adaptation problem by changing the environment in relation to developmental age.

Maria is an 18-month-old girl. She lives with her father, mother, 10-year-old sister Lupe, and 5-year-old brother Anthony. Maria is hospitalized for repair of a club foot. The surgery was yesterday, and she has a cast on her left foot extending from her toes to below the knee. She awakened three times during the night following surgery, crying because her foot hurt. Her postoperative course has been uneventful otherwise. It is morning, and Maria is sitting up in bed eating breakfast. her mother, Irma, is feeding her while sipping a cup of coffee. After breakfast, Irma holds Maria on her lap while they watch Sesame Street, and Maria holds and drinks her bottle of milk (this is a morning routine at home). Maria appears secure, calls "mommy" while Irma leaves the room to go to the bathroom, holds her toy doggy out for the nurse to see and hold, and snuggles up to her mommy every chance that she gets. Irma, in turn, strokes Maria, tickles her, and talks about Daddy and Lupe and Anthony and what they are probably doing right now. She also mentions occasionally that she will be happy when tomorrow arrives and she and Maria may go home. Manuel, the father, brings Lupe and Anthony to visit every evening. The admitting assessment reflects that Irma, her husband, and all three children had participated in

TABLE 24.1
Adaptation Nursing Process Care Plan for Child With Separation Anxiety:
Interdependence Mode

Behaviors	Stimuli

Significant other(s)
  Mother (Irma)
Recipient
  Mother feeds Maria breakfast
  Mother holds Maria while they watch
    Sesame Street and Maria drinks from
    her bottle
  Mother strokes, tickles
  Mother talks about family unit
  Mother tells Maria that they will go home
    soon and be with the family
Contributor
  Calls "mommy"
  Snuggles up to her mommy
Support system(s)
  Father, brother, and sister
Recipient
  Come to visit at hospital every evening
  Picture of family in living room to look
    at
Contributor
  No interaction seen
	Focal: nurturing significant other constantly
	  present in the environment (rooming-in)
	Contextual: developmental tasks, autonomy
	  and becoming a separate person
	  The degree of attachment is intense (this
	    is Irma's "baby" and last child)
	  Previous separations, none; oldest child
	    babysits when necessary
	  Preparation for hospital preadmission
	    class attended by entire family, with
	    concrete sugestions to decrease trauma
	    of hospitalization
	  Homelike environment, favorite dog and
	    blanket brought from home as well as
	    a recent picture of the complete family
	    taken in the living room of their home

Nursing Diagnosis: Maria's affectional needs are being met and separation anxiety has been averted due to the mother's rooming-in; articles brought from home and the family's involvement in the hospital's preadmission class.

Goal: Maria's affectional needs will continue to be met by her mother and family during this hospitalization.

Interventions:
A. Dealing with the stimuli of the nurturing significant other
  1. Provide support to Irma and reinforce what a good job she is doing at mothering during this stressful time.
  2. Supply Irma with any equipment she needs.
  3. Encourage Irma to have a break while the staff or other family members stay with Maria.
B. Dealing with the stimuli of preparation for the hospital
  1. Play out the story of Maria's hospitalization with animals and equipment (begin with the doctor's visit, proceed through the preadmission class, surgery, and conclude with Maria being discharged). Include the mother and, if possible, the rest of the family in this activity. (While this intervention relates to taking on of the sick role, it is useful in this case for its efforts in making the situation more familiar to the child, and thus potentially lessening the effects of the strange environment.)

Evaluation: Assess behaviors and decide if they are congruent with Maria as assessed earlier.

Source: Copyright ©1981 by Mary Poush Tedrow.

the hospital's preadmission class 1 week before surgery. The class emphasizes maintaining the family unit during hospitalization and provides suggestions about how to make the hospital stay more comfortable and less traumatic for the child and family.

Thus we see a child who is at an age to be high-risk for experiencing separation anxiety, hospitalized for surgery and not experiencing separation anxiety. Nursing interventions have prevented problems in the interdependence adaptive mode.

SUMMARY

Separation anxiety is experienced by many people in our society. The incidence is even greater with hospitalized persons or the very young person. Nurses can play a vital role in minimizing the discomfort of the person by using their theoretical understanding of the process involved to plan care based on assessment of behaviors and the factors that influence these behaviors. As distress is relieved or prevented, persons maintain greater integrity and conserve energy for health and growth.

STUDENT LEARNING ACTIVITIES

1. Define separation anxiety.
2. Define bonding/attachment.
3. Discuss or explain Mahler's theory of attachment–separation.
4. Walk down the hall of a pediatric unit between 7 and 8 A.M. or at bedtime. Observe the children and make a list of separation anxiety behaviors according to the three stages defined by Robertson.
5. Select a person who is experiencing separation from his or her significant other and apply the adaptation nursing process in planning his or her care.

REFERENCES

Ainsworth, M. D. S. "Attachment Theory and Its Utility in Cross-Cultural Research," in *Culture and Infancy: Variations in the Human Experience*, P. H. Lerderman, S. R. Tulkin, and A. Rosenfeld, eds. New York: Academic Press, Inc., 1977.

Bowlby, John. *Attachment and Loss*, vol. 1: *Attachment*. New York: Basic Books, Inc., Publishers, 1969.

Bowlby, John. *Attachment and Loss*, vol. 2: *Separation: Anxiety and Anger*. New York: Basic Books, Inc., Publishers, 1973.

Erikson, Erik. *Childhood and Society*. New York: W. W. Norton & Company, Inc., 1963.

Ezor, Patricia Rae. "Student Teacher: Separation Anxiety," unpublished manuscript, Mount St. Mary's College, Los Angeles, 1980.

Klaus, M. H., and J. H. Kennel. *Parent–Infant Bonding*, 2nd ed. St. Louis: The C. V. Mosby Company, 1981.

Mahler, Margaret S. *The Selected Papers of Margaret Mahler*, vol. 2: *Separation–Individuation*, New York: Jason Aronson, Inc., 1979.

Mead, Margaret. *Coming of Age in Samoa*. New York: William Morrow & Company, Inc., 1971.

Robertson, James. "Some Responses of Young Children to Loss of Maternal Care," *Nursing Times*, vol. 49, 1953.

Robertson, James. *Young Children in Hospital*, 2nd ed. London: Tavistock Publications, Ltd., 1970.

Stanford, Gene. *Developing Effective Classroom Groups*. New York: Hart Publishing Company, Inc., 1977

Werner, Emmy Elisabeth. *Cross-Cultural Child Development: A View from the Planet Earth*. Monterey, Calif.: Brooks/Cole Publishing Company, 1979.

ADDITIONAL READINGS

Anthony E. James, and Theresa Benedek. *Parenthood: Its Psychology and Psychopathology*. Boston: Little, Brown and Company, 1970.

Havighurst, Robert J. *Human Development and Education*. New York: Longman, Inc., 1953.

Mahler, Margaret S., Fred Pine, and Anni Bergman. *The Psychological Birth of the Human Infant*. New York: Basic Books, Inc., Publishers, 1975.

Spitz, Rene. "Hospitalism. An Inquiry into the Genesis of Psychiatric Conditions in Early Childhood," in *The Psychoanalytic Study of the Child*, vol. 1, Otto Feinichel et al., eds. New York: International Universities Press, 1945.

Chapter 25

Loneliness

*Sue Ann Brown**

BEHAVIORAL OBJECTIVES

After studying this chapter, the reader will be able to:

1. Define the key concepts of the chapter.
2. Explain the relationship between alienation and loneliness.
3. Compare and contrast aloneness and loneliness.
4. Describe the development of loneliness.
5. List factors influencing loneliness.
6. Discuss behaviors manifesting loneliness.
7. Specify nursing interventions to be used in the problem of loneliness.

KEY CONCEPTS DEFINED

Alienation: a condition or feeling of being estranged or separated from self or others.

Lonely: missing the contact of another who is far from one either by death or other physical separation or emotional separateness.

Lonesome: an adjective used to describe a lonely person.

*Edited for the second edition by Mary Poush Tedrow and Jane Servonsky.

Loneliness: the exceedingly unpleasant and driving experience connected with an inadequate discharge of the need for human intimacy, for interpersonal intimacy.

Aloneness: a chosen state of being by oneself.

There is a saying, "If you can't make it with people, you can't make it." Moustakas (1972, p. 48) points out its corollary, "If you can only make it with people, and not alone, you can't make it."

This precept points out some of the problems that exist in the interdependence mode of adaptation. This chapter will concern itself with one problem of the mode, loneliness.

From the aged client to the infant, from economically privileged person to the more deprived, we see the commonality of this adaptation problem. No one is immunized against loneliness; it is a lifelong struggle for everyone to maintain a balance within interdependent relationships. No one is an island—we need each other. We need to be affiliated with others. To be present to another or to be in contact is a feeling of togetherness or union with self and others. Where presence exists the individual is working to maintain relationships by utilizing receptive and contributive behaviors as each is appropriate. Significant others are able to act as affection suppliers. Consequently, the person who is present to another feels loved and worthwhile and meets affection and affiliation needs. This individual has learned how to build relationships where he or she can love, respect, and value others, and in turn be loved, respected, and valued.

THEORETICAL OVERVIEW OF LONELINESS

Alienation is a condition or feeling of being estranged or separated from self or others. One develops alienated feelings when significant others are not meeting what is expected as one's supplier of affiliation. This deprivation of presence or contact leads to a feeling of being not needed, valued, or appreciated by others, and herein lie the roots of loneliness. The affiliation supplier may or may not be aware of this lack for the other person. Similarly, the alienated one may be asking too much or too little of his or her suppliers. Asking too much is a learned behavior for which the individual has probably been rewarded in the past.

Alienation is a serious problem in contemporary society. Many social theorists have written on its pervasiveness in American life and on the contextual factors, or stimuli, that affect this pattern. Among these stimuli are computerization, diminishing of the family as the basic unit of society, mobility, and urbanization. Contemporary people feel manipulated by others. Every aspect of one's life enhances this feeling. For example, politically one might say "Who can I trust? Being a politician means deceiving others for self-gain." Economically, wages, price controls, strikes, cutbacks, and paybacks all seem to be out of one's control. Socially, friends seem to be transient, families are physically separated, and after all, "Who does care what happens to me?" That alienation exists is undeniable. Particularly because of the contemporary situation, people in our society have a good-to-excellent chance of developing one of the variants of alienation. The major types of alienation were described by Seeman (1959) as: powerlessness, meaninglessness, normlessness, isolation, or self-estrangement. Any of these types of alienation can cause the individual to feel further separated from others.

Some individuals can handle these alienated feelings by innovative ways of building relationships. An example of this is the young adult who appraises the situation and says that things aren't good, aren't the way one would like to have them, but they do not have to remain such, and proceeds to become involved in the change process. This person might join a political campaign with a voice in the platform of the candidate. Another person might pursue an interest in being his or her own boss and have as a management objective that each customer and employee will be treated as an individual.

Others will use less positive means to deal with alienated feelings. These avenues involve a dependency on things or others to ward off alienated feelings. There is a pattern of using "something" to act as a bridge to relationships. These patterns include: (1) dependency on life-style that emphasizes withdrawal and retreatism to feel secure; (2) dependency on performing ritualistic behaviors to deal with anxieties of alienation (chain smoking, overeating, psychosomatic illness, or any activity that is done in excess to stay busy); (3) rebelling against society by joining an altraculture group with subsequent dependency on it (drug culture, alcoholic state, sexual variancy groups—see Chapter 27); and (4) dependency on situations retaining the status quo. This individual sees no possibility for change and looks at the world through pessimistic glasses.

Some of these alternatives can be so ineffective as to stimulate self-concept disruption. An example of this would be the individual who chooses to withdraw from the real world and stay in a fantasy existence. This condition is referred to as self-alienation and can involve a total collapse of one's self-concept.

Alienated feelings lead to ideas of not being accepted or valued or appreciated by others. To develop lonely feelings is the logical next step for the alienated one. Again, to be present to another or to be in contact is the interrelatedness of the person with the society of which all are members. It is possible to be lonely in many different ways. Thus we will review the terminology relating to loneliness.

Being *lonely* is missing the contact of another who is apart from one either by death or other physical separation or emotional separateness. You can probably identify with this feeling since everyone seems to have occasions of being lonely. *Lonesome* is an adjective used to describe a lonely person. Sullivan (in Fromm-Reichmann, 1959) has defined *loneliness* as "the exceedingly unpleasant and driving experience connected with an inadequate discharge of the need for human intimacy, for interpersonal intimacy." This is a severe state unacceptable to most people. It would seem to last longer and be more profound than the state of being lonely. By contrast, *aloneness* is a chosen state, to be by oneself for personal growth, meditation, or for an inspired artistic performance or creative activities. Aloneness is healthy and is to be pursued. From these definitions, one can visualize a continuum as in Fig. 25.1, where aloneness is the most healthy behavior and psychotic loneliness (also termed self-alienation) is at the far-illness end. Midway between these two one finds *lonely*. Contact with others to the left of lonely is definitely healthier. To the right of lonely one finds loneliness and the defenses we have noted as used by some alienated people, and psychotic loneliness.

To be in a state of loneliness is an uncomfortable and unpleasant experience. It hurts—it hurts so badly that one tries distractive measures with an ardent fervor if one is not able to use innovative independency. Moustakas (1972, p. 48) quotes a tenth-grade boy who wrote the following:

> Loneliness is a depressing state of mind that none desires but we all endure. When I'm lonely it's not because of being shut away from human beings physically but when I'm rejected by those I respect and love. If a close friend turns against me I feel hurt and lonely. When I feel like a square block in a round hole, it brings on a form of loneliness. Sometimes my parents seem unfair; there is no one to turn to and I feel desolate, lost. Loneliness comes every day. When someone makes a thoughtless criticism that attacks one of my weaknesses, it takes the wind out of my sails. I wonder if what they say is really true. I get a small feeling and that's a kind of loneliness.

His use of terms are different from ours, but he is saying a lot in these few sentences. Reread his words and see if you can define lonely, loneliness, and aloneness in this quotation. Greenwald (1972) has identified several games

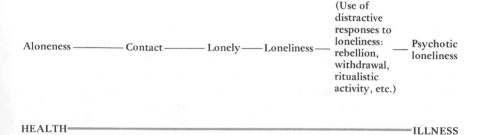

Figure 25.1   Loneliness related to health and illness.

the lonely person plays to maintain dependency on others and one's loneliness. Among them are:

1. *"Someone fill me up" game:* feeling an emptiness in self and looking to others to remedy the situation
2. *"Holier than thou" game:* refusing contact with others since one perceives one's own hang-ups as less than those of others
3. *"Loser-oriented" game:* choosing people for contact who are not what the individual really wants in a relationship of presence
4. *"Being hurt" game:* having more than the average fear of rejection and developing a fantasy of what could happen that is overwhelming and unbearable
5. *"Psycho-anesthesia" game:* using alcohol and drugs to withdraw
6. *"The joker" game:* using humor to keep the situation from hitting relevant issues
7. *"Being present in body only" game:* giving only off-and-on attention to an interaction — daydreaming the contact away
8. *"Busy work" game:* being prevented by activities from experiencing their loneliness and working with it
9. *"Why not ask" game:* learning to ask for everything they want and being insensitive to others and exceeding the other person's desire to give

These games and the behaviors they seem to represent are good criteria to use in assessing a client's communication pattern and interdependency behaviors.

It may seem strange to encourage aloneness and define it at the far healthy end of our continuum. If so, reflect on the precept that begins this chapter. If one always needs others, one is not adaptive. One needs to stand alone at times to be one's own person. If one is only able to define the self as others see him or by that person, he is not in contact with a true self. Moustakas (1972) in his writings advocates the kind of self-encounter and solitude that one experiences when alone. Many individuals today talk of encounters, presence, and groups where one learns to know oneself better. In these groups, however, learning is sometimes restricted to knowing how others see us, not how we see ourselves and how we want to be or to develop. One needs to search one's own mind and experience for direction.

The importance of this state of aloneness may be easier to see if one considers the artist. If a person paints only in the physical or emotional presence of others with their advice, comments, or directions, we are robbed of knowing this artist — of seeing his or her ideas in any kind of pure form — of seeing how one person views the subject. The authentic person is the one who *knows* and *is* his or her true self. This person is like a magnet in that those who come into contact with the individual are attracted. His or her behaviors are genuine; the person is one's own boss in directing this unique life. Because the person is genuine, there is no phoniness and thereby is the attraction for others. Such an individual is far less likely to develop alienated feelings or loneliness. However, even this person may be lonely at times.

DEVELOPMENT OF LONELINESS

The process involved in the development of loneliness can be summarized as outlined in Fig. 25.2. The model depicts the process as often being a circular one. Alienation leads either to reaching-out behaviors — or to feelings of loneliness. The results of each response are very different. Reaching-out behaviors produce positive contact with others. On the other hand, the feelings that loneliness bring may be resolved in a variety of ways. Four of these ways — rebellion, acceptance, withdrawal, and ritualism — have the possible effect of further alienation from others. If help is sought instead of using these behaviors, or if it follows them, the final outcome may be positive contact with others, leading to the ability to establish and maintain effective relationships.

The period of adolescence is used to illustrate the development of loneliness since it has inherent hazards in this direction. Adolescence commences the overt search for identity and independency. Our society emphasizes youth, beauty, the good life, and encourages one to be happy and not necessarily to *be*. When significant others allow adolescents freedom to explore themselves, their goals, and to develop their own route to accomplish these goals, they have a start at becoming genuine persons. Adolescents armed with an instinctual urge to find themselves may meet role models who foster feelings of rejection and ask that they be as that person wants them to be. The young people learn that to be accepted is to be as others want them to be and not as they themselves would like to be. Since exploration of self has resulted in rejection, adolescents can decide not to take further chances but to buckle under. Consequently, the nurse assessing such individuals can find behaviors denoting a dependency on others or things that allow these persons to remain lonely and safe from rebuff. The individual learns that the presence of others and use of others helps decrease feelings of loneliness. All of us learn to use others whether we like to admit it or not. However, think about the difference between your use of your friend to help you complete your chemistry problems, and another person's use of a friend to make parents angry and to obtain some attention.

Take the case of Marcia who uses spectacular behaviors to overcome her loneliness and get her father's attention. Marcia lived with her twice-divorced father and one stepbrother. There were other siblings in other households. Her father was on the verge of his third marriage to an old

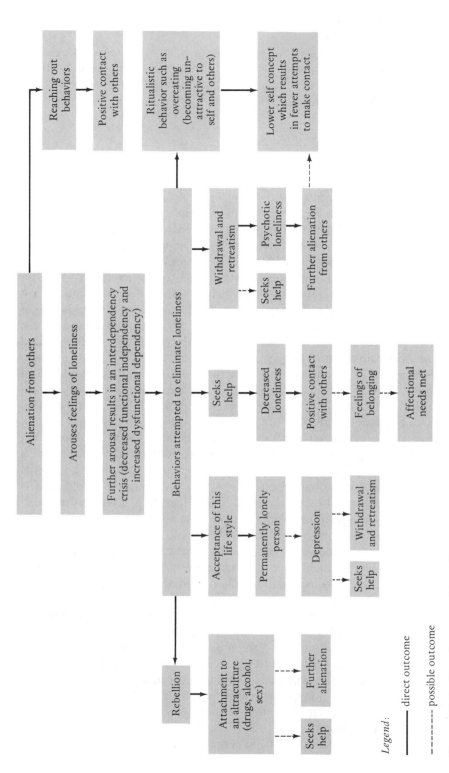

Figure 25.2 Development of Loneliness.

family friend. Marcia had acted during the past year as homemaker and began to feel that her territory was being invaded, and saw not only role loss as an outcome of the pending marriage, but also the loss of a significant other. To call attention to her emerging loneliness caused by role losses, she did the following:

1. Stripped in front of a busy campus center building
2. Wore black clothing and poured water over herself to conserve salt
3. Tried to spread the word among her family that she was having an immaculate conception

These behaviors succeeded in getting her admitted to a psychiatric unit and thereby getting her father's attention, forced a delay in his plans, and reestablished her relationship with him. Marcia used ineffective behaviors to point out her loneliness.

FIRST-LEVEL ASSESSMENT

What, then, can we look for in terms of behaviors in assessing loneliness? The predominant theme that seems to prevail is one of not being able to extend oneself to another for contact. Since the person sees one's own actions as ineffective, motivation to do anything decreases. Nothing matters enough to the individual to require attention. One begins to identify behaviors from other modes—self-esteem diminishes, role failures begin to develop, and phsyical appearance may become neglected. Symptoms of anxiety—that is, the emotional pain a person suffers from viewing one's own dilemma with tunnel vision—will be manifested in different ways by each individual. Another group of symptoms that one could assess revolves around depressive behaviors. How, then, can you distinguish loneliness as an interdependency problem? Once you have made your first- and second-level assessments, it should start to become clear what is the *problem* and what is the *symptom*. Anxiety and depressive behaviors may not be our chief concern when we see in black and white that loneliness is occurring and is the cause of the anxiety or depression.

Behaviors of loneliness might be a contentment to let others care for one, abuse of another person's attempt to help (example: monopolizing a staff person's time), a clinging love relationship, a lack of a broad range of interests, and only a tacit acceptance of those that could be satisfying. Loneliness behaviors are often categorized as recipient and there are fewer or no contributor behaviors. The person who is lonely has learned how to take the nurturing given by others, but for some reason has not learned how to give nurturing effectively or to maintain the relationship.

SECOND-LEVEL ASSESSMENT

The next task in nursing assessment is to cite specific stimuli responsible for the development of behaviors denoting loneliness. In exploring the focal stimulus, the nurse starts by asking these questions: Why is this person lonely at *this* particular time (why *now*)? What is the reason given by the person for the present behavior (what for)? How would the individual rescue the self (what does he or she see as the cause)? What would you eliminate or add to the person's life to help change the situation (what do you see as the cause)?

The major focal stimulus that has been noted in the development of loneliness is one of the variants of alienation. Although a loss, real or imagined, may seem to be the cause of the alienation, the behaviors of loneliness can be more directly connected with the *way* the loss makes the individual feel. In other words, if you identify as focal feelings of despondency about justice or God or life in general following the death of a loved one, it is wiser to view your focal as "feels a great deal of meaninglessness in his present life situation due to concurrent loss" instead of "loss of loved one" as focal. One can work with the focal stimulus of the feeling of alienation to change assessed loneliness behaviors directly rather than altering an event — loss of a loved one. As noted at other points in this text, it is not a concern that the focal stimuli can be a behavior or another problem area; this commonly happens — stimuli for some adaptation problems are behaviors or labels for another adaptation problem. This has been referred to as the kaleidoscopic effect of the way persons function as adaptive systems.

Contextually, the stimuli will also vary widely with the individual. Some areas to explore for possible stimuli are:

1. Family communication: Is the individual hearing them and/or are they truly hearing him? How does the family relate to one another? If unhealthily, is there a family scapegoat? Is there family cohesiveness? In what role does the individual see the self? In what role does the family see the individual?
2. Physical living conditions: Does the person live alone? How far from significant others? Does the individual have or can he or she afford a means of transportation and communication (car, phone, bus, railway, plane)?
3. What are the person's needs or expectations regarding relationships? What kind of behaviors from another would meet the individual's need for affection?
4. Does cultural age separation exist? Today an adolescent spending a day with grandmother would be frowned upon by peers. Peer pressure to stay within certain limits of activity is strong, and consequently one is usually surrounded by individuals of the same age.

5. How are the person's lonely behaviors met? (Loneliness and anxiety are unattractive and contagious and one tends to avoid them.)
6. "Future shock" faces all of us, that is, Toffler's (1970) idea that things are changing so quickly today that the individual cannot adapt to them. How does the individual meet and accept change? Does one try new things, accept new ideas or views?
7. What thing(s) or what person(s) does the individual need? What game(s) is the individual playing to maintain loneliness? What does the person actually know about friendship and how to maintain it?
8. What is developmental age and task of the person? Is there an affectional crisis going on that makes the person more vulnerable to other stimuli?

In considering contextual stimuli it is often the case that although one is not physically removed from others, one may feel lonely in a crowd—the individual may not be able to make contact with anyone. If an individual is a member of many different groups, the chances of finding someone with whom to establish true contact *may* be increased. Both adolescents and adults seem to get into ruts of doing everything with the same people. These are some of the contexts, then, that tend toward loneliness.

Other stimuli one may see in the lonely person are usually related to the inadequate parenting that results in the development of ineffective interactional skills. One important stimuli of which to be aware is interactions tending toward withdrawal from others. Recall that roles exist only when they are identifiable by other's presence; for example, a mother cannot be a mother without a child. Consequently, if another withdraws or society at large withdraws from someone, the individual cannot exist in relationship with the one withdrawing. One has difficulty being in contact with a removed person or thing. Lack of contacts could be an aspect in developing loneliness.

An example of such a withdrawal by society would be a man who is imprisoned. He loses contact with the majority of the population and things that establish feelings of belonging (freedom to be himself, stimulating atmosphere, and so on). This type of withdrawal is overt. Society can unconsciously and covertly also withdraw. Examples of this are seen in reactions of some families to terminal illnesses, disfigurement, or the physically or mentally disabled. In this regard, consider the example of Julie.

Julie is an adolescent who has a cleft lip and palate. Many surgeries have been performed to aid her physical attractiveness and integrity—they have been unsuccessful. Her speech is slurred and one must listen very closely to understand her. I know of no one who knowingly gives her clues of being unwanted. Because of the demands of her position (she is a receptionist) she meets many individuals who unintentionally (or unthinkingly) give facial and bodily clues that they are repulsed by her. Because they reject her, she in turn rejects them—for example, she might remove herself physically each subsequent time they approach her station, or pretend she does not hear their requests. You might rightly conclude that Julie has many problems with her own self-concept and one may ask what gains, primary and secondary, she receives from working in such a situation. However, this example illustrates how interaction affects our presence to one another or disconnectedness.

Related to interaction causing withdrawal is the concept of social disengagement. Social disengagement is thought to be a process identified in the aged to understand both their and society's reaction to becoming older. In this theory the individual is accepting of society's withdrawal and may even prepare for it by developmental and psychological mechanisms (increased preoccupation with self, physical loss of acute awareness—hearing, vision, cohesive speech, and even a decreased interest in significant others). Those opposed to this theory are advocates of the activity theory. This theory proposes that older people have the same needs as middle-aged individuals, and the only reason they experience decreased social interaction is because society withdraws. If you accept the disengagement theory, you will let older people withdraw and take on more aloneness and think that it is natural and right. If you accept the activity theory you will not allow withdrawal and will formulate nursing diagnoses that entail loneliness, and will instead encourage substitute activities, roles, and loved ones when established ones are lost.

CASE STUDY EXAMPLES

Read the following case studies and feel the loneliness that each of these people are experiencing. Then identify the behaviors and stimuli that illustrate loneliness and generate any assessment questions that you would want to ask.

Case 1

Mrs. Sarah Ames is 63 years old and has been a widow for 3 years. She has no children. Until last year when she retired, she worked part time in the cafeteria of the local grade school. Thirty years ago she and her husband built the tiny two-bedroom bungalow she still maintains. When Al was alive, he kept the yard up well, they had three dogs and two cats, and were well liked by the neighbors. Two years ago new huge apartment complexes were built on either side of this house. A brick wall, put up by the developers, completely surrounds the yard. Last year the apartment dwellers complained to the city about the five animals. The city filed a nuisance law regulation against her. Sarah did not get a lawyer and argued the case herself. She lost and was told to get rid of three of the animals, which she did. Sarah does not drive and either walks or takes the bus to get around. Her doctor, an old friend, says that she needs cataract surgery. Sarah rejected his advice and went to an optometrist for bifocals. In an interview with a public health nurse following a referral from the doctor, Sarah said: "It's all so useless; they patch up one thing and then another goes." "Those people (apartment dwellers) don't want an old lady around, messing up 'their block.'" "Oscar and Shadow (the two dogs she got rid of) were really a big part of my life since Al passed on — I needed them." "You know, Al made all the decisions, now I can't decide what to do with the house, or who to call or visit — I just left that up to him." After 2 hours, the nurse tried to close the interview several times, and finally got up saying she had to go. Sarah said, "You must come again and spend the day, I'll fix a nice lunch for you."

Case 2

Ray is a 43-year-old rehabilitation patient with a medical diagnosis of cardiovascular accident. He is slowly regaining his speech and the use of his left side. His family lives a hundred miles from the hospital and usually come to visit him weekly. It has been 6 weeks since his stroke and his progress has been so positive that the doctor anticipates a complete recovery.

Ray has his light on constantly, flirts with all the staff members as best he can, and has developed a meticulous need for his care to be done in a certain way.

Case 3

Linda is a nurse's aide on the surgical floor. She has recently received her final divorce papers. Her marriage was a stormy one that lasted 4 years. She has two children from this marriage.

A new student nurse finds Linda crying in the utility room. Although the student was quite unsure of herself as a practitioner, she felt the need to ask Linda what was wrong and if she could do anything to help. Linda's comments during the ensuring conversation included: "I just feel so let down — I didn't think I'd feel any loss, but I do." "There are a lot of men around who will love me and treat me well — I don't know why I put up with it for even four years." "It's awful at night — when the kids are in bed, it's so quiet it frightens me."

In each of these cases, we see an individual who wants contact (mutual presence with others) but who cannot reach out to the persons they find in their spheres. Sarah is trying to make it all alone. She is at a maturation age when her task is to increase her dependency and decrease her independence from other persons, and yet we find her doing the opposite. Ray and Linda seem similarly involved in a struggle with relationships — Ray being dependent on the staff to meet his affectional needs, and Linda struggling with a need–don't need situation.

The nursing diagnosis, based on the sparse information we have, would stem from behaviors of loneliness. For example, a nursing diagnosis for Linda might be: Linda is manifesting behaviors of loneliness due to the absence of a significant other, a recent divorce after a stormy 4-year marriage, two young children who need a great deal of nurturing. There are, however, many stimuli that need to be assessed in relationship to Linda and her loneliness. Accepted nursing diagnoses labels related to loneliness listed by Gordon (1982) include under the role-relationship pattern:

Communication: impaired verbal
Violence: potential for

and under the activity-exercise pattern:

Diversional activity: deficit

Another accepted diagnosis that might be included in the interdependence mode is:

Noncompliance (specific)

Gordon lists this under the health-perception-health management pattern, but according to our discussion of inability to use support systems, we might include some types of noncompliance as related to the loneliness problem of interdependence.

The goal would be stated: Linda's affectional needs will be met by Linda identifying three people and/or groups that meet some of her nurturing needs and interacting with these people/groups two times a week. The next step in the nursing process is the intervention approach that the nurse uses based on her total assessment.

INTERVENTIONS FOR LONELINESS

The main aim of interventions dealing with loneliness should revolve around the person, decreasing ineffective behaviors and developing instead reciprocal relationships. The person needs to develop contact with others on an adaptive basis to remove feelings of estrangement.

Active friendliness to initiate contact with a lonely person is frequently used as a nursing intervention. In using this method the nurse seeks out the patient to spend time with him or her, although the verbal interaction may be minimal. The nurse does so to increase the person's social confidence and trust in another. Once trust is established by the nurse's *genuine* concern for the individual, the person may feel free to communicate to what degree one is lonely and how helpless it feels. Using this approach the nurse role-models effective communication behaviors and ways of establishing a relationship. Although the one-to-one relationship is the nurse's basic tool, the nurse also encourages rapport with families, neighbors, other patients, or significant persons. This may be done by exploring ways to increase contact in the person's present situation — what happens to make a contact a rewarding or a happy one, what makes it a failure, what does the individual have to offer others, what or for whom is the person lonely, and why.

If an individual is using one of the distractions (of keeping too busy, or joking off interactions, or using any dependent crutches) to ward off loneliness, this can be worked with by the nurse and the whole health team. The person probably is not aware consciously of using these mechanisms. However, when you take something away from a person you *must* help replace it, and the person *must* be ready to let it go and replace it.

Many of the appropriate interventions involve getting the person to see the self as one is and wants to be, and helping the person problem-solve to get there. Think of Sarah, Ray, and Linda. Do they need nursing intervention? If so, what interventions would you supply?

SUMMARY

Loneliness is a miserable state. To be in the state of loneliness is to be unpopular, and to be unpopular relates directly to one's self-esteem. Many people often suffer from this state. If nurses really care about the people they meet and care for, they must consider loneliness a high-priority problem to be analyzed with the nursing process.

As many have said, the antidote for loneliness is not having an answer, but being open, flexible, and finding a way. The same would seem to hold true for the approaches of the caretaker. We can meet the nurturing needs at the root of loneliness and thus help the person promote integrity in the interdependency mode.

STUDENT LEARNING ACTIVITIES

1. Define *alienation*.
2. Define *loneliness*.
3. List five stimuli that can cause or contribute to loneliness.
4. Read the following case study for loneliness. Write out a first- and

second-level assessment using the data in the case study and then postulate a nursing diagnosis. A sample Adaptation Nursing Process Care Plan for a person experiencing loneliness is given in the Appendix.

Case Study

Jim is 15 years old and is in isolation on a medical floor for a staph infection from a wound in his arm. He is not handsome and is 100 pounds overweight. His wound was sustained when his 10-speed bicycle fell apart as he rode home from school. Someone had taken a vital nut off the bike, and Jim, not realizing that anything was wrong, was going fast when the bike fell apart and he went over the handlebars onto the pavement. His jaw is wired and he has many contusions. The infection developed 2 days ago in a large gash in his arm, and at this time he was transferred to isolation. He is a junior in high school, is making poor grades, and has no apparent friends. Nobody can remember ever seeing him with another teenager.

Jim is an only child of a father who is a painter and a mother who is a Ph.D. chemist. The parents are middle-class individuals who are social climbers (throw frequent parties, concerned with having everything the Jones's have, and so on). Both parents say that they are close to Jim. Each has visited him once since his admission 4 days ago, and have phoned once. He spends most of his waking hours watching television. The staff thinks that Jim is a spoiled child since he sulks and makes only minimal response when they are in the room. They feel that he should be doing more of his own care, and do admit to finding him repulsive.

When a student nurse began a relationship with him, he said: "Why do you want me as a patient?" As the relationship progressed, he made these comments: "I need Mother, at least I'm supposed to." "Well, yes, I do, too, have a friend, it's my TV; without it I'd lose my mind." "Who needs friends, anyhow—money can get you what you want."

REFERENCES

Fromm-Reichmann, Frieda. "Loneliness," *Psychiatry*, vol. 22, 1959, p. 3.

Gordon, Marjory. *Nursing Diagnosis: Process and Application.* New York: McGraw-Hill Book Company, 1982.

Greenwald, Jerry A. "Self-Induced Loneliness," *Voices: The Art and Science of Psychotherapy*, vol. 8, 1972, pp. 17–21.

Moustakas, Clark E. *Loneliness and Love.* Englewood Cliffs, N.J.: Prentice-Hall, Inc., 1972.

Seeman, Melvin. "On the Meaning of Alienation," *American Sociological Review*, vol. 24, no. 6, December 1959.

Toffler, Alvin. *Future Shock*. New York: Random House, Inc., 1970.

ADDITIONAL READINGS

Block, E. Wilbur. "Aging and Suicide: The Significance of Marital, Kinship, and Alternative Relation," *The Family Coordinator*, vol. 2, no. 1, January 1972, pp. 71–79.

Burnside, Irene M. "Loneliness in Old Age," *Mental Hygiene*, vol. 55, no. 3, July 1971, pp. 391–397.

Camus, Albert. *The Stranger*. New York: Vintage Books, 1946.

Carlson, Sylvia. "Communication and Social Interaction in the Aged," *Nursing Clinics of North America*, Putting Geriatric Nursing Standards into Practice, Lois Knowles, section editor, vol. 7, no.2, June 1972, pp. 269–279.

Cumming, M. Elaine. "New Thoughts on the Theory of Disengagement," in *New Thoughts on Old Age*, Robert Kastenbaum, ed. New York: Springer Publishing Co., Inc., 1964.

Eisner, Victor. "Alienation of Youth," *The Journal of School Health*, vol. 39, no. 2, February 1969, pp. 81–90.

Francel, Claire G. "Loneliness," in *Some Clinical Approaches to Psychiatric Nursing*, Shirley F. Burd and Margaret A. Marshall, eds. New York: Macmillian Publishing Co., Inc., 1963, pp. 178–183.

Havighurst, Robert J., Bernice T. Newgarten, and Sheldon D. Tobin. "Disengagement and Patterns of Aging," in *Middle Age and Aging*, B. Newgarten, ed. Chicago: University of Chicago Press, 1968, pp. 161–172. (Abridged from an unpublished paper originally presented at the International Association of Gerontology, Copenhagen, 1963.)

Kalish, Richard A. "Of Social Values and the Dying: A Defense of Disengagement," *The Family Coordinator*, vol. 21, no. 1, January 1972, pp. 81–94.

Moustakas, Clark E. *Loneliness*. Englewood Cliffs, N.J.: Prentice-Hall, Inc., 1961.

Peplau, Hildegard E. "Loneliness," *American Journal of Nursing*, vol. 55, no. 12, December 1955, pp. 1476–1481.

Slater, Philip. *The Pursuit of Loneliness: American Culture at the Breaking Point*. Boston: Beacon Press, 1970.

Tietz, Walter, and Sherwyn M. Woods. "Alienation: A Clinical View from Multidisciplinary Vantage Points,"*American Journal of Psychotherapy*, vol. 25, no. 2, April 1970, pp. 296–307.

Part V

Adaptation

Across the Adaptive

Modes or Within Groups

In this section we present five chapters that deal with adaptation across the adaptive modes or within groups. The nurse in clinical practice meets these situations frequently, yet their occurrence is not as common and predictable as those included in Part IV. Furthermore, the ramifications of these problems, for the individual and for a broader circle of people, are more complex. Chapter 26 looks at depressive behavior patterns from the point of view of the Roy Adaptation Model. In chapter 27 the problem of substance abuse is handled in connection with a concept called *insatiable longing*. Life closure, or the unique role of dying persons, and the complementary role of those caring for the dying are explored in Chapter 28.

The authors have incorporated a variety of relevant theories to describe more clearly how the person as an adaptive system is affected across the adaptive modes by each of these situations. Chapter 29 and 30 draw on family and group work theory to address the adaptive functioning of and nursing care according to the Roy Adaptation Model with families and nursing care groups.

Chapter 26

Depression

Nancy S. Taylor and Mary C. Sloper

BEHAVIORAL OBJECTIVES

After studying this chapter, the reader will be able to:

1. Define the key concepts of the chapter.
2. List stresses that can activate the depressive cycle.
3. Identify behaviors in each adaptive mode indicative of depression.
4. Apply the nursing process according to the Roy Adaptation Model to the care of a person with a depressed behavior pattern.

KEY CONCEPTS DEFINED

Depression: a reaction of the person to a real or perceived stress or threat; a coping mechanism in some respects that allows the person some psychic relief due to immobilization and/or distraction from the stress or threat. Occurs within or across the adaptive modes.

Learned Helplessness: a condition in which an individual experiences a trauma over which he or she has no control; then with later trauma, motivation to respond, escape, or control the environment is decreased.

Role Dispute: a conflict with a significant other over the expectations, wishes, or need fulfillment of a particular role.

Depression might be viewed primarily as a psychiatric or at least a medical problem and not the focus for a basic nursing text. However, nurses frequently must deal with depressed people in every area of specialization and in all treatment centers. Depressed people work with us, live with us, and are the recipients of our care. It becomes essential, then, that nurses have the skills to recognize depression and depressive behaviors.

When most nurses are questioned they report that they feel unprepared to deal with depressed people, that this is the role of the psychiatrist or other physician or, at a minimum, someone with advanced education in a psychosocial field. In fact, nurses work without hesitation with many of the components involved in depression. The nursing literature shows that nurses deal with such problems as insomnia, anorexia, feelings of powerlessness, loss, guilt, role inadequacy, and social distance or isolation. In working with these various behavioral patterns and stimuli, they do intervene in the larger problem of depression.

In this chapter we apply the Roy Adaptation Model to the problem of depression. The purpose is not to provide in-depth knowledge about the psychiatric entity of depression, but rather to show how certain clinical entities that affect the person as a whole are examined within the nursing model. We will also develop a format to assist in breaking down the complex problem of depression into smaller units and develop nursing approaches within these units. Based on this overall plan, the nurse can confidently interact with depressed people in an effective manner.

Many theorists in the psychiatric field have identified depression as a problem related to self-concept. Thus we might expect that this text would consider depression as a problem of the self-concept adaptive mode. It is the view of the authors that a disruption in any mode has the potential to lead to depression. Common behaviors manifesting depression may be present regardless of which mode is affected. In addition, there will be other behaviors that are unique and will identify which mode is primarily disrupted. Case studies of depression are included that result from disruptions in each of the four adaptive modes. Theoretical basis for how these depressions develop are included. The authors do not in any way intend to give the impression that the patterns developed in the case studies are inclusive, or even the most commonly seen. Rather, we wish to strongly emphasize that each individual is unique and that a multitude of patterns exist in reality. It is impossible, as well as not germaine to the scope of this text, to cover all possible situations. This chapter is intended to present an application of the Roy Adaptation Model to specific clinical situations. The reader is referred to a basic psychiatric nursing text for a comprehensive review of other theoretical data and mental health principles. It is our hope that the reader, in seeing the variety of patterns we demonstrate, will recognize this and identify further variations in clients in their own case loads. Behaviors for depression that can be assessed in each mode and common stimuli will be presented. The nursing process will be delineated, leading to approaches for nursing care that might be utilized.

THEORY RELATED TO DEPRESSION

"*Depression* is a universal human phenomenon which every person experiences at some level in the course of a lifetime. To love is to experience anxiety and depression; to live with growing technology is to experience these emotions increasingly" (Haber, 1978, p. 307). Existentialists point out that the individual must go through an awareness of hopelessness, and experience emptiness and the concurrent anguish this brings, to become more fully human and the master of one's own future.

Depression, like anxiety, appears to be contagious. Some of the pessimism and negativism that is emitted by a person may be picked up by the nurse without recognizing it. Working with a depressed client, co-worker, or other has the potential to affect the nurse's own self-concept and self-esteem, and thus affect work and interpersonal relationships. Since working with the depressed can have an impact on the care giver, recognizing the dynamics involved becomes an important issue for the nurse, and benefits both personal and professional functioning.

Depression may be the predominant problem that the individual presents, or it may be just one feature in a constellation of physical and/or emotional problems. For example, depression can be secondary to cancer, myocardial infarction, anxiety reaction, or schizophrenia. It may be obvious or the presence of a depression may be subtle.

The representation of depression shown in Fig. 26.1 may help in the understanding of the content to be presented.[1]

Essentially, depression appears to be a reaction to some real or perceived stress or threat. Often the stress is a loss (real, perceived or threatened) which may activate a biochemical or learned response (that is, coping mechanisms, see Chapter 2). Some other significant stresses (stressors) that have been identified are illness, death or threatened death of self or a significant other, body image changes, role changes, role conflicts, and/or social isolation. Internal stresses of high expectations, guilt, and/or a learned pattern of discounting one's accomplishments may also activate the depressive cycle. The threat or stress does not have to be a negative event. What the impact of this threat or stress is expected to be on the person and the response to it are not significant. What is primarily significant is the person's perception. Telling the person that he or she did the best that could be done under the circumstances will have little or no impact on lowered self-esteem.

[1]This diagram was developed over a number of years by several faculty members of the Department of Nursing, Mount St. Mary's College, Los Angeles.

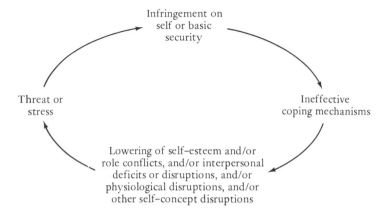

Figure 26.1   Diagram of the Dynamics of Depression.

In some respects, depression might be viewed as a coping mechanism. Psychoanalytic theorists have pointed out that the individual gets some psychic relief from immobilization and/or distraction from conflict. The depression gives the individual a breathing spell from the conflict situation and also warns the individual that something is wrong and needs attention. Generally, it appears that the type of coping mechanisms that are utilized in depression are those related to the flight response rather than the fight response. It is possible that it is the learned use of particular mechanisms that fosters the depression. If the individual faced with the same threat were to activate other coping mechanisms, the depressive cycle might never be initiated. This becomes an extremely important area of consideration both in the area of prevention and nursing research.

The very fact that the coping mechanisms utilized are ineffective, or perceived as such, further perpetuates the disruption. In most cases, there is a lowering of self-esteem as the individual perceives the ineffectiveness of the actions. In addition to this lowered self-esteem, the individual may also demonstrate further disruption within the primary disrupted mode that initiated the depressive cycle. For example, the role conflict may be extended and other areas of role functioning may be affected. Similarly, if the initial disruption were in the interdependence mode, as in the case of the death of a significant other, further disruptions in this mode may develop subsequent to the ineffective coping attempts. Table 26.1 demonstrates that many variations are possible.

It is also possible that the pattern is such that the initial threat is a combination of stresses in the four modes. For example, the initial stress may be a combination of A (disruption in physiologic mode) and B (disruption in self-concept mode), such as the diagnosis of cancer in combination with learned helplessness. Modes C (role function) and D (interdependence) may then be secondarily disrupted as well as further disruptions being present in one or both of the primary modes. It is therefore essential that a careful assessment of each mode be performed to determine the unique pattern being manifested by each client.

TABLE 26.1
Types of Threats and the Disruptions Secondary to Depression

Initial Stress or Threat	*Secondary Disruptions[a]*
1. Biochemical changes (primary disruption in physiological mode)	B. Lowered self-esteem, feels powerless to change situation and/or C. Role distance or failure, limits or stops normal role activities and/or D. Interdependence, social isolation; physically or psychologically distances self from significant other and/or support systems and/or A. Develops a concurrent physiological disorder (e.g., infectious disease) from lowered resistance due to sleep disturbance
2. Learned helplessness activated by conflict (primary disruption in self-concept mode)	A. Any disruption in physiological mode and/or B. Self-consistency problems due to perceived lack of mastery and/or C. Any disruption in role mode and/or D. Any disruption in interdependence
3. Role conflict, dispute over role definition between self and others (primary disruption in role function mode)	A. Any physiological disruption and/or B. Any disruption in self-concept and/or C. Role distance or failure in areas other than the disrupted one, that is, inability to perform work role requirements and/or D. Any disruption in interdependence
4. Interdependence disruption due to depressogenic environment, no adequate support systems (primary disruption in interdependence mode)	A. Any physiological disruption and/or B. Any self-concept disruption and/or C. Any role disruption and/or D. Social isolation from significant other

[a]A, physiological mode; B, self-concept mode; C, role function mode; D, interdependence mode.

CASE STUDY OF PRIMARY DISRUPTION: PHYSIOLOGICAL MODE

Jane S., a married woman of 61, was admitted to the psychiatric unit shortly after her return home from another state. She had been away several weeks caring for her 82-year-old mother, who was ill. Upon her mother's recovery, Jane began to have numerous somatic complaints and within weeks was unable to function in her major role.

Jane's history revealed that she had been married for 39 years. She had three children, ages 30 to 38, all of whom lived away from home, but in the same city. They visited regularly and her husband came daily to the hospital. Jane's marriage had been warm and loving, and continued to be so. She had never worked outside the home and this was agreeable to both her and her husband. They had a fairly active social life, pursued their varied interests, and were looking forward to retirement in the next few years. Jane's history further revealed depressions at ages 44 and 49. She was hospitalized briefly for each episode. There were indications that she may have had another depressive episode in her 20s for which she was not hospitalized. Each episode appeared to resolve completely.

Upon admission Jane complained that she was unable to sleep or eat. She repeatedly stated, "I try to eat, but I can't chew or swallow. I can feel the pill stuck in my throat. My kidneys have stopped working." She complained about shoulder pain, insisting that this pain was caused. by her heart, although x-rays showed some arthritic changes.

The medical diagnosis of endogenous depression was confirmed by a blood test (DST). Jane was placed on an appropriate antidepressant and gradually her eating and sleeping improved. After a period of time her verbal somatic complaints decreased, and she resumed her previous level of functioning.

Problem Identification and Nursing Diagnosis

Researchers for years have looked for a genetic link in depression. While no definite conclusions have been reached, there does appear to be some evidence to sustain this theory. Work in biochemistry has also proceeded. Recent findings have shown that a dexamethasone suppression test (DST) can reliably test for endogenous depression, or what is commonly called melancholia (Carroll et al., 1981). Based on this theoretical understanding and knowledge of the Roy Adaptation Model, the following diagnoses are identified.

Primary Diagnosis: Severe, acute, pervasive depressive behavior pattern related to the physiological factor of biochemical imbalance

Secondary Diagnoses

1. Role failure due to lack of energy to perform role functions
2. Significant other and support system perceived as husband and family, but unable to avail herself of them due to lack of energy
3. Self-concept intact (Perception is that the current state is temporary. Also aware of previous episodes and complete resolution.)

Interventions

Based on the preceding diagnoses, the focal stimuli for this depression is the biochemical disruption. Contextual stimuli to be considered for interventions are coping patterns of somaticizing and withdrawal. Nursing interventions for Jane would focus on supporting her in symptom management and fostering the utilization of the significant other and support systems to demonstrate hope through alteration of symptoms. Health education regarding symptoms, medications, stress level, and habitual coping patterns would be appropriate as Jane improves. Health teaching for the family about Jane's condition would be important as well as support for Jane's husband during her hospitalization.

CASE STUDY OF PRIMARY DISRUPTION: SELF-CONCEPT MODE

When Judy G. was 12 months old, her father abandoned her and her mother. For a time she lived with relatives and eventually returned to her mother. The maternal grandmother also lived in the household, but participated minimally in the emotional life of the family. Judy's mother supported them adequately. The mother enjoyed having a busy social life and frequently went out at night. Judy recalls being very frightened and crying a great deal during her mother's absences. When her mother returned home, she would express a good deal of anger at Judy for not being brave while she was gone. Judy felt "bad" about her mother's absences and "bad" that her mother was angry with her.

At 28, Judy married. The marriage went fairly well for 10 years. They had no children and both husband and wife worked. For no apparent reason, or at least none that Judy could relate, her husband began to go out frequently at night. Judy responded as she had to her mother's absences, with fear and crying at being left alone. Her husband became increasingly intolerant of Judy's behavior, but did not change his own.

Judy became increasingly depressed, feeling that she could do nothing about her plight. She quit her job and in a short time ceased fulfilling her responsibilities in the home. When admitted to the hospital, she was virtually immobilized. Her husband had asked for a separation and a divorce seemed inevitable.

Judy's present behaviors included physically clinging to the staff, inability to make even the simplest decision, and a general look of apathy. She repeatedly asked staff and patients to "Stay with me and tell me what to do" and "Please, help me!"

Problem Identification and Nursing Diagnosis

Learned helplessness (Seligman, 1975) is demonstrated in this case study. Simply stated, it is a learned condition in which an individual experiences a trauma over which they have no control. When a later trauma occurs, the individual's motivation to respond, escape, and/or control the situation is significantly decreased. The individual has a sense of helplessness and therefore does not take any corrective action, for it is deemed as useless. The learned helplessness leads to depression.

Another theoretical influencing factor, or stimulus, demonstrated in Judy's case is the concept of fixation at a particular developmental stage (Bibring, 1953). As discussed earlier in Chapter 4, each phase of development has a goal. The phase at which the individual suffers the first failure will determine the behaviors that are presented clinically in a later difficulty. Thus the predominant behaviors in depression are symbolic of this first failure or loss. According to this theoretical approach, to get affection and to be cared for is the goal of the oral phase. When this goal is not reached, some of the behaviors seen will include dependence, chronic hunger, and demanding narcissistic behaviors. Again, a particular theoretical understanding of the phenomenon of depression is added to knowledge of the Roy Adaptation Model of nursing to state the following diagnoses.

Primary Diagnosis: Severe, acute, pervasive depressive behavior pattern, evidencing learned helplessness and narcissism.

Secondary Diagnoses

1. Role failure and perception that she is incapable of performing roles
2. Social distance from significant other and support system due to hospitalization and impending divorce and excessive dependent demands on hospital and staff
3. Generalized decrease in physiological functioning due to depression

Interventions

The nurse who cares for Judy will need to include the following interventions based on the diagnosis and the identified focal stimuli of learned helplessness. Judy should be involved in a therapy that has a daily program of planned activity in which she can be successful. Judy will need firm pushing and will need to perform the activities repeatedly before she recognizes success (Seligman, 1975). There is often a tendency to overrate emotion and underrate action in depression. Care should be taken that this does not occur, because Judy will require just the opposite, an emphasis on action. Contextual stimuli to be dealt with include Judy's narcissism and demanding behavior. This is further discussed under interventions at the end of this chapter. Other contextual stimuli, such as separation anxiety and the passive coping pattern, need to be identified with Judy and considered in her plan for care.

CASE STUDY OF PRIMARY DISRUPTION: ROLE MODE

Joan M., age 33, married David at 16 because she was pregnant. She subsequently had four children, who now range in age from 11 years to 16. David was, and is, an excellent provider. He worked hard and was quite successful in business. He drank heavily when they were married and gradually his drinking became more and more of a problem for the family. Joan through these years raised the children and maintained the family affairs well. In addition to her home responsibilities, she was active in the community.

Six months ago David joined Alcoholics Anonymous and has remained sober. About three months ago Joan started becoming depressed. She lost 15 pounds and ceased having sexual intercourse with her husband. She voluntarily admitted herself after spending nearly two days in bed because, "I can no longer stand it; I do not know what to do, so I'm doing nothing."

The conflict in the household began when David demanded, after a few months of sobriety, that Joan do things differently, his way. The demands included that Joan was not to drink or have friends over who did, the house was to be kept cleaner, the meals were to be more elaborate and served on a particular schedule. Joan perceived that she was to change to conform to her husband. The children, pleased that Daddy was sober, told her she should do all these things because he had joined Alcoholics Anonymous, and their wish for a happy family would then be fulfilled.

Joan felt strongly that her needs and expectations of the role of wife and mother had been disregarded. She clearly stated, "There is no way I can please them all, yet they all tell *me* I must be different and change what and how I do things."

Problem Identification and Nursing Diagnosis

One reason for the development of depression in women is *role dispute* (Weissman and Paykel, 1974), defined as a conflict with a significant other over the expectations, the wishes, or the need fulfillment of a particular role. The dispute centers around who will define the role—the individual or the significant other. Not agreeing on the role causes conflict which leads to depression of the individual whose role is being disrupted. This concept is closely related to the problem of role conflict described in Chapter 23. Based on this understanding, the nurse identifies the following diagnoses.

Primary Diagnosis: Moderate to severe, acute, pervasive depressive behavior pattern related to role conflict, that is, discrepancy of role definition between the self and significant other.

Secondary Diagnoses

1. Social isolation from family; self-imposed leading to possible alienation
2. Low self-esteem due to guilt feelings that situation must be her fault
3. Sleep disturbance, weight loss, and decreased libido due to depression

Interventions

Interventions based on the nursing diagnosis above would naturally start with altering the identified focal stimuli of role dispute and would include helping Joan to clarify her role and its functions as well as clarification of her feelings about her husband and children. Contextual stimuli that should also be utilized for treatment planning include Joan's poorly developed decision-making skills and nonassertive coping patterns. Joan will need to be supported in decision-making activities. Management of symptoms will need attention and general interventions for low self-esteem must also be included.

CASE STUDY OF PRIMARY DISRUPTION: INTERDEPENDENCE MODE

After 33 years of marriage, Jean B.'s husband died. Five years prior to his death he had suffered a back injury at work. Since then he had not been employed. Jean had cared for him for a year, and when he improved she returned to work to supplement their income. Jean had not worked for 26 years, since the birth of their only child, a son.

During the years Jean worked she called her husband several times a day and remained as the person primarily responsible for all household chores, that is, the cleaning and the preparation of meals. Her husband maintained the garden and they did most of their errands together. They were very active in their church, attending functions at least twice a week. They were well liked in the neighborhood, but very rarely entertained in their home.

When Jean's husband died quite suddenly of an aneurysm, she was devastated. She grieved for him but 16 months later still had not cleaned out his closet or disposed of any of his personal belongings. She continued to work, although her performance suffered. Her son called or visited daily but Jean did not want him as her significant other, and shared little of her feelings with him. She did, however, appreciate his concern and care. She told her co-workers that she was lonely and unhappy and that there were constant reminders of her husband. She heard him snore at night and as a result slept poorly, and often spent several hours at night pacing the house. She often had difficulty deciding what needed to be done around the house and had mild anorexia and a decreased energy level. She felt, and often stated, that if only her husband could be brought back, she would return to being the happy person she had always been.

Problem Identification and Nursing Diagnosis

Women are more prone to suffer interdependence disruption following the loss of a significant other because they bond more strongly with their spouses than men do (Scarf, 1980). From infancy, female children learn to attend to people more than objects. Females form stronger bonds and are very sensitive to any lessening of these bonds. It is felt that because of this close bonding, females suffer frequent and early losses which sensitize them for later losses. Brody and Arieti (1974) point out that men become depressed following a disruption in goal attainment, whereas women more frequently respond to a disruption in a relationship with what he calls the dominant other. Based on this additional theoretical knowledge, the nurse lists the following as diagnoses for Jean.

Primary Diagnosis: Moderate, chronic, intermittent depressive behavior pattern related to death of significant other.

Secondary Diagnoses

1. Anorexia, sleep disturbance, mild agitation, and decreased energy due to depression
2. Anxiety due to disturbance in self-consistency
3. Loss of wife role due to death of spouse, and some diminished work-role function due to decreased energy

Secondary Disruptions of Interdependence, the Primary Role Disrupted

1. Decreased utilization of support system
2. Decreased church attendance and socialization with neighbors

Interventions

The focal stimulus for Jean's depression, that is, the loss of her husband, cannot in itself be altered. However, the meaning of the loss can be altered by using interventions that clarify this meaning and identify any ambivalence that Jean may have about it (see Chapter 18). The particular contextual stimuli of the adaptive coping mechanisms used before the depression are identified and reinforced. The less effective coping patterns of avoidance and isolation are identified and diminished by such interventions as helping Jean develop and carry out a plan to increase her socialization.

THE NURSING PROCESS APPLIED TO PERSONS WITH DEPRESSION

The following sections provide a guide in outline form for applying the nursing process according to the Roy Adaptation Model of nursing to the care of persons with depressed behavior patterns.[2]

---

[2]As developed by faculty members of the Department of Nursing, Mount St. Mary's College, Los Angeles, California.

First-Level Assessment

1. Physiological mode
   (a) *Oxygenation*: shallow breathing; circulatory problems may develop with prolonged chronic depression from nutritional deficits and lack of exercise.
   (b) *Nutrition*: loss of appetite reported; decreased eating and drinking, unpleasant taste in mouth; difficult swallowing reported; occasional pattern of overeating, may appear dehydrated; electrolyte imbalance from poor nutrition.
   (c) *Eliminaton*: constipation; possible diarrhea.
   (d) *Activity and rest*: complains of muscle aches and pains; decrease in physical activity.
   (e) *Skin integrity*: skin dry and scaling.
   (f) *Neurological function*: complains of headaches; decreased coordination; psychomotor retardation; psychomotor agitation; often highly repetitive actions.
   (g) *Endocrine function*: generalized slowing of metabolic processes; decrease in libido; decrease in spontaneity; changes in sexual behavior; menstrual changes; often lengthening of usual cycle or ammenorrhea.

2. Self-concept mode
   (a) *Physical self*: sad, unhappy affect or frozen superficial smile; decreased eye contact; frequent disinterest or decrease in personal hygiene and/or grooming; states that they are "unattractive," focuses on perceived physical defects; states "feels empty, like nothing or numb"; frequent complaints of real or imagined but exaggerated physical ailments; somaticizing; hypochondriasis; states cannot do things, such as make bed, eat, do exercises, and so forth; little or no initiation of conversation; superficial and/or monosyllabic answers to questions; self-mutilation or suicide attempts or actions.
   (b) Personal self
       (1) *Self-consistency*: often ambitious, energetic; overinvolved and competitive individual; somewhat self-absorbed but also sensitive to feelings of others; craves love—but when depressed may avoid others, often making recipient feel guilty; perceives self as a burden on others—rejection proves how bad one really is; anger—after being too patient and accepting, will blow up over something small; demands reassurance for self-accusations but then discounts the reassurance.

(2) *Self-ideal and expectancy*: feels powerless and unable to accomplish what "should" be done; decrease in quality and spontaneity of responsiveness; anticipates failure; discounts any hope; overly concerned with symptoms; little interest in discussing solutions, rather focuses on problems; decreased ambition; lack of goals — or large, unmanageable (global) goals; denies past successes.

(3) *Moral–ethical self*: a general feeling of badness or worthlessness of past behavior and guilt regarding behavior of others; denies past successes; highly developed personal ethics, often inflexible standards; speaks in terms of "should and shouldn't"; very consciencious; ruminates about problems; decreased focusing on solutions except for magical solutions; frequently says, "I feel bad" rather than "I feel sad"; behaviors often take on a moral connotation in situations that are not usually judged by such standards, that is, "I was bad because I didn't fix my husband's breakfast"; pseudo-cheerfulness or a smiling depression.

3. *Role function mode.*   In terms of assigned roles and those based on developmental level, such as husband, mother, breadwinner, housewife, there is a decreasing ability to meet responsibilities associated with role performance. In order to achieve *role mastery*, an individual must have an adequate perception of self, but in depression the individual image is threatened and/or distorted and role functions are inadequate or missing.

a. *Role failure*: often chooses role behaviors that project the negative self-image; decreased role behaviors; lack of motivation, interest, and/or ability to perform simple tasks; may state, "My house started looking terrible, but I was too tired to clean it; I couldn't cook, the kids were driving me crazy, but I just didn't care." Disruptions in this mode relate to disruptions in the personal self of the self-concept mode.

b. *Role distance*: tremendous passivity; does not deny need for help, but does not actively seek it; often lets significant others speak for them as though incapacitated; waits for instructions on where to sit, what projects to do, and so forth; makes little or no attempt to engage in therapeutic process (often sees no hope or value in it) but doesn't resist actively; dependent; takes a long time to do any task.

c. *Role transition confusion* [as in Weissman and Paykel's (1974) *role dispute*]: may not have a clear perception of role boundaries and expectations; may feel role has changed; may no longer have the same expectations as others regarding one's role; may be unwilling to continue role behaviors as defined by others.

4. Interdependence mode
   a. *Personal level*: withdraws from significant other and support system; dependent, clinging behavior often leads to rejection by significant other and support systems; a cyclical situation is set up—depressed individual feels a burden to family and quietly says "I want to be left alone"; significant other and support systems feel that they are causing depression, feel quilty, and therefore agree to leave the individual alone; this withdrawal further deflates self-esteem and increases negative perceptions.
   b. *Societal support systems*: poverty, illness, and changes in community involvement can all lead to a depressogenic environment that has so few stimuli that it fosters the depression.

Stimuli

There is no restrictive list of stimuli that can be presented. An individual can become depressed from a variety of causes and it is imperative that the nurse recognize which stimuli are acting in order to devise effective nursing interventions. Following is a sample of stimuli that will be considered and assessed.

1. Biochemical factors
2. Loss (real, perceived, or threatened)
3. Threat to security
4. Feelings of helplessness and/or learned helplessness and hopelessness
5. Feelings of powerlessness
6. Feelings of ambivalence
7. Anger
8. Anxiety (this can be a defense against a depression, so taking a tranquilizer may escalate or expose a depression)
9. Dependency (real, perceived, or threatened)
10. Guilt (must always assess for the presence of guilt because it increases the tenacity of the depression if not dealt with first)
11. Unrealistically high ideals
12. Low self-esteem
13. Coping patterns of client (predepression and during depression—what does give some relief and/or leads to feelings of success)
14. Who and what is available within the client's environment?
15. Presence of added stressors, such as acute or chronic illness, alcoholism, social stresses in the family, and so forth

Nursing Diagnosis

It is important that the diagnosis communicate something about the client's behaviors and the stimuli that can be the basis for nursing interventions. The term "depression" is acceptable but too broad, so it needs to be qualified in the following manner.

1. Intensity of symptoms: mild, moderate or severe
2. Duration of symptoms: less than 2 weeks; chronic, acute, or recurrent
3. Quality of symptoms: pervasive, intermittent, or able to be distracted
4. Precipitating event, if known
5. Agitated or retarded
6. Primary mode disrupted or major stimuli identified, such as those used in the earlier case studies

An example of such a diagnostic statement is that given on page 468. Severe, acute, pervasive, depressive behavior pattern evidencing learned helplessness and narcissism.

Goals

Goals are prioritized for the behavior to be changed and should bear in mind the following:

1. Safety of client, particularly in mania, agitation, severe retardation, and/or suicidal behaviors.
2. Realistic goal; otherwise, failure can feed into client's negative self-evaluation.
3. Client participation in goal setting, since the nursing goal must be congruent with the client goal or it is doomed to failure.
4. Encouraging hope; for example, often a goal for a behavioral change in the physiological mode, such as increased sleep and eating, can easily be attained and will demonstrate movement to the client and that the situation is not hopeless.
5. Independence and action-oriented goals that move the clients toward their own life goals.

Given these general principles, goals are set with the individual client for promoting the total integrity of the person.

Interventions

For a comprehensive review of interventions the reader is referred to a psychiatric nursing text. These interventions will relate to the stimuli given earlier in the chapter. If the stimulus is identified as focal, it will receive the most direct attention, although creative nursing practice often comes from an intervention that manages multiple stimuli.

1. *Biochemical factors.* Relieve symptoms, leads to hope; time interventions to best time of day for client, diurnal variations; plan assessment for worst time of day—highest suicide risk; health-teaching regarding depression and/or biochemical factors, medications, and treatments.
2. *Loss.* Have client clarify loss; resolve grief, encourage client to talk about loss.
3. *Threat to security.* Have client clarify aspects of threat to security; focus on what client *can* do.
4. *Helplessness or learned helplessness.* Nurse remains hopeful, which can evoke hope in client; using client's anxiety and/or discomfort to motivate problem solving, "You'll feel more comfortable when you have decided about this." Involve client in a daily program of planned activity in which the individual can be successful; strongly encourage client's participation.
5. *Powerlessness.* Action appears to decrease feelings of helplessness; point out the impact the client does have on environment, choices and decisions made.
6. *Ambivalence.* Recognize client's ambivalence and point it out to client; client asks to talk to nurse and then says, "I'd like to be alone." Nurse responds, "It seems that you want to be with me and yet to be alone. I will stay with you for 5 more minutes."
7. *Anger.* Help client recognize feelings of anger when they have occurred in an everyday event. Do not provoke anger. Assist client in problem-solving effective ways to express anger with role playing, and so forth.
8. *Anxiety.* Utilize any of the anxiety-decreasing interventions (see Chapter 19); assist client in recognizing anxiety and identifying ways to decrease it.
9. *Dependence.* Carefully assess what the client can do for self and only provide help in what cannot be done by the client; helpful if nurse maintains an attitude of confidence that client "can do it"; irrational demands should be brought into the open, discussed, and refused.

10. *Guilt.* Do not argue with the client regarding a guilty state—this is the client's view of the self, not the nurse's; do not participate in the client's shoulds and should nots; question where these were learned and in what situation; question client about other options that were available in the situation being discussed; keep goals realistic so that clients cannot feel guilty about not reaching them.

11. *Unrealistically high self-ideals.* Question where high ideals were learned. Does expectation extend to others? If not, why to the client? Point out what factors high self-ideals are unconsciously affecting.

12. *Low self-esteem.* Stay with the client; share (identify) the client's feelings; do not participate in negative evaluations (see Chapter 22).

13. *Coping pattern of client.* Identify any changes in coping patterns that have occurred since the client became depressed; encourage behaviors that do not isolate the client.

14. *Client's environment.* Help the client clarify feelings about significant other; foster communication between client and significant other and support systems; help the client identify other resources available in community.

15. *General.* A nondirective approach is not the best. The client often responds very narrowly and concretely to a nondirective statement. For example, to the question, "What else could you do?" the client may respond, "nothing." Nurse must decentralize the issue and use perspective to assist the client in looking at other stimuli and coping mechanisms.

Evaluation and Modification

Identify any behavioral changes that may have occurred. Point changes out to the client, who may try to negate or discount success, or give credit to others rather than self. Remember that the intervention may have to be performed many times before you see much change.

If the goal is not met, identify the next step. Do you need to assess more? Be sure that all modes were thoroughly assessed. Do you need to identify more stimuli? Does the goal need to be redefined, perhaps narrowed? Is the stimuli focused on the most effective choice? Would dealing with multiple stimuli have the desired effect? Does the stimulus being changed relate to the mode of the primary disruption?

If the goal is met, what becomes the next goal? Remember that sequential short steps are better than a major change. Any intervention may lead to an apparent increase in anxiety. Do not view this as evidence that the intervention is ineffective. Small amounts of energy from anxiety can be used to activate further the client's own coping abilities.

SUMMARY

A disruption in any mode can lead to a depression. By acccurately identifying both the disruption and the subsequent depressive response, the nurse has an opportunity to assist the client in learning new coping patterns that may prevent further disruptions. The depression may be an opportunity for the client to make behavioral changes that can result in a higher state of integration and wellness.

STUDENT LEARNING ACTIVITY

Using the assessment guidelines on pages 473–475, assess a person who expresses feelings of sadness or loss (may be a friend, a co-worker, or a patient). Does he or she exhibit depressive behaviors? If so, clarify a nursing diagnosis for the person's depression.

REFERENCE

Bibring, Edward. "The Mechanism of Depression," in *Affective Disorders*, P. Greenacre, ed. New York: International Universities Press, 1953.

Brody, Eugene B., and Silvano Arieti, eds. *American Handbook of Psychiatry*, 2nd ed., vol. 3. New York: Basic Books, Inc., Publishers, 1974.

Carroll, Bernard J., et al. "A Specific Laboratory Test for the Diagnosis of Melancholia," *Archives of General Psychiatry*, vol. 38, January 1981, pp. 15-22.

Haber, Judith, Anita M. Leach, Sylvia Schudy, and Barbara Flynn Sideleau. *Comprehensive Psychiatric Nursing*. New York: McGraw-Hill Book Company, 1978.

Scarf, Maggie. *Unfinished Business: Pressure Points in the Lives of Women*. New York: Doubleday & Company, Inc., 1980.

Seligman, Martin E. P. *Helplessness: On Depression, Development, and Death*. San Francisco: W. H. Freeman and Company, Publishers, 1975.

Weissman, Myrna, and Eugene S. Paykel. *The Depressed Woman: A Study of Social Relationships*. Chicago: University of Chicago Press, 1974.

ADDITIONAL READINGS

Axelson, L. "The Marital Adjustment and Marital Role Definitions of Husbands of Working and Nonworking Wives," *Marriage and Family Living*, vol. 25, May 1963, pp. 189-195.

Beck, Aaron T. *Depression: Clinical, Experimental and Theoretical Aspects*. New York: Harper & Row, Publishers, 1953.

Cohen, David. "The Link between Self Esteem and Depression," *Psychology Today*, July 1977, pp. 96-99.

Egan, Gerard. *The Skilled Helper: A Model for Systematic Helping and Interpersonal Relating*. Belmont, Calif.: Wadsworth Publishing Company, Inc., 1975.

Ellis, A., and R. A. Harper. *A New Guide to Rational Living*. Englewood Cliffs, N.J.: Prentice-Hall, Inc., 1975.

Flach, Frederic F. *The Secret Strength of Depression*. Philadelphia: J. B. Lippincott Company, 1973.

Freedman, Alfred M., and Harold I. Kaplan, eds. *Comprehensive Textbook of Psychiatry*. Baltimore: The Williams & Wilkins Company, 1967.

Lancaster, Jeanette. *Adult Psychiatric Nursing, Current Clinical Nursing Series*. Garden City, N.Y.: Medical Examination Publishing Co., Inc., 1980.

Morgan, Arthur J., and Judith W. Moreno. *The Practice of Mental Health Nursing: A Community Approach*. Philadelphia: J. B. Lippincott Company, 1973.

Nicholi, Armand M., ed. *The Harvard Guide to Modern Psychiatry*. Cambridge, Mass.: Harvard University Press–Belknap Press, 1978.

Roy, Sister Callista. *Introduction to Nursing: An Adaptation Model*. Englewood Cliffs, N.J.: Prentice-Hall, Inc., 1976.

Schwartz, Morris, and Emmy L. Shockley. *The Nurse and the Mental Patient: A Study in Interpersonal Relations*. New York: John Wiley & Sons, Inc., 1956.

Smith, Mary L. "Depression, You See It, but What Do You Do about It?" *Nursing '78*, vol. 8, September, pp. 43–45.

White, Cheryl. "Nurse Counseling with a Depressed Patient," *American Journal of Nursing*, no. 3, 1978. pp. 436–439.

Chapter 27

Substance Abuse

Mary Hicks

BEHAVIORAL OBJECTIVES

After studying this chapter, the reader will be able to:

1. Define the key concepts of the chapter.
2. Describe the theoretical basis for substance abuse.
3. List the phases of the pattern of substance abuse and identify the nurse's role at various phases.
4. Describe behaviors and factors influencing persons with insatiable longing and substance abuse.
5. Specify the general nursing interventions to be used with persons at crisis points in the substance abuse pattern.
6. Prepare an adaptation nursing process care plan for a person involved in substance abuse.

KEY CONCEPTS DEFINED

Insatiable Longing: vague yearning or gnawing sensation that keeps one in a constant state of anticipation which is difficult to be fulfilled in an ordinary way.

Substance Abuse: the use of chemical substances, drugs or alcohol, to the point of physical and/or psychological dependence.

Physical Dependence: an abnormal state that manifests itself by intense physical disturbances when administration of the drug is suspended.

Tolerance: the process that requires an increase in dosage to obtain the initial pharmacodynamic effect.

Psychological Dependence: a psychic drive that requires periodic and continuous administration of a drug to produce pleasure or avoid discomfort.

Contemporary American society is highly drug oriented, with increasing numbers of persons becoming involved in various forms of substance abuse. The roots, dynamics, and effects of these problems are complex. However, literature in the field cites connections between these problems and what the Roy Adaptation Model calls *unmet interdependency needs.* The complexities of modern society in the industrially developed countries has brought about high levels of stress at the same time that close relationships with others are less available to help individuals cope with these stresses. The breath-taking rate of change, the erosion of family life, and the threat of internal and external hostile political forces are but a few of the factors causing stress. In this situation, the basic need for relating to others in mutual love, respect, and valuing is intensified. When this need goes unmet through a lack of meaningful significant others and support systems, the person may develop a condition known as insatiable longing.

Insatiable longing is a vague yearning or growing sensation that keeps one in a constant state of anticipation which is never fulfilled and which cannot be fulfilled in an ordinary way. The individual with insatiable longing is vulnerable to addiction or being taken over by some substance or activity. People may become dependent on almost anything—morphine, phenobarbital, cocaine, marijuana, alcohol, food, or even work or hobbies (Brown and Fowler, 1969). Once persons are in the condition of insatiable longing, they are likely also to be prone to frustration, anxiety, and depression. Life's experiences for these persons easily become exhaustive and unmanageable and dependence on drugs results when more effective coping mechanisms are not available within the person's cognitive domain.

This chapter provides a theoretical background for viewing the complex problem of substance abuse and applies the Roy Adaptation Model to the nurse's role in prevention and treatment of this condition.

THEORETICAL BACKGROUND

A description of how persons with unmet interdependence needs may choose drugs or alcohol as substitutes for human relationships is shown in Fig. 27.1. This theoretical approach (see Betts and Saletta, 1981) assumes that an individual has previously been exposed to a psychoactive substance

Individual

↕

Stress

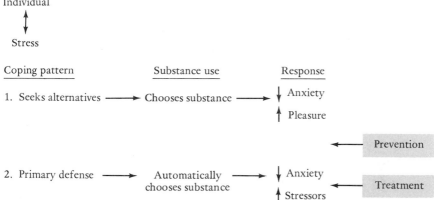

Figure 27.1   Theoretical View of the Substance Abuse. Based on a substantive abuse etiology modes designed by Virginia T. Betts in L. Jarvis, ed. *Community Health Nursing*. Philadelphia: F. A. Davis Company, 1981, p. 546. Used with permission.

and received a pleasurable response, such as a relief of anxiety and/or a thrill of excitement from that substance. When that person later experiences stress, the first coping pattern used is to seek alternatives to deal with the stress. If this person's cognitive–emotive skills are not sufficient to come up with another solution for relief of stress, or if the perceived stress is too great, the individual will choose the substance again. In this instance the use of the substance is perceived as a solution to the stressful situation, with anxiety being lowered and pleasure increased. For a person who is still using this first coping pattern, nursing care can be directed toward prevention of insatiable longing.

There is a second-stage coping pattern in which the individual begins to choose substance use as a primary solution for stress. At this point, from the person's subjective view, the substance use is a positive solution, as it decreases the person's anxiety. Objectively, however, substance use is no solution, as it results in added stressors. A person with this coping pattern can quickly develop insatiable longing and be in need of treatment for substance abuse.

THE NURSE'S ROLE RELATED TO PHASES OF THE SUBSTANCE ABUSE PATTERN

Figure 27.2 extends this theoretical approach and proposes an overview of the various phases in the pattern of substance abuse. Nurses in personal and professional situations are in contact with persons in each of these phases. There are opportunities to intervene at any point; however, too

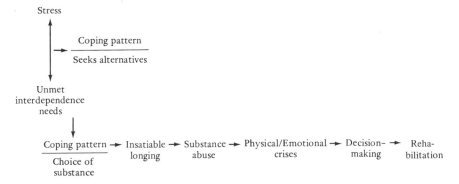

Figure 27.2   Phases in the Pattern of the Substance Abuser.

often persons do not come in contact with the nurse until they reach crisis periods. With concern, thought, and energy, nursing attention can be focused on individual's positive coping that can prevent the substance abuse situation.

The school nurse is in a position to participate in this primary prevention by her consultive, educational, and counseling roles. Education to deter drug abuse is targeted to the vulnerable ages 10 to 13, but is integrated throughout the total curriculum of elementary and secondary schooling. In addition to factual information about drugs, perhaps even more important, the nurse can facilitate education related to coping skills, such as value clarification, decision making, self-acceptance, and stress reduction. These approaches need to be presented in innovative ways to offset the expected counter influences of the need to rebel against authority and to go along with peer group pressures.

The school nurse has her greatest opportunity in secondary prevention. If she is known as a concerned, competent, helping person, students will seek her counsel. Her alertness to subtle and overt behaviors pointing to signs of insatiable longing will lead to assessment and treatment of persons before they reach the stage of substance abuse. Encouraging the student to discuss his or her problem may reveal the important influencing factors. Family discord, difficulties involving the opposite sex and other peers, failing grades, and job problems are all stresses that can cause enough pain to lead to strong feelings of insatiable longing. At this point, the nurse makes every effort to help the student develop an effective coping pattern to deal with these stresses and to find ways to meet interdependency needs (see Chapter 25).

The industrial nurse is also in a position to counsel and to observe early behaviors related to the beginning phases in the process of substance abuse. For example, frequent minor physical complaints and so forth can be further assessed. As interventions, the nurse in this situation often has the added advantage of screening tools, educational media, and treatment programs within the workplace.

Nurses working with obstetrical patients have opportunities for a preventive focus. The growing body of knowledge pointing to the harmful effects of drugs on fetal development may be an important opening for drug abuse teaching. As expectant couples are provided with current prenatal drug information, they may opt to change their substance use habits with carryover into the postpartum and child-rearing years. In addition, when persons do not adjust with needed changed behavior after information is shared and counseling provided, the nurse may have an opportunity for early case finding and referral.

In any area of clinical practice, the nurse is cognizant of the value of prevention and aware of subtle behaviors providing opportunities for teaching, counseling, and positive reinforcement. "What do you think about a small amount of Valium to put me to sleep?" "It's hard for me to lose weight; I think I'll take that 'High Level of Wellness' course at school." "Don't you think the doctor should give me something stronger for pain?" All these are comments that can evoke purposeful responses by the nurse aimed at promoting positive coping and thus preventing progression along the phases related to substance abuse.

As the nurse considers each individual situation, she is aware that at times the inability to develop meaningful relationships and a low tolerance for stress may be rooted in early experiences that might require a psychiatric referral to be dealt with adequately. Such referrals can be another form of preventive intervention.

A person who has used a coping pattern of immediate choice of a substance develops insatiable longing that quickly attaches itself to substance abuse. Vague yearnings keep the person in a constant state of anticipation that can be fulfilled only by the use of the substance that one has found as a solution. The use of a chemical substance, drugs, or alcohol to the point of physical and/or psychological dependence is known as *substance abuse*. The outcome of this stage is often a series of physical and emotional crises. These crises can include bouts of hepatitis and other liver diseases; further alienation from others, including divorce; financial difficulties and job loss; and increasing low self-esteem.

It is the physical and emotional crises that may lead the person to a new point of decision-making. A nurse can exert a crucial influence during these crisis periods. These individuals can begin to see the effects of the substance abuse and consider that they would like to change the way in which they use drugs and/or alcohol. Rehabilitation is the next phase, when persons seek treatment for the substance abuse problem. This phase is of the utmost importance. The altered life-style and abstinence that are the goal of rehabilitation require great commitment on the part of the person. The help and support of the entire health care team, family, and others is needed at this time. This total approach can lead the person to action that moves toward recovery and a healthier and more integrated life for self and society.

Given this broad theoretical overview of substance abuse, and seeing the various points for nurses to play a role in prevention and treatment, we can now discuss the use of the nursing process according to the Roy Adaptation Model in carrying out this role.

FIRST-LEVEL ASSESSMENT: BEHAVIORS

The nurse's assessment for insatiable longing and substance abuse will vary depending on the substance(s) abused and will differ with the individual (Emmel, 1975). There are, however, behavioral manifestations often observed with alcohol dependence. These behaviors can be seen in each of the four adaptive modes. Physiologically, the response of the body to long-term excessive intake causes significant and sometimes fatal damage to the various organ systems.

Alcoholics have extremely high affectional needs and may feel they have never been loved as they should have been or even that they are not worth loving. They may be painfully aware of their excessive needs for affection, attention, praise, and being pampered and babied. They may be chronically angry that these demands are never fully met because significant others are unable to satisfy such demands. Some feel that many alcoholics have never resolved the dependency/independency conflict of early childhood.

A critical variable is the handling of anger toward the self and others. Many alcoholics are very sensitive but when anger builds up, they may withhold feelings and/or lash out. Alcohol aids in releasing angry feelings or in disguising these feelings by euphoria. Grandiosity and aggression may increase to mask feelings of aloneness and the need for affection. The use of alcohol makes the person feel like a champ and a king. With this behavior, the person's mastery of roles becomes increasingly disrupted to the point of role failure in many aspects of the person's life.

Behaviors related to the self-concept include low self-esteem, with a desire to feel powerful and in control of one's destiny, that is, a feeling of omnipotence. Excessive drinking and the feelings of power that alcohol can provide help momentarily to erase feelings of frustration, guilt, and self denigration. When sober thoughts begin to filter through the alcoholic haze, the feelings of failure and self-reproach come to the fore again and can act as the motivation to once more seek that transitory experience of control afforded by alcohol.

The use of denial, rationalization, and projection are frequently encountered. Blame and responsibility are always shifted to someone else. The alcoholic can think of hundreds of logical reasons why he or she needs a drink, but never because he or she has become a victim of insatiable longing and cannot meet interdependence needs. Guilt and shame behaviors are also seen, especially as the alcoholic is sobering up after a drinking bout in which particularly embarrassing behaviors may have been demonstrated.

Behaviors the nurse observes for other substance abusers are often similar to those of the alcoholic. Another behavior or mechanism often observed in drug-abusing persons is manipulation. Manipulation is a mechanism to control or use others to satisfy one's own need without considering the needs, wishes, or values of others. This mechanism is consistent with the dependency characteristic that is frequently associated with persons with insatiable longing. It is an outstanding behavior of the heroin abuser and astute knowledge and skill is required on the part of the nurse to deal with it effectively. One intervention for manipulation is not to accept discrepancies in the person's words and actions, consistently calling this reality to the person's attention.

SECOND-LEVEL ASSESSMENT

In such a complex problem as insatiable longing and substance abuse there are understandably several possibilities for focal stimuli. One focal stimulus for insatiable longing involves the stress experienced by the person and causing the need to seek relief. This individual will attempt to escape or avoid these tense anxiety feelings through the use of drugs or alcohol. The possible stimuli for the nurse to manage can be found by discerning stressful factors contributing to the person's discomfort and related feelings. These stressors include change, conflict, loneliness and deprivation, and peer group pressure.

1. *Change.* Any event that interferes with existing patterns of meeting needs for love, belonging, and self-esteem generates stress and demands coping efforts. Stress and anxiety may arise from new and frightening demands of employment, education, family responsibilities, and maturation as well as situational crises.
2. *Conflict.* Conflict is at the root of most personal and social interactional problems. Conflict can occur interpersonally between parent and child, between spouses, with other significant others, or with an authority figure.
3. *Loneliness.* Glasser (1972) combines the concept of loneliness with self-identity failure as causes of great psychological pain in which persons must become involved with the self. One of these self-involving ineffective solutions is dependency on legal or illegal drugs. "A few questions about the patient's social life and his work can easily reveal whether he is lonely, feels worthless, has few positive involvements. . . ." (p. 53).
4. *Deprivation.* It has been demonstrated that actual physiological

stress can result from crowding. The inner city ghetto's economical and emotional deprivation have frequently been cited as causal stimuli for interdependence problems.

5. *Peer group pressure.* The focal stimulus for insatiable longing in young people is most often peer group pressure. It is well documented that this strong motivational factor in adolescence results from a tendency to rebel against parental and societal values as well as from the need for peer group acceptance and approval.

Professional interviewing techniques and keen observational skills are needed in helping clients discuss factors that cause their discomfort and pain and, more important, to encourage these individuals to express the feelings that have been aroused which lead to insatiable longing.

We may also consider the focal stimuli that cause *continuation* of substance abuse. These include:

1. *Physical dependence,* which involves the development of *tolerance,* physiological dependence on the properties of the drug, and the user's experience with withdrawal phenomena when the intake is decreased or halted.
2. *Positive drug experiences* that provide positive, gratifying, and satisfying sensations, that is, relief from anxiety, euphoria, oblivion, heightened consciousness, and so forth. This experience includes *psychological dependence.*
3. The *life-styles* maintained by some persons dependent on substance abuse serve to reinforce their ineffective dependent behaviors. Distinctive language, rituals of drug administration, and other mores provide a sense of group belonging, but at the same time cut off the individual from other social contacts.

Organic factors have been studied as possibly etiologically related to alcoholism and are worthy of mention. These are: (1) alcoholism is based on a hereditarily transmitted defect in metabolism; (2) alcoholism is due to an allergic hypersensitivity; and (3) alcoholism is based on a hypofunction of the adrenal cortex. These factors might also be considered focal stimuli.

The hereditary factor has received the most merit, partly substantiated by Goodwin's "twin" studies (1971). This theoretical possibility, together with the strong evidence of parental-role-model influencing factors, has implications for preventive measures for vulnerable individuals.

Some contextual factors that the nurse considers in making the second-level assessment include:

1. Self-medication to relieve psychic or physical pain
2. Environmental influence fostered by parental substance use and abuse

3. Rebellion against conventional social values
4. Achievement of social acceptance in some segments of society where illicit drugs are becoming the norm
5. A desire to attain heightened awareness
6. Delinquent behavior and sociocultural pressures

Additional stimuli are the availability of drugs, drug-related literature, and paraphenalia; and the bombardment of mass-media messages of substance use to enhance life and to solve problems.

Residual stimuli for insatiable longing behaviors may be related to inadequate parenting patterns. For example, parents may foster excessive dependency needs, causing corresponding resentment expressed in rage, hostility, and mistrust. These unacceptable emotions are then atoned for later in the guilt, low self-esteem, dependence, and self-destructiveness often characterizing the alcoholic's behavior. Another example of predisposing parenting involve rigid child-rearing practices that retard normal growth patterns and inhibit expressions of anxiety and anger in the child. This parental input prevents the offspring from learning to express or cope with normal feelings, resulting in inability to delay gratification and limited development of coping skills.

Other residual stimuli lie in cultural values; that is, that the Irish are more prone to alcoholism is perhaps related to the value of the male role in drinking, and the low incidence of alcoholism among Jews is perhaps related to drinking behavior ritualized as part of religious and social customs.

CLINICAL EXAMPLES USING THE NURSING PROCESS

The case studies that follow use the theoretical knowledge of this chapter and the nursing process for persons on crisis points of the substance abuse continuum.

Case 1

When making rounds you meet Mr. Adams, a beanpole 42-year-old male who has just been admitted for an elective hernia repair. When you ask about the smell of alcohol on his breath, he replies that he had to see a customer earlier today and had a couple of cocktails. He further volunteers the information that it is necessary for him "to have cocktails with his clients to make the sale." He further states, "I know my limit, though." His wife, who is on her way out and overhears the conversation, states, "You know you continue drinking when you get home." Mr. Adams then says, "Well, I do have a couple of beers to help me unwind." Mrs. Adams replies,

"You don't even eat your dinner anymore; you just sit in front of the television and drink until you pass out." Mrs. Adams stops abruptly, seems embarrassed, and says, "I guess I better leave."

Mr. Adams has an uneventful evening and night, except for needing an additional sedative after an initial medication ordered for sleep. Surgery was postponed until 3 days later.

When you return the next afternoon, you learn that Mr. Adams has been irritable and hostile during the day shift. He refused both meals and did a lot of pacing in the halls. When you see Mr. Adams he appears anxious and agitated; he is perspiring profusely; he begins to tremble and his blood pressure is 150/100, his pulse 112.

Nursing Assessment.   The focal stimuli for the psychomotor agitation is the cessation of alcohol.

Behaviors	Contextual Stimuli
Is irritable	Admits to drinking 3 or more drinks daily
Appears anxious	Wife reports more
Is tremulous and shaking	Denial is a prime defense mechanism for the alcoholic
Has diaphoresis	
BP: 150/100	Probably 24 hours since last drink
P: 112	Potentially excessive stimuli can precipitate seizures and delirium tremens
Demands more sedative medication than ordered	Cross-tolerance for sedative hypnotic
Thin, pale appearance	Alcohol inhibits absorption of essential nutrients
Refuses meals	Alcohol intake and psychomotor agitation deter adequate food intake

Nursing Diagnosis: Acute withdrawal from chemical substance related to hospitalization and denial of dependency problem.

Goals

1. Mr. Adams's psychomotor agitation will reverse and not progress to seizures and/or delirium tremens.
2. Mr. Adams will eat adequate nutrients while in the hospital.
3. Mr. Adams will become more cognizant of his substance abuse problem and consider a referral for help.

Interventions

1. Report findings to physician and continue frequently to monitor vital signs and other signs of impending physiological crisis.

2. Maintain a calm, quiet environment minimizing environmental stimuli.
3. Give adequate sedative and tranquilizing medication as ordered.
4. Encourage and foster adequate nutrition (confer with dietician) and measure intake.
5. When the opportunity permits, discuss substance abuse with Mr. Adams. Help him to look realistically at the consequences of his behavior.

Case 2

Christine Smith is a 45-year-old single female who moved to Los Angeles 20 years ago; she has always lived alone and has worked at a variety of jobs; job change was always an advancement. Christine seemed continually to be striving to move up, but not really formulating concrete goals. She said she was always looking for something in jobs and friends; she dabbled in homosexuality for a while. Christine had experimented with drugs in her teens but during her twenties drank only alcohol socially.

She lost contact with her family and was unable to establish any long-term friends. She sustained several minor illnesses and two minor surgeries at which time barbiturates and sedatives were ordered. Each time, she used the medication longer than prescribed, and during the past 5 years increasingly used barbiturates and sedatives as well as alcohol. She secured medication from physicians and friends.

Christine stated that she began to lose jobs, taking lesser employment and finally becoming unemployable. She stated that she became more lonely and recently has been living a hand-to-mouth existence, eating sparsely and concentrating on getting drugs and/or alcohol. She reported spending much time watching television and said "I talk to it to make myself feel better." She can't understand her life; she always "thought I could get a better job and have lots of friends."

You meet Christine after she accidentally overdoses on phenobarbitol and alcohol and is several days in a coma. She is emaciated, with multiple sores on her extremities.

Christine's basic problem is one of interdependence. Her affectional and nurturing needs have rarely been met. Glasser (1972, p. 44) states that we always need involvement and "we always feel pain when we have none." He further tells us that we replace our pain of failure and loneliness with, among other things, alcohol and legal or illegal drugs.

Christine's past 20 years seemed to be spent searching for involvement with jobs as well as with people to fulfill that unmet need. In a way, she has had insatiable longing throughout her adult life. Certainly anyone so deficient in interdependence needs has a low level of self-esteem, poorly developed interpersonal skills, limited coping mechanisms, and powerlessness. Christine's problems are evident in areas of primary and secondary role functioning. Young adult developmental tasks were never accomplished and progress in mature adult tasks has not occurred.

Physiological problems involve serious ramifications of physical dependence on barbiturate-type drugs. Concomitant behavioral observations encompass severe nutritional deficiencies with yet unknown problems.

Nursing Assessment

Behavior: Comatose from overdose, multiple sores on extremities. The *focal stimulus* for Christine's behaviors is unmet interdependence needs.

Contextual stimuli

1. Estrangement from family
2. Inability to establish meaningful and long-term relationships
3. Increasing responsibility incurred in employment experience
4. Reduced activities due to television watching and minimal nutritional intake
5. Low self-esteem
6. Minor illness and sedative–hypnotic prescriptions
7. Physical dependence on sedative-type drugs

Residual Stimuli

1. Poor early family relationships
2. Inadequate adolescent and young adult task development
3. Probable deception, cunning, and degrading activities necessary in securing drugs

Diagnosis: Insatiable longing and substance abuse related to unmet interdependence needs.

Goals: For Christine, as for most persons with insatiable longing and substance abuse problems, goals must encompass a long-term perspective. The following combine both long- and short-term objectives.

1. Christine will become completely oriented to reality, increase her level of self-esteem, and gain a measure of hope.
2. Christine will demonstrate effective nutritional intake, with improved nutritional status and return to optimum physical health.
3. Christine will examine her feelings of insatiable longing and identify situations and events that trigger stressful feelings.

4. Christine will recognize the coping mechanisms previously used to handle these feelings.
5. Christine will make a commitment to long-term treatment.
6. Christine will begin to interact successfully with others and eventually return to a social and an employment environment.

Interventions: As stated in an earlier chapter, a main intervention for loneliness is *active friendliness.* In using this method, the nurse seeks out the patient and spends time with her so as to increase her social confidence and trust in another. Once trust is established by the nurse's genuine concern for the individual, she may feel free to communicate to what degree she is lonely and how helpless she feels.

Other interventions for Christine are:

1. Assign manageable tasks with probable success value.
2. Establish an activity schedule based on Christine's preferences.
3. Do not allow Christine to isolate herself.
4. Limit television watching—include decreasing amounts of television time in activity schedule with a behavior modification approach.
5. Make suggestions for better grooming.
6. Arrange for loose-fitting long sleeves and slacks to cover sores.
7. Assist in any treatment for sores.
8. Encourage and assist Christine with prescribed nutrition regime: high-protein, high-caloric meals and between-meal nourishment with vitamin supplements.
9. Identify activities Christine likes that would include other people.
10. Discuss Christine's insatiable longing problem, including her overdose and coma episode. Help her to explore feelings, stimuli, and coping mechanisms. Reinforce positive coping mechanisms.
11. Begin resetting career goals and assist with job seeking/career training.
12. Prepare Christine for referral to next step in treatment. A halfway house carefully selected with an outpatient group and individual therapy might be indicated.

Evaluation: Periodically evaluate Christine's progress in relation to the goals set.

SUMMARY

This chapter has looked at the complex problem of substance abuse from a theoretical perspective related to the interdependence mode of adaptation. Based on this understanding, the nurse's role in dealing with persons during various phases related to substance abuse was identified. Clinical examples using the nursing process according to the Roy Adaptation Model were provided to illustrate the role of the nurse with persons facing crises of substance abuse.

STUDENT LEARNING ACTIVITY

Read the following case study and answer the questions below. Check the Appendix for a sample of an Adaptation Nursing Process Care Plan for a person with substance abuse. If your answers do not agree with the sample care plan, provide a rationale for why your answer is different.

Case Study

Karen B., aged 14 years, was admitted to the adolescent inpatient section of a mental health center after becoming ill with nausea, vomiting, agitation, and confusion. She became belligerent when her parents tried to help her. Karen's sister revealed to her mother that Karen was taking "a lot of pills." The family doctor referred Karen to the mental health center when he discerned that Karen was having symptoms of amphetamine intoxication. Besides these behaviors, on admission Karen's symptoms included headache, tachycardia, anorexia, diaphoresis, restlessness, tremors, and some hallucinations.

After palliative measures and a supervised withdrawal period, Karen is now hostile and uncommunicative; she idly sits around the ward. She is poorly groomed, appears physically wasted, and avoids eye contact. She complains of fatigue and eats indiscriminately. When Karen begins to open up to a nurse therapist, she announces that she does not want to go home. "They don't love me anyway. They just want me to work around the house and take care of my sisters and brother. I can't even go out with my girl-friend. Even when my mother does let me out, the kids don't pay much attention to me."

Karen is the oldest of four children. She has sisters aged 9 and 11 and a brother who is 3 years old. Karen is an average student. She is plain and has been chubby. Her only girlfriend is attractive, slim, and popular. As Karen continued to gain weight and was unable to control her snacking, she was glad when her friend gave her some diet pills. She said, "The pills really worked; stopped me from eating, gave me lots of energy. I was getting thinner and the kids began to like me. I guess I got hooked on the stuff and that messed me up."

As Karen markedly increased her drug use, she experienced sleep problems and was a little nervous but apparently maintained herself at school and home at a passable level until her crisis episode.

Karen stated, "My mother constantly picks on me. I have so much work to do—dishes and cooking; I have to look after them (sisters and brother) and when something happens, I get blamed. When I try to explain or even at other times when I give my opinion, she doesn't even listen. She always says I'm the oldest but she doesn't listen to anything I say."

Karen's problem is primarily one of self-concept. She perceives herself as being unloved and used by her parents. It is obvious that she has a poor body image and low self-esteem. Karen's problem with her self-ideal was seemingly remedied with the use of drugs. However, Karen has role conflicts as well, based on her developmental level, regarding herself as a feminine child, sibling, student, and friend. Considering interdependence, Karen's affectional needs are poorly met at best. Behaviors within the physiological mode include fatigue, increased appetite, and psychological dependence on a drug.

Questions

1. What is the focal stimulus for Karen's insatiable longing problem?
2. List other factors influencing the situation.
3. According to the phases in the pattern of substance abuse given in Fig. 27.2, what phase would you identify for Karen at this time?
4. What nursing diagnosis would you state for Karen?
5. What nursing goals and interventions are appropriate?

REFERENCES

Betts, Virginia Trotter, and Anne Wetzel Saletta. "Substance Abuse: Drugs and Alcohol," in *Community Health Nursing*, L. Jarvis, ed. Philadelphia: F. A. Davis Company, 1981, pp. 537–554.

Brown, Martha Montgomery, and Grace R. Fowler. *Psychodynamic Nursing: A Biosocial Orientation*. Philadelphia: W. B. Saunders Company, 1969.

Emmel, Phyllis. "Alcoholism," unpublished paper designed for a student learning module, Mount Saint Mary's College, Los Angeles, 1975.

Glasser, William. *The Identity Society*. New York: Harper & Row, Publishers, 1972.

Goodwin, Donald W. "Is Alcoholism Hereditary?" *Archives of General Psychiatry*, vol. 25, December 1971, p. 545.

ADDITIONAL READINGS

Burgess, Ann Wolbert. *Psychiatric Nursing in the Hospital and the Community*, 3rd ed. Englewood Cliffs, N.J.: Prentice-Hall, Inc., 1981.

Burkhalter, Pamela K. *Nursing Care of the Alcoholic and Drug Abuser*. New York: McGraw-Hill Book Company, 1978.

Fitzpatrick, Eileen. "Primary Nursing Treatment That Works for the Hospitalized Drug Dependent Client," *The Canadian Nurse*, November 1980

Haber, Judith, Anita M. Leach, Sylvia Schudy, and Barbara Flynn Sideleau. *Comprehensive Psychiatric Nursing*. New York: McGraw-Hill Book Company, 1978.

Chapter 28

Life Closure

Marjorie Clowry Dobratz

BEHAVIORAL OBJECTIVES

After studying this chapter, the reader will be able to:

1. Define the key concepts of the chapter.
2. Explain life closure and specify how this varies with each individual life closer.
3. Illustrate the closure continuum and identify behaviors exhibited along the continuum.
4. Make first- and second-level assessments of the life closer.
5. Differentiate focal, contextual, and residual stimuli within life closure.
6. Describe the function of stimuli regulators and list their behaviors, adaptive and ineffective, which affect life closure.
7. Specify the significance of message cues and their purpose in life closure.
8. Describe adaptive life closure.

KEY CONCEPTS DEFINED

Closure: the process of closing or finishing.

Life Closure: a role that concludes and brings together the dimensions of one's life and performing those exhibited behaviors associated with the role according to the uniqueness of each individual life closer.

Life Closer: a person for whom death is pending and who also is approaching the end of the closure continuum.

Stimuli Regulators: individuals who effect adaptive life closure by performing behaviors that help the life closer in role mastery.

Adaptive Closure: behaviors performed by the life closer which maintain the integrity of the individual during life closure.

Stimuli Nonregulators: individuals who effect ineffective life closure by performing behaviors that are detrimental to role mastery.

Ineffective Closure: behaviors performed by the life closer which are disruptive to the integrity of the individual during life closure.

Message Cues: verbal and nonverbal stimuli sent between the life closer and stimuli regulator which act as signals to guide behavior.

Closure Continuum: a continuum that shows a progression through defined and accepted stages of behavior from impending death to finality of life.

Prior to the contributions of Kubler-Ross (1969) there were few identified behaviors and little theoretical background for dealing with the dying person. Death, the most inevitable part of life, outside of birth, remained an uncharted roadway, especially for those who were dying. The work of Kubler-Ross, by identifying a stage theory of dying, provided a theoretical framework which gave structure to both those struggling with the dying process and those giving help and support. With this framework, it became possible to look for signs and guideposts along the way to identify behaviors inherent in the dying process. These expected behaviors were found to be stages through which the dying passed and were adaptive ways of coping with the dying process.

The publication of the Roy Adaptation Model (1970) followed soon after the work of Kubler-Ross and similarly contributed by providing a theoretical framework which gives structure to nursing practice. Assumptions underlying the model are based on the model's approach to the concept of person and the process of adaptation. One of the basic assumptions of the model is that health and illness are an "inevitable" dimension of the person's life (Riehl and Roy, 1980). In order to develop the concept of life closure within the adaptation model, this assumption is broadened to include death. This assumption can be restated by saying that each person is subject to the laws of health, illness, and death. Once the assumption is restated, concepts can be developed within the model in regard to life closure, or the dying process.

In developing the concept of life closure, it is apparent that all four adaptive modes are involved in the dying process. Redman (1974) notes that the greater a life threat to the living system, the more components of the systems are involved in adapting to it. There can be no greater threat to a person than the fact of imminent death and the complexities of the dying process cross all of the adaptive modes. The physiological mode has unending implications regarding physical care and relief of pain. Self-concept is involved, as the greatest loss possible is occurring — oneself. Interdependence is manifested by the need of the dying to relate to others and receive nurturance. The role function mode has been selected as a basis for developing the content of this chapter as a new role must be learned and mastered — life closure. We might say that at this point in the life process, the person is relinquishing secondary and tertiary roles and focusing on the primary role of being a dying person (see Chapter 15). At the same time, the caregiver has to learn the new role of relating to the dying person. This chapter will deal with both of these role changes.

Life closure is defined as a role which concludes and brings together the dimensions of one's life. As in all adaptive processes, performance of this role will be determined by the stimuli present during life closure. The uniqueness of each individual life closer, the disease process, and other persons with whom the dying interact are stimuli that affect the outcome of role performance. Other persons interacting with the dying person will determine if the role of life closure is mastered, if distance occurs, or if failure develops. Life closure is seen as a primary role in that it is a point in the developmental process and the majority of behaviors engaged in by the individual will be toward adaptive or ineffective closure. For the dying person, and others within the situation, this role will take precedence over others. The role of life closure can be performed in a variety of settings, and a life closure assessment, such as that presented below, can be adapted for use in a home or hospice setting, although the focus used here is on the institutional setting.

Two components are necessary to perform a role (see Chapter 15 for a discussion of role theory). First, one holds a position in society. The dying find themselves in a position that is mostly unwanted, feared, and never before experienced. Furthermore, this position has many negative connotations and fears surrounding it. The second component of role performance calls for a pattern of interaction with another person. The person with whom the dying must interact is often inexperienced, ill-equipped, and also fearful. Hoggatt and Spilka (1978) in a study of 207 registered nurses found that only 2.2 percent felt totally capable all the time when dealing with terminally ill patients. They also found that 61.5 percent of the nurses claim that their education was not adequate in teaching them to support and comfort the dying patient. The stage can therefore be set for problems to arise during role performance if one, or both, of the interactors was not able to learn the expected behavior for the role.

Role performance for both the dying person (*life closer*) and interacting persons can be learned. Individuals who interact with the dying person are called *stimuli regulators* (family members, friends, nurse, doctor, and so forth) as they will help the dying person perform the expected behaviors and promote role mastery through effective interactions. They will know which stimuli to change to promote *adaptive life closure.* Individuals who are unable to interact with the life closer in an effective manner (*stimuli non-regulators*) will promote role distance and role failure. They will be unable to manage stimuli to help the life closer learn the role and *ineffective life closure* will result. To lessen the likelihood of one being a stimuli nonregulator, one learns new behaviors for being the interacting person in the helper role.

Interactions with the dying person are different from other types of interactions. Feigenberg and Schneidman (1979) state that a person who systematically attempts to help a dying individual achieve a psychologically comfortable death is acting in a special role. This role differs because a special type of involvement takes place. There is more intensity within the situation, the passage of time is crucial, the goals are also limited, and the possibility of intense transference is present. Once it is understood that a special role is required and appropriate behaviors must be learned for interacting within that role, the behaviors can be introduced and learned.

Studies indicate (Lester et al., 1974; Clowry, 1972) that factors influencing the helper role are educational preparation and exposure to the dying person. Levels of fears of death and dying were decreased as the nurse increased cognitive knowledge regarding death and dying. Diminishing one's own fears of death and dying would lead to more effectiveness in role performance for the helper and less incidence of role distance or failure. Individuals on the helping side of the interaction will be unable to promote adaptive life closure unless they are also mastering their role.

Role performance for the life closer can also be learned. The development of appropriate behaviors within the role is dependent on cues. Roy (1967) found that the nurses' introduction of role cues to the mothers of hospitalized children increased the role adequacy of the mother in dealing with the child. The person with whom the life closer is interacting sends the appropriate cues that promote adaptive life closure. We are calling these cues *message cues* and are including both verbal and nonverbal stimuli that are used to guide behaviors.

This chapter on adaptive life closure defines the role of life closure, how the dying person enters into the role, behaviors exhibited, position on the closure continuum, and interactions with other persons (stimuli regulators) which promote adaptation. Message cues act as guides for learning the role for both the life closer and stimuli regulators. The main goal of life closure is role mastery and the Roy Adaptation Model provides a framework within which assessments can be made. An assessment of the life closer identifies behaviors and other stimuli that are present and affect life closure. Problems in life closure can thus be identified, behavioral outcomes set for the life closer, and stimuli regulated to promote adaptive life closure.

CONCEPT OF LIFE CLOSURE

Role change indicates that a new role must be learned, one that has not been previously encountered during the course of a lifetime. This new role, which the life closer must encounter, has never been experienced and the appropriate behaviors to perform the role are unknown. Life closure means concluding or bringing together the dimensions of one's life. Behaviors associated with the role are exhibited according to the uniqueness of each individual. The important word to be noted is *uniqueness*—the fact that all individual life closers bring with them, into the role, a set of stimuli that differ from those of any other person. As no two individuals live their life in the same manner, no two life closers will perform life closure in the same way. The process of life closure involves all the unique factors in an individual's life which have set them apart. These individual factors, or stimuli, that all life closers bring with them into this process form the basis for nursing assessment. These factors further determine how the role of life closure will be learned.

CONCEPT OF THE CLOSURE CONTINUUM

The *closure continuum* is a progression through the defined and accepted stages of behavior by the life closer and from impending death to finality of life. Figure 28.1 visualizes the closure continuum.

The observations of many persons along the closure continuum have revealed patterns of behaviors which become reference points along the continuum. The behaviors exhibited along the continuum are not to be thought of as fixed points; therefore, the arrows point in both directions. Not all life closers move along the continuum in an orderly progression from denial to acceptance. A life closure may become fixed at any point along the continuum, or may move back and forth along the continuum line. All individual life closers move along the continuum according to their own unique set of stimuli. The behavior patterns have been identified along

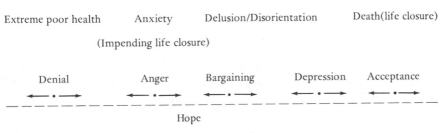

Figure 28.1   Closure continuum on which defined stages of behavior become reference points for the progression of life closure.

the closure continuum as reference points to determine how the individual life closer is progressing with life closure and how the role is being learned.

Stages for the dying process were identified by Kubler-Ross (1969) and were represented as adaptive behaviors that individuals used during dying. These stages are denial, anger, bargaining, depression, and acceptance.[1] The behavior patterns are viewed as adaptive ways of responding and become reference points for assessing behavior along the closure continuum. Underlying the continuum is *hope*, which is present throughout life closure.

The stage theory of dying is currently disputed in the literature. It may be possible to identify other behaviors that are present which the life closer uses as adaptive coping mechanisms. The continuum is not to be thought of as limited to those behaviors placed along the continuum. Any assessed behavior may be placed on the continuum. Delusions have been added to the exhibited behaviors as it has been clinically observed that delusions sometimes occur in persons who are close to the end of the continuum. Delusions at this time seem to be transient in nature and the life closer can be brought in touch with reality with minimal effort. Confusion and disorientation are not uncommon and research needs to be done to better understand these behaviors in the person facing life closure. The following case study presents a life closer who exhibited disorientation followed by paranoid delusions.

EXAMPLE

Mrs. F., a 68-year-old black female, was admitted to the oncology unit with a primary diagnosis of gastric malignancy with secondary hepatic metastasis. She had become severely anorexic and had also developed thrombophlebitis secondary to the increased abdominal pressure and resultant ascites. Respirations were becoming increasingly labored and shallow. There was a history of hypertension and arteriosclerotic heart disease. Student nurses were assigned to Mrs. F. four mornings a week. She tried to help in aspects of her care but could not exert any control over her environment. She was unable to tell the student where she was, or what day it was. At one time, she said she wanted to go home, but otherwise, her responses were in monosyllables of yes and no. Her withdrawal and periods of occasional crying were indicative of depression.

Two days later she became extremely restless and agitated, and refused to take her medications, stating "You're all trying to poison me." She did consent to go to radiotherapy and upon returning said, "The man who works down there is after me." Her family, who was very supportive, became upset with the change in her behavior. After talking to her quietly

---

[1]The reader is asked to read Kubler-Ross (1969, pp. 75–138) for a more thorough explanation of the stage theory of dying.

and reorienting her to reality, she became subdued and consented to take her medication and fell asleep. She later slipped into paranoid delusions accompanied by restlessness and agitation. During this time, she told one of the staff members that she would not be there next week. (The staff member unfortunately did not respond to her statement). Shortly after, she became quiet and peaceful, slipping into a coma, with death occurring a week later, as she had predicted.

A person becomes a life closer when the stage of extreme poor health is reached. This occurs when the process of illness has reached a point of deterioration to the point of impending death. The process of illness cannot be reversed and medical treatment is ineffective. Thompson (1979) describes a person as entering predeath, when behavior is displayed that markedly differs from normal behavior. The behavior changes noted in the individual may include anxiety, anger, depression, or denial. The signs of impending death are recognized by the dying individual and are communicated. At this point one enters into the closure continuum. This entry point signals a change in one's position in society to that of life closer. One must now learn the new role of life closer.

ASSESSMENT OF LIFE CLOSURE

First-Level Assessment

A first-level assessment is made to identify the behaviors exhibited by the life closer. These behaviors differ from the normal behavior of the person and are indicative of the internal struggle that is taking place in the life closer. Leiberman (1965) calls this the experience of "inner disintegration." Imminent death represents an experience of lessened psychological effectiveness, and a decrease in the ability to cope adequately with the environment, particularly because of a lowered ability to organize and integrate stimuli in the environment. This inner experience results in behavioral changes which are exhibited by the life closer. The behavior that is exhibited is identified and assigned to some point along the closure continuum. This determination can be made if denial, anger, bargaining, depression, and acceptance are present. It has been stated that not all life closers progress in the same manner or show the same behaviors. What is seen as universal and identified by Pattison (1977) is that all people involved with dying experience a high degree of stress from which none is immune. Based on this work, the behavior of anxiety has been added to the other behaviors present on the closure continuum. The following behaviors are assessed as adaptive and underlying cues are presented which help in identifying the behavior.

Adaptive Life Closure Behaviors

1. *Fear and anxiety:* present in all life closers and exhibited as a cue to internal disintegration. Exhibits changes in the physiological mode. Behavioral manifestations may be hyperactivity, fatigue, crying, or pseudo-cheerfulness. Apprehensive about what may happen.
2. *Denial:* exhibited by downplaying the illness, making light of it, and treating it as minor. Ignores the symptoms of the disease, changes the subject when approached about the illness.
3. *Anger:* attacks and blames others for happenings, displaces anger or events that occur (anger is out of proportion to cause), demands constant attention, overcontrol of environment.
4. *Bargaining:* attempts to deal with God and others, makes a contract to perform certain behaviors if spared, makes promises to alleviate fear and guilt.
5. *Depression:* begins to decrease external stimuli by withdrawal from environment and others. Frequent crying and self-accusations. Beginning realization of the inevitable. Use of verbal symbolism.
6. *Confusion, disorientation, and delusions:* unable to distinguish time and place and to identify persons and objects. Fails to make distinctions. Displays various persistent beliefs not substantiated by sensory evidence.
7. *Acceptance:* appears serene and passive, control over environment relinquished, retreats into internal self.

Behaviors that are considered ineffective in other situations are considered adaptive during life closure and most behaviors are seen as being adaptive. Behaviors become ineffective when assessed to be excessive, harmful, or fixed at one point along the continuum and the life closer is unable to progress. The nurse or stimuli regulator will intervene to provide safety measures, set limits on behavior, or help the life closer to progress toward adaptive closure.

Ineffective Life Closure Behaviors

1. *Harmful behaviors:* exhibits behavior that will be harmful to the life closer or others, such as striking a nurse out of anger, refusal to eat or receive care, and trying to get out of bed when unable.
2. *Disruptive behaviors:* exhibits behavior that is excessive and disruptive to others in the environment. An example would be excessive yelling or screaming.
3. *Fixed behaviors:* exhibits behavior that is fixed, with no movement seen along the continuum. All behaviors along the continuum are allowed as long as they are not harmful, since they are necessary to

the life closer. The goal of the life closure, however, is to help individuals reach the behavior of acceptance. The helper interacts with the life closer to move the person toward acceptance, or other stages of behavior, when readiness is shown by the life closer.

It is to be remembered that the adaptive and ineffective behaviors, with the exception of a fixed behavior, are in a state of flux and it becomes necessary to assess behavior continually. Once an assessment of behavior is made, a second-level assessment is done to determine the stimuli contributing to the behaviors.

Second-Level Assessment

The first-level assessment identifies the presenting behavior and the second-level assessment determines influencing stimuli for that behavior.

Focal Stimuli.   The focal stimulus is the stimulus most immediately confronting the person, the one to which a response must be made. The focal stimulus confronting the life closer is the nature and progression of the disease state. It is this confrontation with illness that precipitates adaptive responses. Second-level assessments are done to identify the stimuli that influence the nature and experience of dying. The progressive physical deterioration becomes the focal point for the person. In life closure the focal stimulus cannot be removed, although the life closer may attempt to remove the stimuli through denial or bargaining.

The nurse does assess the nature and progression of the disease state. The disease state and its affect on the physiological mode are assessed in conjunction with a life closure assessment. The following aspects of the disease state as a focal stimulus are assessed.

*Questions Related to the Focal Stimulus of the Nature
and Progression of the Disease*

1. Has there been a rapid or lengthy progression of the disease? Has the duration been of sufficient time to allow for life closure?
2. What are the bodily assaults resulting from the disease? Must the life closer deal with repeated treatments or procedures? Have these been of long or short duration?
3. Has the disease affected body image? Must the life closer also deal with altered means of elimination or intake?
4. What other body systems and basic needs are involved?
5. Is pain a constancy to be dealt with?

Contextual Stimuli.   Contextual stimuli are all the other stimuli present in the situation or in the immediate environment confronting the life closer. Contextual stimuli can be validated by the helper as having an effect on the outcome of the situation. The assessment of contextual stimuli includes all the relationships present and the entire immediate environment. The relationships include all persons with whom the life closer comes into contact. These include family, friends, clergy, and professional staff members. These individuals all effect the outcome of life closure by being present within the environment. The second-level assessment includes identifying those persons and the supportiveness of the relationships. Other factors in the person's internal and external environment would be assessed and validated, for example, pain.

Questions Related to Contextual Stimuli

1. What family members are present, and how supportive are they? What are their interactions with the life closer?
2. Has the physician completely informed the life closer of his or her condition? How much disclosure has been made to family members? Is the life closer aware of all aspects of the condition? Is the physician supportive?
3. Is the nursing staff able to deal with their own feelings and fears in regard to life closure? Are they able to interact with the life closer on an individual basis? Are continuous relationships provided for to establish trust and confidence?
4. Is the environment conducive to life closure? Is the life closer allowed to maintain control over the immediate environment? Is the life closer allowed to make decisions that determine life closure?
5. Is there an attempt to deal with life closure within the environment? Is there a thanatology department and/or volunteer program to support family and staff members? Is there an in-service program to deal with life closure? Are staff members encouraged to support each other?
6. Is the life closer able to talk to their minister, priest, or rabbi and receive pastoral counseling and spiritual aid?
7. Is pain eliminated so that the life closer will be able to deal with the psychosocial aspects of life closure?

All of these external factors are involved in making an assessment of the contextual stimuli present. They are part of the present and within the situation of the life closer. In many situations of life closure pain is a significant stimulus. The life closer cannot perform aspects of life closure if pain is an overwhelming concern. Hinton (1963) conducted a very important study using a control group of subjects. In two groups of patients with somewhat comparable physical disorders, the dying patients were much more likely to have unrelieved physical distress than the group that was not dying. Pain control is a contextual stimulus and it must be controlled for the life closer.

Residual Stimuli.   Residual stimuli are those stimuli present which are presumed to affect the current situation. These include attitudes, traits, coping abilities, and other characteristics which, although present, cannot be measured. Whereas contextual stimuli can be thought of as being part of the environment and can be easily identified, residual stimuli are those which cannot be readily seen and can be validated only when the helper interacts with the life closer on a deep, interpersonal level which reveals inner thoughts and feelings. Once these residual stimuli are revealed, they become contextual stimuli, as validation can be made and their effect on the situation is known. The helper, or stimuli regulator, strives for interactions that will reveal the inner self of the life closer so that residual stimuli are revealed. Residual stimuli assume great importance during life closure, since life closure is seen as an internal struggle. Clinical observations on the importance of these stimuli in learning the role of life closure have led to the investigation of certain attitudes and characteristics which effect role closure. The intensity of life closure creates a situation in which the inner self of the life closer is examined and drawn upon to promote adaptation.

Beard (1969) and Pattison (1974) have identified the importance of deep relationships and the ability to use social resources as major factors in adjustment to a terminal disease and an uncertain future. Being able to reach out to significant others and to form relationships are very important residual stimuli to assess in the life closer. These stimuli will contribute greatly to determining the adjustment to the illness and the dying process.

Another residual stimulus identified as promoting adaptation is religion. Castles and Keith (1979) in a study of 33 cancer patients found religion to be the most frequently designated emotional resource. Leming (1980) determined that the highly committed religious person has the least anxiety concerning death. The type of religion did not make a difference, and the most important variable found was strength of commitment. The secular loss is viewed as an eternal gain and provides solace for the life closer. The importance of interpersonal relationships and religious commitment, as residual stimuli, can best be remembered by reference to the Psalm of David: "Yea, though I walk through the valley of the shadow of death, I will fear no evil, for thou art with me." Those persons who are able to reach out to others (thou art with me) will have less fear of death, as inherent within is an act of faith and religious commitment.

There are other residual stimuli which can be assessed. The ability to communicate is very important to the life closer. Coping abilities and previous positive life experiences play a part. If there have been previous difficulties with coping, and life experiences have been unsatisfying, more problems will arise in life closure.

EXAMPLE

Mr. J. was admitted with a diagnosis of lung cancer and pneumonia. He also had a long history of drug and alcohol dependency together with dependency upon his mother. The behavior exhibited by Mr. J. was withdrawal from the environment. He refused to eat or take fluids or communicate — asking only for pain medication. After a few days, his physical condition improved with still no change in behavior. He would stare at the wall and curl up in a fetal position. The student nurses cared for Mr. J.'s physical needs and all attempts were made to give psychological support. Day after day, the food tray was placed in front of him but he refused to eat. One day, the student placed a piece of toast in his hand and he put it to his mouth — a gesture that indicated a change in behavior. He began to trust and improved enough to be discharged to an extended care facility.

Cultural variables are also important in assessing individual stimuli of life closers. Different cultures deal with aspects of life closure in various ways with symbolic meanings within the cultures. The following example illustrates a cultural variable.

EXAMPLE

Mr. S. was suffering from carcinoma of the prostate with metastasis to the spine, producing a symptom of left leg weakness. The family of Mr. S. did not want him to be told of his illness, and this information was to be held from him at all costs. They were of Spanish origin, and he was to remain as the patriarch of the family in spite of his medical condition. Their wishes were respected.

Other residual stimuli that are important are perception of the illness, past experiences with death, the age and sex of the life closer, and pain perception. The following questions are asked to determine residual stimuli that will affect life closure:

Questions Related to Residual Stimuli

1. Is the life closer relating to family and friends in a significant manner? Is closeness and concern or distance reflected? (Interaction can be effective during the withdrawal stage by presence.)
2. Does the life closer express a religious faith and commitment? (God is blamed during the denial stage.)
3. Is the life closer able to communicate his or her wants and needs, and open in levels of communication?
4. Is it possible to ascertain how the life closer has coped with past experiences and problems? Has the life closer directed life or been directed by others?

5. Have previous life experiences been satisfying for the life closer? Is there a sense of accomplishment, of having lived life well, or a sense of failure and disappointment reflected? (Most life closers want to, and need to, talk about their past to bring closure.)
6. What cultural variables are present that would affect the outcome of the life closure?
7. How does the life closer perceive his or her illness? Is it seen as a punishment, or are others blamed? Why has this happened to me?
8. Have past experiences with death been resolved by the life closer? Were these experiences unresolved and unaccepted?
9. Is the age of the life closer such as to have allowed for the finishing of some of life's tasks, or must much unfinished business remain?
10. Is pain perceived and understood with tolerance, or seen as a punishment for wrongdoing?

The purpose of a second-level assessment is to determine which stimuli are present that will effect the outcome of life closure. Table 28.1 summarizes assessment factors in life closure for first- and second-level assessments.

CONCEPT OF MESSAGE CUES

Stimuli are regulated to change the behaviors and enable the life closer to progress toward adaptive life closure along the closure continuum. This is accomplished through message cues. Message cues are verbal and nonverbal stimuli which are sent between the closer and the stimuli regulator.

TABLE 28.1
Assessment Factors in Life Closure

Behaviors	Influencing Factors		
	Focal	*Contextual*	*Residual*
Anxiety	Illness — nature	Family	Significant relationships
Anger	and progres-	Friends	Religious commitment
Denial	sion of the	Nurse	Ability to communicate
Bargaining	disease state	Physician	Coping abilities — self-esteem
Depression		Clergy	Previous life experiences
Disorientation		Thanatologist	Cultural variables
Delusions		Volunteers	Perception of illness
Confusion		Environment	Past experience with death
Acceptance		Freedom from	Age and sex
		pain	Perception of pain
		Mental acuity	

These cues act as messages to guide behavior. Message cues can fall into three categories:

1. Regulator-to-closer cues
2. Closer-to-regulator cues
3. Regulator-to-regulator cues

Regulator-to-Closer Cues

Regulator-to-closer cues are stimuli sent to the life closer which are indicative of availability and presence. A feeling of caring is conveyed and expressed to the life closer. Authorities believe that we are a lot more likely to understand the meaning of death to another person if we give that person the full opportunity to express this meaning. This occurs if we have the ability and willingness to listen. Pattison (1977) goes on to say that there is not so much concern for the issue of how much denial or openness there is, but that there is opportunity, availability, and possibility for open communication with the dying.

A feeling of availability and caring can be conveyed to another person through touch. Touching becomes even more important to the life closer — there is a need for physical contact. This need is called *reverse development* by Benoliel (1981). Persons who undergo prolonged dying become more childlike in their needs and responses to the environment. This need is very similar to that of the newborn infant. Kubler-Ross (1969) mentions a physical similarity when saying that there is a gradually increasing need to extend the hours of sleep very similar to that of the newborn infant, but in reserve order.

In relating to the life closer, one must remember to relate as with any other unique individual. The situation is more intense and the disease state more advanced, but relationships are formed with the life closer as with any other person. The stimuli regulator interacts in the following way to the life closer and sends these regulator cues.

THE CONCEPT OF STIMULI REGULATORS

Stimuli regulators are those individuals who effect adaptive life closure by performing behaviors that help the life closer in role mastery. The function of the stimuli regulator is to promote adaptive closure by regulating focal and contextual stimuli and to help the life closer examine and reflect upon residual stimuli as closure is made. Stimuli regulators act as an external regulatory force to modify the stimuli that affect life closure. Stimuli regulators are all those individuals present in the environment of the life closer who affect the outcome of the situation. They include family members, friends, clergy, physicians, nurses, thanatologists, volunteers, and so forth.

The diagram in Fig. 28.2 helps to illustrate stimuli regulators of life closure. The life closer is at the center, most proximal to the life closer, and encircling is the focal stimulus, a progressive disease state. The outcome of the progression is affected by the contextual stimuli present, of which the stimuli regulator is part. The distal circle represents the residual stimuli. The stimuli regulator is positioned between the focal and the residual stimuli. This position enables the stimuli regulator to regulate stimuli for promotion of adaptive closure. A particular approach to regulating stimuli is the concept of message cues.

Message Cues That Promote Adaptive Life Closure

1. Acknowledges discomfort, looks for expressions of pain, asks if pain is present.
2. Makes eye contact which says that the life closer is acknowledged as a person in spite of a changing body.
3. Involves the life closer in decision making, allows for environmental control, keeps the life closer informed.
4. Listens to what the life closer is saying, does not disregard anything the life closer says. Gives open-ended questions to allow the life closer to reflect and give feedback.

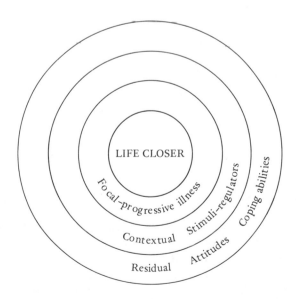

Figure 28.2   Stimuli Regulation of Life Closure.

5. Is available to the life closer when needed and communication is important.
6. Touches the life closer and conveys a feeling of love and caring.
7. Is aware of the mental acuity of the life closer, does not talk about, around, or over the life closer.

The following behaviors by the stimuli regulator are exhibited in response to behaviors observed in the life closer.

1. *In response to anger:* Anger is allowed and it is understood that it is not directed personally at the stimuli regulator, but is a response to the focal stimuli confronting the life closer.
2. *In response to denial:* Denial is also allowed, for the overwhelming aspects of the focal stimulus calls for denial to be used as an adaptive response. Denial can be allowed until it reaches a point of harm and then limits are set.
3. *In response to bargaining:* Allow for contracts to be made with God and others. Guilt and blame are allowed when the contracts cannot be kept. Acknowledge that the life closer tried and did the best possible to keep their end of the contract.
4. *In response to depression:* Allow for crying and expression of sorrow. Acknowledge the sorrow of the life closer. Allow for withdrawal from the environment. Silence becomes important to decrease external stimulation. Touching is more necessary.
5. *In response to acceptance:* Support the life closer to surrender to the internal self. Allow for detachment from the external. A time for touching, caring, and loving.
6. *In response to hope:* Allow for and encourage hope. It is the loss of hope that precedes withdrawal from the external environment.

Stimuli nonregulators are detrimental to life closure by performing those behaviors that prevent role mastery. These behaviors promote distance rather than availability and openness and promote role failure. The following behaviors are indicative of stimuli nonregulators:

Message Cues That Promote Ineffective Life Closure

1. The life closer is avoided, eye contact is not made, the person looks away from instead of toward the life closer. Contact is made only when necessary and then to perform physical tasks — further social isolation results.
2. The life closer is not allowed control of the environment. Decision making is done without input from the life closer. The life closer is

not kept informed of what is happening to him or her. Questions are not directed to the life closer.
3. When the life closer attempts to communicate, conversation is blocked or closed by changing the subject, not answering, or leaving. The life closer is not given a chance to reflect on his or her life. Message cues are missed.
4. The life closer is not acknowledged as a person with any individuality. He or she is talked over, about, and around without any direct reference to him or her as a person and the life closer becomes socially dead.
5. Exhibited behaviors are not understood as being adaptive and are misunderstood, taken personally, and not interpreted as necessary to closure.

Closer-to-Regulator Cues

Closer-to-regulator messages are sent to the stimuli regulator from the life closer. Verbal cues sent to the stimuli regulator indicate a willingness and necessity to talk. These cues occur when the life closer is ready and should not be forced. The life closer will usually send message cues to the stimuli regulator after the regulator has sent cues that indicate a willingness to listen. Verbal cues may also be sent in symbolic form. The importance of these cues are often overlooked. The example of Mrs. F. on page 502 illustrates a cue that was missed when she stated "I won't be here next week." This was spoken clearly and directly and still missed. What the life closer is saying must be listened to. No two life closers will react in the same manner. All of the uniqueness that has set an individual apart in life will be brought out in life closure. Message cues may have a unique form, but if the regulator listens, they generally are present.

Regulator-to-Regulator Cues

It becomes important for the stimuli regulators to be able to reach out to others. The intense emotional demands and complexities of life closure necessitates the need for regulators to have support. The day-in and day-out struggle of life closure is draining emotionally for all concerned. Both staff and family members have a need for supportive relationships. When the life closer begins to withdraw from the external stimuli and environment is the time that those in the immediate situation need the most support and understanding. The stimuli regulators must also draw upon internal stimuli by being able to form interpersonal relationships with others. The following behaviors are indicative of regulator-to-regulator cues.

Regulator-to-Regulator Behaviors That Promote Adaptive Life Closure

1. Exhibit support and understanding for family members in their struggle to allow for closure. Allow verbalization to promote grieving and adaptation following life closure.
2. Is aware of the spiritual needs and concerns for both the life closer and family and seeks counseling and spiritual guidance.
3. Is aware of difficulties that arise between caregivers in dealing with life closure and asks for and gives assistance when needed.
4. Talks to the physician to prevent any problems with disclosure from developing — provides for consistencies.
5. Develops a life closure assessment for each individual life closer.

ADAPTIVE LIFE CLOSURE

Adaptive life closure indicates that behaviors used by the life closer have maintained integrity during life closure. The dying person has been allowed to maintain significant relationships to the end of life, bring closure to these relationships, and supported to express adaptive behaviors. The goal of life closure is to bring each individual life closer to acceptance and the end of the closure continuum. Acceptance (Pattison, 1977) is the surrender to the internal self and allowing the individual to turn away from life. Adaptive life closure promotes behavior indicative of increasing detachment from the external, into the internal, and for the religious person — toward the eternal.

SUMMARY

This chapter has used the Roy Adaptation Model in developing the concept of life closure. Life closure is viewed as the learning of a new role. Variables that effect how the role is learned are given. The concept of the closure continuum is introduced, how a person enters the continuum is described, and behaviors along the continuum are identified. First- and second-level assessments of life closure are made, and the focal, contextual, and residual stimuli are differentiated. Persons interacting with the dying person are identified as stimuli regulators and nonregulators. Behaviors that effect adaptive and ineffective life closure are described. Message cues are explored as signals to guide behaviors and include those that are given from regulator to closer, closer to regulator, and regulator to regulator. Message cues that promote adaptive and ineffective life closure are differentiated.

STUDENT LEARNING ACTIVITY

Based on the following case study, respond to the life closer assessment questions and outline a nursing care plan for Mrs. W. See the Appendix for sample answers and an Adaptation Nursing Process Care Plan.

Case Study

Mrs. W., a 55-year-old black female, was admitted to the oncology unit. A year previous to the admission, she was found to have carcinoma of the right lung. Metastasis to the right femur and frontal skull were found six months later, and she was given another course of radiotherapy, which gave considerable relief from pain, and she was continued on palliative therapy until the time of admission. When admitted, she was found to have lesions in the left femur also, and severe pain prevented her from standing. Anorexia and generalized weakness had also developed. She also had a pathological fracture of the eighth left rib. Frequent coughing was noted and respirations were assessed to be increasing in rate. Hypercalcemia was present due to bone metastasis. Sleep deprivation was evident from dark circles under her eyes, and she stated that she was restless at night and unable to sleep. It was discovered that visual blurring and diploplia were present when she was unable to guide the drinking straw to her mouth.

When the student nurse was first assigned to Mrs. W., she found her crying frequently. One of the staff nurses commended, "She cries all the time, you can't do anything with her." During the morning, she asked what day it was and the student replied, "It's Friday." At that point, she started to cry and stated that she thought it was Sunday. The student asked her if she would like a calendar by her bed to keep track of the days and she declined. There was no further evidence of disorientation to time. When Mrs. W. was encountered, she stated the following: "The nurses don't understand how much pain I'm in." She admitted to the periods of visual blurring and diploplia, but said she hadn't told anyone about it. Along with the frequent episodes of crying, she exhibited the following behaviors: staring into space, and blaming herself for her medical problems by stating, "There's always something wrong with me." She had no concern for her personal care or environment and did not ask about any of her family members. The student was afraid to turn Mrs. W., as she would scream from pain with any movement. Her medication was changed with no decrease in pain level, and it became necessary to begin a continuous drip medication. She became drowsy from the effects of the medication, and barely responded.

Mrs. W.'s several sisters called frequently to check on her condition. The 12 children of her own that she had raised alone visited during the evening. One morning a couple of days after the continuous drip was started, the student nurse came out of the room with tears in her eyes. She had found a beautiful poem left by her sister which expressed all the love from the family to thank her for all the love and caring she had given to others. It was read to Mrs. W. by the student, but she was unable to respond.

First-Level Assessment Questions

1. At what point on the closure continuum would you place Mrs. W. as exhibited by her behavior?
2. Were there other behaviors exhibited?
3. Were the behaviors exhibited by Mrs. W. adaptive or ineffective?
4. Was the student helping Mrs. W. toward adaptive life closure by giving appropriate message cues?
5. Was the staff nurse promoting adaptive life closure?
6. What response would you give to Mrs. W. when she stated that the nurses didn't understand how much pain she was really having?
7. How would you assess the family members as stimuli regulators? Were they helping her toward adaptive life closure?
8. How would you assess Mrs. W.'s coping abilities and means of dealing with life from the information given?
9. What other means of support could be called upon to help her reach life closure in an adaptive manner?
10. What would you assess to be Mrs. W.'s immediate concern—the one to which she was struggling the most to adapt? What could be done by the stimuli regulator?

REFERENCES

Beard, Bruce H. "Fear of Death and Fear of Life," *Archives of General Psychiatry.* vol. 21, no. 3, 1969, p. 80

Benoliel, Jeanne Quintt. Personal correspondence, January 22, 1981 and March 25, 1981.

Castles, Mary R., and Patricia M. Keith. "Patient Concerns: Emotional Resources and Perception of Nurse and Patient Roles," *Omega*, vol. 10, no. 1, 1979, pp. 27–33.

Clowry, Marjorie Dobratz. "Fear of Death and Dying in College Students: A Comparative Study of Nursing Students and Students in Non-Related Fields," master's thesis, Marquette University, 1972, pp. 46–47, 54.

Feigenberg, Loma, and Edwin Schneidman. "Clinical Thanatology and Psychotherapy: Some Reflections on Caring for the Dying Person," *Omega*, vol. 10, no. 1, 1979, pp. 1–8.

Hinton, John M. "The Physical and Mental Distress of the Dying," *Quarterly Journal of Medicine*, vol. 32, no. 3, 1963, pp. 1–21.

Hoggatt, Loretta, and Bernard Spilka. "The Nurse and the Terminally Ill Patient: Some Perspectives and Projected Actions," *Omega*, vol. 9, no. 3, 1978, pp. 225–266.

Kastenbaum, Robert J. *Death, Scoiety, and Human Experience.* St. Louis: The C. V. Mosby Company, 1977, pp. 55, 210–213.

Kubler-Ross, Elisabeth. *On Death and Dying.* New York: Macmillan Publishing Co., Inc., 1969, pp. 34–138.

Leiberman, Morton A. "Psychological Correlation of Impending Death: Some Preliminary Observations," *Journal of Gerontology*, vol. 20, no. 2, 1965, p. 189.

Leming, Michael R. "Religion and Death: A Test of Homan's Thesis," *Omega*, vol. 10, no. 4, 1980, pp. 347–364.

Lester, David, Cathleen Getty, and Carol Kneisel. "Attitudes of Nursing Students and Nursing Faculty toward Death," *Nursing Research*, vol. 23, no. 1, 1974, pp. 50–53.

Pattison, Mansell E. "Psychosocial Predictors of Death Prognosis," *Omega*, vol. 5, no. 2, 1974, pp. 145–160.

Pattison, Mansell E. *The Experience of Dying.* Englewood Cliffs, N.J.: Prentice-Hall, Inc., 1977, pp. 35–46, 305–311.

Redman, Barbara K. "Why Develop a Conceptual Framework?" *Journal of Nursing Education*, vol. 13, no. 3, 1974, pp. 2–10.

Riehl, Joan P., and Sister Callista Roy. *Conceptual Models for Nursing Practice.* New York: Appleton-Century-Crofts, 1980, p. 181.

Roy, Sister Callista. "Role Cues and Mothers of Hospitalized Children," *Nursing Research*, vol. 16, no. 2, 1967, pp. 179–182.

Roy, Sister Callista. "Adaptation: A Conceptual Framework for Nursing," *Nursing Outlook*, March 1970, pp. 42–45.

Thompson, Jan. *Dilemmas of Dying.* Edinburgh: The University of Edinburgh Press, 1979, p. 5.

ADDITIONAL READINGS

Benoliel, Jeanne Q. "Nursing Care for the Terminal Patient: A Psychosocial Approach," in *On Psychosocial Aspects of Terminal Care*, Bernard Schoenberg, ed. New York: Columbia University Press, 1972, pp. 145–161.

Benton, Richard. *Death and Dying: Principles and Practice in Patient Care.* New York: Van Nostrand Reinhold Company, 1978.

Coughill, Rita. *The Dying Patient: A Supportive Approach.* Boston: Little, Brown and Company, 1976.

Davidson, Glenn W. *Living with Dying.* Minneapolis: Augsburg Publishing House, 1975.

Earle, Ann, M. Argondizzo, and A. Kitscher, eds. *The Nurse as Caregiver: for the Terminal Patient and His Family*. New York: Columbia University Press, 1976.

Epstein, Charlotte. *Nursing the Dying Patient*. Reston, Va.: Reston Publishing Co., Inc., 1975.

Feigenberg, Loma. "Care and Understanding of the Dying: A Patient-Centered Approach," *Omega*, vol. 6, no. 2, 1975, pp. 81–94.

Kastenbaum, Robert, and Ruth Aisenberg. *The Psychology of Death*. New York: Springer Publishing Co., Inc., 1972.

Chapter 29

The Family

Joan Hanson

BEHAVIORAL OBJECTIVES

After studying this chapter, the reader will be able to:

1. Define the key concepts of the chapter.
2. Assess the family as a group.
3. Diagnose the level of family functioning based on assessment of the family as a group.
4. Identify the activities of the nurse as she uses her own behavior as a contextual stimuli to change family group behavior.

KEY CONCEPTS DEFINED

Family: a group of two or more persons united by ties of marriage, blood, or adoption. Or, more broadly considered, a group of persons who relate to one another through specified patterns or roles, regardless of ties, and thereby create and maintain a common culture.

Family of Orientation: the family in which persons have grown up and in which they learned their interactional skills.

Group: a group exists whenever three or more individuals are aware of one another, when they are in some important way interrelated in such a way that each individual is changed by its group membership, and when each would be likely to undergo a change as a result of changes in the group.

In this chapter we introduce some of the more recent work in applying the Roy Adaptation Model beyond the care of individuals to groups and in particular to the group of the family. Chapter 4 noted that traditionally a family is defined as a group of persons united through marriage, blood, or adoption. More broadly, a *family* can be considered as a group of persons who relate to one another through specified patterns or roles, regardless of ties, and thereby create and maintain a common culture. Families, then, can include individuals living in communes, close-friend living groups, and so forth.

In community health nursing, the family has long been considered the basic unit to which care is given. Increasingly, other areas of nursing practice are recognizing the importance of focusing on the family as a group in affecting health for individuals and the community. According to the Roy Adaptation Model approach to nursing, the family is considered as a major influencing factor for individual behavior. In Part III we noted particularly that the development of the self-concept, role function, and interdependence modes of adaptation are affected significantly by the family of orientation. The *family of orientation* is the family in which persons have grown up and in which they learned their interactional skills. When adults form a new family, the combination of these learned interactional patterns becomes the skill the family uses in working within the community. A goal of the family is to live successfully within the community. One aspect of this is the family group's interaction with the health care system.

The nurse is often identified in hospitals, clinics, doctor's offices, industrial and student health services, and so forth, as the representative of the health care system. As the nurse deals with the family group, she cannot change the former interactional skills that each person learned in his or her own family of orientation. However, the health care system can be seen as a support to the family group in enhancing its current skill level to function successfully within the community. It is the premise of this author that a major approach to be used in enhancing family skills is the nurse offering her own interactional behavior as a new stimulus for the family to learn skills for interacting. The nurse purposefully manages her own behavior to bring about more mature interactional skills for the family.

This chapter will describe assessment factors within each of the four adaptive modes for the family as a group. In addition, a method for assessing the levels of family skills is described. The nursing activities appropriate for each skill level are identified and illustrated by case examples.

ASSESSMENT OF THE FAMILY GROUP

The family, as a unit, can be assessed in the four adaptive modes: physiological, self-concept, role function, and interdependence. The nurse assesses each family member individually and the family as a unit. Frequently, the family is the stimulus for behaviors assessed in individual members, and similarly behavior of one individual affects the family group. We might note that a *group* exists whenever three or more individuals are aware of one another, when they are in some important way interrelated in such a way that each individual is changed by its group membership, and when each would be likely to undergo a change as a result of changes in the group. In making nursing assessments of family groups, the nurse is aware of this dynamic interactive process.

An example of this process can be seen by observing that the mother of a given family is ill and unable to carry out the function of her role as mother (individual behavior). The major stimulus for the development of this behavior is the family pattern of poor health practices and a lack of plan for preventive or even illness care. In turn, the mother's inability to function due to illness acts as a stimulus to decrease further the family's level of skills in meeting their health care needs (family behavior).

Using group theory, we can think of the family as something more than the sum of its members. The family behavior is even different from the sum of its member's individual behaviors. There is a family spirit, a family mind, and family values. These behaviors are different from the individual's values, spirit, and mind. The family, as with any group, may use more or less coercion to bring about compliance, or compliance may result from a strong "we feeling." Because there is an identifiable family spirit, a family mind, family value, the nurse can assess the family as a unit in the four modes of adaptation.[1]

In the *physiological mode*, the nurse assesses the family's survival needs. The question to ask is how does the family provide for the physical needs of its members? The following behaviors are assessed:

1. The physical maintenance of members:
   a. Food
   b. Clothing
   c. Shelter
2. The allocation of resources for health care needs:
   a. Emergency care
   b. Medical care
   c. Dental care
   d. Preventive care
3. The allocation of space and equipment for:
   a. Rest
   b. Exercise
   c. Aloneness and togetherness

[1]The author wishes to acknowledge that this outline for family assessment was developed in collaboration with Mary Elizabeth Hicks, who taught this content at Mount St. Mary's College.

4. The provision of a safe environment within the home and in the neighborhood
5. The provision for cleanliness and sanitation
6. Accessibility to goods and services, including provisions for transportation

The family unit has a concept of itself as a unit. The behaviors to be assessed in the *self-concept mode* are:

1. The solidarity of the family
2. The social integration of the family into the community. How does the family see itself as part of the community? Clues to watch for are how well are the children prepared to enter school, and adult members the work force?
3. The understanding the family gives to its members
4. The companionship the family provides its members
5 The moral–ethical values of the family
6. The future and present orientation of the family
7. The provision for sexual identity for family members
8. How well does the family defend or stand for its members when a member conflicts with family or community?

The role of the family may be assessed through the communication patterns of the family members. In the *role function mode* the nurse looks at:

1. How are decisions made?
2. Are roles clear and is communication appropriate for these roles?
3. Are role changes tolerated and even assisted?
4. What is the division of responsibility?
5. Is communication clearly understood?

The focus of assessment of the family in the *interdependence mode* is on how successful the family lives within the community. Areas the nurse includes are:

1. What is the interaction of the family with neighbors, government, church, the health care system, and so forth?
2. What are the support systems for the family?
3. Who are the significant others for this family?

The assessment data from this overview within the four adaptive modes can be used to summarize a description of the family's level of functioning. The schema developed by Tapia (1975) is useful in making this summary. The five levels of family functioning that she describes are listed in Table 29.1. At an *infancy* level, the family is chaotic and barely surviving, with inadequate provision of physical and emotional supports. Assessment in the various psychosocial adaptive modes reveals alienation from the community, deviant behavior, distortion and confusion of roles, immaturity, child neglect, depression, and various types of failure.

At the next level, labeled *childhood*, the nurse finds the intermediate family, slightly above survival level. There are variations in economic provisions and alienation, but with more ability to trust. Child neglect is not as great. The family group may be defensive, but is slightly more willing to accept help than at the earlier level.

The third level is called *adolescence* and includes the normal family that has many conflicts and problems. There are still variations in economic levels, but there is greater trust and ability to seek and use help. The parents are more mature but still have emotional conflicts. The family as a group does have successes and achievements and are more willing to seek solutions to problems. They may even be future oriented.

In the level of *adulthood*, the family has solutions and are stable and healthy with fewer conflicts or problems. Members of the family group are very capable providers of physical and emotional supports. The parents in the family are mature and confident. There are fewer difficulties in training of children. The family is able to seek help as needed and are future oriented while enjoying the present.

The last level is labeled *maturity*. The level includes the ideal family, one that is homeostatic with a balance between individuals and group goals and activities. The family group meets its tasks and roles well, and is able to seek appropriate help when needed.

The levels of family functioning are determined by the behaviors of the family. An assessment guideline for describing family behavior according to the Roy Adaptation Model was outlined above. Given this information with an understanding of these levels, it is possible to use the level of the family functioning as a nursing diagnosis; for example: Family is at the adolescent level. According to the diagnostic labels accepted by the North American Nursing Diagnoses Association, and grouped by Gordon (1982) under the functional health pattern of coping-stress-tolerance, related labels would be:

Coping, ineffective family: compromised
Coping, ineffective family: disabling
Coping, family: potential for growth

The nursing diagnosis based on level of family functioning provides direction for nursing intervention. The nursing activities are determined by the skills the nurse brings to the situation to move the family from one level to another. In other words, the assessment data are used to identify the level of interaction that the nurse can develop with the family.

TABLE 29.1

Model for Family Nursing that Assesses Family Level and Identifies the Related Nursing Activities for Intervention

Family Levels:	I. Infancy	II. Childhood	III. Adolescence	IV. Adulthood	V. Maturity
	Chaotic family barely surviving; inadequate provision of physical and emotional supports; alienation from community; deviant behavior, distortion and confusion of roles, immaturity, child neglect, depression and failure	Intermediate family, slightly above survival level; variation in economic provisions; alienation but with more ability to trust; child neglect not as great; defensive but slightly more willing to accept help	Normal family but with many conflicts and problems; variation in economic levels, greater trust and ability to seek and use help; parents more mature but still have emotional conflicts; do have successes and achievements, and are more willing to seek solutions to problems; future oriented	Family has solutions are stable, healthy, with fewer conflicts or problems; very capable providers of physical and emotional supports; parents mature and confident; fewer difficulties in training of children; able to seek help, future oriented, enjoy present	Ideal family; homeostatic, balance between individuals and group goals and activities; family meets its tasks and roles well, and is able to seek appropriate help when needed
Nursing Activities:	Trust	Counseling	Complex of Skills	Prevention	None
	Acceptance and trust, maturity and patience; clarification of role, limit setting; constant evaluation of relationship and progress	Based on trust relationship, uses counseling and interpersonal skills to help family begin to understand itself and define its problems; nurse uses honesty and genuineness, and self-evaluation	Information, coordination, teamwork, teaching; uses special skills, helps family in making decisions and finding solutions	Anticipated problem areas studied; teaching of available resources; assistance in family group understanding, maturity and foresight	

Source: Tapia (1975, p. 327).

NURSING INTERVENTION WITH THE FAMILY GROUP

The work by Tapia (1975) relates levels of nursing activities to the levels of family functioning. These activities include focus on trust, counseling, a complex of skills, or prevention (see Table 29.1). As noted earlier, in applying the Roy Adaptation Model to nursing care of family groups, the nurse is offering her own interactional behavior as a new stimulus for the family to learn skills for interacting and functioning successfully in the community. The nurse selects her own activities along the scale related to the level of family functioning in order to promote forward movement of the family's level of functioning.

When the family is at the infancy level, the nurse focuses activities on *trust*. She shows a great deal of acceptance of the family and seeks their acceptance. The nurse uses her own maturity and patience in clarifying roles and setting limits. Constant evaluation of the relationship and the family's progress is warranted.

At the next level of childhood, the nurse's activities are of a *counseling* nature. Based on the trust relationship established, she uses counseling and interpersonal skills to help the family begin to understand itself and define its problems. The nurse uses her own honesty and genuineness as well as self-evaluation.

When a family can be diagnosed at the adolescent level, the nursing activities involve a *complex of skills*. The nurse may provide information, coordination, and teaching with an emphasis on teamwork. She uses any special nursing skills and helps the family in making decisions and finding solutions.

By the time a family has achieved the level of adulthood, the nurse can focus her interaction on *prevention*. Anticipated problem areas are studied and available resources pointed out. The nurse provides assistance in family group understanding and focuses the interaction on maturity and foresight. For the family at maturity level, no nursing activities are indicated.

Tapia's (1975) model for family nursing gives the nurse a way of summarizing the nursing assessment and selecting appropriate activities for nursing intervention based on the level of family functioning noted. Thus the nurse might use the skills of developing a partnership with the family by simply building trust. The nurse might work in a more developed partnership with the family using counseling skills. More complex skills of using consultation and working as team with the family might be needed if the family shows the ability to identify its conflicts and work toward solutions. The skill of prevention is used with a family who is quite mature in its ability to work within the community. The nurse would probably leave the situation in which the family is able to seek its own solutions and ask for help only when a crisis is anticipated.

Case 1

An example of the nurse using trust-building skills with the family who is assessed as having level 1 skills is as follows:

Behavior Assessed.   Family is living in a crowded three-room apartment. Father's take-home income is $800 a month. Six members in family. Two parents. Three children. Mother's mother. Children are not disciplined. Parents yell at children to give orders. Parents do not converse with one another in front of nurse. Family has no plan for health care. They will use county hospital. Wife would not let community health nurse into apartment. She conversed with nurse at the door of the apartment.

The nurse assesses this family as chaotic. The stimulus which is residual, that is, a hunch based on the theory of the nurse, is that the interactional patterns of this family are limited due to interactional patterns learned in families of origin. The nurse would use her own skills to develop basic trust with this family. The goal is that the family move from the infancy level to the childhood level of interactional skills as evidenced by showing less suspicion of nurse by inviting the nurse into the apartment and sitting down to discuss the family plan for health care.

Case 2

A complete assessment of a more mature family as a unit might show the following:

Behaviors of the Family

Physiological Mode

1. Family meets the basic needs of members: food, clothes, and shelter seem adequate.
2. Family consists of two adults and two children in a four-room apartment. Adequate kitchen and bathroom facilities. Adults have separate bedroom from children. Children share bedroom.

Self-Concept Mode: Adults seem unable to model clear roles for children. Father never disciplines children. He interferes with mother disciplining children with such statements as, "Don't stop them, Angelina, they are too young to understand." (Children jumping from back of sofa onto a table.) Parents speak only Spanish in the home. Father states that he does not wish the children to learn English until they start school.

Role Function Mode: Parents do sit down and talk over the needs of the family. Wife states that her husband makes all the important decisions but he does listen to her before deciding.

Interdependence Mode: Family was hostile to nurse during first visit. Family identifies that they need health care but do not know where to go.

Nursing Diagnosis: Adolescent family level.

Nursing Goal: Family will move from adolescent family level to adult family level as evidenced by:

1. Parents will determine a consistent pattern for training children.
2. Father will assist wife in developing safety measures for children's activities.
3. Parents will look into resources for health care in their immediate neighborhood.

Nursing Interventions:

1. Nurse will teach family about safety for children.
2. Nurse will assist family in planning for health care.
3. Nurse will bring information to family about health care centers in the neighborhood. Also, nurse will provide the names of private doctors who are willing to take families who can pay bills in low monthly payments.

The ultimate goal for all nursing of families is that they become independent of nursing care and that the family will discern its needs for nursing services and, by developing the skills used by the mature family in dealing with problems, the family can apply these skills when interacting with other community support systems.

Case 3

An example of an individual with specific needs that are frequently encountered by the nurse, and also showing the level of family functioning, is given in the following case.

Brief Summary of Demographic Data

Anna R. is a 20-year-old female living in the home of relatives. She came from Mexico a year ago. She speaks limited English. The client's record in the community health agency stated that the client first sought prenatal care in September. Her weight was 98 pounds. Height was 5 feet 2 inches. Last menstrual period was in June. Expected due date is March. Gravida one, para 0.

Weight progression upon each prenatal visit:

Date of Visit	Weight (lb)	
9–19	104¼	
10–28	104½	Hgb: 10.5
11–30	109	

Client mentioned to the nurse that she was unable to sleep because she felt so anxious. The baby's father left her when he learned of her pregnancy. Table 29.2 summarizes the assessment of the client.

SUMMARY

This chapter has combined the Roy Adaptation Model of nursing with a model for family nursing to show how a family group may be assessed according to the four adaptive modes, then a diagnosis of level of family functioning made. The nurse's use of her own interactional skills, selected as appropriate to the level of the family functioning, was seen as the prime approach to managing the context of the situation in such a way as to bring about a more mature interactional skill level for the family. Using this approach, as illustrated in the three case studies, nurses can contribute to the goal of families to live successfully in the community and to use the health care system effectively to meet their needs.

STUDENT LEARNING ACTIVITY

Assess the family of a person that is hospitalized. Diagnose the level of family functioning based on your assessment.

TABLE 29.2
Assessment of Anna R.

| Behaviors | Individual Assessment | | Interventions |
	Stimuli		
Physiological			
Total weight gain at fifth month is 11 pounds. Fundus at umbilicus. BP: 110/70 Hgb: 10.5	E.D.C. 3-22. Fetus is now 19½ weeks. Receives prenatal care from Health Dept. Diet low in iron.		Assess when next prenatal visit occurs. Assess how she gets to clinic. Assess diet.
Self-concept			
Pt. states: "I cannot sleep." Pt. states: "I am afraid." Pt. states: "How shall I manage?"	The father of the child left her 2 months ago.		Assess the significant others in client's life.
Role Function			
Clothes fit too tightly. Wearing loose fitting thongs.	Limited income now that child's father is gone. She has no income for herself.		Assess support systems. Will sister help her with money?
Interdependence			
Pt. states: "I don't have anyone who cares. I live with my sister and her husband. I must find a place to live."	Sister and her husband work all day and leave client in apartment alone. Residual: Sister asking her to leave their apartment.		Plan visit when sister and brother-in-law are at home.

Nursing Diagnosis for Anna R.: Second-trimester pregnancy
Loss of significant other
Anxiety
Mother-to-be role failure

TABLE 29.2 (continued)
Assessment of Anna R.

Goals	Evaluations	Modifications
(These are goals for next home visit, 11/13)	(From home visit 11/13)	(Plans for home visit of 11/30)
Client will successfully complete second trimester as evidenced by:	Client has not gained more weight. BP: 112/74.	Nursing goals: Client will successfully complete first part of third trimester, as evidenced by:
(a) A reasonable weight gain, approximately 10/28 RN visit.	Lips pale pink, nail beds pale. States she feels "so tired."	(a) Talk of baby as person.
(b) BP: 110/70.	States she wants to sleep all day, but cannot sleep when she does lie down.	(b) Increased weight gain of 2 or 3 lb.
(c) Urine negative for sugar and acetone.		(c) BP within normal limits.
(d) Able to sleep through the night and take one nap per day.		(d) Height of fundus above umbilicus.
Has prenatal appointment and a plan to get to appointment.		(e) Wearing loose-fitting clothing and shoes that support feet well.
Client will successfully take on the mother-to-be role as evidenced by:	Client discussed the possible sex of baby. Client spoke of her need for new clothes.	(f) Diet high in iron (she takes ferrous sulfate tablet daily).
(a) Speaking of baby as person.	She said, "Everything feels so tight."	(g) Nurse will discuss signs and symptoms of labor.
(b) Wear loose-fitting clothing.	She stated, "I take my iron tablet everyday when I remember."	(h) Nurse to plan with family for the emergency care for Anna R. Further assessment of brother-in-law and sister's involvement with client.
(c) Wear sturdier shoes for safety.	Plans to use the county hospital for delivery of baby.	
(d) Eat a diet adequate for pregnancy. Has iron tablets from clinic.		
Client will perceive that she has adequate support system.	She stated that her sister will let her stay with them until baby is born.	
(a) She will accept what sister and brother-in-law can give her.	Brother-in-law is 24 years old and works as waiter in restaurant.	
(b) She will work with the nurse in planning care for delivery and baby.	Sister is 18 and cannot speak English.	
(c) She will seek financial counsel from the social worker in health department.		

Family Assessment (Done on home visit 11/30)

Behaviors	*Stimuli*
Physiological Mode	Family are undocumented persons from Mexico.
1. Three adults living in one-room apartment. Two sofas, one makes up into bed. Kitchenette off to one side of room with small gas stove and refrigerator.	New baby is the only person eligible for Medicare benefits. Delivery will cost $1000. Family could receive health care at health department.
2. Brother-in-law works as waiter in nearby restaurant 9:00 P.M. to 3:00 A.M. Sleeps during day.	Total income of family is $600 per month. Couple married 1 year. Couple attended clinic in Mexico.
3. Sister-in-law takes care of two neighbor children in their apartment during the day, 7:00 A.M. to 4:30 P.M.	Family new to community and needs assistance to utilize resources.
4. Family does not have any plans for health care. They do not know of any physician or clinic in immediate neighborhood. Anna R. travels to health department by bus, which takes 1½ hours each way.	
5. Family has an old car.	
6. Family came to the United States 1 year ago.	
7. Brother-in-law speaks limited English, as does Anna R.	
Self-Concept Mode	
Brother-in-law and sister have asked Anna R. to find her own apartment.	
The couple are angry that Anna R. is pregnant. They practice birth-control.	
Brother-in-law stated he will help Anna R. to move and will take her to hospital for delivery.	

531

TABLE 29.2 (continued)
Assessment of Anna R.

Role Function Mode

Brother-in-law makes decisions. He told Anna R. to leave apartment and seek her own.	*Residual:* Brother-in-law may be unaware of limited resources for Anna R.
Brother-in-law introduced Anna R. to baby's father.	*Residual:* Brother-in-law unable to discuss with baby's father his responsibility.
Brother-in-law works with baby's father at restaurant.	

Interdependence Mode

Brother-in-law tells Anna R. what to do. He does not ask her what she would like.	*Residual:* Former communication pattern learned in family of origin. Family not able to take advantage of community resources due to fear of deportation and lack of knowledge of health care system. Family may not be able to discuss their feelings and frustrations with one another.
Sister is very supportive of Anna R. and wants to help her with baby. She has said that she will babysit after the baby is born.	

Diagnosis for Family: Family at childhood level.

Goal: Family will move from childhood to adolescent level of functioning as evidenced by:

1. Meeting everyone's survival needs.
2. Relating appropriate material to the nurse.
3. Seeking health care for all family members.
4. Legitimatizing their presence in the United States.

Interventions

1. Nurse will bring information about health care system to family:
   (a) The limited benefits for mother- to-be when an undocumented person.
   (b) The benefits that will be provided for infant, who will be a U.S. citizen.
   (c) The social services available in the health department.
   (d) The possibility of legitimatizing their status in the United States.
2. Nurse will build trust in family for the nurse and the community health system.
3. Nurse will assist family in working toward supporting Anna R. emotionally as well as providing shelter.
4. Nurse will discuss family with social worker and coordinate a home visit with family.

REFERENCES

Gordon, Marjory. *Nursing Diagnosis: Process and Application.* New York: McGraw-Hill Book Company, 1982.

Tapia, Jayne Anttila. "The Nursing Process in Family Health," in *Contemporary Community Nursing.* Barbara Walton Spradley, ed. Boston: Little, Brown and Company, 1975.

ADDITIONAL REFERENCES

Gilliss, C. L. "The Family as a Unit of Analysis: Strategies for the Nurse Researcher," *Advances in Nursing Science,* vol. 5, no. 3, April 1983, pp. 50–59.

Holman, T., and W. Burr. "Beyond the Beyond: The Growth of Family Theories in the 1970's," *Journal of Marriage and Family,* vol. 42, no. 4, 1980, pp. 729–741.

McCubbin, H., and J. Patterson. "Family Stress Theory, the ABCX and Double ABCX Models," *Systematic Assessment of Family Stress Resources and Coping,* H. McCubbin and J. Patterson, eds. St. Paul: University of Minnesota, 1981, pp. 1–15.

Miller, S. R., and P. Winstead-Fry. *Family Systems Theory in Nursing Practice.* Reston, Va.: Reston Publishing Co., 1982.

Rodgers, R. "Toward a Theory of Family Development," *Journal of Marriage and the Family.* 1964, pp. 202–270.

Roy, S. C. "Roy Adaptation Model," "The Expectant Family—Analysis and Application," and "The Family in Primary Care—Analysis and Application of the Roy Adaptation Model," in Imelda Clements and Florence Roberts, *Family Health: A Theoretical Approach to Nursing Care.* New York: Wiley, 1983.

Sedgwick, R., and S. Hildebrand. "Family Health Assessment," *Nurse Practitioner,* March/April, 1981, p. 374.

Whall, Ann. "Nursing Theory and the Assessment of Families," *Journal of Psychiatric Nursing and Mental Health Services,* 1981, pp. 30–36.

Chapter 30

The Nursing Care Group

Lorraine Ann Marshall

BEHAVIORAL OBJECTIVES

After studying this chapter, the reader will be able to:

1. Define the key concepts of the chapter.
2. Describe disrupted work group behaviors.
3. Describe the groups of stimuli that can contribute to group adaptation or ineffective group functioning.
4. Specify nursing interventions to be used to promote work group adaptations.

KEY CONCEPTS DEFINED

Autonomous Work Group: a self-regulating work system. This group has a primary purpose for existence; it has boundaries allowing regulation of environmental changes; it has the characteristics necessary to maintain a desired steady state; it has goals revolving around the primary purpose; it has regulations for behavior; it has decision-making capacities to enable it to respond to changing situations and to achieve the desired steady state.

Skill Variety: the use of different skills and talents in carrying out one's work.

Task Identity: the extent to which a job allows the worker to do an entire job with a recognizable, meaningful result.

Task Significance: the extent to which a job influences the lives of other people.

Autonomy: the extent to which the job outcome depends significantly upon individual decisions and efforts.

Feedback: the knowledge of results about the effectiveness of one's work activities.

The application of the Roy Adaptation Model to the assessment and nursing care of an individual can be extended to a group setting, specifically to the nursing care group. The nursing care group is continually having to adapt to changing conditions to achieve the desired goals. In order to understand and to be able to effect change on this complex level, one needs a basic understanding of work group functioning. This chapter describes work group functioning, then applies the nursing process of the Roy Adaptation Model to the work group of a clinical nursing unit.

WORK GROUP FUNCTIONING

In hospitals and other health care agencies, the traditional functional division of labor has been organized by tasks and specialization, not always patient needs. In such a system, the registered nurse directs and supervises the care of a group of patients by a group of workers with various skills — licensed vocational nurses, nurses' aides, and ward clerks. Often this approach has resulted in fragmented care. The patient does not know who to rely on for information, support, and assistance. Similarly, the nurse does not receive satisfaction from planning, providing, and evaluating care. Much has been written about this "no win" situation which shows the importance of competent group organization. Thus we will focus on the nursing care group as an important entity in health care. Based on the theoretical approach of the Roy Adaptation Model, the nursing care group will be viewed as an adaptive system.

The very nature of nursing necessitates effective functioning in a complex and changing critical service environment. In this environment, the social or person-related, and technological or thing-related, structures must be smoothly integrated. It is essential for task performance that people relate not only to technology, but also to each other. By means of self-regulating or *autonomous work groups*, technical and social aspects of work can be integrated for goal achievement (Cummings, 1977). An autonomous work group allows the interaction for interdependent tasks to take place. Rather than break down activities to individual tasks, workers are given enough autonomy to master their task environment. On the nursing unit this means that the nurse has a variety of tasks before her that she organizes throughout her shift as she sees fit, thus allowing her to respond to changes or emergencies as necessary. The important factor is that effective group functioning will allow the freedom to cope with change more easily than in a conventional system, where simple task division may provide unnecessary constraints.

According to Cummings (1977), there are certain basic criteria necessary for a group to function sucessfully. These criteria are all present in a nursing care group. There is a primary purpose for the group's existence — and that is effective, efficient patient care. Each nursing unit has its own boundaries; therefore, it can function as a unit to regulate environmental exchanges. By virtue of these boundaries, the unit has the characteristics necessary to maintian a desired steady state within that unit. The unit has a set of goals. The set of goals evolves around patient care. Information is continually available for the system to function from staff, physicians, management, and the patients, as well as reports, charts, and so forth to assist in this goal achievement. Nursing behavior is strictly regulated by procedure codes. In addition, the group has decision-making capabilities which are both necessary and permitted to respond continually to changing situations and to achieve the desired goals. By the group being cognizant of adaptation theory they will find it easier to organize the various tasks as well as the social and technical components of the unit. It is important that nurses continually be conscious of the fact that they comprise one work group. They will work actively as a group to confront, adapt, and respond effectively to problems.

ASSESSMENT OF THE NURSING CARE GROUP

In a nursing care group the possible adaptation problems that might be encountered would be:

Poor patient care or fragmented patient care
Misunderstandings
Decreased communication within the group
Disagreements between staff over routines, patient care, and so forth
Group disorganization
Role identity problems
Self-concept disruption
Low group morale
Low level of job satisfaction

In assessing a disrupted nursing care group, some of the expected behaviors might fall into the following general catgories: (1) anxiety, (2) insecurity, (3) jealousy, (4) fear of the unknown, (5) resentment, (6) frustration, and (7) mistrust. These behaviors apply not only to the nursing staff, but might also be exhibited by patients in response to the type of nursing care they are receiving from the disrupted nursing care group. The following are examples of disrupted behavior:

1. Charge nurse
   (a) A charge nurse who won't help the staff.
   (b) A charge nurse who forgets to provide information: lab results, test results, and so forth.
   (c) A charge nurse who does not plan appropriately for transfer of patients.
   (d) A charge nurse who makes the staff themselves call physicians to get a response to problems.
   (e) A charge nurse who leaves the desk in disarray at the end of the day for the next shift to straighten up.
2. Task responsibilities
   (a) Task division is such that the day shift is left with most tasks to do.
   (b) Rooms are found disorderly in the morning.
   (c) Routine tasks lack standardization of times.
3. Shift-to-shift report
   (a) Language problems — lack of knowledge of English; use of inappropriate language.
   (b) Incoming staff late to start report, makes offgoing staff have to leave late.
   (c) All staff members not listening to the full report, so unaware of patients other than their own as far as conditions and needs.
4. Registry personnel
   (a) Personnel unfamiliar with the unit.
   (b) Personnel do not help others.
   (c) Personnel not allowed to do certain tasks by nature of not knowing hospital policy.
5. Teamwork
   (a) People not answering other people's call lights.
   (b) People often too busy with charts to help each other.
   (c) Unit not understanding of other units' problems when transferring patients (example: patients often transferred just to relieve staffing problem).
6. Physicians
   (a) Lack of orientation to the unit.
   (b) Lack of communication among themselves as far as patient progress.
   (c) Lack of communication to staff of changes in a patient's protocol.

7. Staffing and assignments
   (a) Some people allowed to make schedule switches while other people are not.
   (b) Too many acutely ill patients being given to one staff member consistently.
8. Other behaviors
   (a) Staff members ignoring one another.
   (b) Staff members not answering questions.
   (c) Staff members not providing orientation to new staff members.
   (d) Lack of eye contact when addressing other staff members.
   (e) Staff members making sarcastic statements, showing hostile attitudes, and like responses.

There are many other examples of disruptive group behaviors. The preceding have been identified merely as an outline to begin focusing on the care group and its components.

STIMULI AFFECTING THE NURSING CARE GROUP

Focal stimuli can relate either to the staff members themselves or to their job design. Focal stimuli can fall into four categories: (1) the individual level, (2) job design, (3) team changes, and (4) external factors. A focal stimulus for the staff members on an individual level could be: a new staff member, a difficult or disruptive leadership person (that is, a team leader or head nurse), a particularly ill patient, or a particular staff member who is disruptive.

In assessing job design, one must consider task appropriateness as well as the knowledge and skills required to do the job. If the problems are in job design, they could fall into one of five areas: skill variety, task identity, task significance, autonomy, or feedback (Hackman and Oldham, 1980). Hackman postulates that these five core characteristics contribute significantly to three psychological states—job meaningfulness, feelings of responsibility, knowledge of work effectiveness—which are necessary for work motivation and overall job satisfaction.

Skill variety is the use of different skills and talents in carrying out one's work. Lack of skill variety, such as just being responsible for one or two tasks continually throughout the day (such as linens, blood pressures, vital signs, meals, or medications) can be very disconcerting and lead to lack of meaningfulness in the job.

Task identity is the extent to which a job allows the worker to do an entire job with a recognizable, meaningful result. The inability to see some type of visible outcome of one's work can also contribute to lack of meaningfulness in one's job. The nurse needs to be able to see that a variety of her efforts throughout the day can contribute to a visible difference in the patient's well-being at the end of that day or at the end of a couple of days.

Task significance is the extent to which a job influences the lives of other people. The nurse must perceive that her efforts have an impact on the lives of her patients. This is essential for meaningfulness of the job.

Autonomy occurs when the job outcome depends significantly on individual decisions and efforts. In nursing, increased autonomy therefore contributes not only to accountability as far as the patient is concerned, but also to an increased feeling of responsibility.

In any system, *feedback* is important. One needs to have knowledge of results to be able to assess the effectiveness of one's work activities. Constructive feedback provides actual information that can be used to modify one's performance. These five core characteristics are the focal stimuli that can be modified to influence job design. These characteristics are critical to internal work motivation, and it is internal work motivation that leads to job satisfaction.

The next group of focal stimuli are termed *team changes*, that is, changes at the group level. There will be some crossover between job design and team changes, as they are closely related. In focusing on team changes, understanding how the internal work group functions as a team is very important. Stimuli under this heading would be: the alignment of groupings of the staff against other groups, task division and responsibility, the impact of registry personnel on the unit, the composition of the work group, the norms of the work group, and the levels of effort applied by the work group.

The last grouping of focal stimuli are the external factors. These can be individual or group in nature. Examples of influencing external factors are physicians, ancillary personnel, available resources, and organizational constraints. These are all things that can affect the work group structure.

Contextual and residual stimuli can be many. Contextual stimuli might include threats to self-concept for the team members, threats to role identity, previous experiences with new staff members, threats of disorganization, shift in hierarchy, lack of extensive experience in dealing with students, threat of disruption to the unit, doubt of one another's capabilities, avoidance as a coping mechanism, previous problems with role identity and self-concept, and uncertainty about a new nurse's ability to take charge of the unit or team lead. These factors and others which cannot be validated are classified as residual stimuli.

NURSING INTERVENTION

Following the identification of an adaptation problem in the nursing care group, communication to the entire group is needed. Recall that the overall goal is that the nursing care group function adaptively as a system.

The group needs to analyze the various problems in depth. They must clearly understand the influencing factors or stimuli before they can generate proposals for promoting adaptation.

Next, the various proposals need to be evaluated for the potential of achieving the intended results and the costs, if any, involved. Some proposals will be inappropriate for action on the group level. Once a manageable set of objectives has been selected, an action program for implementation is needed. First, the group must detail how to bring about adaptation. Interventions should focus on the major stimuli areas. On the individual level, interventions such as risk taking, confrontation, and realistic goal setting can be effective. In the area of job design, interventions such as restructuring of tasks and combining tasks to provide a visible outcome of work would be helpful. Interventions on the group level will involve improving communication skills, discussion, coordination of work efforts, reaffirmation of commitment to the group, and positive verbal and nonverbal interaction (that is, encouragement, helping each other with work). Finally, interventions to deal with external factors will revolve around sharing information, and requesting and providing information. Next, the group needs to devise a timetable to introduce the changes. The group must have the understanding that these changes are being attempted on a trial basis. A reasonable period for evaluation of the changes should also be included in the timetable. Specific evaluation mechanisms might be supervisor evaluation, peer review, and checklists by all workers. If particular interventions are found effective, they can be incorporated permanently as part of the nursing care group system. However, the group should be cautioned to maintain an ongoing evaluation process. This will allow the group to continue to make modifications as necessary.

Case Study

Mary and Diane are the RNs on a 20-bed medical/surgical unit. Deedee is the new charge nurse. The staff was very fond of the previous charge nurse who had recently retired. They were very unsure about their bright new charge nurse and avoided interaction with her as much as possible. When contact was made, staff members would often question Deedee's actions.

In the past, Mary and Diane had alternated roles daily. One day Mary would be medication nurse and Diane would do patient treatments, check off lab slips, and help sign-off orders. The next day they would alternate. Similarly, the work of the LVN and nurses' aides was divided up by tasks: baths, linens, vital signs, and so forth. Deedee decided to divide the unit into two permanent miniteams. She made Mary and Diane each a team leader. Deedee believed that this system would allow the RNs to have more patient interaction, ensure patients' continuity in their care, and maintain communication about the patients in an organized fashion among staff, with physicians, and between shifts. By placing the responsibility of coordinating care for a group of patients with the team leaders, some decision making had been decentralized and nursing accountability was built in. Deedee felt that this method would increase the quality of patient care and ultimately would increase the nurse's job satisfaction.

Group I Behaviors	Stimuli
1. RNs ignoring the new charge nurse except when communication absolutely necessary—poor eye contact, rushed verbal responses	*Focal:* new charge nurse *Contextual* 1. Threat to self-concept of staff 2. Threat to role identity 3. Experience with previous charge nurse 4. Uncertainty about Deedee's ability to take charge
2. Nurses' aides questioning the charge nurse's right to change staffing assignments	
3. Staff members excluding charge nurse, making private jokes in front of charge nurse	*Residual* 1. Previous problems with role identity 2. Previous problems with self-concept
4. Staff asking lots of questions about charge nurse's training, theoretical background, and so forth	

Nursing Diagnosis: Anxiety together with frustration related to the presence of a new charge nurse.

Goals: Staff will have a decrease in anxiety and be able to cope with anxiety in more constructive ways.

Interventions:

1. Awareness needed by the charge nurse of the staff's use of avoidance, hostility, humor, and so forth, to cope with anxiety.
2. Use of confrontation by charge nurse to deal with situations as they arise. Verbal confrontation can help to decrease anxiety by getting things in the open and preventing the development of misunderstandings.
3. Encouragement of staff to use confrontation as a coping mechanism.
   a. Encouragement by charge nurse to please ask questions about any issues that arises.
   b. Encouragement by charge nurse to bring out into the open any area of disagreement or uncertainty.
4. Verbal encouragement of staff members. Demonstration by charge

nurse of trust in staff — explaining how she values staff assistance, and so on.
5. Charge nurse spending extra time getting to know staff members and assisting staff members with their work as often as possible.

Group II Behaviors	Stimuli
1. Staff complaining about assignments, lack of variety. 2. RNs often questioning exactly the extent of their responsibilities. 3. RNs unwilling to make decisions on their own. 4. Staff members often forget to do certain tasks.	*Focal:* job redesign *Contextual:* 1. Staff divided into two teams. 2. RNs have increased responsibilities — shift in hierarchy. 3. Tasks have been combined. 4. Threat of disruption to the unit. 5. RNs: Uncertainty about their ability to team-lead. *Residual:* previous problems with role function.

Nursing Diagnosis: Uncertainty by team leaders and staff related to job redesign and the amount of involvement that will now be required of them.

Goals: Team leaders and staff will become more comfortable with their new roles and have increased confidence in their ability.

Interventions

1. Explanation by charge nurse of objectives of team leading — to allow the RNs to have more patient interactions, ensure the patients' continuity in their care, and maintain communication about the patient in an organized fashion among staff, with physicians, and between shifts.
2. In the beginning, charge nurse will explain what the daily activities of the team leaders and the staff members and other staff members are going to be.
3. Staff will be commended by charge nurse when they show effective functioning under new team organization.
4. Frequent conferences by the charge nurse with the team leaders and with the entire staff to discuss any problems developing within the new system and what they can do to resolve them.

This case study represents a few of the many problems that a nursing care group might encounter. The interventions are designed to manage the stimuli on individual and group interaction levels, thereby facilitating individual and group adaptation. To prevent future disruption of group functioning, an assessment of the group norms, regulating functions, socializing patterns, and skill level of the staff members should take place.

SUMMARY

Based on the information presented in this chapter, the nurse should understand the principles that enable the nursing care group to function as an autonomous or self-regulating work group. It is the characteristics of this system that make it suitable for the application of adaptation theory. By successfully incorporating adaptation theory on a group level, the nursing care group will be strong and coherent enough to respond effectively and to bring about change in a smooth, organized, and efficient manner.

STUDENT LEARNING ACTIVITY

Read the case study and complete the assignment below.

Case study

Client.   Staff of a large community hospital, 450 beds, and you will be working with one medical-surgical nursing unit. There are two teams always present, but the team members switch teams weekly. Precipitating event for this situation will be two senior nursing students arriving to do a medical–surgical rotation and to work into team leading in a unit that had not actively had students before.

Theoretical description of the disruption.   The staff of the unit over the past several months have become a very independent close knit group. They had all worked well together and did not have to account frequently to others, as there was no head nurse on the floor. The team leaders were both very comfortable with their roles, as were the team members. There was a strong bond of trust present between all staff members which contributed very importantly to group effectiveness. Team leaders spent time helping staff with patients whenever possible and staff members frequently worked together to increase efficiency. The team functioned in a very set manner.

Everyone seemed to know what was going to happen and when. The staff had not really planned on having to deal with two new students, and the team leaders had not anticipated being involved in teaching students. Thus the presence of two new members was a distinct disruption. The staff did not know what to expect of the students or how they would fit in other than what they had seen from other students on other floors. Because the staff was not fond of the other students, seeing them as interrupting routines and getting in the way, their initial reaction to the new students was a very mixed one. The prevailing feeling was to resist any type of change that might come about. The staff was very wary of any threat to their present organization. They seemed to feel the threats of disorganization, possible shift in hierarchy, confusion, and so on, were bound to become realities with the two students working on the floor. They feared that the students would interrupt the stability of the unit and the set interrelation of the team members' roles. Also, knowing that the students were registered nurse students might have led to questioning by staff members of how they felt about themselves, thus a threat to their self-concept. This caused a lack of warm reception to the students and, in turn, served to increase the students' already present anxiety about entering a new situation. Thus there was a situation present where a change was not only confronting the staff but also the students entering a new rotation; this led to an increased reaction on both sides, resulting in a much higher level of fear and anxiety.

Assignment

Describe the overt behaviors you might expect to follow the disruption described above. What are the possible adaption problems? Next, group your behaviors and decide on the focal, contextual, and residual stimuli that are influencing them. Come up with a nursing diagnosis and devise goals, interventions, and evaluatory mechanisms appropriate to the group.

REFERENCES

Aravjo, Marianne. "Creative Nursing Administration Sets Climate for Retention," *Hospitals*, May 1, 1980, pp. 72–76.

Argyris, Chris. "The Primary Tasks of Intervention Activities," in *Perspectives on Behavior in Organizations*, J. Richard Hackman, Edward E. Lawler III, and Lyman W. Porter, eds. New York: McGraw-Hill Book Company, 1977.

Brooker, Rosemary, D. N. E. Duffield, and Helen Rooke. "There Is a Better Way," *The Australian Nurses' Journal*, vol. 9, no. 3, 1979, pp. 54–56.

Cummings, Thomas G., and Edmond S. Molloy. *Improving Productivity and the Quality of Work Life.* New York: Praeger Publishers, 1977.

Donovan, Lynn. "What Nurses Want (and What They're Getting)," *R.N.*, April 1980, pp. 22–30.

Hackman, J. Richard. "Designing Work for Individuals and for Groups," in *Perspectives on Behavior in Organizations*, J. Richard Hackman, Edward E. Lawler III, and Lyman W. Porter, eds. New York: McGraw-Hill Book Company, 1977.

Hackman, J. Richard, and Gregory R. Oldham. *Work Redesign*. Reading, Mass.: Addison-Wesley Publishing Company, Inc., 1980.

Silber, Mark B. "The Motivation Pyramid in Nurse Retention," *Supervisor Nurse*, April 1981, pp. 45–46.

Timmreck, Thomas C., and P. Joanne Randall. "Motivation, Management and the Supervisory Nurse," *Supervisor Nurse*, March 1981, pp. 28–31.

Wolf, Gail A. "Nursing Turnover: Some Causes and Solutions," *Nursing Outlook*, April 1981, pp. 233–236.

Appendix

Sample Adaptation Nursing Process Care Plans and Sample Student Responses

OXYGEN NEED (Chapter 5)

Adaptation Nursing Process Care Plan Related to Oxygen Need for a Middle-Aged Man Brought to the Hospital with Chest Pain and Shortness of Breath

Behaviors	Influencing Factors		
	Focal	*Contextual*	*Residual*
Anxious expression on face	Damage to cardiac muscle resulting in decreased circulatory effectiveness	Unfamiliar surroundings and people	Obese
Skin pale, cool, and moist		Large amount of activity being carried out in immediate environment	Smoked two packs of cigarettes a day over a 20-year period
BP: 90/40			Sedentary—has not regularly participated in physical exercise
P: 130 and thready		Has had several x-rays, lab tests, and an ECG done since arrival	No previous history of heart disease or hospitalization
Respirations: 30		Attached to cardiac monitor, which can be heard "beeping"	
States pain in left chest area diminished after morphine administration		Has an IV and has been receiving antiarrhythmic medication via the IV	
Insists on being elevated on two pillows "in order to get enough air"; states "I can't get my breath"		Has not seen wife since put in ambulance; has been told she is in waiting room	
Irregular cardiac rhythm		Has had a good response to morphine, which reduces metabolic demands	
Frequently asking where his wife is			

Nursing Diagnosis	*Goal*	*Interventions*	*Evaluations*
Hypoxia due to shock resulting from myocardial damage and decreased circulatory effectiveness	Patient will have improved tissue oxygen perfusion as shown by: 1. Normal skin color	Provide additional oxygen by mask. Monitor response to oxygen and adjust flow rate accordingly.	Facial expression became less tense Skin pink and warm BP: 130/70

Adaptation Nursing Process Care Plan Related to Oxygen Need for a Middle-Aged Man Brought to the Hospital with Chest Pain and Shortness of Breath

Nursing Diagnosis	Goal	Interventions	Evaluations
	2. Disappearance of diaphoresis	Observe closely to be sure airway is kept open.	P: 84
			R: 20
	3. Normal respiratory rate and quality	Explain to patient procedures being performed.	"Dull ache" over left chest relieved
		Reassure him that he will not be left alone.	Monitor showing a normal regular cardiac rate and rhythm
	4. Subjective indication of decreased or absent pain	Act calm and confident and move purposefully.	
		Keep room environment cool and prevent buildup of "clutter" as much as possible.	
		Keep client draped, both for comfort and modesty, as much as possible.	
		Continually monitor vital signs so that appropriate medical therapy can be instituted if the vital signs deteriorate.	
		Give 2-mg increments of morphine IV as per medical order if behaviors indicate increasing pain and increasing shortness of breath.	
		When condition stable, bring wife in, first explaining what she can expect to see.	
		Closely monitor cardiac rhythm to identify recurrences of irregular or otherwise abnormal rhythms.	

ACTIVITY NEED (Chapter 8)

Care Plan for Mrs. L.

Problems

1. Joint contracture
2. Flexion contracture of Achilles tendon (foot drop)
3. Decubitus ulceration on bony prominences
4. Muscle atrophy weakness
5. Urinary tract infection and calculi formation
6. Decreased intellectual capacity and mental confusion
7. Poor tissue healing due to negative nitrogen balance
8. Osteoporosis and fracture of bones

Preventive Nursing Interventions

1. Daily range of motion exercises of all joints and maintenance of good body alignment in all positions at all times
2. Use of foot board
3. Frequent change of position with massaging of all bony prominences
4. Isotonic and isometric exercises of all muscles
5. Adequate fluid intake and upright position whenever possible to facilitate normal urinary flow; intake of fluid which would acidify the urine (cranberry juice)
6. Regularly scheduled visits with a designated person(s) to carry out a purposeful conversation
7. Adequate intake of nutrients, particularly of proteins and calories
8. Imposition of stresses on the bones, such as resistive exercises of extremities whenever possible

SKIN INTEGRITY (Chapter 9)

Adaptation Nursing Process Care Plan Related to Skin Integrity Need for a 76-Year-Old Man Recovering from a Cerebral Vascular Accident

Behaviors	Influencing Factors		
	Focal	*Contextual*	*Residual*
Open skin area 1 cm in diameter noted on the sacrum	Immobility causing anoxia to the tissue	Likes to lie on his back because he can watch television Poor nutritional intake Has difficulty chewing meats Age	Anemia
Skin turgor is nonresilient	Aging process		Fluid intake
Skin is dry and thin		Loss of subcutaneous fat Decreased eccrine sweat glands and decreased output per gland Atrophy of apocrine glands Decreased secretion of the sebaceous glands	
Nails are brittle			
Uneven skin pigmentation with brown spots on the face and arms			Chronic sunlight exposure
Scalp is smooth and clean	Grooming practices		
Hair is thin and gray			

Nursing Diagnosis	Goal	Interventions	Evaluation
The open skin area of 1 cm in diameter on the sacrum is related to immobility causing tissue anoxia.	The client's open skin area on the sacrum will decrease in size within 2 weeks as measured by observation.	1. Change the client's position every 2 hours on the even hour. 2. Turn the bed, enabling the client to watch television from all body positions. 3. Order a soft diet that is high in protein. 4. Keep the client clean and dry. 5. Give a backrub every shift. 6. Apply lotion three times a day and whenever needed.	The open skin area has decreased in size to 7 mm in diameter.

Adaptation Nursing Process Care Plan for a Person With a Head Injury

	Stimuli	
Behaviors	Focal	Contextual
Lethargic; occasionally disoriented to time, place and purpose (oriented to person)	Head injury	Hospital environment; away from home; without significant others; stress of accident
Lethargic; increasingly forgetful; occasionally disoriented; headache; nausea; new complaint of decreased visual acuity	Head injury	

Nursing Diagnosis	Goals	Interventions
Altered level of consciousness and orientation due to head trauma	Patient will be continually oriented to place and time beginning 8 hours from now.	Assess level of consciousness and level of orientation along with other neuro checks every 1–2 hours. Report at once any significant changes in the above. Reorient p.r.n. Open window shades to allow natural light. Keep calendar and clock at bedside. Occasionally turn on radio and/or TV for news or soft music (reorient to time). Ask family for photos of patient with significant others to keep in room.
Possible increasing intracranial pressure due to head injury	Lethargy, forgetfulness, headache, nausea, and visual disturbance will decrease by tomorrow as measured by patient's statements and nurse's observations.	Maintain open airway. Avoid loud noises. Minimize physical and emotional trauma. Keep head of bed elevated 30° with head in alignment with body. Discourage vigorous coughing or straining with BM (follow routine interventions to soften stool). Turn gently. Follow medical orders of osmotic diuretics and fluid limit.

SELF CONCEPT (Chapter 14)

Case Study: Mr. H.

Analysis According to the Adaptation Nursing Process[1]

Behaviors

Physical self
Body sensations
"I'm very tired today."
"My feet are burning."
Body image
"I'm starting to feel old."
Personal self
Self-consistency
"I've always been strong and a hard worker."
"I thought we [wife and self] would live forever."
"I was very happy living here with my wife."
"I have many good memories."
"Somehow I keep on going."
Self-ideal
"I always wanted to get my high school diploma."
"I'd like to have young feet."
Moral–ethical–spiritual self
"I know I've lived my life well."
"I believe in a just God."
"I'm disappointed." (About not getting his high school diploma.)

Stimuli

Perception
Inner cell
1. (+) "I've always been strong and a hard worker." C
2. (+) "I thought we [wife and self] would live forever." C
Perceptual field
3. (−) "It is important to be educated in this country." C

---

[1] +, positive influence; −, negative influence; F, focal stimulus; C, contextual stimulus; R, residual stimulus.

Growth and development
    4. (−)   75 years old.   R
    5. (−)   Has arthritis.   F for physical self-behaviors.
Learning
    6. (+ / −) Must work 3 more months to get his pension (reward).   C
Reactions of others
    7. (−)   Lack of wife due to her death.   C
Maturational crisis — ego integrity versus despair
    8. (+)   Accept help from others as needed — working for pension.   C
    9. (+)   Face the loss of one's spouse — his wife died one year ago; he is able to talk about the loss and the pleasant memories.   C
   10. ( )   Learn new affectional roles with one's children — no data.
   11. ( )   Maintain satisfying relationships outside the family — no data.
Coping mechanisms
   12. (+)   Belief in God helps him keep on going.   C
Other
   13. (+ / −) Worked until nine o'clock last night.   C
   14. ( )   Jewish heritage.   R
   15. ( )   Born in Russia and lived there until 18 years old.   R
   16. (+ / −) Lives alone in home he shared with his wife until her death.   C
   17. (+)   Receiving home visits from a nursing student.   C

Diagnoses

1. Client displays moderate to high self-esteem. Behaviors manifesting moderate to high self-esteem. Talked openly, eager to share as well as listen, sure of his own value, coping with the work world, dealing with the loss of his wife.
2. Client is mastering the task of accepting the loss of one's spouse.

Goals

1. Client will continue to demonstrate moderate to high self-esteem as indicated by his continued ability to talk openly and share his thoughts and feelings during our next interview.
2. Client will continue the process of accepting the loss of his wife. (See the case study at the end of Chapter 19 for the complete goal and interventions).

Interventions

1. Use therapeutic communication techniques of reflecting, para-phrasing, eye contact to encourage further discussion of his thoughts and feelings.   (1,2,3,12,17)*
2. Use therapeutic communication techniques to encourage further discussion of his belief in God. Ask open-ended questions to show interest and encourage discussion.   (12)
3. Point out Mr. H.'s strengths and accomplishments as they come up during the interaction.   (1,3,6,17)
4. Collect more data to determine if a referral to an agency where he can have social interactions is indicated.   (7,11)

Evaluations

Goal 1.   Did the client talk openly and share his feelings and thoughts? List specific behaviors. Make revisions in the goal and approaches as indicated.

Goal 2.   Was the client able to speak easily about his wife? List spe-cific behaviors.

Does he express interest in new relationships or activities to fill the time he used to spend with his wife? List specific behaviors. Revise goal and approaches as indicated.

---

*The numbers following the interventions indicate which stimulus or stimuli are being worked with in that intervention.

SEXUALITY (Chapter 17)

Answer Key to the Sexuality Case Study[a]

Behaviors		*Stimuli*
1. The genital area is free of lesions, nodules, and inflamation.	A	(F) Skin is healthy and free of infection
		(C) Health habits of the client.
2. Occasionally has a small amount of nonodorous, cloudy discharge from the vagina.	A	(F) Normal shedding of cells from the lining of the vagina.
		(C) Hygiene practices.
3. Breast tissue:		
(a) The right breast is slightly larger.	A	(F) Client is right-handed.
(b) Both breasts are symmetrical. No dimpling, rash, nodules, or discharge present.	A	(F) No disease process is evident.
		(C) Client performs a self-breast examination every month.
		(C) Young adult.
		(C) Delivered a child before age 30 and has breast-fed.
		(R) Family history of cancer.
(c) Nipples are slightly inverted.		(F) Own pattern of growth and development.
		(C) Normal shape for client.
		(R) Familial trait.
4. Menstruation:		
(a) Last menstrual period was 12 days ago.	A	(F) Intact and functioning reproductive and neuroendocrine systems.
(1) Menstruates every 26 to 28 days.		
(2) Duration of period is usually 4 to 5 days.	A	(C) Client's normal pattern of menses.
(3) Flow is light to moderate; changes tampons every 3 to 4 hours.	A	
(4) Does not experience vaginal bleeding between periods.	A	
(b) Experiences back pain during menstruation.	I	(F) Menstrual cramps.
		(C) Drinks herbal teas.

[a]A, adaptive behavior; I, ineffective behavior; F, focal stimulus; C, contextual stimulus; R, residual stimulus.

(C) Limited rest and activity pattern.

(C) Lack of knowledge regarding ways to alleviate the pain.

(R) Pain threshold level.

5. Client is the biological parent of one child, age 2 years.   A   (F) Reproductive organs intact with adaptive functioning of the neuroendocrine system.

6. Practices family planning utilizing a diaphragm and condoms.   A   (F) Client wishes to further her education as an architect.

(C) Has nine siblings.

(C) Would like to have a large family.

(C) Cooperation from spouse.

(C) Value of children as viewed from the Mexican American perspective.

7. Sexual intercourse: Enjoys a sexual relationship with her spouse.   A   (F) Status of marital relationship.

(R) Cultural and familial influence on sexuality.

Selected Nursing Diagnosis	*Goal*
The client experiences back pain due to menstrual cramping.	The client's back pain will decrease with her next menses as measured by client statements.

Interventions

1. Reinforce the drinking of herbal teas as a relaxing measure.

2. Suggest to the client the possibility of scheduling less hectic days during the beginning of the menstrual period.

3. Explore various exercise plans with the client such as jogging, bicycle riding, and stretching exercises. A routine exercise pattern seems to decrease the severity of menstrual cramps.

4. Encourage the client to use a heating pad for her lower back and to apply pressure to the area.

5. Suggest a position of relief, such as curling up and bringing the knees to the chest.

6. Suggest to the client that she reduce her intake of coffee and refined foods, especially sugar and white flour. Dolomite calcium or vitamin C tablets, taken for a few days before the start of the period, may be helpful.

Evaluation

The client's back pain has lessened during her menstrual period. Using a heating pad and exercising on a regular basis have been effective.

LOSS (Chapter 18)

Adaptation Nursing Process Care Plan for a Person Experiencing Loss[a]

Behaviors	Focal	Stimuli Contextual	Residual
"I guess I still miss her." Shows SN picture of his wife: "Wasn't she beautiful?" "I think of her often. She was like a part of me. We went through so much together." "I'm not ready yet" (to look around for other people). "Now I just feel lonely." "Mostly I feel too tired to go out."	His wife died a year ago.	Had been married 52 years; lives alone in the house where he lived with wife; goes to the Jewish Community Center at times; son visits him and tells him "look around"; reports he cried in the past when thinking of his wife—in the process of grieving; believes in a just God (from last interview) Receiving home visits from student nurse	Has to work 3 more months to get pension; has arthritis Past experiences with loss and how he resolved them

Nursing Diagnosis	Goals	Interventions	Evaluation
Mr. H. is in the third stage of grief (attempting to deal with the loss) related to the death of his wife of 52 years a year ago.	Mr. H. will continue to move through the grief process as indicated by his verbal expression of feelings about the loss and by talking about pleasant memories of his wife during the next home visit. (short-term) Mr. H. will begin to show an ac-	Ask Mr. H. to talk about how it is for him now that his wife is gone. (stimuli 1, 6, and 11) Ask Mr. H. to talk about how it was for him when his wife was alive. (stimulus 6) Use open-ended questions, silence, reflection, and	The nurse reassesses behaviors related to loss during the next home visit.

[a]Although, the format of the data presentation differs (and stimuli are not numbered), this care plan is based on the same process of analysis shown on pp. 534–556.

LOSS (Chapter 18) *continued*

Adaptation Nursing Process Care Plan for a Person Experiencing Loss

Nursing Diagnosis	Goals	Interventions	Evaluation
	tive interest in interacting with other people by going to the Jewish Community Center weekly, starting in 1 month. (long-term)	paraphrasing to show interest and encourage verbalization. (stimuli 6 and 11) Remind Mr. H. that it takes time to adjust to the loss of a special person and that he is doing well. (stimuli 10 and 6) After doing the above interventions for 2 to 3 weeks, talk to Mr. H. about the need to interact with others. Ask him what programs he would be willing to attend at the Jewish Community Center. Ask him to make the commitment to attend one of those events before the student nurse's next visit.	

LONELINESS (Chapter 25)

Adaptation Nursing Process Care Plan for a Person Experiencing Loneliness

Behaviors	*Stimuli*
1. *Significant other(s)* *Mother and father (parents).*	*Focal* Need for affection.

(1) *Contributor*
        None revealed in data.
	Contextual
	The affectional developmental tasks of a
	  15-year-old male; achieving new and

(2) *Recipient*
        Parents have visited once during
        this hospitalization.
        Parents have called on the
        phone once.
	more mature relations with age mates of
	  both sexes; achieving emotional in-
	  dependence of parents and other adults.
	Accident (4 days ago) and an infection (2
	  days ago) (both increase the need for nur-

2. *Support system(s)*
  a. *No siblings.*
    No friends (peers).
    Nursing staff.
	turing).
	In a private room in isolation, so interac-
	  tions with the staff are decreased.
	Does not know how to establish or main-
	  tain a relationship.

(1) *Contributor*
        "Sulks" when nurses are in the
        room.
        Answers questions with a
        minimal response.
	Residual
	Low self-esteem.
	Parents are busy with their careers and
	  social life. Patient is used to being alone.

(2) *Recipient*
        A feeling of rejection, as they
        feel he should be doing more
        of his care.
        Verbal interaction.
        Physical proximity and touch as
        they give him physical care.	

b. *TV.*	
(1) *Contributor* None.	

(2) *Recipient*
        Watches most of his awake
        time.
        Observes relationships and nur-
        turing among people.	

c. *Student nurse.*	

(1) *Contributor*
        Accepts friendship offered by
        student nurse.
        Shares feelings about friend-
        ship.	

(2) *Recipient*
        Spends time with Jim.
        Talks about feelings related to
        friends and isolation.	

Nursing Diagnosis: Jim is manifesting behaviors of loneliness (minimal or no contributive behaviors) related to not knowing how to establish and maintain a relationship; his developmental crisis to achieve more mature relations with age mates; and his accident and hospitalization.

Goal: Jim will continue to express his feelings about the lack of friendships and learn some effective communication skills.

Interventions
1. Related to hospitalization: Assign to Jim a primary nurse who has effective interactional skills and who likes adolescents.

2. Related to not knowing how to establish and maintain a relationship: Role-model the process of building a trusting relationship; role-play and discuss the feelings associated with the use of ineffective communication.

3. Related to developmental crisis to achieve more mature relations with age mates: As soon as Jim is out of isolation, facilitate interactions with peers of both sexes that should be positive for Jim. Then discuss these interactions and process them with Jim. Provide Jim with community resources that will provide support and/or help as he continues to develop effective interactional skills.

Evaluation: When the nurse evaluates the goals, she asks the questions: Is Jim expressing his feelings about his lack of friendships? Do you assess behaviors that are contributive and that are effective in terms of establishing or maintaining his relationship?

SUBSTANCE ABUSE (Chapter 27)

Adaptation Nursing Process Care Plan for a Person with Substance Abuse

		Stimuli	
Behaviors	*Focal*	*Contextual*	*Residual*
Complains of fatigue. Eats indiscriminately. Appears physically wasted. Poor grooming. Admits she was hooked on diet pills. Expresses the belief that pills were effective for popularity, weight reduction, and energy. Says they (parents) "Don't love me." (Mother) "Picks on me." "Makes me work." "Doesn't listen." "Won't let me go out."	Need for peer group approval	Developmental task: Identify versus Role Confusion. Limited selection of alternatives for coping. Karen is oldest child with siblings 11, 9, and 3. Only girlfriend is slim and popular. Parent–child relationships are strained during the adolescent period. Interested in the nurse therapist. Preoccupied with weight.	Karen may have limited interests and limited coping skills. Possible influence of parental substance use. Karen's mother may be too demanding. Karen's perception of her situation may be faulty.

Nursing Diagnosis	*Goals*	*Interventions*
Physical and emotional crisis of substance abuse related to need for peer group approval. Low self-esteem	Karen will increase activity and decrease caloric intake. Karen will examine her perception of her situation and become aware of the ways in which she copes. Karen will explore her feelings about her family, peers, and herself. Karen will begin to learn to accept herself. Karen will begin to relate to peers in a group situation. Karen's family will see the implications of the family in Karen's problem and agree to family therapy. Karen will incorporate at least one additional interest and achieve some success.	Establish a therapeutic relationship. Practice active friendliness. Help Karen discuss her feelings about family, peers, and herself. Assist her in looking at her past coping mechanisms and identify ways of using the positive ones. Establish an activities schedule considering Karen's interests; include an active sports program. (This should be a program for exercise and also to provide Karen with some success experience.) Provide nutrition counseling with incentives. Consult with Karen's family and suggest family therapy.

LIFE CLOSURE (Chapter 28)

Assessment Responses

1. Mrs. W. was at the depression stage on the life closure continuum, as evidenced by her frequent crying, blaming self for illness, and withdrawal from her environment.
2. Other behaviors exhibited were transient disorientation to time, secondary denial by not letting the staff know about her visual problems, and anxiety as evidenced by her restlessness and inability to sleep.
3. The behaviors exhibited are adaptive and expected at this point on the closure continuum.
4. Yes, for her level of knowledge, she did an excellent job in interacting with Mrs. W. The fear that was displayed in turning Mrs. W. was expected and she was able to ask for support and help. She was able to assess her level of depression and oriented her to reality. She allowed her to express her sorrow. A more experienced stimuli regulator would have given an open-ended statement when she commented "There's always something wrong with me" by stating, "Can you tell me what you mean by that, Mrs. W.?" or "Can you tell me why you feel that way?" Mrs. W. was giving a message cue that she wanted to talk about her illness — which was missed.
5. No, the staff stimuli regulator exhibited behavior indicating frustration in dealing with Mrs. W. Her depression and crying was not accepted as a part of life closure as an adaptive behavior.
6. An acknowledgment of her pain was given, which was what she was wanting and asking for. The level of pain was acknowledged and it was communicated to her that others would be told about her pain and that some measure would be taken to decrease the pain.
7. As being very supportive. The relationship appeared to be very close and a lot of love was evident. The poem left by her sister was her means of bringing closure. Yes, they were very promoting of adaptive closure.
8. Very good — raising 12 children alone would require a lot of strength and ability to cope.
9. Calling in other available stimuli regulators to give added support. A case worker from the Thanatology Program was called to spend time with Mrs. W.
10. The pain level. Her pain was an all-encompassing aspect of her immediate situation. A program to eliminate her pain had to be worked out before she could move to the next stage of life closure. It was impossible for her to deal with anything other than her pain.

Adaptation Nursing Process Care Plan for a Person Experiencing Life Closure

Behaviors	Adaptation Status	Focal	Contextual	Residual
			Stimuli	
Depression, manifested by crying, withdrawal, staring into space	Adaptive	Progressive deterioration—bony metastasis	Family members supportive; promoting adaptation and trying to bring closure	Significant family relationships; not able to bring closure with family
Anxiety, manifested by restlessness, insomnia; transient disorientation	Adaptive		Staff nurse unsupportive—unable to deal with exhibited behavior	Accepting of staff—no hostilities shown
			No control over environment wanted—only concern for control of pain	Unable to cope with pain level; general coping abilities good
Secondary denial	Adaptive		Wanted to talk to student about illness (gave message cue), no mention of wanting to talk about death	Open in desire to talk about illness; visual problem not communicated
			No religious preference given or desire to see clergy; mentally alert	Did not express religious feeling

Nursing Diagnosis

Depression, anxiety, and denial related to progressive disease.

Adaptation Nursing Process Care Plan for a Person Experiencing Life Closure *continued*

Goals	Interventions	Evaluations
Decrease pain level and anxiety.	Change medication.	Pain level unaffected by medication change—necessary to try other methods and reevaluate.
	Give medication 1/2 hour before moving or turning.	Gives reassurance and support to Mrs. W.
	Communicate high level of pain to other staff members.	Staff become more aware of intensity of pain.
	Acknowledge severity of pain.	Developed trust, with Mrs. W. knowing that her pain was understood.
	Allow for rest, which should prevent disorientation.	Disorientation did not occur again.
Support during depressive stage of life closure.	Allow for crying and expression of sorrow.	Crying diminished in intensity.
	Spend time with Mrs. W. and acknowledge her sorrow.	Was responsive to touching and signs of caring.
	Give open-ended answers when she wants to talk about her illness.	Did not talk about her illness, not given adequate support.
	Called case worker from Life Transition Program.	Unable to evaluate.
Move to acceptance on closure continuum.	Decrease pain levels to allow for closure.	Decrease of pain level resulted in clouding of sensorium.
	Allow family to bring closure.	Family able to bring closure. Mrs. W. not able to.
	Develop trust and convey feeling that needs will be met. Spend time with her.	Family members frequently present.

Index

H

I